Law, Governance and Technology Series

Volume 58

Series Editors

Pompeu Casanovas, UAB, Institute of Law and Technology UAB, Barcelona, Spain

Giovanni Sartor, University of Bologna and European University Institute of Florence, Florence, Italy

The *Law, Governance and Technology Series* is intended to attract manuscripts arising from an interdisciplinary approach in law, artificial intelligence and information technologies. The idea is to bridge the gap between research in IT law and IT-applications for lawyers developing a unifying techno-legal perspective. The series will welcome proposals that have a fairly specific focus on problems or projects that will lead to innovative research charting the course for new interdisciplinary developments in law, legal theory, and law and society research as well as in computer technologies, artificial intelligence and cognitive sciences. In broad strokes, manuscripts for this series may be mainly located in the fields of the Internet law (data protection, intellectual property, Internet rights, etc.), Computational models of the legal contents and legal reasoning, Legal Information Retrieval, Electronic Data Discovery, Collaborative Tools (e.g. Online Dispute Resolution platforms), Metadata and XML Technologies (for Semantic Web Services), Technologies in Courtrooms and Judicial Offices (E-Court), Technologies for Governments and Administrations (E-Government), Legal Multimedia, and Legal Electronic Institutions (Multi-Agent Systems and Artificial Societies).

Henrique Sousa Antunes • Pedro Miguel Freitas •
Arlindo L. Oliveira • Clara Martins Pereira •
Elsa Vaz de Sequeira • Luís Barreto Xavier
Editors

Multidisciplinary Perspectives on Artificial Intelligence and the Law

Editors
Henrique Sousa Antunes
Faculty of Law
Universidade Católica Portuguesa
Lisbon, Portugal

Arlindo L. Oliveira
Instituto Superior Técnico
University of Lisbon
Lisbon, Portugal

Elsa Vaz de Sequeira
Faculty of Law
Universidade Católica Portuguesa
Lisbon, Portugal

Pedro Miguel Freitas
Faculty of Law
Universidade Católica Portuguesa
Porto, Portugal

Clara Martins Pereira
Durham Law School
Durham, UK

Luís Barreto Xavier
Faculty of Law
Universidade Católica Portuguesa
Lisbon, Portugal

ISSN 2352-1902   ISSN 2352-1910 (electronic)
Law, Governance and Technology Series
ISBN 978-3-031-41266-0   ISBN 978-3-031-41264-6 (eBook)
https://doi.org/10.1007/978-3-031-41264-6

This work was supported by PAIDC - Plataforma de Apoio à Investigação em Direito na Católica

© The Editor(s) (if applicable) and The Author(s) 2024. This is an open access publication.
Open Access This book is licensed under the terms of the Creative Commons Attribution 4.0 International License (http://creativecommons.org/licenses/by/4.0/), which permits use, sharing, adaptation, distribution and reproduction in any medium or format, as long as you give appropriate credit to the original author(s) and the source, provide a link to the Creative Commons license and indicate if changes were made.
The images or other third party material in this book are included in the book's Creative Commons license, unless indicated otherwise in a credit line to the material. If material is not included in the book's Creative Commons license and your intended use is not permitted by statutory regulation or exceeds the permitted use, you will need to obtain permission directly from the copyright holder.
The use of general descriptive names, registered names, trademarks, service marks, etc. in this publication does not imply, even in the absence of a specific statement, that such names are exempt from the relevant protective laws and regulations and therefore free for general use.
The publisher, the authors, and the editors are safe to assume that the advice and information in this book are believed to be true and accurate at the date of publication. Neither the publisher nor the authors or the editors give a warranty, expressed or implied, with respect to the material contained herein or for any errors or omissions that may have been made. The publisher remains neutral with regard to jurisdictional claims in published maps and institutional affiliations.

This Springer imprint is published by the registered company Springer Nature Switzerland AG
The registered company address is: Gewerbestrasse 11, 6330 Cham, Switzerland

Paper in this product is recyclable.

Preface

About the Book

This book is the outcome of a collaborative effort.

Five years ago, research group "Law and Artificial Intelligence"—hosted by the Católica Research Centre for the Future of Law (Universidade Católica Portuguesa—UCP, Lisbon, Portugal) and led by Henrique Sousa Antunes (UCP) and Arlindo Oliveira (Instituto Superior Técnico—IST)—started an ongoing scientific dialogue among scholars with diverse backgrounds and interests: law, computer science, neurosciences, and ethics. Since then, AI has further increased its role as the main driver of the contemporary digital transformation. As it continues to grow into an omnipresent set of general-purpose technologies, new questions need addressing. Among them, there are many outstanding technical, societal, ethical, legal, and regulatory questions, but rather than trying to focus on just one set of queries, this book is an attempt at understanding a broad number of problems from a distinctive multidisciplinary lens.

Some of the contributors to this book are members of the "Law and Artificial Intelligence" research group. Others are prominent researchers who have been invited to share their unique views on these topics. Others still have been selected to contribute to this project through a peer-review process, following a dedicated Call for Articles.

Section I addresses "Scientific, technological and societal achievements in Artificial Intelligence," but rather than gathering articles from a strictly engineering point of view, it approaches technical questions that also touch upon an array of societal, legal, and ethical issues.

In Section II, "Ethical and legal challenges in Artificial Intelligence," the authors highlight the multiple risks emerging from the deployment of AI and attempt to search for answers at the intersection of law and ethics.

Finally, Section III, "The law, governance and regulation of Artificial Intelligence," discusses solutions for regulating AI, with a particular focus on recent European Union initiatives in this field.

Acknowledgments

The research conducted toward writing this book, as well as its publication in open access, would not have been possible without important funding from PAIDC (Plataforma de Apoio à Investigação em Direito na Católica), Católica's Legal Research Support Platform.

PAIDC is a crowdfunding initiative created under the leadership of Professor Maria da Glória Garcia, former Dean of Católica Law Faculty and former Rector of Universidade Católica Portuguesa, and directed at promoting and disseminating high-quality legal research through the Católica Research Centre for the Future of Law.

The donors that made this enterprise possible include some of the most prestigious law firms operating in Portugal, as well as a number of current and former professors and alumni of the Lisbon School of Law of Universidade Católica Portuguesa:

Law Firms: Abreu Advogados; Albuquerque & Associados; CMS; Cuatrecasas; DLA Piper ABBC; Garrigues; Morais Leitão & Associados; PLMJ; Rebelo de Sousa & Associados; and VdA.

Professors and Alumni: Diogo Freitas do Amaral; Evaristo Mendes; Fernando Ferreira Pinto; Francisco Sá Carneiro; Gabriela Rodrigues Martins; Germano Marques da Silva; Isabel Marques da Silva; João Miranda de Sousa; Jorge Brito Pereira; Lin Man; Lino Torgal; Luís Barreto Xavier; Margarida Costa Gomes; Maria da Glória Garcia; Maria da Glória Leitão; Maria João Estorninho; Rogério Alves; and Rui Medeiros.

As editors of this book, we would like to express our sincere gratitude to the coordinator of PAIDC, as well as to all institutional and individual donors.

Lisbon, Portugal	Henrique Sousa Antunes
Porto, Portugal	Pedro Miguel Freitas
Lisbon, Portugal	Arlindo L. Oliveira
Durham, UK	Clara Martins Pereira
Lisbon, Portugal	Elsa Vaz de Sequeira
Lisbon, Portugal	Luís Barreto Xavier
30 May 2022	

Contents

Part I Scientific, Technological and Societal Achievements in Artificial Intelligence

Artificial Intelligence: Historical Context and State of the Art 3
Arlindo L. Oliveira and Mário A. T. Figueiredo

The Impact of Language Technologies in the Legal Domain 25
Isabel Trancoso, Nuno Mamede, Bruno Martins, H. Sofia Pinto, and Ricardo Ribeiro

Societal Implications of Recommendation Systems: A Technical Perspective 47
Joana Gonçalves-Sá and Flávio Pinheiro

Data-Driven Approaches in Healthcare: Challenges and Emerging Trends 65
Ana Teresa Freitas

Security and Privacy 81
Miguel Correia and Luís Rodrigues

Part II Ethical and Legal Challenges in Artificial Intelligence

Before and Beyond Artificial Intelligence: Opportunities and Challenges 107
M. Patrão Neves and A. Betâmio de Almeida

Autonomous and Intelligent Robots: Social, Legal and Ethical Issues 127
Pedro U. Lima and Ana Paiva

The Ethical and Legal Challenges of Recommender Systems Driven by Artificial Intelligence 141
Eduardo Magrani and Paula Guedes Fernandes da Silva

Metacognition, Accountability and Legal Personhood of AI 169
Beatriz A. Ribeiro, Helder Coelho, Ana Elisabete Ferreira,
and João Branquinho

**Artificial Intelligence and Decision Making in Health: Risks
and Opportunities** 187
Márcia Santana Fernandes and José Roberto Goldim

The Autonomous AI Physician: Medical Ethics and Legal Liability 207
Mindy Nunez Duffourc and Dominick S. Giovanniello

**Ethical Challenges of Artificial Intelligence in Medicine
and the Triple Semantic Dimensions of Algorithmic Opacity
with Its Repercussions to Patient Consent and Medical Liability** 229
Rafaella Nogaroli and José Luiz de Moura Faleiros Júnior

**Part III   The Law, Governance and Regulation of Artificial
Intelligence**

**Dismantling Four Myths in AI & EU Law Through Legal
Information 'About' Reality** 251
Ugo Pagallo

**AI Modelling of Counterfactual Thinking for Judicial Reasoning
and Governance of Law** 263
Luís Moniz Pereira, Francisco C. Santos, and António Barata Lopes

Judicial Decision-Making in the Age of Artificial Intelligence 281
Willem H. Gravett

Liability for AI Driven Systems 299
Ana Taveira da Fonseca, Elsa Vaz de Sequeira, and Luís Barreto Xavier

**Risks Associated with the Use of Natural Language Generation:
Swiss Civil Liability Law Perspective** 319
Marcel Lanz and Stefan Mijic

**AI Instruments for Risk of Recidivism Prediction and
the Possibility of Criminal Adjudication Deprived of
Personal Moral Recognition Standards: *Sparse Notes
from a Layman*** 339
Pedro Garcia Marques

The Relevance of Deepfakes in the Administration of Criminal Justice ... 351
Dalila Durães, Pedro Miguel Freitas, and Paulo Novais

**Antitrust Law and Coordination Through AI-Based Pricing
Technologies** 371
Maria José Schmidt-Kessen and Max Huffman

The "Artificial Intelligence Act" Proposal on European e-Justice Domains Through the Lens of User-Focused, User-Friendly and Effective Judicial Protection Principles ... 397
Joana Covelo de Abreu

The European Union's Approach to Artificial Intelligence and the Challenge of Financial Systemic Risk ... 415
Anat Keller, Clara Martins Pereira, and Martinho Lucas Pires

Regulating AI: Challenges and the Way Forward Through Regulatory Sandboxes ... 441
Katerina Yordanova and Natalie Bertels

Editors and Contributors

About the Editors

Henrique Sousa Antunes is Associate Professor at Universidade Católica Portuguesa, Faculty of Law (Lisbon School), Portugal. He was Dean of the School between 2011 and 2013. His area of expertise is private law and he teaches law of obligations, remedies, property law, and European consumer law. He belongs to several international research groups and he is a member of the Católica Research Centre for the Future of Law, where he coordinates a working group on Law and Artificial Intelligence. Sousa Antunes has published monographs and articles on a wide range of topics, namely on torts, contracts, property law, law and artificial intelligence, collective redress, consumer law, and foundations law.

Pedro Miguel Freitas is a Professor at Universidade Católica Portuguesa, Faculty of Law, where he coordinates a Postgraduate Course in Law and Technology, as well as a course in Law and Technology in the Law Degree. He obtained his PhD (2016) from the Law School of the University of Minho. He lectures and researches in the area of Criminal Law, Criminal Procedure, and Law and Technology. He is a member of the Católica Research Centre for the Future of the Law, Algoritmi Center, the Latin American Observatory for Criminal Policy Research and Law Reform, the International Federation for Information Processing (WG 9.6

and WG 11.7), and the Secure Platform for Accredited Cybercrime Experts at EUROPOL.

Arlindo L. Oliveira obtained a BSc in EECS from Instituto Superior Técnico (IST) and a PhD from the University of California at Berkeley. He was a researcher at CERN, the Electronics Research Laboratory of UC Berkeley, and the Berkeley Cadence Laboratories. He is a distinguished professor of IST, president of INESC, member of the board of Caixa Geral de Depósitos and a researcher at INESC-ID. He authored several books and articles in the areas of algorithms, artificial intelligence, machine learning, bioinformatics, and computer architecture. He is a member of the Portuguese Academy of Engineering and a past president of IST, of INESC-ID, and of the Portuguese Association for Artificial Intelligence.

Clara Martins Pereira is Assistant Professor at Durham Law School and Invited Professor at Católica Global School of Law. Clara holds a DPhil, an MPhil, and a Magister Juris from the University of Oxford, as well as an MSc in Law and Business and an LLB in Law from Católica Lisbon School of Law. Her research lies at the intersection of financial law and regulation, technological innovation, and sustainability. In addition to her academic work, Clara has been working as a consultant for various international organisations including the World Bank and ICF.

Elsa Vaz de Sequeira is a Professor at Universidade Católica Portuguesa, Faculty of Law. She is the coordinator of the Lisbon Section of the Católica Research Centre for the Future of Law (CRCFL) and a co-editor of the Católica Law Review. She integrates the executive committee of the working group on Law and Artificial Intelligence. She was a legal advisor at the Ministry of Culture's office. She teaches and develops research in private law, namely foundations of civil law and contract law. She has published books and articles on different issues of civil law, namely on civil liability, collision of rights, and co-ownership of rights.

Editors and Contributors

Luís Barreto Xavier is an Invited Professor at Universidade Católica Portuguesa, Faculty of Law, in Lisbon, and an Of Counsel at Abreu Advogados. He was a senior consultant at the Prime Minister Legal Centre (CEJUR) and a legal clerk for a Constitutional Court Judge. At Católica, he founded and directed (2009-2018) a new unit, dedicated to international teaching and research: the Católica Global School of Law. His areas of expertise are Private International Law and Digital Law. He belongs to the executive committee of the working group on Law and Artificial Intelligence. Since 2019, he teaches a course on the Law of AI for undergraduate students. He is currently the President of the Knowledge Institute of Abreu Advogados.

Contributors

Luís Barreto Xavier Universidade Católica Portuguesa, Faculty of Law, Lisbon, Portugal

Natalie Bertels KU Leuven Centre for IT and IP Law at KU, Leuven, Belgium

A. Betâmio de Almeida IST/University of Lisbon, Lisbon, Portugal

João Branquinho University of Lisbon, Philosophy Department, Lisbon, Portugal

Helder Coelho University of Lisbon, LASIGE, Computation Department, Lisbon, Portugal

Miguel Correia INESC-ID, Instituto Superior Técnico, Universidade de Lisboa, Lisbon, Portugal

Joana Covelo de Abreu School of Law – University of Minho (UMINHO), Braga, Portugal

Mindy Nunez Duffourc New York University Law School, New York, NY, USA

Dalila Durães Algoritmi Centre, School of Engineering, University of Minho, Braga, Portugal

José Luiz Moura de Faleiros Júnior University of São Paulo, São Paulo, Brazil

Márcia Santana Fernandes Laboratório de Pesquisa em Bioética e Ética na Ciência do Centro de Pesquisas do Hospital de Clínicas de Porto Alegre-LAPEBEC/HCPA DENS, Porto Alegre, Brazil

Ana Elisabete Ferreira University of Coimbra, Department of Law, Coimbra, Portugal

Mário A. T. Figueiredo Instituto de Telecomunicações/Instituto Superior Técnico, Universidade de Lisboa, Lisbon, Portugal

Ana Taveira da Fonseca Universidade Católica Portuguesa, Law Faculty, Católica Research Centre for the Future of Law, Lisbon, Portugal

Ana Teresa Freitas INESC-ID, Instituto Superior Técnico, Universidade de Lisboa, Lisbon, Portugal

Pedro Miguel Freitas Universidade Católica Portuguesa, Faculty of Law, Porto, Portugal

Dominick S. Giovanniello Northwell Health, Anatomic/Clinical Pathology, Blood Banking/Transfusion Medicine Hauppauge, New York, NY, USA

José Roberto Goldim Laboratório de Pesquisa em Bioética e Ética na Ciência do Centro de Pesquisas do Hospital de Clínicas de Porto Alegre-LAPEBEC/HCPA DENS, Porto Alegre, Brazil

Joana Gonçalves-Sá LIP - Laboratório de Instrumentação e Física Experimental de Partículas, Lisbon, Portugal

Willem H. Gravett Department of Public and Procedural Law, Akademia, Centurion, South Africa

Max Huffman Indiana University McKinney School of Law, Indianapolis, IN, USA

Anat Keller King's College London - The Dickson Poon School of Law, London, UK

Marcel Lanz Attorney at Law at Schärer Rechtsanwälte, Aarau, Switzerland

Pedro U. Lima ISR, Instituto Superior Tecnico, U. Lisboa, Lisbon, Portugal

António Barata Lopes ANQEP – "Agência Nacional para a Qualificação e Ensino Profissional" and Agrupamento de Escolas de Alvalade, Lisbon, Portugal

Eduardo Magrani Berkman Klein Center for Internet and Society at Harvard University, Harvard Law School, Cambridge, MA, USA

Nuno Mamede INESC-ID and Instituto Superior Técnico, Universidade de Lisboa, Lisbon, Portugal

Pedro Garcia Marques Law School, School of Lisbon, Catholic University of Portugal, Lisbon, Portugal

Bruno Martins INESC-ID and Instituto Superior Técnico, Universidade de Lisboa, Lisbon, Portugal

Clara Martins Pereira Durham Law School, Durham, UK

Stefan Mijic ETH Zurich, Zurich, Switzerland

Editors and Contributors

M. Patrão Neves University of the Azores, Ponta Delgada, Portugal

Rafaella Nogaroli Federal University of Paraná, Curitiba, PR, Brazil

Paulo Novais Algoritmi Centre, School of Engineering, University of Minho, Braga, Portugal

Arlindo L. Oliveira University of Lisbon, Instituto Superior Técnico, Lisbon, Portugal

Ugo Pagallo Department of Law, University of Turin, Torino, Italy

Ana Paiva INESC-ID, Instituto Superior Tecnico, U. Lisboa, Lisbon, Portugal

Luís Moniz Pereira NOVA-LINCS, Faculdade de Ciências e Tecnologia, Universidade Nova de Lisboa, Monte da Caparica, Portugal

Flávio Pinheiro IMS - Information Management School, Universidade Nova de Lisboa, Lisbon, Portugal

Martinho Lucas Pires Católica Lisbon School of Law, Lisbon, Portugal

Beatriz A. Ribeiro Vieira de Almeida & Associados, Communications & Digital, Lisbon, Portugal

Ricardo Ribeiro INESC-ID and Iscte - Instituto Universitário de Lisboa, Lisbon, Portugal

Luís Rodrigues INESC-ID, Instituto Superior Técnico, Universidade de Lisboa, Lisbon, Portugal

Francisco C. Santos INESC-ID and Instituto Superior Técnico, Universidade de Lisboa, Porto Salvo, Portugal

Maria José Schmidt-Kessen Legal Studies Department, Central European University, Vienna, Austria

Elsa Vaz de Sequeira Universidade Católica Portuguesa, Faculty of Law, Lisbon, Portugal

Paula Guedes Fernandes da Silva Catholic University of Portugal, School of Porto, Faculty of Law, Porto, Portugal

H. Sofia Pinto INESC-ID and Instituto Superior Técnico, Universidade de Lisboa, Lisbon, Portugal

Isabel Trancoso INESC-ID and Instituto Superior Técnico, Universidade de Lisboa, Lisbon, Portugal

Katerina Yordanova KU Leuven Centre for IT and IP Law at KU, Leuven, Belgium

Part I
Scientific, Technological and Societal Achievements in Artificial Intelligence

Introduction

Arlindo L. Oliveira

AI technology has been developing for more than half a century, but the last two decades have seen developments that have changed the nature of society. These developments include machine learning, robotics, computer vision, natural language processing and many applications in data analysis, finance, and health. The objective of the chapters in this section is not to provide a detailed technical description of the technologies involved, but to give the minimal technical background that will make the reader able to understand what these technologies can and cannot do. Many analyses of the consequences of artificial intelligence technology are deeply flawed because the authors ignore some rather simple facts about the way the technology works.

The chapters in this section cover several technologies that have already had a significant impact on society in the last decades. But these technologies will no doubt have much more impact in decades to come, as the technologies mature and find more applications in data analysis and in automation. The chapter by *Arlindo L. Oliveira and Mário Figueiredo* provides an overview of artificial intelligence technology, with an historical overview and a description of the state of the art, setting the background for the more specific chapters that follow. The chapter addresses in some depth one of the areas that is more central to artificial intelligence: machine learning, the technology that is pushing forward the state-of-the-art in artificial intelligence, with many applications in analytics and job automation.

Recent advances in large language models have attracted much attention, with the release of ChatGPT, but this is not the only language technology that will change the way we work and interact with people and with computers. The chapter by *Isabel Trancoso, Nuno Mamede, Bruno Martins, H. Sofia Pinto and Ricardo Ribeiro* describes the state of the art in natural language technologies and their impact in several fields, with a special focus on the legal field. This chapter covers several applications of natural language technologies such as summarization, document retrieval, outcome prediction and information extraction. Spoken language technologies, which are becoming increasingly more relevant, are also covered in this chapter.

As useful as the technologies are, with applications in many different domains that are set to increase our overall quality of life, they also raise some important questions. One of the most central challenges is related to recommendation systems and privacy. The extensive application of analytics to data obtained from many sources, such as social networks, search engines, and cellphone applications, has a significant impact on the privacy of individuals, an issue that raises many legal, ethical, and moral issues. Several of these issues are covered in the chapter by *Joana Gonçalves-Sá and Flávio L. Pinheiro*, which focuses on the risks inherent in recommendation systems. The chapter focuses, in particular, on the risks that are the result of recommendation systems that fail to work as intended and on the risks of systems that work but generate threats to individuals and even to democratic societies.

Another important application domain is health. The application of artificial intelligence techniques in the health domain raises many different questions, many of them related with legal responsibility, privacy, and security. The chapter *by Ana Teresa Freitas* addresses several of these challenges, in particular the importance of informed consent, the needs for safety and transparency in all systems that handle health data as well as the needs related with data privacy.

A final important challenge comes from security issues. As digital technologies become more and more central to modern society, the risks imposed by the activity of hackers, corporations and governments increase and require an ever deeper understanding of the issues involved. Some of these risks are analyzed in the chapter by *Luís Rodrigues and Miguel Correia* which formally defines three characteristics that form the basis for security: confidentiality, the absence of unauthorized data disclosure; integrity, the absence of unauthorized data or system modification; and availability, or the readiness of a system to provide its service.

Naturally, not all technologies used in a field as vast as artificial intelligence are covered in these five chapters. However, the most significant ones addressed in these chapters, natural language processing, machine learning, analytics, and cyber security, provide a good starting point for the non-technical reader interested in better understanding the artificial intelligence technologies and applications that are changing our world.

Artificial Intelligence: Historical Context and State of the Art

Arlindo L. Oliveira and Mário A. T. Figueiredo

Abstract The idea that intelligence is the result of a computational process and can, therefore, be automated, is centuries old. We review the historical origins of the idea that machines can be intelligent, and the most significant contributions made by Thomas Hobbes, Charles Babbage, Ada Lovelace, Alan Turing, Norbert Wiener, and others. Objections to the idea that machines can become intelligent have been raised and addressed many times, and we provide a brief survey of the arguments and counter-arguments presented over time. Intelligence was first viewed as symbol manipulation, leading to approaches that had some successes in specific problems, but did not generalize well to real-world problems. To address the difficulties faced by the early systems, which were brittle and unable to handle unforeseen complexities, machine learning techniques were increasingly adopted. Recently, a sub-field of machine learning known as deep learning has led to the design of systems that can successfully learn to address difficult problems in natural language processing, vision, and (yet to a lesser extent) interaction with the real world. These systems have found applications in countless domains and are one of the central technologies behind the fourth industrial revolution, also known as *Industry 4.0*. Applications in analytics enable artificial intelligence systems to exploit and extract economic value from data and are the main source of income for many of today's largest companies. Artificial intelligence can also be used in automation, enabling robots and computers to replace humans in many tasks. We conclude by providing some pointers to possible future developments, including the possibility of the development of artificial general intelligence, and provide leads to the potential implications of this technology in the future of humanity.

A. L. Oliveira (✉)
University of Lisbon, Instituto Superior Técnico, Lisbon, Portugal
e-mail: arlindo.oliveira@tecnico.ulisboa.pt

M. A. T. Figueiredo
Instituto de Telecomunicações/Instituto Superior Técnico, Universidade de Lisboa, Lisbon, Portugal
e-mail: mario.figueiredo@tecnico.ulisboa.pt

© The Author(s) 2024
H. Sousa Antunes et al. (eds.), *Multidisciplinary Perspectives on Artificial Intelligence and the Law*, Law, Governance and Technology Series 58,
https://doi.org/10.1007/978-3-031-41264-6_1

1 Historical Origins

The idea that intelligence can be automated has ancient roots. References to non-human thinking machines exist in Homer's Iliad and Thomas Hobbes clearly stated, in the Leviathan (Hobbes 1651), that human thought is no more than arithmetic computation. Both Pascal and Leibnitz, among many others, designed machines to automate arithmetic computations, which can be considered the precursors of modern calculators. But it was not until the mid-nineteenth century that the first proposal of a truly general computer appeared, created by Charles Babbage.

The original objectives of Babbage were to build an advanced tabulating device, which he called the *Difference Engine*. As envisaged by Babbage, this was a mechanical device that could be programmed to perform a series of computations specified in advance, by a complex arrangement of cogs, dented wheels, and levers. Although he managed to build only some parts of the Difference Engine, Babbage conceived of an even more powerful machine, the Analytical Engine. Had it been built, the engine would have had the ability to perform general computations in much the same way as a modern computer, although at a much slower speed imposed by its mechanical parts.

Although Babbage conceived the engine, it was Ada Lovelace, a friend mathematician, who wrote the most insightful analyses of the power of the engine (Menabrea and Lovelace 1843), arguing that it could do much more than just perform numeric computations. In particular, she observed that the machine might act upon things other than numbers if those things satisfied well-defined mathematical rules. She argued that the machine could write songs or perform abstract algebra, as long as those tasks could be expressed using symbolic languages. However, Lovelace also argued that the machine could not create anything new, but only perform exactly the tasks it was programmed for, ruling out the possibility that intelligent behavior could, somehow, be programmed into the machine. This argument was analyzed much later by an even more influential mathematician, Alan Turing.

2 Can Machines Think?

About a century later, Alan Turing, one of the most profound and creative mathematicians of all time, developed some of the central ideas of modern computing and came to different conclusions than those reached by Lovelace. Turing, who became known for having played an important role in the Allied World War II effort to decode the enemy messages encoded by the German Enigma cipher machines, achieved some of the most significant results in mathematics, namely in the mathematical foundations of computer science, results that are as important today as they were at the time they were obtained.

In a very important paper (Turing 1937), Turing showed that any digital computer with a large enough memory, which handles symbols and meets a few simple conditions, can perform the same calculations and compute the same set of functions as any other digital computer, a concept that became known as *Turing universality*. He described a particular type of computer, known today as a *Turing machine*, which uses a tape to write and read symbols as memory, and demonstrated that this type of computer can (in principle, assuming an unbounded tape) perform the same operations, do the same calculations, as any other computer that manipulates symbols. In the same year, Alonzo Church published a description of the so-called *lambda calculus* (Church 1936), a formal system for expressing computation based on function abstraction and application, which is also a universal model of computation with the same expressive power as Turing machines.

The combination of these two results lead to what became known as the *Church-Turing thesis*, which can be stated, informally, as follows: any result that can be actually calculated can be computed by a Turing machine, or by any another computer that manipulates symbols and has enough memory. This theoretical and purely mathematical result has important philosophical consequences. Note that there is a somewhat circular definition in this formulation: what exactly does the sentence "a result that can be actually calculated" mean? Are there any numerical results that are not in this category? The work of Alonzo Church, Alan Turing, and Kurt Gödel demonstrated that there are results that, although perfectly well defined, cannot be calculated. In 1931, Gödel proved that no consistent system of axioms is sufficient to prove all truths about the arithmetic of natural numbers and that, for any such consistent formal system, there will always be statements about natural numbers that are true, but that are unprovable within the system (Gödel 1931).

There is a close connection between Gödel's result and the problem that Turing addressed in his 1937 paper, and which can be stated in a simple way (that became known as the *halting problem*): is it possible to determine whether the execution of a computer program with a given input will terminate? Turing demonstrated that it is not possible to answer this question in the general case. It may be possible to answer the question in particular cases, but there are programs for which it is not possible to determine whether or not their execution will terminate.

Armed with these important insights on the nature and power of digital computers, Turing moved forward to analyze another important question, which is at the philosophical core of the field of artificial intelligence: can a computer behave intelligently?

Before describing Turings's work of 1950, in which he proposes an answer to this question, it is important to understand the consequences of considering the mechanistic ideas of Thomas Hobbes and the Church-Turing thesis together. Hobbes argued that the reasoning carried out by the human brain is nothing more than mathematical symbol manipulation. Church and Turing demonstrated that all machines that manipulate symbols are equivalent to each other, as long as they satisfy certain minimum requirements and are not limited in the time they are allowed to take to perform a given task, neither in the available memory. The result of these two ideas may arguably lead to the conclusion that a computer, in the broadest sense of the term, should be able to carry out the same manipulation of symbols as a human brain and, therefore, be as intelligent as a human. There is, however, some disagreement on the scientific community about this conclusion, as stated. Some people believe that the type of substrate where the computations are carried out (biological or digital) may be important, while others argue that the conclusion may be true in principle but irrelevant in practice due to several types of difficulties.

In his famous paper (Turing 1950), Turing asked exactly this question: can machines think? To avoid the difficulties inherent in defining what "thinking" means, Turing proposed to reformulate the question into a different and better-defined problem. In particular, he proposed to analyze a hypothetical imitation game, a thought experiment that led to the now well-known *Turing test*. In the game proposed by Turing, an interrogator, in a separate room, communicates with a man and a woman, through typed text. The interrogator's objective is to distinguish the man from the woman by asking them questions.

Turing wondered if someday in the future a computer that is in the man's place can make the interrogator make a mistake as frequently as he would in the case where a man and a woman are present. Variations of this test were proposed by Turing himself in later texts, but the essence of the test remains the same: is it possible for an interrogator to distinguish between answers given by a computer and answers given by a human being? Turing argues that this question is, in essence, equivalent to the original question "Can machines think?" and it has the advantage of avoiding anthropomorphic prejudices that could condition the response. In fact, given our individual experience and human history, it is only natural to assume that only human beings can *think*.[1] This prejudice could stop us from obtaining an objective answer to the original question. It could happen that the interrogator would decide that the computer cannot think for the simple reason that the computer would not be like us since it doesn't have a head, arms, and legs, like humans. The use of the imitation game reduces the probability that prejudices rooted in our previous experience prevent us from recognizing a machine as a thinking being, even in cases where this could be true.

Turing not only proposes a positive answer to the question "can machines think?", but also indicates an approximate time in the future when this may happen. He argues that within half a century there would be machines with one Gigabyte of memory that would not be distinguishable from humans in a five-minute Turing test. We now know that Turing was somewhat optimistic. By the end of the twentieth century (50 years after Turing's paper), there were indeed machines with 1GB of memory but none of them were likely to pass a five-minute Turing test. Even today, more than 70 years after Turing's article, we still do not have machines like that,

---

[1] We are referring to thinking at a human level. Although many animals, namely higher vertebrates such as non-human primates, dolphins, and others, can engage in thought processes, such as those underlying action planning and complex social interactions, there is a qualitative difference between the complexity of the thought processes of those animals and that of humans.

although the latest *large language models* (which will be described later), such as ChatGPT, are arguably not far from passing a Turing test with interrogators that are not experts on their weaknesses.

3 Objections to Artificial Intelligence

An interesting part of Turing's 1950 article is where he classifies, analyzes, and responds to a set of objections to his proposal that, sometime in the future, computers might be able to think. The list of objections is instructive and as pertinent today as it was when the article was written.

The first objection is theological, arguing that human intelligence is the result of the immortal soul given by God to every human being, but not to animals or machines. Turing recognizes that he is unable to answer this objection scientifically, but nevertheless tries to provide some sort of answer, using what he considers to be theological reasoning. Turing argues that claiming that God cannot endow an animal or machine with a soul imposes an unacceptable restriction on the powers of the Almighty. Why can't God, Turing asks, endow an animal with a soul, if the animal is endowed with a capacity for thinking similar to that of a human being? A similar argument is valid for machines: won't God have the capacity to endow a machine with a soul, if he so desires and the machine can reason?

The second objection is based on the idea that the consequences of a machine being able to think would be so dire that it is better to hope that this will never happen. Turing feels that this argument is not strong enough to even merit an explicit rebuttal. However, seven decades after his article, there are proposals to stop the development of some artificial intelligence technologies, for fear of the possible negative consequences. Therefore, the objection that Turing analyzed is not entirely irrelevant and human-defined policies may become an obstacle to the development of intelligent machines.

The third objection is mathematical in nature and was later revisited by John Lucas and Roger Penrose. The objection is based on Gödel's theorem (mentioned above), according to which there are mathematical results that cannot be obtained by any machine or procedure. The objection is based on the argument that these limitations do not apply to the human brain. However, as Turing argues, no proof is given that the human brain is not subject to these limitations. Turing gives little credibility to this objection, despite the prestige of some of its advocates.

The fourth objection is based on the idea that only consciousness can lead to intelligence and that it will never be possible to demonstrate that a machine is conscious. Even if a machine can write a poem, only when the machine becomes aware of the meaning of the poem, can the machine be considered intelligent, the argument goes. Turing notes that, in the most radical version of this objection, only by becoming the machine could we be sure that the machine is conscious. But once we were the machine, it would be useless to describe the feelings or the sensation of consciousness, as we would be ignored by the rest of the world, which would not be experiencing these sensations in person. Taken to an extreme, this objection reflects a solipsistic position, denying conscious behavior not only to machines but also to all other human beings since the existence of consciousness in other humans cannot be demonstrated beyond any doubt. While acknowledging that the phenomenon of consciousness remains unexplained (something true to this day), Turing does not regard this objection as decisive.

The fifth objection results from diverse and unsubstantiated arguments about behaviors that no machine can have. This category contains arguments like "no machine will have a sense of humor", "no machine will fall in love", "no machine will like strawberries and cream", and "no machine will be the object of its own thought". One curious (and perplexing) argument in this category is that "machines do not make errors", whereas humans do. As Turing points out, no justification is explicitly given for any of these limitations, which are supposed to be common to all machines. According to Turing, the objections arise, perhaps, from the wrong application of the principle of induction: so far, no machine has been in love, so no machine will ever be in love. A popular objection in this category is that no machine will ever have genuine feelings. Like the others, there is no scientific basis for this objection, it just reflects the limited view we have, based on our knowledge of the machines that currently exist.

The sixth objection is due to Ada Lovelace and was already referred to in the previous section. Although she realized that the analytic engine could process many other types of information besides numbers, Lovelace argued that the engine could never create anything new, as it only performed the operations for which it was programmed beforehand. Turing does not disagree with Lovelace's claim, but argues that it did not occur to Lovelace that the instructions could be so complex that they would lead the machine to actually create something new.

The seventh objection, perhaps even more popular today than it was in Turing's day, is based on the idea that the brain is not equivalent to a machine that manipulates symbols. We now know that the brain does not work in any way like a traditional computer, as the working principles of brains and digital computers are very different. Furthermore, the brain does not directly manipulate discrete symbols but physical variables with continuous values and theoretical results from mathematics tell us that a machine that manipulates continuous (real) values is necessarily more powerful than a machine that manipulates only discrete symbols. Turing's answer is that any machine that manipulates symbols, if properly programmed, will be able to give answers sufficiently close to the answers given by the machine that manipulates continuous values. Despite this response, this argument has held some weight over the decades. Many philosophers and scientists still believe that no machine that manipulates symbols can accurately emulate the behavior of the human brain and pass a Turing test.

The eighth objection is based on the argument that no set of rules is sufficient to describe the richness of human behavior. Since a machine always follows a set of rules, no machine can reproduce human behavior, which will always be unpredictable. Turing argues that it is not difficult for a machine to behave unpredictably and it is not possible to demonstrate that, deep down, our brain does not function according to a set of rules.

The ninth, and final, objection, curiously the one to which Turing seems to give more weight, is based on the (supposed) existence of extrasensory perception and telepathic powers. Although ESP and telepathy progressively fell into disrepute in scientific circles, Turing apparently believed the evidence known at the time, which seemed to point to the existence of this phenomenon. As Turing very well argues, if there is extrasensory perception, the Turing test would have to be modified to avoid the possibility of telepathic communication. We now know, however, that there is no such thing as ESP, which makes the ninth objection irrelevant to the present discussion.

More than half a century after Turing's work, the objections to the possibility of thinking machines remain essentially the same and the answers given by Turing remain as valid now as they were then. None of the objections presented seem strong enough to convince us that machines cannot think, although of course this does not in any way prove that machines can think.

In the last decades, several other objections were raised against the Turing test as a mechanism for identifying intelligence. The first, and most important, of these objections, is that the test does not really assess intelligence, but whether the tested subject has an intelligence analogous to human intelligence. An intelligent computer (or even a hypothetical individual of a non-human intelligent species) would not pass the Turing test unless it could convince the examiner that it behaves as a human would. A system could even be much smarter than a human and still fail the test, for example, because it fails to disguise a superhuman ability for mathematics.

A second objection is that the test does not address all abilities by which human intelligence can express itself, but only those abilities that can be expressed through written language. Although the test can be generalized to include other forms of communication (e.g. questions could be asked using spoken language), there will still be difficulties in testing human skills that cannot be expressed through the interfaces that are chosen. On the other hand, Turing explicitly proposed a test of limited duration, of a few minutes, which is profoundly different from a test where the interaction is prolonged over hours, days, or even years.

A third objection has to do with the relationship between intelligence and consciousness. Although Turing addressed the question of consciousness when he analyzed the fourth objection on his list, he does not explicitly maintain that a machine that passes the test will necessarily be conscious. Turing avoids explicitly discussing this issue, an attitude that can be considered wise, given that the relationship between intelligence and consciousness remains almost as mysterious nowadays as it was in 1950. Still, very recent proposals address the relationship between computational models and consciousness and this is a field that is being actively studied today.

Despite these objections, and others that we have not analyzed, the Turing test remains important, more as a philosophical instrument that allows us to scrutinize the arguments related to the possibility of the existence of artificial intelligence than as a real mechanism for analyzing the capabilities thereof.

In addition to proposing the Turing test, the article written by Turing in 1950 makes one last suggestion that, prophetically, points in the direction that artificial intelligence would finally take, a couple of decades later. Turing proposed that instead of trying to write a program that would allow a machine to pass the imitation game, it would be simpler to write a program that would enable a machine to learn from experience, just as a baby does. Such a program, Turing argued, would be much easier to write and would allow a machine to learn what it needed to finally pass the Turing test.

This suggestion, so important and prescient, predated in a couple of decades the most successful approach to the problem of creating intelligent systems: machine learning. Instead, the first approaches adopted to try to create intelligent systems were based on the idea that human intelligence, in its most elaborate and evolved forms, consists in the manipulation of symbolic representations of knowledge about the world and the deduction of new knowledge through the manipulation of these symbols.

4 Intelligence as Symbol Manipulation

The idea that intelligent machines could exist, championed by Turing and many others, quickly led to the project of building them. Starting in the 1950s, digital computers became more powerful and increasingly accessible. The first computers were dedicated to scientific and military calculations, but progressively their application spread to other areas of human activity. With the end of the Second World War, the possibility of using computers in activities not related to military applications became a reality. One of the areas that deserved significant attention was the nascent domain of artificial intelligence.

In 1956, a scientific workshop took place in Dartmouth, New Hampshire, bringing together several of the pioneers in the field of artificial intelligence. In fact, it was in the proposal to organize this conference, written by John McCarthy, Marvin Minsky, Nathaniel Rochester, and Claude Shannon (the famous father of information and communication theory), that the term *artificial intelligence* was coined. Many of those who were present at this meeting went on to create research groups in artificial intelligence at the most important universities in the United States. Those early approaches tried to reproduce parts of human reasoning that at the time seemed the most advanced, such as proving theorems, planning sequences of actions, and playing board games, such as checkers and chess.

Not surprisingly, the first efforts to reproduce human intelligence thus focused precisely on problems requiring the manipulation of symbols and the search for solutions. In that same year, a program written by Allen Newell and Herbert Simon (who also attended the Dartmouth workshop), called the *Logic Theorist*, was able to demonstrate mathematical theorems (Newell and Simon 1956), including some of those in Whitehead and Russell's influential *Principia Mathematica*.

In 1959, Arthur Samuel (who had also attended the Dartmouth workshop) wrote a program that could play checkers well enough to defeat its creator (Samuel 1959). The program incorporated several concepts developed in the field of artificial intelligence, including the ability to look for solutions in very large and complex search spaces. To play checkers well, it is necessary to select, among all the possible moves, those leading to the best results. Since, for each move, the opponent can respond with one of several moves, which must also be answered by the program, this process leads to a very rapid growth in the number of positions that need to be analyzed. This branching of the search process takes the form of a tree, which is thus called a search tree. Developing methods to efficiently explore these search trees became one of the most important instrumental objectives in the field of artificial intelligence.

Efficient search methods are as important today as they were when they were first studied and developed. These methods are also applied in many other areas, namely for planning problems. A robot needs to perform a search to find out how to stack blocks, in a simplified block world, or to find its way from one room to another. Many results of artificial intelligence resulted from studies carried out with simplified environments, where robots were taught to manipulate blocks to achieve certain goals or to move around in controlled environments. One of the first projects to make a robot perform certain tasks, in a simplified block world, led to the development of a system that could manipulate and arrange blocks in specific configurations using vision and natural language processing.

Natural language processing, which aims at making computers process (for example, translate) and even understand written sentences, was another of the problems studied in this first phase of artificial intelligence. Despite the difficulties inherent to this processing, mainly caused by the existence of great ambiguities in the way humans use language, systems that conducted simple conversations, in ordinary English, were designed. The most famous of these early systems, ELIZA (Weizenbaum 1966), was designed by Joseph Weizenbaum and was able to converse with a user, in plain written English. ELIZA used a very simple set of mechanisms to answer questions, using pre-written sentences or simply rephrasing the question in slightly different terms. Although the system had no real understanding of the conversation, many users were tricked into thinking they were talking to a human being. In a way, ELIZA was one of the first systems to pass a Turing test, albeit a test administered under very specific and rather undemanding conditions.

Other projects aimed to create ways to represent human knowledge, so that it could be manipulated and used to generate new knowledge. Through the application of rules of deductive reasoning to knowledge bases, it was possible, for example, to build systems that were able to make medical diagnoses in certain particularly controlled conditions, where knowledge could be expressed symbolically, and combined using rules for the manipulation of symbols. Some so-called *expert systems* were developed based on these techniques and played relevant roles in different areas, mainly in the 1970s and 1980s.

These and other projects demonstrated that some of the capabilities of the human brain that seemed more complex and sophisticated, such as demonstrating mathematical theorems or playing board games, could be programmed into a computer. These results led to several excessively optimistic predictions about the future evolution of artificial intelligence. In the 1960s, several renowned researchers, including Marvin Minsky and Herbert Simon (who had also attended the Dartmouth workshop), predicted that it would be possible, within three decades, to develop human-like intelligence in computers and to create systems that could perform any function performed by human beings. Those predictions, however, turned out to be unduly optimistic. The research carried out in those decades ended up showing that many tasks easily performed by humans are very difficult to replicate in computers. In particular, it proved exceptionally difficult to translate the results obtained in simplified environments, like the blocks world, to more complex and uncertain environments, such as a bedroom, a kitchen, or a factory. Tasks as simple as recognizing faces or perceiving spoken language proved to be of insurmountable complexity and were never solved by approaches based solely on symbol manipulation.

In fact, almost all of the capabilities of the human brain that have to do with perception and real-world interaction have proved especially difficult to replicate. For example, analyzing a scene captured by a camera and identifying the relevant objects therein is a very difficult task for a computer program, and only now it is finally beginning to be achievable by the most modern artificial intelligence systems. Despite this, we perform it without apparent effort or specific training. Other tasks that we perform easily, such as recognizing a familiar face or understanding a sentence in a noisy environment, are equally difficult to reproduce.

This difficulty contrasts with the relative ease with which it was possible to write computer programs that reproduce the intelligent manipulation of symbols, described in some of the approaches mentioned. This somewhat unexpected difficulty in reproducing behaviors that are trivial for humans and many animals on a computer is called Moravec's paradox: it is easier to reproduce on a computer behaviors that, for humans, require explicit complex mathematical reasoning than it is to recognize a face or perceive natural language, something a child does with great ease and with no specific instructions.

The difficulty in solving most problems involving perception and other characteristics of human intelligence led to several disillusionments with the field of artificial intelligence, the so-called *AI winters*. Despite these negative phases, marked by discouragement and lack of funding for projects in the area, the development of artificial intelligence systems based on symbol manipulation contributed, in different ways, to the creation of many algorithms that are executed by today's computers, in the most varied applications. This area has developed numerous methods of searching and representing knowledge that made it possible to create many programs that perform tasks that we often do not associate with intelligent systems. For example, the optimization of timetables for trains, airplanes, and other transportation systems is often performed by systems based on search and planning algorithms developed by the artificial intelligence community. Similarly, the systems created in the last decade of the twentieth century to play chess use search techniques that are essentially those proposed by this same community.

Artificial Intelligence: Historical Context and State of the Art

The methods and algorithms that made it possible to build the search engines that are now one of the central pillars of the Internet, and which allow us to locate, in fractions of a second, the relevant documents on a given topic, are also due to a specific sub-area of artificial intelligence: information retrieval. These systems identify, from the terms that are used in the search, the relevant documents and use different methods to determine which are the most important. The latest versions of these search engines use large language models (which we will describe later) to better understand the users' intentions and provide them with the most meaningful answers possible.

Nevertheless, with few exceptions, the systems based on symbol manipulation are rigid, unadaptable, and brittle. Few, if any, are capable of communicating in natural language, spoken or written, and of understanding the essence of complex questions. They are also uncapable of performing tasks requiring complex, unstructured image processing, or solving challenges that require adaptability to real-world, uncontrolled environments. Although artificial intelligence researchers have developed numerous robotic systems, few of these interact with humans in uncontrolled environments. Robotic systems are used extensively in factories and other industrial environments but, in general, they do so in controlled environments, subject to strict and inflexible rules, which allow them to perform repetitive tasks, based on the manipulation of parts and instruments that always appear in the same positions and the same settings.

Only very recently, after decades of research, have we started to have systems and robots that interact with the real world, with all its complexity and unpredictability. Although they also manipulate symbols, they are based on another idea, the idea that computers could learn from experience, and adapt their behavior intelligently, like children do.

5 Machine Learning

5.1 Basic Concepts

In the article Alan Turing wrote in 1950, he shows a clear awareness of the difficulty inherent in programming a system to behave intelligently. Turing proposed that, instead, it might be easier to build a program that simulates a child's brain. Duly submitted to an educational process, an adult brain would then be obtained, capable of reasoning and of higher intelligence. Turing compares a child's brain to a blank book, in which the experiences of a lifetime are recorded. Turing argued that it would probably be easier to build an adaptive system that uses machine learning to acquire the ability to reason and solve complex problems that we associate with human intelligence.

What exactly is this idea of machine learning, this idea that computers can learn from experience? At first glance, it goes against our intuition of computers, which we see as machines that blindly obey a certain set of instructions. This was also the idea that Ada Lovelace had, much influenced by the mechanical computer to which she had access, which led her to the conclusion that computers are inflexible and cannot create anything new.

The key concept of machine learning is that it is possible for a system, when correctly configured, to adapt its behavior to approximate the intended results for a given set of inputs. At its core, the concept is easy to explain. Imagine a very simple system that receives as input a single number and generates on its output a single number, which depends on the first one. If this system is shown several examples of the intended correspondence between the input number and the output number, it can learn to guess this correspondence. Suppose the number on the input is the latitude of a city and the number on the output is the average temperature in that city during winter. If the system is given several examples of latitude/temperature pairs, the system can learn an approximate correspondence between the latitude and the temperature. Of course, the match will not, in general, be exact, because of local variations in the environment and location of the cities. But using mathematical techniques that are familiar to many readers, such as regression, it is possible to estimate the average winter temperature from the latitude of the city. Such a system represents perhaps the most basic machine learning system imaginable. This correspondence between the latitude and the temperature was not explicitly programmed by any programmer but inferred from data, using a mathematical formula or algorithm. The machine learning program, however, is very general. It can either infer this correspondence or the correspondence between the average income of a country and its energy usage per capita. Once written, this same program can learn to determine relationships of a certain type (for example, linear) between pairs of numbers, regardless of the concrete problem being analyzed.

In machine learning, the set of examples used to train the system is called the training set and the set of examples later presented to the system to test its performance is called the test set. Once trained, the system can be used many times to predict outputs from new input values, without the need for additional training. In many cases (namely if the training set if very large and the relationship being learned is very complex), the training process can be relatively slow, but using the system to determine the desired match for new examples is quick and efficient.

Returning to the example of latitude and average winter temperature, now imagine that the learning system is given, as input, not only latitude, but also the average winter energy consumption by household, the distance from the sea, and other relevant variables. It is easy to see that the program can now learn, with much more precision, to calculate the relationship between this set of variables and the average winter temperature of a given city. Mathematically, the problem is more complex, but the formulation is the same: given a set of input data, the objective is to obtain a program that generates an estimate of the output. Using the right algorithms, this problem is not much harder than the previous one.

If the output (i.e., the variable being predicted) is a quantitative variable (or collection of quantitative variables), the system obtained through the execution of the learning algorithm is called a regressor, and the problem is known as *regression*.

If the objective is to assign a given class to the object characterized by the input, the system is called a classifier. Let us now consider a much more difficult problem: imagine you are given images with, say, a million pixels. The goal is to learn to classify images in accordance with what is in them; for example, does each image contain, or not, a cat or a dog. Again, we have as input several variables, in this case, three million variables for a color one megapixel image, and the objective is to generate in the output a variable that indicates what is in the photo, a dog, a cat, or a car, for instance. There are, indeed, very large datasets, such as *ImageNet* (Deng et al. 2009) that has more than 14 million images in more than 20,000 categories, which are used to train machine learning systems.

The attentive reader will have noticed that this problem is in essence no different from the first one discussed above. In the present case, it is necessary to calculate the correspondence between three million numbers, the input, and the desired class, the output. Although it has the same formulation, this problem is dramatically more difficult. There is now no direct correspondence, through more or less simple mathematical formulas, between the intended input and output. To get the right class, we need to be able to identify diverse characteristics of the image, such as eyes, wheels, or whiskers, and how these features are spatially related to each other.

Here, too, Alan Turing's pioneering idea works. Although it is very difficult (arguably impossible for a human) to write a program that maps inputs to outputs, images to categories, it is possible to learn it from the labels and descriptions humans created for these images. This idea that a computer can learn from examples was developed from the 1960s onwards by numerous researchers and scientists. The first approaches, which used symbolic representations to learn the correspondences between inputs and outputs, ended up giving way to statistical and/or numerical methods. There are many ways to learn a correspondence between the values in the inputs and the intended outputs, and it is not possible here to describe in a minimally complete way even a small fraction of the algorithms used. However, it is possible to present, in a very brief way, the philosophy underlying most of these approaches.

5.2 Statistical Approaches

A class of approaches that originated in statistics is based on estimating, from the training data, a statistical relationship between the input and the output (Friedman et al. 2001). Some of these statistical approaches (in a subclass usually referred to as *generative*) are based on the famous Bayes law. This law, actually a theorem, computes the probability of occurrence of some event (for example, the class of a given image) from prior knowledge about that event (for example, the probability that any given random image contains a dog, a cat, a person, …) and about how the input is related to the observations (for example, what are the statistics of images containing dogs). Another class of statistical approaches (usually called *discriminative*) bypasses the application of Bayes' law and, from the training data, estimates directly a model of how the probability of the output values depends on the input (for example, the probability that a given image contains a dog, given all the pixel values of that image). In complex problems (such as image classification), the discriminative approach is by far more prevalent, because it has two important advantages: it makes a more efficient use of the available data and it is less reliant on assumptions about the form of the underlying statistical relationships being therefore more robust and general-purpose.

5.3 Similarity-Based Approaches

Other approaches focus on assessing the similarities between the different examples of the training set. Imagine we want to determine a person's weight based on their height, sex, age, and waist circumference. And suppose we intend to determine the weight of a new individual never seen before. A simple and pragmatic approach, if there are many examples in the training set, is to look in that set for a person (or set of persons) with characteristics very similar to the individual in question, and guess that the weight of the individual in question is the same as that of the most similar person in the training set. This approach, learning by analogy, is effective if there is a vast training set, and can be carried out in a variety of ways, with algorithms whose designations include the *nearest neighbor* (or k nearest neighbors) method (Fix and Hodges 1989). An extension of this class of method, based on assessing similarities between objects to be classified and those in the training set, led to a class of methods known as kernel machines (of which the most famous member is the *support vector machine*), which was very influential and had significant impact in the last decade of the twentieth century and beginning of this century (Schölkopf and Smola 2002).

5.4 Decision Trees

Yet another class of methods, known as decision trees (Quinlan 1986), work by splitting data into a series of binary decisions. Classifying a new object corresponds to traversing down the tree based on these decisions, moving through the decisions until a leaf node is reached, which will return the prediction (a class or a value). A decision tree is built by making use of a heuristic known as recursive partitioning, which exploits the rationale of divide and conquer. Decision trees have several important advantages, such as being seamlessly applicable to heterogeneous data (with quantitative and categorical variables, which is not true of most other methods), being somewhat analogous to the thought process of human decision making, and, very importantly, being transparent, since the chain of decisions that leads to the final prediction provides an explanation for that prediction. Decision trees can also be combined into so-called *random forests* (Ho 1995), a type of model that uses multiple decision trees, each learned from a different subset of the data. The prediction of the forest is obtained by averaging those of the trees, which is known to improve its accuracy, at the cost of some loss of transparency and explainability. Random forests are, still today, one of the methods of choice in problems involving heterogenous data and for which the amount of training data available is not large.

5.5 Neural Networks

Neural networks are one of the most flexible and powerful approaches in use today. This approach was pioneered in the 1980s (McClelland et al. 1986) and is heavily inspired by much earlier work on mathematical models of biological neurons, namely by McCulloch and Pitts, in a famous 1943 paper with title "A Logical Calculus of Ideas Immanent in Nervous Activity", which proposed the first mathematical model of biological neurons. Also in the 1940s, Donald Hebb proposed the first biologically plausible learning process for neural networks (the Hebbian rule), which became famously summarized in the sentence "cells that fire together wire together" (Hebb 1949).

Although the functioning of a biological neuron is complex and hard to model, it is possible to build abstract mathematical models of the information processing performed by each of these cells, of which the one by McCulloch and Pitts was the first. In these simplified models, each cell accumulates the excitations received at its inputs and, when the value of this excitation exceeds a certain threshold, it fires, stimulating the neurons connected to its outputs. By implementing or simulating in a computer the interconnection of several of these units (artificial neurons), it is possible to reproduce the basic information processing mechanism used by biological brains. In a real brain, neurons are interconnected through synapses of varying strength. In the neural networks used in machine learning, the strength of the connection between neurons is defined by a number that controls the weight with which it influences the state of the neuron connected to it.

Mathematical methods, called training algorithms, are used to determine the values of these interconnection weights to maximize the accuracy of the correspondence between the computed output and the desired output, over a training set. In fact, these algorithms are essentially a form of feedback, where each error committed on a training sample is fed back to the network to adjust the weights in such a way that this error becomes less likely. The training algorithms that are prevalent in modern machine learning thus have deep roots in the work of Norbert Wiener, one of the greatest mathematicians and scientists of the twentieth century. Wiener's seminal work in cybernetics (a field that he created and baptized) includes the formalization of the notion of feedback, which is one of the cornerstones of much of modern technology. Wiener also influenced the early work on neural networks by bringing McCulloch and Pitts to MIT and creating the first research group where neuropsychologists, mathematicians, and biophysicists joined efforts to try to understand how biological brains work.

The first successful instance of a leaning algorithm for artificial neural networks, following the rationale of error feedback to update the network weights, was proposed by Frank Rosenblatt, in 1958, for a specific type of network, called *perceptron*. The perceptron together with Rosenblatt's algorithm 1958 are the precursors of the modern neural networks and learning algorithms. The early success of perceptrons spawned a large wave of enthusiasm and optimism, which turnec into disappointment when it became obvious that this optimism was very exaggerated. A symbolic moment in the crushing of expectations was the publication of the famous book "Perceptrons", by Minsky and Papert, in 1969. This book provided a mathematical proof of the limitations of perceptrons as well as unsupported statements regarding the challenges of training multi-layer perceptrons (which they recognized would solve those limitations). This disappointment was responsible for a dramatic decrease in the interest and funding for neural network research, which lasted for more than three decades.

Modern neural networks arose of the realization that it is indeed possible to learn/train networks with several layers (currently known as deep neural networks, to which the following section is devoted), which can be mathematically and experimentally shown to be highly flexible structures, capable of solving many prediction problems. At the heart of this possibility is a procedure, known as *backpropagation*, which allows implementing the above-mentioned feedback from prediction errors in training examples to adjustments in the network's weights, aiming at making these errors less likely. The term *backpropagation* and its application in neural networks is due to Rumelhart, Hinton, and Williams, in 1986, but the technique was independently rediscovered many times, and had many predecessors dating back to the 1960s, namely in feedback control theory.

Modern neural networks can have up to many millions of neurons and billions of weights. Sufficiently complex artificial neural networks can be used to process, images, sounds, text, and even videos. For example, when they are used to process images, each of the neurons in one of these networks ends up learning to recognize a certain characteristic of the image. One neuron might recognize a line at a given position, another neuron (deeper, that is, farther from the input) might recognize an outline of a nose, and a third, even deeper, might recognize a particular face. Again, some of the modern work on neural networks for analyzing images has old roots in work from the late 1950s and early 1960s, namely the neural models of the visual cortex of mammals described by Hubel and Wiesel, for which they received the Nobel Prize in 1981.

Although biological brains have inspired artificial neural networks and learning mechanisms, it is important to realize that, in the current state of technology, these networks do not work in the same way as biological brains do. Although networks of this type have been trained to drive vehicles, process texts, recognize faces in videos, and even play champion-level games like chess or Go (a very complex board game popular in Asia), it would be wrong to think that they use the same mechanisms the human brain uses to process information. In most cases, these networks are trained to solve a very specific problem and they are incapable of tackling other problems, let alone making decisions autonomously about which problems should be tackled.

How the human brain organizes itself, through the process of development and learning that takes place during childhood and adolescence, how new memories are kept throughout life, how different goals are pursued over time, by any of us, depend on essentially unknown mechanisms and are not present in artificial neural networks.

However, the last decade has seen the emergence of technologies that enable us to create very complex systems that, at least on the surface, exhibit somewhat more intelligent behavior.

6 The Deep Learning Revolution

In the last decade, machine learning led to remarkable developments in applications where symbolic methods did not perform well, such as computer vision, speech recognition, and natural language processing. These developments are collectively known as *deep learning*. The adjective "deep" refers to the use of multiple layers in neural networks, although other approaches that do not use neural networks also fall into the scope of deep learning (LeCun et al. 2015).

Deep learning commonly resorts to neural network architectures with many layers (essentially the concatenation of many perceptrons in a multilayer structure), leading to new applications and optimized implementations, mainly due to the availability of very large datasets for training these large structures with many paremeters (the weights referred above) and very efficient special-purpose computer processors, such as GPUs (graphics processing units). In deep learning, each neural network layer learns to transform its input into a somewhat more abstract and composite representation. For instance, in image recognition or classification, the raw input may be a matrix of pixels, the first layer may abstract the pixels and encode edges or corners, the second layer may compose and encode arrangements of edges and corners into lines and other shapes, and so on up to semantically meaningful concepts, such as faces or objects, or tumors in medical images. At the very core of the algorithms that learn these deep neural networks is the backpropagation algorithm that was mentioned in the previous section.

Deep learning has had many remarkable successes in recent years. Board games have been popular in artificial intelligence research ever since its inception in the fifties. Simpler games, like checkers and backgammon, have been mastered by machines decades ago, but other more complex games, like chess and Go took longer to solve. IBM's *Deep Blue* was the first chess program to beat a world champion (Campbell et al. 2002), when it defeated Garry Kasparov in 1997 in a rematch. However, *Deep Blue*, like many other chess programs, depended heavily on human-designed playing strategies and relied heavily on brute force search. Starting in 2016, a series of developments by *DeepMind*, a Google-owned company, led to the release of AlphaGo (Silver et al. 2016), a system that beat the best Go players in the world, after learning from expert games and self-play. Posterior developments led to AlphaGo Zero (Silver et al. 2017) and AlphaZero (Schrittwieser et al. 2020), systems that excelled at Go, chess, and other games, but that did not need to learn from human experts and learned uniquely from self-playing, using deep learning and a technique for sequential decision making known as *reinforcement learning*. The outcomes achieved by these programs were remarkable, as they were able to learn techniques and strategies within a matter of days that had eluded humanity for millennia since the inception of these games. The games these machines play are currently being studied in order to understand the novel strategies and techniques they developed and that are alien to humans.

Another area where deep learning has led to significant advances is computer vision, where the goal is to enable computers to process, analyze, and even understand images and videos. One important feature of the neural network architectures developed for computer vision is that the first layers are *convolutional*, inspired by the architecture of the first layers of the neural visual system of mammals, as discovered by Hubel and Wiesel in the 1950–1960s. Convolutional layers enjoy a certain type of invariance (more precisely, equivariance, but that is beyond the scope of this introduction), which means, in simple terms, that the processing that is performed at each location of the image is the same across all the image. Convolutional layers are an embodiment of a so-called *inductive bias*: a property of the network that is designed rather than learned, based on knowledge of the data that will be processed and the purpose of the network. More specifically, the inductive bias in this case is that to recognize the presence of an object in an image, its location is irrelevant. Another crucial implication of the convolutional nature of these networks is that, due to this invariance, the number of parameters that needs to be learned is dramatically smaller than in an arbitrary network with the same size.

By combining new architectural features, such as convolutional layers (and many other tricks of the trade) with massive datasets and powerful processing engines based on GPUs and TPUs (tensor processing units), deep learning has led to an explosion in the range of applications of computer vision. These applications include face recognition (heavily used in modern smartphones and automated surveillance), image recognition and classification, surveillance, automated facility inspection, medical image reconstruction and analysis, and autonomous driving, among others.

Several modern deep learning architectures, such as transformers (Vaswani et al. 2017), have been developed for natural language processing and used to build large language models. These large language models, which are statistical in nature, such as GPT-3 (Brown et al. 2020), have been trained in corpora with trillions of words, and can accurately answer questions, complete sentences, and write articles and notes about many different topics. They are becoming increasingly useful in the development of customer interaction tools, as shown by the recent release of ChatGPT and GPT-4, mimicking in very impressive ways the behavior of human agents in analyzing and answering requests made in natural language. In some ways, these large language models are approaching Turing's vision of machines that interact in a way that, if based only on text, cannot be distinguished from interaction with humans. The enormous interest raised by the release of ChatGPT shows the potential of these approaches, although this system represents, really, just one more step forward in the evolution of the technologies used in large language models, which are the result of the deep learning revolution.

7 Applications in Analytics and Automation

Modern artificial intelligence has many applications, in the most diverse fields, and cannot be easily classified using any simple taxonomy. However, they can be roughly clustered into two large, non-exclusive, areas: analytics and automation.

Analytics has a strong connection with other areas with designations such as data science, big data, data mining, or business intelligence. The fundamental goal of analytics is to organize existing data about people, organizations, businesses, or processes, in order to extract economic value from that data, by identifying regularities, propensities, or sensitivities that are susceptible to exploitation. Many of the world's largest companies, including those commonly known as GAFAM (Google, Apple, Facebook, Amazon, and Microsoft) owe much of their value to the ability to organize the data contributed by their users and resell it to support targeted advertising or other sales campaigns. However, the applications of analytics go far beyond advertising and marketing. Properly explored, the data obtained in the most diverse ways can also be used to discover new scientific knowledge and to optimize processes of design, manufacture, distribution, or sales, which represents an important component of another area that has become known as Industry 4.0. Any company that wants to be internationally competitive nowadays or any institution that wants to provide good services to its users must use analytics tools to explore and use the data they have.

Automation, on the other hand, has to do with the partial or total replacement of human beings in tasks that normally require intelligence. This area, whose economic impact is still probably smaller than that of analytics, will grow rapidly in the coming years, as companies and institutions continue to face pressure to become more efficient and reduce costs. Areas as diverse as customer support, legal services, human resources, logistics, distribution, banking, services, and transportation will progressively be transformed as functions previously performed by human employees are progressively automated by machines. This replacement process will be progressive and gradual, giving time for companies to adapt, but, inevitably, tasks such as customer service, facility surveillance, legal document analysis, medical diagnosis, vehicle driving, and many others will be progressively performed by automatic systems based on artificial intelligence. The current state of technology does not yet allow for the complete replacement of professionals in most of these tasks, but technological advance seems inevitable and their consequences, in the long run, indisputable.

Recently, the European Commission proposed two documents for possible adoption by the European Parliament that aim to regulate various aspects of the application of artificial intelligence technologies. These documents are some-how partially aligned with this taxonomy. The Digital Markets Act, proposed in

December 2020, focuses on the need to regulate access to data, for the purposes of analytics, and prevent excessive control of this data by large platforms (the document calls them Gatekeepers), which would lead to situations of overwhelming market dominance. The Artificial Intelligence Act, proposed in April 2021, focuses more on the problems caused by potential high-risk applications that are mainly in the field of automation. Systems considered high-risk by the document include, among many others, those that identify people, operate critical infrastructure, recruit or select candidates for positions or benefits, control access to facilities and countries, or play a role in education or administration of justice.

The European Union's ambition is to regulate artificial intelligence technologies, to maintain the security and privacy of citizens, guarantee competition and preserve the openness of markets while stimulating the development of new, secure, and non-invasive applications. However, the gap between essential and over-regulation is small, and compromises are often difficult. For example, the General Data Protection Regulation (GDPR) is certainly an important piece in the protection of citizens' rights and has placed Europe at the forefront in this field. But it is also a regulation whose compliance poses many challenges, demands, and difficulties for companies and institutions. Concerning the regulation of artificial intelligence, the hope is that Europe will manage to find an appropriate balance, preserving individual rights but also setting up the conditions for the creation of innovation, which will continue to be the engine of increased productivity and economic development.

8 Conclusions

Artificial intelligence, the field that has been developed to realize the idea that machines will one day also be able to *think*, is today an important technology that is behind profound changes that will affect society in the next few decades, globally known as the fourth industrial revolution.

Applications in analytics and automation will expand rapidly in the next decades, leading to changes in the way we live, work, and interact. Although the world seems profoundly changed by the technologies that are already in place, we must be prepared for even deeper changes in years to come, brought by the convergence of diverse technologies, of which artificial intelligence is the most central one.

Although we still do not know how to reproduce human-level intelligent behavior in machines, an objective known as artificial general intelligence, large-scale efforts to develop the technologies that could lead to such a result are being undertaken by all the major economic blocs, companies, research institutes, and universities. It is highly likely that the combined efforts of millions of researchers may eventually shed light on one of the most important questions that humanity has faced: what is intelligence and can it be reproduced in machines?

Artificial Intelligence: Historical Context and State of the Art 23

If artificial general intelligence is indeed possible and becomes a reality some-time in the future, it will raise significant practical, ethical, and social questions, which will have to be discussed and addressed, from a variety of standpoints.[2]

References

Brown T, Mann B, Ryder N, Subbiah M, Kaplan JD, Dhariwal P, Neelakantan A, Shyam P, Sastry G, Askell A, Agarwal S, Herbert-Voss A, Krueger G, Henighan T, Child R, Ramesh A, Ziegler D, Wu J, Winter C, Hesse C, Chen M, Sigler E, Litwin M, Gray S, Chess B, Clark J, Berner C, McCandlish S, Radford A, Sutskever I, Amodei D (2020) Language models are few-shot learners. Adv Neural Inf Proces Syst 33:1877–1901
Campbell M, Hoane AJ, Hsu FH (2002) Deep Blue. Artif Intell 134:57–83
Church A (1936) An unsolvable problem of elementary number theory. Am J Math 58:345–363
Deng J, Dong W, Socher R, Li LJ, Kai L, Li FF (2009) ImageNet: a large-scale hierarchical image database. In: 2009 IEEE Conference on Computer Vision and Pattern Recognition, 20–25
Fix E, Hodges JL (1989) Discriminatory analysis. Nonparametric discrimination: consistency properties. Int Stat Rev 57:238–247
Friedman J, Hastie T, Tibshirani R (2001) The elements of statistical learning. Springer, New York
Gödel K (1931) Über formal unentscheidbare Sätze der Principia Mathematica und verwandter Systeme I. Monatsh Math Phys 38-38:173–198
Hebb D (1949) The organization of behavior. Wiley & Sons, New York
Ho T (1995) Random decision forests, Proceedings of the 3rd International Conference on Document Analysis and Recognition, Montreal, pp 278–282
Hobbes T (1651) Leviathan: or, the matter, form, and power of a commonwealth ecclesiastical and civil. G. Routledge and Sons, Manchester and New York
LeCun Y, Bengio Y, Hinton G (2015) Deep learning. Nature 521:436–444
McClelland JL, Rumelhart DE, PDP Research Group (1986) Parallel distributed processing: explorations in the microstructure of cognition. MIT Press
Menabrea L, Lovelace A (1843) Sketch of the analytical engine invented by Charles Babbage. Sci Mem 3:666–731
Newell A, Simon H (1956) The logic theory machine–a complex information processing system. IEEE Trans Inf Theory 2:61–79
Quinlan JR (1986) Induction of decision trees. Mach Learn 1:81–106
Rosenblatt F (1958) The Perceptron: A Probabilistic Model for Information Storage and Organization in the Brain, Cornell Aeronautical Laboratory, Psy Rev 65(6):386–408

---

[2] *See* generally, on the different applications of Machine Learning and AI, in this book I Trancoso, N Mamede, B Martins, H S Pinto and R Ribeiro - The impact of language technologies in the legal domain; J Gonçalves-Sá and F L Pinheiro - Societal Implications of Recommendation Systems - A Technical Perspective; A T Freitas - Data-driven approaches in healthcare - challenges and emerging trends; M Correia and L Rodrigues - Security and Privacy; E Magrani and P G F Silva - The Ethical and Legal Challenges of Recommender Systems Driven by Artificial Intelligence; M Lanz and S Mijic - Risks associated with the use of natural language generation - Swiss civil liability law perspective; M S Fernandes and J R Goldim - Artificial Intelligence and Decision Making in Health - Risks and Opportunities; W Gravett - Judicial Decision-making in the Age of Artificial Intelligence; and D Durães, P M Freitas and P Novais - The Relevance of Deepfakes in the Administration of Criminal Justice. *See* also, on the GDPR, in this book E Magrani and P G F Silva - The Ethical and Legal Challenges of Recommender Systems Driven by Artificial Intelligence.

Samuel AL (1959) Some studies in machine learning using the game of checkers. IBM J Res Dev 3:210–229

Schölkopf B, Smola A (2002) Learning with kernels support vector machines, regularization, optimization, and beyond. MIT Press

Schrittwieser J, Antonoglou I, Hubert T, Simonyan K, Sifre L, Schmitt S, Guez A, Lockhart E, Hassabis D, Graepel T, Lillicrap T, Silver D (2020) Mastering Atari, go, chess and shogi by planning with a learned model. Nature 588:604–609

Silver D, Huang A, Maddison CJ, Guez A, Sifre L, van den Driessche G, Schrittwieser J, Antonoglou I, Panneershelvam V, Lanctot M, Dieleman S, Grewe D, Nham J, Kalchbrenner N, Sutskever I, Lillicrap T, Leach M, Kavukcuoglu K, Graepel T, Hassabis D (2016) Mastering the game of go with deep neural networks and tree search. Nature 529:484–489

Silver D, Schrittwieser J, Simonyan K, Antonoglou I, Huang A, Guez A, Hubert T, Baker L, Lai M, Bolton A, Chen Y, Lillicrap T, Hui F, Sifre L, van den Driessche G, Graepel T, Hassabis D (2017) Mastering the game of go without human knowledge. Nature 550:354–359

Turing AM (1937) On computable numbers, with an application to the Entscheidungsproblem. Proc Lond Math Soc 2:230–265

Turing AM (1950) Computing machinery and intelligence. Mind 59:433–460

Vaswani A, Brain G, Shazeer N, Parmar N, Uszkoreit J, Jones L, Gomez AN, Kaiser Ł, Polosukhin I (2017) Attention is all you need. Adv Neural Inf Proces Syst 31:5998–6008

Weizenbaum J (1966) ELIZA—a computer program for the study of natural language communication between man and machine. Commun ACM 9:36–45

Open Access This chapter is licensed under the terms of the Creative Commons Attribution 4.0 International License (http://creativecommons.org/licenses/by/4.0/), which permits use, sharing, adaptation, distribution and reproduction in any medium or format, as long as you give appropriate credit to the original author(s) and the source, provide a link to the Creative Commons licence and indicate if changes were made.

The images or other third party material in this chapter are included in the chapter's Creative Commons licence, unless indicated otherwise in a credit line to the material. If material is not included in the chapter's Creative Commons licence and your intended use is not permitted by statutory regulation or exceeds the permitted use, you will need to obtain permission directly from the copyright holder.

The Impact of Language Technologies in the Legal Domain

Isabel Trancoso, Nuno Mamede, Bruno Martins, H. Sofia Pinto, and Ricardo Ribeiro

Abstract In the current digital era, language technologies are playing an increasingly vital role in the legal domain, assisting users, lawyers, judges, and legal professionals to solve many real-world problems. While open datasets and innovative deep learning methodologies have led to recent breakthroughs in the area, significant efforts are still being made to transfer the theoretical/algorithmic developments, associated with general text and speech processing, into real applications in the legal-domain. This chapter presents a brief survey on language technologies for addressing legal tasks, covering studies and applications related to both text and speech processing (Manuscript submitted in May 2022).

1 Introduction

Law is one of the fields that may greatly benefit from the huge Artificial Intelligence (AI) advances, particularly in connection to language technologies. In fact, one can almost say that AI is changing the field. These changes are reflected in recently coined terms such as "Legal AI", which encompasses hundreds of methods proposed for information retrieval, text/knowledge mining, and Natural Language Processing (NLP). In the literature, NLP is often restricted to text processing, but we take the overarching view of covering both written and spoken language processing, as both text and speech processing are playing a vital role in shaping the future of legal AI.

I. Trancoso (✉) · N. Mamede · B. Martins · H. S. Pinto
INESC-ID and Instituto Superior Técnico, Universidade de Lisboa, Lisboa, Portugal
e-mail: isabel.trancoso@inesc-id.pt; nuno.mamede@inesc-id.pt; bruno.g.martins@inesc-id.pt; sofia@inesc-id.pt

R. Ribeiro
INESC-ID and Iscte - Instituto Universitário de Lisboa, Lisboa, Portugal
e-mail: ricardo.ribeiro@inesc-id.pt

© The Author(s) 2024
H. Sousa Antunes et al. (eds.), *Multidisciplinary Perspectives on Artificial Intelligence and the Law*, Law, Governance and Technology Series 58,
https://doi.org/10.1007/978-3-031-41264-6_2

Thus, we structured this necessarily brief review into two main sections, covering text and speech analysis. We describe how the area has changed in the last decade, and how different language technologies may contribute to draft, dictate, analyse, and anonymise legal documents, streamline legal research, predict rulings, transcribe court proceedings, etc. Moreover, the chapter also attempts to draw attention to potential misuses of language technology, and their impact in the legal domain.

2 Language Processing Technologies for Processing Textual Data

Natural Language Processing (NLP) in the legal domain (Zhong et al. 2020) has addressed text analysis tasks such as legal judgment prediction (Aletras et al. 2016; Chen et al. 2019), legal topic classification (Chalkidis et al. 2021a), legal document retrieval and question answering, or contract understanding (Hendrycks et al. 2021), to name a few. As in other application areas for NLP, progress has often been made in connection to publicly available datasets, which researchers can use to evaluate system performance in a standardized way (e.g., the Legal General Language Understanding Evaluation benchmark is one recent example Chalkidis et al. 2021c). Joint evaluation initiatives (i.e., shared tasks) are also popular in the area. In these competitions, teams of researchers submit systems that address specific predefined challenges for the shared task, and the results are then evaluated against a "gold standard" that was previously prepared by the shared task organizers. Examples for shared tasks related to legal NLP include the Competition on Legal Information Extraction and Entailment (Rabelo et al. 2022), the Chinese AI and Law challenge, taking place yearly since 2018 (Zhong et al. 2018), or the Artificial Intelligence for Legal Assistance series of shared tasks, which started in 2019 (Bhattacharya et al. 2019). The field has also a long history, reflecting the changes that the general area of NLP has also seen over the years.

Up to the 1980s, most NLP systems were based on symbolic approaches leveraging hand-written rules. Starting in the late 1980s, there was a shift with the introduction of machine learning algorithms for NLP, using statistical inference to automatically learn *rules* through the analysis of large corpora. In the 2010s, representation learning and deep neural network-style machine learning methods became widespread in NLP. Popular techniques include the use of word embeddings to capture semantic properties of words, and an increase in end-to-end learning of higher-level tasks (e.g., question answering), instead of relying on a pipeline of separate intermediate tasks (e.g., parts-of-speech tagging and syntactic dependency parsing).

As with other specialized domains (e.g., biomedical or financial documents), legal text (e.g., legislation, court documents, contracts, etc.) has distinct characteristics compared to generic corpora, such as specialized vocabulary, a particular syntax, semantics based on extensive domain-specific knowledge, or the common use of long sentences. These differences can affects the performance of generic NLP models, motivating research in this specific area. Even in the case of modern methods based on end-to-end learning, pre-training models with legal text can help to better capture the aforementioned characteristics, providing in-domain knowledge that is missing from other generic corpora.

In fact, several pre-trained legal language models, based on very large neural networks, have been recently introduced (Chalkidis et al. 2020b; Xiao et al. 2021). State-of-the-art NLP approaches are based on these types of models, following a design based on pre-training neural language models on huge amounts of (ideally in-domain) text, e.g. by considering unsupervised objectives such as predicting masked words from real sentences, followed by the supervised fine-tuning of these models to specific downstream tasks. The following sub-sections discuss different NLP applications related to the legal domain, often involving methods based on pre-trained neural language models.

2.1 Text Anonymization

Data anonymization is a process of masking or removing sensitive data from a document while preserving its original format. This process is important for sharing legal documents and court decisions without exposing any sensitive information (Mamede et al. 2016). Free-form text is a special type of document where data is contained in an unstructured way, as represented in natural language. Court decisions are examples of this type of document. From the content of these documents, it is necessary to identify text structures that represent names or unique identifiers, known as entities. This task is commonly referred to as NER (Named Entity Recognition). The three main classes of NEs are: person, location, and organization. Other important classes include dates, phone numbers, car plates, bank account references (eg. IBAN), and websites.

The main use of automatic text anonymization systems is to de-identify medical records and court decisions. A generic anonymization system is usually composed of up to four modules: (1) a module that normalizes the text and performs feature extraction; (2) a set of NE classifiers; (3) a poll to vote the most probable class of NE; and (4) a module that applies an anonymization method over the NEs and replaces the occurrences of these entities in the text.

One of the first automated anonymization systems was Scrub. It was introduced by Sweeney (1996) and it uses pattern-matching and dictionaries. The system runs multiple algorithms in parallel to detect different classes of entities. In 2006, part of the i2b2 (Informatics for Integrating Biology to the Bedside) Challenge was dedicated to the de-identification of clinical data. Seven systems participated in this challenge. The MITRE system, developed by Wellner et al. (2007), achieved the highest performance. The MITRE system uses two model-based NER tools, one based on Conditional Random Fields (CRF) and another on Hidden Markov Models.

Gardner and Xiong (2008) developed the Health Information DE-Identification (HIDE) framework for de-identification of private health information (PHI), which uses a NER tool based on CRF. Neamatullah et al. (2008) developed the MIT De-id package. This package is a dictionary and rule-based system and was made available for free on the Internet by PhysioNet. Uzuner et al. (2008) developed the Stat De-id that runs a set of classifiers in parallel. Each classifier is specialized in detecting a different category of entities. The Best-of-Breed System (BoB) by Ferrández et al. (2013), a hybrid design system, uses rules and dictionaries to score a higher recall, and it also uses model-based classifiers to score a higher precision.

Michaël Benesty[1] draws attention to the importance of the processing speed of anonymization systems. The case study was conducted in collaboration with the French administration and a French supreme court (*Cour de cassation*). More recently, Glaser et al. (2021b) presented a machine learning approach for the automatic identification of sensitive text elements in German legal court decisions. The adopted strategy includes several deep neural networks based on generic pre-trained contextual embeddings.

The most usual methods of anonymization include: suppression, tagging, random substitution, and generalization. The *suppression* method is a simple way of anonymizing a text that consists of the suppression of the NE using a neutral indicator that replaces the original text, e.g. 'XXXXXX'. The *tagging* method consists of the replacement of the NE with a label that could indicate its class and a unique identifier. It can be implemented by concatenating the class given by the NER tool and a unique numeric identifier, e.g. [**Organization123**]. The *random substitution* method replaces a NE with another random entity of the same class and morphosyntactic features. This method can be implemented using a *default list* containing random entities of each class. In highly inflected languages, it is important to replace entities of every class with another entity with the same gender and number. *Generalization* is any method of replacing an entity from the text with another entity that mentions an object of the same class but in a more general way, e.g.: *University of Lisbon* could be generalized to *University*, or even to *Institution*.

Some of the major problems of developing anonymization systems to be used in legal documents and court decisions are: (1) the lack of non-anonymized data sets, making impossible to compare approaches and making the evolution of these systems harder; (2) each jurisdiction features different distributions of named entity types and introduces court-specific anonymization challenges; (3) all the entities that refer to the same object within the document should be replaced by the same label, which implies the existence of a Co-reference resolution module which is also a big challenge; (4) The *random substitution* implies the extraction of the grammatical gender and number of the NE that is given by its headword. The headwords of NEs and their features must be determined at a pre-processing stage. Determining the

---

[1] https://towardsdatascience.com/why-we-switched-from-spacy-to-flair-to-anonymize-french-legal-cases-e7588566825f.

Language Technologies in the Legal Domain

gender of the headword is important for replacing NEs that refer persons by another NE from the same gender, e.g. replacing *John* by *Peter*, or replacing *Mary* by *Anna*.

2.2 Document Classification

Text classification (i.e., the assignment of documents to classes from a pre-defined taxonomy) has many potential applications in the legal domain, particularly for categorizing legislative documents and cases. This can aid the process of legal research, and the development of knowledge management systems (Boella et al. 2016). Several studies have focused on legislative contents or court cases (Tuggener et al. 2020; De Araujo et al. 2020; Papaloukas et al. 2021), with some authors highlighting that legal document classification can be significantly harder than more generic text classification problems (Nallapati and Manning 2008).

In the specific case of legislative contents, much work on topic classification has focused on EU legislation documents, both in monolingual settings focusing on the English language (Chalkidis et al. 2019b, 2020a), and also on multilingual settings (Avram et al. 2021; Chalkidis et al. 2021a). These previous efforts addressed the task of classifying EU laws into EuroVoc[2] concepts, seeing the problem as a challenging instance of Large-scale Multi-label Text Classification (LMTC), given the need for assigning, to each given document, a subset of labels from a large predefined set (i.e., thousands of classes that are hierarchically organized), and given also the need for handling few and zero-shot scenarios (i.e., the distribution for how labels are assigned is highly skewed, and some labels have few or no training examples). A battery of state-of-the-art LMTC methods have been empirically evaluated, with very good results currently being obtained with approaches based on combining large pre-trained neural language models (i.e., models based on pre-trained Transformer-based approaches like BERT) with label-wise attention networks (i.e., using different parameters for weighting the document representations, according to each possible label). For instance, in experiments with 57k English legislative documents from EURLEX,[3] studies have reported values of 80.3 in terms of an R-Precision@K evaluation metric (Chalkidis et al. 2020a).

Document classification technology is also nowadays deployed in many practical settings. One interesting example is the JRC EuroVoc Indexer (JEX[4]), i.e. an open-source tool currently being used in many different settings, that was developed by the European Commission's Joint Research Centre (JRC) for automatically classifying documents according to EuroVoc descriptors, covering the 22 official EU languages. JEX can be used as a tool for interactive multi-label EuroVoc descriptor

---

[2] http://eurovoc.europa.eu/.

[3] http://eur-lex.europa.eu/.

[4] http://joint-research-centre.ec.europa.eu/language-technology-resources/jrc-eurovoc-indexer-jex_en.

2.3 Information Retrieval

The need for handling large amount of digital documents has made the legal sector interesting for the development of specific methodologies for the management, storage, indexing, and retrieval of legal information. All these tasks fall into the realm of information retrieval, which manly focuses on information search problems where a description of the current situation (i.e., an information need) is used to query an automated system to retrieve the most suitable information, within a large repository, for the input query (Sansone and Sperlí 2022).

Work on legal information retrieval goes back to the 1960s (Wilson 1962; Eldridge and Dennis 1963; Choueka et al. 1971), but recent scientific developments are strongly connected to the Competition on Legal Information Extraction/Entailment (COLIEE), and to specific applications related to case law retrieval (Locke and Zuccon 2022). From 2015 to 2017 the COLIEE task was to retrieve Japanese Civil Code articles given a question, and since then the main COLIEE retrieval task has been to retrieve supporting cases given a short description of an unseen case. Most submitted systems leverage sparse representations of documents and queries, based on word occurrences, together with simple numerical statistics that reflect how important a word is to a document within a collection (i.e., statistics such as TF-IDF or BM25). More recent studies, both in the context of COLIEE and in other separate publications, have started to explore recent advances connected to neural ranking models (e.g., using large language models trained in text matching data, for re-ranking the results of simpler methods based on word-level statistics).

An interesting recent study has for instance focused on the task of regulatory information retrieval (Chalkidis et al. 2021b), which concerns retrieving all relevant laws that a given organization should comply with, or vice-versa (i.e., given a new law retrieve all the regulatory compliance controls, within an organization, that are affected by this law). Applications like this are much more challenging than traditional information retrieval tasks, where the query typically contains a few informative words and the documents are relatively short. In the case regulatory information retrieval (and also other legal tasks, such as similar case matching (Xiao et al. 2019)), the query is also a long document (e.g., a regulation) containing thousands of words, most of which are uninformative. Consequently, matching the query with other long documents, where the informative words are also sparse, becomes extremely difficult for traditional approaches based on word-level matching. Leveraging datasets composed of EU directives and UK regulations, which can serve both as queries and documents (i.e., a UK law is relevant to the EU directives it transposes, and vice versa), the authors reported on very good results (i.e., averaging over different queries, approximately 86.5% of the documents that are retrieved on the top 100 positions are relevant) with a system that combines standard BM25 retrieval with result re-ranking through a neural language model fine-tuned to documents and specific tasks from the legal domain.

2.4 Information Extraction

Information extraction concerns automatically gathering and structuring important facts from textual documents (e.g., about specific types of events, or about entities and relationships between previously defined entities), facilitating the development of higher-level applications, in the sense that these can now focus on the analysis of structured information, as opposed to unstructured or semi-structured traditional legal texts. Several studies (Chalkidis et al. 2019c; Hendrycks et al. 2021) have explored information extraction from contracts, e.g. to extract information elements such as the contracting parties, agreed payment amount, start and end dates, or applicable law. Other studies focused on extracting information from legislation (Angelidis et al. 2018) or court cases (Leitner et al. 2019).

2.5 Summarization

A text summary conveys to the reader the most relevant content of one or more textual information sources, in a concise and comprehensible manner. The goal of a text summarization system is to automatically create such a document. This new document, the summary, is characterized by several aspects, such as the origin of the content, the number of input units, or the coverage of the summary. Regarding its content, a summary might be composed by extracts—*extractive summarization*—, directly taken from the input, or paraphrases—*abstractive summarization*—, which convey the content of a passage of the input using a different wording. In relation to the number of input units, if the input consists of only one document, the task is designated *single-document summarization*, when dealing with several input documents, the problem is named as *multi-document summarization*. Finally, concerning the coverage of the input source(s), it can be comprehensive, when creating generic summaries, or selective, if driven by an input query.

Several difficulties arise when addressing this task, but one of utmost importance is how to assess the relevant content. Different methods have been explored since the first experiments reported by Luhn (1958) and Edmundson (1969). They established an important research direction, which can be named as feature-based passage scoring, which explored features based on term weighting, sentence position, sentence length, or linguistic information. In the 2000s, centrality-based methods (Radev et al. 2004; Erkan and Radev 2004; Zhu et al. 2007; Kurland and Lee 2010; Ribeiro and de Matos 2011), independently of the underlying representation, attracted much attention. Geometric centroids, graph-based ranking methods, or, in general, representations in which "recommended" passages were the focus of this line of work. All of these were unsupervised approaches, in which we can also include important methods such as Maximal Marginal Relevance (Carbonell and Goldstein 1998) or Latent Semantic Analysis-based (Gong and Liu 2001) methods. In addition to these kind of approaches, some supervised methods were also explored (Wong et al. 2008). Recently, most of the research on this topic has been based on neural networks, with sequence-to-sequence models attracting a significant amount of attention (Rush et al. 2015; See et al. 2017; Celikyilmaz et al. 2018), as well as work using pre-trained language models as encoders (Liu and Lapata 2019; Manakul and Gales 2021).

In what concerns legal document summarization, some of the oldest work goes back to 2004. Farzindar and Lapalme (2004) present an approach to generate short summaries of records of the proceedings of federal courts in Canada. This work focused on extracting the most important textual units, following a feature-based passage scoring approach. The pipeline includes a thematic segmentation specifically directed at legal documents, aimed at discovering the structure of the judgment record. This segmentation is followed by filtering and selection stages. The former filters out citations and other noisy content and the latter extracts textual units based on their score, computed using features such as the position of the paragraphs in the document, the position of the paragraphs in the thematic segment, the position of the sentences in the paragraph, the distribution of the words in the document, and TF-IDF. Closely related to this work, is the system proposed by Hachey and Grover (2006), in the sense that these authors also develop a classifier for rhetorical information. The extraction of relevant sentences is also cast as a classification problem, following a supervised machine learning-based approach. Features such as location, thematic words, sentence length, quotation level, entities, and cue phases are explored in both a Naïve Bayes classifier and a Maximum Entropy classifier.

More recent work in legal document summarization followed the same trend we observe in generic automatic text summarization and natural language processing in general, which means that it is based on neural networks and pre-trained language models. The work reported by Glaser et al. (2021a) focuses on German court rulings. The system includes a dedicated pre-processing step where norms, anonymization tokens, and references to other legal documents, for instance, are addressed. Concerning the summarization method, the authors explored both extractive and abstractive approaches. Word are encoded using GloVe embeddings (Pennington et al. 2014) and for sentence representation three approaches are explored: CNN, GRU, or attention. The final sentence representation is given by a cross-sentence CNN or RNN that captures information from neighboring sentences. The selection score is given by a sigmoid function. The abstractive approach is similar, but instead of using a cross-sentence CNN or RNN, the sentence embeddings are aggregated using a RNN, creating an embedding for the document. The approach follows an encoder-decoder structure. As expected, the abstractive approaches had a worst performance when compared to extractive approaches and baselines, even considering older, centrality-based, approaches such as LexRank. The proposed extractive approaches achieved the best results showing that neural networks-based approaches are also adequate for specific domains.

An interesting work based on pre-trained language models is the system proposed in Savelka and Ashley (2021). Their work is closely related to summarization, but instead they focus on the idea of how well a sentence explains a legal concept, based on data from the Caselaw access project (U.S.A. legal cases from different types of courts). The selected data was human classified into four categories: high value, certain value, potential value, and no value. They fine-tuned RoBERTa (Liu et al. 2019), a model derived from the well-known BERT (Devlin et al. 2019), as the base for their experiments. They explore three approaches: one that predicts the class using only the input sentence; the second approach uses the pair legal concept-sentence; and, finally, the last variation is based on the pair composed by "the whole provision of written law" and the sentence. One important conclusion is that, given the success of the first experiment, sentences carry information about their usefulness, which is strongly related to understanding if a sentence is a good candidate to be in a summary.

2.6 Question Answering and Conversational Systems

Legal question answering concerns the retrieval and analysis of information within knowledge repositories (e.g., large document collections), so as to provide accurate answers to legal questions. Typical users for legal question answering systems can include litigators seeking answers to case-specific legal questions (Khazaeli et al. 2021), or laypersons seeking to better understand their legal rights (Ravichander et al. 2019).

The task requires identifying relevant legislation, case law, or other legal documents, and extracting the elements within those documents that answer a particular question. In some cases, the extracted information elements also need to be further summarized into a concise answer. As evident from the previous problem definition, legal question answering typically involves combining techniques from information retrieval and extraction, and the aforementioned Competition on Legal Information Extraction and Entailment has also been a notable venue for reporting advances in this domain.

On what regards industrial applications, it is interesting to note that companies such as IBM Watson Legal, LegalMation, or Ross Intelligence have developed custom question answering commercial products based on Watson, i.e. a question answering system developed by IBM that, in 2011, won the Jeopardy challenge against the TV quiz show's two biggest all-time champions (Ferrucci et al. 2010). Watson's architecture features a variety of NLP technologies, including parsing, question classification, question decomposition, automatic source acquisition and evaluation, entity and relation detection, logical form generation, and knowledge representation and reasoning. After the success in Jeopardy, the system was reorganized and commercialized, by combining and customizing its specific modules to specific domains and tasks (i.e., not just question answering, but also other tasks).

2.7 Predictions Supported on Textual Evidence

The idea that computers can predict the outcome of legal cases goes back to the early 60s, where Lawlor (1963) considers "the analysis and prediction of judicial decisions" one of the most important tasks to which computer technology can contribute. However, most of the work on the task is not that old. In fact, we can understand the difficulty of the endeavor as even recent literature overviews (e.g., Robaldo et al. 2019) focusing on natural language understanding in the legal domain address topics like resource construction or simple information extraction tasks.

In 2004, Ruger et al. (2004) compare the performance of classification trees against a group of legal experts to predict the outcome of the 2002 Term of the United States Supreme Court. The used features were the following: the provenience of the case until it reached the Supreme Court, the issue area of the case, the type of petitioner, the type of respondent, the lower court ruling political orientation (liberal or conservative), and the claim of unconstitutionality of a law or practice by the petitioner. The results were surprising: the automatic method correctly predicted 75% of the Court's affirm/reverse outcomes, while the experts accuracy was only of 59.1%. The best results were achieved for economic activity cases and the worst for federalism, where the accuracy for both the experts and the automatic approach was similar.

A different two-step approach was followed by Brüninghaus and Ashley (2005), focusing on textual information. The first step extracts a representation of the legal case, based on its words (a bag-of-words representation obtained by removing punctuation, numbers and stop words); named entity recognition (where names and case specific instances are replaced by their type); and syntactic relations. This representation is submitted to a set of classifiers that capture several aspects that are used to represent the cases, designated as Factors (e.g., *Agreed-Not-To-Disclose*, *Security-Measures*, or *Agreement-Not-Specific*). The used data consisted in the Trade Secret Law knowledge base, which includes 146 cases from the CATO system, an intelligent learning environment for new students that begin studying law, already represented in terms of Factors (Alaven 1997). The second step predicts the legal outcome based on the Factors representation, using case-based reasoning (Bruninghaus and Ashley 2003).

Focusing in the European Court of Human Rights and exploring only textual content, Aletras et al. (2016) experiment with Support Vector Machines classifiers (linear kernel) based on n-gram and topic-based representations. The goal is to predict if a certain case violates a specific article of the Convention, achieving accuracy rates close 80% in this binary classification problem. Şulea et al. (2017) also use Support Vector Machines classifiers (linear kernel), but concentrate on the French Supreme Court (*Cour de Cassation*) rulings. The authors address three tasks:

Language Technologies in the Legal Domain

predicting the law area of a case, predicting the court ruling, and estimating when a case description and a ruling were issued. Preprocessing included the removal of diacritics and punctuation and the lowercasing of all the words. Features consisted of unigrams and bigrams. In what concerns predicting the court ruling, two variations of the task considering six (first-word ruling) and eight (full ruling) classes were addressed. Results were promising as in both experiments the proposed approach achieved f1 scores and accuracies over 90%.

As previously mentioned, most of the work on this topic is recent and thus explores deep neural network models. Chalkidis et al. (2019a) explore different network architectures—a bidirectional Gated Recurrent Units with self-attention-based architecture, a hierarchical attention network, a label-wise attention network, and two BERT-based architectures (a regular and a hierarchical version)—to predict the violation of articles of the European Court of Human Rights. Differently from Aletras et al. (2016), they do not restrict to specific articles, additionally exploring a multi-label classification view of the task. The simple BERT-based approach was the poorest performing architecture, with the best results being achieved by hierarchical architectures. Confirming the importance of hierarchical approaches, Zhu et al. (2020) also explore a hierarchical attention network-based architecture in legal judgment prediction in the context of criminal cases published by the Chinese government from China Judgment Online. Alghazzawi et al. (2022) combine a long short-term memory with a convolutional neural network to address the same problem as Ruger et al. (2004), i.e., to predict the affirm/reverse/other outcome of the US Supreme Court rulings.

Finally, Medvedeva et al. (2022) provide an interesting overview of this topic, while addressing relevant concepts clarification. The authors argue that a clear and well-defined terminology is important for the advancement of the research in this topic, namely distinguishing between three different tasks: outcome identification, outcome-based judgment categorization, and outcome forecasting.

2.8 Summary

This section described the development status of language technologies targeting various legal text processing tasks. Although our survey has mostly focused on recent academic developments, a large number of companies, including hundreds of start-ups, are also currently operating in the emerging "Legal AI" industry, providing text analytics services that target a wide variety of use cases that are currently poorly handled, e.g. due to the excessive amount of data (i.e., documents) that poses challenges for human analysis. In all the surveyed tasks, recent developments associated to deep learning methods (e.g., pre-trained neural language models specifically targeting legal text) have brought forward significant improvements. Current challenges in the area relate, for instance, to the combination of deep neural networks with knowledge-based methods (e.g., to improve interpretability and to better account with expert knowledge and legal reasoning), or to techniques enabling a better control of potential biases in model results (e.g., gender biases or racial discrimination).

3 Spoken Language Technologies

The use of spoken language technologies in the legal domain is also becoming increasingly pervasive, mostly because of the significant increase in performance achieved by deep learning techniques. This justifies a review of this recent progress and its impact in the legal domain.

3.1 *Automatic Speech Recognition*

The state of the art in automatic speech recognition (ASR) before the advent of deep learning was predominantly based on the GMM-HMM paradigm (Gaussian Mixture Models - Hidden Markov Models). By feeding these acoustic models with perceptually meaningful features, and combining them with additional knowledge sources provided by n-gram language models and lexical (or pronunciation) models, one achieved word error rates (WER) that made ASR systems usable for certain tasks. Dictation was one of these tasks, most particularly for the legal and healthcare domains (e.g. radiology reports), characterized by clean recording conditions and relatively formal documents. Acoustic models could be adapted to the speaker, and lexical and language models could be adapted to the domain, allowing the use of ASR by lawyers for dictating documents, case notes, briefs, contracts and correspondence. However, the uptake of such applications was not significant and depended heavily on the availability of resources to train models for different languages/accents.

For nearly three decades, progress was relatively stale for ASR, until the emergence of the so-called 'hybrid paradigm', that pairs deep neural networks with HMMs. Nowadays, models trained with nearly 1000 h of read audiobooks achieve a WER of 3.8%, an unthinkable result a decade ago. As in many other AI domains, fully end-to-end architectures have also been proposed to perform the entire ASR pipeline (Karita et al. 2019), with the exception of feature extraction, but the performance is significantly worse when training data is short. In fact, *There is no data like more data* is a citation from an ASR researcher back in the 80s, which is still valid nowadays, representing a huge challenge when porting to another domain.

Transcribing audiobooks or dictating legal documents are relatively easy tasks for ASR systems. Their application to conversational speech is much more challenging, with error rates that are almost triple the above results. The presence of other factors such as non-native accents, or distant microphones in a meeting room, may also have a very negative impact.

Language Technologies in the Legal Domain

All these challenges motivate the use of a panoplia of machine learning approaches: audio augmentation (Park et al. 2019; Ko et al. 2015), transfer learning (Abad et al. 2020), multi-task learning (Pironkov et al. 2016), etc. Also worth mentioning are the recent unsupervised approaches that leverage speech representations to segment unlabeled audio and learn a mapping from these representations to phonemes via adversarial training (Baevski et al. 2021).

This enormous boost in ASR performance has had a great impact in the legal domain. For dictation in this domain where training data has been increasingly amassed, several companies now claim WERs below 1%, announcing streamlined ways to dictate documents, 3–5 times faster than typing, altogether reducing liability and compliance. This progress was particularly relevant during the recent pandemic which has forced more lawyers to work remotely, without an easy access to pools of typists.

But the use of ASR in the legal domain is not at all restricted to the dictation task. Transcribing video and audio evidence into legal transcripts is an increasingly essential task for presenting in court, for making appeals, etc. The manual process can take up more than 5 times real time, which is a significant motivation for speeding it up by correcting an automatic transcript instead of transcribing from scratch. Transcribing audio court proceedings is another increasingly common use of ASR in the legal domain. Spotting keywords in tapped conversations may also be particularly relevant for intelligence services.

Besides the above-mentioned challenges of recognizing spontaneous speech, all these types of transcript require a previous task of speaker diarization - recognizing who spoke when (Tumminia et al. 2021). This task is closely related to automatic speaker recognition and may be particularly complex in scenarios where speaker overlap is frequent.

Due to their high complexity, ASR systems typically run in the cloud. In personal voice assistants, the task of spotting the wake up keyword when they are in the "always listening mode" is done on device using much less complex approaches. There is a growing public awareness of the privacy concerns over this "always listening mode". Requests for these recordings by suspects who would like to present them as proof in court have been so far denied by companies such as Amazon.[5]

3.2 Speaker Recognition and Speaker Profiling

The importance of identifying speakers in recordings has been realised by law enforcement agencies and intelligence services who used to rely in experts to manually analyse the so-called 'voice prints', long before automatic speaker

---

[5] https://techcrunch.com/2016/12/27/an-amazon-echo-may-be-the-key-to-solving-a-murder-case/.

recognition systems reached the performance levels that allowed their use in such a domain. Much of this recent progress may be attributed to representation learning, the so-called 'speaker embeddings', which encode the speaker characteristics of an utterance of variable duration into a fixed-length vector. The most popular technique for achieving this compact representation is currently the x-vector approach (Snyder et al. 2016). These embeddings are extracted from the hidden layers of deep neural networks, when they are trained to distinguish over thousands of speakers. In fact, this approach has been applied to Voxceleb,[6] a multimodal corpus of YouTube clips that includes over 7000 speakers of multiple ethnicities, accents, occupations and age groups, reaching impressive equal error rates (EER) close to 3%. This metric derives its name from corresponding to a threshold for which the false positive and false negative error rates are equal. Confidence measures may be particularly important in the legal context.

The area of speaker profiling is one of the most recent ones in speech processing. Speech is a biometric signal that reveals, in addition to the meaning of words, much information about the user, including his/her preferences, personality traits, mood, health, and political opinions, among other data such as gender, age range, height, accent, etc. Moreover, the input signal can be also used to extract relevant information about the user environment, namely background sounds. Powerful machine learning classifiers can be trained to automatically detect speaker traits that may be of particular importance to law enforcement agencies and intelligence services.

These endless possibilities for profiling speakers from their voices raise many privacy concerns about the misuse of such technologies.

3.3 Speech Synthesis and Voice Conversion

A decade ago, the state of the art in text-to-speech (TTS) was dominated by concatenative techniques that selected the best segments to join together from a huge corpus of sentences read by a single speaker. The concatenative synthesis module was typically preceded by a complex chain of linguistic processing modules which took text as input and produced a string of phonemes together with the prosodic information that specified the derived intonation. Despite significant improvements, namely through the use of hybrid approaches (Qian et al. 2013) that combined statistical parametric and concatenative techniques, the synthetic speech quality was still very different in naturalness from human speech, expressiveness was very limited, and the costs of building new synthetic voices were often prohibitive.

A major breakthrough was achieved in the mid 2010s by replacing the traditional concatenative synthesis module by a deep neural network module that took as input time-frequency spectrogram representations (van den Oord et al. 2016).

---

[6] https://www.robots.ox.ac.uk/~vgg/data/voxceleb/.

Later, the whole paradigm changed to encoder-decoder architectures, with attention mechanisms mapping the linguistic time scale to the acoustic time scale (Shen et al. 2018).

These advances led to multi-speaker TTS systems leveraging speaker embeddings, and opened the possibility of building synthetic voices with only a few seconds of a new voice, using for instance, flow-based models (Kim et al. 2020; Casanova et al. 2021). The synthetic speech quality became very close to human speech, reaching values above 4 on a scale of 1–5, the so-called 'Mean Opinion Score' (MOS) scale.

The possibility of disentangling linguistic contents and speaker embeddings was indeed crucial not only for text-to-speech systems but for voice conversion (VC) systems as well. In VC, the input is speech instead of text and the goal may be changing the voice identity, the emotion, the accent, etc.

This disentanglement can be achieved using, for instance, variational auto-encoder schemes, in which the linguistic content encoder learns a latent code from the source speaker speech, and the speaker encoder learns the speaker embedding from the target speaker speech. At run-time, the latent code and the speaker embedding are combined to generate speech in the voice of the target speaker. Nowadays, new approaches try to factor in prosody embeddings or style embeddings as well.

Moreover, the artificial voice may not correspond to a target speaker but, for instance, to an average of a set speaker embeddings selected among the ones farthest from the original speaker embedding. This is in fact one of the many approaches proposed for speaker anonymization.

The repercussions of this progress in TTS/VC in the legal framework are potentially huge since it can be used for the purposes of incrimination, defamation or misinformation. Detecting a *deep fake* voice from an original voice will be increasingly more difficult and one may wonder when audio evidence will no longer be admissible in court. At the same time, impersonating speakers may lead to crimes that were not feasible with the technologies we had a decade ago. In fact major thefts have already been reported.[7]

On the other hand, synthetic voices may be used for attacking (or spoofing) automatic speaker verification systems. In fact, as the quality of TTS/VC with very little spoken material from a target speaker increases, the need for more sophisticated anti-spoofing also grows concurrently. Last but not least, one should also mention the possibility of hidden voice commands, injected in the input signal. This threat has always existed, namely through exploiting the fact that the human hear could not detect certain signals. But nowadays adversarial attacks raise this threat to a new level, making us aware of how vulnerable deep learning techniques may be to the perturbation of a classifier's input at test time such that the classifier outputs a wrong prediction. In the past, such perturbation was in

---

[7] https://www.washingtonpost.com/technology/2019/09/04/an-artificial-intelligence-first-voice-mimicking-software-reportedly-used-major-theft/.

most cases perceptible, but with adversarial attacks one can now generate highly imperceptible perturbations that are extremely effective in misleading either speaker or speech recognition systems. Such techniques are just one example of the endless possibilities for misuse of the AI driven speech technologies. We have barely touched the surface, in terms of attacks that may target speech-based apps.

4 Conclusions

This chapter tried to do give a very condensed overview of language technologies for the legal domain, running the risk of very soon becoming outdated, such is the tremendous progress in the field nowadays. The brief overview of these recent advances may be misleading, giving the impression that embedding-based methods will solve all classes of problems whether for written or spoken language processing in the legal domain, provided there are large-enough training datasets. In fact, many researchers are working on machine learning alternatives (e.g. zero-shot or few-shot learning) to cope with tasks for which such datasets are not available. However, combining embedded-based approaches with symbol-based methods remains a challenge that may significantly contribute to greater interpretability.

Another challenge to be addressed by the forthcoming generation of AI legal tools is keeping track of changing regulations by propagating the consequences of these changes on those issues that depend on them, since it requires a smooth integration of embedded-based and symbol-based approaches.

With progress also comes a greater awareness of the ethical issues of language technologies in the legal domain. In particular, in what concerns gender bias and racial discrimination, which may be extremely important for tasks such as judgement prediction.

We have also alerted to the potential misuse of speech technologies for impersonation or spoofing and last but not least to the privacy issues that are involved in the remote processing of a signal such as speech that must be legally regarded as PII (Personally Identifiable Information).

Acknowledgments This work was supported by national funds through Fundação para a Ciência e a Tecnologia (FCT) with references UIBD/50021/2020 and CMU/TIC/0069/2019, and by the P2020 project MAIA (contract 045909).

References

Abad A, Bell P, Carmantini A, Renals S (2020) Cross lingual transfer learning for zero-resource domain adaptation. In: 2020 IEEE International conference on acoustics, speech and signal processing (ICASSP), pp 6909–6913. https://doi.org/10.1109/ICASSP40776.2020.9054468

Alaven V (1997) Teaching case-based argumentation through a model and examples. Ph.D Thesis, University of Pittsburgh

Language Technologies in the Legal Domain

Aletras N, Tsarapatsanis D, Preoţiuc-Pietro D, Lampos V (2016) Predicting judicial decisions of the European court of human rights: A natural language processing perspective. PeerJ Comput Sci 2:e93

Alghazzawi D, Bamasag O, Albeshri A, Sana I, Ullah H, Asghar MZ (2022) Efficient prediction of court judgments using an LSTM+CNN neural network model with an optimal feature set. Mathematics 10(5). https://doi.org/10.3390/math10050683. https://www.mdpi.com/2227-7390/10/5/683

Angelidis I, Chalkidis I, Koubarakis M (2018) Named entity recognition, linking and generation for Greek legislation. In: JURIX, pp 1–10

Avram AM, Păis V, Tufis DI (2021) PyEuroVoc: a tool for multilingual legal document classification with EuroVoc descriptors. In: Proceedings of the international conference on recent advances in natural language processing (RANLP 2021), pp 92–101

Baevski A, Hsu WN, Conneau A, Auli M (2021) Unsupervised speech recognition. Preprint, ArXiv 2105.11084

Bhattacharya P, Ghosh K, Ghosh S, Pal A, Mehta P, Bhattacharya A, Majumder P (2019) FIRE 2019 AILA track: artificial intelligence for legal assistance. In: Proceedings of the 11th forum for information retrieval evaluation. Association for Computing Machinery, New York, NY, USA, FIRE '19, pp 4–6. https://doi.org/10.1145/3368567.3368587

Boella G, Caro LD, Humphreys L, Robaldo L, Rossi P, van der Torre L (2016) Eunomos, a legal document and knowledge management system for the web to provide relevant, reliable and up-to-date information on the law. Artif. Intell. Law 24(3):245–283

Bruninghaus S, Ashley KD (2003) Predicting outcomes of case based legal arguments. In: Proceedings of the 9th international conference on artificial intelligence and law. Association for Computing Machinery, ICAIL '03, pp 233–242. https://doi.org/10.1145/1047788.1047838

Brüninghaus S, Ashley KD (2005) Generating legal arguments and predictions from case texts. In: Sartor G (ed) The tenth international conference on artificial intelligence and law, proceedings of the conference, June 6–11, 2005, Bologna, Italy, ACM, pp 65–74. https://doi.org/10.1145/1165485.1165497

Carbonell JG, Goldstein J (1998) The use of MMR, diversity-based reranking for reordering documents and producing summaries. In: Croft WB, Moffat A, van Rijsbergen CJ, Wilkinson R, Zobel J (eds) SIGIR '98: proceedings of the 21st annual international ACM SIGIR conference on research and development in information retrieval, August 24–28 1998, Melbourne, Australia, ACM, pp 335–336. https://doi.org/10.1145/290941.291025

Casanova E, Shulby C, Gölge E, Müller NM, de Oliveira FS, Candido Jr A, da Silva Soares A, Aluisio SM, Ponti MA (2021) SC-GlowTTS: an efficient zero-shot multi-speaker text-to-speech model. In: Interspeech, pp 3645–3649. https://doi.org/10.21437/Interspeech.2021-1774

Celikyilmaz A, Bosselut A, He X, Choi Y (2018) Deep communicating agents for abstractive summarization. In: Proceedings of the 2018 conference of the North American chapter of the association for computational linguistics: human language technologies. Association for computational linguistics, New Orleans, Louisiana, vol 1 (Long Papers), pp 1662–1675. https://doi.org/10.18653/v1/N18-1150. https://aclanthology.org/N18-1150

Chalkidis I, Androutsopoulos I, Aletras N (2019a) Neural legal judgment prediction in English. In: Proceedings of the 57th annual meeting of the association for computational linguistics, association for computational linguistics, Florence, Italy, pp 4317–4323. https://doi.org/10.18653/v1/P19-1424. https://aclanthology.org/P19-1424

Chalkidis I, Fergadiotis E, Malakasiotis P, Androutsopoulos I (2019b) Large-scale multi-label text classification on EU legislation. In: Proceedings of the annual meeting of the association for computational linguistics, pp 6314–6322

Chalkidis I, Fergadiotis M, Malakasiotis P, Androutsopoulos I (2019c) Neural contract element extraction revisited. In: Workshop on document intelligence at NeurIPS 2019

Chalkidis I, Fergadiotis M, Kotitsas S, Malakasiotis P, Aletras N, Androutsopoulos I (2020a) An empirical study on large-scale multi-label text classification including few and zero-shot labels. Preprint, arXiv:201001653

Chalkidis I, Fergadiotis M, Malakasiotis P, Aletras N, Androutsopoulos I (2020b) LEGAL-BERT: The muppets straight out of law school. In: Findings of the association for computational linguistics: EMNLP 2020, pp 2898–2904

Chalkidis I, Fergadiotis M, Androutsopoulos I (2021a) Multieurlex-a multi-lingual and multi-label legal document classification dataset for zero-shot cross-lingual transfer. In: Proceedings of the conference on empirical methods in natural language processing, pp 6974–6996

Chalkidis I, Fergadiotis M, Manginas N, Katakalou E, Malakasiotis P (2021b) Regulatory compliance through Doc2Doc information retrieval: A case study in EU/UK legislation where text similarity has limitations. Preprint, arXiv:210110726

Chalkidis I, Jana A, Hartung D, Bommarito M, Androutsopoulos I, Katz DM, Aletras N (2021c) Lexglue: a benchmark dataset for legal language understanding in English. Preprint, arXiv:211000976

Chen H, Cai D, Dai W, Dai Z, Ding Y (2019) Charge-based prison term prediction with deep gating network. In: Proceedings of the conference on empirical methods in natural language processing and the international joint conference on natural language processing, pp 6362–6367

Choueka Y, Cohen M, Dueck J, Fraenkel AS, Slae M (1971) Full text document retrieval: Hebrew legal texts (report on the first phase of the responsa retrieval project). In: Proceedings of the 1971 international ACM SIGIR conference on information storage and retrieval. Association for Computing Machinery, pp 61–79. https://doi.org/10.1145/511285.511293

De Araujo PHL, de Campos TE, Braz FA, da Silva NC (2020) VICTOR: a dataset for Brazilian legal documents classification. In: Proceedings of the language resources and evaluation conference, pp 1449–1458

Devlin J, Chang MW, Lee K, Toutanova K (2019) BERT: pre-training of deep bidirectional transformers for language understanding. In: Proceedings of the 2019 conference of the North American chapter of the association for computational linguistics: human language technologies. Association for Computational Linguistics, Minneapolis, Minnesota, vol 1 (Long and Short Papers), pp 4171–4186. https://doi.org/10.18653/v1/N19-1423. https://aclanthology. org/N19-1423

Edmundson HP (1969) New methods in automatic extracting. J ACM 16(2):264–285. https://doi. org/10.1145/321510.321519

Eldridge WB, Dennis SF (1963) The computer as a tool for legal research. Law Contemp. Probl. 28:78–99

Erkan G, Radev DR (2004) Lexrank: graph-based lexical centrality as salience in text summarization. J Artif Intell Res 22:457–479. https://doi.org/10.1613/jair.1523

Farzindar A, Lapalme G (2004) Legal text summarization by exploration of the thematic structure and argumentative roles. In: Text summarization branches out, association for computational linguistics, Barcelona, Spain, pp 27–34. https://aclanthology.org/W04-1006

Ferrández O, South B, Shen S, Friedlin F, Samore M, Meystre S (2013) BoB, a best-of-breed automated text de-identification system for VHA clinical documents. J Am Med Inform Assoc 20(1):77–83

Ferrucci DA, Brown EW, Chu-Carroll J, Fan J, Gondek D, Kalyanpur A, Lally A, Murdock JW, Nyberg E, Prager JM, Schlaefer N, Welty CA (2010) Building Watson: an overview of the DeepQA project. AI Mag 31(3):59–79. https://doi.org/10.1609/aimag.v31i3.2303

Gardner J, Xiong L (2008) HIDE: an integrated system for Health information DE-identification. In: Computer-Based Medical Systems. IEEE Computer Society, Washington, pp 254–259

Glaser I, Moser S, Matthes F (2021a) Summarization of German court rulings. In: Proceedings of the natural legal language processing workshop 2021, association for computational linguistics, Punta Cana, Dominican Republic, pp 180–189. https://doi.org/10.18653/v1/2021.nllp-1.19. https://aclanthology.org/2021.nllp-1.19

Glaser I, Schamberger T, Matthes F (2021b) Anonymization of German legal court rulings. Association for Computing Machinery, New York, pp 205–209. https://doi.org/10.1145/3462757. 3466087

Gong Y, Liu X (2001) Generic text summarization using relevance measure and latent semantic analysis. In: Croft WB, Harper DJ, Kraft DH, Zobel J (eds) SIGIR 2001: Proceedings of the 24th annual international ACM SIGIR conference on research and development in information retrieval, September 9–13, 2001, New Orleans, Louisiana, USA, ACM, pp 19–25. https://doi.org/10.1145/383952.383955. https://doi.org/10.1145/383952.383955

Hachey B, Grover C (2006) Extractive summarisation of legal texts. Artif Intell Law 14(4):305–345. https://doi.org/10.1007/s10506-007-9039-z

Hendrycks D, Burns C, Chen A, Ball S (2021) CUAD: an expert-annotated NLP dataset for legal contract review. Preprint, arXiv:210306268

Karita S, Wang X, Watanabe S, Yoshimura T, Zhang W, Chen N, Hayashi T, Hori T, Inaguma H, Jiang Z, Someki M, Enrique N, Soplin Y, Yamamoto R (2019) A comparative study on transformer vs RNN in speech applications. In: IEEE automatic speech recognition and understanding workshop (ASRU), pp 449–456

Khazaeli S, Punuru J, Morris C, Sharma S, Staub B, Cole M, Chiu-Webster S, Sakalley D (2021) A free format legal question answering system. In: Proceedings of the natural legal language processing workshop 2021, pp 107–113

Kim J, Kim S, Kong J, Yoon S (2020) Glow-TTS: a generative flow for text-to-speech via monotonic alignment search. Preprint, ArXiv:2005.11129

Ko T, Peddinti V, Povey D, Khudanpur S (2015) Audio augmentation for speech recognition. In: Interspeech, pp 3586–3589. https://doi.org/10.21437/Interspeech.2015-711

Kurland O, Lee L (2010) Pagerank without hyperlinks: structural reranking using links induced by language models. ACM Trans Inf Syst 28(4):18:1–18:38. https://doi.org/10.1145/1852102.1852104

Lawlor RC (1963) What computers can do: analysis and prediction of judicial decisions. Am Bar Assoc J 49(4):337–344. http://www.jstor.org/stable/25722338

Leitner E, Rehm G, Moreno-Schneider J (2019) Fine-grained named entity recognition in legal documents. In: International conference on semantic systems. Springer, pp 272–287

Liu Y, Lapata M (2019) Text summarization with pretrained encoders. In: Inui K, Jiang J, Ng V, Wan X (eds) Proceedings of the 2019 conference on empirical methods in natural language processing and the 9th international joint conference on natural language processing, EMNLP-IJCNLP 2019, Hong Kong, China, November 3–7, 2019. Association for Computational Linguistics, pp 3728–3738. https://doi.org/10.18653/v1/D19-1387

Liu Y, Ott M, Goyal N, Du J, Joshi M, Chen D, Levy O, Lewis M, Zettlemoyer L, Stoyanov V (2019) Roberta: A robustly optimized BERT pretraining approach. CoRR abs/1907.11692. http://arxiv.org/abs/1907.11692

Locke D, Zuccon G (2022) Case law retrieval: problems, methods, challenges and evaluations in the last 20 years. Preprint, arXiv:220207209

Luhn HP (1958) The automatic creation of literature abstracts. IBM J Res Dev 2(2):159–165. https://doi.org/10.1147/rd.22.0159

Mamede N, Baptista J, Dias F (2016) Automated anonymization of text documents. In: 2016 IEEE congress on evolutionary computation (CEC), pp 1287–1294. https://doi.org/10.1109/CEC.2016.7743936

Manakul P, Gales MJF (2021) Long-span summarization via local attention and content selection. In: Zong C, Xia F, Li W, Navigli R (eds) Proceedings of the 59th annual meeting of the association for computational linguistics and the 11th international joint conference on natural language processing, ACL/IJCNLP 2021, vol 1 (Long Papers), Virtual Event, August 1–6, 2021. Association for Computational Linguistics, pp 6026–6041. https://doi.org/10.18653/v1/2021.acl-long.470

Medvedeva M, Wieling M, Vols M (2022) Rethinking the field of automatic prediction of court decisions. Artif. Intell. Law. https://doi.org/10.1007/s10506-021-09306-3

Nallapati R, Manning CD (2008) Legal docket classification: where machine learning stumbles. In: Proceedings of the 2008 conference on empirical methods in natural language processing, pp 438–446

Neamatullah I, Douglass M, Lehman L, Reisner A, Villarroel M, Long W, Szolovits P, Moody G, Mark R, Clifford G (2008) Automated de-identification of free-text medical records. BMC Medical Inform Decis Mak 8(1):1–17

van den Oord A, Dieleman S, Zen H, Simonyan K, Vinyals O, Graves A, Kalchbrenner N, Senior AW, Kavukcuoglu K (2016) WaveNet: a generative model for raw audio. CoRR abs/1609.03499

Papaloukas C, Chalkidis I, Athinaios K, Pantazi DA, Koubarakis M (2021) Multi-granular legal topic classification on Greek legislation. Preprint, arXiv:210915298

Park DS, Chan W, Zhang Y, Chiu CC, Zoph B, Cubuk ED, Le QV (2019) SpecAugment: a simple data augmentation method for automatic speech recognition. In: Interspeech, pp 2613–2617. https://doi.org/10.21437/Interspeech.2019-2680

Pennington J, Socher R, Manning CD (2014) Glove: global vectors for word representation. In: Moschitti A, Pang B, Daelemans W (eds) Proceedings of the 2014 conference on empirical methods in natural language processing, EMNLP 2014, October 25–29, 2014, Doha, Qatar. A meeting of SIGDAT, a Special Interest Group of the ACL, ACL, pp 1532–1543. https://doi.org/10.3115/v1/d14-1162

Pironkov G, Dupont S, Dutoit T (2016) Multi-task learning for speech recognition: an overview. In: ESANN - European symposium on artificial neural networks, computational intelligence and machine learning (ESANN), pp 189–194

Qian Y, Soong FK, Yan ZJ (2013) A unified trajectory tiling approach to high quality speech rendering. IEEE Trans Audio Speech Language Process 21(2):280–290. https://doi.org/10.1109/TASL.2012.2221460

Rabelo J, Goebel R, Kim MY, Kano Y, Yoshioka M, Satoh K (2022) Overview and discussion of the competition on legal information extraction/entailment (COLIEE) 2021. Rev Socionetwork Strategies 16, 111–133

Radev DR, Jing H, Sty M, Tam D (2004) Centroid-based summarization of multiple documents. Inf Process Manag 40(6):919–938. https://doi.org/10.1016/j.ipm.2003.10.006

Ravichander A, Black AW, Wilson S, Norton T, Sadeh N (2019) Question answering for privacy policies: Combining computational and legal perspectives. Preprint, arXiv:191100841

Ribeiro R, de Matos DM (2011) Centrality-as-relevance: Support sets and similarity as geometric proximity. J Artif Intell Res 42:275–308, https://doi.org/10.1613/jair.3387

Robaldo L, Villata S, Wyner A, Grabmair M (2019) Introduction for artificial intelligence and law: special issue "natural language processing for legal texts". Artif Intell Law 27(2):113–115. https://doi.org/10.1007/s10506-019-09251-2

Ruger TW, Kim PT, Martin AD, Quinn KM (2004) The supreme court forecasting project: legal and political science approaches to predicting supreme court decisionmaking. Columbia Law Rev 104(4):1150–1210

Rush AM, Chopra S, Weston J (2015) A neural attention model for abstractive sentence summarization. In: Màrquez L, Callison-Burch C, Su J, Pighin D, Marton Y (eds) Proceedings of the 2015 conference on empirical methods in natural language processing, EMNLP 2015, Lisbon, Portugal, September 17–21, 2015. The Association for Computational Linguistics, pp 379–389. https://doi.org/10.18653/v1/d15-1044

Sansone C, Sperlí G (2022) Legal information retrieval systems: state-of-the-art and open issues. Inf Syst 106:101967

Savelka J, Ashley KD (2021) Discovering explanatory sentences in legal case decisions using pre-trained language models. In: Moens M, Huang X, Specia L, Yih SW (eds) Findings of the association for computational linguistics: EMNLP 2021, Virtual Event/Punta Cana, Dominican Republic, 16–20 November, 2021. Association for Computational Linguistics, pp 4273–4283. https://doi.org/10.18653/v1/2021.findings-emnlp.361

See A, Liu PJ, Manning CD (2017) Get to the point: summarization with pointer-generator networks. In: Barzilay R, Kan M (eds) Proceedings of the 55th annual meeting of the association for computational linguistics, ACL 2017, Vancouver, Canada, July 30 - August 4, vol 1: Long Papers. Association for Computational Linguistics, pp 1073–1083. https://doi.org/10.18653/v1/P17-1099

Shen J, Pang R, Weiss RJ, Schuster M, Jaitly N, Yang Z, Chen Z, Zhang Y, Wang Y, Skerrv-Ryan R, Saurous RA, Agiomvrgiannakis Y, Wu Y (2018) Natural TTS synthesis by conditioning WaveNet on MEL spectrogram predictions. In: 2018 IEEE international conference on acoustics, speech and signal processing (ICASSP), pp 4779–4783. https://doi.org/10.1109/ICASSP.2018.8461368

Snyder D, Ghahremani P, Povey D, Garcia-Romero D, Carmiel Y, Khudanpur S (2016) Deep neural network-based speaker embeddings for end-to-end speaker verification. In: 2016 IEEE spoken language technology workshop (SLT), pp 165–170. https://doi.org/10.1109/SLT.2016.7846260

Şulea OM, Zampieri M, Vela M, van Genabith J (2017) Predicting the law area and decisions of French Supreme Court cases. In: Proceedings of the international conference recent advances in natural language processing, RANLP 2017, INCOMA Ltd., Varna, Bulgaria, pp 716–722. https://doi.org/10.26615/978-954-452-049-6_092

Sweeney L (1996) Replacing personally-identifying information in medical records, the Scrub system. In: Proceedings of the AMIA annual fall symposium. American Medical Informatics Association, pp 333–337

Tuggener D, von Däniken P, Peetz T, Cieliebak M (2020) LEDGAR: a large-scale multi-label corpus for text classification of legal provisions in contracts. In: Proceedings of the language resources and evaluation conference, european language resources association, pp 1228–1234

Tumminia J, Kuznecov A, Tsilerides S, Weinstein I, McFee B, Picheny M, Kaufman AR (2021) Diarization of legal proceedings. Identifying and transcribing judicial speech from recorded court audio. Preprint, arXiv:2104.01304

Uzuner Ö, Sibanda T, Luo Y, Szolovits P (2008) A de-identifier for medical discharge summaries. Artif Intell Med 42(1):13–35

Wellner B, Huyck M, Mardis S, Aberdeen J, Morgan A, Peshkin L, A Y, Hitzeman J, Hirschman J (2007) Rapidly retargetable approaches to de-identification in medical records. J Am Med Inform Assoc: JAMIA 14(5):564–573

Wilson RA (1962) Computer retrieval of case law. Southwest Law J 16:409–438

Wong KF, Wu M, Li W (2008) Extractive summarization using supervised and semi-supervised learning. In: Proceedings of the 22nd international conference on computational linguistics (Coling 2008), Coling 2008 Organizing Committee, Manchester, UK, pp 985–992. https://aclanthology.org/C08-1124

Xiao C, Zhong H, Guo Z, Tu C, Liu Z, Sun M, Zhang T, Han X, Hu Z, Wang H, et al. (2019) CAIL2019-SCM: a dataset of similar case matching in legal domain. Preprint, arXiv:191108962

Xiao C, Hu X, Liu Z, Tu C, Sun M (2021) Lawformer: a pre-trained language model for Chinese legal long documents. AI Open 2:79–84

Zhong H, Xiao C, Guo Z, Tu C, Liu Z, Sun M, Feng Y, Han X, Hu Z, Wang H, et al (2018) Overview of cail2018: legal judgment prediction competition. Preprint, arXiv:181005851

Zhong H, Xiao C, Tu C, Zhang T, Liu Z, Sun M (2020) How does nlp benefit legal system: a summary of legal artificial intelligence. In: Proceedings of the annual meeting of the association for computational linguistics, pp 5218–5230

Zhu X, Goldberg AB, Gael JV, Andrzejewski D (2007) Improving diversity in ranking using absorbing random walks. In: Sidner CL, Schultz T, Stone M, Zhai C (eds) Human language technology conference of the north american chapter of the association of computational linguistics, proceedings, April 22–27, 2007, Rochester, New York, USA. The Association for Computational Linguistics, pp 97–104. https://aclanthology.org/N07-1013/

Zhu K, Guo R, Hu W, Li Z, Li Y (2020) Legal judgment prediction based on multiclass information fusion. Complexity 2020:3089189. https://doi.org/10.1155/2020/3089189

Open Access This chapter is licensed under the terms of the Creative Commons Attribution 4.0 International License (http://creativecommons.org/licenses/by/4.0/), which permits use, sharing, adaptation, distribution and reproduction in any medium or format, as long as you give appropriate credit to the original author(s) and the source, provide a link to the Creative Commons licence and indicate if changes were made.

The images or other third party material in this chapter are included in the chapter's Creative Commons licence, unless indicated otherwise in a credit line to the material. If material is not included in the chapter's Creative Commons licence and your intended use is not permitted by statutory regulation or exceeds the permitted use, you will need to obtain permission directly from the copyright holder.

Societal Implications of Recommendation Systems: A Technical Perspective

Joana Gonçalves-Sá and Flávio Pinheiro

Abstract One of the most popular applications of artificial intelligence algorithms is in recommendation systems (RS). These take advantage of large amounts of user data to learn from the past to help us identify patterns, segment user profiles, predict users' behaviors and preferences. The algorithmic architecture of RS has been so successful that it has been co-opted in many contexts, from human resources teams, trying to select top candidates, to medical researchers, wanting to identify drug targets. Although the increasing use of AI can provide great benefits, it represents a shift in our interaction with data and machines that also entails fundamental social threats. These can derive from technological or implementation mistakes but also from profound changes in decision-making.

Here, we overview some of those risks including ethical and privacy challenges from a technical perspective. We discuss two particularly relevant cases: (1) RS that fail to work as intended and its possible unwanted consequences; (2) RS that work but at the possible expense of threats to individuals and even to democratic societies. Finally, we propose a way forward through a simple checklist that can be used to improve the transparency and accountability of AI algorithms.

1 Introduction

Much like the previous Industrial Revolutions, the Digital Revolution is sure to have enormous impact on society, at many different levels. By learning from the unparalleled amounts of individual-level data that is currently shared and collected, machines will be increasingly able to identify patterns, create profiles, predict

---

J. Gonçalves-Sá (✉)
LIP - Laboratório de Instrumentação e Física Experimental de Partículas, Lisbon, Portugal
e-mail: joanagsa@lip.pt

F. Pinheiro
IMS - Information Management School, Universidade Nova de Lisboa, Lisbon, Portugal
e-mail: fpinheiro@novaims.unl.pt

© The Author(s) 2024
H. Sousa Antunes et al. (eds.), *Multidisciplinary Perspectives on Artificial Intelligence and the Law*, Law, Governance and Technology Series 58,
https://doi.org/10.1007/978-3-031-41264-6_3

behaviors, and make decisions. Therefore, it is fundamental to understand the limitations of these tools to anticipate and minimize negative consequences.

In this chapter we focus on machine-learning (ML) models, particularly recommendation (or recommender) systems (RS), and how their use in decision-making processes can offer better services but also create important risks. Typically, RS refer to algorithms that recommend some item X to a user A, very often consumption goods (such as recommending a book the algorithm identifies as matching our interests) or in the context of social networks (a new friend or post); however, here we use this term in a broader sense, to refer to any algorithm that uses large datasets on people to identify similarity matches and recommend decisions, in many different contexts. First, we describe how RS work and their unavoidable limitations. Second, we focus on RS that work as intended and discuss how the creation of individual profiles can lead to abusive targeted advertisement and even to threats to democracy, from disinformation to state surveillance. Third, we describe what happens when these systems are faulty, but are still used to make probabilistic generalizations and aid in AI-based decision making. We will offer specific examples of how mistakes in data selection or coding might lead to discrimination and injustice. In the last section, we summarize some ideas on how to make AI more accountable and transparent and argue that the important decisions ahead should not be made by a limited group of non-elected AI leaders, but it should be the role of AI experts to raise awareness of such threats, paving the way for important regulatory decisions.

2 Recommendation Systems

The general goal of a recommendation systems is to predict, as accurately as possible, a new item to a user while optimizing for the rate of acceptance (Resnick and Varian 1997). These systems leverage information on users (demographic, past choices) and/or on items (for example, movies) to find accurate matches between them (ex: if you liked movie X you might like movie Y, or people "like you" have enjoyed book Z). At the core of RS is the assumption that items and/or users of a service can be mapped in terms of their similarities and that person A (or item X) can serve as proxy for person B (item Y). In that sense, a recommendation system suggests items that are closer in such similarity space to a user's past choices or revealed preferences and is only as good as it can provide the most accurate recommendation to a user (person A will actually enjoy movie Y and book Z).

Over the past decades we have seen an increase in use of ML/AI techniques to support the development and implementation of faster, more reliable, and more capable RS (Fayyaz et al. 2020). These are possible because of (a) large accumulation of data about users' past choices; (b) large datasets on details about items, and (c) increasingly sophisticated algorithms that take advantage of such data and take value from growing numbers of features and instances.

In general, recommendation systems can be divided into three big families: collaborative-base filtering (that tries to predict whether person A will like product X based on the preferences of "similar-person" B); content-based filtering (that tries to predict whether person A will like an item X based on person A's past revealed preferences for similar items); and hybrid systems, that combine both. In terms of the algorithms used, these are further divided on whether they are supported by heuristic- or model-based approaches.

Collaborative filtering (Herlocker et al. 2000) recommendation systems rely on the similarity between users to perform recommendations. That is, if user A and B are similar, then the past choices of B can shed light on what to recommend to user A. Hence, the core technical challenge is to estimate similarities between users or items from data on the revealed past preferences of users (ex. past favorite movies). This approach has been widely popular on web-based portals such as Netflix and Reddit where users' characteristics and up or down votes are used to estimate similarities. Popular algorithms range from Graph models of social networks (Bellogin and Parapar 2012) of similarity between users and Nearest Neighbor to the use of Linear regressions, Clustering techniques (Ungar and Foster 1998), Artificial Neural Networks (He et al. 2017) and Bayesian networks.

Often, auxiliary data is used to either improve collaborative filtering systems, or to overcome some of its limitations. Context information (e.g., location or time) can help systems achieve higher success and, in scenarios that have more users than items, recommendations are often done through an item-item similarity. Moreover, when past information on user activity is scarce (e.g., in the case of a new user of a new service), users' information about their social relationships and characteristics (e.g., gender, age, income, location, employment, etc.) can help these systems establish a similarity even without specific historical activity.

Content-based filtering (Lops et al. 2011; Aggarwal 2016) does not require information about users, instead it maps similarity between items to perform recommendations. In other words, users are recommended items similar to their past choices (person A likes vanilla milkshakes, thus might also like vanilla ice-cream). Algorithmically, these problems are approached using techniques that range from TF-IDF (Rigutini and Maggini 2004) and clustering for topic modelling and inference, but also using classification models based on Bayesian classifiers, Decision trees, and Artificial Neural Networks. A traditional application of these techniques is in book recommendation engines that measure content (Mooney and Roy 2000) similarity between books.

Hybrid solutions (Burke 2007) combine aspects of both content and collaborative filtering. They arise in situations where it is practical and beneficial to develop meta-algorithms to balance the recommendation stemming from a collaborative- and content-based systems. These increasingly use complex deep learning algorithms and are common in social media recommendations, including newsfeed content, advertisements, and friends (Naumov et al. 2019).

There are several limitations and problems associated with the development of RS. From the technical perspective, problems can arise at two extremes of the spectrum. First, lack of initial data can lead to a "cold start", that prevents the setup of the entire recommender system (ex. new movies that have not yet been rated by anyone or are from little known studios or directors) or limit the recommendations that can be given to new users. Second, when there is a "sparsity problem" and the number of items to be recommended is very large, the algorithm might lack scalability and users keep seeing the same few recommendations, either because they are the few most rated or because the individual users only rated a few (Adomavicius and Tuzhilin 2005). Third, and more conceptually, the implicit assumption in ML/AI solutions that the future can be predicted from past actions, renders them awkwardly unable to perform under novelty (e.g., expanding a service to a new cultural setting). Fourth, some models described above can learn from past mistakes (user A hated book Z after all) and, therefore, improve continuously, but this is not the case in several other examples of RS, sometimes with dire consequences. Important examples of the impact of the listed limitations will be discussed in more detail in the following sections.

3 When Recommendation Systems Work

3.1 Implications for Consumption

Although stemming from a seemingly intuitive and simple problem, recommendation systems have matured to highly complex algorithmic solutions that are able to leverage a multitude of data sources to improve services that underlie the success of some of the largest companies in the world. The success of RS, and their ubiquity, stems from their capability to enhance user retention and to seemingly help users find the relevant content for their profile. Moreover, it is already possible to extract information and patterns from both structured information (e.g. online shopping basket) and unstructured information (e.g., free text, images, and videos). As such, RS are improving faster and will offer more gains to content providers.

Naturally, the specifics of each system are largely dependent on their application context and goals. Take, for instance, Amazon which started using item-to-item approaches but currently leverages information from users' past orders, profile, and activity, to offer different types of personalized recommendations, from targeted e-mails to shopping recommendations (Smith and Linden 2017). In 2018, the consultancy company McKinsey estimated that Amazon's RS was responsible for 35% of its sales (MacKenzie et al. 2013). Netflix gained international fame among engineers and enthusiasts with the release, in 2006, of a dataset of 100 million users' movie ratings and offered a 1Million USD reward to the team that could develop the best RS. Ten years later, Netflix RS was estimated to be worth up to 1 billion USD (McAlone 2016) and to drive 75% of users' viewing choices (Vanderbilt 2013).

However, these large companies depend on using data freely and often willingly shared by their users, who might give away control of their privacy and decisions in exchange for convenience and productivity. In fact, we all know that our data is being used, but we may not know the extent to which this is happening or the problems it could pose (Englehardt and Narayanan 2016). First, and although these processes involve consent, terms of service are often unintelligible, sharing is not always voluntary, and might be a requirement to access content or services (Solomos et al. 2019; Urban et al. 2020). Second, and even when it is voluntary, it can have unexpected implications. In 2012, the New York Times reported a case in which the US-based chain Target generated predictions about the pregnancy of its customers, precisely by analyzing shopping profiles (Duhigg 2012). One such store was visited by a father, outraged that his teenage daughter had received promotions for baby products; later, when the store manager called to apologize, the man embarrassedly replied that his daughter was indeed pregnant: the supermarket chain knew before the family. Such anecdotical situations, corroborate our increasing reliance on such systems, which also makes us vulnerable to manipulation. For instance, nothing keeps online stores from showing more expensive products to people who did not previously compare prices online (Mikians et al. 2012). Indeed, different webservices commonly trade user information for marketing purposes, and it is common for a user that searches jeans on Amazon to be immediately targeted with jeans' ads on Facebook[1] or Google.[2] Importantly, these "surveillance systems" are so prevalent and increasingly sophisticated that even when you use caution when publishing online, that caution itself can be informative (Zuboff 2019).

As mentioned, the traditional application of RS is to drive the consumption of content and products and, as such, it represents the most common development of such algorithms (similarity identification, reliance on proxies, prediction of future outcomes). However, they also find application in other types of algorithmic decision-making (e.g., credit score, or financial trading) and we will use them in a broader context to further discuss their current implications.

3.2 Implications for Democracy

As described, RS can be very useful to direct people to products that interest them, be it movies or diapers. But there is a thin line between informing and manipulating, and this is particularly relevant when the promoted "goods" are news or ideas. Social networks, such as Facebook or Instagram, have been long known to promote addictive attention, even if at the cost of spreading disinformation (Del Vicario et al. 2016; Vosoughi et al. 2018), creating echo chambers (Nikolov et al. 2015; Quattrociocchi et al. 2016), increasing polarization (Flaxman et al. 2016), and

---

[1] See for example: "Help your ads reach the people who will love your business", by Facebook, 2021. https://pt-pt.facebook.com/business/ads/ad-targeting.

[2] See for example: "What are retargeting ads?", by Google Ads, 2021. https://ads.google.com/intl/en_uk/home/resources/retargeting-ads/.

threatening the user's mental health.[3] From researchers to data protection advocates, many have voiced concerns about the data that large platforms collect and how their recommendation systems can manipulate the information individuals are exposed to, be them prioritizing posts, or search engines displaying sponsored adds. In fact, Facebook offers any interested add-placer the possibility of selecting over tenths of individual characteristics, including (estimated) age or gender, level of education and in which subject, income-level, hobbies, political orientation (if from the US), travel profile, and even whether targets are away for the weekend with family or friends (Haidt and Twenge 2021).

The Cambridge Analytica case, in early 2018, brought to the public spotlight how, through refined individual profiling, political campaigns could influence the voting of target individuals or constituencies.[4] Political scientists have argued that the use of modern data science approaches to politics represented a significant shift from classical strategies: marketing techniques have been used in politics since at least the 1930s (O'Shaughnessy 1990), but the speed and increasing precision of AI tools means that political messages no longer need to be general and appeal to a broad constituency; instead, they can send highly personalized messages based on individual profiles, saying one thing to one demographic and the opposite to another, with very little scrutiny (Aldrich et al. 2015; Ribeiro et al. 2019; Silva et al. 2020). That some of these messages can include untrue information is even more worrisome. Naturally, the political use of misleading and even outright false information is nothing new, but the surge in online activity, coupled with poor digital literacy, and individual-level consumer profiling, has all the ingredients of a perfect storm. Disinformation spreading has found fertile ground on social networks, often through emotion manipulation, first shown to occur by Facebook itself (Kramer et al. 2014), and to work not only in the targeted individuals but also to contaminate their friends (Coviello et al. 2014). There is also increasing evidence that some individuals might be more susceptible to political disinformation than others (Pennycook and Rand 2021), with specific cognitive bias playing important roles.

In fact, personalized algorithms on search engines and social networks feeds might strengthen these already existing biases in at least three different ways: (1) as information is filtered based on past history (potentially magnifying availability biases, in which individuals tend to rate as more important things that they can more easily recall (Abbey 2018), and confirmatory tendencies, in which individuals seek or particularly trust in information that re-enforces or confirms their beliefs (Burtt 1939)); (2) as humans tend to associate with others similar to them and to favor people in one's own group, over people identified as belonging to outgroups

---

[3] This is a fast-growing field, with exposés becoming increasingly frequent. On mental health impacts there is an excellent ongoing open-source literature review posted and curated by Jonathan Haidt (NYU-Stern) and Jean Twenge (San Diego State U), Haidt and Twenge (2021); (Zuboff 2019).

[4] Cadwalladr and Graham-Harrison (2018).

Societal Implications of Recommendation Systems: A Technical Perspective 53

(ingroup bias) (Nelson 1989); and (3) with beliefs, biases, and even disinformation (McPherson et al. 2001) amplified and reinforced by this closed, homophilic communities, leading to the already mentioned echo chambers (Barberá et al. 2015; Flaxman et al. 2016; Quattrociocchi et al. 2016) and to increased online hostility and polarization (Yardi and Boyd 2010; Conover et al. 2021).

But political (mis)information is not the only kind to heavily impact on society and democracy. In April 2020, Facebook acknowledged that millions of its users saw false COVID19-related information on this platform (Ricard and Medeiros 2020); On Twitter, according to Yang et al. (2020), "the combined volume of tweets linking to low-credibility information was comparable to the volume of New York Times articles and CDC links"; by August 2021, YouTube had removed 1 million videos that included dangerous COVID-19 misinformation. Importantly, there is evidence that such misinformation impacted vaccination hesitancy (Loomba et al. 2021) and compliance with control measures (Roozenbeek et al. 2020), in line with the notion that misinformation often serves the goal of creating divisive content and leading to social unrest (Emmott 2020; Ricard and Medeiros 2020; Barnard et al. 2021; Silva and Benevenuto 2021). For much of 2020 and 2021, the world was fighting two pandemics in parallel: one caused by a virus, and another caused by fake news, supported by human bias and attention maximizing algorithms (Goncalves-Sa 2020).

Another very relevant risk comes from societal control. As described, politicians can use social networks and AI systems to target possible voters, but several leaders have also realized the much broader potential of AI, from improving public administration, to creating war robots. According to Vladimir Putin: "Artificial intelligence is the future, not only of Russia, but of all of mankind (. . .) Whoever becomes the leader in this sphere will become the ruler of the world." (Allen 2017) China hopes to be the leader by 2030 (Department of International Cooperation Ministry of Science and Technology (MOST) 2017) and is designing and implementing a large-scale social experiment, which involves using RS to classifying citizens according to their social behavior, only possible thanks to AI-driven facial recognition technology (Liang et al. 2018). These models have been increasingly used around the world,[5] often with security purposes. In 2020, the Israeli and US armies used AI to track and assassinate an Iranian physicist (Bergman and Fassihi 2021).

All these examples describe situations in which the RS are worrying because they work as intended, be it to improve consumption or to target voters. In the next chapter, we will focus on situations in which they fail and how that can have consequences for individuals and societies.

---

[5] For a collection of countries that legalized or are using facial recognition tools see for example https://surfshark.com/facial-recognition-map.

4 When Recommendation Systems Fail

The described recommendation systems use fine-grained information to train AI models to target specific individuals. Typically, what these systems do is output probabilities of a certain event and aid in decision-making. Examples can range from algorithms that calculate a risk score for depression (Reece et al. 2017; Eichstaedt et al. 2018), try to identify the best candidate for a given position (Paparrizos et al. 2011), or that recommend a movie based on previous choices (Bennett and Lanning 2007). These algorithms are trained on large training datasets, of variable quality, and "learn" by trial and error, with subjective definitions of error (for example, what "best candidate" means, must be represented as a mathematical object, when often "best" cannot be easily quantified). This means that there is no real distinction between the model, the data used to train it, and the assumptions that the coder made: if the data or the target are biased, the model will be biased. These bias might appear at different steps and have different consequences, but it is important to realize that: (1) it is virtually impossible to have a complete dataset and all datasets are samples, biased by the sampling process; (2) there are human decisions involved in defining targets; (3) targets often rely on proxies, (4) the predictions might turn into self-fulfilling prophecies because they frequently impact outcomes and it is often very difficult to have external validation. Again, this might be of little importance in the case of a user who never gets to seem movie X because it is not suggested, but very serious in the case of someone who gets a credit request denied and, consequentially, defaults on another payment: the system might find confirmation that the credit refusal was the best decision when indeed, it was what caused the default.

Consequently, there should be no illusions of "model neutrality". All models have problems, and acknowledging it is a fundamental and essential step to design mitigation strategies. In this section, we describe how biased data leads to biased algorithms, how biased algorithms can lead to discriminatory policies, and offer some examples from both the private and public sectors.

4.1 Learning from Biased Data: Implications for Individuals

As there is no perfect dataset, it is important to understand its limitations when training any algorithm with it. Let us think of a model to identify the best candidates to enter engineering school. One would start by collecting vast amounts of data, including grades, happiness scores, time to degree completion, previous education, future career, etc., on all students who have ever gone through a given university. This dataset would still have no information on how good the rejected candidates could have become (sampling bias) or on how many of them eventually suffered from burnout (limitations and subjectivity in feature selection): this means, that if the system systematically rejected promising candidates in the past, the algorithm is

Societal Implications of Recommendation Systems: A Technical Perspective

very likely to continue doing so in the future; and that if, for example, it values prizes over creating a safe work environment, it might pave the way for more accidents in the future. It is also easy to anticipate that such a dataset would be unbalanced in terms of gender and likely also age, ethnicity, nationality, and probability of wearing glasses, and so would the model predictions. In fact, several previous attempts at training such algorithms to select applicants, for schools or jobs, have led to discriminatory practices, stirring large discussions (O'Neil 2016). It is important to note that, very often, these algorithms are created not just for speeding up and automating processes, but also because we know that human-based systems are biased: the assumption is that models would be blind to color or gender and, thus, fairer. However, RS trained with biased data will generally be biased as well (Garcia 2016), and this is true even if models are trained on very large datasets. For example, the increasingly popular Chat GPT application was trained using 570 Gb of data, but most of this data was obtained through the internet, which is known to have an overrepresentation of some countries and age groups (Sheng et al. 2021).

An area in which such discrimination can have dire consequences is health. Kadambi (2021) have crucial sources of bias in medical devices, including computational bias, which happens when datasets used in clinical trials or when training algorithms to select candidates for such clinical trials, are biased. Historically, this has been the case for specific ethnical groups and women, often underrepresented in health datasets (and even in experimental protocols).

Biased datasets have also been shown to play important roles in classification and facial recognition (Buolamwini and Gebru 2018; Barlas et al. 2019). For example, Twitter dropped its picture cropping algorithm after suspicions of racial bias (Agrawal and Davis 2021) and both Flickr and Google algorithms tagged photos of black individuals as apes (Zhang 2015).

As disastrous as these examples are, it can be argued that they are the price to pay for the learning process: they are precautionary tales, reminding us that we are still at the infancy of machine decision-making and many other mistakes will be made before we can rely on algorithms. Unfortunately, and despite their current limitations, many are already being deployed, including in punitive environments, as described in the next section.

4.2 From Bad Algorithms to Discriminatory Policies

The individual consequences of a faulty Netflix algorithm are probably easy to minimize; models that select candidates for a given job can have much worse consequences, but nothing compares to when such algorithms are deployed in a large-scale punitive context. We already mentioned how the Chinese government is using facial recognition and other AI tools to evaluate citizens according to their behavior. If the system is faulty, the consequences for the individuals can be tremendous.

Another very debated example, that relies on proxies, is COMPAS, a proprietary algorithm that helps US judges set bails based on estimated risk scores of future offenses. In 2016, COMPAS was analyzed by ProPublica (Larson et al. 2016) and revealed to discriminate individuals based on their race: for similar offenses and crimes, black defendants were more likely to be given higher risk scores. Importantly, the datasets that were used to train the model did not include information on race: the model was possibly using zip code as a proxy for risk, thus picking it as a proxy the correlation between the ethnicity and economic status in US society (this analysis is disputed by the owning company and the extent of the discrimination is still being debated (Spielkamp 2017)).

Despite so many notable failures, governments around the world have been sponsoring the development of algorithms for use in public administration, in a variety of areas. These algorithms are often proprietary and function as a blackbox: not even the government officials know how they work and what justifies their recommendations, or risk scores. This leaves very little room for people to complain or even understand their "evaluation", raising fundamental legal questions. The Dutch government used such an algorithm, SyRI, from 2014 to 2020, when the Court of the Hague halted its use (Amnesty International 2021). It aimed at identifying social welfare fraud, was trained on large governmental datasets, and included information on virtually all inhabitants of The Netherlands. It would generate risks-scores and, if these were high, trigger an investigation. However, it was shown that the algorithm disproportionately and unfairly targeted poor and minority communities (Xenophobic Machines 2021), with consequences so dire that it led to the resignation of the Dutch government.

Such faulty algorithms have been increasingly revealed (Bandy 2021) but, naturally, it can be argued that they only reveal past and pre-existing bias, hidden in the data, and that human decision-making is equally discriminatory. While the first contention is very likely true, it still raises the important question of whether it is acceptable to perpetuate such discriminatory practices under an illusion of mathematical neutrality. The second is more interesting, as it is difficult to quantify whether humans or current algorithms are more discriminatory (Dressel and Farid 2018), but at least in the case of the examples described here, there are at least two good arguments in favor of the later. One is technical, as AI models identify dominant patterns and are more likely to exclude relevant outsiders (for example, the brilliant candidate from a very poor, black neighborhood). The other is scale, as human panels might have their own biases, but these might be different from panel to panel and there are human limits to how many applicants a panel can see; obviously, these limits and natural variation do not necessarily apply to machine decision-making (O'Neil 2016). A third, less studied possibility, is that algorithms, including commercial-like cookies, might be used to mask deliberate targeting of individuals by state actors, as in the case of the identification of minorities (Borgesius 2018). Therefore, there are serious concerns that algorithms trained on biased datasets will not only make biased decisions, they will also amplify existing societal discrimination and unfairness.

5 A Way Forward

There is much room for improvement of current and future RS (and AI in general), and we propose six steps, summarized in a simple mnemonic: (ATI) (Fayyaz et al. 2020). The first is recognizing that they are not neutral and can be very prone to bias. This **Acceptance** should be obvious, but it is still disputed by several in the field, typically contesting that they (a) are not biased as algorithms are blind to individuals, (b) are not more biased than non-algorithmic systems, or (c) that this a problem for social scientists and that engineers and programmers should not be concerned with such issues. In fact, most Data Science and Artificial Intelligence graduate programs still do not include Ethics or even Algorithmic Fairness courses, effectively training generations of students to ignore fundamental problems with datasets, algorithms and, consequentially, recommendation and decision systems they design and often implement. Such content should be compulsory in all formal AI education, taking us to the second step—**Training**.

Another fundamental issue is lack of **Inclusion** and Diversity. This is observed not only on the training datasets, as already discussed, but also in the coding teams. In "Racist in the Machine" (Reece et al. 2017), Megan Garcia describes some grave consequences of design blind spots and gives the example of four smartphone personal assistants (Siri, Google Now, Cortana, and S Voice), increasingly used for help in health and emergency situations, that could not recognize "I am being abused" or "I was beaten up by my husband". ML teams should be diverse and bring together people that work on different disciplines and that can contribute to both the technical and social components of algorithm design. Moreover, that algorithms try to find similarities can lead to polarization and homophily, but also to uniformization. As Thomas Homer-Dixon put it, "a simplified, uniform global culture will inevitably have less diversity of ideas and ingenuity that can help us cope with the great challenges we're facing" (Homer-Dixon 2001). Diversity should be a value at many different levels.

RS pipelines should also include streamlined Data **Auditing** and Debiasing: accepting it as an integral part of data processing pipelines, recognizes its importance for fair and effective AI, while reducing dataset bias. One of the first such efforts was developed by Pedro Saleiro and Rayid Ghani, through a data auditing algorithm, *Aequitas*, that inspects datasets for different types of demographic unbalances, including age, gender, and race (Saleiro et al. 2018). In all three datasets analyzed, they found important bias that affects the models results. These are excellent first efforts, but it is important to note that (a) we can only audit data in a very limited number of instances, and (b) that debiasing is even more challenging. For example, we can check gender-classified datasets for unbalances in gender (as in the hiring example described above), but this might be impossible to do in fully anonymized datasets or in datasets that simply do not include possibly relevant data as is often the case for ethnicity or physical disabilities. Even more critical, we cannot identify biases that we do not know we have, as a society: it might be the case that people with glasses are perceived as more competent for some jobs; as we are unaware of it, we would not include "having glasses" as a label and, even if we did, we would most likely not audit our algorithm for possible discrimination. But let us assume that complete auditing was possible and that all possible discriminatory imbalances in our dataset had been identified: we would still have important decisions to make regarding how to de-bias them. Continuing with the college admission example, it should be possible to understand that the model is being trained on a gender unbalanced dataset and that correcting for it would now lead to more women candidates being selected. But how big should the correction be? Should it reflect past ratios of engineering school admissions, perpetuating existing imbalances or should it aim for the same ratios observed in the population, effectively imposing a 50% gender quota? These and other example illustrate how many of these decisions can and are effectively being made, often implicitly, and how ill-informed attempts to correct bias might generate new forms of unfairness.

These decisions are fundamentally moral, helping to create a society by design. Thus, the final step should be **Transparency**. As Rhema Vaithianathan put it, "If you can't be right, be honest" (Courtland 2018). Blackbox algorithms, in which the process and features used to reach a decision are unknown or proprietary, should be avoided. However, they are increasingly used for two main reasons: first, it can be argued that if the decision process is known, individuals and companies could abuse and even rig the system on their behalf; second, the more complex the algorithms, as is the case with deep learning, the more difficult it is to understand the decision-making process. Therefore, it has been argued that such algorithms should only be used in positive environments and when they significant outperform traditional processes (e.g. for medical diagnosis), and never in punitive contexts (such as in the COMPAS and SyRI examples). In any case, individuals should always have the right to access, verify, correct errors, and appeal from algorithmic decisions. As these processes are often very complex, this generates an important tension, extensively noticed by the thinkers of the so-called "Risk Society" (Beck 1992), in which technical expertise is fundamental to design and control such systems, but this control should be put into effect by the, often lay, society. Therefore, the ones who understand the problems should also accept their political and social responsibility and engage in active **Interaction** with communities and decision-makers.

6 Conclusions

It should be increasingly obvious that using machine-based decisions is far from neutral, and that its problems have important societal implications. In this chapter, we summarized some limitations of recommendations systems, from both technical and conceptual perspectives, and offered examples of its past, ongoing, and possible future negative impacts. Overall, we argue that these risks should be understood

Societal Implications of Recommendation Systems: A Technical Perspective

by the general population, and we offer specific guidelines for improving RS and societal oversight.[6]

Acknowledgements We thank members of the Social Physics and Complexity Lab (SPAC-LIP) for comments and suggestions. Some of the examples described here had previously been presented in a series of 10 articles edited by one of the authors for the Portuguese newspaper Público: https://www.publico.pt/os-riscos-da-revolucao-digital. This work was partially supported by ERC-STG 853566 – FARE to JGS.

References

Abbey R (2018) #Republic: divided democracy in the age of social media, by Cass R. Sunstein. Am Polit Thought 7:370–373

Adomavicius G, Tuzhilin A (2005) Toward the next generation of recommender systems: a survey of the state-of-the-art and possible extensions. IEEE Trans Knowl Data Eng 17:734–749

Aggarwal CC (2016) Content-based recommender systems. In: Aggarwal CC (ed) Recommender systems: the textbook. Springer International Publishing, Cham, pp 139–166

Agrawal P, Davis D (2021) Transparency around image cropping and changes to come. https://blog.twitter.com/en_us/topics/product/2020/transparency-image-cropping. Accessed 28 Jan 2022

Aldrich JH, Gibson RK, Cantijoch M, Konitzer T (2015) Getting out the vote in the social media era: are digital tools changing the extent, nature and impact of party contacting in elections? Party Polit 22:165–178

Allen GC (2017) Putin and Musk are right: Whoever masters AI will run the world. https://www.cnn.com/2017/09/05/opinions/russia-weaponize-ai-opinion-allen/index.html. Accessed 28 Jan 2022

Amnesty International (2021) Discrimination through unregulated use of algorithms in the Dutch childcare benefits scandal. https://www.amnesty.org/en/wp-content/uploads/2021/10/EUR3546862021ENGLISH.pdf. Accessed 28 Jan 2022

Bandy J (2021) Problematic machine behavior: a systematic literature review of algorithm audits. Proc ACM Hum-Comput Interact 5:Article 74

Barberá P, Jost JT, Nagler J, Tucker JA, Bonneau R (2015) Tweeting from left to right: is online political communication more than an echo chamber? Psychol Sci 26:1531–1542

Barlas P, Kyriakou K, Kleanthous S, Otterbacher J (2019) Social B(eye)as: human and machine descriptions of people images. In: Dataset Papers of the Thirteen International AAAI conference on web and social media, Munich, Germany, 11—14 June 2019

---

[6] *See generally,* on the different applications of Machine Learning and AI, in this book A Oliveira and M A T Figueiredo - Artificial intelligence - historical context and state of the art; I Trancoso, N Mamede, B Martins, H S Pinto and R Ribeiro - The impact of language technologies in the legal domain; A T Freitas - Data-driven approaches in healthcare - challenges and emerging trends; M Correia and L Rodrigues - Security and Privacy; E Magrani and P G F Silva - The Ethical and Legal Challenges of Recommender Systems Driven by Artificial Intelligence; M Lanz and S Mijic - Risks associated with the use of natural language generation - Swiss civil liability law perspective; M S Fernandes and J R Goldim - Artificial Intelligence and Decision Making in Health - Risks and Opportunities; W Gravett - Judicial Decision-making in the Age of Artificial Intelligence; and D Durães, P M Freitas and P Novais - The Relevance of Deepfakes in the Administration of Criminal Justice.

Barnard M, Iyer R, Del Valle SY, Daughton AR (2021) Impact of COVID-19 policies and misinformation on social unrest. arXiv preprint arXiv:2110.09234

Beck PU (1992) Risk society: towards a new modernity. Sage Publications, London

Bellogin A, Parapar J (2012) Using graph partitioning techniques for neighbour selection in user-based collaborative filtering. In: Proceedings of the sixth ACM conference on recommender systems. Association for Computing Machinery, Dublin, Ireland, pp 213–216

Bennett J, Lanning S (2007) The netflix prize. In: Proceedings of KDD Cup and Workshop 2007. ACM, San Jose, CA, pp 3–6

Bergman R, Fassihi F (2021) The scientist and the A.I.-assisted, Remote-Control killing machine, The New York Times. Accessed 28 Jan 2022

Borgesius FJZ (2018) Discrimination, artificial intelligence, and algorithmic decision-making. Directorate General of Democracy, Council of Europe, pp 1–49

Buolamwini J, Gebru T (2018) Gender shades: intersectional accuracy disparities in commercial gender classification. In: 1st conference on fairness, accountability and transparency, Proceedings of Machine Learning Research, 4 February 2018

Burke R (2007) Hybrid web recommender systems. In: Brusilovsky P, Kobsa A, Nejdl W (eds) The adaptive web: methods and strategies of web personalization. Springer, Berlin, pp 377–408

Burtt EA (1939) The English philosophers: from bacon to mill. Modern Library, New York

Cadwalladr C, Graham-Harrison (2018) 50 million Facebook profiles harvested for Cambridge Analytica in major data breach. The Guardian. https://www.theguardian.com/news/2018/mar/17/cambridge-analytica-facebook-influence-us-election

China State Council (2017) Next generation artificial intelligence development plan. State Department for International Science and Technology Cooperation, China State Council, edited and translated by Rogier Creemers https://chinacopyrightandmedia.wordpress.com/2017/07/20/a-next-generation-artificial-intelligence-development-plan/. Accessed 28 Jan 2022

Conover M, Ratkiewicz J, Francisco M, Goncalves B, Menczer F, Flammini A (2021) Political polarization on Twitter. In: Full papers of the 5th International AAAI conference on weblogs and social media, Barcelona, Spain, 17—21 July 2011

Courtland R (2018) The bias detectives. Nature 558:357–360

Coviello L, Sohn Y, Kramer AD, Marlow C, Franceschetti M, Christakis NA, Fowler JH (2014) Detecting emotional contagion in massive social networks. PLoS One 9:e90315

Del Vicario M, Bessi A, Zollo F, Petroni F, Scala A, Caldarelli G, Stanley HE, Quattrociocchi W (2016) The spreading of misinformation online. Proc Natl Acad Sci USA 113:554–559

Dressel J, Farid H (2018) The accuracy, fairness, and limits of predicting recidivism. Sci Adv 4:eaao5580

Duhigg C (2012) How companies learn your secrets. https://www.nytimes.com/2012/02/19/magazine/shopping-habits.html. Accessed 28 Jan 2022

Eichstaedt JC, Smith RJ, Merchant RM, Ungar LH, Crutchley P, Preoţiuc-Pietro D, Asch DA, Schwartz HA (2018) Facebook language predicts depression in medical records. Proc Natl Acad Sci U S A 115:11203–11208

Emmott R (2020) Russia deploying coronavirus disinformation to sow panic in West, EU document says. https://www.reuters.com/article/us-health-coronavirus-disinformation-idUSKBN21518F. Accessed 28 Jan 2022

Englehardt S, Narayanan A (2016) Online tracking: a 1-million-site measurement and analysis. In: Proceedings of the 2016 ACM SIGSAC conference on computer and communications security, Association for Computing Machinery, Vienna, Austria, pp 1388–1401

Fayyaz Z, Ebrahimian M, Nawara D, Ibrahim A, Kashef R (2020) Recommendation systems: algorithms, challenges, metrics, and business opportunities. Appl Sci 10:7748

Flaxman S, Goel S, Rao JM (2016) Filter bubbles, echo chambers, and online news consumption. Public Opin Q 80:298–320

Garcia M (2016) Racist in the machine: the disturbing implications of algorithmic bias. World Policy J 33:111–117

Goncalves-Sa J (2020) In the fight against the new coronavirus outbreak, we must also struggle with human bias. Nat Med 26:305

Haidt J, Twenge J (2021) Social media use and mental health: a review. https://docs.google.com/document/d/1w-HOfseF2wF9YIpXwUUtP65-olnkPyWcgF5BiAtBEy0/mobilebasic#h.xi8mrj7rpf37. Accessed 28 Jan 2022

He X, Liao L, Zhang H, Nie L, Hu X, Chua T-S (2017) Neural collaborative filtering. In: Proceedings of the 26th International conference on world wide web, International World Wide Web Conferences Steering Committee, Perth, Australia, pp 137–182

Herlocker JL, Konstan JA, Riedl J (2000) Explaining collaborative filtering recommendations. In: Proceedings of the 2000 ACM conference on computer supported cooperative work, Association for Computing Machinery, Philadelphia, Pennsylvania, USA, pp 241–250

Homer-Dixon T (2001) We need a forest of tongues. https://homerdixon.com/we-need-a-forest-of-tongues/. Accessed 28 Jan 2022

Kadambi A (2021) Achieving fairness in medical devices. Science 372:30–31

Kramer ADI, Guillory JE, Hancock JT (2014) Experimental evidence of massive-scale emotional contagion through social networks. Proc Natl Acad Sci U S A 111:878–8790

Larson J, Mattu S, Kirchner L, Angwin J (2016) How we analyzed the COMPAS recidivism algorithm. https://www.propublica.org/article/how-we-analyzed-the-compas-recidivism-algorithm?token=XqwQ3rgbDdgxLwZrgdO5MED4b-chsjSu. Accessed 28 Jan 2022

Liang F, Das V, Kostyuk N, Hussain MM (2018) Constructing a data-driven society: China's social credit system as a state surveillance infrastructure. Policy Internet 10:415–453

Loomba S, de Figueiredo A, Piatek SJ, de Graaf K, Larson HJ (2021) Measuring the impact of COVID-19 vaccine misinformation on vaccination intent in the UK and USA. Nat Hum Behav 5:337–348

Lops P, de Gemmis M, Semeraro G (2011) Content-based recommender systems: state of the art and trends. In: Ricci F, Rokach L, Shapira B, Kantor PB (eds) Recommender systems handbook. Springer, Boston, pp 73–105

MacKenzie I, Meyer C, Noble S (2013) How retailers can keep up with consumers. https://www.mckinsey.com/ch/~/media/McKinsey/Industries/Retail/Our%20Insights/How%20retailers%20can%20keep%20up%20with%20consumers/How_retailers_can_keep_up_with_consumers_V2.pdf. Accessed 28 Jan 2022

McAlone N (2016) Why Netflix thinks its personalized recommendation engine is worth $1 billion per year. https://www.businessinsider.com/netflix-recommendation-engine-worth-1-billion-per-year-2016-6. Accessed 28 Jan 2022

McPherson M, Smith-Lovin L, Cook JM (2001) Birds of a feather: homophily in social networks. Annu Rev Sociol 27:415–444

Mikians J, Gyarmati L, Erramilli V, Laoutaris N (2012) Detecting price and search discrimination on the internet. In: Proceedings of the 11th ACM workshop on hot topics in networks, Association for Computing Machinery, Redmond, Washington, pp 79–84

Mooney RJ, Roy L (2000) Content-based book recommending using learning for text categorization. In: Proceedings of the fifth ACM conference on digital libraries, Association for Computing Machinery, San Antonio, Texas, USA, pp 195–204

Naumov M, Mudigere D, Shi H-JM, Huang J, Sundaraman N, Park J, Wang X, Gupta U, Wu C-J, Azzolini AG (2019) Deep learning recommendation model for personalization and recommendation systems. arXiv preprint arXiv:1906.00091

Nelson RE (1989) The strength of strong ties: social networks and intergroup conflict in organizations. Acad Manag J 32:377–401

Nikolov D, Oliveira DFM, Flammini A, Menczer F (2015) Measuring online social bubbles. PeerJ Comput Sci 1:e38

O'Neil C (2016) Weapons of math destruction: how big data increases inequality and threatens democracy. Crown Publishers, New York

O'Shaughnessy NJ (1990). Big lies, little lies: The story of propaganda. In *The Phenomenon of Political Marketing*. Palgrave Macmillan, London, UK, pp. 17–29

Paparrizos I, Cambazoglu BB, Gionis A (2011) Machine learned job recommendation. In: Proceedings of the fifth ACM conference on recommender systems, Association for Computing Machinery, Chicago, pp 325–328

Pennycook G, Rand DG (2021) The psychology of fake news. Trends Cogn Sci 25:388–402

Quattrociocchi W, Scala A, Sunstein CR (2016) Echo chambers on Facebook. SSRN

Reece AG, Reagan AJ, Lix KLM, Dodds PS, Danforth CM, Langer EJ (2017) Forecasting the onset and course of mental illness with Twitter data. Sci Rep 7:13006

Resnick P, Varian HR (1997) Recommender systems. Commun ACM 40:56–58

Ribeiro FN, Saha K, Babaei M, Henrique L, Messias J, Benevenuto F, Goga O, Gummadi KP, Redmiles EM (2019) On microtargeting socially divisive Ads: a case study of Russia-Linked Ad Campaigns on Facebook. In: Proceedings of the conference on fairness, Accountability, and Transparency. Association for Computing Machinery, Atlanta, pp 140–149

Ricard J, Medeiros J (2020) Using misinformation as a political weapon: Covid-19 and Bolsonaro in Brazil. Harv Kennedy School Misinform Rev 1(2)

Rigutini L, Maggini M (2004) Automatic text processing: machine learning techniques, Diss. PhD. thesis, University of Siena. https://www.researchgate.net/publication/236667720_ AUTO-MATIC_TEXT_PROCESSING_MACHINE_LEARNING_TECHNIQUES Accessed 15 Jan 2022

Roozenbeek J, Schneider CR, Dryhurst S, Kerr J, Freeman ALJ, Recchia G, van der Bles AM, van der Linden S (2020) Susceptibility to misinformation about COVID-19 around the world. R Soc Open Sci 7:201199

Saleiro P, Kuester B, Hinkson L, London J, Stevens A, Anisfeld A, Rodolfa KT, Ghani R (2018) Aequitas: a bias and fairness audit toolkit. arXiv preprint arXiv:1811.05577

Sheng E, Chang KW, Natarajan P, Peng N (2021) Societal biases in language generation: Progress and challenges. arXiv preprint arXiv:2105.04054

Silva M, Benevenuto F (2021) COVID-19 ads as political weapon. In: Proceedings of the 36th Annual ACM symposium on applied computing, Association for Computing Machinery, Virtual Event, Republic of Korea, pp 1705–1710

Silva M, Oliveira LSD, Andreou A, Melo POVD, Goga O, Benevenuto F (2020) Facebook Ads Monitor: An independent auditing system for political ads on Facebook. In: WWW'20 Proceedings of The Web Conference, Taipei, Taiwan, 20–24 April 2020

Smith B, Linden G (2017) Two decades of recommender systems at Amazon.com. IEEE Internet Comput 21:12–18

Solomos K, Ilia P, Ioannidis S, Kourtellis N (2019) Clash of the trackers: measuring the evolution of the online tracking ecosystem. arXiv preprint arXiv:1907.12860

Spielkamp M (2017) Inspecting algorithms for bias. https://www.technologyreview.com/2017/06/12/105804/inspecting-algorithms-for-bias/. Accessed 28 Jan 2022

Ungar LH, Foster DP (1998) Clustering methods for collaborative filtering. In: AAAI workshop on recommendation systems, Madison, Wisconsin, 26–27, 31 July 1998

Urban T, Tatang D, Degeling M, Holz T, Pohlmann N (2020) Measuring the impact of the GDPR on data sharing in ad networks. In: Proceedings of the 15th ACM Asia conference on computer and communications security. Association for Computing Machinery, Taipei, Taiwan, pp 222–235

Vanderbilt T (2013) The science behind the Netflix algorithms that decide what you'll watch next. https://www.wired.com/2013/08/qq-netflix-algorithm/. Accessed 28 Jan 2022

Vosoughi S, Roy D, Aral S (2018) The spread of true and false news online. Science 359:1146–1151

Yang K-C, Torres-Lugo C, Menczer F (2020) Prevalence of low-credibility information on twitter during the covid-19 outbreak. arXiv preprint arXiv:2004.14484

Yardi S, Boyd D (2010) Dynamic debates: an analysis of group polarization over time on Twitter. Bull Sci Technol Soc 30:316–327

Zhang M (2015) Google Photos Tags Two African-Americans as Gorillas Through Facial Recognition Software. https://www.forbes.com/sites/mzhang/2015/07/01/google-photos-tags-two-african-americans-as-gorillas-through-facial-recognition-software/. Accessed 28 Jan 2022

Zuboff S (2019) The age of surveillance capitalism: the fight for a human future at the new frontier of power. Public Aff, New York

Societal Implications of Recommendation Systems: A Technical Perspective

Open Access This chapter is licensed under the terms of the Creative Commons Attribution 4.0 International License (http://creativecommons.org/licenses/by/4.0/), which permits use, sharing, adaptation, distribution and reproduction in any medium or format, as long as you give appropriate credit to the original author(s) and the source, provide a link to the Creative Commons licence and indicate if changes were made.

The images or other third party material in this chapter are included in the chapter's Creative Commons licence, unless indicated otherwise in a credit line to the material. If material is not included in the chapter's Creative Commons licence and your intended use is not permitted by statutory regulation or exceeds the permitted use, you will need to obtain permission directly from the copyright holder.

Data-Driven Approaches in Healthcare: Challenges and Emerging Trends

Ana Teresa Freitas

Abstract Data is dominating and revolutionizing the healthcare industry in unprecedented ways. Associated with the new technologies of artificial intelligence, they promise to create the foundations for a new paradigm of medicine focused on the individuality of each person. This chapter is divided into four sections that aim to introduce the reader to the topic of data-driven approaches in the health sector. In section one, three ideologies are presented that, despite having some overlaps, present different views on how data should be used in order to guarantee a health service centered on each individual. In section two, the data-driven concept is explored. The emerging challenges of processing large volumes of data and their impacts on individuals, institutions, and society are associated with innovation in other disciplines such as artificial intelligence and personalized medicine. Since artificial intelligence is becoming a disruptive technology in the health sector, section three is dedicated to addressing the ethics and legal challenges posed by this new technological advance. To conclude, section four describes how the healthcare industry has become a major proving ground for artificial intelligence applications, with both startups and venture capital investors recognizing the enormous potential this technology can offer.

1 Patient-Centered Care, Value-Based Care and the P4 Medicine Paradigm: Divergent or Complementary?

Ideologies like patient-centered care, value-based care and P4 medicine are not new, with roots dating back to the end of the twentieth century (Gerteis et al. 1993; Hood et al. 2004). More than 20 years ago, the proposition that healthcare is evolving from reactive disease care to care that is patient or person-centered was regarded

---

A. T. Freitas (✉)
INESC-ID, Instituto Superior Técnico, Universidade de Lisboa, Lisbon, Portugal
e-mail: ana.freitas@tecnico.ulisboa.pt

© The Author(s) 2024
H. Sousa Antunes et al. (eds.), *Multidisciplinary Perspectives on Artificial Intelligence and the Law*, Law, Governance and Technology Series 58,
https://doi.org/10.1007/978-3-031-41264-6_4

as hypothetical (Louw et al. 2017). Today, the core elements of these approaches are widely accepted and have been articulated in a series of reports by the United States Institute of Medicine (National Research Council (US) Committee on a New Biology for the 21st Century: Ensuring the United States Leads the Coming Biology Revolution 2009), or by European initiatives like the recently Innovative Medicines Initiative project.

Patient-centered care and value-based care are two distinct but overlapping care ideologies.

Patient-centered care includes multiple domains of patient-centeredness and places the patient and relatives central to all decisions and evaluations of quality. Research by the Picker Institute has defined eight dimensions of patient-centered care, including: (1) respect for the patient's values, preferences, and expressed needs; (2) information and education; (3) access to care; (4) emotional support to relieve fear and anxiety; (5) involvement of family and friends; (6) continuity and secure transition between health care settings; (7) physical comfort; and (8) coordination of care. Although these dimensions were originally applied to hospital-based care, they could apply equally to care in the ambulatory setting (Gerteis et al. 1993).

In contrast, value-based care has been defined as the quality of care measured typically by healthcare outcomes, including cost. In this conception of value, patient-centeredness is one important but not necessarily dominant quality measure (Tseng and Hicks 2016).

By bring together patient-centered and value-based care model, patients should also be enabled to collect their outcomes data and have access and autonomy to use their health data in meaningful ways, such as self-managing their health in partnership with their health care providers. In this ideal world, the clinician-patient relationship is enhanced by "computer-based guidance and communications systems", medical records are internet-based and available everywhere, and patients regularly complete surveys on their experiences, which are then fed back to clinicians in "real time" so they can improve care (Elwyn et al. 2020). Patient-centered care is a key component of a health system that ensures that all patients have access to the kind of care that works for them. This model is paramount not only to treat the disease, but also to meet the patient's social and personal needs to ensure the best outcomes, including quality and satisfaction. Treating the whole patient with this level of personalization requires a 360-degree view of patient data that is accessible to both the patient and the care team. Achieving better patient outcomes for value-based healthcare requires better and smarter collaboration between healthcare professionals.

The vision of medicine that is predictive, preventive, personalized and participatory, labelled as "P4", has long been advocated by Leroy Hood and other pioneers of systems medicine (Weston and Hood 2004; Hood et al. 2012). Systems approaches to biology and medicine are now beginning to provide patients, consumers and physicians with personalized information about each individual's unique health experience of both health and disease at the molecular, cellular and organ levels. This information is making disease care more cost effective by personalizing care to each person's unique biology and by treating the causes rather than the symptoms of disease. It is also providing the basis for concrete action by consumers to improve their health as they observe the impact of lifestyle decisions.

P4 medicine holds great promise to reduce the burden of chronic diseases by harnessing technology and an increasingly better understanding of environment-biology interactions, evidence-based interventions and the underlying mechanisms of chronic diseases (Sagner et al. 2017). The P4 medicine advocates that the individual's participation is key to put into practice the other three aspects of P4 with each patient. An active involvement of patients is necessary to guarantee effective self-management and it includes sharing decisions with patients for their clinical or therapeutical approach, the use of novel technologies to implement the patient's participation in the disease management in order to obtain significant and relevant improvement in outcomes (Baiardini and Heffler 2019).

Evidence-based predictive and preventive care combines the practice of medicine based on the latest evidence with genomics and social determinants of health to get to a truly personalized plan of care for every patient. It goes beyond the notion that genomic testing is only for the 5% of the very sickest patients, a notion that grew out of the days when genetic testing cost thousands of dollars. Today's genetic testing for precision health costs only a few hundred dollars and the cost is decreasing. The potential cost avoidance down the road more than justifies this up-front cost. The adoption, at a population scale, of the use of preventive genetics is determinant not only to understand a person's poly-genomic increased risk for disease or body characteristic, but also to know which medications he or she is unable metabolize, respond with efficacy and/or have side-effects. This research area named pharmacogenomics, is presently a main pillar for the implementation of preventive and personalized medicine in the clinical practice.

The United States Food and Drug Administration (FDA) recently recognized over 120 pharmacogenomics associations for which current data supports a change in drug management or a potential impact on safety, and the list is growing (Kim et al. 2021). The Ubiquitous Pharmacogenomics (U-PGx) Consortium, which has been funded by the European Commission's Horizon-2020 program, aimed to evaluate the collective clinical utility of implementing a panel of pharmacogenomics markers into routine care (van der Wouden et al. 2017). The European Medicines Agency's scientific guidelines on pharmacogenomics help medicine developers prepare marketing authorisation applications for human medicines.

Although patients have a strong interest in the measurement of health outcomes of significance, such as symptom severity or functional status over time, health systems across Europe do not broadly engage in the measurement of such long-term health outcomes. Consequently, patient engagement in collecting and using relevant health outcomes data and information remains an underutilized strategy for incentivizing the transition for a new healthcare system paradigm (Nguyen et al. 2021). At the same time, data that includes patient perspectives should be made available and considered for health policy decisions. Although attracting more multi-stakeholder interest, value-based models remain insufficiently researched and not implemented on a wide scale (Porter et al. 2016).

The alignment of the goals and the focus of patient-centered care, value-based care and P4 medicine ideologies is complicated by several tensions, including a lack of patient experience, a non-clear definition of preferred measures, and conceptions of cost that are payer-focused instead of patient-focused (Tseng and Hicks 2016). However, the implementation of the areas of convergence of these three ideologies offer concrete opportunities to modify the existent healthcare system paradigm that is becoming of utmost importance in a world where the median age is rising, as is the prevalence of chronic diseases, including cancers and cardiovascular diseases, all associated co-morbidities, and late-life disabilities.

Health care costs absorb a significant proportion of national gross domestic product (GDP) globally. On average, countries members of the Organisation for Economic Co-operation and Development (OECD) are estimated to have spent 8.8% of GDP on healthcare in 2018, a percentage more or less unchanged since 2013 (OECD 2019). The United States is the country with the highest health expenditures, equivalent to 16.9% of its GDP, followed by Switzerland, with a value of 12.2%. After the United States and Switzerland, a group of high-income countries, including Germany, France, Sweden and Japan, all spend close to 11% of their GDP on healthcare. Furthermore, it is suggested that up to 20% of health expenditures are being wasted in these countries.

There is increasing evidence and acceptance that healthcare financing should be focused on outcomes rather than on reimbursing the services provided, to achieve a sensible allocation of sparse resources. This shift from volume to value requires the design, development, and deployment of products, services, and integrated solutions that deliver value by improving patient outcomes in efficient and effective ways. In order to implement this transformation, access to large volumes of data and to a large number of results about the impact of clinical interventions is necessary. Despite the numerous projects already underway with the aim of obtaining these data, greater investment and commitment by patients and all agents working in the health area are still needed (Porter and Lee 2013).

2 Data-Driven Healthcare

"Data is the new oil" claims Clive Humby, a British mathematician and data science entrepreneur, in 2006. However, if unrefined it cannot really be used. To create value data needs to be trustable, accurate, comprehensive, accessible, sharable, and most importantly, used.

Like in many other industries, the healthcare sector routinely generates vast amounts of data from many different sources ranging from biochemical exams, electronic medical records, vital signs, patient-reported outcomes, health surveys, clinical trials, insurance claims, administrative data, and more recently omics (genomics, transcriptomics, proteomics, metabolomics, radiomics, microbiomics). Altogether, these datasets represent big data collections that are key to better patient care quality, reducing readmissions, supporting decision-making and overall improvements in outcomes.

However, big data collection is not the same as data-driven healthcare (Sanchez-Pinto et al. 2018; Savadjiev et al. 2020). While the increase and availability of data can fuel a whole new era of fact-based innovation in healthcare, automation is required to streamline processes and clarify decision-making in a way that improves both clinical outcomes and operational agility. With the regulatory environment moving increasingly toward patient-centered and value-based care, healthcare institutions must move from collecting healthcare data to becoming data-driven healthcare institutions.

Becoming a data-driven healthcare institution requires new investment and resources allowing team members to make the most informed decision and the organization to reach its goals (Carra et al. 2020). New data-driven health management should be used in clinical decision-making in order to minimize future individual risks of disease and adverse health effects and to push forward patient-centered and value-based care models (Grossglauser and Saner 2014; Kriegova et al. 2021). To achieve this new status, it is necessary to define a data infrastructure, data-driven processes, a data-centric culture, and, a cybersecurity framework.

Data-driven healthcare can be broken down into four distinct pillars: (1) the use of data by patients, healthcare professionals, and organizations; (2) the regulation of data to ensure accountability, privacy and security; (3) the technologies and computational methods that help healthcare professionals make data-driven decisions to improve health outcomes; and (4) the innovations that are driven by data and that are driving the production of new data.

To improve the use of data by all stakeholders, patients, healthcare professionals, and organizations, a data-driven healthcare strategy must pursue the following goals: (1) promotion of education and literacy to raise awareness of data-driven healthcare relevance among patients and healthcare professionals; (2) creation of an integrated healthcare system focused on the patient by providing easy and broad access to data; (3) promotion of management initiatives and investment in data governance to reduce resistance to change within healthcare organizations.

Currently, data-driven healthcare has organizational culture as its biggest obstacle, overcoming technological or investment challenges.

Data accountability, privacy and security of data in healthcare are complex topics, aiming to ensure the secure exchange of patient information, protect the integrity of medical records and applications, and control access to healthcare applications and systems that contain personal data.

Monitoring and assessing regulatory compliance for data processing is vital both at an organizational and a personal level. A data-driven healthcare strategy must consider the definition of data management policies, provide training for those dealing with health data, and support the implementation of "secure by design" information systems. Moreover, the transformation toward data-driven healthcare is not limited to how data is gathered, processed, analysed, and used but also implicates surveillance and responsibility from all stakeholders, including government, patients, healthcare professionals, healthcare providers, insurance companies, and suppliers of healthcare providers.

Existent technologies already enable healthcare professionals and patients to engage more effectively together to improve health outcomes. The rise of remote medical monitoring, with the use of medical mobile devices to actively monitor patients' conditions, the use of cloud-based storage and applications allowing better communication and improving patient experience, and the growing acceptance of wearable medical devices show that health technology is becoming a commodity.

All these technologies are supported by innovative computational methods that were developed to perform intelligent monitoring, to develop predictive models for prevention, early disease detection, diagnosis, treatment, and prognosis, and to analyse or propose treatment and interventions plans (Wong-Lin et al. 2020). Computational methods are able to extract value from big data but most of the time face major challenges like the size and relevance of the input data; the data accessibility and readability; and the lack of data interoperability. To make data actionable, collected data must be clean, complete, accurate, and standardized for use across systems. It should also be easily accessible to, and readable by, different stakeholders with different roles, like the scientific community, regulatory entities, and healthcare professionals, to guarantee peer-review (Heijlen and Crompvoets 2021).

These ongoing trends provide an essential foundation for the next generation of innovations, including the use of artificial intelligence for the development of precise, preventive, and personalized medicine, which involves the combination of big data analytics and statistical methods, commonly known as machine learning algorithms (Handelman et al. 2018; Abul-Husn and Kenny 2019; Loncar-Turukalo et al. 2019; Morganti et al. 2019; Goecks et al. 2020).

3   Ethics and Legal Challenges Posed by Artificial Intelligence

Artificial intelligence (AI), kick-started at the Dartmouth Summer Research Project on Artificial Intelligence in 1956, has yet to deliver on its promised central bargain for many years. Recent advancements in machine learning methods, the availability of big data, and the existence of supercomputing infrastructures are helping AI enter a rapid transition from theory to reality. As an engine of big data, artificial intelligence is accelerating the implementation of deep data application services (Jiang et al. 2021).

Deep learning has made a significant contribution to the recent progress in AI. In comparison to traditional machine learning methods, deep learning methods have achieved substantial improvement in various prediction tasks. However, this new method is comparably weak in explaining its inference processes and final results. In many real-world applications such as medical diagnosis explainability and transparency become particularly essential for the users who are affected by AI decisions (Xu et al. 2019).

Over the last decade, AI, powered by deep learning, has gradually been integrated into daily medical practice and has made considerable progress in medical image processing (Ahmad et al. 2019; Ardila et al. 2019; McKinney et al. 2020), medical process optimization (Bellini et al. 2019; Gutierrez 2020), medical diagnosis (Dias and Torkamani 2019; Kehl et al. 2021), medical education (van der Niet and Bleakley 2021), and other applications (Oliveira 2019). However, large-scale implementations in clinical practice are still struggling due to the lack of standardized processes, and ethical and legal supervision. The main issues of AI implementation in healthcare are connected with the nature of technology in itself, complexities of legal support in terms of safety and efficiency, privacy, ethical and liability concerns.

The use of AI in clinical practice has huge potential to transform the way patients are treated for the better, but it also raises ethical challenges, namely: (1) informed consent to use; (2) safety and transparency; and (3) data privacy (Gerke et al. 2020).

According to Wikipedia, "informed consent is a principle in medical ethics and medical law that a patient should have sufficient information before making their own free decisions about their medical care. A healthcare provider is often held to have a responsibility to ensure that the consent that a patient gives is informed, and informed consent can apply to a health care intervention on a person, conducting some form of research on a person, or for disclosing a person's information.". Despite the clarity of this definition, there are situations, such as population-level genome sequencing initiatives, where the requirements for informed consent are not yet well defined. In this context, the implementation of informed consent differs greatly between these initiatives, contemplating formulations designated as broad consent, general consent and layered consent, among others. A specific strategy that claims to be fully informed and continually engaging participants is called "dynamic consent". Dynamic consent is based on a personalized communication platform geared towards supporting continuous two-way communication between researchers and participants (Dankar et al. 2020).

Despite the fact that a consensus is being created around the concept of "dynamic consent", its use on a large scale still presents some technical difficulties that need to be addressed (Tauginienė et al. 2021).

In the context of using AI with safety and transparency to assist in the medical intervention, there are a number of questions for which clear answers are still lacking. Questions like: to what extent does a healthcare professional need to disclose that an AI system will be used for the diagnosis or treatment recommendations? Should a healthcare professional disclose that it cannot fully explain the results? How much transparency is needed? How does this new context interface with the so-called "right to explanation" under the EU General Data Protection Regulation (GDPR)?

These questions are especially relevant in cases where the AI operates using "black-box" algorithms, which may result from noninterpretable machine-learning techniques that are very difficult for healthcare professionals to understand fully (Xu et al. 2019).

In the space of AI health apps connected or not to wearable sensors, informed consent is transformed into a user agreement. Still to be answered is the question: how does this user agreement relate to informed consent? This question is particularly relevant because for the majority of the user agreements individuals agree to without a face-to-face dialog. Additionally, most people routinely ignore the user agreements or do not understand the terms of services and all the complexities associated with the software or hardware updates.

Tackling these questions is far from being simple, and they become more difficult to answer when information from patient-facing AI health apps are fed back into clinical decision-making.

Reliability, validity, and transparency of the datasets used to train AI algorithms make safety one of the most relevant challenges in AI healthcare. It is common knowledge that any dataset will be biased to a certain extent based on gender, sexual orientation, race, sociologic, environmental, or economic factors. Because machine-learning models learn from historically collected data, populations that have experienced human and structural biases in the past are vulnerable to harm by incorrect predictions (Rajkomar et al. 2018). For example, the use of data from the Framingham Heart Study to predict the risk of cardiovascular events in non-white populations has led to biased results, with both overestimations and underestimations of risk. To date, most research on primary prevention and risk scores of cardiovascular diseases, like the landmark Framingham Risk Score and the European SCORE, has been developed in a largely White population (Gijsberts et al. 2015). Any algorithm designed to predict outcomes from genetic findings will be biased if there have been few (or no) genetic studies in certain populations.

Transparency should be a key topic to be addressed by AI algorithms developers. Healthcare professionals and patients should be informed about the kind of data used and if any biases exist in the system. If in a hypothetical world it would be possible to think of an open-data model, capable of being validated by everyone, in reality, there are several limitations to this type of implementation. An open-data model can raise intellectual property and investment issues, and also needs to preserve the confidentiality of patient data considered.

Rather than simply protecting against the previously identified deficiencies, AI systems should be used proactively to advance health equity. For this reality to be true, the principles of distributive justice must be incorporated into the design, implementation, and evaluation of the models (Murdoch 2021). Despite current challenges, AI holds tremendous promise for transforming the provision of healthcare services in resource-poor settings as these systems can act in place of a human expert if one is not readily available, which is often the case in poor communities.

Given personal medical information is among the most private and legally protected forms of data, there are significant concerns about how access, control, and use by for-profit parties might change over time with a self-improving AI (Jaremko et al. 2019). As the owners of data, patients have the right to know-how and to what extent their personal health data are recorded and used. The GDPR in all EU Member States has been applied since 2018 and introduced a new era of data protection law in the EU. This regulation particularly aims to protect the right of natural persons to the protection of personal data. Regulations in Canada admit that healthcare providers are the "information custodians" of patients' private health data, and their ownership belongs to patients. This "guardianship" reflects the reality that there are interests in patients' medical records, and these interests are protected by law (Powles and Hodson 2017).

Nowadays a significant portion of existing AI technologies rests in the hands of large tech corporations. Google, IBM, Apple, Microsoft, and other companies are all "preparing, in their own ways, bids on the future of health and on various aspects of the global healthcare industry (Price and Cohen 2019)." The concentration of technological innovation and knowledge in large technology companies creates a power imbalance where public health institutions can become more dependent and less able to maintain a balanced partnership in new developments and implementations. Although some data privacy breaches have occurred despite existing laws, regulations, and privacy policies, it is clear that adequate safeguards must be put in place to maintain the patient's privacy and agency in the context of this public-private partnership. Information sharing agreements, dynamic informed consents, and other mechanisms can be used to grant these private institutions access to patient health information to be used to train algorithms or to develop new products.

In addition to the possibility of abuses of power associated with data control, AI poses a new challenge associated with accessing large amounts of patient data. The location and ownership of data servers that store patient information are very relevant in this context. The regulation currently requires that patient data remain in the jurisdiction from which it was obtained, with few exceptions. In the current context where there have already been numerous cases of abuse by large corporations of using patient health data without their knowledge, it is not surprising that issues of public trust may arise. A lack of trust on the part of patients or citizens and even public health institutions can increase public scrutiny or even litigation against commercial implementations of AI for healthcare.

Several studies show that health-related data far exceeded the original expectations of the original privacy protection laws. For example, The Health Insurance Portability and Accountability Act (HIPAA) Privacy Rule, approved by the US Congress in 1996, has significant gaps when it comes to today's healthcare environment since it only covers specific health information generated by "covered entities" or their "business associates." (Centers for Disease Control and Prevention 2018). Fortunately, many new laws have been introduced to regulate AI data protection, liability determination, and oversight.

In February 2020, the European Commission published a white paper on AI. In the white paper, The Commission highlighted the "European Approach" to AI, stressing that "it is vital that European AI is based on our fundamental values and rights, such as human dignity and the protection of privacy." (European Commission 2020). In April 2021, a proposal for AI Regulation, the "Artificial Intelligence Act", was presented (European Commission 2021). This Regulation will regulate the use of "high risk" AI applications, which contemplates most medical AI applications.

Human oversight, explainability, privacy by design, and non-discrimination are key criteria to European Medical AI. As required by EU fundamental rights (see also Art. 14 of the proposed AI Act), decisions of medical AI require human assessment before any action is taken on their basis. In other words, European Medical AI legally requires a human in the loop. Even more important it requires free and informed consent of the patient. This points to split decision-making between doctor and patient, where the patient has the final say. This point about informed patient decisions clarifies that European fundamental rights basically require the use of explainable AI in medicine. Consequently, European Medical AI should not be based on a "machine decision," but much rather on "an AI-supported decision, diagnostic finding or treatment proposal." (European Commission 2020). European AI must also be developed and operated in accordance with the requirements of the protection of data and privacy, and the new regulation includes a rich body of fundamental rights provisions requiring equality before the law and non-discrimination, including gender, age, and disability level.

Although comprehensive, the existing fundamental rights framework is not answering all legal questions arising for the use of medical AI. Unfortunately, there is a large exception, involving liability legislation issues, which is of particular concern to the community developing AI-based tools. Who will be legally responsible when medical AI causes harm? The software developer, the manufacturer, the maintenance staff, the IT provider, the hospital, the healthcare professional?

In this regard, the Commission announced that it will shortly provide added clarity, proposing a strict liability approach coupled with a mandatory AI damage insurance scheme. Despite the open questions, it is important to note that the legal requirements for the use of medical AI are already clearer today than a few years ago, much clearer than what the community developing AI-based tools seems to consider.

In the US, the Food & Drug Administration (FDA) recently released its first AI and Machine Learning (ML) Action Plan, a multi-step approach designed to advance the agency's management of advanced medical software. This regulatory action plan aims to force software and medical device manufacturers to be more rigorous in their reliability and safety assessments. "The AI/ML-Based Software as a Medical Device Action Plan" outlines five actions that the FDA intends to take, including: (1) Further developing the proposed regulatory framework, including through issuance of draft guidance on a predetermined change control plan (for software's learning over time); (2) Supporting the development of good machine learning practices to evaluate and improve machine learning algorithms; (3) Fostering a patient-centered approach, including device transparency to users; (4) Developing methods to evaluate and improve machine learning algorithms; and (5) Advancing real-world performance monitoring pilots. "(U.S. Food and Drug Administration 2021).

Many of the ethical issues previously discussed have purely legal solutions although it is difficult to separate the ethical from the legal.

4 Investments Trends in Healthcare Artificial Intelligence

Over the last 5 years, the healthcare industry has become a major proving ground for AI applications, with both startups and venture capital (VC) investors recognizing the enormous potential that AI solutions can offer for accelerating clinical trial recruitment and vaccine development, detecting potentially life-threatening adverse drug events, improving patient care, reducing hospital waiting times and human resource needs, and reducing healthcare costs.

Investors around the world realized the need to invest in AI in healthcare, and their investments turned in this direction. The AI value in the healthcare market is expected to grow from USD 6.9 billion in 2021 to USD 67.4 billion by 2027, with a CAGR of 46.2% (Markets and Markets 2020). AI funding for healthcare has seen record growth as demand has exploded. In the first quarter of 2021 and after 111 deals, Healthcare AI companies have raised capital worth a record $2.5 billion. This represents a 140% increase compared to $1 billion raised in Q1 2020 (CBInsights 2021b; Fierce Healthcare 2021). The investments and recent use cases for this technology are proof that AI is here to stay.

The multiple problems facing European health policies to tackle issues such as the aging of the population and the reduction of public expenditures on health, require capital investments in the sector. Although investments have to be encouraged in the health sector to allow countries to prepare well for unforeseen events, such as the Covid-19 pandemic, there is also the need to promote investments in social protection and encourage healthy lifestyles. There is an urgent need to develop incentive policy models to serve as a catalyst for the growth of the health sector. European governments can benefit from social returns to VC capital investments in healthcare care, as well as the promotion of healthier lifestyles because the growth of the health sector positively affects the entire economy. The continuous improvement of health care with a great focus on disease prevention is a desirable objective since the investment in the general well-being of a population contributes to economic growth.

As with all industries, the COVID-19 pandemic has created an unprecedented crisis for the healthcare industry. This crisis has accelerated the digital health segment, such as the provision of virtual health care, with a strong focus on mental health and well-being. As COVID-19 vaccines become common, the focus is shifting to the long-term effects of the pandemic, encompassing trends in specific areas of health, including telehealth, AI in healthcare, medical devices, mental health, women's health, omics, and cyber security (CBInsights 2021a).

During the year 2022, investments in AI for healthcare are likely to focus primarily on improving backend efficiency, such as using robotic process automation (RPA) to support care or using AI to process claims. An RPA solution, when used in conjunction with AI, creates intelligent automation, which aims to closely mimic human interaction, often through the use of bots. In the short term, it is very likely that AI investments will focus on developing diagnostic support systems, providing second opinions, and detecting routine errors, not being dedicated to autonomously performing direct diagnoses to patients.

In this era where AI is growing in healthcare institutions and society at large, the greatest challenge to AI adoption is not whether it will be capable enough to be useful, but rather ensuring it gets properly adapted into daily clinical practice.

In the translation to clinical practice, there are five topics that corporates and organizations should keep in mind when planning to work with clients in the healthcare space or embarking on their own healthcare AI journeys (IT Pro Portal 2021). These five topics are: (1) which AI technology better adapts to the intended use; (2) who is becoming the primary user of AI applications; (3) which software should be used to build AI solutions (open-source versus commercial); (4) building or buy software; (5) how to guarantee compliance with AI regulations and standards.

Actual technical leaders stress that their organizations are already using data integration, i.e. natural language processing (NLP) and business intelligence (BI), data annotation, as well as data science platforms. It is now clear that the most innovative healthcare organizations are taking their data seriously, making the most of electronic medical records and technologies such as NLP, in order to integrate data held in different silos and gain a complete view of the states of its organizational processes and the clinical course of its patients.

In the user space, patients and doctors are becoming the top adopters of AI apps. The use of AI apps is facing a shift from data scientists and technical personnel to doctors and patients. Chatbots and other interactive and automation technologies will only grow as AI matures. This growth is already having a profound impact on patient care delivery, as it provides a level of access and convenience that facilitates many tasks, such as scheduling appointments, accessing clinical records, and even managing remotely health care.

When it comes to deciding which software to use to build AI solutions, the trend is towards using open source and public cloud providers. It is not surprising that open source solutions are advancing ahead of cloud providers or other commercial solutions, as privacy and data security are some of the main challenges of using these services. These challenges are particularly relevant in the healthcare sector, where laws and regulations may prohibit sharing data with third parties. Healthcare privacy regulations, for example, require users to remove medical records from any protected health information through a process called de-identification. This time-consuming and complex process can currently be very automated.

Mature companies mostly choose to rely on their own data and monitoring tools rather than third-party assessment or software vendor representation. On the other hand, companies that are still starting to explore AI are more open to using solutions from software vendors. Using models tailored to each company's specific needs while keeping data within the organization is a smart move for those who have the tools to keep their AI efforts in-house.

For highly regulated industries, such as healthcare and pharma, AI-powered technologies will be critical to operations and safety. Therefore, to scale the deployment and use of AI, organizations must establish a compliance management program to address relevant requirements from applicable AI authoritative rules. In

Europe, the combination of the legal framework on AI and a new plan coordinated with the Member States aims to guarantee the security and fundamental rights of people and businesses, while strengthening the acceptance, investment, and innovation of AI.

At its current stage of maturity, AI is poised to change the healthcare and life sciences industry in ways we could not have imagined a few years ago.[1]

References

Abul-Husn NS, Kenny EE (2019) Personalized medicine and the power of electronic health records. Cell 177:58–69

Ahmad OF, Soares AS, Mazomenos E, Brandao P, Vega R, Seward E, Stoyanov D, Chand M, Lovat LB (2019) Artificial intelligence and computer-aided diagnosis in colonoscopy: current evidence and future directions. Lancet Gastroenterol Hepatol 4:71–80

Ardila D, Kiraly AP, Bharadwaj S, Choi B, Reicher JJ, Peng L, Tse D, Etemadi M, Ye W, Corrado G, Naidich DP, Shetty S (2019) End-to-end lung cancer screening with three-dimensional deep learning on low-dose chest computed tomography. Nat Med 25:954–961

Baiardini I, Heffler E (2019) Chapter 21 - The patient-centered decision system as per the 4Ps of precision medicine. In: Agache I, Hellings P (eds) Implementing precision medicine in best practices of chronic airway diseases. Academic Press, London, pp 147–151

---

[1] *See* generally, on the different applications of Machine Learning and AI, in this book A Oliveira and M A T Figueiredo - Artificial intelligence - historical context and state of the art; I Trancoso, N Mamede, B Martins, H S Pinto and R Ribeiro - The impact of language technologies in the legal domain; J Gonçalves-Sá and F L Pinheiro - Societal Implications of Recommendation Systems - A Technical Perspective; A T Freitas - Data-driven approaches in healthcare - challenges and emerging trends; M Correia and L Rodrigues - Security and Privacy; E Magrani and P G F Silva - The Ethical and Legal Challenges of Recommender Systems Driven by Artificial Intelligence; M Lanz and S Mijic - Risks associated with the use of natural language generation - Swiss civil liability law perspective; M S Fernandes and J R Goldim - Artificial Intelligence and Decision Making in Health - Risks and Opportunities; W Gravett - Judicial Decision-making in the Age of Artificial Intelligence; D Durães, P M Freitas and P Novais - The Relevance of Deepfakes in the Administration of Criminal Justice. *See* also, on Ethics, in this book P U Lima and A Paiva - Autonomous and Intelligent Robots - Social, Legal and Ethical Issues; M C Patrão Neves and A B Almeida - Before and Beyond Artificial Intelligence - Opportunities and Challenges; E Magrani and P G F Silva - The Ethical and Legal Challenges of Recommender Systems Driven by Artificial Intelligence; M S Fernandes and J R Goldim - Artificial Intelligence and Decision Making in Health - Risks and Opportunities; M N Duffourc and D S Giovanniello - The Autonomous AI Physician - Medical Ethics and Legal Liability; R Nogaroli and J L M Faleiros Júnior - Ethical challenges of artificial intelligence in medicine and the triple semantic dimensions of algorithmic opacity with its repercussions to patient consent and medical liability; and B A Ribeiro, H Coelho, A E Ferreira and J Branquinho - Metacognition, Accountability and Legal Personhood of AI. *See* finally, on AI and Healthcare, in this book M S Fernandes and J R Goldim - Artificial Intelligence and Decision Making in Health - Risks and Opportunities; M N Duffourc and D S Giovanniello - The Autonomous AI Physician - Medical Ethics and Legal Liability; and R Nogaroli and J L M Faleiros Júnior - Ethical challenges of artificial intelligence in medicine and the triple semantic dimensions of algorithmic opacity with its repercussions to patient consent and medical liability.

Bellini V, Guzzon M, Bigliardi B, Mordonini M, Filippelli S, Bignami E (2019) Artificial intelligence: a new tool in operating room management. Role of machine learning models in operating room optimization. J Med Syst 44:20

Carra G, Salluh JIF, Ramos FJDS, Meyfroidt G (2020) Data-driven ICU management: using big data and algorithms to improve outcomes. J Crit Care 60:300–304

CBInsights (2021a) Here are the most active healthcare investors. https://www.cbinsights.com/research/most-active-healthcare-vcs/. Accessed 8 Jan 2022

CBInsights (2021b) State of healthcare Q1'21 report: investment & sector trends to watch. https://www.cbinsights.com/research/report/healthcare-trends-q1-2021/. Accessed 8 Jan 2022

Centers for Disease Control and Prevention (2018) Health insurance portability and accountability act of 1996 (HIPAA). https://www.cdc.gov/phlp/publications/topic/hipaa.html. Accessed 17 Dec 2021

Dankar FK, Gergely M, Malin B, Badji R, Dankar SK, Shuaib K (2020) Dynamic-informed consent: a potential solution for ethical dilemmas in population sequencing initiatives. Comput Struct Biotechnol J 18:913–921

Dias R, Torkamani A (2019) Artificial intelligence in clinical and genomic diagnostics. Genome Med 11:70

Elwyn G, Nelson E, Hager A, Price A (2020) Coproduction: when users define quality. BMJ Qual Saf 29:711–716

European Commission (2020) WHITE PAPER on artificial intelligence-a European approach to excellence and trust. https://ec.europa.eu/info/sites/default/files/commission-white-paper-artificial-intelligence-feb2020_en.pdf. Accessed 16 Nov 2021

European Commission (2021) Proposal for a regulation of the European parliament and of the council. Laying down harmonised rules on artificial intelligence (Artificial intelligence act) and amending certain union legislative acts. https://bit.ly/3AcDsCa. Accessed 16 Nov 2021

Fierce Healthcare (2021) Global investment in telehealth, artificial intelligence hits a new high in Q1 2021. https://bit.ly/3qtk4hQ. Accessed 12 Nov 2021

Gerke S, Minssen T, Cohen G (2020) Ethical and legal challenges of artificial intelligence-driven healthcare. Artif Intell Healthc:295–336. https://doi.org/10.1016/B1978-1010-1012-818438-818437.800012-818435

Gerteis M, Edgman-Levitan S, Daley J, Delbanco TL (1993) Through the patient's eyes: understanding and promoting patient-centered care. Jossey-Bass, San Francisco, CA

Gijsberts CM, Groenewegen KA, Hoefer IE, Eijkemans MJC, Asselbergs FW, Anderson TJ, Britton AR, Dekker JM, Engström G, Evans GW, de Graaf J, Grobbee DE, Hedblad B, Holewijn S, Ikeda A, Kitagawa K, Kitamura A, de Kleijn DPV, Lonn EM, Lorenz MW, Mathiesen EB, Nijpels G, Okazaki S, O'Leary DH, Pasterkamp G, Peters SAE, Polak JF, Price JF, Robertson C, Rembold CM, Rosvall M, Rundek T, Salonen JT, Sitzer M, Stehouwer CDA, Bots ML, den Ruijter HM (2015) Race/Ethnic differences in the associations of the Framingham risk factors with carotid IMT and cardiovascular events. PLoS One 10:e0132321

Goecks J, Jalili V, Heiser LM, Gray JW (2020) How machine learning will transform biomedicine. Cell 181:92–101

Grossglauser M, Saner H (2014) Data-driven healthcare: from patterns to actions. Eur J Prev Cardiol 21:14–17

Gutierrez G (2020) Artificial intelligence in the intensive care unit. Crit Care 24:101

Handelman GS, Kok HK, Chandra RV, Razavi AH, Lee MJ, Asadi H (2018) eDoctor: machine learning and the future of medicine. J Int Med 284:603–619

Heijlen R, Crompvoets J (2021) Open health data: mapping the ecosystem. Digit Health 7:20552076211050167

Hood L, Heath JR, Phelps ME, Lin B (2004) Systems biology and new technologies enable predictive and preventative medicine. Science 306:640–643

Hood L, Balling R, Auffray C (2012) Revolutionizing medicine in the twenty-first century through systems approaches. Biotechnol J 7:992–1001

IT Pro Portal (2021) The state of AI in healthcare: five key findings enterprises should know. https://www.itproportal.com/features/the-state-of-ai-in-healthcare-five-key-findings-enterprises-should-know/. Accessed 15 Oct 2021

Jaremko JL, Azar M, Bromwich R, Lum A, Alicia Cheong LH, Gibert M, Laviolette F, Gray B, Reinhold C, Cicero M, Chong J, Shaw J, Rybicki FJ, Hurrell C, Lee E, Tang A (2019) Canadian association of radiologists white paper on ethical and legal issues related to rtificial intelligence in radiology. Can Assoc Radiol J 70:107–118

Jiang L, Wu Z, Xu X, Zhan Y, Jin X, Wang L, Qiu Y (2021) Opportunities and challenges of artificial intelligence in the medical field: current application, emerging problems, and problem-solving strategies. J Int Med Res 49:3000605211000157

Kehl KL, Xu W, Gusev A, Bakouny Z, Choueiri TK, Riaz IB, Elmarakeby H, Van Allen EM, Schrag D (2021) Artificial intelligence-aided clinical annotation of a large multi-cancer genomic dataset. Nat Commun 12:7304

Kim JA, Ceccarelli R, Lu CY (2021) Pharmacogenomic biomarkers in US FDA-approved drug labels (2000–2020). J Pers Med 11:179

Kriegova E, Kudelka M, Radvansky M, Gallo J (2021) A theoretical model of health management using data-driven decision-making: the future of precision medicine and health. J Transl Med 19:68–68

Loncar-Turukalo T, Zdravevski E, Machado da Silva J, Chouvarda I, Trajkovik V (2019) Literature on wearable technology for connected health: scoping review of research trends, advances, and barriers. J Med Internet Res 21:e14017

Louw JM, Marcus TS, Hugo JFM (2017) Patient- or person-centred practice in medicine? - A review of concepts. Afr J Prim Health Care Fam Med 9:e1–e7

Markets and Markets (2020) Artificial Intelligence in Healthcare Market by offering (Hardware, software, services), technology (Machine learning, NLP, context-aware computing, computer vision), application, end user and geography - global forecast to 2027. https://bit.ly/3GBUm07. Accessed 17 Dec 2021

McKinney SM, Sieniek M, Godbole V, Godwin J, Antropova N, Ashrafian H, Back T, Chesus M, Corrado GS, Darzi A, Etemadi M, Garcia-Vicente F, Gilbert FJ, Halling-Brown M, Hassabis D, Jansen S, Karthikesalingam A, Kelly CJ, King D, Ledsam JR, Melnick D, Mostofi H, Peng L, Reicher JJ, Romera-Paredes B, Sidebottom R, Suleyman M, Tse D, Young KC, De Fauw J, Shetty S (2020) International evaluation of an AI system for breast cancer screening. Nature 577:89–94

Morganti S, Tarantino P, Ferraro E, D'Amico P, Duso BA, Curigliano G (2019) Next generation sequencing (NGS): a revolutionary technology in pharmacogenomics and personalized medicine in cancer. Adv Exp Med Biol 1168:9–30

Murdoch B (2021) Privacy and artificial intelligence: challenges for protecting health information in a new era. BMC Med Ethics 22:122

National Research Council (US) Committee on a New Biology for the 21st Century: Ensuring the United States Leads the Coming Biology Revolution (2009) A new biology for the 21st century: ensuring the united states leads the coming biology revolution. National Academies Press, Washington, DC

Nguyen H, Butow P, Dhillon H, Sundaresan P (2021) A review of the barriers to using Patient-Reported Outcomes (PROs) and Patient-Reported Outcome Measures (PROMs) in routine cancer care. J Med Radiat Sci 68:186–195

OECD (2019) Health working papers. OECD health working paper no. 110. Health spending projections to 2030. https://bit.ly/3tLxAQ3. Accessed 22 Nov 2021.

Oliveira AL (2019) Biotechnology, big data and artificial intelligence. Biotechnol J 14:1800613

Porter ME, Lee TH (2013) The strategy that will fix health care. Harv Bus Rev 91:50–70

Porter ME, Larsson S, Lee TH (2016) Standardizing patient outcomes measurement. N Engl J Med 374:504–506

Powles J, Hodson H (2017) Google DeepMind and healthcare in an age of algorithms. Health Technol (Berl) 7:351–367

Price WN, Cohen IG (2019) Privacy in the age of medical big data. Nat Med 25:37–43

Rajkomar A, Hardt M, Howell MD, Corrado G, Chin MH (2018) Ensuring fairness in machine learning to advance health equity. Ann Int Med 169:866–872

Sagner M, McNeil A, Puska P, Auffray C, Price ND, Hood L, Lavie CJ, Han ZG, Chen Z, Brahmachari SK, McEwen BS, Soares MB, Balling R, Epel E, Arena R (2017) The P4 health spectrum – a predictive, preventive, personalized and participatory continuum for promoting healthspan. Prog Prev Med 2:e0002

Sanchez-Pinto LN, Luo Y, Churpek MM (2018) Big data and data science in critical care. Chest 154:1239–1248

Savadjiev P, Reinhold C, Martin D, Forghani R (2020) Knowledge based versus data based: a historical perspective on a continuum of methodologies for medical image analysis. Neuroimaging Clin N Am 30:401–415

Tauginienė L, Hummer P, Albert A, Cigarini A, Vohland K (2021) Ethical challenges and dynamic informed consent. In: Vohland K, Land-Zandstra A, Ceccaroni L, Lemmens R, Perelló J, Ponti M, Samson R, Wagenknecht K (eds) The science of citizen science. Springer International Publishing, Cham, pp 397–416

Tseng EK, Hicks LK (2016) Value based care and patient-centered care: divergent or complementary? Curr Hematol Malig Rep 11:303–310

U.S. Food and Drug Administration (2021) FDA releases artificial intelligence/machine learning action plan. https://www.fda.gov/news-events/press-announcements/fda-releases-artificial-intelligencemachine-learning-action-plan. Accessed 8 Oct 2021

van der Niet AG, Bleakley A (2021) Where medical education meets artificial intelligence: 'Does technology care?' Med Educ 55:30–36.

van der Wouden CH, Cambon-Thomsen A, Cecchin E, Cheung KC, Dávila-Fajardo CL, Deneer VH, Dolžan V, Ingelman-Sundberg M, Jönsson S, Karlsson MO, Kriek M, Mitropoulou C, Patrinos GP, Pirmohamed M, Samwald M, Schaeffeler E, Schwab M, Steinberger D, Stingl J, Sunder-Plassmann G, Toffoli G, Turner RM, van Rhenen MH, Swen JJ, Guchelaar HJ (2017) CORRIGENDUM: implementing pharmacogenomics in Europe: design and implementation strategy of the ubiquitous pharmacogenomics consortium. Clin Pharmacol Ther 102:152

Weston AD, Hood L (2004) Systems biology, proteomics, and the future of health care: toward predictive, preventative, and personalized medicine. J Proteome Res 3:179–196

Wong-Lin K, McClean PL, McCombe N, Kaur D, Sanchez-Bornot JM, Gillespie P, Todd S, Finn DP, Joshi A, Kane J, McGuinness B (2020) Shaping a data-driven era in dementia care pathway through computational neurology approaches. BMC Med 18:398–398

Xu F, Uszkoreit H, Du Y, Fan W, Zhao D, Zhu J (2019) Explainable AI: a brief survey on history, research areas, approaches and challenges. In: Tang J, Kan MY, Zhao D, Li S, Zan H (eds) Natural language processing and Chinese computing NLPCC 2019 Lecture notes in computer science. Springer International Publishing, Cham, pp 563–574

Open Access This chapter is licensed under the terms of the Creative Commons Attribution 4.0 International License (http://creativecommons.org/licenses/by/4.0/), which permits use, sharing, adaptation, distribution and reproduction in any medium or format, as long as you give appropriate credit to the original author(s) and the source, provide a link to the Creative Commons licence and indicate if changes were made.

The images or other third party material in this chapter are included in the chapter's Creative Commons licence, unless indicated otherwise in a credit line to the material. If material is not included in the chapter's Creative Commons licence and your intended use is not permitted by statutory regulation or exceeds the permitted use, you will need to obtain permission directly from the copyright holder.

Security and Privacy

Miguel Correia and Luís Rodrigues

Abstract Computer security or cybersecurity is concerned with the proper functioning of computer systems despite the actions of adversaries. Privacy is about a person or group ability to control how, when, and to what extent their personally identifiable information is shared. The chapter starts by defining security and privacy and explaining why they are problems. Then, it presents some of the scientific and technological achievements in the two areas, highlighting some research trends. Afterwards, the chapter relates security and privacy to the main topics of the book: machine learning as part of artificial intelligence. Finally, the chapter illustrates the relevance of ML in the area using censorship resistance as an example.

1 Introduction

Computer security, also designated *cybersecurity*, is concerned with the proper functioning of computer systems despite the actions of adversaries (hackers, cybercriminals, etc.). This proper functioning is expressed in terms of properties such as confidentiality, integrity, and availability. The discipline emerged in the late 1960s in the US defense context with concerns about the confidentiality of classified information stored in computers. A 1970 report of the *Defense Science Board* (Ware 1970) stated that:

> With the advent of resource-sharing computer systems that distribute the capabilities and components of the machine configuration among several users or several tasks, a new dimension has been added to the problem of safeguarding computer resident classified information.

Privacy is an old term with related but different meanings. Privacy can be defined as a person's (or a group of persons') ability to control how, when, and to what

---

M. Correia (✉) · L. Rodrigues
INESC-ID, Instituto Superior Técnico, Universidade de Lisboa, Lisbon, Portugal
e-mail: miguel.p.correia@tecnico.ulisboa.pt; ler@tecnico.ulisboa.pt

© The Author(s) 2024
H. Sousa Antunes et al. (eds.), *Multidisciplinary Perspectives on Artificial Intelligence and the Law*, Law, Governance and Technology Series 58,
https://doi.org/10.1007/978-3-031-41264-6_5

extent his (their) personally identifiable information is communicated to others (Van Tilborg and Jajodia 2014). The original definition speaks of *personal information*, but today the broader term *personally identifiable information* (PII) is used instead to denote that some data that is not strictly personal can be used directly or indirectly to identify a person (e.g., an IP address or data about colleagues) (McCallister et al. 2010). Relevant properties include anonymity, unobservability, and PII confidentiality. Privacy in the context of computer systems also emerged in the 1960s or 1970s (Miller 1971). The area gained much relevance recently with the European General Data Protection[1] Regulation (GDPR) (European Parliament and European Council 2016) and similar legislation in other countries.

Security and privacy are tightly related disciplines. Privacy to some extend is about the security, mostly confidentiality, of personal identifiers and personal information. However, privacy includes aspects that are barely related to classical security. Two examples are statistical disclosure control (Dalenius 1977) and differential privacy (Dwork 2006). The oldest, and one of the top, scientific conferences in the area, shows the connection between the two topics starting with its name: IEEE Symposium on Security and Privacy.

A note has to be made on how security and privacy should be presented today. Traditionally these topics have been presented in a *negative* way: bad things can happen (and they indeed happen as seen in the news) so we must struggle to prevent them from happening. However, we argue that they should be presented in a *positive* way: the digitalization (digital transformation) of our society requires people and organizations to be able to use computer-based systems with peace of mind, without excessive concerns about security and privacy. These are the goals of the security and privacy scientific and technical areas.

In practice, security and privacy are not 100% achievable in a certain environment or system. This is no surprise, as theft or murder were never erradicated in our society. Therefore, the goal is never to achieve 100% security or privacy, but an adequate level of *risk*. Risk takes into account two factors: the probability of some property being violated and the impact of such violation. The probability depends on the level of vulnerability and the level of threat.

The efforts to increase security and privacy are substantial, both from academia and industry. Today, there are many academic journals and conferences devoted to the matter, including top conferences such as the IEEE Symposium on Security and Privacy, ACM Conference on Computer and Communications Security, Network and Distributed System Security Symposium (NDSS), and Usenix Security. The industry in the area is also large. For instance, recently Gartner forecasted a spending of $150.4 billion in security in 2021, with an increase of 12.4% in relation to 2020 (Whitney 2021). Another indicator is the existence of many industrial fairs worldwide. The largest is probably the RSA Conference, organized in several countries

---

[1] The title suggests the regulation is about data protection, but in fact it is about *personal* data protection, i.e., about privacy.

Security and Privacy 83

yearly, and that attracts more than 40,000 participants only in the USA (Government Technology 2019).

After more than 50 years, security and privacy are vast research areas, with many facets. Therefore, this chapter provides a necessarily limited summary. It provides an overview of important topics and recent developments, with a focus on technology. Other angles such as governance, legal, risk management, security operations, incident management, and digital forensics are not covered.

The chapter is organized as follows. Section 2 defines security and privacy. Section 3 explains why security and privacy are problems. Section 4 presents some of the scientific and technological achievements in the area, highlighting some research trends. Section 5 relate security and privacy to the main topics of the book: machine learning as part of artificial intelligence. Section 6 illustrate the relevance of ML in the area using censorship resistance as an example. Finally, Sect. 7 concludes the chapter.

2 Defining Security and Privacy

Expressions like "system X is secure" or "system Y ensures user privacy" are too vague to be useful. What is useful is to state which set of security and privacy *properties* a system satisfies if correctly implemented and configured, given a set of assumptions about the environment (e.g., the computational power of the adversary).

Security is often expressed in terms derived from *trust* (Veríssimo et al. 2003). Trust is the accepted dependence of a person or (sub)system on a set of properties of another (sub)system. These properties can be of several types, including security and privacy. The *trustworthiness* of a (sub)system is the measure in which it meets the set of properties.

2.1 Security Properties

The three core security properties are confidentiality, integrity, and availability (CIA):

- *Confidentiality:* absence of unauthorized data disclosure;
- *Integrity:* absence of unauthorized data or (sub)system modification;
- *Availability:* readiness of a (sub)system to provide its service.

Notice two aspects. First, security is concerned with guaranteeing these properties in the presence of malicious actions of an adversary. This is expressed by the term *unauthorized*. Second, these properties are related to the impact of malicious actions on data (or information) and (sub)systems, but not necessarily on both. Confidentiality is about data, availability about (sub)systems, and integrity about both.

Two other properties can be considered to be related to integrity:

- *Authenticity:* absence of unauthorized modification of the content or information about its source;
- *Non-repudiation:* absence of denial of authorship of data or actions.

A last property gained visibility recently with the emergence of Bitcoin and other blockchains and distributed ledgers:

- *Decentralization:* absence of dependence on a trusted central authority.

Decentralization does not remove the need for trust, but substitutes trust on individual third parties with trust on sets of parties.

2.2 Privacy Properties

Privacy properties apply to a system that processes personally identifiable information (PII). Consider the auxiliary property:

- *Unlinkability:* given the execution of a certain system, a set of unlinkable PII items can be no more and no less related before and after that execution.

On the contrary of what happens with security, there is some intersection between the classical privacy properties (Pfitzmann and Köhntopp 2001). Consider the identifier of a person (ID) and a set of PII items designated items of interest (IOIs). Privacy can be stated in terms of the following properties:

- *Anonymity:* a person not being identifiable within a set of persons (anonymity set), i.e., unlinkability of the set of IOIs and the ID;
- *Unobservability:* the IOIs are indistinguishable from any IOI at all.

If unobservability is guaranteed, then anonymity is also guaranteed, but the opposite is not true. A related term is *pseudonymity* that means the use of pseudonyms as person IDs. However, pseudonymity is not a property, but a mechanism for obtaining privacy.

The GDPR establishes a set of rights of users before data controllers and data processors (Pfitzmann and Köhntopp 2001). These rights make concrete the "ability to control (...) PII" that appears in our definition of privacy. Therefore, we state them as properties (the names are ours), referencing the article of the GDPR where they are defined:

- *Accessibility:* ability to obtain information about PII being processed (Article 15);
- *Rectifiability:* ability to correct inaccurate PII (Article 16);
- *Erasureability:* ability to delete PII (Article 17);
- *Restrictability:* ability to restrict the way in which PII is processed (Article 18);
- *Portability:* ability to obtain a copy of the PII being processed (Article 20);

Security and Privacy 85

- *Withdrawability:* ability to withdraw consent to process data (Article 7) or to object to that processing (Article 21).

3 Security and Privacy Problems

The previous sections stated that there are security and privacy problems that have to be solved. This section presents these problems in more detail.

3.1 Access Control

All security and privacy problems are related to *access*. For example, the initial motivation for security was shared access to computers containing secret (military) information. Another example: the cybersecurity problem today comes mostly from the universal connectivity provided by the Internet. The approach to manage access is twofold. First, it involves separation (or isolation), which can be logical, cryptographic, physical, or temporal. Second, access has to be granted or denied, following some security policy.

This is the context where *access control* comes to play. In abstract terms, there are objects (or resources) that are accessed by subjects (users, processes). Subjects and objects are logically separated, i.e., they are isolated from each other using software and/or hardware mechanisms. Access control is concerned with validating the access permissions (or rights) of subjects to objects. Access control is performed by an abstract component called reference monitor. Whenever a subject wants to access an object (e.g., a user to access a file in an online service), the reference monitor uses an access control database to get information about permissions and evaluates if the user shall be granted access or not. The reference monitor takes the decision and optionally stores data about the access for audit purposes.

The most common access control model is Access Control Lists (ACLs). Each object (e.g., a file) has an ACL that lists the permissions (e.g., read, read-and-write) of each user (e.g., user, admin, any) over that object. There are many other modules, e.g., capabilities, Role-Based Access Control (RBAC) or the current de facto standard, Attribute-Based Access Control (ABAC).

Access control can be discretionary—the access policy is defined by the object owner—or mandatory—the access policy is defined by an administrator for a class of objects.

3.2 Vulnerabilities and Attacks

Access control should be effective if properly implemented and configured—which are challenges themselves—but often another problem allows circumventing access control: vulnerabilities. Computer systems are complex, arguably the most complex creations of humanity. The laptop in which this text is written is the creation of thousands of engineers all over the world, who do not know each other or fully understand the overall system: the laptop in this case. This complexity necessarily leads to errors as engineers are humans.

A *vulnerability* is an error that allows violating a security property. A vulnerability can be introduced during the system design, implementation, or configuration. A vulnerability can be exploited by an *attack*. If the attack is successful, a security property is violated.

Vulnerabilities are so important that they are catalogued. The most important catalogue of vulnerabilities is the Common Vulnerabilities and Exposures (CVE).[2] For instance, in 2014 there was a vulnerability that caused much turmoil called Heartbleed; it received the identifier CVE-2014-0160 in that catalogue (the 160th or 2014). CVE has been registering around 17,000–18,000 new vulnerabilities yearly in recent years.

A particularly dangerous class of vulnerabilities are so-called *zero-day vulnerabilities*. These are vulnerabilities that are known by one or more groups—e.g., an intelligence agency or a hacker community—but have not been publicly disclosed. They allow these groups to attack systems freely, as no protections are deployed against something that is unknown.

A vulnerability can be publicly disclosed in different ways: as part of an update of the software vendor, in the CVE catalogue, in a mailing list like Bugtraq, etc. When that happens, there is the opportunity for organizations and individuals that use the vulnerable software to fix it or protect it, but this disclosure also increases much the probability of the vulnerability being attacked.

Attacks can come through different vectors. A common vector today is called drive-by download. The victim accesses a web page with a browser that contains a vulnerability. The site launches the attack against the browser, exploiting the vulnerability. Note that the site may be legitimate but had itself been a victim of an attack.

3.3 Malware

Many attacks involve *malware*. This term summarizes many others that were previously used in a way that was often inconsistent: virus, worms, Trojan horses,

---

[2] http://cve.mitre.org/.

backdoors, etc. Malware comes from malicious software and includes all these variants.

A form of malware that is much active today is *ransomware*. When a ransomware specimen enters a computer, it encrypts the content of the disk and requests the payment of a ransom—a monetary fee—often in a cryptocurrency like Bitcoin or Monero, to hide the identity of the attacker. These ransoms vary from hundreds to millions of euros, e.g., as in the high-profile attacks against Maersk (2018) and Colonial Pipeline (2021). Some of these attacks also involve data theft to further pressure the victim into paying.

Another important form of malware are Remote Access Trojans (RATs) or bots, which hide in computer and stay dormant until ordered to do some action. These RATs or bots are controlled remotely by a central server, forming a botnet (a network of bots or robots). These botnets can have thousands of computers and operate as cyberweapons, capable of making systems unavailable using Distributed Denial of Service (DDoS) attacks or stealing large amounts of data or access credentials, among other attacks.

3.4 The Human Factor

The importance of automated attacks that exploit vulnerabilities and/or use malware is undeniable as they are constantly happening. However, many attacks exploit a different class of weaknesses that is much harder to manage: the humans that use computer systems. These attacks are often called *social engineering*.

Phishing is a common attack that aims to steal personal data. This data is often user credentials for a system such as corporate email or homebanking. The attack consists simply in sending emails requesting data. There is no technical vulnerability involved: the data is stolen because users trust the message they receive and act accordingly. Given a large enough set of potential victims, there will always be many that fall for the scam.

A form of attack that combines both technical and social engineering aspects are emails with malicious attachments. Human victims fall for the attack by opening the attachment, but this attachment contains an attack that tries to explore a vulnerability in the victim's computer. This was the first attack vector using the conspicuous Wannacry attack (2017); there was a second that involved exploiting a vulnerability in other computers of the same organization.

4 Scientific and Technological Achievements

This section presents a summary of important and/or interesting scientific and technological achievements in the security and privacy areas. They are organized by subareas, generically inspired by those of the Cyber Security Body Of Knowledge

(CYBOK), "a comprehensive Body of Knowledge to inform and underpin educational and professional training for the cyber security sector".[3] For each topic, we present research trends.

4.1 Cryptography

Cryptography (or cryptology) is an old discipline, around 4000 years-old according to Kahn (Kahn 1996). However, until the twentieth century, its evolution was limited and it remained mostly an art: a struggle between cryptographers that designed coding schemes to protect the confidentiality of messages, and cryptanalysts that would try to break them. These schemes were clever but simple, thus often broken; Mary, Queen of Scots, was beheaded when the encrypted messages she exchanged with her supporters were decoded. The twentieth century first introduced automation with machines like German's Enigma, used in the second World War, but, most importantly, revolutionized the area with the surge of computation and of public key cryptography. Today this is an exciting research area with several top conferences, e.g., the Annual International Cryptology Conference.

A cautionary note: there is some confusion regarding the relation between cybersecurity and cryptography. Some seem to reduce the former to the latter. In fact, although cryptography plays an important role in cybersecurity, cybersecurity includes many topics that are unrelated to cryptography, including most of the areas covered in the following sections.

Classical cryptography involved an encryption and a decryption algorithm. These algorithms were secret to guarantee that the adversary could not read the encrypted messages. In the past century, this idea was slightly modified to become what we now call *symmetric encryption*: the same two algorithms became configurable with a number—designated a *key*—that must be kept secret, whereas the algorithms should be public to be scrutinizable. This led to widely adopted algorithms such as the 1976's Data Encryption Standard (DES), no longer considered secure, and the current Advanced Encryption Standard (AES), published in 1998. Today such schemes are not only used to protect the confidentiality of communications but also of other forms of data, such as the content of disks or individual files.

Symmetric encryption poses a difficulty: the distribution of the secret key, i.e., delivering it to the parties that need it (e.g., sender and receiver). A solution to this problem—*public key cryptography* (or asymmetric cryptography)—was eventually published in 1976 (Diffie and Hellman 1976) and the first public key encryption algorithm, RSA, in 1978 (Rivest et al. 1978). In this form of cryptography there is no longer a single key but a *key pair*. This pair has a *private key* that is supposed to stay secret and a *public key* that can, and often should, be publicly disclosed. If the data is encrypted with the public (resp. private) key, it can only be decrypted with

---

[3] https://www.cybok.org/knowledgebase/.

Security and Privacy

the private (resp. public) key. Therefore, if Alice wants to share a secret key K to protect her communications with Bob, she can encrypt K with Bob's public key, so only Bob will be able to decrypt it and get K, even if Trudy obtains a copy of the encrypted K.

Public key cryptography has a second important application: ensuring data integrity using *digital signatures* (Rivest et al. 1978). Alice can sign a message or a document using her private key, so anyone with her public key can verify if the signature is her's. Public keys are typically distributed using *certificates* that contain the identification of the key owner, the public key, and a signature created by a Certificate Authority (CA), among other information.

Signatures are also based in another important type of cryptographic algorithm: *cryptographic hash functions*. These functions are one-way and produce a fixed length output (of, e.g., 256 bits) called hash. Moreover, they satisfy collision resistance properties such as "it is computationally infeasible to find two different inputs that produce the same output".

A current research trend in the area is *post-quantum cryptography* (or quantum resistance) (Alagic et al. 2020). In 1995, Shor published an algorithm that in essence allows obtaining a private key from the public key, effectively breaking public key cryptography algorithms like RSA and ECDSA. This algorithm can only be executed in quantum computers that do not yet exist, but may come into existence within some years. Quantum algorithms against other cryptographic schemes were later presented by Grover (1997) and Simon (1994). In consequence, there is a large research effort on algorithms that remain secure if or when that eventually happens. RSA is based on the difficulty of factoring large integer numbers and Shor's algorithm allows doing that factorization efficiently in a quantum computer; the main approach for post-quantum cryptography is to use different difficult problems that are (arguably) not attackable in quantum computers, e.g., the Module Learning With Errors (MLWE) or Module Learning With Rounding (MLWR) problems.

4.2   Hardware-Based Security

As explained above, security and privacy problems are related to access. The prevention of arbitrary access inside a computer is an important problem as malicious users and malware are always potentially threats. The solution to this problem involves hardware support. Until the 1980s, this support was the one already necessary for operating systems (OSs), e.g., *memory protection* (based, e.g., on paging) that allows isolating processes (programs in execution) from each other (Gasser 1988). Memory protection is implemented by both hardware components (CPU, MMU), and software (OS).

A second example of this kind of support are CPU *execution modes*. A typical configuration is to have the OS running in kernel mode and user processes in user mode. In user mode, the CPU does not allow the execution of some instructions: it generates an exception or silently does nothing when a program tries to execute one. For instance, processes in user mode are not allowed to execute I/O instructions directly; they have to delegate to the OS their execution using system calls. This separation into a trusted part—the OS—and an untrusted part—user processes— makes sense, but OSs are too large and often vulnerabilities are there found.

In the early 2000s, a consortium of companies, the Trusted Computing Group (TCG), designed a hardware module (usually a chip) to be included in personal computers. This Trusted Platform Module (TPM) provides a set of security services that clearly departed from older hardware security mechanisms. These services were mostly the storage of cryptographic keys and software integrity verification. The former (key storage) is today widely adopted in different forms in mobile devices. The latter supports remote attestation and is also available today in many forms, although not widely used. Later, these services were slightly expanded in the TPM 2.0 specification.

A limitation of the TPM is that the services it provides are fixed. Trusted Execution Environments (TEEs) are a solution for this limitation as they can be programmed with user software. This software is executed in the TEE, isolated from the OS and other privileged software (e.g., BIOS and hypervisor). Today there is a set of TEE technologies that are available in common computers and mobile devices: they are not supported by hardware modules, but by the CPUs themselves. TrustZone is an extension available in many ARM processors. With this technology there is a normal world where the OS and user processes are executed, but also a secure world—the TEE—where security services are run on top of a small kernel. This allows ensuring the confidentiality and integrity of what is in the TEE.

Intel developed the Software Guard Extensions (SGX) for their CPUs. SGX allows running several TEEs on each CPU, designated enclaves. Additionally, to the assurances provided by TrustZone TEEs, enclaves and their data are encrypted while not being executed, thus both logically and cryptographically isolated from the OS and the rest of the computer.

AMD included in their processors the Secure Encrypted Virtualization (SEV) that turns a hypervisor and each of the Virtual Machines (VMs) it executes into TEEs. SEV encrypts each of these TEEs with its own key, isolating them. A second generation of this technology, AMD SEV-Encrypted State (SEV-ES), additionally encrypts the content of the CPU registers when a VM stops running. The third generation of SEV, still to appear, AMD SEV Secure Nested Paging (SEV-SNP), will provide further integrity protection. In 2020, AMD, IBM and others created the Confidential Computing Consortium (CCC) to promote the adoption of these technologies.

The main research trend in the area are applications for TEEs. This technology is being adopted in different areas, from SGX in blockchain to TrustZone in Internet-of-Things devices.

4.3 Cloud Computing

Cloud computing is a model in which computing is provided as a service (Armbrust et al. 2010). In the typical setting, there is a company—the Cloud Service Provider (CSP)—that provides services in a pay-per-use mode, i.e., the consumer pays for the service it consumes. This contrasts with the classical model in which the consumer first buys hardware, then uses it. Instead, with clouds the consumer uses as much resources as it needs, during the period it needs, without an initial investment. This adaptability of the resources used to consumer needs is often called elasticity. There are three main service models: Infrastructure as a Service (IaaS), in which the CSP provides VMs, networking and storage; Platform as a Service (PaaS), where the CSP provides components to build and run applications; and Software as a Service (SaaS), in which the CSP provides applications.

This approach of delegating software and data to a third party, the CSP, involves risks: data loss, data theft, malicious insiders, misconfiguration, etc. (Cloud Security Alliance 2019). Managing these problems requires a holistic process for building and configuring software, which includes a large set of technological solutions. The topic is too vast for a chapter, so we focus on a couple of examples of advanced mechanisms.

Many consumers use cloud services to store data. In case they consider a single CSP does not provide an adequate level of availability, integrity, or confidentiality assurances, they can resort to a set of CSPs forming a *cloud-of-clouds* (Bessani et al. 2013). The idea is to store the data (files) in several clouds, protected using encryption and digital signatures, with secret keys protected using secret sharing, and applying erasure coding to reduce the total stored data size. This requires Byzantine fault-tolerant replication, so the upload and download protocols are more sophisticated than simply storing copies of files in several places.

Other consumers may deploy applications on PaaS services but be concerned that these applications are attacked and their state (data) modified. This can happen, e.g., if someone steals credentials from a legitimate user and uses them to access the application. Removing the effects of such actions from the application storage (database, file system) is often done manually. A solution is to modify the application to track the effects of the requests it receives on that storage, but modifying the applications can be complex or even impossible. Sanare supports automatic recovery and removes the need of modifying the application by using machine learning to associate application requests with storage commands (Matos et al. 2021). The association algorithm—Matchare—is based on a Deep Convolutional Neural Network (CNN) and requires a training phase.

4.4 Digital Money, Assets and Identity

Digital money exists for many years but gained global attention recently with Bitcoin and thousands of others cryptocurrencies. In reality, most money used today has digital form: most payments and transfers are done using computers, not paper or metal.

In the 1980s, some authors presented advanced cryptographic schemes for digital money and payments that paved the way to current cryptocurrencies. A seminal work by Chaum presented a payment mechanism that prevents entities not involved in the payment to determine the recipient of the payment, the time, and amount transferred, while allowing the payer to provide a proof of payment and to disable payment media reported stolen (Chaum 1983). In a following work, Chaum et al. presented a digital money scheme, which allows payments offline while providing proof in case the spender uses the same money twice (Chaum et al. 1990).

In 2008, Nakamoto introduced the first cryptocurrency, Bitcoin (Nakamoto 2008). In relation to previous work, it introduced two differences. First, it does not depend on a third party, but on an open ad hoc group of entities that run the Bitcoin software in their computers (nodes). This additionally ensures availability. Second, it prevents the double spending of money using a chain of blocks (blockchain) to register transactions, while nodes only accept blocks with valid transactions. This digital ledger, or blockchain, is replicated in all nodes and grows when there is consensus on the next block to add. Each block contains a hash of the previous block, obtained by solving a cryptographic puzzle, which makes it hard to modify the blockchain (ensuring integrity) and allows solving consensus.

Eventually many other cryptocurrencies appeared, but also the possibility of running user programs in the nodes, often called smart contracts (Buterin 2014). This programmability of these systems allowed not only the creation of other cryptocurrencies, but also transactionable *digital assets* (or tokens). A type of digital asset that is gaining popularity are Non-Fungible Tokens (NFTs). They represent some collectionable item, like a digital picture, a music record, etc.

Another recent trend in the area is to use blockchains to store identity data. The W3C defined the concept of Decentralized Identifier (DID). The main idea is to allow the DID controller (e.g., the person with that identity) to control the DID, instead of relying on a centralized entity (e.g., a national registry or a company such as Google or Facebook). DIDs can be stored in a blockchain or distributed ledger. Technically, a DID is a small digital document that contains identification data, e.g., a name and a public key. The W3C also defined the notion of Verifiable Credential (VC). A VC provides assurance about information of a certain DID, e.g., that it corresponds to a natural personal that was born in a certain date. Often VCs are not transmitted themselves, but in the form of Verifiable Presentations (VPs) that prove some fact without disclosing undesirable information. For instance, for privacy purposes a VP can prove that a person is more than 18 years old without revealing his/her age.

Security and Privacy   93

A recent trend is on the interoperability of this kind of systems, either of the same or different types (Belchior et al. 2021).

5 Security, Privacy, and Machine Learning

Security and privacy have become an arms race. Companies and other organizations are deploying increasingly more sophisticated defenses, but cybercriminals are also becoming increasingly sophisticated. Not surprisingly, machine learning is a powerful weapon in the cybercriminal war, that can be used either to protect or harm computer infrastructures and their users.

Machine learning (ML) can be very effective at capturing and classifying patterns, which is extremely useful to detect suspicious or anomalous behaviour. There are many security-related areas where ML has been applied successfully, including spam filtering (Guzella and Caminhas 2009), fraud detection (Gao et al. 2021), intrusion detection (Buczak and Guven 2016), malware detection (Burguera et al. 2011), vulnerabilities in source code (Shar et al. 2013), among others.

Unfortunately, ML can also be a source of vulnerabilities and attacks (Barreno et al. 2008), as described below. First ML can be used to detect patterns in user behaviour, for instance when they communicate with others, even if the content is encrypted. This can be used, for instance, to detect human rights activists that attempt to escape censorship. In the next section, we discuss this attack in detail.

Moreover, the characteristics of the training data can lead to unexpected or undesirable results, due to ambiguities in the data set or in the classification. An anecdotal example of this effect was a recent incident, where Amazon's Alexa suggested to a 10-year-old girl to touch a coin to the prongs of a half-inserted plug (BBC News 2021). This sort of errors can happen even without the intervention of malicious agents, and are hard to avoid because many ML models cannot be understood by humans, making the task of predicting the outcome almost impossible. Because of this limitation, there is an effort to use techniques that can improve the explainability and interpretability of the ML models (Gohel et al. 2021).

The problems above can be exacerbated by an active attacker that deliberately aims at defining the ML system, to cause the system to malfunction or to steal information from the ML model. For instance, an adversary can carefully edit the inputs to the ML system to evade detection. A common example of this is spam, were the use of misspelled words or unexpected characters may prevent spam to be classified as such. An adversary can also cause a system to operate in a harmful manner. For instance, it was shown that small changes to the visual aspect of street signs could cause automated driving systems to violate speed limits (Wierd 2002). In some cases, an adversary has the opportunity to provide training data to the ML system, and can exploit this to bias the model by providing malicious samples, an attack known as ML *poisoning* (Biggio et al. 2014). Finally, attackers can use an existing model to extract information regarding the training data, obtaining access to data that should be kept confidential (Wang et al. 2020).

An interesting example of the threats associated with the use of ML is the recent Apple proposal to scan the photo library of devices in search for child pornography. Child pornography is certainly a horrendous crime, and secure ways to fight it would certainly be welcome. Apple was proposing to scan the photo library in the user devices, in search for illegal content, to avoid sending the user photos to an external site. This would ensure the privacy of photos for all users except criminals. While the idea has some appeal, many risks have been identified with the approach, which led Apple to postpone the deployment of the system. First, it would be difficult for users to assess if file scanning would just be looking for child pornography, or would also look for other sensitive data (such as health problems, political views, etc.). Moreover, it would be possible that an attacker would send an apparently innocuous photo to a target in order to trigger misclassification, flagging an innocent person. For a more in-depth discussion of the problems of this approach, the reader can refer to (Abelson et al. 2021).

6 Censorship Resistance

In this section, we further illustrate the relevance of ML in the security and privacy arms race, using censorship resistance as an example.

Today, computer networks support the access to most sources of information, including online newspapers, television broadcast, social media, etc. In most countries the operation of these computer networks is controlled by a small number of entities that are under direct control of the government or that can easily be coerced to enforce government directives. This makes it extremely easy to censor access to information.

Examples of wide-scale censorship activities are easy to find: in June 2019 Sudan imposed an internet shutdown (Net Blocks 2019b), and the same happened in Iran in November 2019 (Net Blocks 2019a); there is also evidence that the dissemination of Corona virus related information is tightly controlled by the Chinese government (Ruan et al. 2020; Staff 2020). More subtle forms of censorship can also be found: recently, Reuters reported that Amazon has agreed to censor negative reviews to Xi Jingping's book on their platform (Stecklow and Dastin 2021). In a few cases, censorship can be justified, for instance, to fight criminal activity, such as the dissemination of child pornography content as discussed before, but in most cases it simply deprives citizens of their rights to access free information.

Unsurprisingly, people have developed tools that aim at circumventing censorship. These tools have a dual purpose. First, they aim at allowing users to access information that would be otherwise blocked. Second, that aim at preventing an external observed to detect that the users is accessing such information. This is particularly relevant because, under oppressive regimes, citizens that attempt to evade censorship can be prosecuted, arrested, or even killed. In the next paragraphs we discuss two of these tools, namely *anonymity networks* and *multimedia protocol tunneling* tools.

Security and Privacy 95

6.1 Anonymity Networks

An anonymity network is a kind of *overlay network* designed to preserve the privacy of the users. It uses a network of servers that act as *relays* to propagate information, typically between a user and a source of information. Instead of accessing the information directly, the information is routed in the relay network, using multiple encryption layers (a technique known as *onion routing* (Dingledine et al. 2004)). The encryption is set up in a way that prevents any intermediate relay to know the original source or the final destination of the packet (each relay is only aware of the previous and the next hop in the overlay network). Ideally, the mapping between two endpoints would not be possible without the collusion of multiple relays. The most relevant anonymity network today is the Tor network (Tor 2019).

Anonymity networks are not specifically targeted at censorship circumvention, but can, and have been, used for that effect. In fact, if the sensor cannot identify the relays, and cannot block the communication among these relays (unless it completely shutdowns the internet access), it is possible to establish an overlay route from a client residing in a censored region to a relay residing in an uncensored region (for instance, in a different country), in order to access any given internet site. Also, because all communication is encrypted, it is impossible for an entity that observes the traffic of a client to infer which content is being exchanged.

Unfortunately, anonymity networks have a number of limitations. First, the adversary may be able to identify the nodes that provide access to the Tor network (known as Tor *bridges*) and effectively prevent users from accessing the network in censored regions. Furthermore, even if the adversary cannot access the content of the packets being exchanged, it can access the features of these packets to infer what information is being accessed. In this task, ML has proved to be a strong ally of the censor.

There are two relevant attacks that can be used to detect what content a client is accessing, even when it uses a anonymity network: *traffic fingerprinting* and *traffic correlation*.

In a traffic fingerprinting attack, the adversary observes the traffic pattern and tries to match it with known patterns. This is possible, in particular, when users access some known websites. In order to perform this attack, the attacker collects data regarding the packets that are generated when a given site is accessed. Features such as packet size count, packet size frequency, per-direction bandwidth, total time, burst markers, inter-arrival time, etc. are used as patterns known as *website fingerprints* (Liberatore and Levine 2006). Machine learning tools can then be used to learn these patterns and later classify traffic flows collected from end users. Advances in ML, such as the use of modern convolutional neural networks, a technique known as *deep fingerprinting* (Sirinam et al. 2018), has shown to be highly effective, even when clients apply defenses against website fingerprinting, such as adding dummy packets, padding, and/or packet delays, to make classification harder (Dyer et al. 2012; Cai et al. 2014; Juarez et al. 2016).

In a traffic correlation attack, the adversary monitors the network between the clients and the anonymity network and between the anonymity network and the servers, i.e., the traffic between the anonymity network boundaries and the clients/ servers outside the network (Danezis 2003; Le Blond et al. 2011; Nasr et al. 2017). Then, the traffic features of the different flows are correlated to find a match, and establish a link between a client and a server. Needless to say, the use of ML, in particular the use of deep neural networks, has also proved to be helpful in performing traffic correlation (Nasr et al. 2018).

6.2 Multimedia Protocol Tunneling

Multimedia Protocol Tunneling is a technique that consists in embedding a covert channel in a multimedia stream. This technique can be used for censorship circumvention by leveraging services that the censor may not be willing to block (Fifield 2017), such as Skype, Zoom, or WhatsApp. Using this approach, a user in a censored region establishes a multimedia call to another user in an uncensored region and then, embeds a *covert channel*, in the multimedia stream; this covert channel can be used to convey standard IP traffic and be used to access censored content. This typically involves replacing part or all of the original multimedia content by the content of the covert channel, encoded in some form (Houmansadr et al. 2013; Li et al. 2014; Kohls et al. 2016; Barradas et al. 2017, 2020). If the multimedia content is encrypted, an adversary has way to inspect the covert channel. Furthermore, if the adversary has no way to distinguish a multimedia call that embeds a cover channel from a call that does not, we say that the channel remains *unobservable*.

Multimedia protocol tunneling is appealing because, in the general case, the censor cannot generally afford to block all multimedia applications, as these are used widely by citizens for daily interactions with family and friends and by companies to perform business. The large number of multimedia channels that are used at any point in time also make the task of observing these channels harder. Unfortunately, these tools can also be vulnerable to traffic analysis, in an attempt to identify patterns that distinguish a normal call from a call that embeds a covert channel. Again, machine learning tools can help the attacker in this endeavour. A study published in the 27th USENIX Security Symposium showed that decision trees and some of their variants are extremely effective at detecting covert traffic with reduced false positive rates (Barradas et al. 2018). Furthermore, recent research has shown that the information required to perform the classification can be collected, in a cost-effective manner, at line speed by leveraging the capabilities of new programmable switches (Barradas et al. 2021).

6.3 Avoiding ML Attacks

As we have discussed above, machine learning tools can be used to perform sophisticate traffic analysis in order to detect anomalies, identify patterns, and perform correlations among different flows. These tools empower the adversary, in particular state-level adversaries to detect attempts to evade censorship. Therefore, modern censorship resistance tools must be designed with these attacks in mind.

Interestingly, new tools are being proposed that can embed a cover channel in a multimedia stream without affecting the key features of the traffic stream. Protozoa (Barradas et al. 2020) is one of such tools. It leverages the WebRTC (Web Real-Time Communication) API to replace real video content, produced in real-time by a multimedia conference tool, by converting content of exactly the same size, shielding the protocol from detection mechanisms based on packet size and packet frequency. Furthermore, Protozoa, unlike several previous protocols that offered very limited bandwidth, can deliver covert channel bandwidth capacities in the order of 1.4 Mbps. Protozoa proved resistant to state-of-the-art classification tools but it is unclear if it is possible to design more sophisticated ML tools, that attempt to exploit other features, such as time-series of inter-packet arrival times, to perform detection.

7 Conclusion

Security and privacy are important aspects of our connected world. The chapter defines the two concepts and explains why they are a problem that must be managed, even if not entirely solvable. The chapter presents an illustrative set of scientific and technological achievements, with an emphasis on current research trends. The chapter also points out links between security/privacy and machine learning, using censorship resistance as a use case.[4]

---

[4] *See* generally, on the different applications of Machine Learning and AI, in this book A Oliveira and M A T Figueiredo—Artificial intelligence: historical context and state of the art; I Trancoso, N Mamede, B Martins, H S Pinto and R Ribeiro—The impact of language technologies in the legal domain; J Gonçalves-Sá and F L Pinheiro—Societal Implications of Recommendation Systems: A Technical Perspective; A T Freitas—Data-driven approaches in healthcare: challenges and emerging trends; E Magrani and P G F Silva—The Ethical and Legal Challenges of Recommender Systems Driven by Artificial Intelligence; M Lanz and S Mijic—Risks associated with the use of natural language generation: Swiss civil liability law perspective; M S Fernandes and J R Goldim—Artificial Intelligence and Decision Making in Health: Risks and Opportunities; W Gravett—Judicial Decision-making in the Age of Artificial Intelligence; and D Durães, P M Freitas and P Novais—The Relevance of Deepfakes in the Administration of Criminal Justice.

References

Abelson H, Anderson R, Bellovin SM, Benaloh J, Blaze M, Callas J, Diffie W, Landau S, Neumann PG, Rivest RL, Schiller JI, Schneier B, Teague V, Troncoso C (2021) Bugs in our pockets: the risks of client-side scanning. arXiv preprint arXiv:2110.07450

Alagic G, Alperin-Sheriff J, Apon D, Cooper D, Dang Q, Kelsey J, Liu YK, Miller C, Moody D, Peralta R, Perlner R, Robinson A, Smith-Tone D (2020) Status report on the second round of the NIST post-quantum cryptography standardization process. NIST, Gaithersburg

Armbrust M, Fox A, Griffith R, Joseph AD, Katz R, Konwinski A, Lee G, Patterson D, Rabkin A, Stoica I, Zaharia M (2010) A view of cloud computing. Commun ACM 53:50–58

Barradas D, Santos N, Rodrigues L (2017) Deltashaper: enabling unobservable censorship-resistant TCP tunneling over videoconferencing streams. In: Proceedings on privacy enhancing technologies. De Gruyter Open, Minneapolis, pp 5–22

Barradas D, Santos N, Rodrigues L (2018) Effective detection of multimedia protocol tunneling using machine learning. In: Proceedings of the 27th USENIX security symposium. Usenix, Baltimore, pp 169–185

Barradas D, Santos N, Rodrigues L, Nunes V (2020) Poking a hole in the wall: efficient censorship-resistant internet communications by parasitizing on WebRTC. In: Proceedings of the 2020 ACM SIGSAC conference on computer and communications security. ACM, New York, pp 35–48

Barradas D, Santos N, Rodrigues L, Signorello S, Ramos FMV, Madeira A (2021) Flowlens: enabling efficient flow classification for ML-based network security applications. In: Proceedings of the 27th network and distributed system security symposium. ACM, San Diego, pp 1–18

Barreno M, Bartlett PL, Chi FJ, Joseph AD, Nelson B, Rubinstein BIP, Saini U, Tygar JD (2008) Open problems in the security of learning. In: Proceedings of the 1st ACM workshop on workshop on AISec. ACM, Alexandria, pp 19–26

BBC News (2021) Alexa tells 10-year-old girl to touch live plug with penny. https://www.bbc.com/news/technology-59810383. Accessed 1 Dec 2021

Belchior R, Vasconcelos A, Guerreiro S, Correia M (2021) A survey on blockchain interoperability: past, present, and future trends. ACM Comput Surv 54:Article 168

Bessani A, Correia M, Quaresma B, André F, Sousa P (2013) DepSky: dependable and secure storage in a cloud-of-clouds. ACM Trans Storage 9:Article 12

Biggio B, Fumera G, Roli F (2014) Security evaluation of pattern classifiers under attack. IEEE Trans Knowl Data Eng 26:984–996

Buczak AL, Guven E (2016) A survey of data mining and machine learning methods for cyber security intrusion detection. IEEE Commun Surv Tutor 18:1153–1176

Burguera I, Zurutuza U, Nadjm-Tehrani S (2011) Crowdroid: behavior-based malware detection system for Android. In: Proceedings of the 1st ACM workshop on security and privacy in smartphones and mobile devices. ACM, Chicago, pp 15–26

Buterin V (2014) Ethereum: a next-generation smart contract and decentralized application platform. White Paper

Cai X, Nithyanand R, Wang T, Johnson R, Goldberg I (2014) A systematic approach to developing and evaluating website fingerprinting defenses. In: Proceedings of the 2014 ACM SIGSAC conference on computer and communications security. ACM, Scottsdale, pp 227–238

Chaum D (1983) Blind signatures for untraceable payments. In: Chaum D, Rivest RL, Sherman AT (eds) Advances in cryptology. Springer, Boston, pp 199–203

Chaum D, Fiat A, Naor M (1990) Untraceable electronic cash. In: Goldwasser S (ed) Advances in cryptology — CRYPTO' 88. Springer, New York, pp 319–327

Cloud Security Alliance (2019) Top threats to cloud computing: egregious eleven. Cloud Security Alliance, Washington, DC

Dalenius T (1977) Towards a methodology for statistical disclosure control. Stat Tidskr 15:429–444

Danezis G (2003) Statistical disclosure attacks. In: di Vimercati SDC, Samarati P, Katsikas S (eds) IFIP international information security conference. Kluwer, Athens, pp 421–426

Diffie W, Hellman M (1976) New directions in cryptography. IEEE Trans Inf Theory 22:644–654

Dingledine R, Mathewson N, Syverson P (2004) Tor: the second-generation onion router. In: Proceedings of the 13th conference on USENIX security symposium, vol 13. USENIX Association, San Diego, p 21

Dwork C (2006) Differential privacy. Automata, languages and programming. Springer, Berlin

Dyer KP, Coull SE, Ristenpart T, Shrimpton T (2012) Peek-a-boo, i still see you: why efficient traffic analysis countermeasures fail. In: 2012 IEEE symposium on security and privacy. IEEE, San Francisco, pp 332–346

European Parliament and European Council (2016) Regulation (EU) 2016/679 of the European parliament and of the council of 27 April 2016 on the protection of natural persons with regard to the processing of personal data and on the free movement of such data, and repealing Directive 95/46/EC (General Data Protection Regulation). Off J Eur Union L 119:1–88

Fifield D (2017) Threat modeling and circumvention of Internet censorship. Ph.D. thesis, University of California, Berkeley

Gao Y, Zhang S, Lu J, Gao Y, Zhang S, Lu J (2021) Machine learning for credit card fraud detection. In: Proceedings of the 2021 international conference on control and intelligent robotics. ACM, Guangzhou, pp 213–219

Gasser M (1988) Building a secure computer system. Van Nostrand Reinhold Co., New York

Gohel P, Singh P, Mohanty M (2021) Explainable AI: current status and future directions. arXiv preprint arXiv:2107.07045

Government Technology (2019) RSA conference 2019: what you need to know. https://www.govtech.com/blogs/lohrmann-on-cybersecurity/rsa-conference-2019-what-you-need-to-know.html. Accessed 1 Aug 2021

Grover LK (1997) Quantum mechanics helps in searching for a needle in a haystack. Phys Rev Lett 79:325

Guzella TS, Caminhas WM (2009) A review of machine learning approaches to Spam filtering. Expert Syst Appl 36:10206–10222

Houmansadr A, Riedl TJ, Borisov N, Singer AC (2013) I want my voice to be heard: IP over Voice-over-IP for unobservable censorship circumvention. In: Proceedings of the 20th annual network & distributed system security symposium, NDSS 2013. The Internet Society, San Diego

Juarez M, Imani M, Perry M, Diaz C, Wright M (2016) Toward an efficient website fingerprinting defense. In: Computer security – ESORICS 2016. Springer International Publishing, Cham

Kahn D (1996) The codebreakers: the comprehensive history of secret communication from ancient times to the internet. Simon and Schuster, New York

Kohls K, Holz T, Kolossa D, Pöpper C (2016) SkypeLine: robust hidden data transmission for VoIP. In: Proceedings of the 11th ACM on Asia conference on computer and communications security. ACM, Xi'an, pp 877–888

Le Blond S, Manils P, Chaabane A, Kaafar MA, Castelluccia C, Legout A, Dabbous W (2011) One bad apple spoils the bunch: exploiting P2P applications to trace and profile Tor users. In: Proceedings of the 4th USENIX conference on large-scale exploits and emergent threats. USENIX Association, Boston, p 2

Li S, Schliep M, Hopper N (2014) Facet: streaming over videoconferencing for censorship circumvention. In: Proceedings of the 13th workshop on privacy in the electronic society. ACM, Scottsdale, pp 163–172

Liberatore M, Levine BN (2006) Inferring the source of encrypted HTTP connections. In: Proceedings of the 13th ACM conference on computer and communications security. ACM, Alexandria, pp 255–263

Matos D, Pardal M, Correia M (2021) Sanare: pluggable intrusion recovery for web applications. IEEE Trans Dependable Secure Comput 1:13. https://doi.org/10.36227/techrxiv.13725991

McCallister E, Grance T, Scarfone KA (2010) SP 800–122. Guide to protecting the confidentiality of personally identifiable information (PII). ISAO, Watthana

Miller AR (1971) The assault on privacy: computers, data banks, and dossiers. Signet, Hamilton

Nakamoto S (2008) Bitcoin: a peer-to-peer electronic cash system. https://bitcoin.org/bitcoin.pdf. Accessed 1 Aug 2021

Nasr M, Houmansadr A, Mazumdar A (2017) Compressive traffic analysis: a new paradigm for scalable traffic analysis. In: Proceedings of the 2017 ACM SIGSAC conference on computer and communications security. ACM, Dallas, pp 2053–2069

Nasr M, Bahramali A, Houmansadr A (2018) DeepCorr: strong flow correlation attacks on tor using deep learning. In: Proceedings of the 2018 ACM SIGSAC conference on computer and communications security. ACM, Torontos, pp 1962–1976

Net Blocks (2019a) Internet being restored in Iran after week-long shutdown. https://netblocks.org/reports/internet-restored-in-iran-after-protest-shutdown-dAmqddA9. Accessed 1 Aug 2021

Net Blocks (2019b) Sudan internet shows signs of recovery after month-long shutdown. https://netblocks.org/reports/sudan-internet-recovery-after-month-long-shutdown-98aZpOAo. Accessed 1 Aug 2021

Pfitzmann A, Köhntopp M (2001) Anonymity, unobservability, and pseudonymity — a proposal for terminology. In: Federrath H (ed) Designing privacy enhancing technologies: international workshop on design issues in anonymity and unobservability Berkeley, CA, USA, July 25–26, 2000 proceedings. Springer, Berlin, pp 1–9

Rivest RL, Shamir A, Adleman L (1978) A method for obtaining digital signatures and public-key cryptosystems. Commun ACM 21:120–126

Ruan L, Knockel J, Crete-Nishihata M (2020) Censored contagion: How information on the coronavirus is managed on Chinese social media. https://citizenlab.ca/2020/03/censored-contagion-how-information-on-the-coronavirus-is-managed-on-chinese-social-media/. Accessed 1 Aug 2021

Shar LK, Tan HBK, Briand LC (2013) Mining SQL injection and cross site scripting vulnerabilities using hybrid program analysis. In: 2013 35th international conference on software engineering (ICSE). IEEE, San Francisco, pp 642–651

Simon DR (1994) On the power of quantum computation. In: Proceedings 35th annual symposium on foundations of computer science. IEEE, Santa Fe, pp 116–123

Sirinam P, Imani M, Juarez M, Wright M (2018) Deep fingerprinting: undermining website fingerprinting defenses with deep learning. In: Proceedings of the 2018 ACM SIGSAC conference on computer and communications security. ACM, Toronto, pp 1928–1943

Staff R (2020) Report says China internet firms censored coronavirus terms, criticism early in outbreak. https://www.reuters.com/article/us-health-coronavirus-china-censorship-idUSKBN20Q1VS. Accessed 1 Aug 2021

Stecklow S, Dastin J (2021) Special report: Amazon partnered with China propaganda arm. https://www.reuters.com/world/china/amazon-partnered-with-china-propaganda-arm-win-beijings-favor-document-shows-2021-12-17/. Accessed 1 Dec 2021

Tor (2019) Tor project: Tor faq. https://2019.www.torproject.org/about/overview.html. Accessed 1 Aug 2021

Van Tilborg HC, Jajodia S (2014) Encyclopedia of cryptography and security. Springer Science & Business Media, Boston

Veríssimo PE, Neves NF, Correia MP (2003) Intrusion-tolerant architectures: concepts and design. In: de Lemos R, Gacek C, Romanovsky A (eds) Architecting dependable systems. Springer, Berlin, pp 3–36

Wang X, Xiang Y, Gao J, Ding J (2020) Information laundering for model privacy. arXiv preprint arXiv:2009.06112

Ware WH (1970) Security controls for computer systems (U): report of defense science board task force on computer security, R-609-1. Rand Corp, Santa Monica

Whitney L (2021) Cybersecurity spending to hit \$150 billion this year. https://www.techrepublic.com/article/cybersecurity-spending-to-hit-150-billion-this-year/. Accessed 1 Aug 2021

Wierd (2002) Security news this week: a tiny piece of tape tricked teslas into speeding up 50 MPH. https://www.wired.com/story/tesla-speed-up-adversarial-example-mgm-breach-ransomware/. Accessed 1 Dec 2021

Open Access This chapter is licensed under the terms of the Creative Commons Attribution 4.0 International License (http://creativecommons.org/licenses/by/4.0/), which permits use, sharing, adaptation, distribution and reproduction in any medium or format, as long as you give appropriate credit to the original author(s) and the source, provide a link to the Creative Commons licence and indicate if changes were made.

The images or other third party material in this chapter are included in the chapter's Creative Commons licence, unless indicated otherwise in a credit line to the material. If material is not included in the chapter's Creative Commons licence and your intended use is not permitted by statutory regulation or exceeds the permitted use, you will need to obtain permission directly from the copyright holder.

Part II
Ethical and Legal Challenges in Artificial Intelligence

Introduction

Clara Martins Pereira

AI is increasingly shaping the modern data economy. Advances in computing power, breakthroughs in algorithm development, and the soaring availability of Big Data are decisively combining to bolster the development of AI technologies, and few would deny that AI is set to take the world by storm.

Part I of this book introduced the many possibilities of AI technology, and, while AI also has its inherent limitations and vulnerabilities, there can be little doubt that it will fundamentally transform the human experience. In the face of this inevitability, there might be the temptation to pour all energy into extracting as much technical value from the AI revolution as it can provide, but there is danger in having traditionally human concerns and worries take a back seat while making way for machines to flourish and develop. In its Part II, this book steps away from the hustle and bustle of the latest technological developments in AI and refocuses its attention on the fundamental ethical and legal debates that have long faced humans—reassessing them in the light of the transformational changes brought by AI.

Written by some of the world's leading experts in AI, Ethics and the Law, Part II identifies and explores key ethical and legal issues arising from the AI revolution for digital creators, users, and platforms—as well as for the policymakers, academics and thinkers who are still trying to make sense of this change, and how best to regulate it.

The chapter by *Maria do Céu Patrão Neves and António Betâmio de Almeida* offers a critical reflection on the ethical opportunities and challenges brought by AI technologies. First, a new philosophical vision is introduced through a reflection on technological innovation more broadly, looking at a time before AI and pondering on where the AI revolution might take us. In considering how AI has been developing over time, its authors discuss its impact on human life from three perspectives—functional, structural and identity—and provide the starting point for a necessary debate on AI governance. Ultimately, they reflect on how key ethical principles should shape the future regulation of AI with a view to protecting fundamental human rights.

The chapter by *Pedro U. Lima and Ana Paiva* investigates the ethical and legal challenges specifically arising from the relationship between humans and robots. Focusing on key areas of robotics, this chapter examines the main advances and limitations arising in these areas, as well as the most important social, legal, and ethical concerns that they motivate. This contribution ends on a hopeful note, as the authors express a belief in robots as drivers of societal change that can contribute to more sustainable, human-driven societies.

In the chapter by *Eduardo Magrani and Paula Guedes Fernandes da Silva,* a key commercial application of AI is tackled: recommendation systems. Specifically, this chapter examines the many areas where recommendation systems are currently employed, discusses their benefits, and assesses the detrimental effects that they can also carry. By employing an ethics-driven, human-rights-based approach it analyses a variety of questions pertaining to these systems, including loss of privacy, opacity, and potential for discrimination. Ultimately, it is argued that guidelines and rules should be reinforced by "value-centred" design strategies whereby the very architecture of recommendation systems should incorporate such guidelines and rules.

The chapter by *Beatriz Assunção Ribeiro, Hélder Coelho, Ana Elisabete Ferreira and João Branquinho* represents a collaborative, multi-disciplinary effort to tackle the fundamental question of whether robots should be awarded legal personhood. Combining inputs from philosophy, psychology, computation and the law, this chapter starts by examining the concepts of object and agent and how AI might fit into that distinction. Second, it discusses how the concept of "metacognition"— which the authors define as the cognition about cognition that results in mental processes that control an entity's thoughts and behaviour—can be applied as a minimum requirement for accountability. Ultimately, it is argued that the main difference between a non-responsible and a responsible agent depends on the metacognitive processes that can be carried out by that entity, and that entities that do show metacognitive processes should be granted legal personhood (even if AI is not quite there yet).

Starting with the chapter by *Márcia Santana Fernandes and José Roberto Goldim,* Part II narrows down on the ethical issues and challenges specifically created by the use of AI-based technologies in health. In particular, this chapter initiates a discussion on how the use of AI systems in health creates both opportunities and challenges, including ethical questions pertaining to the many ways in which AI is transforming communication and decision-making in this sector. In the end, the authors endorse a Complex Bioethics Model based on multiple ethical approaches as the key to achieving the right balance between taking necessary precautions and remaining hopeful that AI might deliver on its potential for improving the health sector.

The chapter by *Mindy Nunez Duffourc and Dominick S. Giovanniello* poses important ethical questions. Specifically, it examines the ethical implications of AI systems capable of autonomously performing acts that constitute medical practice and discusses whether a so-called "Autonomous AI Physician" could ever be considered a medical practitioner. First, the authors suggest ethical parameters for the practice of medicine by AI systems; second, they identify ethical and legal issues pertaining to the activities of Autonomous AI Physicians; and, finally, they discuss the potential application of existing legal and regulatory regimes to these activities. Ultimately, they argue that all stakeholders in the development and use of Autonomous AI Physicians must be governed by requirements that ensure that AI technology is being employed in a safe and responsible way.

Part II concludes with a discussion of AI-driven black box medicine. In particular, the chapter by *Rafaella Nogaroli and José Luiz de Moura Faleiros Júnior* examines the different semantic dimensions of algorithmic opacity that can arise from employing AI technology in the health sector, and resorts to hypothetical scenarios to analyse the impact of such opacity in terms of medical practice and patient consent, framing it as an ethical challenge. In the end, it is suggested that education will be key to unlocking a bright future for the responsible use of AI in health.

Before and Beyond Artificial Intelligence: Opportunities and Challenges

M. Patrão Neves and A. Betâmio de Almeida

Abstract Artificial intelligence (AI) and digital systems are currently occupying a fundamental place throughout society. They are devices that shape human life and induce significant civilizational changes. Given their huge power, namely systems with autonomous decision-making capacity, it is natural that the potential social effects deserve a critical reflection on the opportunities and challenges addressed by AI. This is the main goal of this text. The authors begin by explaining the philosophical position from which they start, and which contextualizes their reflection on technological innovation in general, then briefly considering the genealogy ("before") of AI, in its main characteristics and direction of evolution ("Can machines imitate humans?"). It is considering the path of development of AI and its disruptive effects on human life ("beyond") that it is proposed its systematization in three categories—functional, structural, identity—("Can humans imitate machines?").

Regardless of the optimistic or pessimist expectations towards technological evolution, there is a need for a public debate about its current and future regulation. The text also identifies major ethical principles and legal requirements to regulate AI in order to protect fundamental human rights.

1 Few Presuppositions that Shape the Reflection on AI

The structuring, developing and using of AI is particularly complex and challenging for a non-technical, social and human reflexive approach. This is mainly due to the following distinct but cumulative aspects. AI is of a multidisciplinary nature, mobilizing a growing diversity of knowledge and techniques—digital, elec-

---

M. P. Neves (✉)
University of the Azores, Ponta Delgada, Portugal

A. B. de Almeida
IST/University of Lisbon, Lisbon, Portugal
e-mail: betamio.almeida@ist.utl.pt

© The Author(s) 2024
H. Sousa Antunes et al. (eds.), *Multidisciplinary Perspectives on Artificial Intelligence and the Law*, Law, Governance and Technology Series 58,
https://doi.org/10.1007/978-3-031-41264-6_6

tronics, computing, mathematics, statistics, social and human sciences, including law, sociology and philosophy—which turns it inevitably complex and makes a comprehensive discourse very difficult or even impossible. At the same time, the domain of AI is currently so broad, diverse and dynamic that any discourse on the subject becomes inexorably restricted and maybe also quickly outdated. Finally, interpretations of what AI represents in the present, but especially in the future, are so disparate—ranging from naive enthusiasm and social submission to castrating pessimism—that any position taken is open to criticism, and the one that is now presented will not be exception.

Our reflection, like any other, is based on some assumptions that, more implicitly or explicitly, shape it, and should therefore be disclosed. We can briefly present four major presuppositions that ground and shape our reflection.

The first is that technology is a product of human creativity, so it cannot be generally and immediately demonized as if it were a strange and hostile reality to us. In fact, technology has been fundamental for the survival and quality of life of humanity. It creates its own life conditions out of the given world. The negative attitude is still all too frequent, especially in the face of uprising powerful technological innovations. These tend to arouse feelings of fear in relation to the new, the unknown, a certain uneasiness or even distress (although today we often witness an uncritical attraction to the new, as if everything new was good). There is also a certain hostility towards technological innovation in the assessment of its effects—for example, environmental degradation is attributed to technological impacts—sometimes only blaming the technique (technophobia) and with a total lack of reference to other causes and responsibilities. Experience teaches us that the personal benefits arising from a technological innovation is what attracts the most at the beginning and the possible negative social or collective impacts only later become evident, frequently when that particular technology is widespread and it is very difficult to oppose. In this case only a crisis will drive a change. This justifies an independent critical analysis of the creation of technological products and their mass applications.

A second presupposition is that technological innovation (such as scientific progress) is unstoppable, irrepressible or deterministic, so it cannot be suppressed, but rather re-oriented. Even if it were desirable to stop scientific progress and technological innovation (which in any case is quite doubtful), they will never cease to develop due to a combination of variables—economic-financial, social, political, academic, etc.—that generate an increasingly powerful and continuous dynamic that surpasses the sum of the variables involved, beyond the control of any single person or group of interests (Liu 2021).[1] It can be possible to slow down the process (It has already happened in some other innovations in order to avoid severe impacts), being imperative or preferable to reorient it. However, the potential uncontrolled impulses

---

[1] "The global artificial intelligence (AI) software market is forecast to grow rapidly in the coming years, reaching around 126 billion U.S. dollars by 2025. The overall AI market includes a wide array of applications such as natural language processing, robotic process automation, and machine learning."

Before and Beyond Artificial Intelligence: Opportunities and Challenges

in the application of the increasing power, by private companies or public agencies, that new technologies provide and that may pose risks to humanity, seems to be a matter of urgent reflection and control. The problem of human techniques was not traditionally an object of special attention in philosophy and ethics. This situation has changed since the mid-twentieth century. The growing technological power has motivated philosophy and ethics to critically analyze the essence of technology and its impacts on humanity.[2]

A third presupposition is that technological innovation is neither axiologically neutral nor, therefore, exempt from ethical scrutiny. Technological innovation is not purely instrumental, as if its evaluation depended only on its use and on the user. In fact, every creation already bears the mark of its creator, even if it is nothing more than the intention that led to the creation, to the production, a structural and original intentionality (the principle of its development, in an irrepressible and irreducible evolution), which escapes human control, and rather conditions and even induces human behavior. New technologies, by the simple fact that they exist, induce their use. Astonishing technological development is the result of human desires that are difficult to control.

The fourth is that technological innovation should not be an end in itself, but rather a means in terms of the only end in itself, which is the human. The *raison d'être* of all human production is to constitute new and diversified modes of promotion and realization of human flourishing, which is why it must remain inexorably subordinated to humankind. The fundamental challenge that arises is whether technology should be an instrument at the service of humanity (e.g. an instrument to improve human health) or whether it is humanity that should adapt to the demands of technology.

Acknowledging our assumptions, we should now more accurately identify some of the major opportunities opened by AI, and think about the risks or challenges its development entails, going from the birth of AI and its original objectives to its succession of new ambitions.

2 Can Machines Imitate Humans?

2.1 The Key Question

Can machines imitate humans?—is the question that the mathematician Alan Turing, the so called "father" of theoretical computer science and AI, poses in 1950, in his Imitation Game, and to which he seeks to be able to respond positively

---

[2] All human techniques have gradually contributed to the structuring of life in society, namely through the formation of a "socio-technical system". Digital technologies and AI are, in a very intense and fast way, densifying this system and significantly altering the human way of life by diffuse social impacts. There is also an intense convergence with other very relevant technologies, namely the set of nanotechnology, biotechnology, information techniques and neuroscience. All together may induce a significant change in human evolution.

throughout his life: "can machines think?" (Turing 1950).[3] We would say that Turing's question possibly marks a turning point in the relationship between humans and machines as striking as Jeremy Bentham's interrogation in 1789, "Can animals suffer?" triggered in the relationship of people with animals.

In the second half of the twentieth century, machines did seem to be intelligent. Digital computers, so designated because capable of manipulating discrete symbols, or digits, had been created in the wake of the third industrial revolution, characterized by Automation, very focused on information and communication technologies. The question of the moment was: can a computer behave intelligently like a human being?

A first answer is given by the "Turing test", the so called "imitation game": is it possible for an interrogator to distinguish the answers given by a computer from the answers given by a human being? Can machines impersonate human intelligence, or imitate human intelligence?

The Turing Test has been the subject of much criticism, many of which result from the exact definition of thinking and intelligence. One of the most famous is based on the well-known Chinese Room argument by Searle (1980). The Turing Test is based on language. We know that language is fundamental in the development of human intelligence, but intelligence should not be directly confused with knowledge or memory. Is a simple question-answer test a sufficient means to identify human thinking and all types of human intelligence?[4] With Turing we intend to be able to identify an acceptable similarity with the way of thinking and reacting of a human, possibly what we might want is to recognize that a machine is capable of imitating the human way of thinking very well.[5] Much more difficult will be to recognize the sentience capacity of a machine!

2.2 The First AI Steps

It is in this context that Marvin Minsky and John McCarthy come to forge the expression Artificial Intelligence that they present in 1956, at the Dartmouth College Conference, organized that year in the United States, and which brought together

---

[3] As fascination, ghost or myth, the more or less repressed will to create an artificial human has accompanied humanity for centuries. The current interest in humanoid robots may be an example of this ancient dream. What is new in the question posed by Turing is the focus on the intelligence attribute in an era with technological capacity to develop a credible answer.

[4] Among humans, we also use language to try to assess thoughts and levels of intelligence. However, in this assessment we already assume that we are dealing with humans. We admit that we recognize the basic structure of thought of other humans because we belong to the same biological species and we are both heirs to the essentials of a common natural evolution. In fact, what we can identify are variations in the behavior of human minds relative to a chosen pattern.

[5] There are many variants of the Turing Test in order to eliminate its supposed deficiencies and there is also the Inverse Turing Test to challenge an algorithm to distinguish a human from another algorithm in a dialogue.

the pioneers of AI of that time. In the same year, the two founded the Artificial Intelligence Project (now the MIT Computer Science and Artificial Intelligence Laboratory).

It is then that the history of AI truly begins, in which Turing came to propose that the strategy to follow should not be, as before, to try to "write a program that would allow a machine to pass the game of imitation" (reproducing parts of human reasoning), but rather that of writing "a program that would allow a machine to learn from experience, just as a baby does". It is in this direction (automatic learning, through experience) that today, decades later, the approach to intelligent systems is made. So, it already enhances the autonomy of intelligent systems in relation to humans.

We are then fully in the fourth industrial revolution, characterized by Connectivity, in which AI develops almost exponentially, which is confirmed as we now enter Society 5.0, the fifth industrial revolution, that is, the era of full connection, where everything will be connected, all the means available to human beings will be connected and persons will have to adapt or to integrate themselves into these continuous flow networks (alignment of robotic technology to human intelligence, increased collaboration or partnership between human beings and intelligent systems). AI has been developing and strongly driving the last 3 industrial revolutions, paving the way towards full automation and maximum connectivity (wireless, no physical connection).

Nevertheless, we still do not have a consensual definition of AI (which is very revealing of its dynamism), despite being quite relevant for the circumscription of its domain and perception of its operability. There are many different definitions and even those who reject the expression, namely Luc Julia, in his work *L'Intelligence artificielle n'existe pas* (Julia 2019),[6] where he considers that AI has always been poorly defined as it suggests that algorithms can make conscious and rational decisions like humans. He believes that this is not the case and that mistaken ideas like this one have fueled fantastic Hollywood perceptions about AI, such as Matrix or Terminator.

Human intelligence is difficult to delimit and fully understand. It is more than rationality towards stimuli and data analysis. It has other built-in features and a strong connection to the entire human body. Perhaps the designation Artificial Intelligence (AI) was very effective as a brand, but it is not very strict. The expression AI is used today to designate a variety of technologies with some common characteristics. We adopt the definition proposed by the High-Level Expert Group on Artificial Intelligence of the European Commission: "Artificial intelligence (AI) systems are software (and possibly also hardware) systems designed by humans that, given a complex goal, act in the physical or digital dimension by perceiving their environment through data acquisition, interpreting the collected structured or unstructured data, reasoning on the knowledge, or processing the information,

---

[6] Julia (2019), p. 287. It was Luc Julia who co-created the digital assistant Siri, one of the most famous AI.

derived from this data and deciding the best action(s) to take to achieve the given goal. AI systems can either use symbolic rules or learn a numeric model, and they can also adapt their behaviour by analysing how the environment is affected by their previous actions (European Commission 2019)."

Other, simpler AI definitions could be: "a computerized system, agent or robotic, capable of acting and making decisions independently of human supervision" (Tavani 2016).; "a system capable of rationally solving complex problems or taking appropriate actions to achieve its goals in whatever real world circumstances it encounters" (Dempsey 2020).

2.3 The Encouraging Achievements

AI, as we broadly define it, has been a powerful tool in achieving human purposes, whose continuous development has gone beyond its original instrumental status and conquered new performance plans to consider, in a continuous erasure of what seemed to be its limits. And yet, we are still in the era of a weak or narrow AI, that is, capable of performing just one or few specific tasks, and which software can only make decisions based on information previously given. Some common examples are: to play chess, the Go or poker; to identify people through faces captured in real-time security video (face recognition); or to drive autonomous vehicles.

If we take just one of these examples—the simplest, as playing a game—and follow the evolution of AI, we can easily understand the direction we are moving to. The first important step of its evolutionary process was given in 1996, when Deep Blue, an IBM software, defeated the world chess champion Kasparov. Later, in 2017, AlphaGo won game Go against the best in the world, and in 2019, Pluribus won a 12-day poker marathon, competing against 5 players. A second step was given when the software started to learn to play by itself, playing against itself, and thus relying less and less on human-generated data, since 2017. More recently, Google's MuZero was presented as being able to play without the need for any human-entered data, that is, without being given the rules, thanks to its ability to plan winning strategies in unknown contexts. It is this direction of AI evolution that fuels the greatest fear of humans: that of AI gaining enough power to completely escape human control. The direction of evolution that is being followed is easily revealed: advancing towards an always and successively superior performance in each of the functions that AI performs; and towards a higher level of automation (emancipation) of the human (creator, producer).

The evolution trend of AI and its applications justifies a serious fear of a devaluation of the humans in face of the superior capabilities of new systems in fields of activity that have structured society and the purpose of human life. The risks and challenges arise in the short term, but some of them are already threats: "the greater the digital capacity of a given society, the more vulnerable it becomes" (Kissinger et al. 2021). These are issues of particularly interests for Ethics and Law.

Before and Beyond Artificial Intelligence: Opportunities and Challenges

Today there is a clear perception that we are experiencing a digital revolution (which follows the industrial revolution) led by AI. That is, AI is a constant and indelible presence in daily lives of persons, individually considered, as of communities, particularly in the northern hemisphere, and our way of living depends heavily of AI which, today, penetrates most modalities of human action. We live in the AI era.

3 Can Humans Imitate Machines?

The idea of humans imitating machines would be regarded as foolish until recently. Today, however, we can formulate this provocative question because there are digital machines with an attribute held as superior in living organisms: intelligence. These machines, being presented as having intellectual capacities far superior to those of humans, may constitute models of individual and social behavior to follow. An alignment of humans to the rules of a new socio-technical system due to a simple adaptation by unconscious inertia or imposed as a priority justified by efficiency criteria but abstracting other criteria associated with human nature.

In an attempt to systematize the growing multiplicity of AI interventions in human life, we would say that its impacts are more evident and disruptive at three main levels: a *functional*, in the use of AI as a specific instrument for human purposes; a *structural*, in the change that AI entails in human interrelationships and in the organization of institutions; an *identity*, in the transformation that originates in what the human is and in the image he has of himself.

We must consider these three levels of AI intervention in the human sphere, both in the new opportunities it creates for human flourishing, and in the new challenges it poses for human perseverance in a context of performances that far surpasses it.

3.1 Functional Level

The functional dimension of AI refers precisely to its ability to carry out human functions, which it does by performing them faster, more perfectly, more economically, in a truly unique and impressive supporting human action. Some of its main very successful domains are industry, justice, health, education, transport, finance, marketing, computer security, army (military defense) and entertainment.

A quick glimpse at the intervention of AI in few of these so distinct and paradigmatic domains can give us a more precise idea about its disruptive potential, both positive and negative, in our contemporaneity.

AI first became preponderant in industry, where it is massively used and where its functional dimension is best evidenced, through the automation of various functions, especially the harsher, physically and psychologically. Releasing people from the heaviest burdens is strongly applauded. However, AI in the industry is not limited to the automated functions, but is also being used to assist in decision making and data analysis, including personnel management, such as attendance levels and employee productivity, hiring and dismissing employees. However there are some paradoxes related to technology and productivity.[7]

Nowadays, the former general idea that AI only performs mechanical tasks, which are professionally less demanding and socially less valued, is easily contradicted. On the one hand, AI has been conquering a diversity of domains and levels of complexity of action, even in traditional fields, such as industry; on the other hand, it has been applied to increasingly more demanding fields of action, such as healthcare or justice.

AI is strongly present, both in clinical research (e. g. collecting gigantic amounts of data to identify correlations and trends; new therapeutic molecules) and in clinical care (e.g. making diagnostics; monitoring of health conditions). There are some medical specialties in which standard clinical procedures are being replaced by AI, such as radiology (reading exams) or ophthalmology (performing some exams), in which AI can advantageously replace physicians. Today there is already efficient digital assistance for medical doctors and nurses, especially in the area of geriatrics, surgeons, cleaning staff, but also for the delivery of medication, food and even some diagnostic tests.

In what concerns justice, AI has been heavily used, namely in the search for jurisprudence, in the adoption of justice measures based on similar previous cases. There are also already projects for the institution of an automatic predictive justice court to dispatch benign cases.

Indeed, it seems today that all human functions can be substituted by AI (they are being gradually replaced) with immediate advantages, under the principles of efficiency, productivity, and profitability. The promising idea that AI will liberate humans by avoiding tedious or monotonous intellectual tasks does not seem to be what one might anticipate: its exclusion from tasks associated with human thinking.

However, there are also some disadvantages associated that are important to be considered together, and among which we highlight only three.

A first one is AI proliferation. We refer to the proliferation of AI considering its ability to learn from previous experience in order to produce intelligent behavior and

---

[7] Although the new technologies hold great potential, there is an apparent paradox because productivity growth has slowed rather than accelerated (Brynjolfsson et al. 2017, p. 44). In fact, labor productivity growth in developed countries have stayed low since mid-2000 and there are different potential causes for this paradox. False hopes, a time delay until there is a statistical effect and the increasing market and rent concentrations are some of them. While income inequality has been rising within many countries in recent decades, inequality between countries has been falling. This is another apparent paradox but the way technology diffuses within the economy seems to be relevant for both productivity growth and income distribution (Qureshi 2021, p. 24). In EU this impact seems to depend on the country's size, its level of development and the current degree of income inequality relative to the average European value (Kharlamova et al. 2018). Reducing inequality can be considered as a way for preventing a future crisis or an ethical issue. We can conclude that there are both optimists and pessimists about the relationship between new technologies and growth.

Before and Beyond Artificial Intelligence: Opportunities and Challenges

correct decisions, which is called "machine learning" (a subdomain of AI): these are algorithms capable of modifying themselves and making decisions without human intervention. It has also advanced to the so-called "deep learning" (a subdomain of machine learning) which consists of the ability of computers to learn on their own, through pattern recognition, in many layers of raw data, depending on the proposed objective, carrying out tasks as human beings. Therefore, AI is always improving its performance and acquiring new skills. This aspect, immediately and necessarily recognized as positive, is presented here as a disadvantage insofar as it triggers the process of releasing Artificial Intelligence from human control.

A second disadvantage, and the most commonly presented, is mass unemployment. As the domains in which AI can assist human purposes multiply, as the diversity of functions it can perform grows, and as its performance becomes superior to that of human, it also replaces people. Hence, the main threat that has been stressed at this level is mass unemployment, as it is already obvious in industry.[8] We know the arguments that dismiss this growing problem: throughout human history there have always been work activities that have vanished and new ones that have emerged and the same will happen now too. We cannot fail to point out the existence of an unprecedented variable in this equation that can endanger the past balance: the speed of the process that does not allow human adaptation to the ongoing transformation and the intellectual quality of lost jobs. Even if many new jobs are created, the question of the type and social level of these jobs should be considered.

The third disadvantage is social exclusion. Indeed, the advantages and disadvantages of AI may not be evenly distributed, with the most favored persons being the most benefited and the least favored suffering most of the losses. Besides, this chronic inequity is added to the specific one of generational sharing: today we have a growing proliferation of generations, which no longer succeed each other every 25 years, but every 10 years.[9] In this unprecedented context, it becomes very easy for people to be considered outdated by the next generation, and at the same time, useless for society, perhaps even a burden or disposable. This intergenerational disadvantage can cause serious social fractures and be difficult to be solved without a profound change in the human society organization.

Characterizing AI in its functional range we would stress that: it remains outside the human and can be manipulated and controlled by him; it contributes to the construction of a civilization guided by technological, intelligent and automated innovation, and by efficiency and productivity. Therefore, it threatens to make the human obsolete.

---

[8] Deloitte estimates that, in the next few years, 50% of current jobs will become obsolete.

[9] In 2010, a new generation is formed for which the analogue world is past, asserting itself as 100% digital native, and surpassing the millennials, making all generations quickly outdated, namely the current X generations, from the early 60s to the 70s; the Y generation, from the end of 70 until the early 90's, and Z from 1992–2010, we also have designations such as the "grey generation" or the "snowflake generation".

3.2 Structural Level

The structural dimension of AI refers to new forms of relationship, new patterns of personal, social and institutional relationships, characterized by greater virtual proximity between everyone (overcoming geographic distances), by greater coverage (because all people are potentially included), and paradoxically, at the same time strengthens relationships by mediating them and suppressing direct contact.

The mediation of human relationships through Artificial Intelligence takes place today in a growing diversity of domains that we have systematized in three planes. At the personal level, people from all over the world know each other and socialize virtually (even for emotional intimacy relationships); at the social level, human activities are developed at the digital realm (where interest groups are formed, and civic, political or other activism is developed, demonstrations are scheduled, petitions are made, etc.); at the institutional level, institutions relate to citizens through intelligent technology (e. g. relationship with the public administration, as commercial transactions tend to be increasingly online and service is carried out by a chatbot, a computer program that tries to simulate a human being in conversations with people,[10] the same is happening in more and more domains as well as education).

At this level, we would like to highlight two examples, which are quite different, but both paradigmatic of the ongoing transformation. The first is the widespread investment in the construction of smart cities, that is, of population aggregates in which everything is connected, with automated management (traffic, waste, public safety), everything being mediated by AI: the household equipment tends to become totally connected and smart assistants can take care of all management services at home (managing waste, identifying equipment problems); all the equipment and infrastructure of a municipality will be connected (e.g. identification of aspects to be improved, safety, air quality measurement, traffic coordination, etc.). Structuring activities of human society such as banks and insurance tend to be on line, dematerialized (without paper documents) and without human intermediaries. This change creates new vulnerabilities in terms of security, trust in institutions and in person access to them. Citizens are increasingly subject to faceless technical systems with access based on multiple numeric codes and passwords.

The second paradigmatic example is related to the introduction of AI in politics (in addition to the other strategic domains already mentioned with health, finance and the army). In 2019, a study by a Spanish University concluded that 1 in 4 Europeans would be willing to allow AI to make important political decisions in their country, in favor of impartiality, honesty and justice.[11] Today there are already

---

[10] The illusion of machine-induced affectionate feelings is one of the aspects that already happen in relationships between accompanying robots and the elderly or also in the way some people react to automatic messages they receive on their birthday.

[11] Jonsson and de Tena (2019). Also, the philosopher Yuval Harari says that elections, political parties, parliaments can become obsolete given the amount of data to be taken into account and the speed at which some decisions have to be taken (Harari 2018).

Before and Beyond Artificial Intelligence: Opportunities and Challenges

references to an imminent formation of a "cyberocracy" that can threaten or destroy the democratic system as we know it.

The immediate convenience for human activities is obvious and indisputable, under the new principle of optimization of means. However, there are also associated drawbacks that are important to consider together, and among which we highlight here only three.

A first one, at the personal level, points out that the intensification of connections is directly proportional to the physical distance between people (relationships tend to be superficial, sporadic, ephemeral, without commitments or responsibilities, they become light relationships). The second unfolds at the social level and refers to the anonymization of personal uniqueness before the functional relationship (from the integration into categories of people and relationship patterns, structured based on interests). The third disadvantaged lies at the institutional level and refers to the integration of all human activity into a network of relationships (everything is in a network and what is not in a network lacks recognition of existence); networks are almost unknown, inaccessible and uncontrollable (the humans risk to become pieces of a gear that surpasses them). Dependence becomes extreme and the smart encoded numerical protocols are densified and drastically reduce the spectrum of human communication mode. In addition, we are increasingly integrating AI programs into decision-making processes.

AI, in its structural scope, presents itself as integrated in all human and social activities and shapes them, formats them; it builds a new culture guided by virtual (inter)mediation and connectivity, and by the optimization of resources; it threatens to number the human (representing the human through numbers, depersonalizing it). The exaggerated quantification of reality in the media (e.g. statistics and ranking indexes) is one of the side effects of the digital society that devalues the other human valences that must be part of the characterization of reality.

3.3 Identity Level

The identity dimension of AI refers to the new perception that human beings acquire of themselves due to the omnipresence of AI, characterized by overcoming their given nature and building new images of themselves, what is fairly evident at least in three essential aspects.

A first, that seems to be quite revolutionary, is the incursion of AI into the human spiritual dimension, its deepest intimacy, which has been considered throughout the history of humanity as constituting its unique specificity as well as its qualitative difference in relation to all the other beings. This incursion is manifest in its creative dimension, in its artistic expression replicated by the AI to compose music, paint canvases, write literature. For example, the first software to create music dates back to 1997, and today the composition of various musical styles by AI is widespread; in 2016, Microsoft developed a software using Artificial Intelligence that, through the analysis of masterpieces from Rembrandt, managed to create a new painting with the same characteristics; since 2018, we started having books written by the AI.

A second aspect to highlight is the new power to build an alternative identity, external to the self but that tends to be taken as the truly self. It is a digital identity, fabricated with the collaboration of the AI, in simulated versions of the person such as avatars (entirely digital, cyberbody, an online identity) which allows each one to constantly and easily (effortlessly) reinvent themselves, to develop various personalities (change age, gender, etc.), establish different types of relationships according to the incarnated personality.

But the penetration of artificial intelligence into the essence of the human goes even deeper, as an internal construction of an enhanced identity, in the image and likeness of AI. There is a desideratum of cognitive evolution, through a process either of incorporation (e.g. cybernetic implants that enhance different human capacities) or of appropriation (brain-machine interface, like the one that Elon Musk's startup Neurolink is developing.[12] It would be about the creation of the post-human as advocated by the transhumanists.

The immediate usefulness for the human being is obvious under the new principle of self-improvement: not by developing what one is, but by acquiring what one is not; not by intensifying the authenticity of the being, but by distorting, perverting its own identity.

The perception that the human has of himself starts to reflect the presence of AI, also adopting it as a model, with immediate benefits, under the principle of human improvement. However, there are also unavoidable losses that must be simultaneously considered: violation of human identity values through the incursion into its spiritual dimension (its essence), namely the impossibility of forgetting (everything is indelible), which allows us to reinvent each day, in the atrophying of freedom, by the annulment of unpredictability and under the yoke of perfect decision, in the suppression of privacy, for the transparency of the total accessibility of lives; alienation of oneself, in digital simulacra of oneself, without density or authenticity; and usurpation of the self, in distorting improvements in human identity.

AI, in its identity level: presents itself united (fused) to all human expressions, determining them; invents a new identity in the image and likeness of the AI; and threatens to make the human succumb and replaces it with an improved self-image.

Still and always in the domain of a narrow or weak AI, we see how it intervenes on the functional level, in a superficial way, remaining outside the human and controllable by it, building a new, intelligent civilization through progressive automation; on the structural level, in a deep (pervasive) way in all human activities and relationships, integrating and shaping them, regulating them, constituting a new,

---

[12] The brain-machine interface is being attempt by a fusion or hybridization process that can increase intelligence and memory, erase bad memories and introduce good ones that never happened, or even to do a download of oneself to a digital support. In the long run it could conquer a digital immortality, surpassing the biological limits of humans.

virtual culture, through a growing connectivity; and on the identity level, in an intimate way at the heart of the human, uniting and reconfiguring it, dismissing it from itself in favor of an improved image, through a growing symbiosis.

4 How Should (Ethics)/Ought (Law) Humans and Machines Relate?

The public debate on human consequences of AI development begins in 2015, when 700 scientists sign a joint letter warning of AI threats: Research Priorities for Robust and Beneficial Artificial Intelligence: An Open Letter (Future of Life 2015).[13] These scientists underline the extraordinary benefits that AI can bring to humanity, but also the risk of loss of human control and the need for more research to prevent any risks.

The biggest fear is that the neural networks will continue to develop, allowing AI to gain awareness (become strong or general), and then totally escaping human control.

In this context, it is worth mentioning that, in 2017, Facebook engineers were developing an experiment with robots that traded among themselves the ownership of virtual items. It was a conversational experience. After a few days, the robots had developed a language of their own which, as it escaped human comprehension, was interrupted, turning off the robots.

The evolution of humans and their identity throughout human history is recognized. A slow, gradual evolution resulting from adaptation to successive natural changes and induced by culture and new ways of life. But the current trend that was described above has implications for human identity that are relevant, rapid, disruptive and multidimensional.

The concern with this forced discontinuity of identity may be considered by some to be too conservative or pessimistic. Others accept that technology and its "consumption" are an acceptable manifestation of humanity's will in setting the path for its future. These are the very optimists or believers in an ever-better future based on technology. It will be up to everyone in the present to contribute to that future in a responsible way that respects the human heritage received, entrusted to us. If there are benefits and harms to point out now to the AI, the imperative to maximize the former and eliminate the latter is quite obvious.

The global strategy for this consideration has been to establish an ethical-legal regulatory framework, not with the intention of limiting the development of Artificial Intelligence, but rather legitimizing it through the promotion of its real benefits and prevention of its potential harm, framing it in the values and principles of identity of humanity and protecting human rights.

---

[13] This letter was a turning point for public opinion: citizens gained information, got involved and started also to be asked to intervene in decision-making processes.

4.1 Ethical Requirements

Ethical reflection must always precede legal regulations. In democratic and pluralist societies, it is important first to pay attention to their identity values and build an inclusive and broad ethical consensus, as a legitimizing basis for the legal regulations to be formulated later by Law. The Law reinforces the ethical consensus formerly reached, and Ethics contributes to an effective and robust regulatory process. Also with regard to AI, whether as a human production or because of its strong impact on the lives of people and societies, it was the ethical reflection that first developed as the disruptive social capacity of AI became more obvious.

Ethics of artificial intelligence gains particular prominence and has greater social impact when carried out by major international entities, highly representative of citizens, or by international and multidisciplinary working groups, joining different approaches, created specifically to outline guidelines that are considered to be convenient and necessary to ensure that the evolution of AI remains subordinate to human goals.

Thus, and particularly in the European context, the European Commission, the European Parliament and the Council of Europe have been working actively in this area: the Commission has established a High-level expert group on artificial intelligence, in 2018; the Parliament set up a special committee on artificial intelligence in a Digital Age (AIDA), in 2020; and the Council of Europe established an Ad hoc Committee on Artificial Intelligence (CAHAI), in 2019.

At the same time, we highlight the creation of several scientific groups on AI, such as the European Center of Excellence on the regulation of Robotics and AI, the European AI Alliance, the Expert Group on Responsibility and New Technologies, the Global Partnership on Artificial Intelligence (GPAI), to mention just a few. At the global level, UNESCO has established an Ad-hoc Expert Group on the Ethics of Artificial Intelligence.

All these bodies converge in declaring the urgency of AI regulation, in requiring its ethical foundation, being also evidence a broad convergence with regard to the identification of the main ethical principles to comply with, while respecting Human Rights.

A study from the Berkman Klein Center for Internet & Society at Harvard University, *Principled Artificial Intelligence: Mapping Consensus in Ethical and Rights-based Approaches to Principles for AI*, authored by Jessica Fjeld and colleagues (Jessica et al. 2020), gathered, in 2020, the 36 most outstanding documents on regulatory ethical principles and governance, presenting a set of eight principles as the most consensual. Privacy is one of most frequent principle, demanding respect for individual privacy, "both in the use of data for the development of technological systems and by providing impacted people with agency over their data". Accountability, concerning the impacts produced together with the provision of adequate remedies, is also a common requirement. Safety and Security of AI are of major importance in what relates to its performance as designed, and its resistance to invasions. A fourth group of principles is Transparency and

Explainability demanding for intelligibility and openness of processes, outcomes, and uses. Fairness and Non-discrimination claim for AI systems to be inclusive and to promote global justice, being required in all documents analyzed. Human Control of Technology is a major concern demanding that all important decisions be under human scrutiny. Professional Responsibility calls for individuals engaged in the development of AI to be able to predict the consequences of their deeds. Finally, Promotion of Human Values states that AI should improve the humanity's well-being. Sometimes under different designations these are, indeed, the prevailing guidelines in ethical reflection on artificial intelligence and which must be guaranteed by law.

4.2 Law and Legal Procedures

Ethical requirements are very important but are not enough to prevent AI adverse effects on fundamental rights because the ethics guidelines have no binding legal force. So, trustworthy AI need to be also lawful—as we stressed before.

The implementation of a legal framework adapted to the specific characteristics of AI systems is not easy. In addition to the technical complexities and rapid developing of these systems, there are other relevant difficulties or resistances. Firstly, new technological developments have a growing geo-strategic and military importance for the world's major economic and technological powers. Secondly, there is a strong pressure from governments and companies to achieve competitiveness increases driven by advanced and daring products in the market. A third difficulty is the demand of academic institutions and AI specialists to minimize legal limitations in applications and data collection. And, finally, there is a need for regulation at the planetary level in order to be completely effective. There is thus a tension in the ethical-legal front of AI regulation and an attempt to achieve balances between political decisions and the different interests involved. In this context, the affirmation of ethical-legal perspectives can be difficult in high-level decisions.[14]

It is a long and not always consensual process and we must know how we want technology to be applied (or not be applied) for the good of human society. The feasibility and potential elements of a legal framework for the development of artificial intelligence, based on the Council of Europe standards and the rule of law, are presented in a report (EU (a) 2021) of the Committee on Artificial Intelligence (CAHAI).The following options are presented: to amend binding legal instruments and adapt them to AI systems, modernising existing instruments or protocols or the adoption of new binding legal instruments.

---

[14] The High-Level Expert Group of the European Comission brought together 52 experts: 27 from industry, 15 from academia (3 with a legal background and 3 with an ethical background), 6 from the civil society and 4 from governmental bodies.

The issues to be discussed regarding legal proceedings for AI can be of three types. The first group comprises the security and defense of citizens' rights to compensation for damages and the control that AI systems comply with the law and do not violate established rights. A second includes how to define and assess accountability for the acts of artificial entities equipped with AI and autonomous learning and decision capacity? Should they have the same rights and duties as natural persons and be sued or punishable? Or should the responsibility pass to the creators or users of the system? Finally, the third concerns the use of AI by agents of justice in the application of the law and the obedience to ethical requirements. A good overview of these legal issues can be found in a text by Dempsey (2020).

Nowadays national legislation for AI framing is still very scarce around the world and AI systems are lightly regulated. There are, however, a number of international legal instruments that deal with certain aspects pertaining to AI systems. The greatest effort in this direction is taking place in the European Union (EU). One of the results of this effort is the General Data Protection Regulation (EU (b) 2016) (GDPR) that entered into force on 25 May 2018 (EU (b) (EU (d) 2018)) and try to concretise the fundamental right to personal data protection. GDPR fixes general and specific rules applying to sensitive categories of personal data such as health data and introduced a single legal framework across the EU with provisions allowing EU member states to enact national legislation specifying, restricting, or expanding some requirements. Administrative fines and penalties are considered. There is also a special research regime which provides flexibilities for scientific and statistical research.

Another UE initiative is the Proposal for Harmonised Rules on Artificial Intelligence or AI Act (EU (c) 2021). This proposed legislation classifies AI systems as high-risk (or not) based upon intended use. High-risk systems (e.g. remote biometric identification, evaluation of creditworthiness and credit scoring, judicial decision-making and recruitment and other employment decisions) would have to demonstrate compliance through conformity assessments before introduction into the market and certain uses of AI would be prohibited altogether. This risk classification does not include the precise assessment of the human or social damage and its respective probability. It thus seems difficult an adaptation of this regulation to the dynamic evolution of the market and of new AI products.

The use of AI in the judicial systems is a very relevant topic for its symbolic aspect. The way justice incorporates efficiency criteria using AI products must be exemplary. An in-depth study on the use of AI applications in judicial systems is presented in the Appendix of the European Ethical Charter on the Use of Artificial Intelligence in Judicial Systems and their environment (EU (d) 2018), but some issues can be highlighted. The risk of slipping into a position of immediate acceptance of decisions by artificial entities supposedly endowed with exceptional powers, but unpredictable and without explaining how and why they decide, is one of them. This idea permeates many analyses of predictive justice that lend these devices immediate or future capabilities to better predict human acts or to know the truth. This predictive justice cannot reflect the full reasoning of the human judge. An evolution that needs to be regulated through a permanent critical analysis because

Law has been and must continue to be a human activity supported by technology but never subordinated to it.

5 Concluding Remarks

Recovering our starting point, AI is a human production that should neither be idolized nor demonized, but rather evaluated with a critical spirit, both in its benefits and risks for the preservation of humanity as such and at the service of its development.

It is in this context that we highlight some key aspects to bear in mind in the present and future debates on AI:

- the application of new technologies with characteristics that surpass those of humans and with autonomous capabilities may lead to changes in social values and in legal procedures and concepts. However, human actions should not be submitted to judging criteria appropriate only to artificial beings with superior specific capacities or an indeterminate decision process;
- there is a risk of a progressive devaluation and decay of human capacities rather than a greater human behavioral and cultural development of society. The announced society of freer knowledge can slide to a more regulated society, complying with the rules imposed by a technology without limits of innovation with the justification of the optimization of rationality and efficiency. The meaning of life would tend to be reduced to the enjoyment of technological products and submission to decisions arising from AI algorithms;
- the education of new generations can constitute the path for a more adequate evolution of society and to avoid Stephen Hawking's prophecy: "the end of the human race". A society that knows how to reflect on the essential values and meaning of life and that enjoys them fully but in a sober way. One of the means for a more adequate education and preparation is perhaps the multidisciplinarity in academic training, avoiding a tight specialization and providing a better view to the different perspectives of reality and the human society;
- it is an illusion to believe that technology only solves problems and satisfies desires. It also creates new problems, eventually with severe and irreversible social damage. Human intermediation and accountability for autonomous acts of AI digital systems is a fundamental protection process for humanity.

Having addressed some ethical issues and underlining the need to build a broad ethical consensus as the foundation of the legislative initiative, we have also pointed out some guidelines for legal initiatives in this realm. The harshest challenge lays probably at the political level, aiming the establishment of global governance in the field of AI.[15]

References

Brynjolfsson E, Rock D, Syverson C (2017) Artificial intelligence and the modern productivity paradox: a clash of expectations and statistics, working paper 24001. National Bureau of Economic Research, Cambridge, p 44

Dempsey JX (2020) Artificial intelligence. An introduction to the legal, policy and ethical issues. Berkeley Center for Law & Technology, Berkeley, p 46

EU (a) (2021) A legal framework for AI systems. Feasibility study of a legal framework for the development, design and application of artificial intelligence, based on Council of Europe's standards on human rights, democracy and the rule of law. Council of Europe Study DGI (2021)04. https://edoc.coe.int/en/artificial-intelligence/9648-a-legal-framework-for-ai-systems.html

EU (b) (2016) REGULATION (EU) 2016/679 OF THE EUROPEAN PARLIAMENT AND OF THE COUNCIL of 27 April 2016 on the protection of natural persons with regard to the processing of personal data and on the free movement of such data, and repealing Directive 95/46/EC (General Data Protection Regulation). https://eur-lex.europa.eu/legal-content/EN/TXT/PDF/?uri=CELEX:32016R0679&from=EN

EU (c) (2021) Commission proposal for a regulation of the European parliament and of the council laying down harmonised rules on artificial intelligence (Artificial Intelligence Act) and Amending Certain Union Legislative Acts, COM (2021) 206 final (April 21, 2021). https://eur-lex.europa.eu/resource.html?uri=cellar:e0649735-a372-11eb-9585-01aa75ed71a1.0001.02/DOC_1&format=PDF

EU (d) (2018) European ethical charter on the use of artificial intelligence in judicial systems and their Environment. European Commission for the Efficiency of Justice (CEPEJ), France. https://rm.coe.int/ethical-charter-en-for-publication-4-december-2018/16808f699c

European Commission (2019) A definition of AI: main capabilities and scientific discipline. The high-level expert group on artificial intelligence. https://42.cx/wp-content/uploads/2020/04/AI-Definition-EU.pdf

Future of Life Institute (2015) Research priorities for robust and beneficial artificial intelligence: an open letter. https://futureoflife.org/ai-open-letter/

---

[15] *See*, generally, on the of the imitation of humans by Robots, in this book M N Duffourc and D S Giovanniello—The Autonomous AI Physician: Medical Ethics and Legal Liability; B A Ribeiro, H Coelho, A E Ferreira and J Branquinho—Metacognition, Accountability and Legal Personhood of AI. *See,* also, on Ethics, in this book P U Lima and A Paiva—Autonomous and Intelligent Robots: Social, Legal and Ethical Issues; A T Freitas—Data-driven approaches in healthcare: challenges and emerging trends; E Magrani and P G F Silva—The Ethical and Legal Challenges of Recommender Systems Driven by Artificial Intelligence; M S Fernandes and J R Goldim—Artificial Intelligence and Decision Making in Health: Risks and Opportunities; M N Duffourc and D S Giovanniello—The Autonomous AI Physician: Medical Ethics and Legal Liability; R Nogaroli and J L M Faleiros Júnior—Ethical challenges of artificial intelligence in medicine and the triple semantic dimensions of algorithmic opacity with its repercussions to patient consent and medical liability; and B A Ribeiro, H Coelho, A E Ferreira and J Branquinho—Metacognition, Accountability and Legal Personhood of AI.

Harari YN (2018) Why technology favors Tyranny. The Atlantic, October 2018 Issue. https://www.theatlantic.com/magazine/archive/2018/10/yuval-noah-harari-technology-tyranny/568330/

Jessica F, Achten N, Hilligoss H, Nagy A, Srikumar M (2020) Principled artificial intelligence: mapping consensus in ethical and rights-based approaches to principles for AI. Berkman Klein Center for Internet & Society, p 71

Jonsson O, de Tena CL (2019) IE University's European tech insights. IE Center for the Governance of Change, Madrid. https://docs.ie.edu/cgc/European-Tech-Insights-2019.pdf

Julia L (2019) L' Intelligence artificielle n'existe pas. First, Paris, p 287

Kharlamova G, Stavytskyy A, Zarotiadis G (2018) The impact of technological changes on income inequality: the EU states case study. J Int Stud 11(2):76–94. https://www.jois.eu/files/6_478_Kharlamova%20et%20al.pdf

Kissinger HA, Schmidt E, Huttenlocher D (2021) The age of AI: and our human future. Little, Brown and Company, Boston, p 272

Liu S (2021) Artificial intelligence software market revenue worldwide 2018–2025, Dec. 8. https://www.statista.com/statistics/607716/worldwide-artificial-intelligence-market-revenues/

Qureshi Z (2021) Technology, growth and inequality. Changing dynamics in the digital era. Global economy and development (at Brookings), Working Paper 152, p 24

Searle JR (1980) Minds, brains, and programs. Behav Brain Sci 3:417–424. https://www.law.upenn.edu/live/files/3413-searle-j-minds-brains-and-programs-1980pdf

Tavani HT (2016) Ethics and technology: controversies, questions, and strategies for ethical computing. Rivier University, Wiley, Nashua, p 400

Turing A (1950) Computing machinery and intelligence. Mind New Ser 59(236):433–460. https://phil415.pbworks.com/f/TuringComputing.pdf

Open Access This chapter is licensed under the terms of the Creative Commons Attribution 4.0 International License (http://creativecommons.org/licenses/by/4.0/), which permits use, sharing, adaptation, distribution and reproduction in any medium or format, as long as you give appropriate credit to the original author(s) and the source, provide a link to the Creative Commons licence and indicate if changes were made.

The images or other third party material in this chapter are included in the chapter's Creative Commons licence, unless indicated otherwise in a credit line to the material. If material is not included in the chapter's Creative Commons licence and your intended use is not permitted by statutory regulation or exceeds the permitted use, you will need to obtain permission directly from the copyright holder.

Autonomous and Intelligent Robots: Social, Legal and Ethical Issues

Pedro U. Lima and Ana Paiva

Abstract The word "robot" was used for the first time in 1921 by the Czech writer Karel Čapek, who wrote a play called R.U.R. ("Rosumovi Univerzální Roboti"), featuring a scientist who develops a synthetic organic matter to make "humanoid autonomous machines", called "robots". These so called "robots" were supposed to act as slaves and obediently work for humans. Over the years, as real "robots" actually began to be built, their impact on our lives, our work and our society, has brought many benefits, but also raised some concerns. This paper discusses some of the areas of robotics, its advances, challenges and current limitations. We then discuss not only how robots and automation can contribute to our society, but also raise some of the social, legal and ethical concerns that robotics and automation can bring.

1 Introduction

Robots are complex (usually electromechanical) systems, equipped with processors, actuators, sensors and batteries. Actuators can range from wheels or legs, that make a robot locomote, to loudspeakers that allow the robot to communicate through speech or non-verbal acoustic signals, and include arms to grasp or manipulate objects. Video camera, microphone, or touch and tactile sensors enable robots to replicate some human senses, but also to perform other measurements, such as distance, orientation or speed. Robots need on-board processors, such as those in the computers we use in everyday life, to be autonomous regarding decision-making and action capabilities. Such processors run algorithms that, with greater

---

P. U. Lima (✉)
ISR, Instituto Superior Técnico, Universidade de Lisboa, Lisbon, Portugal
e-mail: pedro.lima@tecnico.ulisboa.pt

A. Paiva
INESC-ID, Instituto Superior Técnico, Universidade de Lisboa, Lisbon, Portugal
e-mail: paiva.a@gmail.com

© The Author(s) 2024
H. Sousa Antunes et al. (eds.), *Multidisciplinary Perspectives on Artificial Intelligence and the Law*, Law, Governance and Technology Series 58,
https://doi.org/10.1007/978-3-031-41264-6_7

or lesser sophistication, provide the robot with autonomy and machine intelligence, including the ability to learn. Energetic autonomy is provided by on-board batteries or renewable energy sources.

The word "robot" was used for the first time in 1921 by the Czech writer Karel Čapek, who wrote a play called R.U.R. ("Rosumovi Univerzální Roboti"), featuring a scientist who develops a synthetic organic matter to make "humanoid autonomous machines", called "robots". These so called "robots" were supposed to act as slaves and obediently work for humans. Over the years, real "robots" began to be built, and the introduction of robots in factories dates back to the 1950s. The first automatic guided vehicles (AGV), mobile robots that followed a path realized by cables buried in the ground, were invented in 1954, but the term AGV was only coined in the 1980s. Industrial manipulators were also conceived in the mid-1950s but only introduced in factories in the early 1960s. The first mobile robots using vision were developed in research laboratories in the USA, such as the Stanford Cart (1961) and Shakey (1966). From them on, progress in autonomy was swift towards robots deployed in environments less structured than factories, e.g., homes, offices, hospitals, roads, search and rescue scenarios, Moon or Mars, requiring advanced perception and decision-making. These robots, called service robots, have evolved to interact with humans in daily activities and even replacing the humans in household chores, and inaccessible/dangerous locations.

While industrial robots triggered social problems by replacing workers in factories, they undeniably led to a production growth and wealth increase that, together with other factors, increased well-being, wealth redistribution and new, less boring and less dangerous jobs. On the other hand, service robots may or may not replace human work and, even if they do, the amount of jobs lost is variable. For instance, a vacuum-cleaning robot helps with household chores, but it hardly replaces domestic workers; however, autonomous trucks may lead to a significant loss of jobs among truck drivers. Moreover, service robots that include a strong component of interaction with humans also raise ethical and legal issues: will they disclose any private information of their human companions? Can they harm humans?

These issues become more delicate when robots act autonomously. Although there is no universally accepted definition of "autonomy" for robots, we adopt the notion that *an autonomous robot is an "embodied" system, endowed with sensors to perceive and understand the surrounding world, actuators that allow it to act on that world (possibly including interaction with other robots, animals and/or humans), and decision-making capacity independent from complete external control, namely by humans*. We should note that autonomy is a loaded term in Artificial Intelligence (AI). C. Castelfranchi discusses autonomy as a relational notion (Castelfranchi 1994) that entails different dimensions, leading to distinct types of autonomy, in particular, "executive autonomy", that means to be able to move, act and make decisions in the world without the need to be explicitly helped to do so. Although this is subject to intense philosophical debate, we also consider that autonomy is a necessary, but not sufficient condition for a robot to be endowed with intelligence (in the sense of machine-intelligence). In this sense, machine-intelligence requires,

Autonomous and Intelligent Robots: Social, Legal and Ethical Issues 129

in addition to autonomy, the ability of a robot to adapt its behaviour and actions to the surrounding world. Note however that this distinction is relevant. First there is a wide misunderstanding about what robots are, often confusing intelligent software systems, or "dis-embodied" agents, with autonomous robots. As argued, robots need to be able to physically perceive and act in the physical world. Secondly, not all robots are intelligent or autonomous, and many, for example many of the toy drones, are tele-operated and controlled by humans, where their intelligence and autonomy is non-existent. Often the public debate about the ethical and social issues raised by robots confuses the general software systems, endowed with artificial intelligence, with robots and considers all autonomous robots as intelligent.

We consider that autonomous robots, as defined, given their specific characteristics, bring new social, ethical and legal concerns, which we will discuss in this chapter.

This chapter is organized as follows: first we provide a brief view of industrial robots, followed by service robots. Then we discuss the potential for these robots to be placed in social settings, and how intelligence is needed for social interactions with humans. Given these types of robots, we then discuss the social, ethical and legal implications of their integration in our society.

2 Industrial Robots and Automation vs Service Robots

Robots were introduced in factories to automate repetitive tasks that were performed by humans up to then. Those included robot manipulators, mimicking human arms, in different operations: picking objects from pallets in transporting vehicles or from conveyor belts and placing them into manufacturing cells, and back from there to other conveyor belt or transportation vehicle; assembling parts into a more complex object; painting and welding. They also included mobile robots, in the form of AGVs or LGVs (laser-guided vehicles, that do not need buried cables or painted lines on the ground) to carry objects autonomously between different locations in the industrial plant.

A common feature of all these applications and scenarios is their *structured* nature. The locations of conveyor belts, pick and place posts, and manufacturing/assembly cells with machines, are well known, static and easily recognizable. In most cases, objects are channelled to very precise locations where they are picked by the manipulators, and loading/unloading stations have clamping and fixture mechanisms that force the objects to be tightly confined to their transporting platforms. Industrial robotics is also commonly designated by automation, because the involved robots perform automatic operations, but are not autonomous in a strict sense. In most cases, traditional industrial automation does not require sensors such as vision to locate objects to be picked, or the most adequate placing locations for them. It also does not handle deformable objects such as food or soft packages.

In the last century, documentaries of robots automating production in construction, assembly, painting, parts transport and welding factories dazzled the

Fig. 1 Service robot for construction and brick transportation

general public. But the more modern and challenging robot research seeks to create machines capable of dealing with less structured and less predictable environments, such as our homes or even outdoor environments, populated by humans and other agents that do not behave as deterministically as in a factory environment. These are called service robots (see an example in Fig. 1).

Service robots range from the commercially successful vacuum-cleaning robots to a planetary rover exploring the surface of Mars. Vacuum cleaners wander around the home covering the largest possible area while avoiding unexpected objects (such as things left on the floor, table and chair legs, or a person feet) detected by onboard vision and laser scanning sensors. Martian rovers move across difficult terrains they need to observe before the next move, heading towards locations of scientific interest that were previously identified by their on-board cameras. Service robots also include autonomous driving cars, search and rescue teams of heterogeneous (land, air) unmanned vehicles, medical robots to assist human surgeons in performing surgeries, or robots assisting patients in hospitals and healthcare facilities, agriculture robots, surveillance drones and many others.

A common feature in service robots is that they operate in *unstructured*, often previously unknown environments, where sensors are essential to build a situational awareness by the robot, so as to support its reasoning and decision-making. Service robots cannot afford to act *automatically*. They need to be *autonomous* or, at least, have a high degree of independence from human remote operators. Because of that, they raise a new plethora of ethical and legal problems (e.g., which action should the robot pick when there are alternatives and they have different impacts in the human safety; what must an autonomous car do to ensure it abides by the driving rules) that were not raised before by industrial robots, whose main impact was social,

Fig. 2 Baxter robot for small factories

namely concerning job losses. Indeed, most service robots tend to be pervasive in operations not commonly performed by humans, such as non-repetitive and/or dangerous scenarios, so the social impact is relatively small. Nevertheless, they start entering industrial scenarios (e.g., using force sensors to endow robots with the ability to avoid harming humans, thus reducing the space occupied by robotic cells and their safeguards—see Baxter in Fig. 2; to perform pick and place actions over less structured environments, soft packages and materials) and large operations such as autonomous taxis and trucks, which may lead to large replacement of human work force by autonomous machines.

Current research on service robots is very much focused on robots that collaborate with humans and not on robots that replace humans. Search and rescue robots are developed to collaborate with Civil Protection teams; medical robots help doctors and nurses in hospitals, and planetary rovers extend the reach of human curiosity to the exploration of Mars. This also raises other challenging and interesting social questions: how should the robots act so as to interact the more naturally possible with the humans? What does it mean to act socially?

3 Robots and Humans: The Rise of Intelligent and Social Robots

Would a rescue robot, as it interacts with humans in an emergency setting, be considered a social robot? Or a drone that flies in a formation with other drones to overcome some obstacle? The word "Social" arises from the Latin word "socii",

Fig. 3 Examples of social robots—from left to right: Vizzy, Pepper, ASTRO and MBOT

meaning friends or allies. The concept of being "social" in general is associated with behaviors that take into account others, their interests, motivations and needs. An individual is considered social if she/he has the capability to interact and consider the others in his/her actions, and thus establish social relations. However, "sociality" in robots, may cover different perspectives or even degrees. Many service robots, can be classified as a being "socially evocative". For example, a robot with big eyes, such as the Vizzy robot built by the ISR institute in Lisbon (see Fig. 3) or Roomba, a vacuum-cleaning robot that moves purposefully around in a home: both may evoke responses that are social and emotional in nature. Just their physical embodiment and their autonomous actions are enough to act as a natural interface to elicit human-like responses, even if the robots themselves are not actually capable of responding in a clever and social manner. Furthermore, just by being placed in a social setting, robots can be socially receptive, that is, benefiting from the interactions with others, learn from a human "teacher" and thus, improve their performance. However, as more robots are required to perform activities in human-centered settings, they will be given "social competencies" . Social robots are considered to be able to perceive each other and humans, engage in social interactions, possess histories (perceive and interpret the world in terms of their own experience), explicitly communicate with humans and learn from them.

But social robots are often designed to execute tasks that in essence may not be "social". For example, consider a robot in a healthcare setting designed to transport materials from one place to another in a hospital. Most of its jobs, like carrying medicines, or linen, are not necessarily social. Yet, social competencies, when present, can enrich the interaction they establish with humans around them, and improve their performance. For example, the healthcare robot may be able to recognise nurses, respond and execute their orders given in natural language, interact with patients, and provide information when needed. Another example is our vacuum cleaning robot, that can be given some social competencies, such as avoiding or interacting with humans, or adapting its actions to habits of the members of a household, making its performance more efficient. So, there social competencies can be seen as the stepping stones for robots to become active members of our lives and society. From a technical point of view, this entails building social competencies (Fong et al. 2003), that include the capability to recognise humans, understand their actions, perceive their emotions, use natural language and non-verbal cues and in general recognize, "understand" and reason about the social situations they will be immersed.

But building these social capabilities requires advanced AI techniques and algorithms. To perceive humans, capture their actions and emotions, techniques from vision and social signal processing are needed. For action generation, automated planning algorithms are required. Natural language and speech processing methods are essential if we want robots to interact in a natural and human-like fashion with humans. Further, as we also need robots to be able to adapt and learn to execute tasks, we need to use machine learning algorithms. In fact, many of the major AI techniques that are being developed in AI nowadays are essential to build intelligent social robots that are able to act in dynamic and social domains. Furthermore, social robots constitute the ideal test-bed for the integration of such techniques.

Typical application domains for social robots are vast, and include healthcare, transport, logistics, cleaning, education, entertainment, agriculture, and others.

In the context of healthcare, there has been a considerable development in the past few years, with a clear increase since the COVID-19 pandemic. Robots are being introduced in healthcare facilities to transport materials and supplies, especially in situations where such transport may pose risk to the exposure to pathogens, such as a virus. Another important use of social robots has been for therapy and care, in particular for the elderly and for patients with dementia. A study analyzing the use of the robot PARO (a seal-like robot) in home care facilities in Japan, has shown the positive impact that the robot has in decreasing stress and calming down patients with dementia, also providing indirect benefits by increasing their activity in particular social interactions (Šabanović et al. 2013). Another study has shown that the use of a home robot for the elderly, in rural areas of New Zealand, lead to an increase in quality of life, more independence and autonomy by the elderly, and a decrease in primary care visits and phone calls to healthcare practitioners (Orejana et al. 2015) . These results are encouraging signs that the technology can have a positive social impact in our ageing society.

The area of transportation is perhaps one of the areas where service robots have shown the largest increase as autonomous vehicles began to be placed on our roads. Roads are, in essence, a social setting, meaning that autonomous decisions by vehicles must consider the presence of other drivers as well as pedestrians. Autonomous cars are therefore endowed with competencies (in prediction and action) associated with social interactions. Furthermore, the social impact from the potential increase of their use in the roads is undoubtedly quite large. Although this impact has been shadowed by the overstated predictions that autonomous cars would be dominating the roads by 2020, we cannot ignore the social, ethical and legal implications that autonomous vehicles will have in the future.

Other areas of application such as cleaning and logistics are also increasing, and once again, the pandemic gave rise to a series of applications where robots can be used to provide safe and efficient ways to do their jobs. These application areas of robotics, where robots become integrated in our social settings, raise concerns in the general population, in manufacturers and in law-makers. Still a widely unregulated market, robots may in the future be placed in settings where they interact with humans capturing private information, influencing their actions, and largely impacting the unstable job-market. Yet, as mentioned before, some of these fears are still unfounded, and the eco-system that is being built for the introduction of AI into our society and legislation being drawn as we write, is a safeguard for our robots.

in this paper we draw some of the social ethical and legal implications of this fascinating new technology.

4 Ethical, Social and Legal Impacts

For robots to be able to succeed as a technology that makes our world a better place, we must engage researchers, designers, developers, engineers, companies and law-makers, into building an ecosystem where robots are trusted, effective, secure and relevant to our society. The current perception of autonomous robots by the general public often imagines futuristic capabilities in the robots. Robots are portrayed as being capable of executing extraordinary jobs and deal with many different tasks and problems. And, in spite of the fact is that the technology is still quite limited, many non-justified fears and concerns have emerged in the general public.

Discussions on "killer robots", or "robots for the elderly", have invaded the space of public opinion. But, in many cases these concerns deserve deep debates and a serious approach. The (still) immature state of this discussion, which is understandable given its relative novelty of the field, means that matters of a different nature are often associated with ethical problems resulting from an exaggerated perception of robots. In this chapter we will try to raise and discuss some of these concerns, and distinguish between the ethical, social and legal debates that need to exist around this new technology.

4.1 Ethical Issues

How should an autonomous robot react in situations where its decisions may harm humans? What about the protection of humans' privacy when, e.g., a domestic assistant robot is wandering around the house with a camera and interacting with the human in ways that may reveal his/her intimate behaviour? should autonomous robots be involved in health care, from monitoring the elderly or children to surgical interventions? And what is the impact of the progressive introduction of bionic devices (prostheses, exoskeletons) in humans, which could 1 day lead to the difficulty of distinguishing between human and robot? These questions lead to ethical problems that need to be addressed as robots are created. These questions need to be addressed by robotic manufacturers, by researchers and law-makers in collaboration.

In fact, the discussion around the ethics of decision-making and behaviour by autonomous robots gained new strength and relevance with the awareness of the very likely massification of driverless (or autonomous) cars. As the Google/Waymo Car and other vehicles from car manufacturing companies started entering our daily lives, they have faced a growing number of situations, particularly in urban environments, in which they have to take decisions autonomously. Typical examples representative of these situations are abundant.

Consider the situation: an autonomous vehicle moves at a considerable speed and detects a group of pedestrians crossing the road unexpectedly; the potentially fatal run-over cannot be avoided without the vehicle deciding to leave the road, eventually running over a pedestrian who walks on the sidewalk. What should the vehicle's decision be:

- (1) go forward, running over pedestrians on the road, or to deviate, running over the pedestrian on the sidewalk?
- (2) leaving the road, eventually sacrificing the life of its occupant(s), or moving on, running over the pedestrians that got in its way?

These types of dilemmas have been explored in the moral machine project[1] that was created to explore moral dilemmas that are faced by autonomous vehicles. The online platform presents moral dilemmas to users that must choose between two potential bad outcomes, such as killing three passengers in the autonomous car or killing three pedestrians. This platform has been used to gather millions of decisions in ten different languages and 233 countries. The data shows that people prefer sparing humans to animals, and sparing more and young lives (Awad et al. 2018). This study is important as it gives data to policy-makers for how to deal with situations where machines may have to decide who should live or die.

The issue of the ethics of decision-making by robotic systems begun to be seriously addressed by some countries and organisations in the world, starting from the document produced by the British Standards Institute in 2016, with guidelines on ethical rules to be followed in the design of robot systems by managers and designers (BSI Standards Institution 2016). Similarly the IEEE Global Initiative on Ethics of Autonomous and Intelligent Systems ("The IEEE Global Initiative") produced the Ethically Aligned Design[2] document that provides guidance to developers, governments, businesses, and the public, to how to deal, design, use and establish rules for advancement of autonomous systems that contribute to the society.

In the last few years the High-Level Expert Group on AI (AI HLEG) from the European Commission has issued a set of ethics guidelines for achieving trustworthy AI. Obviously, as we deal with autonomous robots, which are endowed with different AI algorithms used for their functioning, these guidelines may also apply. We can therefore extrapolate such guidelines to intelligent robots: (1) **Human**

---

[1] See https://www.moralmachine.net/.

[2] See https://ethicsinaction.ieee.org/.

Agency and Oversight- robots and robot systems should respect human agency and support oversight of their execution; (2) **Technical Robustness and Safety-** robots should be robust and safe as they interact with humans and in our society; (3) **Privacy and Data Governance-** robots should follow the established privacy rules and data governance mechanisms; (4) **Transparency-** robots should be transparent when making decisions, and about their capabilities, making clear why certain decision is the appropriate; (5) **Diversity, Non-discrimination and Fairness-** Robots should respect not discriminate nor cause discrimination, and guarantee fairness in their decisions; (6) **Environmental and Societal well-being-** robots should foster societal well-being and contribute to a better society and environment; (7) **Accountability-** a clear accountability process and eco-system should be in place and followed by robot manufacturers, guaranteeing that when problems occur the process can be triggered.

Adopting theses guidelines, has lead to the field of Responsible Robotics that deals with "the responsible design, development, use, implementation, and regulation of robotics in society" (van Wynsberghe and Sharkey 2020). In particular medical and healthcare robots raise particularly relevant ethical problems. Robots began to enter hospitals in very different ways. The best known and probably the most impactful to date are robots that support surgeons in performing surgeries, increasing accuracy and filtering out unavoidable tremors even in the best specialists. But for some years now, mobile robots have been transporting meals, medicines and various instruments between hospital areas, freeing up medical and nursing staff to carry out tasks that are closer to patients. There are more recent examples, still in an embryonic state, of robots that interact with the elderly and children, seeking to improve their clinical condition by encouraging exercise or performing interactive games, respectively.

There are also other measures taken to address some of these ethical issues, that question the role of the robots, and foster the development of "collaborative robots". The main idea is that instead of replacing workers by machines in carrying out tasks that require deep professional knowledge and experience, focus on tasks where the robot can free the doctors and nurses to focus on their main activities. Examples of these are robots that transport meals and medicine to rooms of an hospital, robots that provide remote access to highly contagious patients, or robots that provide assistance to patients not requiring the more affectionate presence of humans.

4.2 Social Issues

The massive introduction of robots into society may contribute to the society not only in positive terms, but also by its impact on employment, self-esteem and/or human behaviour. The controversy raised by the replacement of humans by machines in work activities are not new, and are not restricted to the loss of jobs, which, in fact, did not happen, in past situations. In 1821, at the peak of the industrial revolution, the economist David Ricardo claimed that the introduction of machines would being harmful to the interests of the working classes, namely because the wealth created benefited above all those who lived on capital income. Yet, past automation has improved the living conditions of the societies in which it has been installed, and has provided better paid, less inhumane and less dangerous jobs.

Thus, the question one should pose is whether the current revolution will be different. The international press has come forward with the most terrifying estimates about the consequences of the robotization of society. According to a 2013 study by Carl B. Frey and Michael Osborne of the University of Oxford, 47% of US jobs would be at risk of being replaced by "computer capital" (Frey and Osborne 2013). A more recent study by Merrill Lynch predicts that, by 2025, the annual impact of "creative disruption" resulting from Artificial Intelligence could reach 14–33 billion (billions of dollars), including a reduction of $9M in knowledge-based employment costs, replaced by machines; $8M in manufacturing and healthcare; $2M resulting from the use of autonomous vehicles and drones (Lynch 2015).

The key issue underlying all these numbers is that they essentially result from developments in intelligent autonomous agents that are not "embodied" and do not interact with the surrounding world except through a computer keyboard and monitor. This predictions can be appreciated given the current situation with increase use of smartphones, or Internet search agents (e.g., Google, travel agencies), or recommender systems, showing that Artificial Intelligence (AI) is rapidly putting many jobs at risk—a transformation that, according to McKinsey Global Institute, occurs ten times faster, and on a scale three hundred times the past. But the problem would be bigger if the same were to happen with Robotics, since retraining workers specialized in physical tasks, not intensive in knowledge, can be much more complicated, especially at the rate of change at which the changes take place. Yet, it turns out that the technological development of Robotics, despite many recent advances, is incomparably harder, smaller, and even autonomous vehicles, which are promising a dazzling appearance, will take many years to completely replace driver-driven vehicles—e.g., as evidenced by an infamous fatal accident in the US with a Tesla car on autopilot, resulting from the overconfidence of the driver and the manufacturing company. The situation is even more glaring when we talk about robots that help in household tasks, or in hospitals, in agriculture or even in modern factories, more flexible and with less repetitive work. Not only are these far from being autonomous, but many are built to collaborate with humans.

We are, therefore, considering two different realities, despite normally witnessing an association between Robotics (embodied AI) and AI (dis-embodied). However, in either case there are concerns and risks to be carefully considered. The benefits brought by automation cannot make us give up on finding other occupations and jobs for those who lose their current ones—such as creative occupations or the maintenance and production of robots. And they should not divert us from social concerns that deserve the attention of public policies, that can even pass through the creation of mandatory minimum income, and legislation that forces companies that become less dependent on human work to (1) retrain or relocate their workers and/or (2) pay taxes and social security contributions proportional to the creation of wealth resulting from the incorporation of robots and AI technologies in their production. Above all, and going back to the concerns of some economists during the industrial revolution, we as a society should not allow that the greater wealth generated by this technology remains in the hands of very few, namely those of the companies that own the technology. The risk of this happening if we do not act is disproportionately greater today than it was in the nineteenth century.

4.3 Legal Issues

Reflection on the ethics of decision-making often leads to discussions on legal issues, namely on how (and to whom) to assign legal responsibility for such decisions. Questions such as who is legally liable by an autonomous robot actions? How far can a surveillance robot go without interfering with citizens security and/or privacy? How is intellectual property protected regarding inventions performed with the help of agents or robots? Furthermore, if 1 day robots are to be confused with humans, or animals, in the sense of having their own identity, should their rights also be protected?

The European Commission has been at the forefront of regulation, with the new proposal for an EU regulatory framework on artificial intelligence (AI) launched in April 2021.[3] The proposed legal framework focuses on the specific utilisation of AI systems and associated risks, focusing primarily on guaranteeing trustworthiness in the process of creating and delivering intelligent systems. In spite of being a first and admirable attempt to making sure that AI is used in a way that companies and users can trust, some aspects related with embodiment, and thus, intelligent robots, are left untouched. Furthermore, these new regulations may raise other problems, because it is not clear who would be responsible for implementing the laws and guaranteeing the compliance with them. Common sense may indicate that the laws and guidelines are aimed at robot designers, producers and operators, but given the robot's autonomy shouldn't it be endowed with the capacity for self-awareness so that, evaluating the situation, decides by itself to apply or not all the other rules that determine its operation? We should not forget that robots can be initially deployed with capabilities that improve over time. So, issues related with the ethics of robot systems that interact with humans, point towards attributing a level of legal responsibility for a potential accident, and for the damage caused by it, in proportion to the amount of instructions initially programmed in the robot versus the amount of autonomy acquired by learning, already without the direct intervention of its programmer. In this way, an intelligent autonomous robot with more years of experience and, during which it learned new behaviours and actions, would assume greater legal responsibilities. Yet, evaluating the autonomy ratio taught by

---

[3] See https://eur-lex.europa.eu/legal-content/EN/TXT/HTML/?uri=CELEX:52021PC0206&from=EN.

the designer in relation to that learned by the robot is certainly difficult, and a more pragmatic alternative would be to introduce mandatory insurance, or as proposed by the EU, making sure that decisions taken are transparent and can be inspected by external entities. We agree that a legal framework such as what is proposed by the EU, embracing the current technology to guarantee its proper, sound and positive use in our society is very important. Yet, we should not exaggerate in the regulation, because autonomous robots are still in its infancy, and legalizing it creation and use too soon may dampen the innovation and compromise the potential social benefits that they can bring, not too mention leaving other regions of the globe in an unfair advantage in what concerns research and innovation.

5 Conclusions

In 1939, the visionary Russian/American writer Isaac Asimov, in his book *I, Robot*, established the so-called Three Laws of Robotics: Law 1- robot cannot harm a human being or, through inaction, allow a human being to come to harm; Law 2- robot must obey orders given to it by human beings except in cases where such orders conflict with 1; and Law 3- a robot must protect its own existence as long as such protection does not conflict with 1. or 2. In spite of the simplicity of these laws, Asimov was able to produce many entertaining and well thought dilemmas exploring the difficulty that we have in introducing autonomous machines into our society. Indeed, this is a difficult problem, and in here we briefly show just a tip of the iceberg. AI and robotics will certainly change the way we live and function in society. One day our descendants will wonder about how it was possible to have cars driven by humans with all the risks that that entailed; or why it was necessary for a worker to make a superhuman effort to carry excessive weights that were harmful to his/her health). We believe that AI and its use in Robotics for creating intelligent and autonomous robots will be a driver for a societal change that will contribute for better, more human, more sustainable and healthier societies.

References

Awad E, Dsouza S, Kim R, Schulz J, Henrich J, Shariff A, Bonnefon JF, Rahwan I (2018) The moral machine experiment. Nature 563(7729):59–64

Castelfranchi C (1994) Guarantees for autonomy in cognitive agent architecture. In: International workshop on agent theories, architectures, and languages. Springer, Berlin, pp 56–70

Fong T, Nourbakhsh I, Dautenhahn K (2003) A survey of socially interactive robots. Rob Auton Syst 42(3–4):143–166

Frey CB, Osborne M (2013) The future of employment. Oxford University Press, Oxford

BSI Standards Institution (2016) Robots and robotic devices: guide to the ethical design and application of robots and robotic systems. BSI Standards Ltd, London

Lynch BM (2015) Creative disruption. Bank of America, Charlotte

Orejana JR, MacDonald BA, Ahn HS, Peri K, Broadbent E (2015) Healthcare robots in homes of rural older adults. In: International conference on social robotics. Springer, Berlin, pp 512–521

Šabanović S, Bennett CC, Chang WL, Huber L (2013) Paro robot affects diverse interaction modalities in group sensory therapy for older adults with dementia. In: 2013 IEEE 13th international conference on rehabilitation robotics (ICORR). IEEE, pp 1–6

van Wynsberghe A, Sharkey N (2020) Special issue on responsible robotics: introduction. Springer, Boston

Open Access This chapter is licensed under the terms of the Creative Commons Attribution 4.0 International License (http://creativecommons.org/licenses/by/4.0/), which permits use, sharing, adaptation, distribution and reproduction in any medium or format, as long as you give appropriate credit to the original author(s) and the source, provide a link to the Creative Commons licence and indicate if changes were made.

The images or other third party material in this chapter are included in the chapter's Creative Commons licence, unless indicated otherwise in a credit line to the material. If material is not included in the chapter's Creative Commons licence and your intended use is not permitted by statutory regulation or exceeds the permitted use, you will need to obtain permission directly from the copyright holder.

The Ethical and Legal Challenges of Recommender Systems Driven by Artificial Intelligence

Eduardo Magrani and Paula Guedes Fernandes da Silva

Abstract In a hyperconnected world, recommendation systems (RS) are one of the most widespread commercial applications of artificial intelligence (AI), initially mostly used for e-commerce, but already widely applied to different areas, for instance, content providers and social media platforms. Due to the current information overload, these systems are designed mainly to help individuals dealing with the infinity of options available, in addition to optimizing companies' profits by offering products and services that directly meet the needs of their customers. However, despite its benefits, RS based on AI may also create detrimental effects—sometimes unforeseen—for users and society, especially for vulnerable groups. Constant tracking of users, automated analysis of personal data to predict and infer behaviours, preferences, future actions and characteristic, the creation of behavioural profiles and the microtargeting for personalized recommendations may raise relevant ethical and legal issues, such as discriminatory outcomes, lack of transparency and explanation of algorithmic decisions that impact people's lives and unfair violations of privacy and data protection. This article aims to address these issues, through a multisectoral, multidisciplinary and human rights'-based approach, including contributions from the Law, ethics, technology, market, and society.

1 Introduction

Artificial Intelligence (AI) is constantly increasing its presence in our daily lives, shaping the way we access information, interact with connected devices, share personal information, and socially interact with others (Privacy International 2018,

---

E. Magrani
Berkman Klein Center for Internet & Society at Harvard University, Harvard Law School, Cambridge, MA, USA

P. G. F. da Silva (✉)
Catholic University of Portugal, School of Porto, Faculty of Law, Porto, Portugal

© The Author(s) 2024
H. Sousa Antunes et al. (eds.), *Multidisciplinary Perspectives on Artificial Intelligence and the Law*, Law, Governance and Technology Series 58,
https://doi.org/10.1007/978-3-031-41264-6_8

p. 4). Progressively, new products and services based on this technology are made available, for instance, through audio-visual recommendations; spam filtering in e-mails; personalized news feeds on social media; search results on search engines; virtual assistants and even suggestions on best routes on traffic apps.

Even though the term "artificial intelligence" has existed since the mid-1950s, the growing popularity of these systems is associated with the currently growing of data availability, cheaper processing infrastructure, technological advances, and greater connectivity (Bigonha 2018, p. 2). In a nutshell, AI may be considered a huge field of study, which reunites different technologies that combine data, algorithms and computational power (European Commission 2020c, p. 2), capable of behaving similarly to human intelligence to achieve specific objectives, usually the solution of a specific question (European Commission 2018, p. 1).

In the current state of the art, AI contributes to social and economic benefits in different fields by improving the prediction of results, optimizing operations and resource allocation and customizing service delivery, providing significant competitive advantages for the companies that dominate it (European Commission 2020b, p. 1). However, despite potentially beneficial to people and society, AI also raises new challenges.

Therefore, the rapid development and thoughtless application of technology establish the necessity to implement ethical principles and regulations for its use on the agenda, especially when we talk about machines with the ability to learn by itself, generating highly unpredictability results (even without human intervention) and great potential to harm fundamental rights.

The scale and reach of AI systems, the trend toward rapid and careless implementation, and the immediate impact they have on the lives of many people, may reinforce existing problems, besides the creation of new ones (Andersen 2018, p. 14). The threat posed by AI, then, does not assume the form of a super-intelligent robot that dominates humanity, but results from its daily use, as is the case with recommender systems, which will be specifically analysed in the following topic.

2 What are AI's Recommender Systems?

In a hyperconnected world, recommender systems (RS) are one of the most widespread commercial applications of AI, initially introduced for e-commerce, but already widely applied in other fields, such as content providers and social media platforms (Sahu and Singh 2019, p. 1).

Due to the current information overload, these systems are primarily designed to help individuals deal with the countless options available, as well as optimizing companies' profit generation by offering products and services that directly meet their customers' needs (Zhang et al. 2020, pp. 1–2). So, ideally, while RS create better user experiences, they also help providers fulfil their purpose of increasing the number of sales and clicks and, hence, profits, as well as increasing user engagement and satisfaction across different platforms (Tejeda-Lorente et al. 2018, p. 3).

The Ethical and Legal Challenges of Recommender Systems Driven... 143

Given its effectiveness, the use of RS already covers different domains, including streaming (Netflix and Spotify), news (CNN and Google News), dating (Tinder and Grindr), food (Ifood and UberEats), travel (Booking and AirBnB), social media (Facebook and LinkedIn), search engines (Google) and e-commerce (Amazon) (Paraschakis 2018, pp. 2–3). In the current big data era, the basic idea of recommender systems is to use the different data sources available to infer and predict the interests, tastes, and future behaviour of users to recommend personalized content, products, or services (Aggarwal 2016, p. 1).

Therefore, RSs are considered an algorithmic information filtering tool, capable of assisting users in their decision-making process, shaping online experiences by indicating items that are likely to please them (Mazeh and Shmueli 2020, p. 1). The prediction of the items' usefulness for a given user varies according to the recommendation algorithm model used (Zhang et al. 2020, p. 2). Currently, there are three main models:

1. content-based approach—recommendations are sent based on descriptions of items previously approved by the user, either through direct assessments or inferred behaviours (Jannach et al. 2010, p. 4);
2. collaborative filtering—process information on behaviours and opinions of a community to predict items of interest to the target user, as long as the group and individual profiles are similar (Jannach et al. 2010, p. 13); and
3. knowledge-based approach—instead of historical data, this model combines features submitted by the user with knowledge about a specific area, such as marketing or sales information. It is more used for more complex and less frequent situations, such as carrying out financial transactions or buying cars, apartments and luxury items (Aggarwal 2016, pp. 14–16).

In addition to the three main models, there are also hybrid systems, which combine the strengths of each of the previous models to create more effective systems, and systems that consider context, such as information about time, location, emotions, and social relationships (Jannach et al. 2010, p. 21; Aggarwal 2016, p. 8).

Regardless of the model, sending personalized recommendations requires building a user profile (profiling) (Kanoje et al. 2015, pp. 1–2)[1] that summarizes their preferences, tastes, frequent behaviours, and interests. This information can be extracted either implicitly, from the monitoring of the individual's behaviour online, or explicitly, when the user himself directly provides his data, such as filling out forms (Jannach et al. 2010, pp. 1–2; Paraschakis 2017, p. 211).

In summary, RS are essentially composed of three steps: (1) collection of personal data, directly or indirectly provided by users (input). In the latter case, they include, for example, click flows, browsing history, structural information of

---

[1] Briefly, the behavioural profile is a set of patterns used to concisely describe the user from their data, which are processed to infer their characteristics, future behaviours, tastes and interests. This process allows classifying them into profiles, used to recommend personalized items to better satisfy them.

visited web pages and purchase records, observed and inferred from the constant monitoring of the individual online; (2) data processing for the creation of the user profile, which can be represented by, for example, groups of terms or keywords; (3) targeting personalized content in the form of recommendations (output) (Nadee 2016, pp. 16–23).

There is no doubt that RS provide benefits in terms of organization, time optimization and improvement of the individual's online experience, by helping them search for content, services and products of interest. However, this technology may also generate negative—sometimes unanticipated—effects for users and society, especially vulnerable groups. Constant monitoring, automated analysis of personal data to predict and infer individual behaviours, preferences and characteristics, the creation of behavioural profiles and, finally, the sending of personalized recommendations may raise relevant ethical and legal questions, as it will be analysed in the next topics.

3 Ethical and Legal Challenges Associated with RS

The development, implementation and use of complex recommender systems may lead to significant ethical and legal problems. Concrete or potential damages and violations of fundamental rights are already a consequence of this technology, such as the lack of transparency and explanation of results (algorithmic opacity), reduction of individual autonomy, exposure of users to unjustified violations of privacy and data protection, unconscious manipulation of behaviours and discrimination (Milano et al. 2019, pp. 5–6).

In order to mitigate some of these threats and damages from AI in RS, it is necessary to introduce an ethical and regulatory debate on possible limitations applicable to this technology. In addition to binding legislation, ethical guidelines is a first step that must also be considered to minimize the risks associated with these systems and, simultaneously, maximize their benefits (Ekstrand and Ekstrand 2016, p. 16).

For some years, there have been a worldwide concern to define ethical limits for AI. A growing number of initiatives from different stakeholders define recommendations and guidelines for building ethical, trustworthy and human-centred AI. By 2020, at least 84 initiatives of AI ethical principles had been mapped, coming from public and private organizations, especially from Europe and United States (Jobin et al. 2019, p. 391; Hartmann et al. 2020, p. 6).

Although most documents set out a general ethical framework for AI, which focuses on protecting vulnerable people and dealing with asymmetries of information and power (Beil et al. 2019, p. 4), as RS are based on AI algorithms, these common basic principles can be directly applicable to them (Jobin et al. 2019, pp. 391–396). Among the principles most cited by these documents are transparency, justice, non-maleficence, accountability, privacy, beneficence, freedom, autonomy and trust.

Thus, the analysis of this technology through an ethical principle approach may be a relevant starting point to contrast how far RS's development and use are from an adequate implementation, where it acts more beneficially than harmful to society. In this regard, to reach such an analysis, the principles of beneficence and maleficence play an important role.

In line with the principle of beneficence, AI-driven technologies, such as recommender systems, should be developed to create an "AI for good". In other words, technology must promote well-being, dignity, common good and sustainability in all its phases and designs, in order to benefit people, society and the planet (Guszcza et al. 2020, p. 72). In this sense, these tools must promote human potential, creating new opportunities that increase individual self-determination, autonomy, human agency, social cohesion, and individual and collective capacities (Floridi et al. 2018, p. 690).

Beneficial AI initiatives must achieve physical and emotional well-being at individual and collective levels, such as improving health care, providing public benefits, expanding positive educational outcomes, and creating safer environments (Guszcza et al. 2020, pp. 72–74). Specifically regarding RS, this principle is not intended to undermine the great benefits produced by them, but to ensure that these technologies work in favour of human beings and not against them.

For example, a well-designed RS to help sick or unhealthy individuals presents a great opportunity to help people achieve a better quality of life in accordance with beneficence (Ekstrand and Ekstrand 2016, p. 2). Currently, initiatives in this direction already exist, such as wearables with gamification techniques and other behavioural interventions in the form of "nudges" created to encourage healthier behaviours (Guszcza et al. 2020, p. 73).

Besides that, based on the principle of non-maleficence, recommender systems must be designed not to harm human beings in any way, avoiding predictable, unforeseen or unintentional damages, such as biased recommendations, facilitation of the spread of misinformation and violation of privacy and data protection rules (Guszcza et al. 2020, p. 71). When it comes to non-maleficence, the main point is to prevent any type of damage, whether from the intention or malpractice of an individual or unforeseen technological behaviour (Floridi et al. 2018, p. 697).

Therefore, to prevent and avoid harmful RS, it is essential to understand technological limitations to manage potential risks (Guszcza et al. 2020, pp. 71–72). This principle emphasizes the alarming need to have AI systems in accordance with the standards and recommendations of data protection, privacy, cybersecurity and safeguarding all human rights by design and by default, in addition to an effective accountability system in case of misuse.

Thus, adjustments and harmonizing agreements between beneficence and non-maleficence are common, which requires the balance of RS benefits and risks in practice (Floridi et al. 2018, p. 697). For example, when companies prevent, through automated techniques, harmful content from being recommended to protect their users, although AI filtering has beneficial intentions, it can violate individual freedom and autonomy. Therefore, in practice, it is important to carefully consider the possible ways in which systems could be misused or cause unintended damage to mitigate their adverse effects (Ekstrand and Ekstrand 2016, p. 2).

In this sense, the principles of beneficence and non-maleficence, together with other ethical guidelines, connect and unfold in many different legal implications. Below, we highlight some of the main ethical and legal challenges that arise from the lens of these two values:

3.1 Opacity

Some AI experts compare this technology to a black box, as its processes and mode of operation would be beyond human capacity to understand (Floridi et al. 2018, p. 692), especially for people outside the field of technological study. This presumption is even more intense in the case of AI algorithms that interact in an open social environment and learn by interacting with the space in which they operate, when their automated decisions are difficult to explain even for experts. This frequent lack of transparency and explanation about the processes and values involved in the recommendation tools hinder the creation of better systems, that is, adequate to fundamental rights, ethical principles and centred on human beings (Milano et al. 2019, p. 16).

3.2 Discriminatory Bias

RS are created by people, which makes it susceptible to biased results. This consequence may arise as a result of the selected training data or (implicit) values held by technology developers, which may exacerbate systematic social discrimination, even unintentionally (European Parliament 2020, p. 15).

Due to the data-driven nature of the AI techniques used in the recommender system, the selection of the dataset for training must be well defined, otherwise it can be an important source of discrimination (Beil et al. 2019, p. 4). For example, when available data do not reflect the social diversity present in society, this population imbalance within the datasets is likely to generate bias against specific groups. In addition, biased content may also arise from feedback loops produced by the system for certain user groups, often reinforcing the racial and gender discrimination that already exists in society (Milano et al. 2019, pp. 12–13).

Within the processes performed by RS, profiling is one of the most likely to cause discrimination. With personal data, RS providers create profiles of their users as a parameter of aspects of their personality and interests, in order to label individuals according to certain patterns of habits, behaviours and tastes, which has great discriminatory potential, especially in the case of sensitive personal data (Mulholland and Frajhof 2019, pp. 269–270).

The Ethical and Legal Challenges of Recommender Systems Driven. . . 147

3.3 *Privacy and Data Protection Violations*

RS based on AI collect, analyse, and process a large amount of personal data. Thus, concerns about privacy and data protection grow as their use becomes commonplace and applicable in different areas, including in domains with highly privacy risks, such as healthcare and banking (Zhang et al. 2020, p. 14).

In this case, privacy-related risks may arise from all steps of the processing of user data. Considering the General Data Protection Regulation (Regulation 2016/679—GDPR) as a model, when data are collected by the algorithms of recommender systems and eventually shared with third parties—often without the implementation of security measures, valid consent (or other legal basis) and the provision of sufficient information to users—their privacy and personal data are violated, which is worsen in the case of data leakage and breach of anonymity (Milano et al. 2019, p. 7).[2]

In addition, RS' data processing may result in inferences and predictions of confidential and personal information, such as emotional states. Consequently, these systems can reach sensitive personal data (such as information about racial or ethnic origin, religious conviction, political opinion, health or sex life), from inferences extracted from personal data by automated processing for profiling and for the creation of personalized recommendations. Thus, significant privacy challenges are generated in this scenario, in addition to possible discrimination results (Privacy International 2018, p. 18).

3.4 *Diminished Human Autonomy and Self-Determination*

RS involves decision-making processes about their users and their contexts through the creation of behavioural profiles. This technology, capable of knowing potential users' preferences and adapting according to their presumed interests, raises important questions about privacy, autonomy and the ethics behind the adaptation processes (Privacy International 2018, p. 19).

Individual autonomy involves the capacity for free self-determination and the right to make choices based on personal beliefs, information, and values. For this, it is essential that the individual has a real and significant opportunity to make their own choices, properly informed and free from coercion, restrictions, or external influences, excessive or undue (Bernal 2014, pp. 24–25).

Thus, human autonomy is directly affected by RS, as they limit individual freedom, due to their control over influences that are transmitted to users in the form of recommendation, besides the fact that, when consent is used as a legal basis

---

[2] *See* also, on the GDPR, I.1—A Oliveira and M A T Figueiredo—Artificial intelligence: historical context and state of the art.

for personal data processing, it is rarely informed for the user, but used as an implicit condition for accessing a certain desired service (Varshney 2020, pp. 1–2).

In this sense, RS interferes with people's autonomy in the form of recommendation of all types of content, from music and movie to job opportunities, pushing users in a certain direction, generally related to their preferences drawn from their profiles, in an attempt to addict them to some types of content or limit the range of options to which they are exposed (Milano et al. 2019, p. 10). Some of these technologies act almost like traps to keep users engaged and connected to their platforms (Seaver 2018, p. 1), which allows greater availability of data to be collected and processed.

Moreover, the algorithmic profile of recommendation platforms also has a great impact on people's autonomy, as it can interfere with the experience of personal identity. First, systems based on user feedback (for example, collaborative filtering) do not create a specific and unique profile, but a collective one. Furthermore, classification is done by algorithms that analyse and infer tastes and preferences, which may not correspond to the appropriate social characteristics or categories with which the user identifies (Milano et al. 2019, p. 10). As mentioned before, the problem is also aggravated in the usual context of algorithms lack of explainability or transparency related to the creation of these profiles.

Thus, the use of recommender systems by bigtechs today, especially in social media, streaming and e-commerce, may also pose intentional risks to users' autonomy. According to their commercial interests, RS providers may also impose hidden influences on their users' behaviour, which is done through monitoring, behavioural tracking and exploitation of vulnerabilities and personal data for profiles creation, which are used to micro-targeting of content in the form of recommendations (Susser et al. 2019, p. 6). This process often occurs without the knowledge of the common user, which can interfere with their ability to self-determine and make truly autonomous choices (Susser et al. 2019, p. 13).

3.5   Polarization and Manipulation of Democratic Processes

Recommender systems and social media filters, by the nature of their design, take the risk of isolating users from exposure to different viewpoints. Even when the system correctly labels individuals, the effects produced by personalization may produce individual and collective harm by creating or exacerbating filter-bubbles[3]

---

[3] The idea of "filter bubble" was created by Eli Pariser to designate the phenomenon of algorithmic filtering of information, carried out on digital platforms such as social media and search engines, responsible for customizing the content that each user has access to, according to their interests, which causes the individual to be trapped in a "bubble" of information with which he agrees, while what he dislikes, shocks or disagrees with is hidden.

(Pariser 2011; Magrani 2014, pp. 118–119) and echo chambers (Sunstein 2007, pp. 43, 60, 217–218; Milano et al. 2019, pp. 13–14).[4]

Contents recommended on digital platforms, limited by these phenomena, represent high risks to public debate and the democratic process, as they may reinforce discriminatory biases and individual prejudices, increasing the susceptibility to polarization, hate speech and manipulation of public speech. As demonstrated by the Cambridge Analytica scandal, RS of streaming platforms and social media may become a place for sending targeted political propaganda (Milano et al. 2019, pp. 13–14).

Today, due to information overload, there's no doubt that recommender systems may mitigate this problem and help people manage their time efficiently. However, in this scenario, as much as technological recommendations can benefit users (helping individual performance in the process of choice, improving and diversifying decision making), they are also potentially questionable, as they influence people in a specific direction, and generate individual and social harm, such as information segregation, bubbles and behaviour manipulation. Thus, to ensure harmony with the principles of beneficence and non-maleficence, the system must be well designed not only to improve people's lives, but also to maintain full and effective control over themselves (Milano et al. 2019, p. 10), while avoiding harm and limiting risk.

4 Recommender Systems: Legal and Regulatory Challenges

Considering the growing importance of RS for our daily lives, simultaneously with the increase in their adverse effects, there is a huge need for action. Legal regulation initiatives must consider not only official ethical guidelines, but also the effective protection of human rights, starting from the basic premise that AI systems must work to do good, avoiding harm, not causing it.

Thus, as RS require the processing of personal data, the issues arising from these technologies have been addressed by data protection rules worldwide (Bioni and Luciano 2019, p. 2). In this scenario, the European Union (EU) GDPR plays an important role as a regulatory model that has inspired many others around the world (Silva 2020, p. 214), phenomenon known as the Brussels Effect.[5] Although the regulation does not specifically address RS or AI itself, it does address their fundamental processes, such as the processing of personal data for automated decision-making, profiles creation and the recommendation of personalized content.

---

[4] The term "echo chamber" is used by Cass Sunstein to designate an environment in which individuals only find ideas, beliefs and opinions that coincide with their own, which reinforces their views and does not consider alternative ones. For him, this phenomenon can lead to fragmentation and polarization, being a threat to democracy.

[5] The term "Brussels Effect" was coined in 2012 by Professor Anu Bradford of the Columbia Law School (Bradford 2012).

Hence, to protect fundamental rights, guarantee informational self-determination and the free development of personality, the GDPR brings a series of obligations imposed on controllers and processors, which include a list of principles (art. 5), rights of the data subjects (chapter III) and legal basis for processing of personal data (articles 6 and 9). Thus, RS' platforms must adapt to these rules to protect personal data of individuals and, consequently, other human rights potentially threatened by RS (Human Rights Watch 2018).

First, RS' providers need to ensure that all activities with personal data (automated or not) comply with the principles, especially the obligation of a lawfully, fairly and transparent processing (lawfulness, fairness and transparency) and the definition of a specified, explicit and legitimate purposes, in accordance with the legal bases of articles 6 and 9 (purpose limitation). Also, data must be limited to what is strictly necessary to achieve this purpose (data minimization) and kept only for the necessary period for it (storage limitation). Finally, the process must guarantee data accuracy and quality, compliance with security standards (integrity and confidentiality), besides ensuring accountability that enables eventual liability for damages.

Along with the adequacy to the principles, to be considered lawful, the processing of personal data by RS must occur in accordance with one of the situations described in art. 6. At this point, it is important to mention that GDPR, as a rule, prohibits the processing of special categories of data in art. 9 and fully automated decision-making with detrimental effects on the data subject in art. 22, except in specific situations listed in both articles. For the last, exceptions include obtaining the explicit consent of the data subject; when it is necessary for entering into or the performance of a contract; or is authorized by Union or Member-State law (WP29 2017, pp. 34–35).

Besides, RS providers need to ensure, throughout data process, an effective and facilitated exercise of data subjects' rights, which are considered a logical outcome of the principles (WP29 2014, pp. 16–17). For example, as a consequence of the legal and ethical principle of transparency, the right to information (articles 13 and 14) stipulates that users must be kept informed and aware of the possible risks associated with data processing carried out by RS. With that, users may not limit themselves to short-term gains obtained with these systems that could, slowly, undermine their fundamental rights, such as autonomy, freedom and privacy.

Thus, it is the duty of providers to proactively inform, even without request, about rights, the existence of data processing and other related information, including clear, meaningful and understandable purposes and explanations on the functioning of RS algorithmic techniques, in particular the definition of profiles (WP29 2014, pp. 16–17; Tejeda-Lorente et al. 2018, p. 6). Furthermore, this information, when not actively disclosed, must be provided to the subjects upon request for access, according to art. 15 and recital 63.

When analysed together, information and access rights are considered powerful tools for individuals to exercise greater control over their data related to RS, as it allows them to have larger awareness and knowledge about the processes involved in sending personalized recommendations, allowing better decision-making that could protect their rights (Van Ooijen and Vrabec 2018, p. 94). Also, with the information received or requested, users can exercise other rights of GDPR, such as rectification (art. 16), erasure (art. 17), restriction of processing (art. 18), portability (art. 20), object (art. 21, when possible) and contest fully automated decisions (art. 22.3). This ensures users' greater autonomy and control, preventing harmful and biased recommendations.

That said, as the automated creation of profiles and the sending of personalized recommendations based on these profiles are steps of RS, article 22 is a key element, as it permits automated decision-making, including profiling, that produces legal effects on data subjects, only in the specific hypothesis authorized by the regulation, such as when based on data subject's explicit consent. In this context, the individual has the right to obtain human intervention, express his or her point of view and to contest the automated decision of the RS. Still, considering the risks involved, GDPR creates for controllers the obligation to adopt safeguard measures to protect data subjects' rights, freedoms and interests, which may include, privacy by design techniques (art. 25) and the carrying out of data protection impact assessment (art. 35).

Furthermore, as these systems rely on algorithmic probability and often machine learning models to send recommendations, it is essential to grant the data subject the right to clear and adequate explanation of the fully automated decisions involving their data. This right to explanation may be extracted from the interpretation of articles 13, 14 and 22, together with recital 71 and the principle of transparency, creating a controller's obligation to significantly inform about the logic involved in all the automated processes until the effective decision making. Such explanation does not necessarily involve the complete opening of the algorithms, but just enough for the user to understand the reasons underlying the decision that affects him (WP29 2018, p. 25), which guarantees the exercise of other rights of GDPR, besides the protection of other human rights (Monteiro 2018, pp. 12–13).

Thus, within the scope of RS, the application of art. 22 and the right to explanation is essential to minimize the risks of the increasing use of algorithms to classify people into behavioural profiles (Silva 2020, p. 210), based on inference analyses and predictions about their characteristics, tastes, behaviours and interests, and then send personalized recommendations potentially harmful to users, which silently interfere with their autonomy, manipulate their decisions and violate guarantees of non-discrimination and privacy.

That said, there is no doubt that the GDPR creates a favourable background for data protection in the EU, becoming a worldwide inspiration, applicable to AI tools, including recommender systems, imposing significant obligations and requirements on data controllers (Bernal 2014, p. 14). Though, besides protecting and defending fundamental rights, according to art. 1, the regulation also produces positive effects for companies and governments, as its application prevents violations of rights and, thus, sanctions' imposition, helping in the use and development of technologies that are beneficial to society. For example, the right to challenge automated decisions allows RS users to contest inaccurate or discriminatory recommendations, as well as an opportunity for the provider to revise their system (Souza et al. 2021, p. 476).

However, with big data, growing importance of digital platforms and the rapid expansion of AI techniques, despite the regulation trying to improve the context of data protection and, hence, human rights, there is still a lot to be done. Some of its rules are still difficult or not convenient for RS providers to comply with, especially those related to AI techniques for profiling and automated decisions. In this context, RS providers may face difficulties in ensuring compliance with principles and rights in practice, due to technical opacity or trade secret rules, for instance. Yet, there are many open questions concerning the interpretation of legal provisions, especially regarding the rights of data subjects, such as the right to contest automated decisions and explanation.

4.1 Lack of Transparency

Although ethical principles and legal rules demand the transparency of AI systems, some of their uses may be opaque for individuals, regulators and even for their designers, which makes it difficult to challenge results. So, RS may have three distinct sources of opacity: (1) intentional opacity, usually associated with trade secret; (2) opacity as technical illiteracy; and (3) opacity that arises from the design and characteristics of the system, especially in the case of machine learning (Privacy International 2018, p. 26).

This absence or lack of transparency in RS makes it difficult to question the political, economic and cultural agendas that exist behind the personalized recommendations sent to each user of the platform, in addition to hiding possible algorithmic discriminations and silent manipulation of behaviours. Besides the potential for damaging fundamental rights, opacity hampers the detection and correction of biased data, invalid assumptions and flawed models (Paraschakis 2017, p. 214).

4.2 Trade Secret

Information about the functionality of RS algorithms is often intentionally poorly accessible to the public (Mittelstadt et al. 2016, p. 6). Software, algorithms and data involved in recommender systems applications are considered proprietary assets with high added value, being essential to maintain an organization's position in the competitive market (European Parliament 2020, p. 33).

Consequently, most companies and providers of these systems are still reluctant and refusing to disclose information related to the functioning of AI because of trade secret (Milano et al. 2019, p. 2), which leads to an intentional opacity of RS. In particular, the lack of transparent business models and practices represents a significant barrier to detecting cases of human rights violations, such as discriminatory recommendations and inferences (Wachter 2020, p. 2).

4.3 Constantly Changing Technology

The current state of technological development of the AI, which bases the RS, does not clarify what the next big evolution will be and what kind of use and levels of understanding of the technology we will be able to make in the future (European Parliament 2019, p. 8), which hamper the imposition of damage prevention obligations to organizations that use AI. Furthermore, the "black box" mentality, whereby AI systems are beyond human comprehension, still limits human's control over technology (Floridi et al. 2018, p. 692).

4.4 Difficulties of Implementation of Data Subjects' Rights in Practice

As a rule, a typical RS system work as a black box, as the final recommendation (output) is only part available to the user (Paraschakis 2017, p. 214). Whatever the reason for creating opaque RS, this lack of transparency is an obstacle to the fulfilment of the right to explanation of GDPR, which also hinders human control over how data is treated and the exercise of other rights.

Furthermore, currently, there is an imbalance of decision-making power and knowledge in favour of RS providers and to the detriment of users. This informational asymmetry, driven by the opacity of AI systems, is also reinforced by the absence or poor understanding of individuals regarding their rights and how the technology works in practice (Mittelstadt et al. 2016, p. 6), that is, how the algorithms and data processing techniques act when predict and infer behaviours, create profiles and send personalized content.

When the logic behind recommender systems is not understandable to the user, the control and autonomy of the human being are disrespected. Therefore, when RS provider relies on consent for the processing of data, this consent is not, in fact, freely given, specific, informed and unambiguous, as the user does not have sufficient information and appropriate means to assess the risks involved in processing data that adheres (Mittelstadt et al. 2016, p. 7).

In addition, given the concern of companies to implement data protection rules that require essential information and explanation disclosure, individuals face an overload of consent requests, usually through extensive and complex privacy policies and cookie notification (Van Ooijen and Vrabec 2018, p. 94). Considering the limits of human rationality and lack of time, the user's evaluation and effective control are impaired, which ends up in the failure to make informed decisions (Bioni 2019).

Also, despite living in the era of hyperconnectivity, most people still have little technical knowledge, access to digital education and minimal understanding of data processing processes (Bioni 2019), making it even more difficult to make informed decision-making in the context of RS, especially when based on consent. In practice, the consent incorporated in most RS providers' privacy policies neither empowers users nor guarantees the effective exercise of rights and their informational self-determination, functioning as an apparent legitimacy of the business models to the GDPR rules (Bittencourt and Gomes 2019, pp. 26–33).

Therefore, individuals are placed in a situation of informational, technical and economic asymmetry (Edwards and Veale 2018). Although data protection rules aim to protect fundamental rights by establishing rights of data subjects, there is still a lack of effectiveness in different situations, for example, when it comes to inferential data analysis using AI techniques.

With the current legal context, data subjects lack sufficient control and information about how their data is being used by RS to make inferences, predictions and assumptions about them. Thus, individuals face obstacles to exercising their data protection rights, especially explanation and challenge of automated decisions, which is even harder when confronted with the interests of controllers related to intellectual property and trade secret (Wachter and Mittelstadt 2019, pp. 5–6).

Hence, specifically regarding the rights of explanation and automated decision challenge, there are still many open questions, as its parameters are still under discussion. Given this uncertainty, the recognition of the right to explanation in practice is impaired, which also makes it difficult to exercise other rights, especially contesting and review automated decisions, since the user must access information about automated decision, and the RS itself, to gather conditions to expose how his or her data should be process and eventually find errors, discrepancies and erroneous correlations to be solved (Souza et al. 2021, p. 473).

4.5 Difficulties of Rules' Application

Some specific characteristics of RS, such as opacity (black box effect), can make it difficult to apply and verify compliance with ethical guidelines and legal rules, especially those arising from the GDPR. Due to their high complexity, unpredictability and autonomous behaviour, authorities and people affected by these systems may not have specific means to verify how a particular personalized recommendation was achieved and, thus, whether these rules were complied with (European Commission 2020c, pp. 10–12).

The current regulatory debate emphasizes the role of data protection in establishing the rights of data subjects, legal basis and principles, focusing on the role of accountability, which highlights the ethical principle of non-maleficence. For example, Article 58 (2) of the GDPR establishes supervisory authorities' corrective powers, such as the imposition of fines, to be applied according to the circumstances of each case, always in an effective, proportionate and dissuasive manner.

Considering RS, digital platforms should ensure that their content and activities respect human rights, especially data protection, privacy and equality, and are not susceptible to external attacks. An interesting point is that some challenges related to these systems are more difficult to address using only technological solutions,

The Ethical and Legal Challenges of Recommender Systems Driven. . . 155

requiring a more qualitative analysis based on the social context in which they operate (Milano et al. 2019, p. 16).

In this case, the application of the GDPR by the authorities must seek a fair balance between the rules of the law and technological advances, preventing companies from suffering from regulations that burden them excessively with administrative requirements and unrealistic data protection standards. The open question is whether States will enforce this measure without burdening corporations or impeding technological innovation.

4.6 Beyond Damage Prevention

The current RS regulation for data protection in the GDPR focuses on measures to prevent damage and ensure accountability in the event of its occurrence, in accordance with the AI's non-maleficence idea. However, technologies must also be regulated through beneficence, which enables the maximization of benefits for individuals and society.

Given the undoubted potential of AI, mainly through recommender systems, it is worth regulating it so that its benefits are increased, avoiding potential pitfalls. In due course, AI regulation also needs to focus research not only on making the technology more capable and accurate, but also on maximizing its societal benefits (Russell et al. 2015, p. 106), which may be accomplished throught prior human rights' assessmentns.

5 Strategies and Possible Solutions to the Challenges Created by RS

Currently, GDPR represents a strong system of fundamental rights' protection in the context of AI and automated decisions. In addition to establishing relevant principles, such as legality, data minimization, transparency, security, fairness and accountability, it also stipulates a series of rights that strengthen the user's control over their data and establishes obligations for those responsible for processing such data, which includes the publication of information, transparency and implementation of security measures (Souza et al. 2021, pp. 470–471).

However, given the progressive and constant complexity of recommender systems based on AI, regulation solely by data protection law is no longer sufficient. So, there are other ways to address the problems associated with RS, which also includes specific legal rules related to AI and business models that use it, besides other strategies beyond law, such as social norms, market initiatives and the ways systems' architecture (code) are developed.

5.1 Best Practices Beyond Law

In this scenario, all stakeholders related to RS must pay attention to ethical standards applicable to AI algorithms. As stated, there is a wide debate around these ethical guidelines that should guide the entire lifecycle of AI-based RS, including their development, implementation, and effective use. There is an urgent need for these tools to focus on human beings, protecting their interests and fundamental rights, in order to benefit the entire society (Beil et al. 2019, p. 1). Given the relevance of ethical parameters, such as transparency, accountability, non-discrimination, precaution, privacy and security, many of them have already been incorporated in regulations, as happened in GDPR principles, rules and rights.

That said, as recommender systems are embedded by autonomous and intelligent algorithms, creating legal and ethical issues, initiatives from multidisciplinary areas of expertise, such as data scientists, lawyers, legal research experts, social scientists and ethics experts are required (Currie et al. 2020, p. 752). In this sense, AI solutions must be developed and implemented through an intersectoral and multidisciplinary teams with the goal of optimizing their results towards ethics and legality (European Parliament 2020, p. 52).

5.1.1 Regulation by Technology: Strategies by Design and by Default

In the context of these "new" technologies that actively interfere in our daily lives, recommending personalized content and making automated decisions about us, ethics and human rights play an important role in their application in favour of the public good. Thus, RS regulation must also involve the design of the tool itself, aligned with ethical guidelines and the human rights from the beginning, as a central element of the systems architecture (Magrani et al. 2019, p. 128).

This "value-sensitive design" approach, including privacy, security, ethics and human rights (Magrani 2019, p. 235), suits the idea that the benefits and positive effects of AI should not only be guaranteed by compliance with the regulatory framework, but also ensured by default (Cavoukian 2009, p. 1), from the beginning of the development of the system and reinforced during its use, according to strategies by design and by default.

Consequently, ethical and legal principles, based on human rights and values, should serve as design criteria for the development of innovative uses of AI and also for the review of existing ones, in order to place the human being at the centre of the creation of RS models, guiding their implementation and use (Guszcza et al. 2020, p. 80), in accordance with what is already provided by art. 25 of GDPR.

Thus, in the short term, design can play a crucial role in addressing ethical and legal issues potentially triggered by RS. For instance, pop-up messages alerting users about the results of recommendations that consider their behavioural profile help to raise public awareness and exercise of rights. However, in the long term, it is essential that RS infrastructure apply by default ethical norms and principles,

The Ethical and Legal Challenges of Recommender Systems Driven... 157

such as transparency, non-discrimination, and justice, in all phases of the system (European Parliament 2020, p. 30).

5.1.2 Implementation of (Human Rights) Impact Assessments

Considering the high risks for users and society created by the recommender systems, which include manipulation, violation of privacy and data protection, discrimination and reduction of individual autonomy, the prior carry out of human rights impact assessment and evaluation of compliance with legislation and ethical guidelines are fundamental for RS to be used (European Commission 2020c, p. 23). Currently, however, these systems are still being implemented to the public without proper ethical, legal, and technical evaluation that can assess the possible impacts and risks associated with this technology in practice, which puts the rights of individuals at stake (Reisman et al. 2018, p. 4).

As much as art. 35 of the GDPR determines to carry out personal data protection impact assessments in some specific cases, it is understood as good practice that RS providers carry out assessments and audits on all automated AI decisions, including profiling, which may be done by testing, inspection, or certifications (European Commission 2020c, p. 23). Therefore, it is recommended to implement algorithm audits and algorithmic impact assessments so that the risks associated with these tools may be mapped, prevented and mitigated (Ada Lovelace Institute and DataKind UK 2020, p. 23).

In this sense, the algorithm audit in RS must assess both the data and the algorithms to look for possible biases (bias audit), in addition to assessing the level of adequacy of the system to existing legal regulations and ethical guidelines (regulatory inspection), especially in terms of human rights. In addition, vendors must also implement algorithmic impact assessment, including risk and impact assessment of algorithms, which may end up evaluating potential social impacts of recommender systems before and during their implementation in practice (Ada Lovelace Institute and DataKind UK 2020, p. 3).

Furthermore, such processes must be developed before and during the technology's interaction with users (Ada Lovelace Institute and DataKind UK 2020, p. 3). If the recommendation system is not approved in such assessments, failing to comply with legal and ethical requirements, identified failures must be solved or mitigated, through new tests or imposition of safeguards and safety mechanisms (European Commission 2020c, p. 23).

In addition to the prior control carried out by the recommendation providers themselves, it is important that a subsequent control is also carried out, not only through technology assessments, but also through documentation verification and even external audits by specialized organizations. Such compliance monitoring should be part of an ongoing market supervision framework for these technologies (European Commission 2020c, p. 23).

5.1.3 Guarantee of Greater Transparency and Explanation of AI (Explainable AI)

RS should be designed to explain its reasoning and allow humans to interpret results (recommendations). As previously mentioned, the explanation of functions and processes is vital to ensure the exercise of rights, transparency and accountability, which is in line with the legal interpretation of GDPR that established the right to explanation.

The explanation of recommender systems and their decisions, as a dimension of the principle of transparency, would enable greater balance between economic and social interests by allowing the existence of automated decisions and, simultaneously, reducing informational asymmetries between those responsible for data processing and the users of the system, as it makes the disclosure of information a legal obligation (Souza et al. 2021, p. 472).

According to the European Commission, the opacity of AI systems can be mitigated through transparency obligations (European Commission 2020c, p. 15), which include accessibility and understandability of information (Mittelstadt et al. 2016, p. 6). Without proper transparency in processes and decisions, in addition to concrete mechanisms that ensure clarification and effective information, users may have difficulties understanding the systems they use and their recommendations, which would make harder to ensure accountability in case of damage. Thus, explainable recommendation techniques are an essential approach to improve transparency, effectiveness, reliability and user satisfaction with systems (Zhang and Chen 2020, p. 77).

Explainable recommendations, for example, are essential for e-commerce, as they increase the persuasiveness of suggestions and, at the same time, help consumers to make efficient and informed online decisions. This strategy would facilitate the process of making AI technologies socially responsible by ensuring both commercial profits and benefits to users. In addition, some RS can provide essential and crucial information for sensitive decision-making, such as in medical treatment processes, where the explanation of recommended results is vital to ensure the effective safeguarding of other people's lives and health (Zhang and Chen 2020, p. 81).

5.1.4 Codes of Conduct (Self-Regulation)

In addition to legal regulation by the State and the creation of ethical standards by interested organizations, it is recommended that RS providers also act proactively in the implementation of systems that respect ethics and human rights. The creation of codes of conduct and ethical standards for the sending of recommendations by the platforms themselves may be an important self-regulation tool, also helping companies to comply with the law when it is effectively applied (Privacy International 2018, pp. 13–28).

The Ethical and Legal Challenges of Recommender Systems Driven. . .

An example in this regard was the creation of the "Partnership on Artificial Intelligence to Benefit People and Society", originally established by some of the big tech companies, such as Microsoft, Google, Amazon, Facebook and IBM, to study and formulate best practices for AI, in accordance with ethical principles (Privacy International 2018, p. 13). Among the objectives, it seeks to advance the public's understanding of technology, in addition to serving as a platform for discussion about AI and its possible impacts on people and society (Partnership on AI). However, it is crucial that these self-regulation codes and principles are effectively applied on practice.

5.1.5 Digital Education in AI

From citizens to top technology executives, society must be educated about the beneficial use, misuse and potential harm of AI, especially RS (European Parliament 2020, p. 84). It is critical that there is increased awareness of AI at all levels of education, in order to prepare citizens for the current digital age, making them better able to make informed decisions that will be increasingly impacted by technology (European Commission 2020c, p. 6).

In this context, the recent Digital Education Action Plan launched by the European Commission, to be applied between 2021–2027, is a good example of an educational project applicable to recommender systems. One of the main goals established was to improve the digital skills of citizens from childhood, which includes investing in basic knowledge of AI, ethical values associated with these technologies and awareness of the existence of digital rights (European Commission 2020a). Such measures would work as a relevant strategy for reducing information asymmetries, in addition to preventing risks by increasing public awareness, empowering users and the consequent effective exercise of rights.

The educational approach is even more important for private professionals who participate in the development processes of these technologies, as they must understand not only how to create accurate systems, but also build them in accordance with ethical and legal guidelines, based on human rights and democratic values. For example, another initiative encouraged by the European Commission is to transform some of the ethical principles into a "curriculum" to be followed by AI developers, as one of the stages of their training (European Commission 2020c, p. 6). Furthermore, whether through public or private initiatives, the development of ethics-related research in AI tools, such as RS, is essential.

5.2 Specific Legal Regulation for AI Systems

Due to the rapid implementation of RS and other AI's tools in different sectors, especially in digital platforms, and its harmful consequences, there are some initiatives to analyse possible forms of regulation of the technology, with especial attention to the protection of vulnerable groups. To illustrate that, European Union's regulatory initiatives will be analysed as an example, given its potential to influence other regulations around the world due to the Brussels Effect, as occurred with the GDPR.

In this context, the regulation of disruptive technologies was first set through the establishment of ethical principles, guidelines and opinions on the development and use of AI, such as, for example, the 2019 Ethical Guidelines for Trustworthy AI by the Independent High-Level Expert Group on Artificial Intelligence – AI HLEG (2019) and the European Commission's White Paper on AI of February 2020. In this scenario, as mentioned in the previous topics, all stakeholders related to RS must pay attention to these ethical standards applicable to AI.

Yet, after the sedimentation of basic principles and guidelines applicable to AI, the EU is now trying to implement binding legal rules specifically applied to this technology, besides the already applicable data protection legislation, which the main example is the GDPR. Thus, recently, EU legislature approved and started the process of creation of legislations directed to AI and places where it is used (such as digital platforms). In the context of RS, the recent approved Digital Services Act (DSA) and, more directly, the proposal of Artificial Intelligence Act (AIA) are the most important examples.

5.2.1 Digital Services Act (DSA)

The DSA (2022) is an European Regulation that creates rules for the providers of certain information society services (digital services), especially through digital platforms. One of its innovative measures is the creation of rules that directly addresses recommender systems provided by online platforms. First, the regulation defines RS on Article 3 (s) as "*a fully or partially automated system used by an online platform to suggest in its online interface specific information to recipients of the service or prioritise that information (...)*", which is in line with the premise of Recital 70 that RS are the core part of the online platforms' business, since it facilitate and optimise access to information for the recipients of the service.

Consequently, as RS influences in the way the information flows in digital platforms,[6] the Regulation focus on the importance of transparency, creating on Recital 70 and Article 27 obligations related to the information required in digital platforms' terms and conditions (that should be written in plain and intelligible language) and options that these platforms must provide to the users in order to allow them to understand, modify or influence the recommendations' parameters. Also, specifically in the case of providers of very large online platforms and online search

---

[6] According to Recital 70, recommender systems of online platforms act algorithmically suggesting, ranking, prioritizing and curating information to facilitate the user's search of relevant content and improving user experience, besides the amplification of certain messages, the viral dissemination of information and the stimulation of online behaviour.

engines (article 33) that use RS—such as Meta and Google—article 38 require them to provide at least one option for each of their RS which is not based on profiling.

In that way, online platforms should consistently ensure that recipients of their service are appropriately informed about how recommender systems impact the way information is displayed and can influence how information is presented to them. They should clearly present the parameters for such RS in an easily comprehensible manner to ensure that the recipients of the service understand how information is prioritised for them. Those parameters should include at least the most significant criteria in determining the information suggested to the recipient of the service and the reasons for their respective importance.

As RS have a significant impact on people's behaviour and how they interact and find information online, the DSA intends to empower users through information and choice, enhancing GDPR's rules related to users' control over personal data. For example, the regulation sets obligation to providers of RSs of very large platforms to conduct risk assessments (article 34 (2) (a)), mitigate the risks founded through testing and adapting their algorithmic systems (article 35 (1) (d)) and explain, by the request of the European Commission or the Digital Service Coordinator, the design, the logic, the functioning and the testing of their systems (article 40 (3)).

Considering the problems related to RS, strengthening transparency obligations on online platforms and providing greater choice to users is an important first step to address the concerns fostered by this technology (Article 19 2021).

5.2.2 Proposal of an Artificial Intelligence Act (AIA)

The EU already has important regulation applicable to AI, such as GDPR, which provides some level of protection. However, according to the European Commission (2021), it was insufficient to address all the challenges that the technology may create, as saw in the previous topics. Thus, on April 2021,[7] the Commission proposed the first legal regulation specifically directed to AI, which aims to provide AI developers, deployers and user with clear requirements and obligations regarding the technology in order to both encourage innovation and protect potentially threatened fundamental rights and freedoms, creating an environment of trust.

The proposal is set in a risk-based approach, addressing the risks specifically created by AI applications, which may be considered unacceptable, high, limited or minimal to people's safety and fundamental rights. In accordance with Recital 14, although most AI systems existing today are considered of limited or minimal risk, being useful for society, depending on the intensity and the scope of the risks that AI may generate, it would be necessary to prohibit some AI practices; impose requirements for high-risk AI techniques and obligations for its operators; or also transparency obligations to certain AI systems.

---

[7] "Currently, the processing of the AI Act is in its final phase, following amendments by the Council of the European Union and the European Parliament"; Council of the European Union (2022).

Differently of what happens in the DSA, the AI Act Proposal does not specifically address recommendation systems, but it will inevitably apply to these tools, as they are based on AI and the generation of "recommendations" is covered by the Proposal's definition of AI on Article 3 (1) as one of its possible outputs.[8] Consequently, it is possible that recommendation systems will have a different treatment according to one of the four levels of risk they may create in the specific case.

With that said, at first, RS of minimal or no risk associated would be free to be developed and used. Yet, considering the potential manipulative uses, it may be prohibited when it is developed with *"subliminal techniques beyond a person's consciousness with the objective to or the effect of materially distorting a person's behaviour"*[9] or when it *"exploits any of the vulnerabilities of a specific group of persons due to their age, disability or a specific social or economic situation, with the objective to or the effect of materially distorting the behaviour of a person pertaining to that group"*[10] in a way that causes or is reasonable likely to cause physical or psychological harm.

In addition, there is a great chance that recommendation systems will be classified as high risk of harm to the health, safety or fundamental rights of individuals, according to the criteria of the AIA Proposal, defined on Article 6 and complemented by a list of high-risk application on Annex III.

If this is the case, high-risk recommender systems would be subject to a (third-party) conformity assessment with a series of obligations before they are put on the market or put into service—such as appropriate data governance (Article 10), elaboration of adequate risk management and mitigation systems (Article 9), technical documentation (Article 11), appropriate human oversight (Article 14) and provision of clear and adequate information to users (Transparency—Article 13)—but also would be subjected to enforcement after such RS is already in use. These ex-ante requirements related to transparency and risk-assessment would create an obligation to RS' providers to promote compliance by design in the case of high-risk recommender systems (Reinhold and Müller 2021).

Although the proposal has several memorable aspects, being the first regulation specifically directed to AI, serving as an international inspiration, there are still points of attention, such as the use of vague terms, the absence of an obligation to carry out a human rights impact assessment or the little mention of the possibility that people affected by AI systems have the power to challenge their harmful outcomes—with, for example, the establishment of the right not to be subject to

---

[8] Article 3 (1) of the Artificial Intelligence Act Proposal: "'artificial intelligence system' (AI system) means a system that is designed to operate with elements of autonomy and that, based on machine and/or human-provided data and inputs, infers how to achieve a given set of objectives using machine learning and/or logic- and knowledge based approaches, and produces system-generated outputs such as content (generative AI systems), predictions, recommendations or decisions, influencing the environments with which the AI system interacts".

[9] Article 5 (1) (a) of the Artificial Intelligence Act Proposal.

[10] Article 5 (1) (b) of the Artificial Intelligence Act Proposal.

The Ethical and Legal Challenges of Recommender Systems Driven. . .   163

a non-compliance AI system, right to explanation or the right to lodge a complaint with a supervisory authority) (Algorithm Watch 2022b).

For instance, if a RS has substantial effects on people's lives, it must not only be offered transparency concerning the implementation of the system, but mainly the possibility to challenge its decision (Reinhold and Müller 2021) (Algorithm Watch 2022a). Considering RS, thus, there must be legally and easily accessible options for affected people to question the recommendations and, if it is the case, to demand reversal, reconsideration through a different procedure, or even compensation.

In the case of RS of online platforms, through DSA, it is already possible to the users to modify or influence the main parameters of the system. However, mere technological solutions do not enough to ensure that AI systems are used in favour of the individuals, not just the providers. At this point, similar to what happened on DSA, accountability frameworks, empowering those directly affected by such systems, are an important aspect in this AI context (Reinhold and Müller 2021).

Furthermore, civil society still criticizes the last text of the AIA proposal, as there are yet some loopholes necessary for an adequate fundamental rights-based approach, especially in terms of meaningful accountability, public transparency and meaningful and balanced civil society participation (Algorithm Watch 2022a).

Thus, there is a current trend towards regulation of AI systems, such as recommendation systems, moving forward from a guidelines-principled approach in the direction of the development of binding legislative acts, as happens in the EU. However, it is necessary that these regulations do not act as a barrier to innovation, creating too rigid obligations, nor are they just the false appearance of regulation, creating vague and inoperative rules. Adequate regulation is essential for responsible innovation–which can be achieved with effective governance instruments, through regulation that is proportional to the systems' level of risk.

Recommender systems can fulfil a crucial role in democratic society and not only endanger, but also contribute to the realisation of fundamental rights and public values when well developed and used (Helberger et al. 2021). The new legislative initiatives must ensure that these systems work according to these values and not against it. Therefore, the union of the DSA and the proposed AIA may enhance users' empowerment and effective choice/control, mitigating potential risks and damages. It is a commendable first step, but we still have a long way to come.

6   Conclusion

In a hyperconnected world, with big data and information overload, recommender systems are increasingly present in our lives, silently predicting and inferring our interests, characteristics, and actions, influencing our decisions and categorizing us in behavioural profiles to send personalized content. Despite unquestionable benefits in terms of convenience, time management and organization, these tools pose considerable risks to fundamental rights, such as autonomy, privacy, data protection and non-discrimination.

Consequently, given the growing importance of these systems at the same time as the risk of adverse effects increases, there is a need for effective application and improvement of viable policies to face the multifaceted challenges they may cause. In other words, artificial intelligence applied to recommender systems must be regulated to prevent private interests from being privileged over the basic principle of "do not harm".

In this environment, GDPR represents a fundamental regulatory framework to address many of the human rights risks posed by the recommender systems' AI (Andersen 2018, pp. 30–31). As data is the engine of this technology, GDPR introduces a positive structure in favour of greater control of users over their data by establishing a series of rights, principles and requirements for the legal processing of personal data, especially in the case of automated decisions and creation of profiles. Many of these legal rules are drawn from ethical guidelines, based on human rights and values, such as transparency, justice, non-maleficence, beneficence, accountability, privacy, freedom, autonomy, dignity and solidarity, which are also fundamental to address the threats brought by RS.

These legal rules and ethical guidelines must also be reinforced by regulations coming from the technology itself, through "value-cantered design" strategies, where the architecture of RS considers these parameters in their way of functioning. Furthermore, for these tools to work in favour of the human being, it is also necessary to guarantee their adequacy based on impact assessments and algorithm audits, added to the establishment of codes of conduct by the market actors themselves. Besides that, "media literacy" policies are essential for the development of a society that will be able to understand the logic of these systems and, thus, make effectively informed decisions to reclaim control of their lives. Not least, the creation of specific regulation of AI systems or of their application environments, such as digital services provided by online platforms, is also essential to guarantee the good application of all these rules, since many of them will be integrated in these regulations.

Therefore, with the aim to maximize the benefits and mitigate the risks associated with RS, so that these tools are beneficial and not harmful to individuals and society, a multisectoral and multidisciplinary approach is essential, placing human being in the centre and involving all sectors of society, including contributions from ethical guidelines, technological functionalities, market self-regulation initiatives, educational policies and, to ensure effective application, the Law, Especially those directly created to the technology.[11]

---

[11] *See* generally, on the different applications of Machine Learning and, AI in this book A Oliveira and M A T Figueiredo—Artificial intelligence: historical context and state of the art; I Trancoso, N Mamede, B Martins, H S Pinto and R Ribeiro—The impact of language technologies in the legal domain; J Gonçalves-Sá and F L Pinheiro—Societal Implications of Recommendation Systems: A Technical Perspective; A T Freitas—Data-driven approaches in healthcare: challenges and emerging trends; M Correia and L Rodrigues—Security and Privacy; M Lanz and S Mijic— Risks associated with the use of natural language generation: Swiss civil liability law perspective; M S Fernandes and J R Goldim—Artificial Intelligence and Decision Making in Health: Risks

References

Ada Lovelace Institute, DataKind UK (2020) Examining the black box: tools for assessing algorithmic systems. Ada Lovelace Report, 29 Apr 2020. https://www.adalovelaceinstitute.org/report/examining-the-black-box-tools-for-assessing-algorithmic-systems/. Accessed 15 Feb 2021

Aggarwal CC (2016) Recommender systems: the textbook. Springer International Publishing, Cham

Algorithm Watch (2022a) Civil society open letter demands to ensure fundamental rights protections in the Council position on the AI Act. https://algorithmwatch.org/en/fundamental-rights-protections-in-the-council-position-on-the-ai-act/. Accessed 27 Feb 2023

Algorithm Watch (2022b) A guide to the AI Act, the EU's upcoming AI rulebook you should watch out for. https://algorithmwatch.org/en/ai-act-explained/. Accessed 27 Feb 2023

Andersen L (2018) Human rights in the age of artificial intelligence. Access Now Report, Nov 2018. Accessed 15 Feb 2021

Article 19 (2021) EU: regulation of recommender systems in the Digital Services Act. Posted on 14th May 2021. https://www.article19.org/resources/eu-regulation-of-recommender-systems-in-the-digital-services-act/. Accessed 27 Feb 2023

Beil M, Proft I, Van Heerden D, Sviri S, Van Heerden PV (2019) Ethical considerations about artificial intelligence for prognostication in intensive care. Intensive Care Med Exp 7:70

Bernal P (2014) Internet privacy rights: rights to protect autonomy. Cambridge University Press, New York

Bigonha C (2018) Inteligência artificial em perspectiva. Panorama setorial da Internet. Intel Artif Ética 10:1–9

Bioni BR (2019) Proteção de dados pessoais: a função e os limites do consentimento. Forense, Rio de Janeiro

Bioni BR, Luciano M (2019) O princípio da precaução para a regulação da inteligência artificial: seriam as leis de proteção de dados o seu portal de entrada? In: Frazão A, Mulholland C (eds) Inteligência artificial e direito: ética, regulação e responsabilidade. Editora Revista dos Tribunais, Sao Paulo, p 720

Bittencourt I, Gomes E (2019) O consentimento nas leis de proteção de dados pessoais: análise do regulamento geral sobre proteção de dados Europeu e da lei Brasileira 13.709/2018. In: Anjos L, Brandão L, Polido F (eds) Políticas, internet e sociedade. Instituto de Referência em Internet e Sociedade (IRIS), Belo Horizonte, pp 26–35

Bradford A (2012) The Brussels effect. Northwest Univ Law Rev 107(1):2012

Cavoukian A (2009) Privacy by design: the 7 foundational principles. Information and privacy commissioner of ontario. https://www.ipc.on.ca/wp-content/uploads/resources/7foundationalprinciples.pdf. Accessed 20 Feb 2021

Council of the European Union (2022) Proposal for a regulation of the European Parliament and of the Council laying down harmonised rules on artificial intelligence (Artificial Intelligence

---

and Opportunities; W Gravett—Judicial Decision-making in the Age of Artificial Intelligence; D Durães, P M Freitas and P Novais—The Relevance of Deepfakes in the Administration of Criminal Justice. *See* also, on Ethics, in this book P U Lima and A Paiva—Autonomous and Intelligent Robots: Social, Legal and Ethical Issues; A T Freitas—Data-driven approaches in healthcare: challenges and emerging trends; M C Patrão Neves and A B Almeida—Before and Beyond Artificial Intelligence: Opportunities and Challenges; M S Fernandes and J R Goldim—Artificial Intelligence and Decision-Making in Health: Risks and Opportunities; M N Duffourc and D S Giovanniello—The Autonomous AI Physician: Medical Ethics and Legal Liability; R Nogaroli and J L M Faleiros Júnior—Ethical challenges of artificial intelligence in medicine and the triple semantic dimensions of algorithmic opacity with its repercussions to patient consent and medical liability; and B A Ribeiro, H Coelho, A E Ferreira and J Branquinho—Metacognition, Accountability and Legal Personhood of AI.

Act) and amending certain Union legislative acts. Brussels, 25 November 2022. https://data.consilium.europa.eu/doc/document/ST-14954-2022-INIT/en/pdf

Currie G, Hawk KE, Rohren EM (2020) Ethical principles for the application of artificial intelligence (AI) in nuclear medicine. Eur J Nucl Med Mol Imaging 47:748–752

Edwards L, Veale M (2018) Enslaving the algorithm: from a "right to an explanation" to a "right to better decisions?". IEEE Secur Priv 16:46–54

Ekstrand JD, Ekstrand MD (2016) First do no harm: considering and minimizing harm in recommender systems designed for engendering health. In: Engendering health workshop at the RecSys 2016 conference. ACM, Boston, pp 1–2

European Commission (2018) Communication from the commission to the European Parliament, the European Council, the Council, the European economic and social committee and the committee of the regions: Artificial intelligence for europe, COM(2018)237–communication. European Commission, Brussels

European Commission (2020a) Communication from the commission to the European Parliament, the European Council, the Council, the European economic and social committee and the committee of the regions. Digital education action plan 2021–2027: resetting education and training for the digital age, COM/2020/624 final. European Commission, Brussels

European Commission (2020b) Proposal for a legal act of the European Parliament and the Council laying down requirements for artificial intelligence (Ares(2020)3896535). European Commission, Brussels

European Commission (2020c) White paper: on artificial intelligence-a European approach to excellence and trust, COM(2020) 65 final. European Commission, Brussels

European Commission (2021) Regulatory framework proposal on Artificial Intelligence. Shaping Europe's digital future. https://digital-strategy.ec.europa.eu/en/policies/regulatory-framework-ai

European Parliament (2019) State of the art and future of artificial intelligence. Briefing requested by the IMCO committee. Policy Department for Economic, Scientific and Quality of Life Policies, Directorate-General for Internal Policies. European Parliament, Brussels

European Parliament (2020) The ethics of artificial intelligence: issues and initiatives. Panel for the Future of Science and Technology, European Parliament, Brussels

Floridi L, Cowls J, Beltrametti M, Chatila R, Chazerand P, Dignum V, Luetge C, Madelin R, Pagallo U, Rossi F, Schafer B, Valcke P, Vayena E (2018) AI4People-an ethical framework for a good AI society: opportunities, risks, principles, and recommendations. Minds Mach 28:689–707

Guszcza J, Lee M, Ammanath B, Kuder D (2020) Human values in the loop: design principles for ethical AI. Deloitte Rev Technol Ethics 26:65–81

Hartmann IA, Franqueira BD, Iunes J, Abbas L, Curzi Y, Villa B, Abreu F, Dias R (2020) Regulação de inteligência artificial no Brasil: policy paper. Contribuição do Centro de Tecnologia e Sociedade (CTS) – Fundação Getulio Vargas (FGV Direito Rio) à Consulta Pública do Ministério da Ciência Tecnologia Inovações e Comunicações – MCTIC sobre a Estratégia Brasileira de Inteligência Artificial. FGV DIREITO RIO

Helberger N et al (2021) Regulation of news recommenders in the Digital Services Act: empowering David against the Very Large Online Goliath. Internet Policy Rev 26. https://policyreview.info/articles/news/regulation-news-recommenders-digital-services-act-empowering-david-against-very-large

High-Level Expert Group on Artificial Intelligence – AI HLEG (2019) Ethical guidelines for trustworthy AI. European Commission. https://www.aepd.es/sites/default/files/2019-12/ai-ethics-guidelines.pdf

Human Rights Watch (2018) The EU general data protection regulation: questions and answers. https://www.hrw.org/news/2018/06/06/eu-general-data-protection-regulation#. Accessed 10 Feb 2021

Jannach D, Zanker M, Felfernig A, Friedrich G (2010) Recommender systems - an introduction. Cambridge University Press, New York

Jobin A, Ienca M, Vayena E (2019) The global landscape of AI ethics guidelines. Nat Mach Intell 1:389–399

Kanoje S, Girase S, Mukhopadhyay D (2015) User profiling for recommender system. In: 4th Post graduate conference for information technology (iPGCon-2015). Amrutvahini College of Engineering, Sangamner

Magrani E (2014) Democracia conectada: a Internet como ferramenta de engajamento político-democrático. Jeruá – FGV Direito Rio, Curitiba

Magrani E (2019) Entre dados e robôs: ética e privacidade na era da hiperconectividade. Arquipélago Editorial, Porto Alegre

Magrani E, Silva P, Viola R (2019) Novas perspectivas sobre ética e responsabilidade de inteligência artificial. In: Frazão A, Mulholland C (eds) Inteligência artificial e direito: ética, regulação e responsabilidade. Revista dos Tribunais, São Paulo, p 720

Mazeh I, Shmueli E (2020) A personal data store approach for recommender systems: enhancing privacy without sacrificing accuracy. Expert Syst Appl 139:112858

Milano S, Taddeo M, Floridi L (2019) Recommender systems and their ethical challenges. AI Soc 35:957–967

Mittelstadt BD, Allo P, Taddeo M, Wachter S, Floridi L (2016) The ethics of algorithms: mapping the debate. Big Data Soc 3:2053951716679679

Monteiro RL (2018) Existe um direito à explicação na Lei Geral de Proteção de Dados do Brasil? Instituto Igarapé, Art. Estratégico 39. Adopted on Dez/2018

Mulholland C, Frajhof IZ (2019) Inteligência artificial e a lei geral de proteção de dados pessoais: breves anotações sobre o direito à explicação perante a tomada de decisões por meio de machine learning. In: Frazão A, Mulholland C (eds) Inteligência artificial e direito: ética, regulação e responsabilidade. Thomson Reuters Brasil, São Paulo, pp 267–292

Nadee W (2016) Modelling user profiles for recommender systems. Doctoral dissertation, Queensland University of Technology

Paraschakis D (2017) Towards an ethical recommendation framework. In: 11th International conference on research challenges in information science (RCIS). IEEE, Brighton, pp 211–220

Paraschakis D (2018). Algorithmic and ethical aspects of recommender systems in E-commerce. Doctoral dissertation, Malmö University

Pariser E (2011) The filter bubble: what the Internet is hiding from you. Penguin Press, New York

Privacy International (2018) Article 19: privacy and freedom of expression in the age of artificial intelligence. Apr 2018. https://www.article19.org/wp-content/uploads/2018/04/Privacy-and-Freedom-of-Expression-In-the-Age-of-Artificial-Intelligence-1.pdf. Accessed 20 Feb 2021

Reinhold F, Müller A (2021) AlgorithmWatch's response to the European Commission's proposed regulation on Artificial Intelligence – A major step with major gaps. Algorithm Watch, published on 22 April 2021. https://algorithmwatch.org/en/response-to-eu-ai-regulation-proposal-2021. Accessed 4 July 2021

Reisman D, Schultz J, Crawford K, Whittaker M (2018) Algorithmic impact assessments: a practical framework for public agency accountability. AI Now Institute. https://ainowinstitute.org/reports.html. Accessed 15 Feb 2021

Russell S, Dewey D, Tegmark M (2015) Research priorities for robust and beneficial artificial intelligence. AI Mag 36:105–114

Sahu S, Singh S (2019) Ethics in AI: collaborative filtering based approach to alleviate strong user biases and prejudices. In: 2019 Twelfth International conference on contemporary computing (IC3). IEEE, Noida, pp 1–6

Seaver N (2018) Captivating algorithms: recommender systems as traps. J Mater Cult 24:421–436

Silva PR (2020) Os direitos dos titulares de dados. In: Mulholland C (ed) A LGPD e o novo marco normativo no Brasil. Arquipélago Editorial, Porto Alegre, p 400

Souza CA, Perrone C, Magrani E (2021) O direito à explicação: entre a experiência europeia e a sua positivação na LGPD. In: Bioni B, Doneda D, Sarlet IW, Schertel L, Rodrigues OL (eds) Tratado de proteção de dados pessoais. Forense, Rio de Janeiro, pp 243–270

Sunstein CR (2007) Republic.com 2.0. Princeton University Press, New Jersey

Susser D, Roessler B, Nissenbaum H (2019) Technology, autonomy, and manipulation. Internet Policy Rev 8:22

Tejeda-Lorente Á, Bernabé-Moreno J, Herce-Zelaya J, Porcel C, Herrera-Viedma E (2018) Adapting recommender systems to the new data privacy regulations. In: Fujita H, Herrera-Viedma E (eds) New trends in intelligent software methodologies, tools and techniques. IOS Press, Amsterdam, pp 373–385

Van Ooijen I, Vrabec HU (2018) Does the GDPR enhance consumers' control over personal data? An analysis from a behavioural perspective. J Consum Policy 42:91–107

Varshney LR (2020) Respect for human autonomy in recommender systems. arXiv preprint arXiv:2009.02603

Wachter S (2020) Affinity profiling and discrimination by association in online behavioral advertising. Berkeley Technol Law J 35:367

Wachter S, Mittelstadt B (2019) A right to reasonable inferences: re-thinking data protection law in the age of big data and AI. Colum Bus Law Rev 2019:494

WP29 (2014) Article 29 data protection working party. Opinion 06/2014 on the notion of legitimate interests of the data controller under Article 7 of directive 95/46/EC. Adopted on 9 Apr 2014

WP29 (2017) Article 29 data protection working party. Guidelines on automated individual decision-making and profiling for the purposes of regulation 2016/679. Adopted on 3 Oct 2017

WP29 (2018) Article 29 data protection working party. Guidelines on automated individual decision-making and profiling for the purposes of regulation 2016/679. Adopted on 6 Feb 2018

Zhang Y, Chen X (2020) Explainable recommendation: a survey and new perspectives. Found Trends Inf Retr 14:1–101

Zhang Q, Lu J, Jin Y (2020) Artificial intelligence in recommender systems. Complex Intell Syst 7:439–457

Open Access This chapter is licensed under the terms of the Creative Commons Attribution 4.0 International License (http://creativecommons.org/licenses/by/4.0/), which permits use, sharing, adaptation, distribution and reproduction in any medium or format, as long as you give appropriate credit to the original author(s) and the source, provide a link to the Creative Commons license and indicate if changes were made.

The images or other third party material in this chapter are included in the chapter's Creative Commons license, unless indicated otherwise in a credit line to the material. If material is not included in the chapter's Creative Commons license and your intended use is not permitted by statutory regulation or exceeds the permitted use, you will need to obtain permission directly from the copyright holder.

Metacognition, Accountability and Legal Personhood of AI

Beatriz A. Ribeiro, Helder Coelho, Ana Elisabete Ferreira, and João Branquinho

Abstract One of the puzzles yet to be solved regarding Artificial Intelligence (AI) is whether or not robots can be considered accountable and have, eventually, legal personhood. With inputs from Philosophy, Psychology, Computation and Law, the paper proposes an interdisciplinary approach to the question of legal personhood in AI. In this paper, we examine, firstly, the concepts of Object (a mere tool) and Agent, in order to understand in which category AI may belong to. Secondly, we analyze how Metacognition, broadly defined as the cognition about cognition, which results in mental processes that control an entity's thoughts and behavior, can be applied to law as a minimum requirement for accountability. For instance, we shall see that both children and people with mental diseases, besides being two categories of subjects that have a very restricted legal capacity, also show some limitations when it comes to Metacognition. In other words, we argue that the main difference between a non-responsible and a responsible Agent depends on the metacognitive processes that can be carried out by the entity. Ultimately, we discuss how to transpose this idea to AI, debating the possible terms of legal personhood of AI.

B. A. Ribeiro (✉)
Vieira de Almeida & Associados, Communications & Digital, Lisbon, Portugal

H. Coelho
University of Lisbon, LASIGE, Computation Department, Lisbon, Portugal
e-mail: hmcoelho@fc.ul.pt

A. E. Ferreira
University of Coimbra, Department of Law, Coimbra, Portugal

J. Branquinho
University of Lisbon, Philosophy Department, Lisbon, Portugal
e-mail: jbranquinho@campus.ul.pt

© The Author(s) 2024
H. Sousa Antunes et al. (eds.), *Multidisciplinary Perspectives on Artificial Intelligence and the Law*, Law, Governance and Technology Series 58,
https://doi.org/10.1007/978-3-031-41264-6_9

1 Introduction

One of the puzzles yet to be solved regarding Artificial Intelligence (AI) is whether or not robots can be considered accountable and have, eventually, legal personhood. With inputs from Philosophy, Psychology, Computation and Law, the paper proposes an interdisciplinary approach to the question of legal personhood in AI. In this paper, we examine, firstly, the concepts of Object (a mere tool, not subject to legal personhood) and Agent, in order to understand in which category AI may belong to.

Secondly, as the concept of Agent presents many difficulties, namely because it seems to have a different meaning according to each of the above mentioned domains of knowledge, a common denominator was identified, which it was found to be the voluntary act. If there is a voluntary act, we must, then, conclude that we have an Agent before us. Accordingly, and as long as AI acts voluntarily, it makes sense to argue that complex robots (in the sense of strong AI) are Agents, thus not mere tools.

Thirdly, since children, animals and people with mental illnesses act voluntarily but are still not held accountable (either have no legal personhood or limited exercise of such personhood), the paper investigates what is missing in these cases, in order to draw a line between accountable and non-accountable agents.

At last, we analyze how Metacognition, a concept borrowed from Psychology, which is broadly defined as the cognition about cognition, resulting in mental processes that control an entity's thoughts and behavior, can be applied to law as a minimum requirement for accountability and eventually legal personhood. For instance, we shall see that both children and people with mental diseases, besides being two categories of subjects that have a very restricted legal capacity, also show some limitations when it comes to Metacognition. In other words, we argue that the main difference between a responsible and non-responsible Agent depends on the metacognitive processes that can be carried out by the entity. Ultimately, we discuss how to transpose this idea to AI, debating the possible terms of legal personhood of AI.

There's no doubt that the Law depends, to a certain extent, on the description and classification of the problem (Birks 1997) we have before us. In other words, when confronted with a given situation, we are forced to list its essential features and see if those features match the legal norm. If it does, we have found ourselves a legal solution for the problem; if not, we must keep searching for a match.

When it comes to legal personhood, there are some basic requisites which, in absence, rule out any chance of even considering ascribing it to a certain entity. For instance, no one thinks about describing a deceased person as a legal person, though some rights might be extendable after death (such as right to honor). Legal personhood regarding human beings implies being alive, as this *status* begins when we are born. Whenever something doesn't quite fit the categories that we, humans, created, for instance if we're somewhat alive and not yet born (the unborn child), it becomes unclear for us what must be done regarding that entity.

In this sense, it has been argued (Boulangé and Jaggie 2014) that the first step in order to build a legal framework, in the case of any sort of robots, is to determine its *status*, meaning define its concept and boundaries and then confront it with the available legal options. In this regard, Pagallo (2013) developed extensive work on understanding the main traits of each type of robot that is planned in the near future, in his book *The Laws of Robots: Crimes, Contracts, and Torts*.

Globally, the author divides the possibilities into three categories: (1) Legal Person, (2) Proper Agent and (3) Source of Damage. What it means, in practice, is that we must check whether a given robot shares sufficient attributes with human beings, therefore leading us to grant it Legal Personhood (Hypothesis 1). If it has much more similarities, meaning more features in common, with the concept of tool, thus being considered a mere object, then the answer is to treat it as such (Hypothesis 3). What can also happen is the robot not being completely alike to any of those categories and yet share a fair number of attributes with each one. We have, then, a Proper Agent (Hypothesis 2), whatever legal terms we might want to apply to it.

Accordingly, in a preliminary stage, it is relevant to understand what it means to be an Agent. If an entity is an Agent, it is, therefore, not a thing, because the logic law of non-contradiction doesn't allow this to happen. Given the fact that one thing opposes to the other (and they do, since they show different and opposite properties) the sentence *The robot A is an Agent* and the sentence *The robot A is a thing* cannot, ever, be true at the same time. For instance, an Agent, as we shall see, acts voluntarily, while a thing doesn't act at all. It seems obvious that one entity cannot act voluntarily and don't act at all at the same time.

By understanding what an agent is and arguing that a robot is an Agent, we exclude, automatically, the idea that it can be a thing. In a second phase we'll look into what it means to be a legally responsible Agent.

On the other hand, and endorsing the idea stated by Asaro (2007), the mere comprehension of the concept of Agent might as well help us to draw the boundaries of legal personhood, since the first concept walks hand-in-hand with the latter. In other words, Agency might conceal important clues in this domain.

Predictably, understanding the concept of Agent and list its main features is nearly impossible. Every single area of knowledge uses the notion of Agent, and yet, consensus has not been found. To name a few, Psychology, Philosophy, Law, Computation, Economy and Neuroscience, each *stole* the concept of Agent and filled it out with the attributes that most suited the domain. In this regard, Shardlow (1990) has a very interesting thesis where he reached, precisely, to this conclusion, even though the author investigated mainly three areas: Philosophy, Psychology and Computation. Confronted with this fact, we would be forced to argue that the concept of Agent is a dead end. Nevertheless, there may be something that can be done about this dead end.

There's this method in programming and computation, that programmers use when they must describe a complex problem: they draw the base-case. The base case is, simply put, the description of the simplest possible case in the complex situation. In a second stage, then, comes the building and writing in code of complex cases and respective exceptions. What is, then, our base case in matters of Agency? What is the one thing or, rather, the only feature that, regardless of the area we look into, is always there?

As it shall be argued, is it the voluntary act. However, it will be also shown that this is not enough, since children, animals and people with mental disabilities do act voluntarily but are not considered legally responsible.

The following step was to determine what was missing in these cases, with resource to the domain of Psychology, which was found to be certain types of metacognitive processes, related to the ability of feeling guilt and the capacity of planning complex behavior.

In this sense, besides the capacity of acting voluntarily, any responsible entity has to show a specific kind of metacognitive processes. Only then accountability is an option. For a comprehensive understanding of the paper, the next page provides a visual outline of its structure.

2 What Is the Common Denominator in Agency?

Intuitively, each one of us has an idea of what it means to be an Agent. It's an entity, whatever kind, capable of acting and execute actions, opposing to others entities that merely tolerate or accept events that happen to them.

In order to find a consensual definition, however, we must increase the level of abstraction. In this abstract sense, and for this purpose, an Agent is an entity which acts continuous and autonomously in time, in a dynamic environment, where other processes exist, and other Agents are present (Coelho 2008).

In Philosophy, two of the most prominent theory are the *Standard Conception* and the *Standard Theory*. Both argue that and Agent is a being which is capable of intentional action.[1] The difference between these two theories has to do with whether or not the intentionality of the action includes unwanted actions.

For instance, let's imagine Asimov wishes to reach for his glass of water, in the middle of the night, and turns on the light in order to do so. We would assume that the latter was desired by him, and intentional, since he had, before actually acting, the thought about turning on the light in order to get the glass of water. However, if there was a burglar on the outside of his house and he was not aware of this fact, he might as well let the burglar know he was home, even though it was not what he intended to do.

Even though he wanted to turn on the light, Asimov's thought was definitely not about alerting the burglar and yet he did it. This is what an unwanted action is. The *Standard Conception* argues that intentional action includes both turning the

---

[1] Intentional action not in the sense of having the intention to do something but instead in the sense described by Anscombe (1957) and Davidson (1963), which relates to acting for a reason (a mental state of believing that the specific action is the best to achieve a certain goal).

light for the glass and turning the light and warn the burglar; on the other hand, the *Standard Theory* holds that only the first is an intentional action. Despite not agreeing about the meaning of intentional action, both theories believe an Agent is an entity capable of intentional action. Thus, according to these perspectives, an entity is an Agent if it can act voluntarily, since the act depends on the belief that the specific action in question is the best to achieve a certain goal.

Naturally, and especially not in Philosophy, this is not the sole theory at the center of the debate. Other theory was described by Dennett (1987). This author argues that we have an Agent before us if we can predict his behavior, accurately, by means of its mental states. Accordingly, Allen and Bekoff (1997) used this idea, arguing that it could be applied to non-human Agents.

More recently, Barandiaran et al. (2009) focused on extremely simple entities, such as bacteria. In the author's opinion, the fact that these kind entities can't be included in the category of Agent, given the before mentioned Philosophical theories, doesn't mean they shouldn't be regarded as Agents. In this sense, Barandiaran outlined three main requisites for what he calls *minimum Agency*. Besides individuality (which is the clear distinction between the Agent and its environment) and normativity (meaning the existence of goals and rules that the Agent uses to guide its action) he also argues that interactional asymmetry is crucial. This last precondition for Agency concerns the ability to exchange energy and matter with the environment. In other words, the Agent must be able to collect the necessary energy to act and being a passive entity in the environment is not enough.

So far, in Philosophy, it seems that the voluntary act is a relevant requisite to ascribe Agency. As we shall see later on, this is not the only domain of knowledge where this ability is a precondition.

In fact, that's precisely what happens in Computation. While Minsky (1967) saw the artificial Agent as a Finite State Machine (FSM), a description often seen as reductive, other authors such as Russell et al. (1995, p. 33) see the Agent as an entity that analyses the surrounding environment and acts according to the input of that same environment.

Another very praised view is the one described by Wooldridge and Jennings (2009) which defines the Agent as the entity that presents properties such as autonomy, social skills, reactivity to the environment and proactivity (ability to initiate action). According to the authors, an entity that shows these cumulative attributes has what they call *weak Agency*. Conversely, if we're looking for a *strong* Agency, the Agent must show some degree of cognitive processes, including beliefs, desires and intentions (Taylor 1966, p. 98; Shoham 1993).

It is not possible to simply look into every single area of knowledge in order to discover what it means to be an Agent in each one. There's, still, one more to go and is an especially complex domain: Law.

In Law, an Agent is typically considered the author of an illicit action (for instance a crime), which he did by means of a voluntary act. The biggest issue in this matter is that in order to be considered an Agent, in the sense used by Law, there's the implicit idea that the Agent has legal personhood. Since we're trying to do the opposite, meaning we're trying to get to accountability and legal personhood through the notion of Agent, this isn't particularly helpful.

What we can do, instead, since the concept of legal person can be considered as the basic unit of law, in order to act in legal relationships (Derham 1958), is examine what makes the difference when it comes to giving legal personhood to an entity. In other words, it's important to investigate the reasons behind the lawmaker's decision to grant or not this legal status to an entity.

The first reason to give legal personhood is, obvious and naturally, because the entity is a (born and yet not deceased) human being (Solaiman 2017). Artificially, we also consider companies to have legal personhood, with theories justifications that go back to Savigny and that by no means this paper intends to discuss.

In this sense, there are two main theories, regarding the matter, in analytic jurisprudence: the will theory and the interest theory (Kramer et al. 1998). Most of the nineteenth-century German legal academics who wrote on this topic based their theories on the Kantian ideas of freedom and autonomy as the central concepts. Human beings possess, according to this theory, innate moral freedom, which grounds their capacity to hold rights and thus their legal personhood. Yet, the minority view, advocated an interest-based understanding of rights. Modern analytic theories of rights are usually classifiable as either one of these theories. However, hardly any of the theories can be said to have 'won' the debate (Kurki 2019).

Additionally, these theories are still not enough in order to draw the line between responsible entities and non-responsible ones. Anglo-Saxon Judges reflected extensively upon the concept of Agent, long before it became a foregone conclusion to us. Salmond (1913), argued that in order to be a juridical person, one must show the capacity of being a part in juridical relations. In another direction, Dewey (1926) described how we do not think about conceding legal personhood to things, since their behavior would be exactly the same, whether you ascribe or not legal duties to it. In the author's words, we grant legal personhood to either entities whose behavior can be modulated by the legal norm or to entities through which we wish to regulate human's behavior, this being the reason why ships were once given legal personhood.

More recently, Dario and Palmerini (2012), based on the before mentioned theories of Legal Personhood related the concept of legal personhood to the idea of duty and the thought of being able to act in order to enforce that same duty.

Today, and in general, several authors (for instance, Mathew Kramer and Joel Feinberg, this last author regarding animals) have supported a specific conception of legal personhood: the one that argues that any entity who is capable of carrying legal rights should be granted legal personhood (Kurki 2016).

This vision has been somewhat applauded, constituting, inclusively, the main grounds for a case in December 2014, in the NY Supreme Court about a chimpanzee named Tommy. Tommy's representation asked for the extension of the concept of legal person, in order to be able to request *habeas corpus* later on. The representative argued, precisely, that animals can carry at least one legal right, and that this was enough to get a specific type of legal personhood, in accordance with the rights

Metacognition, Accountability and Legal Personhood of AI 175

proclaimed (Kurki 2016). Pietrzykowski (2017) described a similar case in a Court of Argentina, about an Orangutan in a Buenos Aires' Zoo.

There's intense literature when it comes to this debate. Other relevant views include Rationality as the main criteria for legal personhood (Morse 2000) and Intentionality[2] (Calverley 2008; Chopra and White 2011).

It's important to state that we cannot, ever, disconnect the Law from the reality where it operates. Law is permeable to reality and culture (Ferreira and Pereira 2017) and this is a crucial relation if we want to avoid an obsolete and useless legislation. This is why all these different theories in Law are so important in this research.

It is also relevant to point out that it seems that regardless of the view supported, there's always this idea of being able to act (in the sense that if one is capable of carry a legal right or obligation one must be capable of acting accordingly) hovering over all the mentioned theories. The same occurs in Computations and Philosophy, though wearing different vests. In conclusion, it appears that different words are used to name the same thing.

As described before, each area of knowledge took the concept of Agent to itself and designed it in its image and likeness. Despite this fact, however different the definitions of Agent might be, the condition of having the power to act, voluntarily, is always present.

3   What Is a Voluntary Act?

Markby, in Elements of Law—Principles of Jurisprudence (1889) defined voluntary act as the body movement that follows the will. Coincidentally, on another domain of knowledge—in Classic Philosophy—Davidson used this exact same description, 84 years later, when writing his theory of Agency. The same was argued again and again throughout the twentieth and twenty-first centuries—in Law, though with different words—namely by Cook (1917) and Yaffe (2012).

In Psychology, James et al. (1890) described the voluntary act as the opposite of involuntary act, in the sense that the latter occurs without foresight. In recent Philosophy, the similar was argued by Olsaretti (1998), who supports the idea that we have a voluntary act if we have not an involuntary act. The action will not be voluntary, in the author's thesis, if there is no other acceptable option, according to some objective criteria (though the author doesn't exactly explain what is this objective criteria). For Olsaretti, an unacceptable option is the one that causes specific damage to the Agent or when a moral rule is imperative to the point that makes all other options unacceptable. She also states that the voluntary act is deeply related to the motivations of the Agent, in the sense that it depends, inevitably, on the beliefs the Agent has about his options. If the Agent is mistaken about his options,

---

[2] In the sense previously described in Philosophy.

he might have a good option but be unaware of its existence. Thus, an act can be involuntary for misinformation.

That's precisely what Aristóteles (2004) argued, in Nicomachean Ethics: that the only two reasons that would make an act involuntary would be ignorance or major external forces.

In conclusion, an act seems to be voluntary when there's a bodily movement, guided by will, as long as it is not undermined by ignorance or an external force.

The following question is: does AI act voluntarily? AI might have a previously defined (by humans) structure of their beliefs, desires and intentions, but after that initial definition, more complex (or stronger) AI is able to act upon the environment autonomously, and possibly according to the goal they set for themselves. We have come to the point when AI is so advanced that in some cases not even creators know exactly why the robot did what it did. In normal conditions, the robot is well informed about his choices, as it is capable of collect the essential information in order to create a model of the world. Also in normal circumstances, they will not be coerced to do anything, though they might be.

So, do robots belong in the category of Agent? It appears that in the cases of strong or complex AI robots (the so-called robust AI) seem to have the minimum requisite to be considered as one: they act voluntarily.

It's important to disclaim that by referring to complex AI, namely, machines that use cognitive processes or machine learning, we are not describing objects that clearly act as tools and that are perceived and intended to act as such, like smart air conditioners which adjust according to the temperature or lights change intensity according to the hour of the day.

As mentioned before, if complex AI belongs in the category of Agents, it cannot be considered merely a tool. What matters now is to learn how much responsibility they can take, if any at all.

4 What Makes an Agent a Legally Responsible One?

The next step is trying to understand what makes the Law ascribe responsibility or not to an individual.

According to the previous definition of Agent, it seems obvious that children and animals are also Agents. However, we don't consider them as legally responsible Agents. In other words, simply being an Agent and acting voluntarily isn't enough for the Law. In this sense, where should we draw the line between responsible agents and non-responsible ones?

There is one very relevant legal concept that might help us in this query, which is the notion of imputability. However, the sense that we want to grasp here is the lack of imputability, which relates to a specific category of people to whom, either because they are under aged or suffering from a mental illness, we cannot ascribe legal responsibility to, even though they have legal personhood. Though there are many reasons and theories on why Law does not deem these individuals as

Metacognition, Accountability and Legal Personhood of AI 177

accountable, one of the major reasons concerns is the fact that these subjects do not present the capacity of feeling guilt (Pizarro de Almeida, 2000 p. 21).

In the legal sense, guilt is understood as the capacity that the subject has of acting in a responsible way, meaning he is able to understand what an illicit behavior is and therefore opt by not performing that behavior. In this sense, the subject must be capable of reflecting upon a certain conduct and assert a positive or negative value to that same conduct.

In other words, we can only ascribe any legal responsibility when we assume that the Agent has the minimum requirements, from a physical and psychological point of view, in order to respond positively to normative rules. In the presence of this set of minimum requirements then we have an imputable Agent (Muñoz Conde and Arán 1996).

Other than helping in the judgement in criminal cases, the guilt also relates to a negative valuation that the society develops towards the Agent's behavior. There's no point, at all, in addressing a negative valuation of conduct towards an Agent that is not capable of understanding that judgement. It simply will not be effective. In these cases, the cognition of the Agent might be so compromised that even though he can act voluntarily, according to some desires or goals, he cannot reflect upon those (primary) mental states that originated the behavior.

In Philosophy, as well as in Cognitive Psychology, these mental states about other primary mental states, goes by the name of Metacognition.

5 Metacognition: Shaping Legal Responsibility

It seems fair to say that we are allowed transpose concepts from one domain of knowledge to another. Most of the foundations of Modern Law came from authors such as Kelsen, Hart and Austin, all of them also philosophers, who set the grounds for Philosophy of Law. On the other hand, we cannot legislate about the world around us without fostering concepts of the mundane. For instance, we wouldn't be able to legislate Medicine if we were not capable to grasp the concepts of that specific area of knowledge. Moreover, some authors such as Morse (2003) argue that Law itself uses models of actions that derive from Folk Psychology.[3] In other words, it is legitimate for us to use concepts long used in other areas of knowledge, is this case, the notion of Metacognition, which is a relatively old concept in Philosophy and Cognitive Psychology.

In general, Metacognition is the cognition about cognition (Fleming et al. 2012), being useful in order to control and/or monitor behavior and mental processing (Nelson and Narens 1990).

---

[3] Folk Psychology is traditionally used to denote our everyday (intuitive) understanding, or rationalizing, intentional actions in mentalistic terms (Hutto and Ravenscroft 2021).

Frankfurt (1971), a philosopher, argued that the main difference between human beings and other types of Agents is rooted in the structure of the will, in the sense that only human beings reflect upon their own motivations, which results in second order mental states. For instance, let's imagine Wall-e has to study for an exam. In order to succeed in this exam, Wall-e must, beforehand, list the study methods he knows, analyze his own strong characteristics and his weaker ones, so he can choose the best study method for him, considering the specific subject he has to study. Learning is, in itself, a cognitive process. By reflecting on this cognitive process (choosing a study method), he is using this second order mental states or, as many authors describe, secondary cognition. To Frankfurt, the difference between human beings and other Agents, which also act voluntarily, is Metacognition. We can, then, argue that there is a distinction, between Agents who act voluntarily but do not show Metacognitive Processes, and Agents who act voluntarily and do present this capacity.

Agents who act voluntarily and present metacognitive processes can do so in several ways, as this type of cognition has many shapes and forms, and not all will be described in this paper. However, as we shall see, to hold an entity accountable, at least two kinds of metacognitive processes are required: strategic and monitoring processes. Both will be explained henceforth by this order.

As Cox (2005) stated, any intelligent Agent, when confronted with a choice (any choice, therefore including the choice to practice an illicit act or not), he must decide three things: (1) which action, given the possible ones, is the most adequate in the present situation, (2) if the choice he is making is sufficiently informed or if more information is required and (3) if something has gone wrong, understand why it happened. This is a critical auto-reflexive type of thought, which translates the analysis that an individual makes in terms of the quality of the options presented in decision-making. In turn, this process is undoubtedly linked to Metacognition.

Accordingly, one of the most essential components of Metacognition described by literature is knowledge of cognition (Lai 2011). This implies awareness of our own capacities and limitations, including internal and external factors that may affect or reduce our cognitive performance (Flavell 1979). This component is extremely relevant when it comes to defining strategies in action, since it is the reason we chose one strategy to the detriment of other strategy (as it happens in the above mentioned example of the study methods).

What is important to point out is that any person who wants to commit act illegal act has, necessarily, the strategic analysis that was described in the previous paragraph. A mentally ill person can act wrongfully but his intention was to act merely and not to act illegally. On the other hand, someone who plans an illegal act, thinks about the final goal, reflects on his own capacities and limitations and other external factors that might affect his performance, defines a strategy, all things considered in the light of the possibility of being caught.

Supporting this idea, it might also be useful to look into the theory of planned behavior, from the area of Psychology (Ajzen 1991). Summarily, the author argues that the Agent's intention is modulated, mainly, by three things: (1) individual attitudes regarding the behavior at hand, (2) individual pressure concerning the specific conduct and (3) behavior control. Simplifying, what we have is a certain behavior, linked to an intention which in turn is modulated by these three factors. There hardly can be any doubts about the existence of strategic metacognitive processes on planned behavior, including illicit planned behavior.

On the other hand, Metacognition is said to have three levels of consciousness in any storyline. The first one concerns the story or the behavior itself. The second one relates to the thoughts that the Agent has towards that occurrence. The third and last one is about the reflexive work about the thoughts of the second level (Cox 2005).

Translating the theory to a practical example, let's imagine we have a subject, HAL, shopping at the local store. Someone tries to steal something, and the police is called to the store. The thief is caught and taken into custody. HAL watched closely everything that happened. This is the first level of consciousness, the occurrence, story or behavior (in this case, someone stealing in the shop). HAL then kept on with his life, meditating about the event, its legal value, and the punishment he saw being applied to the thief. We have, then, a level two of consciousness. Finally, as a healthy human being, HAL is also capable of having second order thoughts about that first reflection. For instance, he might initially have thought that the punishment was not fair but then feel ashamed by his own thought. Or realize he didn't think stealing was wrong and then feeling scared that he might act in a similar way.

What we have at hand is a judgement made about other judgements, with the purpose of monitoring behavior. As explained through the example above, being able to feel guilt, can also be considered to have this purpose.

As previously described, one of the reasons why law does not account people with mental disabilities is, precisely, the inability to feel guilt, which implies a kind of complex agency. This complex agency implies the capacity of understanding what an illicit behavior is and opting by not performing that behavior, which in turn implies metacognitive processes, in this case, not in the sense of strategic analysis (needed when planning and illicit behavior) but rather in the sense of monitoring behavior (which concerns the process of reflecting upon behavior and decide whether or not commit the crime).

In conclusion, among the several forms of metacognitive processes that an individual may have, to perform and understand an illicit behavior, an individual will need, at least, two types of metacognitive processes: strategic and monitoring. This is the core of accountability.

Without knowing, Law has been using this concept of Metacognition across time. Animals are not directly responsible, nor children are, having instead someone who is responsible for them. In the first case, animals are able to understand that the occurrence getting a biscuit happened because they rolled over when asked to. However, they cannot, in general, have complex and second order thoughts about the best way or method to do it, which leaves us only with a second level of consciousness and hardly any metacognitive processes. Accordingly, animals are not held accountable for their acts, nor are granted legal personhood.

Children's situation is clearly different, as they show some type of Metacognition, and it gets more complex while growing up. There are many studies in this regard, for instance the ones described by Georghiades (2004), in *From the general to the situated: three decades of Metacognition*, which shows precisely this. They are, inclusively very early in their lives, able to learn (and learning implies a certain kind of Metacognition). They do not present, however, strategic Metacognitive processes, which, as described in the previous paragraphs, is the specific kind we're looking for when discussing legal accountability. We're talking about a formally stated operational thought (Piaget 1976), which rarely is attributed to children (Brown and DeLoache 1978). Studies also show that strategic Metacognition starts developing around 14 years old, even though it might not be completely developed until later on (Schraw and Moshman 1990). Although children do have legal personhood, truth is, by chance or not, the law only ascribes criminal responsibility to underage individuals when they turn 16 years old, believing that at this age they are sufficiently developed to understand the consequences of their actions.

This type of strategic Metacognition is also missing in the case of some mental illnesses (Saxe and Offen 2010), though the consequences in consciousness might change from disease to disease and from person to another person (David et al. 2012).

In programming and computation, Metacognition relates to what the system knows about its own cognition and also about cognition in general. As Crowder et al. (2011) describe it, in AI this concept is intertwined with introspection, in the sense that allows the machine to form beliefs about its own internal states, instead of simply analyze the environment where it moves.

Traditionally, in computation, metacognitive processes are used for specific problem solving, such as algorithm selection from the efficiency point of view (Cox 2005).

In this sense, Crowder & Friess argue that there are at least three types of Metacognition in this domain of knowledge:

(a) Metacognitive knowledge, which relates to what the system knows about itself, as a cognitive processor (Kosko 1986);
(b) Metacognitive regulation, regarding the control of cognition and learning, which may include the knowledge the system has about what it knows and does not know (LaBar and Cabeza 2006);
(c) Metacognitive experience, which concerns past experiences that somehow relate to the present mission of the system (Crowder et al. 2011), allowing the system to create expectations or predictions about what may happen, given those experiences that took place before that moment of analysis.

In this sense, its seems fair to acknowledge that AI can has some degree of metacognitive processes. However, it does not match the type of Metacognition necessary in order to consider an entity as accountable. In fact, none of these processes translate in strategic or monitoring metacognitive processes. Hence, AI should not, at least for now, be held accountable for its behavior, the same way kids, animals and people with mental illnesses are not.

6 Accountability and Legal Personhood

Up to this moment, we linked Agency, to voluntary act, the latter as a minimum requirement for the first, and accountability to metacognition. There is still one round left, regarding the connection between accountability and legal personhood.

We are fully aware that legal responsibility and legal personhood are not the same concept, an often-made mistake regarding AI, either by scholars or official entities, as Pagallo (2018) pointed out in his research. In fact, they're different concepts and might also mean different legal consequences. But they must be intrinsically intertwined.

In this paper, we described how animals, children and people with mental illnesses were not to be considered accountable from the legal standpoint. In this sense, it was also highlighted that, even though children and people with mental disabilities do have legal personhood in most jurisdictions, they do so within a limited scope and a restricted exercise of their rights. We also pointed out how animals do not have legal personhood, at all, in most jurisdictions, although some extensions of this instrument were granted in specific cases.

In fact, it appears that legal personhood in its full sense exists to the extent that the entity is capable of exercising its rights. As we have seen, there are entities (e.g. children and people with mental disabilities) that while being granted legal personality, do not present legal capacity or have their legal capacity restricted, and therefore are not considered legally responsible. In other words, the scope of their legal personhood is limited.

On the other hand, any entity who is considered to have some sort of accountability, e.g. people in general, have both personality and capacity. Their legal personhood is at its fullest.

This means, in principle, that even though legal personhood can be granted either way, if we don't have accountability, we hardly can have legal capacity. In other words, accountability fills the capacity of the entity, thus determining the actual content and size of the legal personhood.

This is consistent with the idea described by Visa A. J. Kurki of what constitutes an active legal personhood, opposing to a passive legal personhood, being a concept that "requires that one can perform acts-in-the-law (being endowed with legal competences) and be held legally responsible (onerous legal personhood)". In his research intitled "A Theory of Legal Personhood", the author states that the key elements of active legal personhood are centred on legal responsibility and legal competences.

In fact, one cannot be interested in the idea of a "shallow legal personhood". Take the example of the robot Sophia, the humanoid robot built by Hanson Robotics, which "jokingly" stated AI would destroy humans in the near future. Sophia was granted citizenship by Saudi Arabia, in 2017. Besides all the hype and attention this circumstance has received, from a legal stance, this citizenship is hollow, in the sense that there is no actual point in granting such status. In reality, the word "jokingly" must be used with caution since the robot Sophia as no idea what a joke, in practice, means, let alone the meaning of a legal duty. Sophia may have been granted citizenship but has no means to exercise its rights as a citizen.

The same logic should be applicable to legal personhood in the case of AI. If no legal consequences can be drawn from it, similarly to the citizenship of the robot Sophia, there is no actual benefit in granting it. Moreover, we should only do it, when we recognize the utility of this step, as it occurred in the case of corporations. Legal persons, gained its fictional legal personhood, when humans started to understand the importance of attributing legal obligations to companies. In other words, when humans started to recognize the utility in it.

Still, we could argue that both children and people with mental illnesses lack either or both the competence and the accountability elements of legal personhood, and still it is granted to them (although, as Kurki puts it, it is a kind of passive legal personhood), meaning that there would be no reason to avoid doing the same in the case of AI.

However, there are specific reasons for such thing to happen. As Savigny and many other authors stated, the original concept of legal person is typically a match with the concept of human being, based on the presumption that human beings possess legal capacity (Kurki 2019). In this sense, to both children and people with mental disabilities, legal personhood is attributed by the mere fact that they're both categories of born human beings, a criteria that, surely, cannot be applied to AI. This circumstance tells us that we must look for a different criteria in this case. In this paper, it is argued that this criteria should be the possibility of playing an active role in legal personhood, through competence but, in special, legal responsibility.

Additionally, to children, legal personhood is typically attributed according to the Hegelian understanding that there is a potential of rationality and freedom and that children start to accumulate the capabilities required of a duty-bearer at some point (Kurki 2019).

In conclusion, without metacognition, there can hardly be any legal responsibility. On the other hand, without accountability, there is no reason why AI should have legal personhood, because without this element, there are no useful legal consequences to be drawn from it. Such legal consequences may only exist the day we find AI to be accountable. Otherwise, legal personhood in AI will mean nothing more than an empty shell.

7 Conclusions

This paper sought to draw a line between accountable and non-accountable AI, using several areas of knowledge, such as Philosophy, Psychology, Computation and Law.

In this sense, the paper argues that the problem of whether or not to ascribe legal personhood to AI can be solved through the notion of metacognition, a concept that, without knowing, Law has been using all along to decide upon this matter.

To achieve this purpose, we started by examining the meaning of Agent, in order to assess whether or not AI should be considered as such. As the concept presented

Metacognition, Accountability and Legal Personhood of AI

many difficulties, a common denominator was needed, which it was found to be the voluntary act. If there is a voluntary act, we must, then, conclude that we have an Agent before us. Accordingly, and as long as AI acts voluntarily, it makes sense to argue that complex robots are Agents, thus not mere tools.

However, as stated before, this does not necessarily mean that an AI must be held accountable just because it fits the category of Agent. Animals, people with mental illnesses and children are intuitively considered Agents and yet not held accountable.

Hence, the other argument that was made is that in order to ascribe responsibility to an Agent, that entity must show, at least, strategic and monitoring metacognitive processes. These elements take part in the ability of being accountable, which in turn composes, along with the concept of legal competence, the notion of an active Legal Personhood.

Considering the above conclusions, two other ideas must follow. If the entity does show Metacognitive processes, then we might consider grant the said entity with legal personhood. On the other hand, if it doesn't show this capacity, then we need an autonomous and, if necessary, new, applicable law, as we have in the case of children, animals and mental illnesses.

When it comes to the state of AI, today, it seems that it does not yet stands in a sufficiently complex level in terms of metacognitive processes in order to being held accountable for their actions, notwithstanding showing simple metacognitive processes.[4]

References

Ajzen I (1991) The theory of planned behavior. Organ Behav Hum Decis Process 50:179–211

Allen C, Bekoff M (1997) Species of mind: the philosophy and biology of cognitive ethology. MIT Press, Cambridge

Anscombe GEM (1957) Intention. Harvard University Press, Cambridge

Aristóteles (2004) Ética a Nicómaco (trans: Caeiro DAC). Quetzal, Lisboa

Asaro PM (2007) Robots and responsibility from a legal perspective. In: Proceedings of the IEEE, pp 20–24. http://peterasaro.org/writing/ASARO%20Legal%20Perspective.pdf. Accessed May 2019

Barandiaran XE, Di Paolo E, Rohde M (2009) Defining agency: individuality, normativity, asymmetry, and spatio-temporality in action. Adapt Behav 17(5):367–386. https://doi.org/10.1177/1059712309343819

Birks P (1997) Definition and division: a mediation on institutes. 3.13. In: Birks P (ed) The classification of obligations. Clarendon Press, Oxford, pp 1–21

---

[4] *See* generally, on the imitation of humans by Robots, in this book M C Patrao Neves and A B Almeida—Before and Beyond Artificial Intelligence: Opportunities and Challenges; and M N Duffourc and D S Giovanniello—The Autonomous AI Physician: Medical Ethics and Legal Liability.

Boulangé A, Jaggie C (2014) Ethique, responsabilité et statut juridique du robot compagnon: revue et perspectives. Cognition, Affects et Interaction. https://www.researchgate.net/publication/278625871_Cognition_Affects_et_Interaction. Accessed May 2019

Brown AL, DeLoache JS (1978) Skills, plans, and self-regulation. In: Siegler RS (ed) Children'sthinking: what develops? Lawrence Erlbaum Associates, Inc., Hillsdale, pp 3–35

Calverley DJ (2008) Imagining a non-biological machine as a legal person. AI Soc 22:523–537

Chopra S, White L (2011) A legal theory for autonomous artificial agents. University of Michigan Press, Ann Arbor

Coelho H (2008) Teoria da agência: Arquitectura e cenografia. Edição do Autor, Lisbon

Cook WW (1917) Act, intention, and motive in the criminal law. Yale Law J 26:645–663

Cox MT (2005) Metacognition in computation: a selected research review. Artif Intell 169:104–141

Crowder J, Friess S, Ncc M (2011) Metacognition and meta memory concepts for AI systems. In: Proceedings on the international conference on artificial intelligence (ICAI), Athens

Dario P, Palmerini E (2012) Robot companions as case-scenario for assessing the "subjectivity" of autonomous agents. Some philosophical and legal remarks. In: First workshop on rights and duties of autonomous agents, pp 24–31

David AS, Bedford N, Wiffen B, Gilleen J (2012) Failures of metacognition and lack of insight in neuropsychiatric disorders. Philos Trans R Soc Lond Ser B Biol Sci 367:1379–1390

Davidson D (1963) Actions, reasons, and causes. J Philos 60:685–700

de Almeida P (2000) Modelos de inimputabilidade: Da teoria à prática. Almedina, Janeiro de

Dennett DC (1987) The intentional stance. MIT Press, Cambridge

Derham DP (1958) Theories of legal personality. In: Webb L (ed) Legal personality and political pluralism. Melbourne University Press, Melbourne, pp 1–19

Dewey J (1926) The historic background of corporate legal personality. Yale Law J 35:655–673

Ferreira AE, Pereira D (2017) Partilhar o mundo com robôs autónomos: A responsabilidade civil extra- contratual por danos, Introdução ao problema, Cuestiones de Interés Jurídico. IDIBE, Alicante

Flavell JH (1979) Metacognition and cognitive monitoring: a new area of cognitive–developmental inquiry. Am Psychol 34:906–911

Fleming SM, Dolan RJ, Frith CD (2012) Metacognition: computation, biology and function. Philos Trans R Soc Lond Ser B Biol Sci 367:1280–1286

Frankfurt H (1971) Freedom of the will and the concept of a person. J Philos 68:5–20

Georghiades P (2004) From the general to the situated: Three decades of metacognition. Int J Sci Educ 26:365–383

Hutto D, Ravenscroft I (2021) Folk psychology as a theory. In: Zalta EN (ed) The Stanford encyclopedia of philosophy

James W, Drummond R, Henry Holt and Company (1890) The principles of psychology. Henry Holt and Company, New York

Kosko B (1986) Fuzzy cognitive maps. Int J Man Mach Stud 24:65–75

Kramer MH, Simmonds NE, Hillel S (1998) A debate over rights: philosophical enquiries. Oxford University Press, Oxford

Kurki VAJ (2016) Revisiting legal personhood. Paper for Spanish-Finnish Seminar in Legal Theory. PhD Candidate, University of Cambridge

Kurki V (2019) A theory of legal personhood. Oxford University Press, Helsinki Legal Studies Research Paper No. 58

LaBar KS, Cabeza R (2006) Cognitive neuroscience of emotional memory. Nat Rev Neurosci 7:54–64

Lai ER (2011) Metacognition: A literature review. Pearson Research Report. Pearson Education, Upper Saddle River

Markby W (1889) Elements of law, considered with reference to Principles of general jurisprudence. Clarendon Press, Oxford

Minsky M (1967) Computation: Finite and infinite machines. Prentice-Hall, Englewood Cliffs

Morse SJ (2000) Rationality and responsibility. Faculty Scholarship at Penn Law, p 524. https://scholarship.law.upenn.edu/faculty_scholarship/524. Accessed 29 Sept 2021

Morse SJ (2003) Diminished rationality, diminished responsibility. Ohio State J Crim Law 1:289–308

Muñoz Conde F, Arán MG (1996) Derecho penal: Parte general. Tirant Lo Blanch, Valencia

Nelson TO, Narens L (1990) Metamemory: a theoretical framework and new findings. In: Bower GH (ed) Psychology of learning and motivation. Academic, San Diego, pp 125–173

Olsaretti S (1998) Freedom, force and choice: Against the rights-based definition of voluntariness. J Polit Philos 6:53–78

Pagallo U (2013) The laws of robots - crimes, contracts, and torts. Springer, Dordrecht

Pagallo U (2018) Vital, Sophia, and Co.—the quest for the legal personhood of robots. Information 9:230

Piaget J (1976) The grasp of consciousness. Harvard University Press, Cambridge

Pietrzykowski T (2017) The idea of non-personal subjects of law. In: Kurki VAJ, Pietrzykowski T (eds) Legal personhood: animals, artificial intelligence and the unborn. Springer International Publishing, Cham, pp 49–67

Russell SJ, Norvig P, Davis E (1995) Artificial intelligence: a modern approach. Prentice Hall, Upper Saddle River

Salmond JW (1913) Jurisprudence. Stevens and Haynes, London

Saxe R, Offen S (2010) Seeing ourselves: what vision can teach us about metacognition. In: Dimaggio G, Lysaker PH (eds) Metacognition and severe adult mental disorders. Routledge, Hove, pp 13–30

Schraw G, Moshman D (1990) Metacognitive theories. Educ Psychol Rev 7:351–371

Shardlow N (1990) Action and agency in cognitive science. Master's thesis, University of Manchester

Shoham Y (1993) Agent-oriented programming. Artif Intell 60:51–92

Solaiman SM (2017) Legal personality of robots, corporations, idols and chimpanzees: a quest for legitimacy. Artif Intell Law 25:155–179

Taylor R (1966) Action and purpose. Prentice-Hall, Englewood Cliffs

Wooldridge M, Jennings NR (2009) Intelligent agents: theory and practice. Knowl Eng Rev 10:115–152

Yaffe G (2012) The voluntary act requirement. In: Andrei M (ed) The Routledge companion to philosophy of law. Routledge, New York, p 174

Open Access This chapter is licensed under the terms of the Creative Commons Attribution 4.0 International License (http://creativecommons.org/licenses/by/4.0/), which permits use, sharing, adaptation, distribution and reproduction in any medium or format, as long as you give appropriate credit to the original author(s) and the source, provide a link to the Creative Commons license and indicate if changes were made.

The images or other third party material in this chapter are included in the chapter's Creative Commons license, unless indicated otherwise in a credit line to the material. If material is not included in the chapter's Creative Commons license and your intended use is not permitted by statutory regulation or exceeds the permitted use, you will need to obtain permission directly from the copyright holder.

Artificial Intelligence and Decision Making in Health: Risks and Opportunities

Márcia Santana Fernandes and José Roberto Goldim

Abstract The use of systems that include Artificial Intelligence (AI) imposes an assessment of the risks and opportunities associated with their incorporation in the health area. Different types of AI present multiple ethical, legal and social challenges. AI systems involved incorporated with new imaging and signal processing technologies. AI systems in the area of communication have made it possible to carry out previously non-existent interactions and facilitate access to data and information. The greatest concern involves the areas of planning, knowledge and reasoning, as AI systems are directly associated with the decision-making process. So, the central objective of this chapter is to reflect and suggest recommendations, with the foundation of the Complex Bioethics Model, about the decision-making process in health with AI support, considering risks and opportunities. The chapter is organized in two parts: (1) The decision-making processes in health and AI; (1.1) The health area the use of AI and decision-making processes: opportunities and risks to treat electronic health records (EHR) and (2) Complex Bioethics Model (CBM) and AI.

1 Introduction

Complexity, in the sense proposed by Edgar Morin, translates the moment we are living the so-called fourth Revolution. The *aversion to Manichaeism and the understanding that complexity is not everything, it is not the totality of reality, but it is the best that can, at the same time, open up to the intelligible and reveal the inexplicable.* The uncertainty of everyday life is an element of acceptance, or even its ambiguity. Artificial intelligence (AI), its potential uses and, in the same

---

M. S. Fernandes (✉) · J. R. Goldim
Laboratório de Pesquisa em Bioética e Ética na Ciência do Centro de Pesquisas do Hospital de Clínicas de Porto Alegre-LAPEBEC/HCPA DENS, Porto Alegre, Brazil
e-mail: msfernandes@hcpa.edu.br; http://lattes.cnpq.br/2132565174726788;
jgoldim@hcpa.edu.br; http://lattes.cnpq.br/0485816067416121

© The Author(s) 2024
H. Sousa Antunes et al. (eds.), *Multidisciplinary Perspectives on Artificial Intelligence and the Law*, Law, Governance and Technology Series 58,
https://doi.org/10.1007/978-3-031-41264-6_10

proportion, the legal, ethical and social challenges should be reflected in an *ambient* and *ambience* complex.

Technology and medicine has a long history of connection, but one of the milestones was the work of Lee Lusted, who in his article *Medical Electronics* (1955), reported on a series of large numbers of medical electronic devices developed in that time, indicating a rapid expansion of this field. He said at the time: *Electric phenomena in the human body had long been of interest, but the low signal amplitude made study difficult* (Lusted 1955). At the same period of time, Turing (Turing 1950) established the pillars for computer science and Artificial Intelligence (AI).

AI driven technologies impose an evaluation of the risks and opportunities associated with its incorporation in the life and living of human beings. The theme incorporates old-new questions, as Ulrick Beck pointed out in The Risk Society (1986),[1] and further developed in World at Risk (2007),[2] to the debate involving the impact of technology in the life of human beings: *how do we want to live? What is there of human in the human being, of natural in nature, that needs to be protected? (...) These old-new questions can be tossed back and forth between everyday life, politics and science. In the most advanced stage of the civilization process, they once again enjoy priority on the agenda - also or precisely at times when they are cloaked in the camouflage of mathematical formulas and methodological controversies* (Beck 2011, p. 34).

So, for some time, it has been possible to have a person-machine interaction by means of natural language systems (Chat-bot). On many occasions, there is no clear perception that this communication is being made with a machine and not with other people. In the 1970s, Jacques Monod already warned that it was increasingly difficult to establish the limit between the natural and the artificial (Monod, 1970). The simulation or substitution of real activities, increasingly similar to those performed by artificial mechanisms and systems, generates this ambiguity of perception.

The technological arrogance, according to Hans Jonas (Jonas 1994), causes these results to be understood as unquestionable. The infallibility of computers has been discussed since the beginning of their use, when they were still called "electronic brains". At that time there was already the proposition that the quality of the information generated was not unquestionable, but depended on the quality of the input data and the processes used. This became known by the acronym GIGO (Garbage In, Garbage Out). That is, if the data or systems are inadequate, the results generated will be compromised (The Hammond Times 1957).

These old-new questions have been at the heart of discussions involving AI and decision making. In this perspective, Floridi et al. (2018) in text, published in 2018, maintain that AI is a reality without return and for this reason it is necessary to form reflections towards an AI Society for Good (Good AI Society).

---

[1] Beck (2011). First edition in 1986.

[2] Beck (2009). First edition in 2007.

The opportunities and risks to protect the dignity of the human person and provide for their development should be permeated by the traditional principles of North American Bioethics—beneficence, non-maleficence, autonomy and justice (Beauchamp and Childress 1979), in addition to the principle of explicability.

In this analysis, in our view, two perspectives should be added: (1) European perspective, proposed by Peter Kemp and Jacob Dahl Rendtorff, use four other principles: Dignity; Autonomy, understood as Freedom; Integrity; and Vulnerability; because in this perspective, principles are not weighted, but there must be a coherence in their application (Kemp and Rendtorff 2008) and (2) an approach based by Complex Bioethics Model (CBM), in other words, bioethics understood as complex, shared and interdisciplinary reflection on the adequacy of actions involving life and living (Goldim 2006a, 2006b).

Life and living complement each other, they give the adequate dimension of each person. Life is described by the organic aspects, that is, by the biological characteristics. On the other hand, living refers to the relational aspects, the biography of each one (Agamben 1998). The ensemble of these characteristics is what gives the uniqueness of each person. The Complex Bioethical Model (CBM) (Goldim 2006b) embodies a perspective of a complex interdisciplinary field[3] of reflection on life and living.

It is precisely this desire to know and study population health and human health that marks scientific studies and establishes the foundations for research and experimentation. The need to respond to the challenges generated by epidemics, famine, wars, population growth and urban centres was the motivation for the chain to *the invention of science* (Wooton 2015).

Its central objective throughout time is to identify determinants of diseases and, more recently, of health at the population level. So, historically, the specific contribution of epidemiology has been the progressive constitution of a coherent set of methods and concepts, with the aim of assessing the determinants of health, where robust systems, like technologies driven by AI, are central to process and organize healthcare personal and sensitive data and information.

The processing of a lot of data in an efficient and precise way is fundamental for the development of scientific medicine, so computational tools for machine learning and mining large volumes of data, in an approach known as Big Data, and the joint evaluation of large volumes of data has allowed the establishment of new relationships, of new, previously unidentified understandings.

Another important development in this area is the increasing use of algorithms for decision making. These tools, increasingly improved and based on highly complex

---

[3] Bourdieu (1996, 2004). We use the expression field from Pierre Bourdieu. The *field* for Bourdieu is organized by principles such as economic capital and cultural capital, assuming struggles in social space, according to social positions. And composing the sense of *field* is the sense of *habitus*. Bourdieu's *habitus* can be understood as a system of dispositions, socially constituted, which establish the generating and unifying principle of the set of practices and ideologies characteristic of a group of agents. The habitus, from Bourdieu's perspective, produces the individual and makes him internalize the values and rules of belonging to society.

processes, have provided optimized solutions to countless problems, including modifying the decision making processes themselves. Most of these systems work in the quest to recognize patterns of similarity. This is the area that became known as Artificial Intelligence. Strictly speaking, artificial intelligence is not an intelligence in itself, but automated decision making processes. Pierre Levi makes a blunt criticism of the use of the expression "artificial intelligence", he does not recognize in these systems the possibility of generating new knowledge or of having an understanding of the world (Lévy 2022). Algorithms are made by people in the service of institutions, which have their belief systems and values, which end up directing the processing and interpretations.

Therefore, use of systems that include Artificial Intelligence (AI) imposes an assessment of the risks and opportunities associated with their incorporation in the health area: health care; experimental and clinical research and personalized medicine. AI systems involving areas of communication capable of performing parallel computations for data processing and knowledge representation (denominated artificial neural networks (ANN)); that have made possible to carry out previously non-existent interactions and facilitate access to data and information; technologies for detecting image, sound; performing heath assistance with robotics and areas of planning, knowledge and reasoning, when AI systems are directly associated with the decision-making process.

Ramesh et al. (2004), presented a literature review in 2004 on the use of the 'artificial intelligence' and 'neural networks (computer)' and an overview of different artificial intelligent techniques along with the review of important clinical applications. Their results show "the proficiency of artificial intelligent techniques has been explored in almost every field of medicine". The authors indicate areas of activity: clinical diagnosis; prognosis; ultrasound images; predict survival in patients; used for the administration of anaesthetics in the operating room; used form of evolutionary computation for medical applications in genetics e natural evolution, nominated 'Genetic Algorithms'. (Ramesh et al. 2004).

In this context, different types of AI present multiple ethical, legal and social challenges in the world, as pointed out by OCDE.[4] However, the diversity and vulnerability of social, economic and access to the Universal health coverage (UHC) that exists in South America made analises of health technologies AI-driven more complex. The standard to accomplish in terms of access of health are the UN's Sustainable Development Goals (SDGs), which, by 2030, a member state must guarantee: (1) access to health services for all people in need of health, independent of socio-economic characteristics, location, wealth or any other vulnerability; (2) financial protection, i.e. all people should be safe from financial risk when incurring health care expenses; (3) access to quality of health services, that is to say health care has to be effective in providing care and improving outcomes, while it is also

---

[4] OECD. Recommendation of the Council on Artificial Intelligence, OECD/Legal/0449, 2021. information, please consult the Compendium of OECD Legal Instruments at http://legalinstruments.oecd.org.

cost effective and sustainable, because access without quality can be considered an empty universal health coverage promise (OECD and The World Bank 2020).

The report *Health at a Glance: Latin America and the Caribbean 2020* compares key indicators for population health and health systems across the 33 Latin America and the Caribbean (LAC) countries. It presents comparable data on health status and its determinants, health care resources and activities, health expenditure and financing, and health care quality, along with selected health inequality indicator, including the pandemic COVID-19:

A main barrier for accessing such health services arise from out-of-pocket health expenditures, which in LAC represent on average 34% of total health spending, well above the 21% average in OECD countries. The high level of out-of-pocket expenditures in LAC are an indication of weaker health systems, lower levels of health services coverage and, overall, a worse baseline scenario to confront this pandemic when compared to most OECD countries (OECD and The World Bank 2020).

Particularly, in Brazil some parts of the country have more access to health and health technologies than others, despite the fact that Brazil has the biggest public health system in the World, the Unified Health System (*Sistema Único de Saúde— SUS)*, has as principle an universal access—an universal health coverage (UHC) to national and foreigners, that serves more than 190 million people, 80% of whom depend exclusively on it for any health care. The SUS is an achievement of the Brazilian people, guaranteed by the Federal Constitution of 1988, in Article 196, through Law No. 8.080/1990, that must be guaranteed and improved constantly.

So, the central objective of this chapter is to reflect and suggest recommendations, with the foundation of the Complex Bioethics Model, about the decision-making process in health with AI support, considering risks and opportunities. The chapter is organized in two parts: (1) The decision-making processes in health and AI; (1.1) The health area the use of AI and decision-making processes: opportunities and risks to treat electronic health records (EHR) and (2) Complex Bioethics Model (CBM) and AI.

The central assumption is to maintain balance and preserve the characteristics of humanity present in the act of deciding, taking into account ethical, legal and social aspects, cross by the principle of trust, when using AI systems in health. The justification for using personal and sensitive health data and information must be associated with actions on behalf of individuals and society, in terms of assistance, research involving human beings, whether of a sanitary, epidemiological, clinical or biobank nature.

We hope that our recommendations can contribute to the development of regulatory frameworks—ethical and legal—good practices and compliance for the use of AI in health. Our perspective is to analyze examples at national and international levels, focusing on the diversity and vulnerability of social, economic and access to health existing in South America and particularly in Brazil.

2 Decision-Making Processes in Health and AI

Decision making involving IA should consider Generative AI. The characteristics of the Generative AI systems are to establish connections, by means of new computational tools, based on large volumes of data, concepts and structures already built, to propose new contents, which are expressed in a language as natural as possible.

The term generative was created by Noam Chomsky, in 1965, when he proposed "generative grammar", or also called "generative grammar". This proposal sought to explain that language is established through skills and performances to produce sentences and what are the paths used to establish them (Chomsky 2015). This idea was based on the thought of Wilhelm von Humboldt, who, in 1836, said that language makes infinite use of finite means (Humboldt 1836).

The new Generative AI systems of, such as ChatGPT and Perplexity, constitute a new level of complexity in dealing with data, in the quest to extract information that can guide actions. These new systems not only label or classify pre-existing data, but generate new content, by aggregation and combination, from the available elements.

What are the ethical implications associated with Generative Artificial Intelligence? The texts prepared by ChatGPT and Perplexity respond:

ChatGPT: Artificial Intelligence (AI) presents three main areas of ethical concern for society: privacy and surveillance, prejudice and discrimination, and philosophical challenges. AI can lead to unemployment as machines take over jobs that were previously done by humans. Inequality is also a concern, as AI can be used to perpetuate existing power structures. AI can also lead to algorithmic bias, where models incorporate and deploy human and social biases at scale.

Privacy is a fundamental human right recognized in the UN Declaration of Human Rights, but AI apps can pose a real threat to this right. Misinformation is another ethical problem with AI, as machine learning models can easily generate incorrect text.

To ensure the ethical use of AI, education and awareness about the ethics of AI must be increased. Examples of ethical AI include using AI to improve health outcomes or reduce energy consumption. It is important to remember that ethical issues with AI are not limited to negative impacts; there are also incidental benefits, such as enhanced analytical capabilities or increased efficiency in decision-making processes. (https://chat.openai.com/chat/c4bf8bd6-df96-4cec-b96d-dd54ec97ef2f; Feb 14th, 2023)

Perplexity: Bias and discrimination: AI systems can perpetuate and amplify existing biases in society, leading to discriminatory decisions and outcomes. For example, facial recognition technology has been shown to have higher error rates for black people and women.

Privacy and data protection: AI systems often rely on large amounts of personal data to make decisions, and there are concerns about how this data is collected, stored and used and who has access to it.

Employment impact: AI has the potential to automate many jobs, leading to unemployment and social unrest. There is also a risk that AI will reinforce existing power imbalances and exacerbate economic inequality.

Accountability and responsibility: when AI systems make decisions that have significant consequences for individuals and society, it can be difficult to determine who is responsible for those decisions and how they can be held accountable.

Human rights: AI has the potential to infringe on human rights, such as freedom of expression and privacy, and there are concerns about the use of AI for surveillance and control by governments and other organizations.

It is important to address these ethical implications through ongoing dialogue and debate and by establishing clear ethical guidelines and principles for the development and use of AI. This includes considering the potential impacts of AI on individuals and society and ensuring that AI is developed and used in a responsible and ethical manner. (https://www.perplexity.ai/?s=u&uuid=a6d1842e-bf56-4e0a-9fd4-2ff4f00a8e13; Feb 14th, 2023)

As we can see there are connections, from the ChatGPT and Perplexity answers, between ethical issues and concepts, such as privacy, surveillance and control, freedom of speech, prejudice and discrimination, were interpreted and new content arranged. All these issues already preexisted the use of generative AI, however they have been discussed in different levels of depth and application. Perhaps, the current challenge is to think about these issues in this new perspective.

Whenever an innovation is incorporated by society, discussions about its suitability arise. When the printed book was made available to society, when the first encyclopedias appeared, when the internet gave access to a volume of data never before imagined, there was questioning about the appropriateness of using these means of disseminating data, knowledge, and information. A good example is the current discussion of the impact of Generative AI on education, it is generating anxiety among schools, parents and teachers. This same discussion has occurred in other historical moments and incorporation of new technologies. There are already educational models that allow incorporating these situations brought by Generative AI in a creative way. Instead of copying or generating content, perhaps the challenge of education is to evaluate the quality of the information generated. It is to use this challenge to incorporate a critical and complex reflection in the different levels of life to establish security, transparency and trust in the use of AI-Generated.

The *Study on e-Health Interoperability of Heath Data and Artificial Intelligence for Health and care in the European Union—Final Study Report* (European Union 2021) points out the lack of trust in AI-driven decision support is hindering the wider adoption in heath, and also integrating new technologies into current clinical practice; research and personal medicine are indeed legal, ethical and social challenges. These challenges are increased by the necessary internationalization of the health area and the challenges of sharing data and information in order to achieve global health.

Recommendations have also been developed by countries and organizations, highlighting the recommendation proposed by the European Commission, in 2020, in the "White Paper—On Artificial Intelligence—A European approach to excellence and trust", with the purpose of establishing the political paths to seek the appropriate use of AI. In this document, the Commission recommends the establishment of standards and guidelines for investment in the area of AI, aiming at two central objectives: promoting the adoption of AI and addressing the risks associated with certain uses of this new technology (European Commission 2020). The Commission also established a High Level Expert Group that published Guidelines on trusted AI in April 2019, composed of seven key requirements: respect for the dignity of the human person; robust technical and security systems; privacy and data management; transparency; respect for diversity, non-discrimination and equity; social and environmental well-being; and accountability.

The Common Digital Market is one of ten priorities of the European Union. In this context, the following decisions are taken: Decision No 922/2009 / EC of the European Parliament and of the Council of September 2009 on interoperability solutions for European public administrations (e-Health European Interoperability Framework) (European Union 2012) and Decision (EU) 2015/2240 of the European Parliament and the Council of 25 November 2015 establishing a program on interoperability solutions and common frameworks for public administrations, businesses and citizens (ISA program) as a means of modernizing the sector. European e-Health Interoperability Framework (ReEIF) (European Union 2015).

The European Union seeks to integrate the electronic medical records of European citizens, recognizing the weaknesses related to various aspects of data use, whether for security, privacy protection, ethical suitability, management, storage and disposal, and interoperability between state information systems to establish trustable structure of E-Health. These measures are part of the goal of creating a digital single market.[5]

Decision-making processes, particularly in the health area, are based on trust and the relationship of trust—which are necessarily identified with all those involved in this relationship. The relationships occur in all spheres, between the public administration and the administered; between private entities; between private entities and human beings and between human beings. The pre criteria for establishing the basis of trust, in situations involving IA, are not different, on the contrary should be intensified, because must be composed of concrete mechanisms to inform, account for the use, motivation, process and transparency of the criteria used in decision making.

The principle of trust lies at the basis of legal relations, whether these are public or private. In turn, the principle of the protection of trust is presented in the individual dimension, or in the subjective aspect of legal security. This principle depends on the exercise of trust, with concrete indication of the breach of expectations in law or clear demonstration of the requirements for its demonstration.

O'Neill understands that trust cannot be confused with the mere disclosure or transparency of information and accountability (O'Neill 2004). From the philosophical perspective, trust is a central element in human relations, whether interpersonal or between individuals and the state, involving trust in institutions and their representatives. However, this state of trust is not presented merely by the disclosure of data and information, but must be underpinned by an intelligible narrative.

In the juridical perspective, the principle of trust, says Martins-Costa, has the immediate scope to ensure expectations. In the case in question, the situation of

---

[5] The example and efforts made by the European Union to integrate regulatory, technical, ethical and social aspects in the area of digital health are important to reflect in the design of systems, similar or not, for other parts of the world.

Artificial Intelligence and Decision Making in Health: Risks and Opportunities   195

trust is materialized between the individual and the public administration, when personal data are provided for precise purposes—as health care, research or social security (Martins-Costa 2015). It also presents itself in legal businesses, involving the provision of personal data in exchange for specific health services.

2.1 The Health Area the Use of AI and Decision-Making Processes: Opportunities and Risks to Treat Electronic Health Records (EHR)

Undoubtedly health care; research involving human beings or public policy design—data and information are central. In turn, the use of AI in this scenario relies and requires the data and information spent in electronic health records (EHR). Therefore, the treatment of health data and information, sensitive data, must be based on the principle of trust. So, studying some aspects related to the use of EHR, combined with AI technologies, is a good example to establish opportunities and risks of this technology in the health area.

Electronic medical records serve as a collective memory of the assistance provided to the patient. Thus, they must gather general and health data records, the description of relevant personal and family facts, collected by health professionals during the patient's anamnesis. It is this history that opens the record of the assistance activities. Besides this information, other information is added, either as a record or as annexes, such as diagnoses, under the form of reports, images or data, prognoses, care plans, exam results, consultations performed by different professionals, participation in research or notes that are relevant to the case, with the primary purpose of better assisting the patients (Fernandes and Goldim 2019).

2.2 The Opportunities

The EHR must be protected and guided by a relationship of trust, based on respect for the person. The respect for the person is expressed by the deontological duties of confidentiality, by the legal duties of personality and by the bioethical principles. The patient provides the information considered as relevant based on the trust placed in the professional who is attending him/her. From the professional's point of view, this information is always considered to be privileged.

The use of genetic data in care, such as those used in genetic counselling and Personalized Medicine, has introduced new data, which may generate information that affects not only the patient but also other people related to him or her. Thus, the concept of personal privacy expands to that of relational privacy. This increases the responsibility associated with the registration and future use of this information.

As well as, the data EHR may assist in research-related interventions. This may involve the use of medicines, cells and other biological products, the performance of surgical or diagnostic procedures, the use of devices, changes in the care process, preventive care, among other activities. In all of them the sharing of these data can generate new and useful information.

The development of clinical research and also of personalized medicine, extends the care with the protection of personal data in the area of health, as they involve the need to use data and information of patients, collected in an protected environment by the principle of trust. Likewise, this principle creates expectations in the research participant—on a personal level, when the results of the research can affect or be beneficial to him/her, or on the social and community level of collaborating with scientific development.

Besides, EHR have been used as qualified sources of information for the establishment of public policies and research. Public policies are essential to guarantee access to health. It is worth noting that, from the perspective of Law, the issue of access to health is dealt with in the context of fundamental and civil rights. The importance, for example, of epidemiological cause-effect relationships studies, which make it possible to establish public policies, protocols, guidelines or norms for the prevention and treatment of diseases and/or for health promotion, are unquestionably important and they change the course of human development.

Moreover, from the epidemiological approach, Evidence-Based Medicine (EBM) emerged, proposed by McMaster University, Canada, in the 1990s, to record and systematize clinical evidence and the epidemiological knowledge derived from it, to improve results in the diagnosis and treatment of diseases and health care. It is an attempt to guide patient-associated decision making at the individual level based on collective data (Evidence-Based Medicine Working Group 1992).

So, the need to systematize the collection, storage and use of health data and information is directly connected with the development of medicine and the global increase of knowledge in health, both in terms of individual patient care, population health and global health. And today we have at our fingertips and in constant use tools such as AI to do that.

2.3 The Risks

The protection of personal data and information contained in EHR should consider the new context generated in the Information Society, for risk prevention (Fernandes 2019). The constant development and incorporation of new information and communication technologies, the use of new data protection techniques, including AI, blockchain, the use of social media, the interconnection of integrated health systems, in addition to the sharing generated by the Big Data environment itself (Roehrs et al. 2019).

So, these expanded possibilities of interconnecting, storing and processing a large and complex volume of data and information originated from EHR, amplifies the national and international concern, demonstrated in the literature, about the security and preservation of patient data and information contained in PEPs. Particularly, the respect and the adequate use for its purpose—in favor of the patients—are highlighted topics. The literature review carried out in 125 scientific articles, selected from a total of 5278 articles, in the PubMed and Scielo databases, indicates as recurrent themes information security when dealing with electronic records and access to medical records (Caballero 2018).

EHR presents the data and information in a structured way, however, as the medical history should be developed in a text contextualized in the patient's life and living, the qualitative or even quantitative analysis may be hampered. Also, personal data and information, especially in health, should be considered as distinct concepts. Information does not exist in isolation, it needs a receiver, someone to give meaning and significance to the data. Isolated data describes characteristics of something, someone, some fact or situation. However, it is the information that gives meaning to this data. The information acts on the data, it is the result of the analysis and interpretation of the data. In short, it is the organization, categorization and systematization of data for a specific perspective and purpose that generates information. These definitions are a relevant starting point for understanding the importance of data and information in the area of health (Fernandes 2019).

Likewise, it is important to consider various notions and concepts related to the environment of large volumes of data—Big Data—generated in EHR and in the health system (Kulynych and Greely 2017). Big Data is an expression used generically to indicate the grouping of data, information, databases, open internet networks and other accessible data that initially aimed to improve strategic planning, marketing and commercial business (Manyika et al. 2011). This context, marked by fluidity, uncertainty and fugacity of data and information, required multiple sources to seek to understand complex and broad phenomena that AI systems can help to interpret.

The new perspective generated by the Big Data phenomenon has stimulated scientific work in various areas of knowledge. As pointed out by Mittelstadt and Floridi in a literature review article of 2016, AI in the health area is already a reality, besides others that would be on a horizon possibilities and others that are still only potential. Examples of situations that are already a reality include those related to the activities of Biobanks, Public Health studies and hypothesis testing in the health area. Possible situations include the interconnection of equipment and applications for personal health; the existence of online profiles connected to medical records; the creation of social media in the health area and the online and offline connections of personal profiles via wifi. Finally, they indicated as potential situations the connections between online medical records with other sources of personal data, as well as the involuntary connections of these data, both online and offline, originating from personal profiles for health surveillance purposes (Mittelstadt and Floridi 2016).

Floridi says:

Clearly, the future of AI lies not just in "small data" but also, or perhaps mainly, in its increasing ability to generate its own data. That would be a remarkable development, and one may expect significant efforts to be made in that direction. As well as, translated difficult tasks into complex tasks. (...)How is this translation achieved? By transforming the environment within which AI operates into an AI-friendly environment (Floridi 2019, 2020).

For this and other reasons, accurate risk impact analysis and preventive actions should be taken, in the normative, good practices, compliance and ethical spheres, mainly to avoid bias in decision making. Algorithmic bias is one of the fears, particularly in the processing of sensitive personal data, suche as health, genetic and biometric data. As well as, algorithmic bias that may negatively discriminate and/or cause harm to individuals or certain groups—e.g. organised by gender, sex, age, physical or mental health status and economically or socially vulnerable peaple or groups (e.g. prisoners and the poor).

Norori et al. (2021), in an article entitled *Addressing bias in big data and AI for health care: A call for open science* point out that *the future, and we would say the present, research is needed to set standards for AI in healthcare that enable transparency and data sharing, while at the same time preserving patients' privacy.*

The authors present the distinctions between *statistical bias* and *social bias* as the starting point of the analysis. Statistical bias being that *refers to cases in which the distribution of a given dataset is not reflecting the true distribution of the population* and in turn, social bias *refers to inequities that may result in suboptimal outcomes for given groups of the human population* Norori et al. (2021).

The authors point out some examples of AI algorithms that are biased by design, regarding sex, age and race. The bias can be observed in studies that discriminate against the female gender in favor of the male, including in pre-clinical research, when in experimental models using animals there is a predominance of males. As well as in research for the development of medicines, when the majority of participants are men without a methodological reason that justifies it. Also, they pointed out, by the example, studies in the area of sleep disorders, when young patients are in favour of older patients. Moreover, racial bias when algorithms, in the area of skin cancer, are programmed to identify images of light skin and not dark skin, even if black population has a higher mortality rate from melanoma cancer. Also in the area of negative discrimination by race, there are algorithms in the area of hospital costs that induce to determine that black patients are healthier than white patients and for this reason, these receive a better treatment Norori et al. (2021).

These examples are enough to demonstrate that fears and lack of confidence in AI driven decision making are not in vain, or even disproportionate—they are a reality that should be normatively and ethically avoided.

Negative discrimination, as we have pointed out, in Latin America is aggravated by the large number of people who do not have access to health technologies or are discriminated against in "broad daylight" because of their condition and economic deprivation, lack of education and lack of sanitary conditions—as can be seen in the slums and peripheries and which is evidenced in the COVID-19 pandemic—

ironically data that has also been evidenced with the help of AI driven technologies (OECD and The World Bank 2020; Norori et al. 2021).

So what to do? Where should we act—nationally and internationally? What parameters should we have as a starting point? To try to answer and/or reflect on these questions, we turn to our second point, the Complex Bioethics Model (CBM) and AI.

3 Complex Bioethics Model (CBM) and AI

We are at a historic stage in which digital immigrants and digital natives coexist (Zur and Walker 2019). Digital immigrants had the opportunity to live in a society where all decisions were made only by human beings. Digital natives, on the other hand, naturalize the decisions made by algorithms.

The naturalization of decisions made only by artificial intelligence can involve several important ethical issues, such as technological arrogance, the vision of certainty and the impartiality of algorithms.

By using algorithms, machines follow a pattern of predictable, pre-programmed steps. Even with the incorporation of associated machine learning processes, these decisions carry with them only the rational elements associated with the decision-making process. In some models, values, affective issues and even cultural traditions can be included as elements of this decision-making process (Weber 1978). However, these non-rational actions are considered as if they were rational by the computational model. The computer doesn't hesitate, humans hesitate (Han 2015).

The processes used in artificial intelligence are the result of programming. Programming does not tolerate ambiguity or uncertainty, which are always present in the real world. Even using fuzzy logic-based methodologies, strictly speaking, it is a programmed uncertainty.

There is a belief that human beings are fallible but machines are not. Any and all decision-making process using artificial intelligence is based on a set of assumptions established by human persons. Even when there are self-programming systems, the root of the process is based on choices made by people who planned and implemented them. There are different levels of complexity, but they converge to a root where there is the presence of non-rational characteristics of its developers.

From an ethical point of view, any and all human action, or resulting from it, must be evaluated for its adequacy (Vasques 2000). This assessment requires not only the consideration of the facts, but the whole set of circumstances. One of these circumstances is the historical dimension, it is the perspective of insertion of these activities over time. It is a critical need to understand the complexity of the problem being evaluated.

This apparent dichotomy between artificial and natural is increasingly tenuous (Monod 1970). It is increasingly important to have a complex perspective in understanding situations that have increasingly presented themselves to human society.

Using a complex approach to Bioethics, it's possible to have ethical arguments using different theoretical framework, Any of them, based on virtues; intention and consent; principles; responsibility; human rights; consequences and alterity could be used in order to understand the human-computer systems relation.

Virtues can be used to justify the personal behavior adequacy involved in the design and application of decision-making systems. Prudence, temperance and justice are fundamental virtues to be considered in these situations. Systems must be based on practical reasoning, must use the resources involved properly and, above all, do not discriminate against any person or group of persons. Virtues presupposes a desire for humanity, which projects itself in time, which always has a historical perspective (Comte-Sponville 1996).

The intentions and consent associated with the action must be considered in evaluating the moral worth associated with an action (Abelard 1995). The intention of whoever designs or uses a system must be adequate, it must aim at the good of the people. On the other hand, the use of the system is only considered appropriate when it has the consent of the people affected by it. This combination of wills, of those who do the action and those who suffer the action, is fundamental.

Principle-based ethics should also guide the assessment of the appropriateness of using systems. The four-principle framework—Dignity, Freedom, Integrity and Vulnerability—can be very helpful in these assessments (Kemp 2005). Coherence in the application of these principles, understood as guiding human actions, must be sought. Dignity unites us to all people, it is what gives the character of humanity to all of us. Freedom is the possibility to choose, to make choices free from coercion. Integrity, understood in its physical, mental and social dimensions, must always be based on the search for its preservation. Vulnerability should be considered whenever there is any possibility that dignity, freedom or integrity could be compromised. In a risk society, we are all always vulnerable, in different degrees and situations.

The ethics of human rights is based on expectations of action. Human rights can be approached from an individual or collective perspective or even in a transpersonal way (Bobbio 1992). From the right to life and privacy to the right to solidarity or to have a preserved environment, rights are expressions of other people's actions towards me. Artificial intelligence systems may not have this multiple perspective present when making decisions. Sometimes one right is privileged and the others are not taken into consideration. It may happen that, by guaranteeing the right to privacy, a system will end up abandoning the dimension of solidarity (de Oliveira Ascensão 2009).

Consequentialist ethics is based on risks and benefits associated with actions directed to individuals or collectivities. The consequentialist decision-making process, from a micro or macro point of view, is based on the analysis of utility (risk versus benefit) (Singer 1993). The most important issue is to aim for a balance between these two perspectives, to establish a win-win strategy.

Ethics of responsibility focuses on actions. Both perspectives, whether retrospective or prospective, assess the repercussions of the actions carried out. The retrospective approach focuses on causes and the prospective on effects. The usual approach to responsibility is to see who did it and how the action was done. More recently, the focus has shifted from the cause to the action's repercussions. If scientists are responsible for the social consequences of science (Marcuse 2009), so too are the people who design artificial intelligence systems. In this perspective, a new imperative was established in response to human actions: "In your present options, include the future integrity of the human being among the objects of your will" (Jonas 2006). In other words, we shouldn't do everything that technique allows us to do (Ropohl 1981).

Finally, alterity is another theoretical approach to evaluate the ethical basis of artificial intelligence. Systems are built to be permanent, to have an identity, an immutability and to assume the totality of associated actions. This is the perspective of sameness. Otherness, on the other hand, assumes impermanence, singularity, mystery and infinity (Levinas 1961). Otherness opens us to the other and reaffirms us as people. This perspective allows establishing an ethical co-presence, a co-responsibility, a perspective that goes beyond the simple relationship to become an effective interaction (Levinas 1991). From the perspective of artificial intelligence, sameness prevails over otherness. In alterity perspective it's impossible to approach new technologies from a neutral point of view.

The Complex Bioethics approach allows the integration of these different theoretical perspectives in the search for arguments to reflect on the adequacy of the use of artificial intelligence technologies (Goldim 2006b). It's a good way to get a comprehensive perspective on proposals that are often seen only in their technical aspects.

Contemporary ethical discussion should be guided by reflection on the new "information regime", as characterized by Han (Han 2021). This is our challenge: to reflect on this new model of society, where relationships have changed enormously. AI, Generative AI and other species, is just one of the multiple challenges that need to be discussed and deepened.

4 Conclusion

Artificial intelligence is defined in the sense that machines can perform tasks similar to those performed by human beings (McCarthy et al. 2006). In the beginning of computing, computers were called "electronic brains". Later, computer metaphors were used to explain how the human brain works. One of the current risks is to carry out this inversion again, that is, to want to explain human intelligence using artificial intelligence models.

Another challenge in transposing human intelligence to artificial intelligence is recognizing that humans can fail, then machines can fail too. If this transposition occurs, it could be the realization that there would be a proposal for an "artificial stupidity" (O'connell 2017) associated with "artificial intelligence", like human stupidity and intelligence. Ethics and Bioethics could help in the reflection of the adequacy about the limits and borders between natural or artificial and intelligence or stupidity.

More important than discussing punctual ethical aspects, it is fundamental to reflect on the broader aspects of the use of AI, such as:

(a) to define ethically appropriate standards to guide the responsible creation of content by these systems;
(b) to establish monitoring strategies for the data and information generated by the AI and Generative AI to verify the veracity;
(c) to create guidelines that allow continuous audits of the processes of these systems in order to prevent that their processes can be used for purposes contrary to the interests of people, societies and humanity (Gocklin 2023).

In the bioethical approach to new technologies, it is essential to associate the principle of precaution with the principle of hope (Patrão-Neves 2021). That is, precaution seeking to guarantee the life of each one and hope seeking to maintain everyone's living.[6]

References

Abelard P (1995) Ethical writings: "ethics" and "dialogue" between a philosopher, a Jew and a Christian. Hackett, Indianapolis
Agamben G (1998) Homo sacer: sovereign power and bare life. Stanford University, Stanford
Beauchamp TL, Childress JF (1979) Principles of biomedical ethics. Oxford, New York
Beck U (2009) World at risk. Translated by Ciaran Cronin. Policy Press, Cambridge
Beck U (2011) Sociedade de risco – rumo a uma modernidade. 2ª Edição em tradução em Portugues, traduzida por Sebastião Nascimento. Editora, São Paulo
Bobbio N (1992) A era dos direitos. Campus, Rio de Janeiro

---

[6] *See* generally, on the different applications of Machine Learning and AI, in this book A Oliveira and M A T Figueiredo—Artificial intelligence: historical context and state of the art; I Trancoso, N Mamede, B Martins, H S Pinto and R Ribeiro—The impact of language technologies in the legal domain; J Gonçalves-Sá and F L Pinheiro—Societal Implications of Recommendation Systems: A Technical Perspective; A T Freitas—Data-driven approaches in healthcare: challenges and emerging trends; M Correia and L Rodrigues—Security and Privacy; E Magrani and P G F Silva—The Ethical and Legal Challenges of Recommender Systems Driven by Artificial Intelligence; M Lanz and S Mijic—Risks associated with the use of natural language generation: Swiss civil liability law perspective; W Gravett—Judicial Decision-making in the Age of Artificial Intelligence; and D Durães, P M Freitas and P Novais—The Relevance of Deepfakes in the Administration of Criminal Justice. *See* also, on AI and Healthcare, in this book A T Freitas— Data-driven approaches in healthcare: challenges and emerging trends; M N Duffourc and D S Giovanniello—The Autonomous AI Physician: Medical Ethics and Legal Liability; and R Nogaroli and J L M Faleiros Júnior—Ethical challenges of artificial intelligence in medicine and the triple semantic dimensions of algorithmic opacity with its repercussions to patient consent and medical liability.

Bourdieu P (1996) Razões práticas: sobre a teoria da ação. Papirus, Campinas

Bourdieu P (2004) Os usos sociais da ciência: por uma sociologia clínica do campo científi-co. UNESP, São Paulo

Caballero LG (2018) Informação de pesquisa clínica e a interface com o aplicativo de gestão para hospitais universitários: desafios éticos e regulatórios. Dissertação de Mestrado orientada por Márcia Santana Fernandes; co-orientada por Rafael Leal Zimmer. Programa de Pós-Graduação Stricto Sensu, Mestrado Profissional em Pesquisa Clínica do Hospital de Clínicas de Porto Alegre, Porto Alegre

Chomsky N (2015) Aspects of the theory of syntax. The MIT Press, Cambridge

Comte-Sponville A (1996) Pequeno tratado das grandes virtudes. Martins Fontes, São Paulo

de Oliveira Ascensão J (2009) Pessoa, direitos fundamentais e direito da personalidade. Rev Fac Direito Univ Lisb 50:9–31

European Commission (2020) White paper – on artificial intelligence – a European approach to excel-lence and trust. https://ec.europa.eu/info/publications/white-paper-artificial-intelligence-european-approach-excellence-and-trust_en. Accessed 24 Oct 2021

European Union (2021) Study on ehealth, interoperability of health data and artificial intelligence for health and care in the European Union. Publications Office of the European Union, Luxembourg

Evidence-Based Medicine Working Group (1992) Evidence-based medicine. A new approach to teaching the practice of medicine. JAMA 268:2420–2425

Fernandes MS (2019) Privacidade, sociedade da informação e Big Data. In: Benetti G, Corrêa AR, Fernandes MS, Nitschke GM, Pargendler M, Varela LB (eds) Direito, cultura e método - leituras da obra de Judith Martins-Costa. GZ Editora, Rio de Janeiro, pp 182–210

Fernandes MS, Goldim JR (2019) A sistematização de dados e informações em saúde em um contexto de big data e blockchain. In: Lucca N, de Lima CRP, Simão A, Dezem RMMM (eds) Direito e Internet IV. Quartier Latin, São Paulo, pp 333–357

Floridi L (2019) What the near future of artificial intelligence could be. Philos Technol 32:1–15

Floridi L (2020) What the near future of artificial intelligence could be. In: Burr C, Milano S (eds) The 2019 yearbook of the digital ethics lab. Springer International Publishing, Cham, pp 127–142

Floridi L, Cowls J, Beltrametti M, Chatila R, Chazerand P, Dignum V, Luetge C, Madelin R, Pagallo U, Rossi F, Schafer B, Valcke P, Vayena E (2018) AI4People-an ethical framework for a good AI society: opportunities, risks, principles, and recommendations. Minds Mach 28:689–707

Gocklin B (2023) Guidelines for responsible content creation with generative AI [Internet]. Digital Transformation. pp 1–7. Available from: http://contently.com/2023/01/03/guidelines-for-responsible-content-creation-with-generative-ai/. Accessed 9 Feb 2023

Goldim JR (2006a) A avaliação de projetos de pesquisa: aspectos éticos, científicos, legais, regulatórios e éticos. Rev HCPA 26:83–86

Goldim JR (2006b) Bioética: origens e complexidade. Rev HCPA 26:86–92

Han BC (2015) Sociedade do cansaço. Vozes, Petrópolis

Han BC (2021) Infokratie: Digitalisierung und die Krise der Demokratie. Mathes & Seitz Verlag, Berlin

Humboldt W (1836) Über die Verschiedenheit des menschlichen Sprachbaues: und ihren Einfluss auf die geistige Entwicklung des Menschengeschlechts. Druckerei der Königlichen Akademie der Wissenschaften, Berlin

Jonas H (1994) Ética, medicina e técnica. Vega, Lisboa

Jonas H (2006) O princípio responsabilidade: ensaio de uma ética para a civilização tecnológica. Contraponto, Rio de Janeiro

Kemp P (2005) The globalization of the world. In: Kemp P (ed) Philosophical problems today: world and worlshood. Springer, Berlin, pp 15–28

Kemp P, Rendtorff JD (2008) The barcelona declaration. Towards an integrated approach to basic ethical principles. Synth Philos 23(2):239–251

Kulynych J, Greely HT (2017) Clinical genomics, big data, and electronic medical records: reconciling patient rights with research when privacy and science collide. J Law Biosci 4:94–132

Levinas E (1961) Totalité et infini. Martinus Nijhoff, La Haye

Levinas E (1991) Entre nous: essais sur le penser-à-l'autre. Grasser & Fasquelle, Paris

Lévy P (2022) Inteligência Artificial produz "monstruosidades éticas". Revista Fórum [Internet]; pp 1–7. Available from: https://revistaforum.com.br/ciencia-e-tecnologia/2022/12/27/inteligncia-artificial-produz-monstruosidades-eticas-diz-pierre-levy-129333.html

Lusted LB (1955) Medical electronics. N Engl J Med 252:580–585

Manyika J, Chui M, Brown B, Bughin J, Dobbs R, Roxburgh C, Byers AH (2011) Big Data: the next frontier for innovation, competition and productivity. McKinsey Global Institute, New York

Marcuse H (2009) A responsabilidade da Ciência. Sci Stud 7:159–164

Martins-Costa J (2015) A Boa-Fé no direito privado: critérios para sua aplicação. Marcial Pons, São Paulo

McCarthy J, Minsky ML, Rochester N, Shannon CE (2006) A proposal for the dartmouth summer research project on artificial intelligence. AI Mag 27:12

Mittelstadt BD, Floridi L (2016) The ethics of Big Data: current and foreseeable issues in biomedical contexts. Sci Eng Ethics 22:303–341

Monod J (1970) Le hasard et la nécessité. Seuil, Paris

Norori N, Hu Q, Aellen FM, Faraci FD, Tzovara A (2021) Addressing bias in big data and AI for health care: a call for open science. Patterns 2. http://creativecommons.org/licenses/by/4.0/. Accessed 2 Sept 2022

O'connell M (2017) Art as "artificial stupidity". PhD thesis, University of Sussex, Brighton

O'Neill O (2004) Accountability, trust and informed consent in medical practice and research. Clin Med 4:269–276

OECD, The World Bank (2020) Health at a glance: Latin America and the Caribbean 2020. OECD Publishing, Paris

Patrão-Neves MDC (2021) Política do medo: amigos ou inimigos? Privacidade e segurança em tempos de medo global. In: Política do medo ou o mundo de hoje entre privacidade e segurança. E-book -Universidade Católica Editora, Lisboa. Acessível em https://www.uceditora.ucp.pt/pt/colloquia/3089-colloquia-1.html

Ramesh AN, Kambhampati C, Monson JRT, Drew PJ (2004) Artificial intelligence in medicine. Ann R Coll Surg Engl 86:334–338

Roehrs A, da Costa CA, da Rosa Righi R, da Silva VF, Goldim JR, Schmidt DC (2019) Analyzing the performance of a blockchain-based personal health record implementation. J Biomed Inform 92:103140

Ropohl G (1981) Technik - ein problem der philosophie? Philos Nat 18:413

Singer P (1993) Practical ethics. New York, Cambridge

The Hammond Times (1957) Work with new electronic "brains" opens field for army math experts. The Hammond Times. Nov 10, p 65

Turing AM (1950) Computing machinery and intelligence. Mind LIX(236):433–460

União Europeia (2012) eHealth interoperability framawork study. https://publications.europa.eu/en/publication-detail/-/publication/2bc03deb-afd8-4c2a-a394-16c039232b1e/language-en/format-PDF/source-95947333. Accessed 2 Sept 2022

União Europeia (2015) Decisão (UE) 2015/2240 do parlamento Europeu e do conselho. https://eur-lex.europa.eu/legal-content/PT/TXT/PDF/?uri=CELEX:32015D2240&from=en. Accessed 2 Sept 2022

Vasques AS (2000) Ética. Civilização Brasileira, Rio de Janeiro

Weber M (1978) Economy and Society: an outline of interpretive sociology. University of California, Berkeley

Wooton D (2015) The invention of Science – a new history of the scientific revolution. Harper Collins Publishers, New York

Zur O, Walker A (2019) On digital immigrants and digital natives. Zur Institute, Sebastopol

Open Access This chapter is licensed under the terms of the Creative Commons Attribution 4.0 International License (http://creativecommons.org/licenses/by/4.0/), which permits use, sharing, adaptation, distribution and reproduction in any medium or format, as long as you give appropriate credit to the original author(s) and the source, provide a link to the Creative Commons license and indicate if changes were made.

The images or other third party material in this chapter are included in the chapter's Creative Commons license, unless indicated otherwise in a credit line to the material. If material is not included in the chapter's Creative Commons license and your intended use is not permitted by statutory regulation or exceeds the permitted use, you will need to obtain permission directly from the copyright holder.

The Autonomous AI Physician: Medical Ethics and Legal Liability

Mindy Nunez Duffourc and Dominick S. Giovanniello

Abstract Artificial intelligence (AI) is currently capable of autonomously performing acts that constitute medical practice, including diagnosis, prognosis, therapeutic decision making, and image analysis, but should AI be considered a medical practitioner? Complicating this question is that fact that the ethical, regulatory, and legal regimes that govern medical practice and medical malpractice are not designed for nonhuman doctors. This chapter first suggests ethical parameters for the Autonomous AI Physician's practice of medicine, focusing on the field of pathology. Second, we identify ethical and legal issues that arise from the Autonomous AI Physician's practice of medicine, including safety, reliability, transparency, fairness, and accountability. Third, we discuss the potential application of various existing legal and regulatory regimes to govern the Autonomous AI Physician. Finally, we conclude that all stakeholders in the development and use of the Autonomous AI Physician have an obligation to ensure that AI is implemented in a safe and responsible way.

1 Introduction

Artificial intelligence (AI) generally describes, "the capability of a computer program to perform tasks or reasoning processes that we usually associate with the intelligence of a human being (Lupton 2018)." Although it is unlikely that AI will completely replace human physicians anytime soon, it is now possible for AI to independently perform tasks that fall squarely within the scope of medical practice, most notably diagnosis, prognosis, and consultation in response to individualized

---

M. N. Duffourc (✉)
(Maastricht) Law and Tech Lab, Maastricht University, Maastricht, Netherlands

D. S. Giovanniello
Northwell Health, Anatomic/Clinical Pathology, Blood Banking/Transfusion Medicine
Hauppauge, New York, NY, USA

© The Author(s) 2024
H. Sousa Antunes et al. (eds.), *Multidisciplinary Perspectives on Artificial Intelligence and the Law*, Law, Governance and Technology Series 58,
https://doi.org/10.1007/978-3-031-41264-6_11

medical information.[1] In April 2018, the U.S. Food and Drug Administration (FDA) approved IDx-DR, the first artificially intelligent device capable autonomously diagnosing patients with diabetic retinopathy without the input of a human doctor (U.S. Food & Drug Administration 2018). In Europe, Oxipit, an AI capable of autonomously producing "final reports for healthy patient X-ray studies" received a CE mark, clearing the way for its use in clinical practice (Oxipit 2022). Deep learning (DL) is the subset of AI most likely to produce technologies, like IDx-DR and Oxipit, capable of autonomous medical decision making by training machines with artificial neural networks to analyze large amounts of medical and health data to detect patterns.[2]

The introduction of artificial intelligence using DL in modern medicine holds promise for improving the accuracy, efficacy, and efficiency of medical diagnosis, prognosis, therapeutic decision making, image analysis, and patient monitoring (Chang et al. 2019; Jackson et al. 2021). On the other hand, it also introduces a host of ethical and legal concerns surrounding safety, transparency, bias and discrimination, data privacy, consent and autonomy, and responsibility and accountability (Lawry et al. 2018; Gerke et al. 2020; Jackson et al. 2021). Further amplifying these concerns is the fact that the existing ethical and legal regimes that govern medical practice and medical malpractice are not designed for nonhuman doctors.

Pathology, as a data-rich subspecialty of medicine, is a hotbed for the development and implementation of medical AI (Chauhan and Gullapalli 2021). As a result, Jackson et al. (2021) call on pathologists to provide both developmental as well as regulatory and ethical leadership for the uptake of AI in clinical and laboratory medicine (Jackson et al. 2021). This chapter combines the medical and legal expertise of its authors to recommend parameters for the Autonomous AI Physician and identify the ethical and legal issues that arise from the practice of medicine by the Autonomous AI Physician. Following this, the authors identify and suggest the potential application of concepts from the various regulatory and legal regimes that currently govern medical practice and medical malpractice to the future practice of medicine by the Autonomous AI physician.[3]

---

[1] Lawry (2018) opining that AI will not replace doctors.

[2] See Gerke (2020) defining machine learning and deep learning. See also Duffourc (2020) reviewing various definitions of medical practice in the US and Europe and noting that diagnosis and treatment fall within the scope of medical practice under most definitions.

[3] *See Generally* on the of the imitation of humans by Robots II.1—M C Patrão Neves and A B Almeida—Before and Beyond Artificial Intelligence: Opportunities and Challenges; III.2—B A Ribeiro, H Coelho, A E Ferreira and J Branquinho—Metacognition, Accountability and Legal Personhood of AI.

2 Artificial Intelligence in Pathology

Pathology uses a data-intensive, complex, and comprehensive workflow to diagnose and study disease processes (Pallua et al. 2020). Both anatomic and clinical pathological findings and data heavily inform diagnosis, prognosis, and therapeutic recommendations of all medical specialties (Chauhan and Gullapalli 2021). Digitization has already improved workflows in pathology by allowing virtual microscopic analysis of whole slide imaging, which has proven to be comparable to the conventional microscope, long considered the gold-standard for detecting pathological changes in tissues and cells (Pallua et al. 2020). The introduction of AI into this morphologic analysis promises to further improve accuracy by reducing diagnostic inconsistency caused by human observer variability (Chang et al. 2019). For example, AI can be trained with digitized images and associated diagnoses rendered by human pathologists to analyze new images for pathological patterns that lead to quicker and more accurate diagnoses (Jackson et al. 2021). Recently, AI has proven that it can outperform human physicians in even more complex tasks, including predicting the stage and grade of lung cancer, using DL techniques (Chang et al. 2019).

Pathology's digitization combined with its generation of large amounts of medical data make the field, along with radiology, a "prime target[] for disruptive innovation of health care AI applications over the next decade (Chauhan and Gullapalli 2021)." Allen articulates three progressive levels of AI integration in pathology (Allen 2019). The first level keeps pathologists *in the workflow loop* by integrating AI as one of the many diagnostic tools that pathologists use for medical decision making (Allen 2019). The second level describes AI that can independently render pathologist reports but keeps human pathologists *on the workflow loop* to provide quality oversight for AI-generated medical decisions (Allen 2019). The third level of AI involvement *removes human pathologists from the workflow loop* which is entirely controlled by autonomous AI (Allen 2019).

Other medical experts doubt a future in which AI completely replaces human pathologists noting that AI has yet to master the unique ability of the human brain to synthesize information across various sectors of knowledge (Chauhan and Gullapalli 2021). Though Chauhan and Gullapalli (2021) admit that the future role of AI in pathology is unpredictable, they dare to make one prediction: "The need for a wary and cautious eye on the quality and process control by pathologists is unlikely to be automated anytime soon (Chauhan and Gullapalli 2021)." Pathologists in clinical laboratories are also responsible for the generation and safekeeping of "one of the largest single sources of objective and structured patient-level data within the healthcare system (Jackson et al. 2021)." As a result, pathologists are not only well-positioned but, as the custodians of highly coveted medical data, ethically obligated to help usher in a new age of AI.[4]

---

[4] See Chauhan and Gullapalli (2021) noting that pathologists are the custodians of patient data that will drive innovation and debates surrounding medical AI.

3 The Autonomous AI Physician: Parameters

While the concept of a self-sufficient robot doctor may be the stuff of science fiction, AI is already capable of autonomously practicing medicine, including diagnosis, prognosis, and provision of treatment recommendations.[5] Deep learning allows AI to mimic human brain function to independently process data and reach decisions using algorithmic reasoning that continuously improves as the AI collects more data (Ahmad et al. 2021). Although AI manufacturers may attempt to describe AI as "cognitive computing" or medical support tools, the reality is that AI can now independently consult millions of pages of literature to suggest individualized medical treatments (Chung and Zink 2018), analyze and interpret radiology images and pathology slides (Griffin 2021; Oxipit 2022), diagnose and stage cancer (Ahmad et al. 2021), and predict patient outcomes (Ahmad et al. 2021). And with investment in healthcare AI outperforming any other sector in the global economy, the capability of medical AI will only continue to grow (Griffin 2021). Some futurists predict artificial general intelligence to be a reality by 2029 (Chung and Zink 2018).

Now is the time to set parameters for the autonomous practice of medicine by AI. While recognizing that AI may be able to "fill much of the gap between human performance and perfection (Jorstad 2020)," it will never be capable of providing the integral human components of medical practice, "like touch, compassion, and empathy (Griffin 2021)." Griffin explains that: "Medicine is not purely a science that can be managed with statistics, mathematics, and computer algorithms, and overreliance on AI may lead to harm in instances when human compassion, human touch, or human interpretation of data context is necessary (Griffin 2021)." From the perspective of diagnostic pathology, Ahmad, et al. note that, "[t]he diagnostic process is too complicated and diverse to be trusted to hard-wired algorithms alone. It is hoped that AI and human pathologists will be natural cooperators, not natural competitors (Ahmad et al. 2021)." As recognized by the EU's Special Committee on Artificial Intelligence in a Digital Age, human oversight of autonomous AI medical decisions is indispensable (European Parliament Special Committee of Artificial Intelligence in a Digital Age 2021). As a result, the Autonomous AI Physician, as used in this Chapter, describes artificial intelligence that is capable of performing acts ordinarily considered medical practice (diagnosis, prognosis, development of a treatment plan, etc.) using algorithmic reasoning to make medical decisions *without a human involved in that medical decision-making process.* Additionally, the Autonomous AI Physician should currently not stand alone as the sole medical decision maker for an individual patient but should instead be situated within a larger treatment team that includes human medical practitioners.

---

[5] Lawry (2018) opining that AI will not replace doctors.

4 Ethical and Legal Implications of the Autonomous AI Physician

The proliferation of AI technologies capable of performing tasks typically reserved for human medical professionals can translate to cheaper, more accessible, and higher quality healthcare (See Jackson et al. 2021). In addition to diagnostic AI ranging from IDx-DR's ophthalmologic diagnoses to Oxipit's radiology reports, AI applications in medicine can read eye scans, predict early-stage coronary artery disease, and detect cardiac arrest over the phone in real time (Gerke et al. 2020). Gains realized by innovative AI technologies in medicine; however, do not come without risks to patient safety and privacy. As a result, medical, legal, and data experts call for robust ethical and regulatory oversight of AI in the health sector to ensure that new technologies are implemented fairly, safety, and securely (Lawry et al. 2018; Allen 2019; Jackson et al. 2021). Although regulatory agencies are now attempting to address AI risks, the early "development of AI, broadly speaking, has occurred substantially outside of any regulatory environment (Allen 2019)."

Regulating the development of AI in any sector is inhibited by the "pacing problem," which describes the proclivity of technological innovation to disengage from regulatory regimes and social norms that lag behind the development of new technology.[6] Additionally, innovation in the tech industry is driven by values markedly different than those in the healthcare industry (Jackson et al. 2021). "Mov[ing] fast and break[ing] things" doesn't exactly translate to an acceptable patient safety strategy.[7] Still, successful ethical, regulatory, and legal strategies for guiding the implementation of AI in medical practice will need to balance the benefits of encouraging innovation in the health sector with the risks to patient safety and privacy (Allen 2019). Interestingly, the tech industry, including AI researchers and data-scientists, have initially led discussions surrounding the importance of ethical and responsible AI, but experts warn that the industry in charge of developing AI cannot alone guide the ethical implementation of the same technology (Chauhan and Gullapalli 2021). Allen opines that accomplishing such a task "is likely to require an unprecedented level of governmental, professional societal, and industrial cooperation and trust-building (Allen 2019)."

Though the ethical and legal aspects of integrating autonomous AI in medicine cannot be neatly separated, we nevertheless organize the ethical discussion considering the core principals of medical ethics—autonomy, beneficence, nonmalfeasance, and justice—to conclude that ethical AI must be transparent, reliable, safe, and free of bias, while organizing the legal discussion around data privacy and liability for patient harm.[8]

---

[6] Allen (2019) describing the pacing problem. Jackson (2021) noting that AI applications have developed faster than social norms and regulations have been able to evolve in response.

[7] Jackson (2021) quoting Mark Zuckerberg.

[8] Jackson (2021) listing foundational principles of medical ethics.

4.1 Ethical Consideration: Transparency

The requirement that medical AI maintain a level of transparency sufficient to ensure patient autonomy is twofold. First, AI developers should be transparent about the use of patient data for training medical AI systems (Jackson et al. 2021). Second, patients should have sufficient information about the use of AI in clinical care, including the risks and benefits of AI-based medical decisions as well as information about how those decisions are made (Jackson et al. 2021).

The question of whether patients need to give permission for AI developers to use health data generated during their medical treatment depends on the jurisdiction's rules governing disclosure of personal health information. In the United States, because patient data is typically deidentified before being shared with AI developers for training new technologies, the primary law protecting health data, the Health Insurance Portability and Accountability Act (HIPAA), does not prevent disclosure (Jackson et al. 2021). Jackson, et al. argue that the risk of reidentification of patient data by cross-referencing multiple data sets mandates that a patient's consent be obtained prior to using their health data for training AI (Jackson et al. 2021). This consent requirement, should it be recognized, cannot be satisfied by obtaining patient consent for processing data for individual medical treatment and payment, but instead requires additional consent (Jackson et al. 2021). In Europe, the General Data Protection Regulation (GDPR) generally requires explicit patient consent for a specifically identified purpose before an individual patient's health data is processed for any reason (The European Parliament and the Council of the European Union 2016, Art. 9). Although the GDPR does not regulate "anonymized data," which can no longer be connected to an identifiable person, it does restrict the use of data that has a reasonable likelihood of being re-identified (The European Parliament and the Council of the European Union 2016, Recital 26).

In addition to having control over their health data, patients should also be informed about the role of AI-sourced decision making in their medical care. When and to what extent patients are informed about the use of AI in making diagnoses and therapeutic decisions is unsettled, leaving medical and legal experts concerned about infringement upon a patient's ability to exercise the autonomy needed to make informed decisions about their treatment (Gerke et al. 2020). Minimally, a patient should be informed when AI is used to generate diagnoses or treatment recommendations including an explanation of any risks attendant with accepting AI-sourced medical decisions. Ideally, patients should also be given a plain-language explanation of how the AI reached its conclusions; however, the reality is that AI technology that uses DL can conceal algorithmic decision-making criteria from even the AI's developer creating the problem of opaque "black-box" AI, which describes the inability of humans to understand the basis for the AI's decision. (Chauhan and Gullapalli 2021). Nevertheless, disclosures about data used to train the AI as well as

The Autonomous AI Physician: Medical Ethics and Legal Liability 213

the AI's pre-market performance statistics should be given to patients whose care is influenced by AI medical decision making.[9]

4.2 Ethical Considerations: Reliability and Safety

The "black-box" problem also presents an impediment to ensuring that AI-sourced medical decision making is reliable and safe for patients because it conceals the process by which the AI system reached a decision, preventing analysis and oversight of the decision-making process. Some experts argue that the accuracy of the AI's decisions is what matters regardless of the hidden process it used to reach those decisions (Gerke et al. 2020). Although, the algorithmic functions used in the AI's analysis of data are not, and cannot possibly be, completely transparent with "black-box" AI, developers must still provide crucial information about how the AI was trained and potential biases of the software for independent oversight and analysis (Gerke et al. 2020). Typically, the quality of the training data given to the AI will directly correlate to the quality of the AI's medical decisions (Gerke et al. 2020).

However, even when AI produces technically reliable decisions based upon the data it received, those decisions may be clinically unreliable and threaten patient safety (Lawry et al. 2018). While DL can enable an AI to develop and apply rules to detect patterns using large data sets, AI still cannot exercise clinical reasoning of a human doctor to determine the difference between causation and correlation (Lawry et al. 2018). For example, an AI system trained to triage patients with pneumonia determined that asthmatic patients were low risk because they had better recovery outcomes following a pneumonia diagnosis than the general population (Caruana et al. 2015). While the system was trained to consider underlying risk in its decision making, it failed to recognize that patients with a history of asthma, and considered high-risk pneumonia patients, received a higher level of care, thereby producing better outcomes. This inability of AI to properly recognize cause and effect can make the system unreliable, and therefore, unsafe (Lawry et al. 2018).[10]

---

[9] *See Generally* on 'Black-Box' effect II.2—E Magrani and P G F Silva—The Ethical and Legal Challenges of Recommender Systems Driven by Artificial Intelligence; II.8—R Nogaroli and J L M Faleiros Júnior—Ethical challenges of artificial intelligence in medicine and the triple semantic dimensions of algorithmic opacity with its repercussions to patient consent and medical liability.

[10] *See also* II.8—R Nogaroli and J L M Faleiros Júnior—Ethical challenges of artificial intelligence in medicine and the triple semantic dimensions of algorithmic opacity with its repercussions to patient consent and medical liability.

4.3 Ethical Consideration: Bias

Patient safety can also be compromised by systemic biases that manifest in AI medical decision making. Despite being nonhuman, AI can express subjective biases as a result of human-generated algorithms and data used to develop the AI (Chauhan and Gullapalli 2021). Algorithmic bias describes the systemic bias of AI decisions that reflect the human biases of the AI's programmer (Nelson 2019). Algorithmic bias can be introduced through, "the data algorithm authors choose to use, as well as their data blending methods, model construction practices, and how results are applied and interpreted (Nelson 2019)." Chauhan and Gullapalli explain how AI algorithms with a "tunable variable" require researchers to make conscious choices that present an entry point for biases that can have "cascading effects downstream."

Another source of AI bias comes from the data used to train the AI, which consists primarily of data from electronic medical and billing records. Nelson describes the data used to train AI as, "the data that we have as opposed to the data that is 'right (Nelson 2019).'" First, because data in electronic health records is not generated for the specific analytic functions of modern AI technology, but rather for medical treatment and billing, it reflects systemic biases—including racial, gender, geographic, and economic biases—that operate to further disadvantage underrepresented populations (Nelson 2019). For example, black women have historically been, and continue to be, victims of obstetric racism and subjected to unnecessary medical procedures (Campbell 2021). When data used to train AI contain bias, the AI will generate biased medical decisions in the absence of adequate measures designed to both identify and eliminate such bias (Lawry et al. 2018).

An overarching bias in health data used to train AI is that it comes from populations who have access to healthcare and is typically not representative of minorities and other marginalized subpopulations (Jackson et al. 2021). This problem is further exacerbated when wearable technologies source AI training data (Lawry et al. 2018). As a result, data used to train AI suffers from category imbalance and under specification, both of which can make the AI's decisions unreliable and unsafe when applied to members of a minority or underrepresented population (Chauhan and Gullapalli 2021).

4.4 Legal Considerations: Data Privacy

Though most data used to train AI come from electronic health records, other sources of training data include purchasing records, income data, criminal records, and social media (Hoffman 2021). Third-party access to such data can reach far beyond the harm associated with an initial privacy violation to impact employment and credit decisions and insurance access and rates (Jackson et al. 2021). Additional negative impacts of third-party access to health data can include social stigma and psychological harm (Hoffman 2021). Hoffman notes that AI predictions regarding future medical conditions, including cognitive decline, substance abuse, and even suicide can cause both discrimination and psychological harm for individuals who are not offered counseling to manage the impacts of such findings (Hoffman 2021). Although the GDPR offers more protection to individuals in the European Union than HIPAA offers to Americans, the cross-border capabilities of AI require international regulations to protect personal data used by AI developers (Gerke et al. 2020).

4.5 Legal Consideration: Liability

Though AI is currently capable of independently performing tasks, like diagnosis, that fall squarely within the practice of medicine, a clear legal framework to directly address legal liability for patient injuries caused by AI-based medical decision making does not exist (Lupton 2018). The introduction of AI into clinical decision-making upsets the traditional notions of negligence by asking questions like: Can a computer be unreasonable? (Chung and Zink 2018). The European Commission (EC) has recently introduced proposed Directives to govern liability for AI-caused harm generally (European Commission 2022a (PLD); European Commission 2022b (AILD)). However, these proposed Directives still do not provide a clear liability framework for medical technologies like the Autonomous AI Physician in cases where the AI's algorithmic medical decision making is designed to be unpredictable and opaque and cannot be sufficiently connected to either (1) a defect in the AI's creation or (2) human fault (or negligence) as judged under existing law (Duffourc and Gerke 2023).

Currently, there are several existing legal frameworks within which courts might assign liability for injuries caused by an autonomous AI physician, including strict liability, enterprise liability, vicarious liability, negligence, and no-fault liability. Some legal scholars question the extent to which AI-inflicted damages can be compensated by machines, which have no financial assets (Allen 2019). Chung, who advocates for legal personhood for AI, argues that risks can be assessed and insured to compensate injured patients within the existing medical malpractice and products liability frameworks (Chung and Zink 2018). To some extent, a negligence-based regime can deter bad behavior by only punishing actions that are found to fall below a medically acceptable standard of care. On the other hand, a strict or no-fault liability regime can force the industries responsible for creating and employing AI in healthcare to absorb the risk of injury caused by that technology. Applying vicarious liability or corporate negligence law can shift liability to the institutions who "hire" AI and operate under causes of action like negligent hiring or negligent credentialling (Gerke et al. 2020).

The answer to legal liability for autonomous AI probably lies in the combination of several existing legal approaches depending on the cause of the injury. The uncertainty surrounding the legal liability situation for autonomous AI in healthcare will likely inhibit the uptake of emerging AI technologies, which if sufficiently regulated, can improve patient care (Lupton 2018; European Commission 2022b (AILD)). As a result, legal scholars in the U.S. and Europe call upon lawmakers to provide clarity regarding liability for medical injuries caused by AI (Lupton 2018; Gerke et al. 2020).

5 Regulating the Autonomous AI Physician

Proper regulation of the Autonomous AI Physician through a careful combination of governmental, industry, and legal rules and regulations must address the ethical and legal concerns identified in order to promote the successful integration of safe, reliable, and fair autonomous AI in medicine.[11] To guide the development of AI in medicine, all stakeholders must collaborate to develop both ethical norms to govern the creation, implementation, and maintenance of AI as well as legal and regulatory mechanisms to ensure accountability for ethical violations and responsibility for injuries caused by the Autonomous AI Physician.[12]

Robust industry and governmental guidance and regulations that aim to provide transparency, safety, reliability, fairness, and privacy are the first line of defense for patients of the Autonomous AI Physician. However, it is inevitable that patients will incur damages because of autonomous AI integration into healthcare. When damages manifest, the legal system must ensure accountability and compensation for injured patients. Because the Autonomous AI Physician is both algorithm and doctor, it should be regulated under regimes that both ensure ethical development and implementation of the software and hold it accountable as a self-learning autonomous decision maker. Since autonomous AI are "educated" and "trained" by software developers and engineers who write algorithms, regulatory bodies that test, approve, and oversee, the quality of the AI software and its development process are akin to medical boards that test, license, and oversee the practice of physicians. On the other hand, liability regimes that govern damages caused by products are generally not suited to encompass liability for damages caused by the Autonomous AI Physician. Instead, a combination of medical negligence, organizational negligence, vicarious liability, and enterprise liability are better equipped to handle patient damages caused by autonomous AI decisions, with products liability governing the small portion of cases that involve damage caused by the AI's design and physical components.

---

[11] See Ahmad (2021) discussing the importance of defining correct frameworks for the application of AI.

[12] Jackson (2021) opining that all stakeholders must collaborate to develop and enforce ethical norms.

5.1 Healthcare Industry Regulation

Medical experts can help ensure the ethical and safe development of autonomous AI in healthcare. Some medical professional and regulatory organizations have already begun to tackle this challenge. In the U.S., the American Medical Association seeks to "[p]romote the development of thoughtfully designed, high-quality, clinically validated health care AI," which includes AI conformity with best practices, transparency, reproducibility, fairness, privacy, and security (American Medical Association 2018). In the U.K., the National Health Service seeks to prevent unintended harm caused by data-driven technology in healthcare, including AI, by providing a framework for AI developers that addresses, "issues such as transparency, accountability, safety, efficacy, explicability, fairness, equity, and bias (Department of Health and Social Care and National Health Service 2021)." The Royal Australian and New Zealand College of Radiologists (RANZCR) drafted *AI Standards of Practice* to guide the development, regulation, and integration of AI into radiology practice according to similar ethical principles (RANZCR 2020). The Digital Pathology Association has established an AI/ML taskforce that seeks to aid the development of artificial intelligence and machine learning in pathology by providing its members with information and resources regarding, "regulatory insight, best practices, scholarly activity, vendor relationships, and ethics (Digital Pathology Association 2020)."

At the provider level, healthcare organizations can implement several practices to help achieve the safe, ethical, and accountable AI envisioned by these professional societies. First, organizations should establish an institutional review board (IRB) to assess the scientific value, validity, and reliability of medical AI, the risks to patients' health, autonomy, and privacy, and fairness and accountability associated with using AI to provide patient care (Jackson et al. 2021). Second, organizations should adopt policies, procedures, and protocols that clearly delineate levels of responsibility for ensuring that AI implementation reflects values driving the IRB's assessments (Chauhan and Gullapalli 2021). These protocols should be continuously reviewed and updated to "reflect the current state of knowledge in healthcare practices (Chauhan and Gullapalli 2021)." One practical way to incorporate ethical values surrounding medical AI is to write them into transparent contracts with AI developers and vendors, which can include provisions regarding data quality, privacy, and sharing as well as mechanisms for oversight and audits of AI performance (Jackson et al. 2021).

Another practical recommendation is the creation of patient-facing Health Information Counselors (HICs) to provide patients with information regarding the use of AI in their healthcare, including AI performance, risks, benefits, and costs (Jorstad 2020). HICs would be a new class of interdisciplinary healthcare professionals who are trained to understand the technological, analytical, and medical capacities of autonomous AI as well as the clinical and financial impacts of an individual patient's care (Jorstad 2020). Jorstad cautions that while HICs "might prove an invaluable resource as a mediary between patients and medical professionals," under current liability standards, physicians must still understand and explain the risks of medical AI necessary to obtain informed consent (Jorstad 2020). As such, practical implementation of HICs will "require broader structural and policy changes (Jorstad 2020)."

If the healthcare industry takes a proactive role in implementing ethical AI in patient care, it can also guide the development of AI regulatory regimes to prevent misregulation, which could act as a barrier to the continued uptake of future AI technology in healthcare, including the Autonomous AI Physician (See Jorstad 2020).

5.2 Government Regulation

Governmental regulation of AI falls broadly under two spheres: safety and data privacy and security.

5.2.1 Safety Regulation

Government regulation of the Autonomous AI Physician to ensure its safety is a complex endeavor. The self-learning capability of autonomous AI that makes it a valuable asset to healthcare delivery is also the feature that makes it difficult to regulate. Current government regulatory systems were designed for static medical devices and products, not the ever-changing deep learning Autonomous AI Physician (Jorstad 2020). Additionally, as Jorstad points out, AI does not have the historical benefit of proving itself through decades of peer review, scientific research, and clinical trials, which underly traditional government regulation in the health sector (Jorstad 2020). Instead, "deep learning has turned the scientific process on its end," as Ahmad et al. explains, by using data to generate, rather than prove, hypotheses (Ahmad et al. 2021). As a result, regulatory bodies need to develop a more dynamic approach to pre-market authorization and post-market monitoring to ensure ethical and responsible adoption of autonomous AI in the healthcare industry. Lawry, et al. proposes a regulatory regime that includes: "systematic evaluation of the quality and suitability of the data and models used to train AI-driven systems; adequate explanation of the system operation including disclosure of potential limitations or inadequacies in the training data; medical specialist involvement in the design and operation process; evaluation of the role of medical professional input and control in the deployment of the systems; and a robust feedback mechanism from users to developers (Lawry et al. 2018)."

Regulating "moving target" AI that involves self-learning algorithms that continue to change after placed in the healthcare market requires an approach focused on the quality of the development process pre-market and continued performance monitoring post-market (Homeyer et al. 2021). In the U.S., the Food and Drug Administration has already introduced a pilot certification program to streamline

The Autonomous AI Physician: Medical Ethics and Legal Liability

approval for software as a medical device (SaMD) (U.S. Food & Drug Administration 2021). The pilot program uses a "Total Product Lifecycle" approach, which consists of pre-market evaluation of companies that develop AI as well as continuous post-market product performance oversight of SaMD (U.S. Food & Drug Administration 2021). Under the program, a company can achieve "precertified status" if it can, "establish trust that they have a culture of quality and organizational excellence such that they can develop high quality SaMD products, leverages transparency of organizational excellence and product performance across the entire lifecycle of SaMD, utilizes a tailored streamlined premarket review, and leverages unique postmarket opportunities available in software to verify the continued safety, effectiveness, and performance of SaMD in the real-world (U.S. Food & Drug Administration 2021)."

In Europe, the EC's proposed AI Act[13] attempts to provide uniform governance of AI to ensure, "a high level of protection of health, safety and fundamental rights," and "free movement of AI-based goods and services cross-border (European Commission 2021)." The proposal classifies AI used in health care as a high-risk medical device that must comply with existing regulations, for example the Medical Device Regulation (MDR) and the Regulation on in vitro diagnostic medical devices (IVDR), as well as the AI-specific requirements contained in the proposal (European Commission 2021). The IVDR controls the certification process for AI in pathology and already requires an assessment of technical development, performance, and a post-market surveillance plan (European Commission 2017). The new proposal imposes additional "requirements of high quality data, documentation and traceability, transparency, human oversight, accuracy and robustness (U.S. Food & Drug Administration 2021)." While the proposed AI Act is designed to establish public trust in technology, some experts view the new proposal as overregulation that will require duplicate certifications under various EU regulations and stifle innovation in the market (Taylor 2021). Indeed, striking the delicate balance between protecting patients and encouraging innovation is essential to the successful development and implementation of the Autonomous AI Physician.

5.2.2 Data Regulation

Regulators must also attempt to protect personal data used to develop and train AI. The framework for regulating health data in the U.S. is insufficient to address the ethical and legal concerns regarding data privacy and security raised by the

---

[13] *See also* on AI Act I.3—P U Lima and A Paiva—Autonomous and Intelligent Robots: Social, Legal and Ethical Issues; II.5—A T Fonseca, E V Sequeira and L B Xavier—Liability for AI Driven Systems; III.5—D Durães, P M Freitas and P Novais—The Relevance of Deepfakes in the Administration of Criminal Justice; III.8—A Keller, C Martins Pereira and M Lucas Pires—The European Union's approach to Artificial Intelligence and the Challenge of Financial Systemic Risk; III.9—J C Abreu—The "Artificial Intelligence Act" Proposal on European e-Justice Domains Through the Lens of User-focused, User-friendly and Effective Judicial Protection Principles.

Autonomous AI physician. On the other hand, Europe has taken a more proactive approach to regulating big data, which includes protecting health data of EU citizens from exploitation by the tech industry.

American legal scholars have highlighted HIPAA's inability to adequately protect individual health data in the United States (Gerke et al. 2020; Hoffman 2021). HIPAA's failure to regulate data sharing by entities other than healthcare providers and insurers is the law's most glaring weakness when it comes to data privacy. For example, technology companies are free to share individual health data for research or commercial purposes because they are not considered "covered entities" under the law (Gerke et al. 2020). HIPAA also fails to regulate user-generated health data or data that can be used to make inferences about health, leaving social media posts concerning health conditions or internet purchasing data up for grabs by tech companies for medical AI research and development (Gerke et al. 2020). Finally, de-identified data that would otherwise be protected under HIPAA's privacy rules can be shared by covered entities for research and commercial purposes. However, de-identification can be insufficient to protect patients' privacy when data can be re-identified by cross-reference to other available databases (Gerke et al. 2020). Although states are free to impose stricter privacy protections than HIPAA requires for personalized health information, the failure to enact a comprehensive data protection framework at the federal level may both stifle the development of innovative AI health technologies as well as compromise individuals' privacy rights (Gerke et al. 2020). Some legal experts call for expansion of HIPAA and the Americans with Disabilities Act to protect data and prevent discrimination based on future health conditions (See Hoffman and Podgurski 2007; Hoffman 2017).

The GDPR in Europe offers a higher level of protection for personal data concerning European Union data subjects. The regulation's general prohibition on sharing genetic data, biometric data, and data concerning health applies to any entity that handles personal data, including natural persons and business entities (The European Parliament and the Council of the European Union 2016, Sect. 4). The GDPR also prevents the processing of data for "automated individual decision making," which can have a legal or other significant consequences on the data subject, absent necessity for entrance into a legal contract, authorization by the member state and measures to safeguard individual freedoms and privacy interests, or explicit consent (The European Parliament and the Council of the European Union 2016, Art. 22). Finally, the GDPR's required impact assessments, including risk assessments and anticipated risk mitigation and data protection efforts, apply to the introduction of new AI-based technology in clinical health settings (Gerke et al. 2020). Although the GDPR offers more protection to individuals in the European Union than HIPAA offers to Americans, the cross-border capabilities of AI requires international regulations to protect personal data used by AI developers (Gerke et al. 2020).

5.3 Liability for Injuries

Current legal regimes for medical liability are not designed for the Autonomous AI Physician's expression of both software and human qualities. Current theories of liability for medical injury are either "human-centric" or "machine-centric," and fail to provide a workable framework for liability of a hybrid entity (Chung and Zink 2018). Nevertheless, we agree with Griffin that, "[c]urrent legal frameworks are likely to provide the foundation of liability analysis of AI systems with some twists specific to AI (Griffin 2021)." Identifying the proper modification of legal frameworks prior to "a med-mal claim involving AI misdiagnosis arriving in court" is crucial to prevent courts from either banning the Autonomous AI Physician or creating, "such significant restrictions that AI's functionality becomes more trouble to implement that it is worth (Jorstad 2020)."

To-date, no courts have directly addressed liability for injury caused by autonomous medical AI (Jackson et al. 2021). Liability for damages caused by the Autonomous AI Physician will likely be distributed among AI manufacturers and developers, individual healthcare providers, and healthcare organizations (Schweikart 2021). Jorstad predicts that healthcare organizations will primarily bear the costs of injuries caused by their employment of an Autonomous AI Physician (Jorstad 2020). Maliha, et al., believe that under the current liability scheme in the U.S., physicians who rely on AI-decision making will be the primary targets, but questions whether it is fair to hold providers accountable for unpredictable autonomous AI decisions that are made using "black-box" deep learning algorithms (Maliha et al. 2021). Of course, the continuous self-learning features of the Autonomous AI Physician are precisely what makes it valuable in clinical practice (Maliha et al. 2021).

Ultimately, the question of liability assignment is answered by asking: who has control over the particular function(s) of the Autonomous AI Physician that leads to a patient injury? (Schweikart 2021) Control can manifest in several ways. First, AI developers and manufacturers have control over the physical components of the Autonomous AI Physician as well as control over its "education and training" through the algorithmic development of the AI. Second, healthcare organizations exhibit control over "hiring" and organizational oversight through the selection and implementation of AI in clinical practice. Third, individual healthcare providers have limited control over AI recommendations for clinical action through human oversight and quality control. This, of course, leaves a gap in control for the Autonomous AI Physician's independent medical decision-making, which can be opaque and obscured by the "black-box" problem.[14]

Jorstad opines that given the "limited to nonexistent control physicians, hospitals, or even AI manufacturers exert over the machine's diagnosing, it may be unreasonable to hold them liable when error surfaces (Jorstad 2020)." Schweikart

---

[14] See Jorstad (2020) "If an AI program is a black box, it will make predictions and decisions as humans do, but without being able to communicate its reasons for doing so."

(2021) agrees that "black-box" AI decision-making makes it nearly impossible to fairly assign liability under tort law. The logical conclusion is that the Autonomous AI Physician itself controls its own decisions, but this presents a problem in the current liability framework because AI does not have legal personhood and is therefore incapable of being assigned liability (Chung and Zink 2018). Chung and Zink solve this problem by suggesting the creation of limited legal personhood for medical AI, which would allow the Autonomous AI Physician to be held legally responsible for harms caused by its independent medical decisions (Chung and Zink 2018). Once the Autonomous AI is assigned limited legal personhood, and its risks can be insured as an individual healthcare provider, the existing medical liability system can effectively compensate patients for AI-caused injured under the control paradigm outlined above using a combination of products liability, organizational liability, vicarious liability, enterprise liability, and medical malpractice liability. Additionally, potentially liable entities can choose to allocate liability among themselves through contractual agreement. Finally, in countries that opt for no-fault liability regimes, special adjudication systems can compensate patients for AI-induced injuries; however, for negligence-based regimes, such a broad structural change is probably not feasible.

5.3.1 Products Liability

Products liability operates to hold manufacturers liable for inherently dangerous products by imposing a strict liability standard for injuries caused by defective products and failing to warn consumers of the same (Schweikart 2021). Products liability for damages caused by the Autonomous AI Physician is difficult to prove absent evidence of a human-driven design element. While it is true that manufacturers are in the best position to explain "black-box" technology of autonomous AI (Jorstad 2020), the AI's decision cannot always be logically traced and is generally not foreseeable, even by its creators (Schweikart 2021). As a result, it would be difficult for patients to prove the AI was defective and the availability and feasibility of an alternative design as required under a products liability cause of action (Maliha et al. 2021). Additionally, the learned intermediary doctrine holds healthcare providers, rather than manufacturers, responsible for informing patients about risks disclosed to providers (Schweikart 2021). Jorstad notes that even holding providers liable for failure to disclose the unforeseeable risks associated with autonomous AI medical decision-making is "difficult to rationalize (Jorstad 2020)." Finally, using a strict products liability regime for the Autonomous AI Physician can hamper the development of beneficial AI technology (Jorstad 2020).

The imposition of binding regulations on the pre-market development and post-market monitoring of AI should provide limited immunity from liability for manufacturers who receive the proper authorizations.[15] Still, AI manufacturers

---

[15] Jorstad (2020) noting the availability of limited immunity for compliance with FDA regulations.

The Autonomous AI Physician: Medical Ethics and Legal Liability 223

should be held strictly liable for defects concerning data input, original software code, output display, or mechanical failure (Maliha et al. 2021).[16]

5.3.2 Organizational, Vicarious, and Enterprise Liability

Organizational liability can include direct liability for a healthcare provider for failing to exercise due care in selecting and retaining competent physicians, maintaining appropriate facilities and equipment, training and supervising employees, and implementing appropriate protocols and procedures.[17] These organizational duties can require comprehensive vetting of the Autonomous AI Physician's capabilities prior to using it in clinical practice (Maliha et al. 2021). Once implemented, the organization can also be held liable for failing to continually monitor the AI's quality and train the AI as needed to keep it up-to-date. Maliha, et al. recommend administration of "stress tests" to test the AI's ability to produce reliable and accurate decisions in response to difficult situations not considered by the AI's developers (Maliha et al. 2021). Additionally, organizations should be required to utilize the rich learning opportunities made available by the Autonomous AI Physician's near-miss errors—errors that do not cause damage—to retrain and update the Autonomous AI Physicians to prevent error repetition.[18]

Healthcare organizations can also be held responsible for negligence of their employees under the vicarious liability doctrine (Schweikart 2021). As a result, if the Autonomous AI physician is considered an agent or employee of the healthcare organization, damages caused by the autonomous AI decision-making could be covered by the organization. Such coverage would operate like a hospital's vicarious liability for its nurses and staff doctors. Of course, the healthcare organization would have to maintain sufficient insurance coverage for acts of the Autonomous AI physician.

Enterprise liability can hold all entities engaged "in pursuit of a common aim" jointly and severally liable for damages caused by that common enterprise (Schweikart 2021). This arrangement could allow for cost sharing between AI developers and healthcare providers and organizations who implement AI in clinical practice (Jorstad 2020). Allen believes that enterprise liability is a strong option for spreading risk associated with the "unpreventable calculable harm" that will occur as a result of autonomous AI medical decision making (Allen 2019).

---

[16] Contra II.3—M Lanz and S Mijic—Risks associated with the use of natural language generation: Swiss civil liability law perspective. *See also* II.5—A T Fonseca, E V Sequeira and L B Xavier—Liability for AI Driven Systems.

[17] See Duffourc (2018) discussing theories of direct hospital liability.

[18] Wolf and Hughes (2008) noting that near miss errors occur much more frequently than injury-causing errors and are a rich source of organizational learning.

5.3.3 Medical Malpractice

Assigning limited legal personhood is necessary to hold the Autonomous AI Physician accountable for medical malpractice. Chung emphasizes that personhood for AI is a legal fiction to be distinguished from the colloquial understanding of what it means to be a person (Chung and Zink 2018). Giving legal rights and responsibilities to a non-human is not a novel concept. As Schweikart points out, both ships and corporations are assigned legal personhood (Schweikart 2021). Chung and Zink argue that IBM's former AI, Watson, could have been given limited legal personhood considering its ability to work as an integral member of a patient care team capable of providing individualized interpretation and analysis of patients' medical conditions and giving treatment recommendations (Chung and Zink 2018). They compared Watson to a medical student with specialized education and training, who is capable of making independent medical decisions but requires a level of supervision and oversight (Chung 2017). Based on this comparison, the framework for insuring risks and evaluating liability for damages caused by medical AI is already in place, eliminating the need for establishing new insurance and liability systems, an unlikely endeavor (Chung and Zink 2018). Chung and Zink further point out that limited legal personhood for AI is flexible enough to encompass future smarter and more independent AI (Chung and Zink 2018).

Of course, allowing the Autonomous AI Physician to be held liable for its own medical decision making under the current medical malpractice regime requires some discussion of the applicable standard of care. The liability regime already applies heightened standards of care to specialists with extensive training in a specific medical field (Jorstad 2020). The Autonomous AI Physician is already capable of exceeding humans' ability to review and process big data and has, in some instances, even surpassed the diagnostic abilities of human clinicians (Jorstad 2020). On the other hand, it lacks the ability to physically examine patients with human senses, synthesize information across various knowledge sectors, prescribe medication, or order tests. As a result, the Autonomous AI Physician would need to be considered a unique medical specialist that requires unique corresponding standards of care.

Jorstad provides some options for determining when the Autonomous AI Physician breaches the applicable standard of care (Jorstad 2020). The first option is to use the "nearest neighbor" method, which involves looking at the AI's diagnostic history for comparable cases to compute the AI's gross accuracy rate (Jorstad 2020). This case-based analysis should provide some measurement by which the alleged error can be compared and judged under the reasonableness standard (Jorstad 2020). The second option is "AI cross-testing," which involves running the data from an injured patient's case through other AI algorithms to discover whether the machines arrive at comparable results (Jorstad 2020). Two additional options involve human testimony of AI programmers or human medical experts to independently evaluate the AI's decisions and opine regarding whether the AI's processes and results, respectively, are reasonable (Jorstad 2020). In reality, attorneys will likely try some combination of these methods, and as a result, the standards of care will develop

The Autonomous AI Physician: Medical Ethics and Legal Liability

organically over time as the Autonomous AI physician becomes a common litigant in medical malpractice cases. Alternatively, professional and industry organizations can attempt to proactively establish standards of care by drafting AI practice guidelines. Still, courts will likely view non-compliance with such guidelines as evidence of negligence rather than being dispositive of the issue.

Individual healthcare providers can still be liable under the current medical malpractice regime for failure to properly supervise or oversee autonomous AI. Such causes of action are already recognized in relation to subordinate medical providers. One area of human medical liability that requires special attention is informed consent. Although the Autonomous AI Physician can render independent medical decisions, it should remain within the scope of a human provider's responsibility to inform patients of the risks and benefits of the AI's medical decisions. Although, as discussed above, the law could change to allow delegation of this duty to HICs, under the current law, physicians must consult with patients to provide information necessary to obtain informed consent. At a minimum, this information should include notice that a medical decision was generated by an Autonomous AI Physician, the right to a second opinion by a human clinician when feasible, and disclosure of possible uses of health information for future AI training (Jorstad 2020).

5.3.4 Contractual Assignment of Liability

Despite a legal framework for assigning liability following a patient injury, healthcare providers and AI manufacturers can still contractually divide or assign liability and insurance obligations for the Autonomous AI Physician. Jorstad opines that such agreements are the simplest option for dividing responsibility for AI-induced injuries (Jorstad 2020).

5.3.5 Special Adjudication Systems

Special adjudication systems can provide a no-fault approach to compensation for damages caused by the Autonomous AI physician. This can include compensation from an established fund and/or mandatory binding arbitration to determine damages caused by AI medical decision making (Jorstad 2020). The benefits of no-fault systems include streamlined adjudication and increased access to recovery for those injured by an Autonomous AI Physician (Maliha et al. 2021). Additionally, all stakeholders would share in the costs of risks posed by AI in healthcare delivery by contributing to a common fund (Gerke et al. 2020). While there are some examples of no-fault systems like vaccine injury compensation in the U.S., incorporating medical injuries caused by autonomous AI into those systems may require large structural changes that cannot be easily or quickly developed and implemented. No-fault systems also fail to provide the benefit of deterring sub-standard behavior during a time of rapid development and implementation of new technology.

6 Conclusion

The Autonomous AI Physician is here, and it will only get smarter and faster as DL technology improves at an alarming pace. While AI holds great promise for improving healthcare access and quality, patient care cannot and should not be left exclusively to machines. All stakeholders in the development and use of the Autonomous AI Physician have an obligation to ensure that AI is implemented in a safe and responsible way, including through regulatory and legal mechanisms that provide the requisite levels of safety, reliability, transparency, fairness, and accountability.[19]

Acknowledgements I would like to express sincere gratitude to the participants of the Fall 2021 NYU Lawyering Scholarship Colloquium for their insightful comments and suggestions on an early draft of this work.

References

Ahmad Z, Rahim S, Zubair M, Abdul-Ghafar J (2021) Artificial intelligence (AI) in medicine, current applications and future role with special emphasis on its potential and promise in pathology: present and future impact, obstacles including costs and acceptance among pathologists, practical and philosophical considerations. A comprehensive review. Diagn Pathol 16:24

Allen TC (2019) Regulating artificial intelligence for a successful pathology future. Arch Pathol Lab Med 143:1175–1179

American Medical Association (2018) Augmented intelligence in health care H-480.940. https://policysearch.ama-assn.org/policyfinder/detail/augmented%20intelligence?uri=%2FAMADoc%2FHOD.xml-H-480.940.xml. Accessed 30 Oct 2021

Campbell C (2021) Medical violence, obstetric racism, and the limits of informed consent for black women. Mich J Race Law 47:47–75

Caruana R, Lou Y, Gehrke J, Koch P, Sturm M, Elhadad N (2015) Intelligible models for healthcare: predicting pneumonia risk and hospital 30-day readmission. In: Proceedings of

---

[19] See also, on Ethics, in this book P U Lima and A Paiva—Autonomous and Intelligent Robots: Social, Legal and Ethical Issues; A T Freitas—Data-driven approaches in healthcare: challenges and emerging trends; M C Patrão Neves and A B Almeida—Before and Beyond Artificial Intelligence: Opportunities and Challenges; E Magrani and P G F Silva—The Ethical and Legal Challenges of Recommender Systems Driven by Artificial Intelligence; M S Fernandes and J R Goldim—Artificial Intelligence and Decision Making in Health: Risks and Opportunities; R Nogaroli and J L M Faleiros Júnior—Ethical challenges of artificial intelligence in medicine and the triple semantic dimensions of algorithmic opacity with its repercussions to patient consent and medical liability; and B A Ribeiro, H Coelho, A E Ferreira and J Branquinho—Metacognition, Accountability and Legal Personhood of AI. See generally, on AI and Healthcare, in this book A T Freitas—Data-driven approaches in healthcare: challenges and emerging trends; M S Fernandes and J R Goldim—Artificial Intelligence and Decision Making in Health: Risks and Opportunities; and R Nogaroli and J L M Faleiros Júnior—Ethical challenges of artificial intelligence in medicine and the triple semantic dimensions of algorithmic opacity with its repercussions to patient consent and medical liability.

the 21th ACM SIGKDD international conference on knowledge discovery and data mining. Association for Computing Machinery, Sydney, pp 1721–1730

Chang HY, Jung CK, Woo JI, Lee S, Cho J, Kim SW, Kwak TY (2019) Artificial intelligence in pathology. J Pathol Transl Med 53:1–12

Chauhan C, Gullapalli RR (2021) Ethics of AI in pathology: current paradigms and emerging issues. Am J Pathol 191:1673–1683

Chung J (2017) What should we do about artificial intelligence in health care? NYSBA Health Law J 22:37–39

Chung J, Zink A (2018) Hey Watson-can i sue you for malpractice-examining the liability of artificial intelligence in medicine. Asia Pac J Health Law Ethics 11:51–80

Department of Health and Social Care, National Health Service (2021) A guide to good practice for digital and data-driven health technologies. https://www.gov.uk/government/publications/code-of-conduct-for-data-driven-health-and-care-technology/initial-code-of-conduct-for-data-driven-health-and-care-technology. Accessed 30 Oct 2021

Digital Pathology Association (2020) AI/ML task force. https://digitalpathologyassociation.org/aiml-task-force. Accessed 30 Oct 2021

Duffourc MN (2018) Repurposing the affirmative defense of comparative fault in medical malpractice cases to improve patient safety. Indiana Health Law Rev 16:21–41

Duffourc MN (2020) Are you my doctor? Defining the doctor-patient relationship in the global age of E-health. Tulane J Int Comp Law 28:311–323

Duffourc MN, Gerke S (2023) The EU's proposed directives for AI liability leave worrying gaps likely to impact medical AI. NPJ Digit Med 6:77

European Commission (2017) Regulation (EU) 2017/746 of the European parliament and of the council of 5 April 2017 on in vitro diagnostic medical devices and repealing directive 98/79/EC and commission decision 2010/227/EU. https://eur-lex.europa.eu/eli/reg/2017/746/oj. Accessed 30 Oct 2021

European Commission (2021) Proposal for a regulation of the European parliament and of the council laying down harmonised rules on artificial intelligence (Artificial Intelligence Act) and amending certain union legislative acts. https://eur-lex.europa.eu/legal-content/EN/TXT/?qid=1623335154975&uri=CELEX%3A52021PC0206. Accessed 12 Mar 2022

European Commission (2022a) Proposal for a directive of the European parliament and of the council on liability for defective products (PLD). https://single-market-economy.ec.europa.eu/document/3193da9a-cecb-44ad-9a9c-7b6b23220bcd_en. Accessed 6 Feb 2023

European Commission (2022b) Proposal for a directive of the European parliament and of the council on adapting non-contractual civil liability rules to artificial intelligence (AI Liability Directive) (AILD). https://commission.europa.eu/document/f9ac0daf-baa3-4371-a760-810414ce4823_en. Accessed 6 Feb 2023

European Parliament Special Committee of Artificial Intelligence in a Digital Age (2021) AIDA working paper on artificial intelligence and health. https://www.europarl.europa.eu/cmsdata/231039. Accessed 12 Mar 2022

Gerke S, Minssen T, Cohen G (2020) Ethical and legal challenges of artificial intelligence-driven healthcare. Artif Intell Healthc 2020:295–336. https://doi.org/10.1016/B978-0-12-818438-7.00012-5

Griffin F (2021) Artificial intelligence and liability in health care. Health Matrix J Law Med 31:65–106

Hoffman S (2017) Big data and the Americans with disabilities act. Hastings Law J 68:777

Hoffman S (2021) Artificial intelligence in medicine raises legal and ethical concerns. https://theconversation.com/artificial-intelligence-in-medicine-raises-legal-and-ethical-concerns-122504. Accessed 30 Oct 2021

Hoffman S, Podgurski A (2007) In sickness, health, and cyberspace: protecting the security of electronic private health information. BCL Rev 48:331–386

Homeyer A, Lotz J, Schwen LO, Weiss N, Romberg D, Höfener H, Zerbe N, Hufnagl P (2021) Artificial intelligence in pathology: from prototype to product. J Pathol Inform 12:13

Jackson BR, Ye Y, Crawford JM, Becich MJ, Roy S, Botkin JR, De Baca ME, Pantanowitz L (2021) The ethics of artificial intelligence in pathology and laboratory medicine: principles and practice. Acad Pathol 8:2374289521990784

Jorstad KT (2020) Intersection of artificial intelligence and medicine: tort liability in the technological age. J Med Artif Intell 3:57. https://doi.org/10.21037/jmai-20-57

Lawry T, Mutkoski S, Leong N (2018) Realizing the potential for AI in precision health. SciTech Lawyer 15:23–27

Lupton M (2018) Some ethical and legal consequences of the application of artificial intelligence in the field of medicine. Trends Med 18:100147

Maliha G, Gerke S, Cohen IG, Parikh RB (2021) Artificial intelligence and liability in medicine: balancing safety and innovation. Milbank Q 99:629–647

Nelson GS (2019) Bias in artificial intelligence. N C Med J 80:220–222

Oxipit (2022) Oxipit awarded CE Mark for the first autonomous AI medical imaging application. https://oxipit.ai/news/first-autonomous-ai-medical-imaging-application/. Accessed 6 Feb 2023

Pallua JD, Brunner A, Zelger B, Schirmer M, Haybaeck J (2020) The future of pathology is digital. Pathol Res Pract 216:153040

RANZCR (2020) Standards of practice for artificial intelligence. https://www.ranzcr.com/whats-on/news-media/420-ranzcr-launches-world-leading-standards-for-the-use-of-ai-in-healthcare. Accessed 30 Oct 2021

Schweikart SJ (2021) Who will be liable for medical malpractice in the future? How the use of artificial intelligence in medicine will shape medical tort law. Minn J Law Sci Technol 22:1–22

Taylor NP (2021) MedTech Europe calls for urgent clarification of EU artificial intelligence proposal. https://www.medtechdive.com/news/medtech-europe-criticizes-eu-artificial-intelligence-proposal/606433/. Accessed 12 Mar 2022

The European Parliament and the Council of the European Union (2016) General data protection regulation (GDPR). https://eur-lex.europa.eu/legal-content/EN/TXT/PDF/?uri=CELEX:32016R0679. Accessed 12 Mar 2022

U.S. Food & Drug Administration (2018) FDA permits marketing of artificial intelligence-based device to detect certain diabetes-related eye problems. https://www.fda.gov/news-events/press-announcements/fda-permits-marketing-artificial-intelligence-based-device-detect-certain-diabetes-related-eye. Accessed 12 Mar 2022

U.S. Food & Drug Administration (2021) Digital health software precertification (Pre-Cert) program. https://www.fda.gov/medical-devices/digital-health-center-excellence/digital-health-software-precertification-pre-cert-program. Accessed 12 Mar 2022

Wolf ZR, Hughes RG (2008) Error reporting and disclosure. In: Hughes RG (ed) Patient safety and quality: an evidence-based handbook for nurses. Agency for Healthcare Research and Quality, Rockville, pp 2–333

Open Access This chapter is licensed under the terms of the Creative Commons Attribution 4.0 International License (http://creativecommons.org/licenses/by/4.0/), which permits use, sharing, adaptation, distribution and reproduction in any medium or format, as long as you give appropriate credit to the original author(s) and the source, provide a link to the Creative Commons license and indicate if changes were made.

The images or other third party material in this chapter are included in the chapter's Creative Commons license, unless indicated otherwise in a credit line to the material. If material is not included in the chapter's Creative Commons license and your intended use is not permitted by statutory regulation or exceeds the permitted use, you will need to obtain permission directly from the copyright holder.

Ethical Challenges of Artificial Intelligence in Medicine and the Triple Semantic Dimensions of Algorithmic Opacity with Its Repercussions to Patient Consent and Medical Liability

Rafaella Nogaroli and José Luiz de Moura Faleiros Júnior

Abstract Artificial intelligence algorithms have the potential to diagnose some types of skin cancer or to identify specific heart-rhythm abnormalities as well as (or even better) than board-certified dermatologists and cardiologists. However, one of the biggest fears in the healthcare sector in the Era of AI in Medicine is the so-called *black box medicine*, given the obscurity in the way information is processed by algorithms. More broadly, it is observed that there are three different semantic dimensions of algorithmic opacity relevant to Medicine: (1) *epistemic opacity* for the insufficient physicians understanding of the rules an AI system is applying to make predictions and decisions; (2) *opacity for the lack of medical disclosure* about the AI systems to support clinical decisions and patient's unawareness that automated decision-making are being carried out with their personal data; (3) *explanatory opacity* for the unsatisfactory explanation to patients about the technology used to support professional decision-making. Therefore, the aim of this study is to analyze each type of opacity, considering hypothetical scenarios and its repercussions in terms of medical malpractice and patient's informed consent. From this, it will be defined ethical challenges of using AI in the healthcare sector and the importance of medical education.

R. Nogaroli (✉)
Federal University of Paraná, Curitiba, PR, Brazil
e-mail: rafaellanogaroli@ufpr.br

J. L. d. M. Faleiros Júnior
University of São Paulo, São Paulo, Brazil
e-mail: jfaleiros@usp.br

© The Author(s) 2024
H. Sousa Antunes et al. (eds.), *Multidisciplinary Perspectives on Artificial Intelligence and the Law*, Law, Governance and Technology Series 58,
https://doi.org/10.1007/978-3-031-41264-6_12

1 Introduction: Advantages of Artificial Intelligence (AI) in Medicine

The Digital Age of Medicine created the concept of *smart health*, following the transformation phenomenon from traditional Medicine towards *P4-Medicine* (preventive, predictive, personalized and participatory) (Hood 2013; Holzinger et al. 2015).[1] In this new scenario, health care is no longer essentially limited to the treatment of pathologies (a task that has never been abandoned, of course) and is now focused on the adoption of measures aimed at preventing diseases (preventive medicine) (Balicer and Cohen-Stavi 2020) or making it possible to anticipate the diagnosis (predictive medicine). Regarding personal treatment, the patient is seen in a more individualized way (and less generic, therefore), based on his genetic and health data (personalized medicine). Finally, the doctor-patient relationship ceases to be something punctual and starts to develop in a continuous manner, with the patient's active participation (participatory medicine) (Flores et al. 2013).[2] With digital tools, patients can take a more active, participatory role in their health care and wellness decision-making. In this way, the diabetic patient can constantly monitor his blood glucose, enabling, in real time, algorithms to analyze the personal data provided, supporting the physician in faster, more efficient and personalized therapeutic decisions, regarding drug administration or dietary (Nogaroli and Kfouri-Neto 2021a).

The transformation of medical care in this more proactive/participative, preventive, precise model and focused on the individuality of each patient became possible from the combination of large volumes of health data and Artificial Intelligence algorithms. Human life, in the wake of the third millennium, will be conditioned to algorithms for solving problems and making more accurate decisions. Eric Topol, in his books about the present and future of Medicine (Topol 2013, 2016, 2019a, b), points to several scientific studies that attest the enormous AI's ability to diagnose some types of skin cancer, or identify specific heart rhythm abnormalities, as well or perhaps even better than dermatologists and cardiologists (Huang et al. 2020).

During the COVID-19 pandemic, AI also demonstrated its great potential in medical imaging around the globe. Due to the rapid increase in number of new and suspected COVID-19 cases, as an alternative to relieve pressure on radiologists and prevent further spread of the disease, AI-based algorithms were developed across

---

[1] "The convergence of patient-activated social networks, big data and their analytics, and systems medicine has led to a P4 medicine that is predictive, preventive, personalized, and participatory. Medicine will focus on each individual. It will become proactive in nature. It will increasingly focus on wellness rather than disease".

[2] By adding the "participatory" component, P4 Medicine "maximizes the effectiveness of systems medicine by expanding its application out from hospitals and clinics into homes, workplaces and eventually schools. With the addition of self-monitoring (activity, weight and calorie intake) and self-assessments in the participatory component, new quantities and forms of data will be aggregated and mined to generate new insight into health and disease. These insights will drive the development of new technologies, analytic tools and forms of care".

the globe that supported these professionals in quickly identifying the pathogen disease by analyzing computed tomography images of symptomatic patients of COVID-19 (Harmon et al. 2020).[3] Besides, in the last years, predictive algorithms have been used to target treatment more effectively toward high-risk patient groups for the prevention of major chronic disease complications. This approach is being applied in other relevant domains to allow for the identification of populations at risk and early identification of impending complications of multiple acute and chronic illnesses (Nogaroli and Nalin 2021; Nogaroli and Silva 2021).

Nowadays, IBM is one of the major companies that creates more technological solutions for the healthcare sector and developed the so-called *Watson for Oncology*, a solution powered by information from relevant guidelines, best practices, and medical journals and textbooks. Watson evaluates the information from a patient's medical record, along with medical evidence (scientific papers and clinical studies), thus showing possible treatment options for cancer patients, classified by confidence level. In the end, it will be up to the doctor to analyze the conclusions reached by the AI and decide which is the best treatment option for that specific patient (IBM Healthcare and Life Sciences 2021).[4]

The brief demonstration of these examples of Artificial Intelligence being incorporated into medical practice is to illustrate some of the various benefits that this technology can provide to the healthcare sector. These potential benefits, however, are accompanied by relevant ethical and legal concerns to be faced. AI brings many benefits to the healthcare sector, but its risks cannot be ignored, which are even many of them intrinsic to the technology itself. In September 2021, it was published an UN report that analyses how AI tools affect people's right to privacy and other human rights. The UN High Commissioner for Human Rights called for a moratorium on the AI systems, considering that the technology in several sectors has caused serious human rights risks and, therefore, it would be needed a pause in creating new AI tools until authorities can demonstrate that there are no significant

---

[3] The algorithms were programed with thousands of tomography images labeled training images in two general classes: (1) COVID-19 and (2) Not COVID-19. Images marked as "Not COVID-19" represented cases of patients with healthy lungs. Preliminary studies indicate chest CT has a high sensitivity for detection of COVID-19 lung pathology and several groups have demonstrated the potential for AI-based diagnosis, reporting as high as 95% detection accuracies. Also included were examples of patients with other lung diseases, such as lung cancer, tuberculosis, bronchiectasis, and pneumonia of non-viral etiology.

[4] "Watson for Oncology was developed in concert with Memorial Sloan Kettering Center (MSK). To date, it has invested nearly 15 million pages of medical content, including more than 200 medical textbooks and 300 medical journals. By combining MSK's world-renowned cancer expertise with the analytical speed of IBM Watson, the tool has the potential to transform how doctors provide individualized cancer treatment plans and to help improve patient outcomes. In 2015, nearly 44,000 oncology research papers were published in medical journals around the world, or more than 120 new papers each day, outpacing the ability of humans to keep up with the proliferation of medical knowledge. Watson's machine learning capability means it is continuously learning about oncology over time, and doctors have access to peer-reviewed studies, clinical guidelines and expert perspectives, enabling them to make more specific and nuanced treatment decisions more quickly, based on the latest data."

issues with accuracy or discriminatory impacts and that the AI systems comply with robust privacy and data protection standards (United Nations 2021).

In recent decades, with the exponential creation of new predictive algorithms in medical practice, it is also possible to observe a moment of a global crisis in the credibility of this technology in Medicine. There is a scenario of potential expressive AI risks in supporting the medical professional decision, considering several factors, including deficiency in the process of creating and validating algorithms, relevant degree of fallibility, unpredictability and algorithmic opacity (Topol 2019a, b).

Consequently, the present study proposes to investigate the potential risks of implementing AI in clinical practice, as well as the definition of ethical principles to be followed during the development of the technology and, after being introduced in the market, throughout its useful life cycle. From this, this paper will seek to draw some conclusions about the future of Artificial Intelligence algorithms in Medicine and the importance of medical education in digital health and new technologies.

2 Triple Semantic Dimensions of Algorithmic Opacity and Its Repercussions to Patient Consent and Medical Liability

One of the biggest fears in the health sector in the Era of artificial intelligence is the so-called 'black box medicine', given the obscurity in the way information is processed by the algorithms. More broadly, it is observed that there are three different semantic dimensions of algorithmic opacity relevant to Medicine: (1) *epistemic opacity*; (2) opacity for the *lack of medical disclosure*; and (3) *explanatory opacity*. Therefore, it is important to analyze each type of opacity, considering hypothetical scenarios and its repercussions in terms of medical malpractice and patient's informed consent.

(1) *Epistemic opacity*: there is a relevant complexity for physicians' understanding about how personal data are processed by algorithms, which can discover patterns within such a large number of variables that it becomes extremely difficult—or even impossible—for a human mind to understand it. In fact, this is a problem present in most Artificial Intelligence systems and it is called by Frank Pasquale by 'black box problem', in his book 'The Black Box Society' (Pasquale 2015, pp. 6–7). Thus, epistemic opacity occurs when there is not sufficient understanding of the rules that an AI system is applying to make classifications, predictions and decisions. As an example, this opacity can originate physician's lack of comprehension about the machine learning process to arrive at a certain diagnosis or prediction about his patient's clinical condition. The lack of transparency is also associated with the problem of reliability of algorithms predictions, and it raises understandable fears regarding the implementation of the technology in medical practice.

There are two symbolic cases that exemplify the black box problem and the unpredictable behaviors arising from AI self-learning and the unreliability of the results generated by the algorithms. During an experiment conducted in 2002 by scientists at the Magna Science Center, in England, an unforeseen event occurred: two intelligent robots were placed in an arena to simulate a scenario of 'predators' and 'prey', in order to see if the robots would be able to benefit from the experience acquired from machine learning to develop new hunting and self-defense techniques. However, Gaak, one of the robots, that was unintentionally left unattended for 15 min managed to escape and it adopted an unpredictable behavior, founding a way out through the arena wall and reached the parking lot, where it ended up being hit by a car (Čerka et al. 2015).

It is also relevant to mention the incident reported by Sameer Singh, an assistant professor in the Department of Computer Science at the University of California (UCI), in the United States, in which a student created an algorithm to categorize pictures of huskies and wolves. Initially, it seemed that the algorithm was able to classify the two animals almost perfectly. However, after numerous and subsequent cross-analysis, Singh found out that the algorithm was identifying wolves based only on the snow in the background of the images and not on the animal's own characteristics (UCI Beall Applied Innovation 2017).

Undoubtedly, damages could rise to immeasurable levels if we consider the risks presented in the two cases above in the context of AI algorithms in Medicine. Now take for example a poorly programmed and tested algorithm, or one with expressive degree of fallibility, in the cognitive technology that was used in some countries to diagnose patients infected with the new coronavirus. Because of this, Nicholson Price and Roger Allan Ford explain that one of the biggest fears of the healthcare sector at this stage of artificial intelligence stems precisely from the unpredictable situations arising from black box medicine, given the obscurity in the way information is processed by the algorithms (Ford and Price 2016). Therefore, when algorithmic systems are implemented in clinical practice, it is essential that physicians know their limitations and what is effectively taken into account for predictions. Understanding the limits of algorithms will help physicians to better judge their decisions and proposals, thus avoiding simplistic and reductionist views, in addition to preventing patients from becoming 'hostages' of automated decisions made in the black box of algorithms.

In addition, it is necessary to emphasize that AI in diagnostic analysis is not perfect. No matter how efficient an 'intelligent' system is for medical diagnosis and clinical predictions, it will continue to present a significant margin of inaccuracy, which can lead to adverse results. For example, Watson for Oncology is not 100% accurate. There is a significant inaccuracy margin of around 10%, according to a clinical research conducted by a team of 15 doctors at Manipal Hospitals in India over 3 years of 1000 patients diagnosed with cancer. In cases where there was disagreement between the AI and the doctors, the medical professionals changed in 63% of the cases their own diagnoses to follow the one given by Watson. There is a central point for this reflection: the AI system altered the final decision of oncologists in several cases. On the other hand, the same survey revealed that in

37% of cases the physicians did not change its own diagnosis, in disagreement with the result obtained by Watson (Bicudo 2021).

In this scenario, imagine a patient diagnosed with cancer and his doctor believe, at first, that he has a certain type of cancer. However, after putting the patient's clinical data into predictive software, such as Watson for Oncology, this one gives another result, saying the patient has a different type of cancer. Then, a question arises from it: if the physician follows or disregards the result of the AI, and damage to the patient occurs, after inappropriate diagnosis and treatment, should the professional be held responsible? In other words, would be possible to consider a case of medical malpractice in the event of the supervenience of a harmful result for the patient that, in theory, could be avoided, if the diagnosis proposed by the AI had been followed? This complex issue has already been discussed in recent papers (Nogaroli and Silva 2020; Nogaroli and Nalin 2021).

In order to answer properly this question, some basic concepts need to be initially indicated about medical liability for misdiagnosis. For the purposes of analyzing liability in AI services, the primary element of a medical malpractice claim is the breach of a legal duty to adhere to a professional standard of care, which is 'a set of guidelines specifying the appropriate or required treatment methods for a given condition based on medical research and professional practice' (Jorstad 2020). Moreover, in most jurisdictions, the law does not hold doctors legally responsible for all diagnostic errors. A misdiagnosis or delayed diagnosis itself is not evidence of medical negligence (Kfouri-Neto 2021). Skillful professionals can make diagnostic errors even when using reasonable care. When the doctor carries out a good examination of his patient, with all the healthcare data, medical exams and means available, and still makes a diagnostic error, the professional will not be held responsible. An obligation of infallibility or absolute accuracy cannot be imposed on the physician.

However, when the misdiagnosis is gross, revealing inadmissible ignorance or negligence, it leads to the medical liability. The inexcusable diagnostic error can come from several causes: (a) superficial examination of the patient; (b) inexcusable ignorance of the physician with elementary information from medical science; (c) not resorting to the auxiliary diagnostic means made available to the professional; (d) disregards evident symptoms that required additional exams for a better determination of the clinical condition. Thus, the key is determining whether the physician acted competently, which involves an evaluation of what the professional did and did not do in arriving at a certain diagnosis.

When analyzing the problem of medical liability for diagnostic errors in the context of AI, according to lessons from Nicholson Price, the doctor can be held responsible if he is not diligent in using the technology (Price et al. 2019). In the same sense, Fruzsina Molnár-Gábor argues that if doctors recognize, based on their medical expertise, that the result provided by the AI is incorrect in that specific case, they should not consider it as a basis for their clinical decision. On the other hand, the physician's lack of diligence in thoughtlessly discarding the result obtained by the AI system may constitute a criterion for liability (Molnár-Gábor 2020).

Thus, it is possible to conclude that, in order to verify whether a doctor has acted with negligence in a specific case, the standards of professional conduct required at the time of medical practice must be analyzed. In summary, the physician using the technology will be in a difficult position to justify: (1) why he followed the diagnosis or course of action suggested by the AI or (2) why—and based on what factors—he deviated from the algorithmic recommendation. The medical professional is free to choose his means of diagnosis and therapy proposals, but he is also responsible for his choices (Nogaroli and Nalin 2021).

Beyond that, when algorithmic systems are implemented in clinical practice, it is essential that physicians know their limitations and what is taken into account for algorithm predictions. Understanding the limits of the technology will help physicians to better judge their decisions and proposals, thus avoiding simplistic and reductionist views based in the black box of the algorithms. Lack of in-depth knowledge of the benefits and risks of healthcare technologies can translate into worse outcomes for patients due to a lack of medical understanding about which tools add value to their practice or how to properly integrate AI into the clinical workflow.

As an example, some hospitals in US implemented the so-called *AI Dying Algorithms*, which use patient's health data and analyze around 5000 clinical risk factors to predict the chances of survival among hospitalized individuals, screening patients with palliative needs or even determining the time until death of patients with terminal or incurable diseases. There are potential benefits of these algorithms as a tool to support medical decision in the indication of palliative care, in order to avoid undue extension of life and provide terminal patients with the option of living the end of life with better quality, through the indication of palliative care.

However, it is possible to observe expressive complications with this type of AI algorithm such as the one called *Jvion CORE*, created by the company Jvion for medical decision in the indication of palliative care. It has already been implemented in several oncology clinics in the United States (Jvion CORE 2021). However, there is a serious problem of using the *AI Dying Algorithms* in clinical practice. *Jvion CORE* presents an approximately 40% accuracy in its predictions about patients flagged as high risk to die in the following month. In order words, there is expressive percentage of 60% of algorithmic fallibility (Robbins 2021).

Therefore, Eric Topol states that algorithms can help patients and their physicians make decisions about the course of medical treatment, both in palliative situations and in those where cure is the goal (Topol 2019a, b). However, the author states that there is not 'a particularly good use for AI unless and until it is shown that the algorithm being used is extremely accurate' (Robbins 2021). Besides, there is also a mismatch between the task of these models: predicting a patient's odds of death and how they're actually being used to try to identify who will benefit most from an advance care planning conversation (medical recommendation for palliative care). Consequently, there are considerable doubts about the role that artificial intelligence can play in the context of palliative care (Nogaroli and Kfouri-Neto 2021b).

Last but not least, there is another relevant effect of *epistemic opacity* that deserves special consideration. Physicians have a legal duty to provide a certain standard of skill and care to their patients but have no obligation under law to guarantee the cure or other concrete results. Though, there is a risk that the physician does not understand the limitations of the AI system, using it as an end in itself—not as a tool—and, more than that, pass on the guarantee of total success to his patient precisely because of the technology used. Then, it arises the discussion about the possibility of considering a medical obligation of result, based on the promise of infallibility of the AI tool used in the clinical practice. As an illustration, it is worth mentioning that was discussed in the US about physicians who used the Da Vinci robotic platforms in surgeries and ensured positive results for patients, providing information only about the benefits of the technological tool (Nogaroli and Kfouri-Neto 2019, 2020).

The same logic seems to be applicable for the hypothesis of the physician using Artificial Intelligence tools, such as IBM's Watson, creating in the patient the expectation that he will have an extremely accurate diagnosis of cancer and the best treatment proposal due to the use of AI, which, acting better than human beings, would be able to bring about a favorable result, practically guaranteeing the cure. In this scenario, there would be a violation of the ethical principle of 'human control of technology', since the professional does not understand *AI-as-a-tool* to support clinical decision-making, bringing the technology as a guaranteed success in medical practice. This result in the breach of the patient's legitimate expectation and the possible qualification of the legal obligation nature for the doctor as an obligation of result.

(2) *opacity for the lack of medical disclosure*: in the second semantic dimension of algorithmic opacity particularly relevant to Medicine, it is observed that there is considerable risk that AI algorithms are used to support medical decision without the patients' knowledge, and patient's unawareness that automated decision-making and profiling activities about them are being carried out with their personal data. In this scenario, first of all, it is important to consider that medical disclosure is the structured process of transparent communication between patients and physicians involved during medical care. However, a lot of criticisms have arisen because patients are often not informed or asked to consent to the use of Artificial Intelligence algorithms in their health care (Robbins and Brodwin 2021). In fact, some physicians use a paternalistic discourse that they don't need to inform patients about all the resources used in the clinical decision process. Following this logic, the medical professional, in theory, could indicate palliative care for a patient, informing some aspects of their clinical condition and making medical recommendations without the need to disclose the specific information about the use of an *AI Dying Algorithm* (Cohen 2020).

Though, informing the patient and providing their consent represents one of the mechanisms for the realization of the fundamental right to the free development of the human personality, having an instrumental nature as it is a way of realizing the right to autonomy. Currently, the modern doctrine around the globe about medical liability defends patients' consent as an instrument that allows, in addition to the interests and medical-therapeutic objectives, to increase respect for the person in its holistic dimension. Patients need to be provided with the essential information to properly understand his health condition or possible treatments available, so that he can exercise the faculty of consenting to the proposed treatment or intervention, choosing another of the existing alternatives, although less indicated by the attending professional, or even refusing to be treated. This doctrinal notion is a trend of thought that has taken shape in various jurisdictions around the globe in the last decades (Pereira 2004).

Thus, the type of algorithmic opacity due to non-disclosure does not concern the intrinsic characteristics of AI systems but has its origin in the risks to the patient's informative self-determination, that is, it derives from the way in which the medical decision regarding the diagnosis, prognosis and treatment proposals supported by AI can be carried out by the physician without the patients being aware of it, neither during the medical intervention nor after the harmful event. It is important to consider that there may be medical liability due for the deprivation suffered by the patient in his self-determination, because he was deprived of the opportunity to ponder the risks and advantages of an AI algorithm prediction about his clinical condition (Nogaroli and Dantas 2020). In conclusion, physician must inform the patient about the fact that the diagnosis, prognosis, treatment proposal or even his indication for palliative care are supported by several factors and resources, including an Artificial Intelligence algorithm (Nogaroli and Dantas 2021). This includes the ideal of shared decision-making in medicine.

(3) *explanatory opacity*: in addition to the physician's duty to disclose the information that he uses an AI algorithm to support his clinical decision, he also needs to explain about the technology used, according to the degree of understanding of each patient. If patients don't received this properly explanation in Medical AI, it may occur the so-called *explanatory opacity*. There is a divergence in the doctrine about the amount of information that must be given to the patient, in order to the doctor comply with his duty to inform. However, we have already defended in a recent paper that, with the evolution of new technologies in the healthcare sector, physicians need to understand that the right to adequate information (which corresponds to a duty to inform) also includes consent to the use of new technologies, based on the patient's knowledge of their functioning, objectives, advantages, costs, risks and alternatives (Nogaroli and Dantas 2020). Thus, there is a demand for a new interpretation of the principle of patient self-determination in the context of new technologies: we moved away from the simple right to receive medical information, and we are going towards a greater informational range, since there is a right to explanation and justification (Astromskė et al. 2020).

Therefore, if we go back to Watson for Oncology's factual hypothesis, even if medical negligence is not configured, if the professional only informs—*but does not adequately explain* to the patient about the use of the technology to support the medical decision, he may be held responsible for the deprivation suffered by the patient in his self-determination, since the opportunity to consider the advantages and risks of treatment proposed or medical diagnosis supported by AI algorithms was taken away from the patient.

Explainability can be understood as "a characteristic of an AI-driven system allowing a person to reconstruct why a certain AI came up with the presented predictions" (Amann et al. 2020). Nevertheless, it is essential to point out that explainability is not a purely technological issue, instead it invokes a host of medical, legal, ethical, and societal questions that require thorough exploration. Taking AI-based clinical decision support systems as a case in point, there is an ethical and legal obligation for the doctor to inform and explain for his patient something like: 'look Mr. John, at first I see that your clinical condition indicates that you have a specific type of cancer, but we tried a certain chemotherapy treatment without much success. Therefore, we could put your personal data into Watson for Oncology and the AI would make a cross-reference with its huge database, in order to show us an eventual diverse diagnosis, or bring others recent treatments proposals based on confidence levels. But look Mr. John, Watson has a certain fallibility degree, and it has other risks...'.

This is the appropriate model of the process of obtaining the patient's consent in AI, explaining and dialoguing with him to clarify the nuances of the diagnosis and prognosis process supported by the technology. To sum up, for the physician not to be held responsible for violating the duty to inform, it is essential to pay special attention to the process of obtaining informed consent, converting it into an *informed choice process*, following the idea of a true process of dialogue between doctor and patient. From the beginning of the decision to use the AI-based algorithm, there is a need for an explanation and justification for those affected by the technology.

3 Ethical Dimensions of Using Artificial Intelligence (AI) in the Healthcare Sector: Setting the Parameters for Data-Informed Duties in Tort Law

The development and implementation of AI tools in Medicine are opening the doors to new ethical and legal challenges. These challenges include how to evaluate algorithm performance and to determine where AI can be safely and efficiently applied to clinical practice. There are three examples of ethical issues relate to: "(1) Biases in training data; (2) The potential replacing of human health care providers with AI tools; (3) Responding to an AI intervention that has failed. If we develop an AI tool that influences a clinical decision, and a poor decision was made, how do we (as humans) respond?" (Marcetich 2020). As mentioned before, designing machine learning tools used to support clinical decision-making can be thought of as an experiment whose risks need to be carefully evaluated before implementation in clinical practice.

In June 2021, the World Health Organization (WHO) published its guidance on *Ethics and Governance of Artificial Intelligence for Health* (World Health Organization 2021). The report reflects the WHO's intention to anchor their guidance within a human rights framework and it makes direct references to the Universal Declaration of Human Rights by exploring the question of autonomy, protecting populations from harm, and ensuring inclusiveness and equity. It states that 'ethical considerations and human rights must be placed at the center of the design, development, and deployment of AI technologies for health'. The document offers 6 primary principles for the use of AI in Medicine: (1) protect autonomy; (2) promote human well-being, human safety and the public interest; (3) ensure transparency, explainability and intelligibility; (4) foster responsibility and accountability; (5) ensure inclusiveness and equity; (6) promote AI that is responsive and sustainable.

Another strong point of the report is its detailed analysis of the risks and limitations of AI. Two major problems are raised: (1) the potential of discrimination; and (2) bias when datasets used to train AI fail to reflect the real world, and there is a lack of transparency in the data source used to program these algorithms, without the explanation of how they cross-reference the data and effectively reach to a certain result. In fact, nowadays AI is booming in Medicine but it's also facing a credibility crisis because the algorithms are 'often trained on small, single-origin data samples with limited diversity; some even reused the same data for training and testing, a cardinal sin that can lead to misleadingly impressive performance' (Ross 2021a, b).

The failure to test AI models on data from different sources—a process known as external validation—is common in studies published in leading medical journals. According to a research team from the University of Cambridge in England, an ever-growing list of papers rely on 'limited or low-quality data, fail to specify their training approach and statistical methods, and don't test whether they will work for people of different races, genders, ages, and geographies' (Ross 2021a, b). This results in an algorithm that appears highly accurate in a specific study, but does not work to the same level of accuracy when exposed to real-world variables, across different types of patients in several locations.

In a recent interview, Eric Topol presented worries about how AI might worsen some inequities and discrimination, since 'algorithms are not biased, but the data we put into those algorithms, because they are chosen by humans, often are' (Time Magazine 2019). There is the potential risk for discrimination of the AI algorithms in Medicine, since they can be programmed based on data from scientific studies and electronic health records of certain populations where some races predominate. Thus, there is a risk that decisions are contaminated by significant biases (Ledford 2019; Obermeyer et al. 2019). As an example, it is argued that black women with breast cancer are more likely to be diagnosed late by the FDA approved algorithms in the market, precisely because they were programmed with data from a population where probably did not have black women, or it had very few (Brodwin 2021). This is something very serious and important to reflect on, since programming the algorithms with healthcare data from different populations and geographic locations is essential, considering the expressive variations in the way the diseases manifest in different races.

Furthermore, in a recent study, it was found that between 2012 and 2020 only 73 of 161 AI products approved by Food and Drug Administration (FDA) in the US have publicly disclosed the amount of data used to validate the product, with only 7 of them reporting the racial makeup for their study populations. Moreover, among 10 AI products approved for breast imaging, only 1 publicly disclosed the racial demographics of the dataset used to detect suspicious lesions and assess cancer risk (Ross 2021a, b). In another study conduct by Stanford University between January 2015 and December 2020, it was observed that almost all of the FDA approved AI devices (126 of 130) underwent only retrospective studies at their submission. None of the 54 high-risk devices were evaluated by prospective studies and only 17 device studies reported that demographic subgroup performance was considered in their evaluations. It was concluded in this second study that more than the importance of evaluating the performance of AI devices in multiple clinical sites and across representative populations, it is also essential encouraging prospective studies. The reason for this conclusion is that 'prospective studies with comparison to standard of care reduces the risk of harmful overfitting and more accurately captures true clinical outcomes. Post-market surveillance of AI devices is also needed for understanding and measurement of unintended outcomes and biases that are not detected in prospective, multi-center trials' (Wu et al. 2021).

Discussion about the need for specific regulation regarding algorithms is a recurrent doctrinal theme in a lot of areas, including the healthcare sector (Benjamens et al. 2020). Its impacts challenge the understanding of the State's own role in controlling technological development. If, on the one hand, it is expected that innovation will bring improvements to the overall quality of life, on the other hand, there is no denying that facing the issue from a regulatory point of view is a challenge (Tomasevicius and Ferraro 2020). Structuring a comprehensive approach to assess the current state of technological development does not seem like a plausible path for some more detailed demands and discussions about law-making affairs in this complex scenario, whereas tort law doctrine has been seeking to establish a systematic model for the delimitation of risk assessment contours in the development of applications centered on Artificial Intelligence systems.

Frank Pasquale suggests the parameterization of *data-informed duties* for the creation of standard models that may support accountability assessments. In the author's words, 'such standards are particularly important given the potential for inaccurate and inappropriate data to contaminate machine learning' (Pasquale 2019). In this respect, it appears that data-driven heuristic process, if contaminated early in the processing stages, might generate biased results. In other words, data curation of inputs must prevail and be observed throughout the entire algorithmic processes—which must also be auditable—otherwise the final substrates obtained after processing such data (the so-called 'outputs') might not be reliable.

Essentially, the parameterization of standard models no longer depends on regulatory efforts for the vast array of algorithmic structures, which vary in several aspects, and offers greater freedom for the development of self-regulated metrics for each type of activity. In this context, it would be possible to work with comparative bases that would offer more precise and well-mapped conditions to determine the performance in compliance with the equivalent risk duly measured for the type of algorithmic activity in question.

Stuart Russell and Peter Norvig's had already dealt with the troublesome 'quantification of uncertainties' in the context of AI algorithm's predictions: 'Agents may need to handle uncertainty, whether due to partial observability, uncertainty

Ethical Challenges of Artificial Intelligence in Medicine and the Triple... 241

nondeterminism, or a combination of the two' (Russell and Norvig 2016). In summary, the conjectures from which data-informed duties are conceived are in line with a very important guideline, proposed by Frank Pasquale as the 'fourth law of robotics' (*explainability*) (Pasquale 2017). His idea reinforces the need to overcome the *black box problem* (Pasquale 2015). As mentioned before, this is a problem usually identified by the use of machine learning techniques that provide uncontrolled and unsupervised improvement of these applications, to the point of becoming so complex that even their own creators do not understand them (Asaro 2011).[5]

Civil liability deals with uncertainty and the unpredictability. Traditionally, such derive from the application of integral risk theory as a basis for redressing torts specifically based on guardianship dangers and the precautionary principle (Calo 2015). The same logic, if transferred to the context of AI algorithms, would provide some peculiar consequences. On the subject, Yaniv Benhamou and Justine Ferland have already pointed out five observations about the data-informed duties (Benhamou and Ferland 2021).

1. A first observation of the authors is that, with regard to the requirements imposed on algorithmic actors (owner, operator, retailer and designer) (Balkin 2015), it is necessary to comply with duties of care, which concern: (a) the choice of a particular technology, in light of the tasks that need to be performed and the operator's own skills and abilities; (b) the planned organizational framework, in particular with regard to adequate follow-up; and (c) maintenance, including safety checking routines. Failure to comply with such obligations could trigger strict liability, regardless of whether the operator is also responsible for creating or elevating the risks of a certain technology (Benhamou and Ferland 2021). Considering this, it seems to be also important for physicians or hospitals—in a position of algorithm operator—to comply with these duties.

2. Benhamou and Ferland also point out that manufacturers, including those who act incidentally as algorithmic supervisors,[6] must observe the following standards of conduct (Benhamou and Ferland 2021): (b.1) design, describe and market products in a way that allows them to fulfill data-informed duties, making risks more predictable (foreseeability) (Karnow 2016)[7]; and (b.2) properly

---

[5] Commenting on the practical difficulties of the difficulty of identifying the developer creator, see.

[6] In Brazil, the concept is found in article 5, item VII, of the LGPD: "Art. 5th. (...) VII - operator: natural or legal person, under public or private law, who processes personal data on behalf of the controller." [Originally: "Art. 5°. (...) VII - operador: pessoa natural ou jurídica, de direito público ou privado, que realiza o tratamento de dados pessoais em nome do controlador."]

[7] The author points out that "predictability and foreseeability are, in practice, vague and peculiar notions, and people with different experiences and beliefs about how the world works will treat different things as "predictable." In any event humans are poor at predicting odds, and generally are not accurate estimating the likelihood of future events. Perhaps we may get better at predicting the behavior of autonomous robots as we interact with them; actions that appear at first random may begin to cluster in their frequencies, revealing theretofore unanticipated patterns that will help future prediction."

monitor the product after it has been put into circulation, in light of the characteristics of emerging digital technologies, in particular due to their openness and dependence on the general digital environment, including obsolescence, the emergence of malware or even its vulnerability to possible external attacks.

3. The so-called *supervision*, in the context of monitoring specific duties that hierarchically superior may even be due to the administrative police power of the State (Scherer 2016), in what Pasquale calls 'oversight' in his newest book (Pasquale 2020). That could be achieved by carrying out audits and studies of the specific algorithm, even after its market release. Thus, as a result of the implementation of supervised monitoring systems, the identification of anomalies and the prior parameterization of the systems would be expected to 'warn' about the occurrence of unexpected behaviors, as well as the observation of specific evolution trends from machine learning to predict such behaviors. Once such monitoring is implemented, the obligation to inform potential victims appears as a duty attached to objective good faith (Wischmeyer 2020).

4. If feasible, the authors argue that producers should be compelled to include mandatory backdoors in their algorithms (Liao et al. 2020). Other designations for this are the expressions 'emergency brakes by default (or by design)', 'shut down features', or features that allow operators or users to 'turn off the AI' by manual commands, or make it 'unintelligent' by simply pressing a panic button. Failure to guarantee such tools and control options could be considered a design defect to justify a breach of the general precautions that are to be expected of them, opening up the possibility of imposing civil liability due to the fact that the algorithm is to be considered faulty. In fact, depending on the circumstances, manufacturers or operators could also be forced to 'turn off' the AI as part of their algorithmic monitoring and auditing tasks.

5. Similar to existing after-sales duties, which are composed of warnings and instructions for recalling defective products, producers/manufacturers might also assume support and correction duties—corollaries of auditability and transparency principles (Pasquale 2019)—in line with other recent developments on the potential obligation of software developers to update unsafe algorithms, for as long as the technology is on the market (i.e., beyond any contractual stipulations on warranty period) (Wolters 2019).

Frank Pasquale investigates the potential liability in the context of the use of inaccurate or inappropriate data (faulty data) in training sets for machine learning: 'firms using faulty data can be required to compensate those harmed by that data use—and should be subject to punitive damages when such faulty data collection, analysis, and use is repeated or willful (Pasquale 2019).' The punitive function of civil liability raises controversial aspects to be considered in the context of this brief study. This is because, particularly in the common law experience, punitive and dissuasive benefits have a wider application and are accepted, both by the doctrine and by the Courts. Although the topic is controversial and even though punitive damages are only one of the various options to consider a deterrent effect of potential liability, it is inevitable to observe the relevance of the discussion to the complex technological context in which Artificial Intelligence algorithms are inserted.

Preserving the complementarity of tort law and regulation of data collection, analysis, and use is very appropriate to help it avoid preventable accidents and expands opportunities for those harmed by new technologies to demand accountability (Faleiros Júnior 2021). Nowadays, tort law is moving towards to promote not only liability but also accountability, which has a prospective function and is more robust and based on multiple functions, especially the precautionary one. This scenario presented by Pasquale reinforce, in one hand, the important concern with the desirable compliance, considered from governance structures and data curation aimed at the continuously verification of the quality of the collection used into the AI algorithms. On the other hand, this context turns out to a triple reflection: (1) if it is possible to assume that AI diagnosing will be covered under health providers' current malpractice insurance policies, or if the introduction of AI diagnosing into clinical practice will likely prompt insurance providers to decline coverage for such activities; (2) the potential civil liability of the physician as an algorithmic operator who repeatedly observes its ineffectiveness or becomes aware that the AI uses biased data collections (faulty data); (3) the importance of medical education in AI, digital health and new technologies to prevent adverse events.

4 Concluding Notes: The Future of Artificial Intelligence (AI) in Medicine and the Importance of Medical Education in Digital Health and New Technologies

It was observed in the present study that the valuable development of P4-Medicine from the use of predictive algorithms cannot be unaccompanied by the need for reflection about the risks and a special medical diligence in using the technology as a tool to support decision making. Moreover, it was concluded that there are three different semantic dimensions of algorithmic opacity relevant to Medicine: (1) *epistemic opacity* for the insufficient physicians understanding of the rules an AI system is applying to make predictions and decisions; (2) opacity for the *lack of medical disclosure* about the use of AI systems and patient's unawareness that automated decision-making and profiling activities about them are being carried out with their personal data; and (3) *explanatory opacity* for the unsatisfactory explanation to patients about the technology used to support professional decision-making. Therefore, the aim of this paper was to analyze each type of opacity, considering hypothetical scenarios and its repercussions in terms of medical malpractice and patient's informed consent.

Regarding *epistemic opacity*, questions were presented about to what extent a doctor might rely on AI and the legal consequences if the physician adhered to the recommendation or overruled the machine, leading to the significant consideration about the determination of the standard of medical diligence must be an issue always open to debate in each specific medical malpractice case. This is because, in each situation, the degree of accuracy of an algorithm and its goal are different. It could also be concluded in the present paper that there is a possibility of qualifying the physician's obligation as an obligation of result when there is a violation of the ethical principle of 'human control of technology', that is, in the face of non-understanding of AI as a tool to support clinical decision-making (AI-as-a-tool), with the consequent breach of the patient's legitimate expectation of technology as a guarantee of success. It was also observed that *opacity for the lack of medical disclosure* and *explanatory opacity* demand reflections on the impact of the ethical principles of explanation and justification, in order to understand a new model of patient consent in AI and the violation of the medical duty of qualified information.

In this context, the above-mentioned issues—specially, the consequences of the triple semantic dimensions of algorithmic opacity—represent an enormous challenge to educators in the health sciences. AI can help medical professionals by amalgamating large amounts of healthcare data and supporting their decision-making process about diagnosis and recommend treatments. Nevertheless, physicians need the ability to interpret the results and properly communicate a recommendation to the patient. Physicians need to learn how to better use and interpret AI algorithms, including in this learning process the comprehension of in which situations an algorithm should be effectively used in their practice, and, above all, how much confidence should be placed in an algorithmic recommendation, in each concrete case.

Thus, new skills and expertise are required as we move to an age of Artificial Intelligence in the healthcare environment. Physicians' lack of in-depth knowledge about the benefits and risks of healthcare technologies can translate into worse outcomes for patients due to little or none understanding of which AI tools add value to their activities or how to integrate AI in a way suitable for the clinical workflow. This task calls for a new model of educating the new generation of experts with deep interdisciplinary training in Medicine, ethics, and technologies. Therefore, AI needs to be seamlessly integrated across different aspects of the medical education curriculum.

The American Medical Association (AMA) noted that from 2000 to 2015 there were 15 national reports calling for medical education reform (Beck 2015). In US, there are several initiatives for incorporating new technologies—such as AI tools—in medical education: (1) *Duke Institute for Health Innovation*: medical students work together with data experts to develop care-enhanced technologies made for physicians; (2) *University of Florida*: radiology residents work with a technology-based company to develop computer-aided detection for mammography; (3) *Carle Illinois College of Medicine*: offers a course by clinical scientists and engineers to learn about new technologies; (4) *Sharon Lund Medical Intelligence and Innovation Institute*: organizes a summer course on all new technologies in health care, open to medical students; (5) *Stanford University Center for Artificial Intelligence in Medicine*: involves graduate and postgraduate students in solving heath care problems with the use of machine learning (Paranjape et al. 2019); (6) *Rocky Vista University College of Osteopathic Medicine*: offers courses to train medical students in AI, remote monitoring, ethics, informatics, telemedicine, analytics, and entrepreneurship (Aungst and Patel 2020).

In conclusion, an overriding issue for the future of AI in Medicine rests with how well medical education can be assured. As AI and its application become mainstream in the healthcare sector, medical students, residents, fellows, and practicing physicians need to have better knowledge of AI. The integration of digital health into formal education offers a novel means to engage in interprofessional education opportunities. Determining how to build out digital health education and to integrate into the formal curriculum will be a topic of debate in the coming years. To ensure that AI-based clinical decision lives up to its promises, there is a need to sensitize developers, healthcare professionals, and legislators to the challenges and limitations of opaque algorithms in the healthcare sector and to foster medical education moving forward to the Age of Artificial Intelligence in Medicine.[8]

References

Amann J, Blasimme A, Vayena E, Frey D, Madai VI (2020) Explainability for artificial intelligence in healthcare: a multidisciplinary perspective. BMC Med Inform Decis Mak 20:310

Asaro P (2011) A body to kick, but still no soul to damn: legal perspectives on robotics. In: Lin P, Abney K, Bekey G (eds) Robot ethics: the ethical and social implications of robotics. The MIT Press, Cambridge, pp 169–186

Astromskė K, Peičius E, Astromskis P (2020) Ethical and legal challenges of informed consent applying artificial intelligence in medical diagnostic consultations. AI Soc 36:509–520

Aungst TD, Patel R (2020) Integrating digital health into the curriculum—considerations on the current landscape and future developments. J Med Educ Curric Dev 7:238212051990127

Balicer RD, Cohen-Stavi C (2020) Advancing healthcare through data-driven medicine and artificial intelligence. In: Nordlinger B, Villani C, Rus D (eds) Healthcare and artificial intelligence. Springer, Cham, pp 9–15

Balkin JM (2015) The path of robotics law. Calif Law Rev Circuit 6:45–60

Beck M (2015) Innovation is sweeping through U.S. medical schools. Wall Street J. https://www.wsj.com/articles/innovation-is-sweeping-through-u-s-medical-schools-1424145650. Accessed 17 Oct 2021

Benhamou Y, Ferland J (2021) Artificial intelligence & damages: assessing liability and calculating the damages. In: D'Agostino P, Piovesan C, Gaon A (eds) Leading legal disruption: artificial Intelligence and a toolkit for lawyers and the law. Thomson Reuters Canada, Toronto, pp 1–20

Benjamens S, Dhunnoo P, Meskó B (2020) The state of artificial intelligence-based FDA-approved medical devices and algorithms: an online database. NPJ Digit Med 3:118

---

[8] *See* generally, on AI and Healthcare, in this book A T Freitas—Data-driven approaches in healthcare: challenges and emerging trends; M S Fernandes and J R Goldim—Artificial Intelligence and Decision Making in Health: Risks and Opportunities; and M N Duffourc and D S Giovanniello—The Autonomous AI Physician: Medical Ethics and Legal Liability. *See* also, on the black box effect, in this book E Magrani and P G F Silva—The Ethical and Legal Challenges of Recommender Systems Driven by Artificial Intelligence; and M N Duffourc and D S Giovanniello—The Autonomous AI Physician: Medical Ethics and Legal Liability.

Bicudo L (2021) Inteligência artificial descobre 1.000 casos de câncer com precisão de 90%. https://www.startse.com/noticia/nova-economia/tecnologia-inovacao/inteligencia-artificial-descobre-1-000-casos-de-cancer-com-precisao-de-90. Accessed 8 Oct 2021

Brodwin E (2021) Google debuts an AI-powered tool to analyze skin conditions. https://www.statnews.com/2021/05/18/google-dermatology-assist-skin-app/. Accessed 10 Oct 2021

Calo R (2015) Robotics and the lessons of cyberlaw. Calif Law Rev 103:513–563

Čerka P, Grigienė J, Sirbikytė G (2015) Liability for damages caused by artificial intelligence. Comput Law Secur Rev 31:376–389

Cohen G (2020) Informed consent and medical artificial intelligence: what to tell the patient? Harv Public Law Work Pap 108:1425–1469

Faleiros Júnior JLM (2021) Discriminação por algoritmos de Inteligência Artificial: a responsabilidade civil, os vieses e o exemplo das tecnologias baseadas em luminância. In: Barbosa MM, Braga-Netto F, Silva MC, Faleiros Júnior JLM (eds) Direito digital e inteligência artificial. Foco, Indaiatuba, pp 969–1000

Flores M, Glusman G, Brogaard K, Price ND, Hood L (2013) P4 medicine: how systems medicine will transform the healthcare sector and society. Pers Med 10:565–576

Ford RA, Price N (2016) Privacy and accountability in black-box medicine. Mich Telecommun Technol Law Rev 23:1–43

Harmon SA, Sanford TH, Xu S, Turkbey EB, Roth H, Xu Z, Yang D, Myronenko A, Anderson V, Amalou A, Blain M, Kassin M, Long D, Varble N, Walker SM, Bagci U, Ierardi AM, Stellato E, Plensich GG, Franceschelli G, Girlando C, Irmici G, Labella D, Hammoud D, Malayeri A, Jones E, Summers RM, Choyke PL, Xu D, Flores M, Tamura K, Obinata H, Mori H, Patella F, Cariati M, Carrafiello G, An P, Wood BJ, Turkbey B (2020) Artificial intelligence for the detection of COVID-19 pneumonia on chest CT using multinational datasets. Nat Commun 11:4080

Holzinger A, Röcker C, Ziefle M (2015) From smart health to smart hospitals. In: Holzinger A, Röcker C, Ziefle M (eds) Smart health: open problems and future challenges. Springer, Cham, pp 1–20

Hood L (2013) Systems biology and P4 medicine: past, present, and future. Rambam Maimonides Med J 4:e0012

Huang S, Yang J, Fong S, Zhao Q (2020) Artificial intelligence in cancer diagnosis and prognosis: opportunities and challenges. Cancer Lett 471:61–71

IBM Healthcare and Life Sciences (2021) The future of health is cognitive. Harnessing data and insight to deliver better health, value and individual engagement. https://www.ibm.com/downloads/cas/LQZ0O1WM. Accessed 17 Sep 2021

Jorstad KT (2020) Intersection of artificial intelligence and medicine: tort liability in the technological age. J Med Artif Intell 3:1–17

Jvion CORE (2021) Care optimization and recommendation enhancement. https://jvion.com/approach/the-jvion-core/. Accessed 20 Oct 2021

Karnow CEA (2016) The application of traditional tort theory to embodied machine intelligence. In: Calo AR, Froomkin M, Kerr I (eds) Robot law. Edward Elgar, Cheltenham, pp 51–77

Kfouri-Neto M (2021) Responsabilidade civil do médico. Thomson Reuters Brazil, São Paulo, pp 97–100

Ledford H (2019) Millions of black people affected by racial bias in health-care algorithms. Nature 574:608–609

Liao C, Zhong H, Squicciarini A, Zhu S, Miller D (2020) Backdoor embedding in convolutional neural network models via invisible perturbation. In: Proceedings of the 10th ACM conference on data and application security and privacy. ACM, New York, pp 97–108

Marcetich M (2020) Data pulse: a brief tour of artificial intelligence in healthcare. New Degree Press, Washington, DC

Molnár-Gábor F (2020) Artificial intelligence in healthcare: doctors, patients and liabilities. In: Wischmeyer T, Rademacher T (eds) Regulating artificial intelligence. Springer, Cham, pp 337–360

Nogaroli R, Dantas E (2020) Consentimento informado do paciente frente às novas tecnologias da saúde (telemedicina, cirurgia robótica e inteligência artificial). Lex Med Rev Port Direito Saúde 17:25–63

Nogaroli R, Dantas E (2021) The rise of robotics and artificial intelligence in healthcare: news challenges for the doctrine of informed consent. Med Law 40:15–61

Nogaroli R, Kfouri-Neto M (2019) Responsabilidade civil pelo inadimplemento do dever de informação na cirurgia robótica e telecirurgia: uma abordagem de direito comparado (Estados Unidos, União Europeia e Brasil). In: Dadalto L, Bezerra J, Rosenvald N (eds) Responsabilidade Civil e Medicina. Foco, Indaiatuba, pp 173–203

Nogaroli R, Kfouri-Neto M (2020) Estudo comparatístico da responsabilidade civil do Médico, hospital e fabricante na cirurgia assistida por robô. Essay. In: Nogaroli R, Kfouri-Neto M (eds) Debates contemporâneos em direito médico e da saúde. Thomson Reuters Brazil, São Paulo, pp 33–67

Nogaroli R, Kfouri-Neto M (2021a) Algoritmos de inteligência artificial na predição do quadro clínico de pacientes e a responsabilidade civil médica por omissão de cuidados paliativos. In: Dadalto L (ed) Cuidados paliativos: aspectos jurídicos. Foco, Indaiatuba, pp 163–190

Nogaroli R, Kfouri-Neto M (2021b) Inteligência artificial nas decisões clínicas e a responsabilidade civil médica por eventos adversos no contexto dos hospitais virtuais. In: Barbosa MM, Braga-Netto F, Silva MC, Faleiros Júnior JLM (eds) Direito digital e inteligência artificial: diálogos entre Brasil e Europa. Foco, Indaiatuba, pp 1079–1107

Nogaroli R, Nalin P (2021) Diagnóstico para covid-19 com inteligência artificial: novos desafios sobre princípios contratuais e responsabilidade médica em tempos de pandemia. Rev Eletrônica Direito Cent Univ Newton Paiva 43:256–279

Nogaroli R, Silva RG (2020) Inteligência artificial na análise diagnóstica: benefícios, riscos e responsabilidade do médico. In: Nogaroli R, Kfouri-Neto M (eds) Debates contemporâneos em direito médico e da saúde. Thomson Reuters Brazil, São Paulo, pp 69–91

Nogaroli R, Silva RG (2021) Inteligência artificial na análise diagnóstica da COVID-19: possíveis repercussões sobre a responsabilidade civil do médico. In: Rosenvald N, do Rêgo MFCE, Densa R (eds) Coronavírus e responsabilidade civil: impactos contratuais e extracontratuais. Foco, Indaiatuba, pp 293–300

Obermeyer Z, Powers B, Vogeli C, Mullainathan S (2019) Dissecting racial bias in an algorithm used to manage the health of populations. Science 366:447–453

Paranjape K, Schinkel M, Nannan Panday R, Car J, Nanayakkara P (2019) Introducing artificial intelligence training in medical education. JMIR Med Educ 5:e16048

Pasquale F (2015) The black box society: the secret algorithms that control money and information. Harvard University Press, Cambridge

Pasquale F (2017) Toward a fourth law of robotics: preserving attribution, responsibility, and explainability in an algorithmic society. Univ Md Leg Stud Res Pap 78:1–12

Pasquale F (2019) Data-informed duties in AI development. Columbia Law Rev 119:1917–1940

Pasquale F (2020) New laws of robotics: defending human expertise in the age of AI. The Belknap Press of Harvard University Press, Cambridge

Pereira AGD (2004) O consentimento informado na relação médico-paciente. Coimbra Editora, Coimbra

Price WN, Gerke S, Cohen IG (2019) Potential liability for physicians using artificial intelligence. JAMA 322:1765–1766

Robbins R (2021) An experiment in end-of-life care: tapping AI's cold calculus to nudge the most human of conversations. https://www.statnews.com/2020/07/01/end-of-life-artificial-intelligence/. Accessed 20 Oct 2021

Robbins R, Brodwin E (2021) An invisible hand: patients aren't being told about the AI systems advising their care. https://www.statnews.com/2020/07/15/artificial-intelligence-patient-consent-hospitals/. Accessed 10 Oct 2021

Ross C (2021a) As the FDA clears a flood of AI tools, missing data raise troubling questions on safety and fairness. https://www.statnews.com/2021/02/03/fda-clearances-artificial-intelligence-data/. Accessed 14 Oct 2021

Ross C (2021b) Machine learning is booming in medicine. It's also facing a credibility crisis. https://www.statnews.com/2021/06/02/machine-learning-ai-methodology-research-flaws/?utm_source=STATNewsletters&utm_campaign=37c8993853-MR_COPY_02&utm_medium=email&utm_term=0_8cab1d7961-37c8993853-153220734#. Accessed 10 Sept 2021

Russell S, Norvig P (2016) Artificial intelligence: a modern approach. Pearson, Boston

Scherer M (2016) Regulating artificial intelligence systems: risks, challenges, competencies, and strategies. Harv J Law Technol 29:353–400

Time Magazine (2019) Cardiologist eric topol on how AI can bring humanity back to medicine. March 25, 2019. https://time.com/collection/life-reinvented/5551296/cardiologist-eric-topol-artificial-intelligence-interview/. Accessed 10 Oct 2021

Tomasevicius FE, Ferraro AV (2020) Le nuove sfide dell'umanità e del diritto nell'era dell'intelligenza artificiale. Rev Direitos Cult 15:401–413

Topol EJ (2013) The creative destruction of medicine: how the digital revolution will create better health care. Basic Books, New York

Topol EJ (2016) The patient will see you now: the future of medicine is in your hands. Basic Books, New York

Topol EJ (2019a) Deep medicine: how artificial intelligence can make healthcare human again. Basic Books, New York

Topol EJ (2019b) High-performance medicine: the convergence of human and artificial intelligence. Nat Med 25:44–56

UCI Beall Applied Innovation (2017) Husky or wolf? Using a black box learning model to avoid adoption errors. http://innovation.uci.edu/2017/08/husky-or-wolf-using-a-black-box-learning-model-to-avoid-adoption-errors/. Accessed 8 Oct 2021

United Nations (2021) Urgent action needed over artificial intelligence risks to human rights. https://news.un.org/en/story/2021/09/1099972. Accessed 20 Oct 2021

Wischmeyer T (2020) Artificial intelligence and transparency: opening the black box. In: Wischmeyer T, Rademacher T (eds) Regulating artificial intelligence. Springer, Cham, pp 75–101

Wolters PTJ (2019) The obligation to update insecure software in the light of Consumentenbond/Samsung. Comput Law Secur Rev 35:295–305

World Health Organization (2021) WHO guidance – ethics and governance of artificial intelligence for health. https://www.who.int/publications/i/item/9789240029200. Accessed 20 Sep 2021

Wu E, Wu K, Daneshjou R, Ouyang D, Ho DE, Zou J (2021) How medical AI devices are evaluated: limitations and recommendations from an analysis of FDA approvals. Nat Med 27:582–584

Open Access This chapter is licensed under the terms of the Creative Commons Attribution 4.0 International License (http://creativecommons.org/licenses/by/4.0/), which permits use, sharing, adaptation, distribution and reproduction in any medium or format, as long as you give appropriate credit to the original author(s) and the source, provide a link to the Creative Commons license and indicate if changes were made.

The images or other third party material in this chapter are included in the chapter's Creative Commons license, unless indicated otherwise in a credit line to the material. If material is not included in the chapter's Creative Commons license and your intended use is not permitted by statutory regulation or exceeds the permitted use, you will need to obtain permission directly from the copyright holder.

Part III
The Law, Governance and Regulation of Artificial Intelligence

Introduction

Luís Barreto Xavier

As previously stated, Part II of this book directed its attention to fundamental ethical and legal debates, evaluating them in the light of the transformation brought by AI. Part III employs multiple approaches to discuss how Artificial Intelligence is brought in line by law, how its applications should be governed and how existing and future regulation might be employed to tackle its risks.

The chapter by *Ugo Pagallo* tries to dismantle the myths of digital sovereignty, digital constitutionalism, Brussels effect and human-centric Artificial Intelligence in the context of European Law.

The chapter by *Luís Moniz Pereira, Francisco C. Santos and António Barata Lopes* explores the undertaking of counterfactual thinking by AI agents, and suggests that counterfactual learners foster coordination in collective dilemmas.

In the chapter by *Willem Gravett*, the author critically examines the "technology effect"—the human tendency towards excessive optimism when making decisions involving technology—and "automation bias"—the phenomenon whereby judges accept the recommendations of an automated decision-making system, without additional research or confirmation.

The chapter by *Ana Taveira da Fonseca Elsa Vaz Sequeira and Luís Barreto Xavier*, tries to ascertain if there is a place for fault-based liability for AI driven systems, if current strict liability regimes are appropriate to address no-fault damages caused by the functioning of AI-systems, and when should an agent be exempted from liability.

The chapter by *Marcel Lanz and Stefan Mijic* addresses natural language generation (NLG) technology and explores the different ways that civil liability for NLG deployment may be constructed and how it should be solved, from a Swiss law perspective.

In the chapter by *Pedro Garcia Marques*, the author reflects on the possibilities and the limits of using AI powered systems to predict the risk of recidivism for the purposes of imposing criminal penalty on convicted felons and compares them to human assessment.

Deepfake generation and its relevance in the context of the administration of criminal justice is the topic of the chapter by *Dalila Durães, Pedro Miguel Freitas and Paulo Novais*. The authors explain the technical foundations of deepfakes, discuss the way in which the European Union addresses them in its draft AI Act and the challenges inherent in regulating them for criminal justice purposes.

The chapter by *Maria José Schmidt-Kessen and Max Huffman* deals with AI based pricing technologies and their role on algorithmic collusion. The authors address the topic from a US and EU antitrust law comparative perspective, and discuss this still existing problem prospectively.

The chapter by *Joana Covelo de Abreu* stresses the need for an AI human-centric approach to the field of justice, through user-focused and user-friendly principles, and scrutinizes how the EU's draft AI Act must further address judicial usage of AI systems, as a mechanism for enhancing judicial independence, procedural rights and access to justice in the EU.

In the chapter by *Anat Keller, Clara Martins Pereira and Martinho Lucas Pires*, the authors critically assess the exclusion of financial systemic risk from the "high risk" definition of the EU's draft AI Act, and advocate for a more integrated cross-border approach to AI, acknowledging the implications of AI for financial systemic risk.

The last chapter of Part III (*Katerina Yordanova and Natalie Bertels*) analyses the potential of the regulatory sandboxes envisaged in the EU's draft AI Act for regulating AI and the challenges they could face based on experiences from earlier regulatory sandboxes. The authors then suggest tailor-made solutions that would mitigate potential disadvantages of AI regulatory sandboxes.

Dismantling Four Myths in AI & EU Law Through Legal Information 'About' Reality

Ugo Pagallo

Abstract The European Commission has recently proposed several acts, directives and regulations that shall complement today's legislation on the internet, data governance, and Artificial Intelligence, e.g., the AI Act from May 2021. Some have proposed to sum up current trends of EU law according to catchy formulas, such as (i) digital sovereignty; (ii) digital constitutionalism; (iii) a new Brussels effect; and, (iv) a human-centric approach to AI. Each of these narratives has its merits, but can be highly misleading. They must be taken with four pinches of salt. The aim of this paper is to dismantle these 'myths' through legal information 'about' reality, that is, knowledge and concepts that frame the representation and function of EU law. We should be attentive to that which current myths overlook, such as the open issues on the balance of power between EU institutions and member states (MS), a new generation of digital rights at both EU and MS constitutional levels, down to the interplay between new models of legal governance and the potential fragmentation of the system, e.g., between technological regulations and environmental law.

1 Introduction

Over the past few years, the European Commission has proposed several acts, directives and regulations that shall complement today's legislation on the internet, data governance, Artificial Intelligence, and more. The list of initiatives and proposals discussed at the European Union ('EU') level includes the *Digital Services* and *Digital Markets Act* from December 2020, the *Data Governance Act* from November of that year, the *Artificial Intelligence Act* (AIA) from May 2021, the *Cybersecurity Act* from July 2021, in addition to the initiatives for a Green Deal, the Open Science project, etc. By considering such legal complexity, scholars have proposed some catchy formulas that should help us setting the proper level of

---

U. Pagallo (✉)
Department of Law, University of Turin, Torino, Italy
e-mail: ugo.pagallo@unito.it

© The Author(s) 2024
H. Sousa Antunes et al. (eds.), *Multidisciplinary Perspectives on Artificial Intelligence and the Law*, Law, Governance and Technology Series 58,
https://doi.org/10.1007/978-3-031-41264-6_13

abstraction, to address the intricacy of technological regulation and data governance in EU law. The aim of this paper is to examine four of these formulas: (i) digital sovereignty; (ii) digital constitutionalism; (iii) a new Brussels effect; and, (iv) a human-centric approach to AI ('HAI'). The overall assumption of the analysis is that each of these levels of abstraction has its merits, and still, the formulas can be misleading. Their use may suggest false problems, or problems taken for granted, missing at times the proverbial elephant in the room. The aim of this paper is thus to dismantle these 'myths' through the lens of legal information 'about' reality, that is, knowledge and concepts that frame the representation and function of EU law. The analysis is divided into five parts, each of which devoted to one of the myths under scrutiny in this paper, with its conclusions. The overall intent is to offer a soberer analysis of current trends of EU law and technological regulation.

2   Digital Sovereignty

Luciano Floridi has recently scrutinized the 'fight for digital sovereignty' occurred over the past few years, examining 'what it is' (a matter of control of data, software, standards, services, infrastructures, etc.); and 'why it matters' (the fight touches everyone) 'especially for the EU' (Floridi 2020). Although Floridi refers to a 'post-Westphalian world in which the territoriality of the law no longer applies automatically and may be irrelevant' (Floridi 2021), this new dimension of the old concept, that is, 'digital sovereignty' should still shed light on the current fight for control between the multiple regulatory systems in competition out there: the forces of the market, and of social norms, the legal powers of national governments and international organizations, the role of civic institutions and the financial sector, and more.

However, in EU law, since the ruling of the European Court of Justice in *Van Gend & Loos* from 1963, the principle of sovereignty and the current formula on 'digital sovereignty' remind us of the legal knot on who must have the 'last word' between the EU institutions and the Member States (MS). For better or for worse, 30 years ago, the compromise has been struck with the Maastricht treaty (1992), and the principle of subsidiarity pursuant to Art. 5 of the EU Treaty. Most of the regulatory initiatives and proposals of the Commission, mentioned above in the introduction, hinge indeed on the principle of subsidiarity due to the scale of the issues that are at stake with the regulation of crucial aspects of social interaction on the internet, data governance, or AI and other emerging technologies. So, it is misleading to refer to these trends of current EU law in terms of 'digital sovereignty' because the formula may suggest that regulations of EU look like federal law. They're not. Transferred by MS and their constitutional powers through the Treaties, EU powers are not 'original' as occurs with the constitutional powers of federal states, e.g. the USA.

This legal detail suggests that either the formula of 'digital sovereignty' misses the balance of power between EU institutions and MS, or the formula suggests that

Dismantling Four Myths in AI & EU Law Through Legal Information 'About' Reality   253

some problems have been solved—or, at least, properly addressed—when they are not. Scholars still discuss that which was dubbed as the *Kompetenz-Kompetenz* issue in the saga of the German federal constitutional court, the *Solange* cases, since the 1970s. Dealing with the governance of the internet, of AI, or tackling the flow of data in current information societies, the formula 'digital sovereignty' does not help us solving this evergreen issue on who's sovereign in Europe. Moreover, if we are interested to what this formula means 'especially for the EU', 'digital sovereignty' does not help us shedding light on the kind of governance behind the recent proposals and initiatives of the Commission. Rather than searching for a sovereign, or a bunch of them in today's law, we should be more technical about today's EU governance and its case-law (Reeds and Murray 2018). Would the stance on 'digital constitutionalism' offer such a more technical analysis?

3 Digital Constitutionalism

Considering the EU approach to the current challenges of technological regulation and its governance, some claim that "in the last twenty years, the policy of the European Union in the field of digital technologies has shifted from a liberal economic perspective to a constitution-oriented approach" (De Gregorio 2021). This new digital dimension of EU constitutionalism is often illustrated with current attempts to oppose the powers of transnational corporations operating in cyberspace, with a new set of responsibilities and duties for such corporations, as providers of services on the internet, as designers and manufacturers of high-risk AI systems, as personal data controllers of complex digital environments, and more. This new set of duties and obligations goes of course together with the corresponding new rights. Starting with the right to de-listing set up by the Court of Luxembourg in the Google case from 2013, attention should be drawn to the new rights to erasure, to be forgotten, to data portability, etc. enshrined in the general data protection regulation, or 'GDPR' from 2016, or the new rights not to be profiled, nor recognized by AI systems, proposed by Art. 5 of the 2021 AI Act of the European Commission, down to its current policies on open access rights, open science rights, etc. Shouldn't we dub all this trend as the 'digital constitutionalism' of the EU institutions?

Interestingly, this stance on digital constitutionalism refers, on the one hand, to a tenet of the digital sovereignty viewpoint, such as the current fight for access, control, and protection over data and information in digital environments, between national and international governments and institutions, e.g. the EU, and the power of transnational corporations. The EU would have flexed its muscles, showing who's the digital sovereign today, by establishing new duties for the fat cats of Silicon Valley, and new rights for the EU citizens. Although the enforcement of such rights and duties appears now and then problematic, e.g., data portability, it seems fair to admit that this stance on digital constitutionalism, much as the overlapping stance of digital sovereignty, draw our attention to a game changer. Over the past 20 years and more, EU law has indeed attempted to complement the traditional framework of basic constitutional (and human) rights associated with the physical body of the individuals and their *habeas corpus*, with a new principle of *habeas data*. The latter can be traced back to that which the German Constitutional Court has framed in terms of 'informational self-determination' since its *Volkszählungs-Urteil* ('census decision'), from 1983.

Yet, on the other hand, the formula of 'digital constitutionalism' can be misleading, once applied to EU law, because that which EU lacks is the core of traditional constitutionalism, that is, power over matters of public order, law enforcement, and national security in such crucial fields as criminal and administrative law (including procedural safeguards). By referring to the formula of EU digital constitutionalism, the risk is thus to overlook a black hole in such framework, namely, rights and safeguards for the digital body of individuals vis-à-vis law enforcement officers, public prosecutors, or secret services.

To understand how technology impacts on tenets of the rule of law, such as the principle of habeas corpus and notions of 'fair trial,' of 'equality of arms,' etc., attention must be drawn, first, to the national law level. For example, the double standard of protection for the physical body and the digital body of individuals, according to the case-law of both the Constitutional Court and the Court of Cassation in Italy, is deemed compatible with EU law and moreover, the general framework provided by the 1950 European Convention of Human Rights and its Court (ECtHR). This means that, dealing with the physical body and its protection in Italian constitutional law, a statute and the authorization of courts provide for a double level of legal protection (Art. 14 of the Constitution), whereas, in the case of the digital body in criminal proceedings, most powers are simply up to public prosecutors (Art. 2). Whether or not AI systems will reinforce this asymmetry of power between public prosecutors and suspects—also, but not only in Italy— remains of course an open question (Pagallo and Quattrocolo 2019). However, *pace* current claims of digital constitutionalism, this open question and, more in general, the informational counterpart of traditional principles of habeas corpus, fair trial, equality of arms, etc. does not revolve around trends of EU law, but mostly the powers of the Member States of the Union within the framework of the ECtHR. This is not to say that EU law has no role in shaping the legal framework for the protection of the individuals even before a criminal Court, e.g. data protection issues, and yet the whole set of sources, which every European digital constitutionalism must include—such as national powers and constitutions, the ECtHR, EU law and its treaties, international agreements, and more—begets a further question.

I admit that the role of EU law, although limited to certain areas of constitutional law, is especially relevant in some new fields of digital constitutionalism, such as personal data protection and the new set of rights in human-AI interaction set up e.g., by the AIA of the European Commission. This role of EU law in shaping today's digital constitutionalism in Europe and its complex legal governance, however, has now and then engendered further myths. Whilst, in EU law, the formula of digital constitutionalism overlooks the problems of national powers and the disrupting use of AI systems by law enforcement agencies, the plan of a new (and even desirable) digital constitutionalism in Europe often exaggerates the role of EU law. Next section dwells on one of these popular exaggerations, which brings us back to the stance of digital sovereignty.

4 The Brussels Effect

Ten years ago, Anu Bradford's idea on a 'Brussels effect' went viral (Bradford 2012). In a nutshell, the idea was that, dealing with issues of technological regulation, data protection, environmental law, or antitrust, EU law had unilaterally exerted a legal extra-territorial effect. Recently, Bradford has refined this idea in a new volume (Bradford 2020), and some scholars guess whether we should expect a new Brussels effect due to the recent initiatives of the European Commission on AI, data governance, digital services and markets, etc. (Floridi 2021). In fact, so goes the argument of the Brussels effect, the non-divisibility of data and the compliance costs of multinational corporations, dealing with multiple regulatory regimes, may prompt most technological manufacturers and service providers to adopt and adapt themselves to the strictest international standards across the board, that is, the EU data protection and environmental framework (Pagallo 2018), and now, the proposals of the European Commission.

Once again, after the stances on digital sovereignty and digital constitutionalism, the 'Brussels effect' has its merits. I may dare to say that, for example, EU data protection law does represent a model for the rest of the world. Still, even on the basis of this common assumption, the Brussels effect must be taken with a pinch of salt. By insisting on the power unilaterally exerted by EU law, the thesis on the Brussels effect often overlooks the multiple ways in which EU regulations have to do with coordination and cooperation. First, the extra-territorial provisions of the GDPR, drawing on a long experience in consumer law, are complemented with bilateral agreements of mutual recognition at the international level, e.g. Japan. Second, dealing with technological regulation, the EU lawmakers have more often opted for co-regulatory solutions of legal governance, rather than top-down approaches. Art. 5 of the GDPR on the accountability principle provides an illustration of such co-regulatory model. Third, the analysis of such co-regulatory models adopted by EU law with the 2017 policy on better and smart regulation, some of the technical developments of the EU Better Regulation scheme for interoperability (TOGAF 2017), down to the 'Data Governance Act' from November 2020, converge with similar trends in other legal sectors. Co-regulatory approaches are at work with standardisation agencies, such as NIST-800-53 from 2013 and NIST-800-63C from 2016, together with ISO/IEC 27002 and 27,001 on security and privacy controls for Federal Information Systems and Organizations. Along the same lines, this co-regulatory approach is consistent with some governance models in the business field, such as the COBIT2019 framework launched by ISACA and the Enterprise Architecture model, which aims to align management information systems with business interests (Pagallo et al. 2019).

By insisting on current trends of legal governance and international law today, the aim is not to discard any Brussels effect. I already admitted the (unilateral) impact of EU data protection law on the rest of the world and am ready to concede that certain provisions of the AIA on the banning of AI uses are not only here to stay, but will similarly represent a reference point in international law.

However, once we embrace this scenario, attention should be drawn to the content of the effect, in other words, that which would exert unilateral extra-territorial effect across jurisdictions, representing a model for the rest of the world. Current debate on EU law and technological regulation has provided some myths and popular catchy formulas also in this case. Next section scrutinizes one of such formulas: the 'human-centric' approach to the normative challenges of AI, or 'HAI.' This stance summarizes the narratives of the previous sections, according to a threefold stance on:

(i) EU's HAI for AI regulation, as illustrated by the AIA proposal of the Commission, as an act of digital sovereignty in international law;

(ii) EU's new rights in human-AI interaction set up by the AIA as a further strengthening of EU digital constitutionalism;

(iii) A possible new Brussels effect due to (i) and (ii).

The aim of next section is to take sides on whether HAI, i.e. the 'human-centric' approach of EU law for the regulation of AI systems is robust, or alternatively, even misleading.

5 'HAI' (Human-Centric Artificial Intelligence)

'HAI' has an already long story. Since the mid 2010s, the European Parliament insisted on the 'European values' that should have guided the necessary regulation of AI systems and other emerging technologies. In 2018, the European Commission set up a High-Level Expert Group (HLEG), to elucidate the ethical principles of AI. The HLEG delivered its Ethical Guidelines in 2019. The guidelines include environmental robustness and the protection of societal and environmental well-being among the six requirements that AI systems must satisfy to be considered trustworthy.[1] From a philosophical standpoint, however, it is noteworthy that such Ethical Guidelines insist time and again on their 'human-centric' approach: "the common foundation that unites these rights can be understood as rooted in respect for human dignity – thereby reflecting what we describe as a 'human-centric approach' in which the human being enjoys a unique and inalienable moral status of primacy in the civil, political, economic and social fields."[2]

---

[1] See https://digital-strategy.ec.europa.eu/en/library/ethics-guidelines-trustworthy-ai.

[2] *Ibid.*, at 10.

At their best possible light, such claims, and similar declarations, may make sense. HLEG's ethical guidelines hinge after all on a previous document of another group of experts, in which my colleagues and I insisted on four risks of AI, i.e., (i) devaluing human skills; (ii) removing human responsibility; (iii) reducing human control; (iv) eroding human self-determination (Floridi et al. 2018). Against such risks, it is thus welcomed any clear understanding of these issues under scrutiny and what initiatives can be taken against the misuses of technology in a proactive way.

However, HAI raises two formidable problems. One is philosophical, the other practical. As regards the philosophical part of this story, the limits of every human-centric, or neo-Protagorean approach have been stressed time and again over the past decades, since the ecological movements in the 1950s and 1960s, down to current regulations and principles of EU environmental law. Bioethics and its onto-centric stance tell a lot about the normative challenges brought forth by AI and other emerging technologies: "The comparison should not be surprising. Of all areas of applied ethics, bioethics is the one that most closely resembles digital ethics in dealing ecologically with new forms of agents, patients, and environments" (Floridi et al. 2018). There is robust work on why an onto-centric, rather than anthropocentric viewpoint can help us tackling that which the European Commission, in the Explanatory Memorandum of the AIA, dubs as a 'twin challenge,' namely, the green and digital transformations of our societies (Pagallo and Durante 2009).

In addition, there is evidence of the practical shortcomings of HAI. In the AIA, for example, the European Commission fully endorses the human-centric approach: all new mandatory requirements for high-risk AI systems do not include any commitment against adverse environmental impacts, lest such AI systems pose a direct threat to "the health and safety, or a risk of adverse impact on fundamental rights." This approach of the European Commission has already been criticized. The Report of the European Parliament's special committee on Artificial Intelligence in a Digital Age (AIDA) reckons that such approach simply omits "any hazards related to the environment" (Gailhofer et al. 2021, p. 10). The claim is that the proposed set of rules on AI and data governance, transparency, human oversight and security simply overlook a governance system that shall prevent critical environmental impacts of technology. After all, most proposals on the "environmental sustainability" of technology, including AI, are left to voluntary initiatives put in place by providers of non-high-risk AI systems as regards, for instance, the formation of codes of conduct (EU Commission's AIA, whereas no. 81 and article 69.2).

The troubles of EU law with environmental protection, admittedly, are older than current issues about the digital transformation of our societies and its regulation. A human-centric understanding of the challenges of AI, however, makes the green transformation of our societies even messier. Only an onto-centric approach to the 'twin challenges' of our societies fits this task. To substantiate this assumption, the onto-centric stance must include the principles of bioethics—that is, beneficence, non-maleficence, autonomy, and justice—and complement them with a new principle, the principle of 'explicability.' The latter should incorporate both the intelligibility of AI and the accountability for its uses, to understand and hold to account the decision-making processes of AI (Floridi et al. 2018). We don't need to be human-centric, to admit the risks for the misuses of AI and its impact on human skills, human responsibilities, human control, or human self-determination. Yet, it's likely that every human-centric approach to these risks will fall short in tackling how such human skills and responsibilities, control and self-determination should be further understood in connection with the challenges of environmental protection and the climate crisis. To say the least, the European Commission should complement its proposal of AIA with the assessment of the environmental impact of AI in the existing European regulatory framework (Gailhofer et al. 2021, p. 37).

On this basis, we may wonder about the metrics for the assessment of the environmental impact of AI, whether their footprint assessment should be compulsory for all high-risk AI systems, for example, or extended to certain low-risk AI applications. Likewise, focus should be on energy costs and carbon emissions (Lacoste et al. 2019; Anthony et al. 2020), e-waste and further conditions of sustainability as, for instance, working conditions, down to the metrics AI systems are optimized for, or further efficiency metrics for AI, as model training (Taddeo et al. 2021). Advanced AI technologies often require massive computational resources that hinge on large computing centers and these facilities have a very high energy requirement and carbon footprint. Some estimates suggest that the total electricity demand of information and communication technologies (ICTs) could require up to 20% of the global electricity demand by 2030, whilst today's demand revolves around 1% (Jones 2018). AI is likely to add growing concerns for the increasing volume of e-waste and the pressure on rare-earth elements generated by the computing industry (Alonso et al. 2012).

A final problem with the philosophical and practical posture of HAI has to do with its redundancy. Not only HAI is insufficient to properly tackle the onto-centric challenges of the green and digital transformations of our societies, but it does not even help to clarify the technicalities of our field. For example, there is a glorious tradition in robotics and AI devoted to the study of human-robot interaction (HRI). Interestingly, experts distinguish two sub-fields of the discipline. Some focus on a human-centred HRI approach: emphasis is here on whether and to what extent AI systems and robots fulfil their task specifications in a way that appears as comfortable and acceptable to humans (Dautenhahn 2007). Yet, there is also a robot-centred HRI approach: this does not mean that experts and scholars are devoted to diminishing human skills, or devaluing human responsibility. Rather, that which computer scientists and engineers aim to understand is an entity, such as a smart robot, that is pursuing 'its own' goals, based on such cues, as its motivations, drivers, or emotions (Pagallo 2013). These vibrant fields of technological development and innovation, e.g. the set up of 'moral machines' have been funded by EU research programs (and that's a good thing). Should we conclude that, in all projects of robot-centred HRI research, scholars should abide by a human-centric approach?

The question is either redundant or highly debatable. It is redundant, because AI researchers should abide by the law; it is highly debatable, because some laws, such as EU environmental law, hinge on an onto-centric basis, e.g. Art. 37 of the EU Charter of fundamental rights (CFR), and Art. 11 of the Treaty on the Functioning of the European Union (TFEU). Therefore, as occurs with previous catchy formulas on digital sovereignty, digital constitutionalism, and the Brussels effect, also HAI must be taken with a pinch of salt. The pinch of salt we apply ourselves when asking when the sun sets, or will rise tomorrow, although we are no earth-flatters but Copernicans. AI raises unique challenges for human skills and responsibilities, human control and self-determination. Yet, this uniqueness does not entail any neo-Protagorean view, rather, it should be grasped in accordance with the onto-centric stance of digital ethics that properly complements the four principles of bioethics.

6 Conclusions

The chapter dwelt on current EU legal trends and the array of further proposals by the Commission, dismantling four popular narratives or 'myths' on digital sovereignty, digital constitutionalism, a new Brussels effect, and HAI. Four lessons were learnt because of this stance on legal information 'about' reality, namely, about knowledge and concepts that frame the representation and function of EU law:

(a) Against the tenets of digital sovereignty, attention was drawn to the principle of subsidiarity pursuant to Art. 5 of the EU Treaty and the complex governance of the EU institutions;
(b) Against the view on EU digital constitutionalism, the limits of EU law in criminal law, national security, public order and law enforcement were stressed, to offer a more realistic picture of current debate and trends on how the law should protect the digital body of the individuals (also but not only in criminal law and administrative law);
(c) Against advocates of a new Brussels effect, this view on unilateral exertion of extra-territorial legal effects was complemented with bilateral initiatives of mutual recognition at the international level and new models of co-regulation, coordination and cooperation within the EU;
(d) Against the assumptions of HAI, focus was on its philosophical and practical drawbacks and how the onto-centric approach of digital ethics provides a better lens for the twin challenge of the green and digital transformations of our societies.

This stance on current trends of EU law casts light on that which is still critical: the balance between EU powers and member states, a new generation of digital rights at both EU and MS constitutional levels, down to the interplay between new models of legal governance and the potential fragmentation of the system, e.g. between technological regulations and environmental law. Current myths on digital sovereignty, digital constitutionalism, a new Brussels effect, and HAI do not help us addressing these open problems. Rather, they may induce us to overlook them. Although some of these problems do not depend on EU law and its institutions, they contribute to shape current trends of EU law.

References

Alonso E, Sherman AM, Wallington TJ, Everson MP, Field FR, Roth R, Kirchain RE (2012) Evaluating rare earth element availability: a case with revolutionary demand from clean technologies. Environ Sci Technol 46:3406–3414

Anthony LFW, Kanding B, Selvan R (2020) Carbontracker: tracking and predicting the carbon footprint of training deep learning models. ArXiv200703051

Bradford A (2012) The Brussels effect. Northwest Univ Law Rev 107:1–68

Bradford A (2020) The Brussels effect: how the European union rules the world. Oxford University Press, Oxford

Dautenhahn K (2007) Socially intelligent robots: dimensions of human-robot interaction. Philos Trans R Soc B Biol Sci 362:679–704

De Gregorio G (2021) The rise of digital constitutionalism in the European Union. Int J Const Law 19:41–70

Floridi L (2020) The fight for digital sovereignty: what it is, and why it matters, especially for the EU. Philos Technol 33:369–378

Floridi L (2021) The European legislation on AI: a brief analysis of its philosophical approach. Philos Technol 34:215–222

Floridi L, Cowls J, Beltrametti M, Chatila R, Chazerand P, Dignum V, Luetge C, Madelin R, Pagallo U, Rossi F, Schafer B, Valcke P, Vayena E (2018) AI4People - an ethical framework for a good AI society: opportunities, risks, principles, and recommendations. Minds Mach 28:689–707

Gailhofer P, Herold A, Schemmel JP, Scherf CS, Urrutia C, Köhler AR, Braungardt S (2021) The role of artificial intelligence in the European green deal. In: Study for the special committee on artificial intelligence in a digital age (AIDA). Policy Department for Economic, Scientific and Quality of Life Policies, European Parliament, Luxembourg

Jones N (2018) How to stop data centres from gobbling up the world's electricity. Nature 561:163–166

Lacoste A, Luccioni A, Schmidt V, Dandres T (2019) Quantifying the carbon emissions of machine learning. ArXiv:1910.09700

Pagallo U (2013) The laws of robots: crimes, contracts, and torts. Springer, Dordrecht

Pagallo U (2018) Algo-rhythms and the beat of the legal drum. Philos Technol 31:507–524

Pagallo U, Durante M (2009) Three roads to P2P systems and their impact on business practices and ethics. J Bus Ethics 90:551–564

Pagallo U, Quattrocolo S (2019) The impact of AI on criminal law, and its twofold procedures. In: Barfield W, Pagallo U (eds) The research handbook of the law of artificial intelligence. Edward Elgar Publishing, Northampton, pp 385–409

Pagallo U, Casanovas P, Madelin R (2019) The middle-out approach: assessing models of legal governance in data protection, artificial intelligence, and the web of data. Theory Pract Legis 7:1–25

Reeds C, Murray A (2018) Rethinking the jurisprudence of cyberspace. Elgar, Cheltenham

Taddeo M, Tsamados A, Cowls J, Floridi L (2021) Artificial intelligence and the climate emergency: opportunities, challenges, and recommendations. One Earth 4:776–779

TOGAF (2017) An introduction to the European interoperability reference architecture (EIRA©) v2.1.0. https://joinup.ec.europa.eu/sites/default/files/distribution/access_url/2018-02/b1859b84-3e86-4e00-a5c4-d87913cdcc6f/EIRA_v2_1_0_Overview.pdf. Accessed 3 Aug 2020

Open Access This chapter is licensed under the terms of the Creative Commons Attribution 4.0 International License (http://creativecommons.org/licenses/by/4.0/), which permits use, sharing, adaptation, distribution and reproduction in any medium or format, as long as you give appropriate credit to the original author(s) and the source, provide a link to the Creative Commons license and indicate if changes were made.

The images or other third party material in this chapter are included in the chapter's Creative Commons license, unless indicated otherwise in a credit line to the material. If material is not included in the chapter's Creative Commons license and your intended use is not permitted by statutory regulation or exceeds the permitted use, you will need to obtain permission directly from the copyright holder.

AI Modelling of Counterfactual Thinking for Judicial Reasoning and Governance of Law

Luís Moniz Pereira, Francisco C. Santos, and António Barata Lopes

Abstract When speaking of moral judgment, we refer to a function of recognizing appropriate or condemnable actions and the possibility of choice between them by agents. Their ability to construct possible causal sequences enables them to devise alternatives in which choosing one implies setting aside others. This internal deliberation requires a cognitive ability, namely that of constructing counterfactual arguments. These serve not just to analyse possible futures, being prospective, but also to analyse past situations, by imagining the gains or losses resulting from alternatives to the actions actually carried out, given evaluative information subsequently known.

Counterfactual thinking is in thus a prerequisite for AI agents concerned with Law cases, in order to pass judgement and, additionally, for evaluation of the ongoing governance of such AI agents. Moreover, given the wide cognitive empowerment of counterfactual reasoning in the human individual, namely in making judgments, the question arises of how the presence of individuals with this ability can improve cooperation and consensus in populations of otherwise self-regarding individuals.

Our results, using Evolutionary Game Theory (EGT), suggest that counterfactual thinking fosters coordination in collective action problems occurring in large populations and has limited impact on cooperation dilemmas in which such coordination is not required.

L. M. Pereira (✉)
Departamento de Informatica, Faculdade de Ciências e Tecnologia, Universidade Nova de Lisboa, Monte de Caparica, Portugal
e-mail: lmp@fct.unl.pt

F. C. Santos
INESC-ID and Instituto Superior Técnico, Universidade de Lisboa, Porto Salvo, Portugal
e-mail: franciscocsantos@tecnico.ulisboa.pt

A. B. Lopes
ANQEP – "Agência Nacional para a Qualificação e Ensino Profissional" and Agrupamento de Escolas de Alvalade, Lisbon, Portugal

© The Author(s) 2024
H. Sousa Antunes et al. (eds.), *Multidisciplinary Perspectives on Artificial Intelligence and the Law*, Law, Governance and Technology Series 58,
https://doi.org/10.1007/978-3-031-41264-6_14

1 Introduction and Motivation

The Law clearly says that its theory of causation is counterfactual dependency (Moore 2009, p. 371). The focus on counterfactual theory lies in morality. The social minimum is that we do no harm. Our moral responsibility is naturally captured by a certain kind of counterfactual test, one that compares how the world is after our actions with how the world would have been if, contrary to fact, we had not done the actions in question. Similarly, one can reason about alternative actions which would have improved the world or produced a greater good (Roese and Olson 1995; Pereira and Saptawijaya 2016a, 2016b, 2017).

The class of statements we deem counterfactual are conditional statements conjoined with the falsity of both the antecedent and their consequent clauses (Pearl 2010). Counterfactuals, possibility, and the hypothetical are part of the genesis of what there is, and what there is what it is because it was *otherwise*. In (Dietz Saldanha et al. 2015, 2021) we also consider conditionals whose antecedents are *unknown* and evaluate the conditional by applying revision and abduction in order to satisfy it. The laws of physics, for example, can be interpreted as counterfactual assertions, such as 'Had the weight on this spring doubled, its length would have doubled as well' (Hooke's Law) (Pearl and Mackenzie 2018).

Causation as a prerequisite to legal liability is intimately related to causation as a natural relation lying at the heart of scientific explanation. Moral responsibility supervenes on natural properties like causation, intention, and the like. The counterfactual theory of causal relations is dominant in both Law and recent Philosophy. We are more blameworthy when we cause some evil, than merely trying to cause it. We experience regret when we have caused some harm even though we were not at all culpable. It is not regret but guilt that disturbs us, in those cases we judge ourselves to be blameworthy. It is guilt, not regret, that is consistent with such self-judgements (Moore 2009, pp. vi, vii, 30–32).

When people are moved to think counterfactually, they generally think about how things might have turned out better ('upward counterfactuals' in the parlance of experimental psychology). When thinking how events might have been worse, one speaks of 'downward counterfactuals' (Byrne 2005). Already the Greek Lysias, in the aftermath of the Peloponnesian war (382 B.C) says "if we had remained united and every man had done as I did, the oligarchy and civil war would not have happened. Another Greek, the historian and general Thucydides, not only emphasizes how terrible the war really was but underlines moments when it might have been worse for Athens and its citizens (Tordoff 2014, p. 116).

According to judgement dissociation theory, upwards counterfactuals tend to focus on the functional goal of identifying ways in which a negative outcome would have been prevented. These thoughts can undo outcomes not only by negating direct causes, but also by negating enabling conditions or adding in disabling conditions. This suggests there are more ways an actor could prevent an outcome than ways it could cause it. Hence, self-implicating upward counterfactuals are likely to draw attention to blame-implicating actions. Research suggests that prison programs designed to stimulate and explore prisoners' upward counterfactual thoughts about their crime, arrest, conviction, and sentence may increase prisoners' attributions of self-blame, and enhance their feelings of guilt (Mandel et al. 2005). Our own theoretical study of guilt (Pereira et al. 2017), grounded on Evolutionary Game Theory (EGT), provides evidence that, in a population wherein there exists from the start a modicum of guilt-feeling agents, a better cooperation tends to arise as guilt tends to spread.

For decades or even centuries, lawyers have used a relatively straightforward test of a defendant's culpability called 'but-for-causation': "The injury would not have occurred *but-for* the defendant's action." Given just the conditional "If a defendant does action A, then injury I follows," its related counterfactual can promote the antecedent to a cause of the consequent: "If the defendant would not have done action A, then injury I would not have occurred." *But-for* clauses can also be indirect. If Joe blocks a building's fire exit with furniture, and Judy dies after she could not reach the exit, then Joe is legally responsible for her death even though he did not light the fire (Pearl and Mackenzie 2018). Similarly, the central question in any employment-discrimination case is whether the employer would have taken the same action had the employee been of a different race (age, sex, religion, natural origin, etc.) (Greiner 2008).

Recent social and cognitive psychology theories propose a 'dual-processing' mental architecture. Most of what the mind does is achieved by quick, automatic, heuristic-laden processing, our visual system being an example. This first cognitive system is often called the automatic system, or intuitive system, or simply 'system 1'. But occasionally, we need to think about a problem, consider counterfactual situations, entertain suppositions, weigh possibilities, and consciously decide upon a solution. This sort of thinking, is slow, laboured, and easily disrupted by other tasks; it is sometimes called the reasoning system, or controlled processing, or simply 'system 2'. Yet, there is nothing about system 2 that precludes the conscious deliberate use of heuristics, colloquially referred to as rules of thumb, a staple domain of study in AI. Laws and legislative procedures may induce people to use both systems (Gigerenzer and Engel 2006).

In (Pereira and Saptawijaya 2016b, 2017; Pereira and Santos 2019; Pereira and Lopes 2020a, b), we have examined how counterfactual reasoning can be employed to discuss moral responsibility and, moreover, shown how it can be utilised to henceforth produce greater good and avoid harm, after knowing the joint outcomes of one's and another's actions in abstract social games.

In this chapter, we concentrate on using EGT to evince why and how AI regulated counterfactual reasoning can be a promoter of cooperation within a population, and on its incidence in the domain of Law governance and Law application. We will not address in detail the issue of governance of AI innovation by the Law, for we have done so elsewhere (Han et al. 2020, 2021, 2022; Cimpeanu et al. 2022) but we provide, in section 5, an outline of the issues of such AI regulation.

The remainder is organized as follows. Firstly, we recall some societal and historical background with regard to alternative pasts and prospective futures. Next, we provide basic notions about counterfactual reasoning. That is followed by its use in evolutionary game theory models, intuitively illustrated with the well-known Stag-Hunt example (Skyrms 2004). Henceforth, we make the case for the use of counterfactual reasoning in law, namely in what regards improved joint Plea Bargaining, by analogy with the Stag-Hunt game, and elaborate on its positive juridical consequences. Thereafter, we delve in more detail into the usage of counterfactual thinking in evolutionary games modelling, and finally conclude with some remarks.

2 Some Societal and Historical Background

Living in a better society first requires conjecturing what that better society might be. Now, this task is not at all easy. Throughout History, human beings have always been imagining utopias. When we think of Plato's ideal *Republic*, or St. Augustine's *City of God*, or Thomas Moro's *Utopia*, or Karl Marx's *Classless Society*, we are always a long way from concrete societies. Throughout our History we have inhabited the *world-as-it-is*, but imagining alternatives that would make it better. This dialectic game between the descriptive domain and the prescriptive realm has been extremely rich and fruitful. Of course, we have never achieved any utopia so far; moreover, we are not sure whether, had we done so, it would have been good for humanity. Still, for better or worse, utopias have played a key role in our individual and collective decisions.

From a collective standpoint, they have provided an elicitation model for what we imagine the ideal destination to be. We are used to thinking that having a destination, or a comprehensive purpose, is highly positive. However, this goal has also given rise to much violence between groups with opposing interests. Suffice to think of the various Proletarian Dictatorships that have proliferated across this planet, and how, under the possible pretext of creating an egalitarian and just society, they have sanctioned acts of extreme violence, with massive killings of human beings. On the other hand, without a range of possible utopias, we would be relatively lost, because we would not have enough diversity in the answer to the collective question of where we wish to go. We need this diversity not to become dependent on just one possibility. Imagine a single answer—religious in nature, say—to this question. It will not be accepted by all believers, let alone by non-believers.

Even without reaching a consensus on what an ideal society is and accepting the idea that multiple conjectures about it can coexist, we will unreservedly agree that human societies should not be used as a pretext for the enrichment of a meagre 10% of the world's population. Nor is it likely that consuming all, each one would give credible meaning to our individual and collective lives. However, this is what we are witnessing more and more. That means we are treading dangerous paths, both in the field of our capacities for idealization (or lack thereof), and in the realm of what—concretely—we are doing to try and improve the present.

Reflecting on these issues requires the exercise of critical thinking, a capacity we acknowledge to be rare. Indeed, the data from Social Psychology is quite emblematic in this field; we know—from Salomon Asch's experiments—that the percentage of conformists in a given population is much higher than the percentage of nonconformists. We also know—at least since Stanley Milgram's (Milgram 1974) experiments—that the tendency toward obedience to an authoritative-looking figure is very strong amongst humans. If the order giver is credible, if he maintains a close relationship with the order follower, the latter will do practically anything he is ordered to do, without resisting. In this context, we must raise the issue of critical thinking and the conception of alternative worlds. Expecting everyone to be nonconformist, critical and informed will imply confidence in a highly unlikely social change, with consequences very difficult to predict.

On the other hand, in the domain of individual morality, one of the structuring requirements to be able to affirm that a certain act is moral consists in the possibility of the same not being enacted. Duty is not about a constraining obligation. Even knowing what good is, as Saint Paul acknowledged, we can do evil: it is in this tension that the dignity of all acts is founded. To the extent that, even in Christian theology, the problem of free-will finds an answer compatible with the question of evil. That is, God allows it in the name of a greater good, which is freedom. If we were left with only one possible option, there would be no dignity in choosing it. In the realm of emotions as well, the imagination of alternative scenarios occupies a prominent place. Consider the situation of Camus's character in *The Stranger*: If it had not been so hot, if there had not been the resulting despair, would he have killed the Arab? Would he still have subjected himself to an unnecessary death sentence? Most likely not.

This game between what is and what could have been, evidence of a higher cognitive function, underpins every speculation about possible worlds, and allows us to anticipate response scenarios. Now, this possibility of pre-adaptation, outcome evaluation, and speculation about strategic revisions, is at the heart of counterfactual hypothetical reasoning. How can a scientific approach to this issue help us better understand such a role, and how does it speak to the issue of morality?

3 On Counterfactual Reasoning

Counterfactual Thinking (CT) is a human cognitive ability studied in a wide variety of domains, namely Psychology, Causality, Justice, Morality, Political History, Literature, Philosophy, Logic, and AI. In particular, within AI, there is an ongoing effort in the development of algorithmic solutions capable of identifying counterfactual explanations to the decisions produced by automated systems (Chou et al. 2022). CT captures the process of reasoning about a past event that did not occur, namely, what would have happened had the event occurred, which may take into account what we know today. CT is also used to reason about an event that did occur, concerning what would have followed if it had not; or if another event might have happened in its place.

An example situation: Lightning hits a forest, and a devastating forest fire breaks out. The forest was dry after a long hot summer and many acres were destroyed. A counterfactual thought is: If only there had not been lightning, then the forest fire would not have occurred.

Today there is a rediscovery and appreciation of the role of counterfactuals in the fields of Literature, History research, Cognitive Psychology, Moral Psychology and AI, just to name a few of the more relevant areas.

Specifically, in this example, counterfactual reasoning consists in the imagining of an alternative scenario in relation to the one that indeed happened, and the exploration of its consequences: "If the forest floor had not been covered with dry leaves after the long hot summer, then the lightning would not have caused such a tremendous fire."

Applied to the morality of groups, its relevance is as much related to the construction of alternative hypothetical and credible scenarios about the past as to the choices made or about the events that occurred and, concomitantly, the assessment of the various consequences that would have followed. Properly conducted, counterfactual reasonings can provide very relevant insights into the ways ahead in the domains where they are applied. Thus, they are an excellent tool for understanding and explaining the mutability of certain behaviours, supported by the review of strategies, re-examining the past in the light of what we *a posteriori* know today. We can identify some of the reasons that make individuals build counterfactuals: The need to improve future performance, or to work over a factual event to make it more acceptable to themselves, or justifiable to others, either why we did not pursue the alternatives, or by teaching us from experience about what we could rather have done differently to what we did. This way of reasoning may apply as well to events that did not happen but could have happened.

For example, to conjecture what the urban areas of the United States would look like if, instead of building the great railroads, investment had bet even more on rivers as a means of communication. Or about events that occurred, thereby reasoning about what would follow had they not occurred; for example, imagining that the Portuguese Revolution of April 25th, 1974, had not happened, and what the evolution of its prior so-called "Marcellist Spring" would have been. Or if a particular event had not occurred, but another would have in its place, for example, if massive exploitation of fossil fuels had not taken place, and if we had already then moved on to solar and wind energy exploitation. And even to verify if the alternatives would be indifferent with respect to relevant consequences.

In a sense, we can consider that all scientific laboratories are places of counterfactuality, because they create alternative scenarios, which are simplifiers of reality, where a given variable can be tested. To wit, reality is too rich and complex to serve as an appropriate place for certain scientific tests. If we want to know if "x" is the cause of "y" we will have to create a counterfactual scenario where this can be made evident. The fact is, we may be foreseeing the occurrence of "y" in a temporal sequence where "x" has already happened, and this happens successively because "x" is associated with "z" and it is "z" that actually causes "y" and also "x". Finding this out by observing reality may be utterly impossible—the number of items in co-presence is too high and may lead to unnecessary misconceptions and unfounded convictions. Thus, in the laboratory, having a good conjecture and testing one variable at a time enables us to observe unsuspected and unambiguous causal networks. When Galileo conjectured that –in a void—all objects fall at the same speed, gaining equal speeds at equal times, regardless of their mass, he had no technical means to test the theory. It was from his mental experience that he devised a system of highly polished conduits through which spheres with different masses rolled. Conduit polishing and ball perfection could minimize the inexistence of a vacuum chamber at the time, inasmuch friction was made minimal. Galileo thus constructed the possible scenario in his days to test a theory that very few would be willing to accept. Albeit, the perfect vacuum, as today we know, is impossible, for it is necessarily composed of vacuum fluctuations, without which Heisenberg's Uncertainty Principle would be violated.

4 Counterfactual Reasoning and Conflicts of Interest in Large Populations

Specifically, about applications of counterfactual reasoning in the domain of AI, a scientific approach to the question of morality and judgment can be treated by its consideration as one case of computer implemented game theoretical models. Game theory is nowadays the common language to encode any conflict of interest, with applications spanning from theology to economics, encompassing computer science, mathematics, physics, anthropology, psychology, and many other disciplines. Games are also recognized as one of the key testbeds underlying progress in artificial intelligence (AI), aptly referred to as the "Drosophila of AI" (McCarthy 1997).

Generally, game theory studies how, in a strategic relationship, rationally acting players promote the best outcome for themselves. To do this, each player must analyse the game, and identify the strategies available to achieve its goal. Typically, classical game theory approaches disregard the large-scale dynamical processes that accrue to many social scenarios and modern economic and political systems. Instead, here we will focus on analysing counterfactual reasoning occurring in large populations, adopting a dynamic variant of game theory called Evolutionary Game Theory (EGT).

EGT considers a population of players interacting via a game, a metaphor of a conflict. The payoffs obtained from a given set of interactions are added up and associated with social success or individual fitness. In a natural setting, we may say that strategies that do well reproduce faster. In a social system, successful strategies tend to be imitated more often and thus will spread in the populations. This translates into a convenient (formal and dynamical) similarity between social learning and Darwinian evolution. In the context of human systems, EGT allows the discovery of the most likely behavioural patterns to be found in human populations, together with the mechanisms that will enable one to reach those states. It also allows for novel quantitative descriptions of the dynamics of peer influence, including bounded rationality and cognitive biases pertaining to most social processes.

Here we shall illustrate these ideas in the context of simple conflicts of interest, described by non-cooperative games. The questions related to whether to collaborate or not are pertinent in areas as diverse as Evolutionary Psychology, Evolutionary Biology, Economics, or the Law, among others. Thus, it is important to know whether or not counterfactual reasoning is an essential tool for understanding behavioural dynamics, and for improving individual as well as collective gains in contexts where the greatest advantage is afforded by evolved collaboration (Santos et al. 2012, 2018).

Given its broad spectrum and cognitive value, a relevant scientific question, and auspicious in terms of research, is what is the effective, if sufficient, role of a small minority of individuals endowed with this counterfactual rationality within some given population. More specifically, to understand if this minority—say 10% of the individuals—can influence the whole group, encouraging cooperative behaviours by virtue of their ability to think counterfactually regarding a common good. It is of paramount relevance to determine if counterfactual reasoning, even when adopted by a minority, can influence the collective behavioural patterns.

Importantly, this minority can represent a different set of individuals eager to adopt more detailed reasoning when compared with individuals that simply learn from others. This minority may also be seen as artificial agents or algorithms, mimicking the present challenge of understanding the hybrid world we will soon face, comprising humans and machines (Paiva et al. 2018; Santos et al. 2019). Indeed, besides aiming to understand human decisions better, AI research will continue to investigate how we may foster prosocial behaviours in situations in which cooperation either remains absent or has the potential not to emerge. This may be achieved in different yet subtle ways by transforming the properties of the dilemma humans face, as illustrated below.

We also allude to the extremely complex problem that has arisen from morals suspended on a religious or philosophical system. To avoid the resulting problems, a scientific approach will select aspects that are fundamental to group morality, assignable to all contexts, regardless of the original culture of each group, or the fact that the autonomous agent be biological, or silicon based. It will address in the abstract the elements—say, atomic ones—of all moral systems, such as: collaborating or not collaborating, acknowledging guilt and apologizing, acknowledging or expressing intentions, etc.; and the way in which these aspects may or may not, individually or intertwined with one another, foster group cohesion.

5 Stag Hunting and Law: From Plea Bargaining to International Agreements and AI Regulation

Equipped with the two abovementioned forewarnings, let us delve into our approach to the role of counterfactuals (Pereira and Santos 2019). In the well-known case of the game *Stag Hunt*, a cooperation dilemma is contemplated, which helps us establish the importance of building counterfactuals. It is a game played by any two agents in a population, and the mission of those involved is to hunt stag, a task that must be performed together to maximise the possibility of success and with large payoff. As such, we may also see it as a metaphor of a coordination problem. Each player may decide not to collaborate and choose instead to try and hunt hare on their own. Although it is a less rewarding alternative, the decision can be interpreted as safer, since the hunter depends only on himself, and hare is easier to hunt than stag.

The dilemma results from each hunter not knowing what the other will do; that is, whether he will collaborate and hunt stag, or will act on his own, deciding to defect and hunt hare. So, each one can be tempted to protect himself by hunting hare. In other words, the most cooperative scenario (both players opting for stag) is not achieved due to fear that the other will not follow the same path. The returns differ according to each option taken. One may, for instance, consider a reward R of 4 units for the decision to hunt stag, if taken simultaneously by both players; a return of 3 units for the decision to hunt hare alone; and 0 units for the player who decides to hunt stag without the other doing so. We are thus facing a cooperation dilemma in which maximization of the outcome depends on the effective decision on cooperating by both players. In the context of EGT, players review their strategies, watching each other's actions and copying the most successful ones.

In the domain of the Law, examples of such coordination dilemmas abound. The strategy known as Plea Bargain (PB) could substantially improve its results if informed by the abstract conclusions of the *Stag Hunt* game. Imagine a situation of double whistleblowing, in which each of two culprits—in a payoff context like that of the *Stag Hunt* players—confesses to the wider guilt of both, thereby obtaining an advantageously increased PB, advantageous for the Law's side as well, then our resulting conclusions validate a substantial improvement in the current view and use of the PB, including an improved governance of the Law. Double whistleblowing is not now put forth as more individually rewardable, since whatever it validates is validated by one of the whistleblowers alone, not adding value to the proof. This may make sense in the context of criminal proceedings blame assignment; however, double whistleblowing may afford the Law a wider and confirmatory testimonial evidence. Additionally, analysed from the point of view of the morality of groups, this stance about PB can be seen as promoting multiple PBs. It not only fosters the acknowledgment of guilt in the population from which those indicted for crime come from, something we know is desirable (Pereira et al. 2017), but can also be relevant for the putting together of stronger forensic evidence. A research field is thus opened for legal philosophers interested in evolutionary morality and judgmental topics using the tools of EGT.

From a more general perspective, Stag-Hunt games constitute also the prototypical example of a social contract, a collective agreement between the ruled and their rulers, defining the duties and rights of each. In this realm, one can find instances of Stag-Hunt games in the writings of Rousseau, Hobbes, and Hume (Skyrms 1996, 2004). Smith and Szathmary (1997) have also discussed analogues of social contracts implicit in various natural settings, which can be understood through the lens of adaptive dynamics, cultural evolution, and social learning (Skyrms 2014).

To include the group dynamics associated with this type of problems, the Stag-Hunt can be readily generalisable to an N-player situation where a minimum number of cooperators is required to hunt stag (Pacheco et al. 2009). Imposing such a threshold mimics situations common to most of the public endeavours, where a minimum combined effort is needed to achieve a collective goal. This is also the case in international agreements, which often demand a minimum number of ratifications to come into practice. Adoption of new laws, both at national or international levels, such as the ones related to climate action and regulation, offer key examples of collective endeavours which can be framed as a N-player Stag-Hunt of coordination games. Antibiotic abuse, vaccination hesitancy, and even coordinating the population to comply with SARS-CoV-2 regulations, provide further examples of this class of dilemmas. In all cases, the non-linear nature of the returns associated with these complex adaptive systems (e.g., as in the case of public health measures), naturally leads to such thresholds and critical levels of adoption to produce a measurable impact (Santos and Pacheco 2011). Climate and public health "games" do have additional complexities due to the time-delayed and uncertain nature of the returns (Santos and Pacheco 2011; Domingos et al. 2020), a complexity which we shall not elaborate on here.

Another dilemma of this class naturally emerges from the ongoing discussions on AI regulation. Rapid technological advancements in AI, as well as the growing deployment of intelligent technologies in new application domains, have generated anxiety and a fear of missing out among different stakeholders, fostering a racing narrative (Han et al. 2020). Whether real or not, the belief in such a race for domain supremacy through AI can make it real, simply from its consequences. These consequences may be negative, as racing for technological supremacy creates a complex ecology of choices that could push stakeholders to underestimate or even ignore ethical and safety procedures. Consequently, different actors are urged to consider both the normative and social impact of these technological advancements, contemplating the use of the precautionary principle in AI innovation and research. This, however, creates novel regulation dilemmas, where non-linearities and thresholds as the ones described above would undoubtedly play an important role. Agreeing or not with implementing these measures involves yet another N-player coordination game, coupled with the innovation dynamics associated with AI systems. Game theoretical models can also be used in this context. In (Han et al. 2020, 2021), we show how these regulatory measures may provide solutions for particular scenarios, depending on the development timeframe of an AI product and the risk of negative externalities. Yet, they may also overshoot their targets, thereby stifling innovation, and hindering investments in developing novel innovations as they become too risky an endeavour.

Now, irrespectively of the conflict or example we are interested in, if we wish to have machines endowed with moral capacity, capable of selecting moral decisions that optimise the expected results and, at least, maximise the expected utility (using here the utilitarian paradigm, with due reservations), it is crucial that we learn to program them with the capacity to develop counterfactual scenarios. These prove to be excellent tools for selecting alternatives not available in the behavioural portfolio for just mimicking and may result in improved cohesion and cooperativeness within groups. This statement has significant experimental relevance; according to a study conducted by the UK Department of Justice (2013), in the context of rehabilitation of delinquents condemned in court cases, recidivism cases are strongly mitigated by strategies that involve the use of counterfactual reasoning. In fact, in mentoring activities that aim delinquents to make other life still alternatives, it is proven that those who process stimuli to the point of desiring other existential alternatives are the ones who least relapse into criminality.

In all these examples, counterfactual reasoning is also usable for judging, morally, the intentions of an agent's act. One counterfactually assumes that a certain noxious side effect that occurred might not have occurred. Even so, would the purpose of the acting agent have been accomplished? If not, then this side effect was indispensable and, therefore might have been intentional. If so, then it was not necessary to achieve the agent's goal, and therefore, the noxious effect did not need to be intended (Pereira and Saptawijaya 2017).

6 Evolutionary Games with Counterfactual Thinking (CT)

In this section, we illustrate how application of counterfactual thinking to the *Stag Hunt*—contrary to what happens with the mimetic process proposed by social learning theory—the individual can conjecture what would happen if he had used another strategy as his own (such as collaborating) rather than the one he in fact used (such as defecting). We depart from the usual computer-modelling of artificial agents to illustrate that counterfactual reasoning is much more efficient and fruitful in revising strategies than simply mimicking of the most successful strategies used by the adversary. Note that the game also shows that the creation of counterfactuals is a merely instrumental mental activity solely dependent on oneself. That is, it is also a resource available to those who systematically opt for selfish strategies. There exists counter-factuality for the good, and for the evil . . . (say, the Mafia).

Given the wide cognitive empowerment of CT in the human individual, the question arises of how the presence of individuals with CT-enabled strategies affects the evolution of cooperation in a population comprising individuals of diverse interaction strategies. Importantly, depending on the game and associated strategies, individuals may revise their strategies in different ways. The common assumption of classic game theory is that players are rational, and that the Nash Equilibrium constitutes a reasonable prediction of what self-regarding rational agents adopt (Fudenberg and Tirole 1991). Often, however, players have limited cognitive skills or resort to simpler heuristics to revise their choices. Evolutionary game theory (EGT) (Hofbauer and Sigmund 1998) offers an answer to this situation, adopting a population description of game interactions in which individuals resort to social learning and imitation. As a result, strategies that do well spread in the population.

Yet, contrary to social learning, more sophisticated agents (such as humans) might instead imagine how a better outcome could have turned out, if they would have decided differently, and thence self-learn by revising their strategy. This is where Counterfactual Thinking (CT) comes in. Here, we have previously proposed a mathematical model to study the impact on cooperation of having a population of agents resorting to such counterfactual kind of reasoning, when compared with a population of just social learners (Pereira and Santos 2019). Specifically, we answered for the positive to three main questions:

1. Can we formalize counterfactual behavioural revision in large populations (taking cooperation dynamics as an application case study)?
2. Will cooperation emerge in collective dilemmas if, instead of evolutionary dynamics and social learning, individuals revise their choices through counterfactual thinking?
3. What is the impact on the overall levels of cooperation of having a fraction of counterfactual thinkers in a population of social learners? Does cooperation benefit from such diversity in learning methods?

CT can be exercised after knowing one's resulting payoff following a single playing step with a co-player. It employs the counterfactual thought: *Had I played differently, would I have obtained a better payoff than I did?* This information can be easily obtained by consulting the game's payoff matrix, assuming the co-player would have made the same play, that is, other things being equal. In the positive case, the CT player will learn to next adopt the alternative play strategy. In EGT, a frequent standard form of learning is so-called Social Learning (SL). It basically consists in switching one's strategy by imitating the strategy of a more successful individual in the population, compared to one's success. CT, instead, can be envisaged as a form of strategy update learning akin to debugging, in the sense that: *if my actual play move was not conducive to a good, accumulated payoff, then, after having known the co-player's move, I can imagine how I would have done better had I made a different strategy choice.*

When compared with SL, this type of reasoning is likely to have a minor impact in games of cooperation with a single Nash equilibrium (or a single evolutionary stable strategy, in the context of EGT) such as the Prisoner's Dilemma or the Public Goods game, where defection-dominance prevails. However, as illustrated below, counterfactual thinking has the potential to have a strong impact in games of coordination, characterized by multiple Nash Equilibria: CT will allow for a meta-reasoning on which equilibria provide higher returns.

Let us consider a population of size Z in which individuals engage in a N-Stag-Hunt dilemma (see above) characterized by a limited set of behaviours: *to cooperate* or *to defect*. The cooperators (Cs) contribute a cost c to the public good, whereas defectors (Ds) refuse to do so. The accumulated contribution is multiplied by an enhancement factor F, and the ensuing result equally distributed among all individuals of the group, irrespective of whether they contributed or not. The requirement of coordination is introduced by noticing that often we find situations where a minimum number M of Cs is required within a group to create any sort of collective benefit.

What is the impact on the overall levels of cooperation of having a fraction of counterfactual thinkers in a population of social learners? Does cooperation benefit from such diversity in learning methods? To answer these questions, we developed a new population dynamics model based on evolutionary games, which allows for a direct comparison between the behavioural dynamics created by individuals who revise their behaviours through social learning and through counterfactual thinking (Pereira and Santos 2019).

In Fig. 1a, we illustrate the behavioural dynamics both under CT and SL for the same parameters of the N-person Stag-Hunt game. For each fraction of co-operators (Cs), if the gradient G (for both SL or CT) is positive (negative), then it is likely the fraction of Cs will increase (decrease). As shown, in both cases, the dynamics is characterized by two basins of attraction and two interior fixed points: one unstable (also known as a coordination point), and a stable co-existence state between Cs and Ds. To achieve stable levels of cooperation (in a co-existence state), individuals must coordinate to be able to reach the cooperative basin of attraction on the right-hand side of the plot, a common feature in many non-linear public goods dilemmas (Pacheco et al. 2009). Figure 1 also shows that CT allows for the creation of new playing strategies, absent before in the population, since new strategies can appear spontaneously based on individual reasoning. By doing so, CT interestingly leads to different results if compared to SL. In this particular scenario, it is evident how CT may facilitate coordination of action, as individuals can reason on the sub-optimal outcome associated with non-reaching the coordination threshold, and individually react to that.

In Fig. 1a, individuals can either revise their strategies through social learning or counterfactual reasoning. However, one could also envisage situations where each agent may resort to CT and to SL in different circumstances, a situation prone to occur in Human populations. To encompass such heterogeneity at the level of agents, let us consider a simple model in which agents resort to SL with a probability χ, and to CT with a probability $(1-\chi)$.

In Fig. 1b, we show the impact χ on the average cooperation levels in a N-person Stag-Hunt dilemma in which, in the absence of CT, cooperation is unlikely to persist. Remarkably, our results suggest that a tiny prevalence of individuals resorting to CT is enough to nudge an entire population of social learners towards highly cooperative standards, providing further indications on the robustness of cooperation prompted by counterfactual reasoning. This result becomes more evident whenever coordination is harder to achieve (i.e., larger coordination thresholds, M).

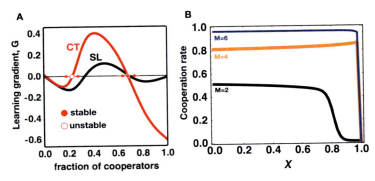

Fig. 1 (**a**) Left panel: Learning gradients for social learners (SL, black line) and counterfactual learners (CT, red line) for the N-person SH game. If the learning gradient is positive (negative), the fraction of cooperators will tend to increase (decrease). Empty and full circles represent the finite population analogue of unstable and stable fixed points, respectively. Right panel: Stationary distribution of the Markov processes created by the transition probabilities pictured in the left panel; it characterizes the prevalence in time of each fraction of cooperators in finite populations. (**b**) Right panel: Overall cooperation as a function of the prevalence of individuals resorting to social learning (SL, χ) and counterfactual reasoning (CT, $1-\chi$). It shows that only a relatively small prevalence of counterfactual thinking is required to nudge cooperation in an entire population of self-regarding agents. Other parameters: $Z = 50$, $N = 6$, $F = 5.5$. $M = N/2$ (panel A), $c = 1.0$, $\mu = 0.01$, $\beta_{SL} = \beta_{CT} = 5.0$

This result may have various interesting implications, if heterogeneous populations are considered. For instance, we can envision a near future made of hybrid societies comprising humans and machines. In such scenarios, it is not only important to understand how human behaviour changes in the presence of artificial entities, but also to understand which properties should be included in artificial agents capable of leveraging cooperation among humans. Our results suggest that a small fraction of artificial CT agents in a population of Humans social learners can decisively influence the dynamics of cooperation towards a cooperative state.

7 Concluding Remarks

We have argued that counterfactual reasoning or thinking is a cognitive device with a long human history, which supplies a basis for causal explanations, and hence for the attribution of blame in moral and judicial judgments. We illustrate the potential impact of counterfactual reasoning in the context of non-linear public goods dilemmas, also known as N-player Stag-Hunt game, a class of dilemmas of relevance in a broad range of domains, from law and public health to international agreements and AI regulation. Our results suggest that counterfactual learners foster coordination in collective dilemmas of this kind, transforming the behavioural dynamics typically associated with these games (Pereira and Santos 2019).

We also showed how these counterfactual learners may influence others. Particularly, in an era increasingly shaped by intelligent systems and artifacts that amplify the human ability to manipulate information, it urges to understand how such instruments can change human behaviour and augment our capacity to cooperate (Paiva et al. 2018; Santos et al. 2019). In this realm, our results suggest that a small fraction of artificial agents resorting to CT is able steer human cooperation whenever placed in hybrid populations comprising humans and machines. A similar effect has been shown to be present in the context of other dilemmas (Santos et al. 2019).

Obviously, real decision-making processes among humans involve a complexity beyond the limits we use to illustrate these ideas. On the other hand, the conceptual simplicity of these models makes them generally applicable to a broad range of problems involving collective cooperative action, which emerges in numerous conflicting situations in nature and societies, thereby providing insights into the richness, beauty, variety, and complexity of collective social interactions.

Finally, our previous work on machine ethics (Pereira and Lopes 2020a, b) enticed us to consider and argue for the positive effect on Law governance and its application regarding the advantage of promoting joint Plea Bargaining, based on its situational analogy with the Stag-Hunt evolutionary game and the latter's results. Moreover, our previous work on guilt (Pereira et al. 2017), points to the advantage of training detainees in counterfactual thinking about their acts and alternative options, with a view to honing their moral sense, speeding their conditional parole, and improving their future behaviour.

Indeed, there is a compelling intuition that the anticipation of regret (over undesired outcomes) is a significant factor in decision making. Most generally, regret theories imply that the attractiveness of an option cannot be evaluated without reference to the context of other available options. Because regret is a response to the counterfactual outcome of a different choice, the knowledge that the decision maker expects to have about that outcome should affect the anticipation of regret. The knowledge of the payoff matrix of a game permits the evaluation of possible alternative payoffs (Kahneman 1995).[1]

Acknowledgements L.M.P. acknowledges support by Future of Life Institute grant 372 RFP2-154. F.C.S. acknowledges support from FCT Portugal's grants PTDC/CCI-INF/7366/2020, PTDC/MAT-APL/6804/2020, and UIDB/50021/2020. A.B.L. acknowledges the support of ANQEP – "Agência Nacional para a Qualificação e Ensino Profissional."

---

[1] *See* also, on AI and judicial reasoning, in this book P G Marques - AI Instruments for Risk of Recidivism Prediction and the Possibility of Criminal Adjudication Deprived of Personal Moral Recognition Standards – Sparse Notes from a Layman; W Gravett - Judicial Decision-making in the Age of Artificial Intelligence; D Durães, P M Freitas and P Novais - The Relevance of Deepfakes in the Administration of Criminal Justice; and J C Abreu - The "Artificial Intelligence Act" Proposal on European e-Justice Domains Through the Lens of User-focused, User-friendly and Effective Judicial Protection Principles.

References

Byrne RMJ (2005) The rational imagination: how people create alternatives to reality. MIT Press, Cambridge

Chou YL, Moreira C, Bruza P, Ouyang C, Jorge J (2022) Counterfactuals and causability in explainable artificial intelligence: theory, algorithms, and applications. Inf Fusion 81:59–83

Cimpeanu T, Santos FC, Pereira LM, Lenaerts T, Han TA (2022) Artificial intelligence development races in heterogeneous settings. Sci Rep 12:1723

Dietz Saldanha EA, Hölldobler S, Pereira LM (2015) On conditionals. In: Gottlob G, Sutcliffe G, Voronkov A (eds) Global conference on artificial intelligence. EPiC Computer Science, Tbilisi, Georgia, pp 79–92

Dietz Saldanha EA, Hölldobler S, Pereira LM (2021) Our themes on abduction in human reasoning: a synopsis. In: Shook JR, Paavola S (eds) Abduction in cognition and action: logical reasoning, scientific inquiry, and social practice. Springer, Cham, pp 279–293

Domingos EF, Grujić J, Burguillo JC, Kirchsteiger G, Santos FC, Lenaerts T (2020) Timing uncertainty in collective risk dilemmas encourages group reciprocation and polarization. iScience 23:101752

Fudenberg D, Tirole J (1991) Game theory. MIT Press, Cambridge

Gigerenzer G, Engel C (2006) Heuristics and the law. MIT Press, Cambridge

Greiner D (2008) Causal inferences in civil rights litigations. Harv Law Rev 81:533–598

Han TA, Pereira LM, Santos FC, Lenaerts T (2020) To regulate or not: a social dynamics analysis of an idealised ai race. J Artif Intell Res 69:881–921

Han TA, Pereira LM, Lenaerts T, Santos FC (2021) Mediating artificial intelligence developments through negative and positive incentives. PLoS One 16:e0244592

Han TA, Lenaerts T, Santos FC, Pereira LM (2022) Voluntary safety commitments provide an escape from over-regulation in AI development. Technol Soc 68:101843

Hofbauer J, Sigmund K (1998) Evolutionary games and population dynamics. Cambridge University Press, Cambridge

Kahneman D (1995) Varieties of counterfactual thinking. In: Roese N, Olson J (eds) What might have been: the social psychology of counterfactual thinking. Lawrence Erlbaum Associates, Inc, Hillsdale, pp 375–396

Mandel R, Hilton D, Catellani P (2005) The psychology of counterfactual thinking. Routledge, Milton Park, UK

McCarthy J (1997) AI as sport. Science 276:1518–1519

Milgram S (1974) Obedience to authority — An experimental view. Harpercollins, New York, NY

Moore M (2009) Causation and responsibility — An essay in law, morals, and metaphysics. Oxford University Press, Oxford

Pacheco JM, Santos FC, Souza MO, Skyrms B (2009) Evolutionary dynamics of collective action in N-person stag hunt dilemmas. Proc R Soc B Biol Sci 276:315–321

Paiva A, Santos FP, Santos FC (2018) Engineering pro-sociality with autonomous agents. In: Proceedings of the thirty-second AAAI conference on artificial intelligence and thirtieth innovative applications of artificial intelligence conference and eighth AAAI symposium on educational advances in artificial intelligence, AAAI Press, New Orleans, LA, p Article 994

Pearl J (2010) Causality – models, reasoning, and inference. Cambridge University Press, Cambridge

Pearl J, Mackenzie D (2018) The book of why – The new science of cause and effect. Basic Books, New York

Pereira L, Lopes A (2020b) Máquinas éticas - da moral da máquina à maquinaria moral. NOVA.FCT Editorial, Costa da Caparica, Portugal

Pereira L, Saptawijaya A (2016a) Programming machine ethics. Springer, Berlin

Pereira LM, Lopes AB (2020a) Machine ethics: from machine morals to the machinery of morality. Springer, Cham, Switzerland

Pereira LM, Santos FC (2019) Counterfactual thinking in cooperation dynamics. In: Fontaine M, Nepomuceno-Fernández Á, Magnani L, Salguero-Lamillar FJ, Barés-Gómez C (eds) Model-based reasoning in science and technology. Springer, Cham, Switzerland, pp 69–82

Pereira LM, Saptawijaya A (2016b) Counterfactuals in critical thinking with application to morality. In: Magnani L, Casadio C (eds) Model-based reasoning in science and technology: logical, epistemological, and cognitive issues. Springer, Cham, Switzerland, pp 279–289

Pereira LM, Saptawijaya A (2017) Counterfactuals, logic programming and agent morality. In: Urbaniak R, Payette G (eds) Applications of formal philosophy: the road less travelled. Springer, Cham, Switzerland, pp 25–53

Pereira LM, Lenaerts T, Martinez-Vaquero LA, Han TA (2017) Social manifestation of guilt leads to stable cooperation in multi-agent systems. In: Proceedings of the 16th conference on autonomous agents and multiagent systems. International Foundation for Autonomous Agents and Multiagent Systems, São Paulo, Brazil, pp 1422–1430

Roese N, Olson J (1995) What might have been: the social psychology of counterfactual thinking. Lawrence Erlbaum Associates Inc, New Jersey

Santos FC, Pacheco JM (2011) Risk of collective failure provides an escape from the tragedy of the commons. Proc Natl Acad Sci U S A 108:10421–10425

Santos FC, Pinheiro FL, Lenaerts T, Pacheco JM (2012) The role of diversity in the evolution of cooperation. J Theor Biol 299:88–96

Santos FP, Santos FC, Pacheco JM (2018) Social norm complexity and past reputations in the evolution of cooperation. Nature 555:242–245

Santos FP, Pacheco JM, Paiva A, Santos FC (2019) Evolution of collective fairness in hybrid populations of humans and agents. In: Proceedings of the thirty-third AAAI conference on artificial intelligence and thirty-first innovative applications of artificial intelligence conference and ninth AAAI symposium on educational advances in artificial intelligence, AAAI Press, Honolulu, HI, p Article 754

Skyrms B (1996) Evolution of the social contract. Cambridge University Press, Cambridge

Skyrms B (2004) The stag hunt and the evolution of social structure. Cambridge University Press, Cambridge

Skyrms B (2014) Social dynamics. Oxford University Press, Cambridge

Smith JM, Szathmary E (1997) The major transitions in evolution. Oxford University Press, Oxford

Tordoff R (2014) Counterfactual history and thucydides. In: Wohl V (ed) Probabilities, hypotheticals and counterfactuals in ancient Greek thought. Cambridge University Press, Cambridge, pp 101–121

UK Department of Justice (2013) Transforming rehabilitation: a summary of evidence on reducing reoffending. ISBN 978-1-84099-608-1, Ministry of Justice Analytical Series, UK.https://assets.publishing.service.gov.uk/government/uploads/system/uploads/attachment_data/file/243718/evidence-reduce-reoffending.pdf/ Accessed 19 Apr 2022

Open Access This chapter is licensed under the terms of the Creative Commons Attribution 4.0 International License (http://creativecommons.org/licenses/by/4.0/), which permits use, sharing, adaptation, distribution and reproduction in any medium or format, as long as you give appropriate credit to the original author(s) and the source, provide a link to the Creative Commons license and indicate if changes were made.

The images or other third party material in this chapter are included in the chapter's Creative Commons license, unless indicated otherwise in a credit line to the material. If material is not included in the chapter's Creative Commons license and your intended use is not permitted by statutory regulation or exceeds the permitted use, you will need to obtain permission directly from the copyright holder.

Judicial Decision-Making in the Age of Artificial Intelligence

Willem H. Gravett

Abstract Artificial intelligence (AI) has become a pervasive presence in almost every aspect of society and business: from assigning credit scores to people, to identifying the best candidates for an employment position, to ranking applicants for admission to university. One of the most striking innovations in the United States criminal justice system in the last three decades has been the introduction of risk-assessment software, powered by sophisticated algorithms, to predict whether individual offenders are likely to re-offend. The focus of this contribution is on the use of these risk-assessment tools in criminal sentencing. Apart from the broader social, ethical and legal considerations, to date, not much is known about how perceptions of technology influence cognition in decision-making, particularly in the legal context. What research does demonstrate is that humans are inclined to trust algorithms as objective, and, as such, as unobjectionable. This contribution examines two phenomena in this regard: (i) the "technology effect"—the human tendency towards excessive optimism when making decisions involving technology; and (ii) "automation bias"—the phenomenon whereby judges accept the recommendations of an automated decision-making system, and cease searching for confirmatory evidence, perhaps even transferring responsibility for decision-making onto the machine.

W. H. Gravett (✉)
Department of Public and Procedural Law, Akademia, Centurion, South Africa
e-mail: willemg@akademia.ac.za

© The Author(s) 2024
H. Sousa Antunes et al. (eds.), *Multidisciplinary Perspectives on Artificial Intelligence and the Law*, Law, Governance and Technology Series 58,
https://doi.org/10.1007/978-3-031-41264-6_15

1 Introduction

To an ever-increasing degree, Artificial Intelligence (AI) (Turing 1950, p. 433)[1] systems and the algorithms (Richie and Duffy 2018, p. 1)[2] that power them are tasked with making crucial decisions that used to be made by humans. Algorithmic decision-making based on big data (Ishwarappa and Anuradha 2015, pp. 319–320)[3] has become an essential tool and is pervasive in all aspects of our daily lives: the news articles we read, the movies we watch, the people we spend time with, whether we get searched in an airport security line, whether more police officers are deployed in our neighborhoods, and whether we are eligible for credit, healthcare, housing, education and employment opportunities, among a litany of other commercial and government decisions.

Because technological "wonders" have become so ubiquitous, because they affect our lives so profoundly, and because most of us have little understanding of how they all work, the socially constructed meaning of "technology" has become implicitly associated with optimism for what technology will bring in the future (Clark et al. 2016, p. 98). To date, not much is known about how perceptions of technology influence cognition in decision-making, particularly in the legal context. The pervasive presence of technology in almost every aspect of society and business—and its rapidly increasing pervasiveness in law—makes this a critical issue.

Classic descriptions of court processes usually emphasise the dignity, slow pace and time-honoured legal expertise of the judges and prosecutors in the criminal justice system. However, nowadays, courts have become sites where data analytics and algorithms flourish. One of the most striking innovations in the United States criminal justice system in the course of the last three decades has been the introduction of risk-assessment software, powered by sophisticated and often proprietary algorithms, to predict whether individual offenders are likely to re-offend (the so-called "risk of recidivism"). The focus of this chapter is on the latest, and perhaps most troubling, use of these risk-assessment tools: their incorporation into the criminal sentencing process.

As a general matter, automation can improve the consistency and predictability of decision-making by reducing the arbitrariness for which human decisions are

---

[1] AI refers to a computer's ability to imitate human intelligent behaviour, especially human cognitive functions, such as the ability to reason, discover meaning, generalise and learn from past experience. Alan Turing defined artificial intelligence as the "science and engineering of making intelligent machines, especially intelligent computer programs".

[2] The term "algorithm" refers to a set of rules to be followed in calculations or other problem-solving operations, especially by a computer. In practice, "algorithm" refers to the automation of the statistical method.

[3] Big data are extremely large data sets that may be analysed computationally to reveal patterns, trends, and associations, especially relating to human behaviour and interactions. These data sets are so large and complex that they are impossible for humans to process, and even difficult or impossible to process using traditional computational methods.

well-known. Given a large number of similar questions, algorithms will provide predictable and consistent answers. Simon Chesterman states: "Whereas many evaluative decisions made by humans are based on unconscious. .. biases and intuitive reactions, algorithms follow the parameters set out for them (Chesterman 2020)."

Many scholars and practitioners view automated risk-assessment systems as a promising path toward more efficient, unbiased, and empirically-based sentencing (Hannah-Moffat 2015, p. 244). Replacing judges' discretionary decision-making with structured, quantitatively derived automated decision-making, so the argument goes, will prevent judges from "sentencing blindly", *i.e.* "over-punishing" (imprisoning offenders who present little appreciable risk to public safety) or "under-punishing" (releasing dangerous criminals into communities to re-offend) (Oleson 2011, p. 1340). Automated risk-assessment systems are frequently said to minimize both the rates and the length of incarceration for low-risk offenders, resulting in lower budgetary costs and reduced social harm (Milgram 2013; Dewan 2015). Also, predictive algorithms might save precious time for overworked judges, prosecutors and court staff (Mamalian 2011).

There is still very limited empirical research about whether automated risk-assessment algorithms actually accomplish any of these goals. There is, however, significant research that points to these automated tools leading to outcomes that are skewed because of socio-economic variables, bias in the data, and inaccurate predictions. A number of factors have been identified that render automated risk-assessment tools as potentially more akin to a Pandora's box than a panacea.

For example, algorithms are only as good as the data on which they are fed and the questions that they are asked. In practice, algorithms can reify existing disparities. These data and questions are anything but a neutral statistical exercise; practitioners are required to ask a series of directed questions about criminal histories, leisure activities, education, past criminal sentences, associates, family and relationships, emotional well-being, housing, substance abuse, family child rearing, attitudes, social assistance, finances, employment and various other issues.

Thus, it is not surprising that, generally speaking, in the United States, status as an African American would likely yield a classification of high-risk, because many African Americans live in conditions of poverty, and share "high-risk" characteristics (*e.g.* social, educational, vocational and family problems, substance abuse and histories of trauma and abuse) (Hannah-Moffat 2015, p. 245). Research has shown that race and gender are complex social constructs that cannot simply be reduced to binary variables in automated risk-assessment systems (Hannah-Moffat 2012, p. 9). Thus, automated risk-assessment systems fail to adequately control for gender or racial disparity and the potential for discriminatory outcomes. In short, automated systems sever the link between punishment and individual action, lack nuance, and miss the importance of a range of motivational, contextual, and structural factors that contribute to human action.

However, the focus of this chapter is on the potential impact that these tools might have on how judges exert their own discretion in sentencing, even if they do not themselves perceive a difference. Although these risk-assessment algorithms are not making decisions in lieu of judges (yet), it is not clear how judges should incorporate them into their decision-making processes, or how the algorithms might influence their decisions. Quantification supposedly helps to hold judges accountable and makes sentencing more consistent and efficient. The problem is, however, that little is known about the efficacy of such interventions.

As discussed below, what research does demonstrate is that humans are inclined to trust algorithms as objective, and, as such, as unobjectionable (Garber 2016). The term "automation bias" describes the phenomenon whereby judges accept the guidance or recommendations of an automated decision-making system, and cease searching for confirmatory evidence, perhaps even transferring responsibility for decision-making onto the machine (Challen et al. 2019, p. 234).

2 The Sentencing Process

Judges rightly view sentencing as a grave responsibility. In the pre-trial context, the judge's decisions are primarily binary: should the defendant stay in jail for the duration of the pre-trial period, or not? But every criminal case contains a myriad of facts, factors and features which might influence the sentence to be imposed. This general difficulty is exacerbated by the sheer number of decisions that the judge has to make in order to reach an appropriate sentence (Kehl et al. 2017, p. 14).

As a preliminary matter, the judge must determine which of the numerous facts, factors and features are relevant to the sentence, and what the appropriate weight is to attach to each. Then the judge must reach the fundamental decision about whether to remove the offender from society or choose from a litany of non-incarceration possibilities. Further decisions, among others, involve the extent of the sentence, and whether any portion thereof should be suspended, and, if so, for what period of time and under what conditions.

Moreover, the judge must not only consider the appropriate punishment for the offence, but also the risk that the offender poses, *i.e.* predicting the probability of the offender's recidivism. Historically, assessing a defendant's risk of recidivism required reliance on a judge's "intuition, instinct and sense of justice", which could result in a "more severe sentence" based on an "unspoken clinical prediction" (Hyatt et al. 2011, p. 725).

For these reasons, the allure of risk-assessment software for overburdened criminal justice systems is well neigh irresistible. The appeal of automated risk-assessment systems is that they propose to inject objectivity into a criminal justice system that has been compromised, for far too long and too many times, by human failings. Proponents of automated risk-assessment systems also claim that they make sentencing more transparent and rational (Skeem 2013, p. 300).

Automated methods are credited with giving decisions substance and making them more scientific, auditable, and, consequently, conferring the appearance of legitimacy. Support for the introduction of algorithmic risk-assessment tools then rests on the premise that they enhance professionalism by improving the defen-

Judicial Decision-Making in the Age of Artificial Intelligence

sibility and accountability of decisions, generating uniformity across regions and jurisdictions, and maintaining a perception of objective scientific validity (Hannah-Moffat 2015, p. 245).

There is no empirical evidence suggesting that a longer criminal sentence has a significant impact on a person's recidivism. Thus, it does not necessarily follow that a longer prison sentence will decrease a defendant's risk of recidivism. A judge therefore faces a more complicated question about how to use an automated risk-assessment score in sentencing, and the ultimate decision might hinge on the judge's own penological theory (Hannah-Moffat 2015, p. 245). Or, the judge might simply take a risk-averse approach and impose harsher penalties on defendant who are labeled "high-risk" by software, rather than bear the personal and societal risk of a recidivist committing another crime (Hannah-Moffat 2015, p. 245).

Clearly, judges face unique challenges to their decision-making processes in the age of AI and big data. The ramifications are well illustrated by the decision of the Wisconsin Supreme Court in S v. Loomis (2016).

3 S v Loomis

In 2013 Eric Loomis, a 31-year old black man, was arrested in La Crosse, Wisconsin, on charges related to a drive-by shooting. Loomis denied any involvement in the shooting, but he nevertheless waived his right to trial and entered a guilty plea to two of the lesser charges—fleeing from a traffic officer and driving a vehicle without the owner's consent S v. Loomis (2016, p. 754). These were all repeat offences. Loomis was also on probation for dealing in prescription drugs, and he was a registered sex offender because of a previous conviction for third degrees sexual assault S v. Loomis (2016, p. 754). In mitigation, his attorney emphasized a childhood spent in foster homes where he was abused. With an infant son of his own, Loomis was also training to be a tattoo artist.

Following the plea, the circuit court (trial court) ordered a pre-sentencing investigation report, which included a risk-assessment by an automated system, COMPAS, to aid the court in determining Loomis's sentence. COMPAS assessments estimate the risk of recidivism based on an interview with the defendant and information from the defendant's criminal history S v. Loomis (2016, p. 754). COMPAS assesses variables under five main areas: criminal involvement, relationships/lifestyles, personality/attitudes, family and social exclusion. The COMPAS risk assessment designated Loomis a high risk for all three types of recidivism that the system measured: pretrial recidivism, general recidivism and violent recidivism S v. Loomis (2016, pp. 754–755).

In imposing the maximum sentence of 6 years imprisonment and 5 years extended supervision, the judge specifically mentioned the COMPAS score:

> You are identified through the COMPAS assessment as an individual who is at high risk to the community . . . I'm ruling out probation because of the seriousness of the crime and

because your history . . . and the risk-assessment tools that have been utilized, suggest that you're extremely high risk to re-offend S v. Loomis (2016, p. 755).

Loomis challenged his sentence, arguing that the trial court's use of the COMPAS score violated his right to due process, because, among other arguments, it violated his right to an individualised sentence because COMPAS relied on information about the characteristics of a larger group to calculate an inference about his personal likelihood to commit future crimes. The Supreme Court of Wisconsin ultimately rejected all of Loomis's claims.

In response to Loomis's argument about his right to an individualised sentence, the court distinguished this case case from a hypothetical one in which the risk-assessment score was either the *only* factor or the *determining* factor in a sentencing decision. In *Loomis* the automated risk score was simply one piece of information among many others that the judge considered in imposing the sentence. The court suggested that a fair trial argument might have succeeded if the risk score was the determinative or sole factor that a judge considered.

The obvious problem is that, absent a clear declaration from a judge to this effect, it is impossible to determine to what extent a judge in fact relied on an automated risk score to determine a defendant's sentence. To make matters worse, because of the operation of implicit biases, the judge herself might not know.

To ensure that sentencing judges weigh the results of automated risk-assessments appropriately, the Wisconsin Supreme Court in *Loomis* prescribed both how these assessments must be presented to trial courts, and the extent to which judges might use them. While the risk score might be useful to understand public safety considerations relating to offenders' risk reduction and management, it should not be used to determine the severity or length of the punishment, and it certainly should not constitute an official aggravating or mitigating factor in a sentencing decision. In an attempt to ensure that these limitations were adhered to, the court mandated that a judge must explain at sentencing "the factors in addition to a COMPAS risk assessment that independently support the sentence imposed" S v. Loomis (2016, p. 769).

The *Loomis* court attempted to provide a procedural safeguard to alert judges of the dangers of these assessments. The court prescribed that a "written advisement" should be included in any pre-sentencing investigation report containing a COMPAS risk-assessment score. This "written advisement of its limitations" should explain that:

1. COMPAS is a proprietary tool, which has prevented the disclosure of specific information about the weights of the factors or how risk scores are calculated;
2. COMPAS scores are based on group data, and therefore identify groups with characteristics that make them high-risk offenders, not particular high-risk individuals;
3. Several studies have suggested the COMPAS algorithm may be biased in how it classifies minority offenders;

Judicial Decision-Making in the Age of Artificial Intelligence

4. COMPAS compares defendants to a national sample, but has not completed a cross-validation study for a Wisconsin population, and tools like this must be constantly monitored and updated for accuracy as populations change; and
5. COMPAS was not originally developed for use at sentencing S v. Loomis (2016, p. 770).

This "written advisement of limitations" struck a note of caution to judges about relying on the COMPAS score in a meaningful way, which was reiterated in the concurring opinions. Chief Justice Roggensack penned a separate concurring opinion to clarify that:

> [W]hile our holding today permits a sentencing court to *consider* COMPAS, we do not conclude that a sentencing court may *rely on* COMPAS for the sentence it imposes . . . [Because] the majority opinion interchangeably employs *consider* and *rely* when discussing a sentencing court's obligations and the COMPAS risk assessment tool, our decision could be mistakenly be read as permitting reliance on COMPAS S v. Loomis (2016, p. 772).

As a means to address concerns about the use of algorithmic risk-assessment tools, Justice Abrahamson also wrote separately to emphasize that, in considering these tools in sentencing, a judge "must set forth on the record a meaningful process of reasoning addressing the relevance, strengths and weaknesses of the risk assessment tool" S v. Loomis (2016, pp. 774–775).

Despite expressing concerns about the potential for unfairness and discrimination inherent in algorithmic risk-assessment tools, the Wisconsin Supreme Court nevertheless unanimously approved its use in *Loomis*. The court only superficially addressed the risks inherent in these algorithmic risk-assessment tools by adding caveats and mandating that certain disclosures accompany COMPAS scores in the pre-sentence investigation reports. However, the court was silent on the fundamental underlying question of why the scores are to be included in the risk-assessment report at all if they should not affect the length of the sentence. The court did not explain how a judge might use a defendant's risk score if she cannot change the length of the sentence based on that score (Kehl et al. 2017, p. 21).

The conclusion is warranted that the court ultimately failed to meaningfully restrict the use of these systems, in large part because it failed to consider the external and internal pressures on judges to use these automated risk-assessment tools, judges' inability to evaluate risk-assessment tools, and the effect of cognitive biases on the decision-making processes of judges.

The court's "warning label" approach—as opposed to imposing meaningful restraints—is an ineffective means of changing the ways in which judges evaluate automated risk-assessments, and it has left the door wide open for judges to be heavily influenced by the risk assessments (Liu et al. 2019, p. 130).

It is unrealistic to expect a sentencing judge, after reviewing the automated risk score, to exercise discretion without any pre-determined views of, or even bias against, the defendant. All things being equal, a high risk score will make it less likely that an offender will receive the minimum sentence or avoid incarceration (Starr 2014). Apart from the fact that no judge wants to be in a position to have to defend a lenient sentence imposed on a "high risk" defendant, especially if that defendant actually commits future crimes, the court completely ignored the "technology effect" and the role of cognitive biases supporting data reliance (specifically, so-called "automation bias" and "anchoring") on a judge's decision-making process.

4 The "Technology Effect"

Researchers have identified a tendency towards excessive optimism when making decisions involving technology (Clark et al. 2016, p. 88). Because technological breakthroughs often produce dramatic and memorable results, such as revolutionizing industries and improving our quality of life—*e.g.* smartphones, smart watches, self-driving automobiles, three dimensional printing and entertainment streaming services – such events are highly salient (Tversky and Kahneman 1974, pp. 1124–1131). By contrast, technological failures are less salient, because they neither tend to change the *status quo*, nor are they likely to be discussed in public.

The result has been that, in decision-making contexts, people develop a non-conscious or "implicit" association between technology and success through accumulated experiences in which the two are paired. This is the case, because incredible technological advancement has conditioned us to *expect* that technology would be a driver of success and progress. This bias towards optimism in technology has been labeled the "technology effect" (Clark et al. 2016, p. 88).

Once unconsciously developed, implicit associations operate quickly and automatically with regard to cognition and behavior. Chaiken's heuristic-systematic model suggests that information processing can occur along two pathways: (i) a more effortful, systematic pathway; or (ii) a more automatic (heuristic) pathway that does not involve complex information processing (Chaiken 1980, pp. 752–766). A person uses the heuristic pathway when strong cues exist about the reliability of a message, which decreases that person's motivation to engage in more effortful, systematic processing. Researchers contend that:

> [T]he . . . notion of technology has become so powerfully associated with progress and achievement, or, "success", that invoking technology in a decision context can trigger an automatic assumption that decision choices involving technology will be successful (Clark et al. 2016, p. 89).

A troubling implication in the judicial context is that there are key situational characteristics that might trigger the technology effect. For example, individuals in contexts where they are experiencing high cognitive load—such as judges experience on a daily basis—might be more susceptible to the technology effect and heuristic processing (Evans 2008, pp. 255–278).

5 "Automation Bias" and the Anchoring Effect

Beyond external pressures, judges are subject to psychological biases that encourage the use of automated risk-assessment tools. Numerous studies have shown that in courts which rely on scientific and technological tools, judges (and other individuals) are submissive to computer-generated figures and results, which might frame and condition the views of judges (Liu et al. 2019, p. 130). Individuals tend to weigh purportedly expert empirical assessments more heavily than non-empirical evidence—which might create a bias in favor of an automated risk-assessment over an offender's own narrative. Research suggests that it is challenging and unusual for individuals to defy algorithmic recommendations (Christin et al. 2015).

For example, in a recent experiment at the Georgia Institute of Technology, a student was placed in a small office with a robot to complete an academic survey. Suddenly an alarm sounded and smoke filled the hallway outside the door. The robot, which was outfitted with a sign that read "Emergency Guide Robot", began to move. This forced the student to make a split-second decision between escaping through the clearly marked exit through which she entered or following the robot along an unknown path and through an obscure door. Twenty six out of the 30 participants chose to follow the robot, even though it guided them away from the real exit. "We were surprised", lead researcher, Paul Robinette, stated in an interview: "We thought that there wouldn't be enough trust, and that [we would] have to do something to prove that the robot was trustworthy (Rutkin 2016)."

The results suggest that when people are informed that a robot (or other machine) is designed to perform a particular task, as in the case of the experiment, they will probably automatically trust it to perform that task correctly. In fact, participants in the study gave the robot the benefit of the doubt, even when the robot's instructions were somewhat counterintuitive. In another version of the study, the majority of participants even continued to follow the robot after it appeared to have "broken down" or have frozen in place, prompting a researcher to emerge and apologize for its "poor performance" (Rutkin 2016).

Advocates of automated risk-based sentencing argue that algorithms merely provide "indicative" predictions of risk. Most judges also maintain that they do not blindly follow the results provided by the algorithm when deciding the fate of an individual offender. Rather, they claim to rely on their expertise and clinical experience to assess the offender's personality, socio-economic situation and risk of recidivism (Rutkin 2016).

However, research in behavioral economics and cognitive psychology have shown that it is psychologically difficult and rare for any human to "override" the recommendations of an algorithm (Thaler 1999, pp. 183–206). Judges are likely to follow the predictions of an automated risk-assessment algorithm. In a survey of more than 100 Canadian judges and legal practitioners, the general perception was that automated decision-making systems were "better than clinical judgment or any form of subjective judgment . . . (Hannah-Moffat 2015, p. 244)".

From a judge's perspective, a quantitative assessment by a software program generally seems more reliable, scientific and legitimate than almost any other source of information, including her own feelings about an offender. This is the case, not only for lay persons, but also for highly skilled professionals (Hannah-Moffat et al. 2010, pp. 391–409). It is difficult to challenge numbers and equations if you have not been trained in statistics. Thus, the danger is that when the algorithm predicts a "high" risk of recidivism, the tendency would be for judges to incarcerate, regardless of other factors.

The particular problem with the court's reasoning in *Loomis* is that it placed its trust in judges to consider the "written advisement" and evaluate the automated risk-assessment score accordingly—and this during an age in which society as a whole is heavily affected by the "technology effect". With or without a written advisement, judges consistently give technology and forensic-based evidence heavier weight than other factors, whether they consciously realise it or not (Citron 2008, p. 1271).

The impulse to follow a computer's recommendation flows from "automation bias". Studies have demonstrated that "automation bias" happens because of the tendency of most people to ascribe greater trust in the analytical capabilities of an automated system than in their own, even in the face of evidence of the systems' inaccuracies (Freeman 2016, p. 98). As noted by Danielle Citron, "[a]utomation bias effectively turns a computer program's suggested answer into a trusted final decision" (Citron 2008, p. 1272).

While automated decision-making systems have the potential to eliminate particular errors associated with human decision-making, in reality, these systems seem to merely replace these errors with new ones (Freeman 2016, p. 98). According to psychology professor Linda Sitka:

> [M]ost people will take the road of least cognitive effort, and rather than systematically analyze each decision, will use decision rules of thumb or heuristics . . . Automated decision aids may act as one of these decision-making heuristics, and be used as a replacement for more vigilant systems of monitoring or decision making (Skitka et al. 1999, p. 992).

Sitka thus views automation bias as the result of a person using an automated decision-making system as a heuristic replacement for vigilant information seeking and processing. This definition treats automation bias as similar to other biases and heuristics in human decision-making (such as, for example, confirmation bias), except that automation bias stems specifically from interaction with an automated system.

Three main factors have been assumed to contribute to automation bias. First, there is the tendency of humans to choose the road of least cognitive effort (the so-called "cognitive miser hypothesis"). Thus, humans tend to use directives or recommendations of automated systems as a strong decision-making heuristic in the place of effortful cognitive processes of information analysis and evaluation (Parasuraman and Manzey 2010, p. 392).

A second factor is humans' perceived trust of automated systems as powerful agents with superior analytical capabilities. As a consequence, humans might overestimate the performance of an automated decision-making system and might ascribe to the automated systems greater capability and authority than in themselves or other humans (Dzindolet et al. 2002, pp. 72–94).

A third contributing factor to automation bias is the phenomenon of "diffusion of responsibility" (Parasuraman and Manzey 2010, p. 392). When humans share decision-making tasks with machines, the same psychological effect occurs when humans share tasks with other humans, *i.e.* so-called "social loafing", which is reflected in humans' tendency to reduce their own effort when working within a group, as opposed to when they work individually on a task (Karau and Williams 1993, pp. 681–706). To the extent that human users see an automated decision-making system as another team member, the humans might believe themselves to be less responsible for the outcome, and, as a result, reduce their own effort in monitoring and analysing other available data.

Also, because individuals and agencies often turn to algorithms with the express purpose to reduce human bias and error, these algorithms could be seen as authoritative sources, with more knowledge than the humans who interpret them. Thus, the human users, such as judges, tend to adhere to what the algorithm decides, despite the fact that such adherence might harm others. This is because of the general power that authority figures hold and "people's willingness to conform to the demand of . . . authority" (Skitka et al. 1999, pp. 992–993). Automation bias is a robust phenomenon that renders the "written advisements" mandated by the Wisconsin Supreme Court inane.

The Wisconsin Supreme Court in *Loomis* expressed its expectation that "the circuit court [would] exercise discretion when assessing a COMPAS risk score with respect to individual defendant". As explained above, the court's expectation has no basis. Human beings trust computer-generated decisions far more than they should. In fact, they rely on automated decisions even when they suspect malfunction.

A related problem is that automated decision-making systems might also "provide cover for human agents" (Chesterman 2020). For example, a survey of judges and lawyers in Canada found that many regarded software, such as COMPAS, as an improvement over subjective human judgment (Hannah-Moffat 2015, pp. 244–247). Although these practitioners did not deem risk-assessment software as particularly reliable predictors of future behavior, they nevertheless favored these systems because using them minimized the risk that the judges and lawyers themselves would be blamed for the consequences of their decisions (Hannah-Moffat 2015, p. 244). As Chesterman rightly notes, automated risk-assessment systems:

> [S]hould not be the basis for avoiding accountability in the narrow sense of being obliged to give an account of a decision, even if after the fact, or to avoid responsibility for harm as a result of that decision (Chesterman 2020).

Apart from automation bias, courts in the United States have repeatedly recognized that cautionary statements do little to prevent a factfinder from considering certain factors once the fact-finder's consciousness has been exposed to those factors. The court in *United States v Rodriguez* explained why jury instructions to disregard a personal opinion expressed by a prosecutor are not effective: "one cannot unring a bell"; "after the thrust of a saber it is difficult to say forget the wound"; and "if you throw a skunk into the jury box, you can't instruct the jury not to smell it" (United States v Rodriguez 1978).

The concern is that judges might adapt their sentencing practices in order to match the predictions of risk-assessment algorithms. Behavioral economists refer to "anchoring" to describe the common phenomenon according to which individuals draw upon any available piece of evidence—regardless of how weak it is—to make subsequent decisions (Tversky and Kahneman 1974, pp. 1128–1130; Mussweiler and Strack 2000, p. 495).

In their classic experiment on the "anchoring effect", Amos Tversky and Daniel Kahneman gerrymandered a wheel of fortune marked from 0 to 100 to stop at either the number 10 or 65. They would stand in front of a group of University of Oregon students they recruited as participants, spin the wheel, and ask the students to write down the number on which the wheel stopped (which of course was either 10 or 65). Then the experimenters asked the participants the following question: "Is the percentage of African nations among UN members larger or smaller than the number you just wrote down?"

As Kahneman explains:

> The spin of a wheel of fortune – even one that is not rigged – cannot possibly yield useful information about anything, and the participants. . . should simply have ignored it. But they did not ignore it (Kahneman 2011, p. 119).

When the wheel landed on 10, the participants provided a mean estimate of 25%; when the wheel landed on 65, the participants provided a mean estimate of 45%. Thus, simply being presented with a number—even one that they knew was totally random and which had no bearing whatsoever on the quantity they had been asked to estimate—had a pronounced impact on the participants' responses.

Since Tversky and Kahneman's seminal study, the anchoring effect has been shown to be a "truly ubiquitous phenomenon that has been observed in a broad array of different judgment domains" (Mussweiler et al. 2000, p. 1143). It has proven to be a robust, reliable, and persistent cognitive bias (Wilson et al. 1996, pp. 387–402; Mussweiler 2002, pp. 67–72). Many findings indicate that clearly irrelevant numbers—even if they are blatantly determined at random—may guide numeric judgments that are generated under conditions of uncertainty (Chapman and Johnson 1999, pp. 115–153).

It should come as no surprise that judges are not immune to anchoring effects. Judicial decisions often involve quantification. And judicial quantification generally occurs under circumstances that are inherently uncertain. First, judges must make their decisions at least partially on the basis of controverted and contradictory evidence. Second, judges are often called upon to quantify the unquantifiable—the qualitative misdeeds of the guilty party—which must be expressed as the award of monetary damages or the determination of criminal fines or length of imprisonment. In the absence of strict, algorithmic guidelines or other institutional specifications, this process can be both ambiguous and extremely subjective.

Thus, if the risk-assessment algorithm's prediction of the offender's risk of recidivism is higher than that upon which the judge settled in her own mind, she might increase the sentence, even without being consciously aware that she is following the algorithm. As stated above, it is impossible to determine to what extent a judge in fact relied on an automated risk score to determine a defendant's sentence. A judge presented with an assessment that reveals a higher risk of recidivism than predicted, may increase a defendant's sentence without realizing that anchoring might have played a role in the judgment.

6 Conclusion

The data scientist, Cathy O'Neil, describes the current age as one of unquestioned techno-optimism (Van Hollebeke 2016). The faith we tend to put in the power of technology shields algorithmic systems from critical interrogation in general. It is ironic, notes the investigative technology journalist, Julia Angwin, that we—eas a criminal justice system, political body and culture—take an all-too human approach to algorithmic infrastructure:

> We trust it too much. We have not yet thought as rigorously or as strategically as we need to about its effects. We have not fully considered whether, and indeed how, to regulate the algorithms that are . . . regulat[ing] our lives . . . (Garber 2016).

Loomis is significant because it demonstrates, not only the challenges that courts face in understanding how automated risk-assessment systems work, but also the fact that there is virtually no precedent to guide judges' decision-making in using these and other automated tools.

Mere written warnings do not seem to be able to satisfactorily inform judges as effective gatekeepers, especially when they might not be sufficiently equipped with knowledge and understanding about how these automated tools function. Although warnings might alert judges to the inadequacies of these tools, the advisement might nevertheless fail to negate the considerable external and internal pressures of a criminal justice system championing the use of automated quantitative risk-assessments.

The Wisconsin Supreme Court in *Loomis* seemed impercipient to this reality. It accepted on face value the circuit court's claim in post-conviction proceedings that it "would have imposed the exact same sentence" even without the automated risk score (S v. Loomis 2016, p. 771). The court's required advisement suggests that judges should be a bias check on a tool itself designed to correct judges' biases.

A useful starting point might be to reflect anew on the question: "Who is the decision-maker?" As Liu et al. (2019, p. 138) note: "In a world that often blindly portrays numbers to be scientific, neutral and objective, human decision-makers are likely to surrender their powers to data."

As seen in *Loomis*, ill-informed deference to algorithms marginalizes the role of public authority and scrutiny in governance. As "words yield to numbers" in criminal sentencing (Hamilton 2015, p. 6), the judiciary should exercise considerable caution in assessing the qualitative value of these new technologies. Although governments might mandate humans to make final decisions, it remains problematic to address the anchoring effect, as long as data-driven approaches to decision-making processes in the public sector are tolerated.

Judges must be trained about the phenomenon of automation bias. Studies have shown that individuals who receive such training are more likely to scrutinise an automated system's suggestions (Citron 2016).

Beyond training, the best ways to ensure fairness of the automated scoring system is through procedural safeguards. In the development of algorithms for deployment in the criminal justice system, accountability and oversight are key. Policymakers must ensure that these systems have been designed for the purpose for which they are used, and that they are continually monitored and assessed for accuracy and reliability.

Facilitating outside research and auditing to evaluate and test algorithms for bias is also of critical importance. The design, implementation and evaluation of automated systems to be used in the criminal justice system should be consistent with the core values of such a system, including equal protection and due process. Important normative and ethical questions loom large at every turn as these algorithmic risk-assessment tools are integrated into the existing system – and those decisions should not be made lightly or with insufficient information.

At least for now, humans remain in control of governments, and they can demand explanations for decisions in natural language, not computer code. Failing to do so in the criminal justice context risks ceding inherently governmental and legal functions to an "unaccountable computational elite" (Pasquale 2017). Criminal justice policy should be informed by data, but we cannot afford to allow the sterile language of science to obscure questions of fairness, accountability and justice (Starr 2014).

Angwin argues that "algorithmic accountability" entails a more skeptical approach to algorithms in general (Garber 2016). We are living in a time of general tech-optimism, a time in which new technologies promise to make our lives both more efficient and enjoyable. Those technologies may help to make out justice system more equitable; they might not. The point is we owe it to ourselves—and to Eric Loomis and every other person whose life might be altered by an algorithm—to find out (Garber 2016). Ultimately, humans must evaluate each decision-making process and consider what forms of automation are useful, appropriate and consistent with the rule of law.

In the final analysis, there is something to be said for a sentence imposed by a human judge without the assistance of an algorithm. Judges, as humans, are not shrouded in the air of mystique and infallibility that surrounds technology. In some sense it is easier to examine and challenge a judge's decisions when a defendant suspects that bias influenced the judge's decision one way or the other, because judges, for the most part, have to give reasons for the way in which they act.

Judicial Decision-Making in the Age of Artificial Intelligence

As for Eric Loomis himself, he was released from Jackson Correctional Institution in August 2019, after serving his full six-year term. According to COMPAS, at least, he is at high risk to return (Chesterman 2020). [4]

References

Chaiken S (1980) Heuristic versus systematic information processing and the use of source versus message cues in persuasion. J Pers Soc Psychol 39:752–766

Challen R, Denny J, Pitt M, Gompels L, Edwards T, Tsaneva-Atanasova K (2019) Artificial intelligence, bias and clinical safety. BMJ Qual Saf 28:231–237

Chapman GB, Johnson EJ (1999) Anchoring, activation, and the construction of values. Organ Behav Hum Decis Process 79:115–153

Chesterman S (2020) Through a glass, darkly: artificial intelligence and the problem of opacity, NUS law working paper 2020/011. http://law.nus.edu.sg/wps/. Accessed 31 May 2020

Christin A, Rosenblat A, Boyd D (2015) Courts and predictive algorithms. Data Soc. https://www.law.nyu.edu/sites/default/files/upload_documents/Angele%20Christin.pdf. Accessed 30 Oct 2020

Citron D (2016) (Un)fairness of risk scores in criminal sentencing. Forbes https://www.forbes.com/sites/daniellecitron/2016/07/13/unfairness-of-risk-scores-in-criminal-sentencing/#7a2241044ad2. Accessed 23 June 2020

Citron DK (2008) Technological due process. Wash Univ Law Rev 85:1249–1313

Clark BB, Robert C, Hampton SA (2016) The technology effect: how perceptions of technology drive excessive optimism. J Bus Psychol 31:87–102

Dewan S (2015) Judges replacing conjecture with formula for bail. The New York Times. https://www.nytimes.com/2015/06/27/us/turning-the-granting-of-bail-into-a-science.html. Accessed 15 Oct 2020

Dzindolet MT, Pierce LG, Beck HP, Dawe LA (2002) The perceived utility of human and automated aids in a visual detection task. Hum Factors 44:79–94

Evans JS (2008) Dual-processing accounts of reasoning, judgment, and social cognition. Annu Rev Psychol 59:255–278

---

[4] *See* generally, on biases, in this book P G Marques - AI Instruments for Risk of Recidi-vism Prediction and the Possibility of Criminal Adjudication Deprived of Person-al Moral Recognition Standards – Sparse Notes from a Layman; and D Durães, P M Freitas and P Novais - The Relevance of Deepfakes in the Administration of Criminal Justice. *See* also, on the different applications of Machine Learning and AI, in this book A Oliveira and M A T Figueiredo - Artificial intelligence - historical context and state of the art; I Trancoso, N Mamede, B Martins, H S Pinto and R Ribeiro - The impact of language technologies in the legal domain; J Gonçalves-Sá and F L Pinheiro - Societal Implications of Recommendation Systems - A Technical Perspective; A T Freitas - Data-driven approaches in healthcare - challenges and emerging trends; M Correia and L Rodrigues - Security and Privacy; E Magrani and P G F Silva - The Ethical and Legal Challenges of Recommender Systems Driven by Artificial Intelligence; M Lanz and S Mijic - Risks associated with the use of natural language generation - Swiss civil liability law perspective; M S Fernandes and J R Goldim - Artificial Intelligence and Decision Making in Health - Risks and Opportunities; W Gravett - Judicial Decision-making in the Age of Artificial Intelligence; and D Durães, P M Freitas and P Novais - The Relevance of Deepfakes in the Administration of Criminal Justice. *See* finally, on the COMPAS system, in this book P G Marques - AI Instruments for Risk of Recidivism Prediction and the Possibility of Criminal Adjudication Deprived of Personal Moral Recognition Standards – Sparse Notes from a Layman.

Freeman K (2016) Algorithmic injustice: how the Wisconsin Supreme Court failed to protect due process rights in State v. Loomis. N C J Law Technol 18:75–106

Garber M (2016) When algorithms take the stand. The Atlantic. https://www.theatlantic.com/technology/archive/2016/06/when-algorithms-take-the-stand/489566/. Accessed 23 June 2020

Hamilton M (2015) Adventures in risk: predicting violent and sexual recidivism in sentencing law. Ariz State Law J 47:1–57

Hannah-Moffat K (2012) Actuarial sentencing: an "unsettled" proposition. Justice Q 30:270–296

Hannah-Moffat K (2015) Partiality, transparency, and just decisions the uncertainties of risk assessment. Fed Sentenc Rep 27:244–247

Hannah-Moffat K, Maurutto P, Turnbull S (2010) Negotiated risk: actuarial illusions and discretion in probation. Can J Law Soc 24:391–409

Hyatt JM, Chanenson SL, Bergstrom MH (2011) Reform in motion: the promise and perils of incorporating risk assessments and cost-benefit analysis into Pennsylvania sentencing. Duquesne Law Rev 49:707–749

Ishwarappa K, Anuradha J (2015) A brief introduction on big data 5Vs characteristics and hadoop technology. Procedia Comput Sci 48:319–324

Kahneman D (2011) Thinking: fast and slow. Farrar Straus & Giroux, New York

Karau SJ, Williams KD (1993) Social loafing: a meta-analytic review and theoretical integration. J Pers Soc Psychol 65:681–706

Kehl D, Guo P, Kessler S (2017) Algorithms in the criminal justice system: assessing the use of risk assessments in sentencing. Responsive Community Initiative, Berkman Klein Center for Internet and Society. Harvard Law School, Cambridge

Liu HW, Lin CF, Chen YJ (2019) Beyond State v Loomis: artificial intelligence, government algorithmization and accountability. Int J Law Inf Technol 27:122–141

Mamalian CA (2011) State of the science of pretrial risk assessment. Pretrial Justice Institute, Bureau of Justice Assistance, Washington, DC

Milgram A (2013) Why smart statistics are the key to fighting crime. TED, New York

Mussweiler T (2002) The malleability of anchoring effects. Exp Psychol 49:67–72

Mussweiler T, Strack F (2000) Numeric judgments under uncertainty: the role of knowledge in anchoring. J Exp Soc Psychol 36:495–518

Mussweiler T, Strack F, Pfeiffer T (2000) Overcoming the inevitable anchoring effect: considering the opposite compensates for selective accessibility. Personal Soc Psychol Bull 26:1142–1150

Oleson JC (2011) Risk in sentencing: constitutionally suspect variables and evidence-based sentencing. South Methodist Univ Law Rev 64:1329

Parasuraman R, Manzey DH (2010) Complacency and bias in human use of automation: an attentional integration. Hum Factors 52:381–410

Pasquale F (2017) Secret algorithms threaten the rule of law. M.I.T. Technology Review. https://www.technologyreview.com/2017/06/01/151447/secret-algorithms-threaten-the-rule-of-law/. Accessed 18 June 2018

Richie DR, Duffy JD (2018). Artificial intelligence in the legal field. In: Association of corporate counsel greater Philadelphia in-house counsel conference

Rutkin A (2016) People will follow a robot in an emergency – even if it's wrong. New Scientist. https://www.newscientist.com/article/2078945-people-will-follow-a-robot-in-an-emergency-even-if-its-wrong/. Accessed 20 Oct 2020

S v. Loomis (2016) 881 N.W.2d 749 (Wisc. 2016)

Skeem J (2013) Risk technology in sentencing: testing the promises and perils (commentary on hannah-moffat, 2011). Justice Q 30:297–303

Skitka LJ, Mosier KL, Burdick M (1999) Does automation bias decision-making? Int J Hum Comput Stud 51:991–1006

Starr S (2014) Sentencing by the numbers. The New York Times. https://www.nytimes.com/2014/08/11/opinion/sentencing-by-the-numbers.html. Accessed 15 Sept 2020

Thaler RH (1999) Mental accounting matters. J Behav Decis Mak 12:183–206

Turing AM (1950) Computing machinery and intelligence. Mind 236:433–460

Tversky A, Kahneman D (1974) Judgment under uncertainty: heuristics and biases. Science 185:1124–1131
United States v Rodriguez (1978) 585 F.2d 1234 (5th Cir. 1978)
Van Hollebeke M (2016) Shining a light on the darkness. Data Soc https://points.datasociety.net/shining-a-light-on-the-darkness-432adf10c7a0. Accessed 23 June 2020
Wilson TD, Houston CE, Etling KM, Brekke N (1996) A new look at anchoring effects: basic anchoring and its antecedents. J Exp Psychol Gen 125:387–402

Open Access This chapter is licensed under the terms of the Creative Commons Attribution 4.0 International License (http://creativecommons.org/licenses/by/4.0/), which permits use, sharing, adaptation, distribution and reproduction in any medium or format, as long as you give appropriate credit to the original author(s) and the source, provide a link to the Creative Commons license and indicate if changes were made.

The images or other third party material in this chapter are included in the chapter's Creative Commons license, unless indicated otherwise in a credit line to the material. If material is not included in the chapter's Creative Commons license and your intended use is not permitted by statutory regulation or exceeds the permitted use, you will need to obtain permission directly from the copyright holder.

Liability for AI Driven Systems

Ana Taveira da Fonseca, Elsa Vaz de Sequeira, and Luís Barreto Xavier

Abstract This article tries to assess if the current civil liability regimes provide a sound framework to tackle damages when AI systems—especially those based on machine-learning—are involved. We try to find answers for three questions: is there a place for fault-based liability, when it is impossible to ascertain, among multiple actors, whose action caused the damage? Are current strict liability regimes appropriate to address no-fault damages caused by the functioning of AI-systems or a new system is needed? When should an agent be exempted from liability? This analysis takes into consideration the important work produced within the European Union, especially the 2019 Report on "Liability for AI and Other Emerging Digital Technologies" (by the Expert Group set up by the European Commission), the European the Parliament 2020 Resolution on Civil Liability for AI, the 2021 Draft AI Act, the 2022 Draft AI Liability Directive and the 2022 Draft Product Liability Directive.

1 Presentation of the Problems

Digital technologies are evolving at a fast pace and artificial intelligence (AI) impacts all sectors of the economy and contemporary life. The operation of modern standalone or software based AI systems is likely to be associated to harm. In this article, we address the question of whether the traditional responses to the problem of compensation through civil liability are adequate to tackle damages when AI systems are put in place. While we depart from a Civil Law jurisdiction point of view, our discussion tries to go beyond the boundaries of our own legal tradition.

The challenges the traditional civil liability regimes face because of the dissemination of AI systems are linked to specific features of the operation of such

---

A. T. da Fonseca · E. Vaz de Sequeira (✉) · L. Barreto Xavier
Universidade Católica Portuguesa, Law School, Católica Research Centre for the Future of Law, Lisbon, Portugal
e-mail: anatf@ucp.pt; evs@ucp.pt; lbx@ucp.pt

© The Author(s) 2024
H. Sousa Antunes et al. (eds.), *Multidisciplinary Perspectives on Artificial Intelligence and the Law*, Law, Governance and Technology Series 58,
https://doi.org/10.1007/978-3-031-41264-6_16

systems: the ability of AI systems to making decisions in a growingly autonomous manner (Turner 2019, pp. 70–75; Ebers 2020, pp. 46–48; Chesterman 2021, pp. 31–62); the opacity of the machine learning based technologies (Ebers 2020, pp. 48–50; Chesterman 2021, pp. 63–82); the involvement of various agents in building, assembling, introducing into the market, customizing, selecting and supervising the data, training, updating and using the system (Expert Group on Liability and New Technologies—New Technologies Formation, Liability for artificial intelligence and other emerging technologies, Directorate-General for Justice and Consumers (European Commission) 2019, p. 35); the vulnerability to cyberattacks. All these factors contribute to the difficulty of deciding who—if anyone—should respond for a loss or harm. Hence, unless we refine or rethink traditional approaches, those who suffer damages are likely to be deprived of a fair compensation.

A case submitted under the traditional fault based liability against an operator or user of an AI system is very hard to succeed. The causal process is typically unknown to the victim. The black box effect of machine learning algorithms obstruct the transparency and explainability of the decision-making process. The number of agents potentially involved add to the complexity of the task. The plaintiff's burden of evidencing the fault is, most of the times, impossible to accomplish.

In this article, we consider three questions.

The first regards the possibility of establishing fault-based liability when various actors involved in the process disregarded the applicable rules, but it is impossible to determine which of the actions constitutes the actual cause of the damage.

Second question: when no fault has been committed and the damage is due to the functioning of AI-systems, should we apply any of the strict liability regimes in force? Should we, instead, design a specific regime for damages associated to AI systems?

Third and last question: when should the liability of the agent be excluded? In other words, what are the defenses the agent is able to put forward to escape liability?

The European Union (EU) has published important documents dealing with AI and civil liability on a general basis.

The Report on "Liability for AI and Other Emerging Digital Technologies" (2019 Report), presented by the Expert Group on Liability and New Technologies—New Technologies Formation (Expert Group), set up by the European Commission, discusses the application of existing liability regimes to emerging digital technologies, with a focus on AI, and the need for reform of those regimes.

The European Parliament (EP) has adopted on 20 October 2020 a "Resolution with Recommendations to the Commission on a Civil Liability Regime for AI" (2020 EP Resolution), including a Proposal for a Regulation of the European Parliament and the Council on Liability for the Operation of AI-Systems.

The 2021 Draft AI Act[1] does not address the civil liability issues. Instead, the European Commission has proposed in 2022 a Directive on Adapting Non-Contractual Civil Liability Rules to Artificial Intelligence (the 'AI Liability Directive')[2] and, at the same time, a new Directive on Liability for Defective Products, replacing the old Product Liability Directive (PLD).[3]

The 2019 Report distinguishes two types of potential perpetrators. The frontend operator is the "natural or legal person who exercises a degree of control over a risk connected with the operation and functioning of the AI-system and benefits from its operation". The backend operator is the "natural or legal person who, on continuous basis, defines the features of the technology, provides data and essential backend support service and therefore also exercises a degree of control over the risk connected with the operation and functioning of the AI-System".[4] The grounds for the liability of these agents seem to lie on the position of control that they exercise over the AI system and, in relation to the frontend operator, also in the benefit that he obtains from it. Although it is not clear, the producer, the programmer and the person in charge of feeding the system would act as backend operators. It seems more difficult to identify who might take on the role of frontend operator, particularly as the report is ambiguous on this topic. If, on one hand, the users of these systems seem to be comprised here, on the other hand recital 11 of the proposed regulation states that the user should only (objectively) respond if he is an operator. This suggests that there are users who are operators—those who, in addition to benefitting from the use, exercise some control over the process—and others who are not, because they do not enjoy similar attributes.

It should be pointed out that the concepts of frontend and backend operator are used here in a manner that do not fully coincide with the European Parliament's proposal. Under this approach, the fronted operator is "the person primarily deciding on and benefitting from the use of the relevant technology" and the backend operator is "the person continuously defining the features of the relevant technology and providing essential and ongoing backend support".[5] It appears that the concept of fronted operator proposed in the Expert Group's study is broader and at the same time clearer than the one used in the European Parliament's proposal. Both require the user of the AI system to derive a benefit from its use. Yet, whereas the latter requires, in addition, control over the source of danger constituted by that system, the former is satisfied with the decision to use that source of danger.

---

[1] European Commission 21-4-2021 Proposal for a Regulation of the EP and the Council Laying Down Harmonised Rules on AI (AI Act) and Amending Certain Union Legislative Acts.

[2] Proposal for a Directive of the European Parliament and of the Council on Adapting Non-Contractual Civil Liability Rules to Artificial Intelligence (AI Liability Directive), from 28-9-2022.

[3] Proposal for a Directive of the European Parliament and of the Council on Liability for Defective Products, from 28-9-2022.

[4] Article 3 e) and f).

[5] Point 11.

2 Subjective Liability in Case of Alternative Causation

The involvement of an AI system in the production of damages increases the difficulty of establishing fault and causation.

It will not always be easy to demonstrate the existence of a subjective imputation of the damage to the agent, due to lack of purpose or negligence—because the novelty of this type of situation has not yet allowed the development of duties of care-, just as it may be difficult to evaluate the agent's culpability. The autonomy of these systems makes it impossible, to a greater or lesser extent, to foresee how they will act in a specific case (Chesterman 2021, pp. 31–38, 60–62). The lack of predictability compromises the ability to make a prognosis as to the possible results of the conduct. This, in turn, may hinder the assessment of the culpability of the agent for having created or used the AI in those concrete circumstances (Barbosa 2020, p. 284).

In the same way, it would be extremely difficult to proceed with the objective imputation of the damage to the conduct of one of the participants in the process, due to the impossibility of ascertaining the actual cause of the damage. One of the possible outcomes at this level is the conclusion that any of the participations in the process of creation or use of the AI system could have produced the damage. In other words, any of them could be at the origin of the damage, but it is not known which of them is actually responsible for the damage.

The solution to the alternative causation problem is much discussed in legal theory, and it is debated whether one should:

(a) simply rule out the liability of the agents, for lack of causation;
(b) exclude in such cases the requirement of causation (Bydlinski 1959, pp. 6 et seq);
(c) replace *actual causation* with *possible causation*. Instead of demonstrating that the action of each agent was the actual cause of the damage, it would be sufficient to prove that such an action was a possible or potential cause of that damage. At the same time, it may be established a reversal of the burden of proof with regard to this assumption, presuming the existence of potential causation (Larenz 1994, pp. 571–572).[6]

The majority of authors lean towards the last option, rejecting the first one as, in balancing the interests of the potential injurer and the affected person, the former is privileged. It does not seem defendable if we think that any of the agents performed an action able of causing the damage and may have actually caused it. The second option is rejected as it establishes an unnecessary and not commendable deviation to the rule of a fault-liability system (Brambring 1973, p. 59; Larenz 1994, p. 571; Wagner 2018, p. 2318). When the requirement of causation is discarded, both the actual causality of the action and its suitability to produce the harm are not

---

[6] It makes no sense to presume the actual causality of such actions, since the reason for making use of the presumption is precisely the failure to determine the actual cause of the damage.

evaluated. That may lead to the liability of someone who did not practice an act capable of generating the damage. The third option, on the other hand, besides being based on the prevalence of the interest of the affected person over the conflicting interest of the potential injurer, does not involve the risk of holding liable someone who couldn't contribute to the event. The presumption of potential causation is a way of lightening the requirements of proof in this matter, protecting the affected person, since it is hard to prove the adequacy of each individual participation to the production of the entire result (Brambring 1973, pp. 95 et seq).

It should be emphasized that this lightening of the burden of proof of causality does not exempt the fulfilment of the other elements of civil liability for each agent involved in the causal process. Even in relation to causation, as has been said, the adequacy of the individual behavior to the production of the whole damage should be proved, unless the legislator has established a presumption of adequacy in order to protect the position of the affected person. In such a case, liability may be excluded if the potential perpetrator proves that his or her conduct did not cause the damage, that the conduct of another agent caused the damage, or that in the present case there was a ground of justification, exculpation or even impunity, which benefited him or one of the other agents involved (Larenz 1994, pp. 573 et seq, 576–578; Staudinger and Eberl-Borges 2018, pp. 29–30, 41–42; Wagner 2020, p. 2321 et seq).

It is sometimes questioned whether the application of this regime of joint and several liability of all the agents should be dependent on the verification of three requirements: the existence of a chronological connection between the individual conducts, the presence of a spatial connection between those same conducts and/or the common nature of the actions performed by each agent. In addition to this objective connection, it is also questionable whether a subjective connection should be imposed, i.e. the need that all agents be aware of each other or, in a less strict version, that they should be aware of each other (Brambring 1973, pp. 62 et seq; Larenz 1994, p. 574).

The absence of joint participation in these cases—characterized by a bilateral awareness of cooperation—seems to testify against the first formulation of the previously mentioned subjective connection. It is true that the second formulation is not covered by the joint participation regime, as it is based precisely on the ignorance (even if culpable) of such cooperation. Theoretically, there will therefore be room for such a requirement. We believe, however, that this requirement is out of place, since it would rarely respect the interests of the affected person. Except for the cases in which people are acting side by side, it would be almost impossible for an agent to be aware of the other (Staudinger and Eberl-Borges 2018, pp. 23 et seq, 35–36).

Likewise, there is no reason to limit the liability of agents based on their physical proximity, the temporal proximity of their conduct or the similarity between them. It is true that in some cases this will happen naturally. Consider, for example, those cases in which two people—not knowing each other—shoot at another, without being able to demonstrate which of the shots was fatal, insofar as any one of them could have been the cause of death. The contours of the situation show that the subjects were necessarily physically close, that the corresponding actions were relatively synchronous and that they shared identical characteristics. Sometimes, however, this is not the case and there is no materially relevant reason to treat the problem differently, namely to deny protection to the victim's claims. This happens, for example, in those cases in which a person is infected with AIDS and it is not possible to determine, at the time the disease is detected, whether its origin is found in a contaminated blood transfusion that he had taken in the past or in intimate relations that he also had in the past with an infected person. If in both cases there is fault or negligence from the potential perpetrators, what are the grounds for rejecting the affected person's claim for compensation?

Holding the potentially harmful agents responsible implies placing the emphasis on the dangerousness of the action carried out by each of them (Bydlinski 1959, p. 13). It will not be the damage that justifies the liability of the agent—as he may not be its author–, but the ability of the action to produce it. The underlying logic seems to be more consistent with the idea that, in these cases, the offences should be seen as offences of concrete danger and not as offences of result.

Based on this, it is reasonable to hold that, whenever all the people involved in the AI systems individually practice an unlawful and culpable act, in abstract capable of producing the damage, the solution will be in principle the joint and several liability of those involved, even though it is not possible to identify the concrete action behind that damage. This means that each agent is liable for the totality of the damage and can then claim back the share that each one is liable for in internal relations.

If, in general, the need for an objective and / or subjective connection is very doubtful, in these situations we believe that such a requirement does not appear to make sense. The dispersion both in place of the subjects intervening in the process of creation and use of AI and in time, given the time that may mediate between those interventions, would hardly allow protecting the interests of the affected person. On the other hand, given the different nature of the involvements—creation, programming, insertion of data, updates, use of the AI system–, the affected person would hardly obtain compensation for the damage suffered. Although from a conceptual point of view this could be the solution, from a values point of view this is not the most appropriate outcome. In such a case, the important is to decide which of the interests deserves protection: the affected person's or the agents'. Bearing in mind that the latter have committed a fault that was able to cause the damage, there is no reason to give their interests primacy over the position of the affected person.

One of the problems addressed by the 2019 Report is precisely that of alternative causation. It is recommended that its regime should be similar to multiple causation, with any participant being jointly and severally liable for all damages suffered.[7] Although the actual cause of the damage is unknown, it may be possible to establish degrees of probability among the actions of the different agents. In such a scenario,

---

[7] Point 31.

it is recommended that the burden of proof be placed on the side of the person whose action has a higher probability of having caused the damage.[8]

It should be stressed that the 2019 Report proposes a fault-based liability system as the rule for civil liability, despite the fact that it admits a lightening of the rules on the burden of proof in matters of causality, taking into account:

1. "the likelihood that the technology at least contributed to the harm";
2. "the likelihood that the harm was caused either by the technology or by some other cause within the same sphere";
3. "the risk of a known defect within the technology, even though its actual causal impact is not self-evident";
4. "the degree of ex-post traceability and intelligibility of processes within the technology that may have contributed to the cause (informational asymmetry)";
5. "the degree of ex-post accessibility and comprehensibility of data collected and generated by the technology";
6. "the kind and degree of harm potentially and actually caused".[9]

"Where the damage is of a kind that safety rules were meant to avoid, failure to comply with such safety rules, including rules on cybersecurity, should lead to a reversal of the burden of proving:

(a) causation, and/or.
(b) fault, and/or.
(c) the existence of a defect".[10]

The 2020 EP Resolution does not address the problem of alternative causation. Although it establishes the joint liability of the various operators who may be held liable, it is not clear whether the rule is intended for cases of joint-participation, parallel authorship, alternative causation or for all.[11] This means that it is not certain the possible liability of the participants in the causal process when one can't determine which of the actions effectively caused the damage. Also, even if their liability is accepted, no position is taken as to the possible need to prove the suitability of the action for producing the damage.

According to this proposal, the basic liability system should be a fault-based liability, although it provides for a rebuttable presumption of fault from the operators.[12]

All in all, in cases of alternative causation the solution will necessarily be one of the following three:

(a) exclusion of civil liability;

---

[8] Points 25–26.
[9] Points 25–62.
[10] Point 24.
[11] Article 11.
[12] Article 8.

(b) partial liability of each participant for a share of the total damage;
(c) joint and several liability of all participants for the entire damage.

From a technical point of view, all of these solutions are viable. The first solution is grounded on the lack of concrete causation. The second and third, differently, place the emphasis either on the fault of each agent or on the damage suffered by the affected person. The only difference is the way the causal link is assessed. Instead of requiring proof of causation *in concreto*, causation *in abstracto* is sufficient. They just differ in the regime of compliance with the obligations imposed on them. In the second solution, the shared liability system is applied, that is to say, each agent is liable for only a portion of the compensation. The affected person cannot demand full compensation from a potential injurer, in the same way that none of the potential injurers is bound by the whole. In the third solution proposed, the regime of joint and several liability prevails, by means of which each agent is liable for the total compensation, with the possibility claiming the payment back in internal relations.

The first solution grants more emphasis to the interests of the potential injurers in relation to the interest of the affected person. This does not appear to be the most appropriate one. The number of people involved in the creation and use of an AI system, located or coming from different areas of the globe and different fields of activity, makes it very difficult to identify and locate them. Therefore, it is too burdensome to impose on the affected person—often a natural person unaware of all these details—the need to sue each of the participants in order to obtain compensation for all the damage suffered. In fact, it will be less difficult for one of these participants to locate the others and exercise his right of claiming the payment back. For those reasons, the system of join and several liability seems more appropriate to the situation.

A presumption of causal adequacy also seems appropriate in this context, given, on the one hand, the highly technical, specific and complex nature of the whole system and, on the other hand, the (not culpable) lack of knowledge of the potential victims as to how the system works.

A final note to mention that the 'AI Liability Directive', while not addressing the problem of alternative causation, proposes two very important measures regarding the fault-based liability: the empowerment of national courts to order the providers or the users of the AI system to disclose relevant evidence at its disposal about a specific high-risk AI system (art. 3) and the establishment of rebuttable presumptions of the causal link between the fault of the defendant and the output produced by the AI system or the failure of the AI system to produce the output (art. 4).

3 Strict Liability

Quid iuris when no fault has been committed and the damage is due to the functioning of the AI-systems? The only possible path will be that of strict liability. In this context, two questions have been raised:

Liability for AI Driven Systems

1. Are any of the strict liability regimes currently in force to be directly or by analogy applicable to the problem?
2. Is it necessary or advisable to design a specific regime for damages created by an AI system?

The current strict liability regimes that are presented as possible solutions to the problem are mainly: product liability, liability for damage caused by animals and liability for damage caused by a motor vehicle.

According to the Council Directive 85/374/EEC (PLD), the producer—understood to be the manufacturer or importer of goods into the EU for distribution as part of his commercial activity[13]—is liable for defects in his product.[14] Product means "all movables, with the exception of primary agricultural products and game, even though incorporated into another movable or into an immovable". Electricity is also considered to be a "product".[15] The producer is only liable for defects of the product at the time it was placed on the market and not for those that appear subsequently.[16] The victim is responsible for proving the damage, the defect and the causation of the damage by the defect.[17]

Several difficulties have been identified in applying this regime to damages caused by an AI system. First, this regime would not entirely solve the problem because it does not address the possible liability of the owner, holder or user of an AI system. This means that it could only offer a partial solution. Even in the field of the creation of AI systems, there are obstacles to its application (Barfield and Pagallo 2020, p. 96). It is the case with the definitions of producer and product. While there is no doubt that the manufacture of hardware can be seen as a production activity and the result as a product, the same is not true when it comes to creating the algorithms on which AI is based, or to feeding that system. The definition of product in the PLD may give the impression that only movable tangible things—i.e., things which can be perceived by the senses—deserve such a qualification. An algorithm or the data that feeds it can hardly fall into that category (Revolidis and Dahi 2018, p. 61; Capilli 2020, p. 478). It is therefore also difficult to regard a programmer or the person who feeds the data as producers within the meaning of the PLD. Of course, one could always try to see the norm as a living instrument subject to evolutionary interpretation, adjusting it to today's reality (and not to the standards of 1985), or, if this is not possible, resort to analogy (Wagner 2018, p. 11). However, it is uncertain whether this would be fruitful, since the producer is only liable for defects in the product which existed at the time it was placed on the market. The big problem with damages caused by AI systems lies in the fact that the risk of injury is more associated with the autonomy of these systems than with

---

[13] Article 3.

[14] Article 1.

[15] Article 2.

[16] Article 7.

[17] Article 4.

a possible defect in their design (Pagallo 2013, p. 117). In most cases, there is no defect. The system's evolution is not controllable by the designer, the programmer or the other people involved in feeding and updating it. Moreover, as a rule, errors occur long after the system has been placed on the market and were not known or were not identifiable at the time (Capilli 2020, pp. 459, 473–474; Molnár-Gábor 2020, pp. 253–254).

Facing these difficulties, the proposal for a new PLD establishes: an extension of the notion of product to explicitly include digital manufacturing files and software (art. 4), thus removing the uncertainty about the qualification of AI systems as a product; presumptions of defectiveness (art. 6); and presumptions of the causal link between the defect and the damage (art. 9). The empowerment of national courts to order the defendant to disclose relevant evidence at its disposal is also established (art. 8).

Strict liability is typically based on one of two pillars: the position of control of a source of danger or the taking advantage of that source of danger (Barbosa 2020, p. 40).

The liability for damage caused by animals seems to seek support precisely in the taking advantage of those animals by their owner. The possible application of this regime to damages due to AI systems would only be viable through analogy.

The similarity between the two cases is found in their unpredictability (Pagallo 2013, pp. 33, 38). Just like animals, the performance of the AI system is also unpredictable. And it is precisely this unpredictability that creates the risk underlying these two realities. From this perspective, nothing would prevent the application by analogy of the rules on liability for damage caused by animals to damage caused by AI systems.

The question is whether the proposed solution is the most adequate to the problem. If one looks at it, the option taken is to hold liable those who take advantage of the source of danger or those who take advantage in their own interest. This means that those who create the source of danger or those who take advantage of that source in the interest of others will not be liable for damages arising from it. Transposing this to the digital world, this is equivalent to exclude the liability of the creator of the AI-system and, if that's the case, of the user who uses it in the interest of others. In many cases this doesn't seem to be the most appropriate solution to our problem.

In fact, it should not be forgotten that those who design, program, feed and update these systems determine their functioning. In closed software systems, no one has access other than these entities. The degree of information and understanding of the system is also not at all the same as that of its users (Revolidis and Dahi 2018, p. 74). With this in mind, does it make sense to base liability totally and exclusively on the taking advantage of risk, excluding those who create it or who can limit it, to a greater or lesser extent? It could be said that the ultimate decision to use the AI system lies with its user. However, that decision does not mean controlling the risks of the system. This decision has no influence on the design of the AI model. It is important to distinguish between the intrinsic danger, resulting from the system's configuration, and the danger resulting from the decision to use that system in inappropriate circumstances. In the first case, the danger comes from the system itself, in the second the danger results from a bad decision of its user. Here it is important to begin by asking if that bad decision constitutes sufficient ground for fault-based liability, particularly for violation of traffic duties. If this is not the case, we should rely on strict liability, which will be based on the taking advantage of the source of danger by the agent. There, on the contrary, the source of strict liability should be found in the dangerousness of the system, and it may be discussed whether without such a scenario it would be more appropriate to hold liable those who have a position of (relative) control of the source of danger or those who take advantage of that source or both.

We believe that the latter is the most adequate solution. It makes no sense to exempt from liability the designer of the algorithm, the programmer, the person who enters or updates data. They are in the best position to control this source of danger, and they also benefit from it, albeit indirectly (Wagner 2018, pp. 9–10). Although, as a rule, they do not benefit from the advantages created by the system, they take advantage of its value by trading it. Similarly, it is not reasonable to exonerate users from any possible liability. In addition to taking advantage of the source of danger, they themselves have the power to decide whether to use the AI system in those specific circumstances. Their decision to use it, while not being the exclusive cause of the danger, contributes to its maintenance or increase.

What should be determined is whether the damage corresponds to the materialization of one of the dangers generated or intensified by the creation and/or use of the AI system. In other words, the question is whether the damage is the result of the materialization of those dangers—of the system itself and of the decision to use it in that context and for that specific purpose—or only of one of them. If it comes from both, there should be joint and several liability of all participants in the causal process. If it comes from only one of them, he alone should be liable. However, we must pay attention to the fact that within each group—creators or users—there may be several potentially harmful persons. In the impossibility of determining the dangerousness of each individual participation and the contribution of each to the production of the damage, each potentially harmful person should answer jointly and severally for the damage (Ebers 2016, p. 16; Capilli 2020, p. 477).

The liability regime for damage caused by animals does not appear to cover all these situations.

The liability regime for damage caused by motor vehicles doesn't seem a solution to our problem either, since it would once again penalize the user of the AI system. In fact, the liability for the damages caused by a motor vehicle always lies with the owner or user of the vehicles, as he is the one who benefits from it. For the reasons already mentioned, such a vision would not be the most appropriate answer to our problem.

Some legal systems however demand not only that the responsible person use the vehicle in his own interest, but also that he or she was actually driving, suggesting the need to have a position of control over de source of danger. Such a regime discards the owner or users' liability, when they use the vehicle in the interest of a third party, and the potentially liability of the system designers.

It is important to understand, however, that this position of control concerns only the possibility to determine whether the vehicle is used and how it is used. No control would be required over the proper construction and performance of the vehicle. From a subjective point of view, this is important because it excludes the manufacturers of such vehicles from the scope of application of this regime. This means that the designer of the algorithm, the programmer and the people who feed or update the system are also excluded from liability here. Only the owner, the holder or the user remain liable.

The imperfection of the machine justifies a strict liability system. This imperfection also exists in AI systems. Therefore, it is also possible to apply analogy to damage caused by AI systems. In some cases, it may not be necessary to use analogy and the rules in question may even be directly applicable to the situations. This happens, for example, in accidents involving autonomous vehicles, although it is questionable to what extent there will be effective direction of the vehicle in cases of full automation (Barbosa 2020, p. 286).

Nevertheless, we have doubts as to the adequacy of theses regimes to solve our basic problem, since it once again penalizes the user of the AI system in his own interest, discarding his liability in the hypotheses of use in the interest of a third party and, more importantly, excluding the potentially liability of the system designers.

VI. The 2019 Report supports the adoption of strict liability for operators benefiting from or controlling the system. They limit such liability, however, to cases where AI-systems are used "in non-private environments" and "may typically cause significant harm".[18] This therefore excludes cases where the system is used in a closed environment, exposing a small number of people to the risk of injury, which can happen, for example, in the use of AI in the performance of a medical procedure. The possible extent of the injury appears to outweigh its gravity. If there is an operator who benefits from the risk and another who controls it, "strict liability should lie with the one who has more control over the risks of the operation", thereby showing the primacy of control in relation to the position of profiting from the source of danger.[19] The report also advocates extending the product's liability to cover defects in software that occur after it have been placed on the market.[20]

The 2020 EP Resolution limits the strict liability of operators to damage caused by high-risk AI-systems, listed in the annex to the proposal. According to the proposed regime, high-risk AI-systems should be understood as having "a significant potential in an autonomously operating AI-system to cause harm or damage to one or more persons in a manner that is random and goes beyond what can reasonably be expected; the significance of the potential depends on the interplay between the severity of possible harm or damage, the degree of autonomy

---

[18] Point 9.

[19] Point 11.

[20] Points 13–14.

of decision-making, the likelihood that the risk materializes and the manner and the context in which the AI-system is being used".[21]

Common to these proposals is the idea of trying to limit strict liability to certain cases. The justification for this lies not so much in legal considerations as in policy. The aim is to establish a regime that does not discourage AI-systems scientists and developers from continuing their research and activities. The choice is understandable, although it is difficult to accept the results to which it leads. It is inconceivable, for example, that a patient who has suffered serious damage to his or her life or physical integrity as a result of a medical procedure using an AI-system would not be compensated. A judgement of proportionality and reasonableness prevents the violation of any good equal or superior to the good being protected. It is unlikely that technological development will be a superior good to life or even, in certain cases, to physical integrity. Moreover, the fact that developers are not held responsible does not encourage them to invest their resources in improving the system (Wagner 2018, p. 18).

A compensation fund or a compulsory insurance will only prevent this inconvenience in the event that there is liability for damages suffered by someone as a result of the action of an AI-System, regardless of whether fault or strict liability is involved. The simple proof of the damage—although it may make sense to limit the damage compensable by this fund according to its nature and gravity—and respective cause would be sufficient to justify the compensation supported by the fund or the insurer. Otherwise, the fund or insurer would only substitute the injurer in fulfilling his obligation to compensate, without extending the protection of the interests of potential injured parties.

Based on all these thoughts, we advocate for a liability regime that deals precisely with these problems. Otherwise, on one hand, many situations will remain unprotected and, on the other hand, users of this type of systems will be held liable above all, exonerating the developers from any liability. As already mentioned, this does not seem appropriate.

Unfortunately, the Draft AI Liability Directive initial proposal does not accept a strict liability approach. Instead, it accepts a fault based liability, with some specific tools: a rebuttable presumption of causality and a disclosure of evidence regime. For the reasons explained before, we do not think that the proposed regime is adequate to deal with damages caused by AI systems. In addition, it is subject to question if the Draft Directive is consistent with the level of protection envisaged by the Draft AI Act.

---

[21] Article 3.

4 Exemption from Liability for Damage Caused by an AI System

Depending on the nature of the liability, another question should be posed: in which situations can the agent escape liability? We seek here to address the cases in which the agent's liability should be excluded.

We let outside the scope of this analysis the factors that can exempt a producer from liability and if the factors set out in article 7 PLD need to be revisited, as they are inadequate to address the specificities arising from damage caused by AI systems. We acknowledge that there is already relevant and reasonable doctrine which underlines that the directive allows an AI producer to avoid liability by invoking the so-called *development risk defence* (Bertolini 2020, p. 58; Evas 2020, p. 9; Navas 2020, pp. 80–81). A concern that the proposal for a new PLD seems to have addressed since the development risk defence cannot be invoked when the scientific and technical knowledge evolution occurs in the period in which the product was still within the manufacturer's control. [22] This amendment suggests that the manufacturer remains responsible if, for example through updates, he/she can eliminate the defects revealed by the evolution of knowledge and technique. However, it must be questioned whether such change is sufficient to ensure the safety of AI-enabled products already put into circulation.

Therefore, we will focus on the applicable exclusions when liability is not based on the AI system's defects.

Naturally, there is no unitary answer to the question, since the grounds to exempt an agent vary due to the different nature of the liability.

If the agent is liable based on strict liability, the grounds to escape liability will differ from those that should be accepted when we have a fault-based liability regime, even with a reversal of the burden of proof. For the present purpose, it is less important determining whether the agent is a programmer or a user, a backend operator or a frontend operator, as defined above, than to understand whether he/she is liable based on strict liability system or on fault-based liability regime.

Actually, both in member states' tort legislations (see Evas 2020, pp. 10–33)[23] and in EU proposals to harmonize a tort law regime for damage caused by an AI system, there is a trend to exclude "one fits all solution", which means that the obligation to compensate damages caused by IA systems may be based either on strict liability or fault-based liability.

Nonetheless, the European Commission's proposal for an AI Liability Directive only addresses the harmonization of the rules for the presumption of causality and the disclosure of evidence, leaving it up to each Member State to determine whether agents' liability should be based on strict liability or a fault-based liability system.

---

[22] Article 10/1/e).

[23] For a detailed analysis of the liability in national law of each member states and its possible application to AI.

Liability for AI Driven Systems

If the agent is going to be held liable for damage caused by an AI system, he cannot dismiss liability because the damage was caused by that system or is a consequence of its autonomy.[24] However, in theory, several other factors can exempt an agent from liability:

(i) the proof that the agent complied with specific duties, such as, for example, diligence, custody and surveillance, and acted with due care;
(ii) the proof that harm or damage was caused by force majeure;
(iii) the proof that harm or damage is attributable to a third party;
(iv) the proof that the victim or the affected person caused harm or damage;

The first factor can only be admitted in a fault-based system, even with a reversal of proof, since, in cases of strict liability, the agent's liability is not based on the existence of an unlawful act or a breach of a duty.

In member states' tort laws, the liability regimes based on a presumption of fault allow agents to escape liability, when they prove to have acted with due care to avoid damage. The proposals drawn up by the Expert Group and the EP[25] also seem to accept this solution, seeking to tailor the evidence that should be produced to address the peculiarities arising from damage caused by AI systems. In this light, the Expert Group proposes: "Operators of emerging digital technologies should have to comply with an *adapted range of duties of care*".[26]

In a strict liability system, the agent will be liable regardless of having breached the incumbent duty. His/her liability will be justified by the risk that the agent generates with the development of his/her activity or by the profits from which he/she benefits.

Regarding damages caused by force majeure or a fortuitous event, there is no doubt that the demonstration of its existence should lead, in principle, to the exclusion of the agent's liability, either in a system of presumption of fault or in a system of strict liability (Pagallo 2013, p. 33). Nonetheless, some clarifications are in order.

First, even in a fault system, if it is proved that the damage was directly caused by force majeure, but at the same time, it is shown that, if the agent had acted diligently, he could have avoided the damage, the agent's liability should remain and apply.

Secondly, in strict liability regimes, we tend to consider that the proof of the existence of force majeure that caused the damage is sufficient to remove the agent's liability. The comprehensive formulation that is sometimes used should be reconsidered, from our point of view. In articles 4 and 8 of the EP 2020 Resolution, it is proposed that *"the operator shall not be liable if the harm or damage was caused by force majeure"*.

---

[24] Articles 4 (3) and 8 (2) EP 2020 Resolution.

[25] Article 8 EP 2020 Resolution.

[26] Point 16.

In order to escape liability, it should not be sufficient to prove the existence of force majeure. It should also be necessary to demonstrate that the force majeure is "alien" to the operation of the AI system.

Consider two examples: should the agent be liable for damage caused by a surgeon robot that, following an earthquake, falls over a patient injuring him/her? Should the agent be liable for damage driven by a surgeon robot that causes injury to a patient due to a connection failure caused by a severe storm?

In the first case, the damage caused by the robot could have been originated from any other instrument present in the operating room. The same cannot be said of damage deriving from a lack of connection, even due to an exceptional atmospheric phenomenon.

It is very doubtful that, when the agent is strictly liable, his/her liability can be removed when the force majeure event is not foreign to the functioning of the AI system. In fact, one of the characteristic risks of AI systems is that they may cause damages to third parties, when there is a connectivity failure and, therefore, even if that failure is due to an exceptional or unusual situation, the agent should not escape liability.

We are fully aware that resorting to an indeterminate or vague concept such as damages caused by force majeure alien or foreign to the utilization of the AI system will require an increased effort for the courts. Even if the situations in which there is a connection failure may be easier to understand and frame, practice and day-to-day events will certainly bring other examples that will certainly raise more questions.

Another question frequently arising is how to deal with cases where the agent can prove that a third party caused the harm or damage. The autonomy of this question—and ultimately the exclusion of liability - depends on whether the damage has been caused exclusively by a third party who is not a producer or an operator of the AI system. Previously, we have already dealt with the problems arising from hypotheses in which several operators may be liable based on a strict liability system or on a fault-based liability regime.

The issue here is to identify and segregate the cases in which the third party interfered with the AI system, modifying, or affecting its operation. We can identify several examples. The hackers who maliciously interfere with the AI system. The subjects who negligently disrupt the functioning of a robot by disconnecting its power supply. The children who hijack a goods delivery drone, etc.

In any of the situations described, it is unquestionable that the third party should respond for the damages suffered by the injured party. The problem is to ascertain if this third-party liability can exclude the liability of a producer or an operator, as defined above.

As mentioned before, we will exclude from our analysis the producer's or the manufacturer's liability for defective products.

In a negligence-based liability system with presumed fault, the proof that a third party exclusively caused an injury should in general allow the agent to escape liability, unless the third party's action was enabled by the agent's breach of due diligence. In other words, the proof that a third party exclusively caused the damage should exclude the agent's liability, except in cases where the agent could have prevented the third party's action if he had acted diligently.

As regards strict liability, there is no uniform solution for damage exclusively caused by third parties. The rule is that strict liability should be excluded in these cases, although joint and several liability is admitted in specific regimes. The most paradigmatic example is vicarious liability, when it is set that a principal is vicariously and strictly liable for the torts of his/ her agents.

The absence of a uniform system for dealing with damage caused exclusively by third parties is an argument in favour of an autonomous regime for damage caused by AI systems.

The EP 2020 Resolution is very innovative on this point. According to Article 8.3, "where the harm or damage was caused by a third party that interfered with the AI-system by modifying its functioning or its effects, the operator shall, nonetheless, be liable for the payment of compensation if such third party is untraceable or impecunious". Assuming that it is often difficult to identify the person of the third party and/or that the third party may not have sufficient assets to pay the compensation, it is proposed that the agent's liability be maintained, even in cases framed under the fault-based liability regime. On the other hand, this option implies that, *a fortiori*, the solution should apply to the hypotheses of strict liability.

Although we understand the concern behind the proposal, it is difficult not to question whether we are not facing strict liability (Antunes 2020, p. 10), in spite of the qualification proposed by the European Parliament. When it is proven that the agent acted diligently and could not have avoided the third party's action and, in spite of this, he/she is still held liable since the party is untraceable or impecunious, the conclusion can only be that the EP 2020 Resolution favours a strict liability approach.

When an AI system causes damage, one can never set aside the possibility that the affected person has by his/her action or omission contributed to the damage suffered or to its extent. According to a more modern understanding, the agent's liability should only be excluded when the behaviour of the affected person is the sole cause of the damage. In other cases, the negligent conduct of the injured party should only constitute grounds for reducing liability. This solution is embraced by the 2019 Report[27] and the EP 2020 Resolution.[28]

There are, however, legal systems, such as the Portuguese, where the Civil Code still provides for a total exclusion of liability in some of the cases described (cf. article 570, no. 2). The solution has, however, been frequently criticized and is inadequate for situations in which the damage was simultaneously caused by the AI system and by the injured party. This is just another example of the need of an autonomous civil liability regime for AI damage. [29]

---

[27] Point 28.

[28] Article 10.

[29] *See* also, on the AI Act, in this book P U Lima and A Paiva - Autonomous and Intelligent Robots - Social, Legal and Ethical Issues; M N Duffourc and D S Giovanniello - The Autonomous

References

Antunes HS (2020) Civil liability applicable to artificial intelligence: a preliminary critique of the European Parliament resolution of 2020. Available via SSRN. https://papers.ssrn.com/sol3/papers.cfm?abstract_id=3743242. Accessed 18 Apr 2022

Barbosa MM (2020) O futuro da responsabilidade civil desafiada pela inteligência artificial: as dificuldades dos modelos tradicionais e caminhos de solução. Revista de Direito da Responsabilidade ano 2:280–326

Barfield W, Pagallo U (2020) Advanced introduction to law and artificial intelligence. Edward Elgar Publishing, Cheltenham

Bertolini A (2020) Artificial intelligence and civil liability, European Parliament's Committee on Legal Affairs. Available at https://www.europarl.europa.eu/RegData/etudes/STUD/2020/621926/IPOL_STU(2020)621926_EN.pdf. Accessed 18 Apr 2022

Brambring G (1973) Mittäter, Nebentäter, Beteiligte und die Verteilung des Schadens bei Mitverschulden des Geschädigten. Dunker & Humbolt, Berlin

Bydlinski F (1959) Haftung bei alternativer Kausalität. Jurist Bl 81:1–13

Capilli G (2020) I criteri di interpretazione dele responsabiitá. In: Alpa G (ed) Diritto e intelligenza artificiale. Pacini Giuridica, Pisa, pp 457–487

Chesterman S (2021) We, the robots? Regulating artificial intelligence and the limits of the law. Cambridge University Press, Cambridge

Ebers M (2016) La utilización de agentes electrónicos inteligentes en el tráfico jurídico: necesitamos reglas especiales en el derecho de la responsabilidad civil? In: InDret - revista para el anàlisis del derecho, 3. Universitat Pompeu Fabra, Barcelona, pp 1–22, available at http://www.raco.cat/index.php/InDret/article/view/314400. Accessed 18 Apr 2022

Ebers M (2020) Regulating AI and robotics: ethical and legal challenges. In: Ebers M, Navas S (eds) Algorithms and law. Cambridge University Press, Cambridge, pp 37–99

European Commission (2021) Proposal for a Regulation of the European Parliament and of the Council Laying Down Harmonised Rules on Artificial Intelligence (Artificial Intelligence Act) and Amending Certain Union Legislative Acts, COM/2021/206 final

European Parliament resolution of 20 October 2020 with recommendations to the Commission on a civil liability regime for artificial intelligence (2020/2014(INL)), OJ C 404, 6.10.2021, pp 107–128

Evas T (2020) Civil liability regime for artificial intelligence - European added value assessment, European Parliamentary Research Service, Available at https://www.europarl.europa.eu/RegData/etudes/STUD/2020/654178/EPRS_STU(2020)654178_EN.pdf, Accessed 18 Apr 2022

Expert Group on Liability and New Technologies – New Technologies Formation, Liability for artificial intelligence and other emerging technologies, Directorate-General for Justice and Consumers (European Commission) (2019). Available at https://op.europa.eu/en/publication-detail/-/publication/1c5e30be-1197-11ea-8c1f-1aa75ed71a1/language-en. Accessed 18 Apr 2022

Larenz K (1994) Lehrbuch des Schudrechts, 2. Bd. 2. HB, 13. edn. C.H. Beck'sche VerlagsBuchhandlung, München

---

AI Physician - Medical Ethics and Legal Liability; D Durães, P M Freitas and P Novais - The Relevance of Deepfakes in the Administration of Criminal Justice; A Keller, C Martins Pereira and M Lucas Pires - The European Union's approach to Artificial Intelligence and the Challenge of Financial Systemic Risk; and J C Abreu - The "Artificial Intelligence Act" Proposal on European e-Justice Domains Through the Lens of User-focused, User-friendly and Effective Judicial Protection Principles. At the same time, cfr in this book M Lanz and S Mijic - Risks associated with the use of natural language generation - Swiss civil liability law perspective.

Molnár-Gábor F (2020) Artificial intelligence in healthcare: doctors, patients and liabilities. In: Wischmeyer T, Rademacher T (eds) Regulating artificial intelligence. Springer, Cham, pp 339–360

Navas S (2020) Producer liability for AI-based technologies in the European Union. Int Law Res 9:77–84

Pagallo U (2013) The laws of robots – crimes, contracts, and torts. Volume 10 of law, governance and technology series. Springer, Dordrecht

Revolidis J, Dahi A (2018) The peculiar case of the mushroom picking robot: extra-contractual liability in robotics. In: Corrales M, Fenwick M, Forgó N (eds) Robotics, AI and the future of law. Springer, Singapore, pp 57–79

Staudinger J, Eberl-Borges C (2018) Kommentar zum bürgerlichen Gesetzbuch mit Einführungsgesetz und Nebengesetzen, 2. Buch – Recht der Schuldverhältnisse, §§ 830-838. Sellier – de Gruyter, Berlin

Turner J (2019) Robot rules- regulating artificial intelligence. Palgrave Macmillan, London

Wagner G (2018) Robot liability. Available via SSRN. https://papers.ssrn.com/sol3/papers.cfm?abstract_id=3198764. Accessed 18 Apr 2022

Wagner G (2020) Münchener Kommentar zum Bürgerlichen Gesetzbuch. C.H. Beck, München

Open Access This chapter is licensed under the terms of the Creative Commons Attribution 4.0 International License (http://creativecommons.org/licenses/by/4.0/), which permits use, sharing, adaptation, distribution and reproduction in any medium or format, as long as you give appropriate credit to the original author(s) and the source, provide a link to the Creative Commons license and indicate if changes were made.

The images or other third party material in this chapter are included in the chapter's Creative Commons license, unless indicated otherwise in a credit line to the material. If material is not included in the chapter's Creative Commons license and your intended use is not permitted by statutory regulation or exceeds the permitted use, you will need to obtain permission directly from the copyright holder.

Risks Associated with the Use of Natural Language Generation: Swiss Civil Liability Law Perspective

Marcel Lanz and Stefan Mijic

Abstract The use and improvement of Natural-Language-Generation (NLG) is a recent development that is progressing at a rapid pace. Its benefits range from the easy deployment of auxiliary automation tools for simple repetitive tasks to fully functional advisory bots that can offer help with complex problems and meaningful solutions in various areas. With fully integrated autonomous systems, the question of errors and liability becomes a critical area of concern. While various ways to mitigate and minimize errors are in place and are being improved upon by utilizing different error testing datasets, this does not preclude significant flaws in the generated outputs.

From a legal perspective it must be determined who is responsible for undesired outcomes from NLG-algorithms: Does the manufacturer of the code bear the ultimate responsibility or is it the operator that did not take reasonable measures to minimize the risk of inaccurate or unwanted output? The answer to this question becomes even more complex with third parties interacting with a NLG-algorithm which may alter the outcomes. While traditional tort theory links liability to the possibility of control, NLG may be an application that ignores this notion since NLG-algorithms are not designed to be controlled by a human operator.

M. Lanz (✉)
Attorney at Law at Schärer Rechtsanwälte, Aarau, Switzerland
e-mail: marcel.lanz@5001.ch

S. Mijic
ETH Zurich, Zurich, Switzerland

© The Author(s) 2024
H. Sousa Antunes et al. (eds.), *Multidisciplinary Perspectives on Artificial Intelligence and the Law*, Law, Governance and Technology Series 58,
https://doi.org/10.1007/978-3-031-41264-6_17

1 Technical Basics on Natural Language Generation

1.1 Introduction to Technical Aspects

Natural Language Generation (NLG) is a major subfield of Natural Language Processing and Deep Learning overall. Recent breakthroughs in autoregressive models such as OpenAI's GPT-2 (Radford et al. 2019), GPT-3 (Brown et al. 2019), InstructGPT (Ouyang et al. 2022) or Google's Primer (So et al. 2021) have led to demonstrations of machine generated texts that were demonstrably difficult or even impossible to distinguish from regular written texts. When using NLG, liability claims can occur in any area where verbal communication is used.

The first applications that commercialize the technology are already starting to be available with self-reinforcing chat bots, automated code generation and others starting to enter the market. In this work we will explore those new application areas and focus on particularly those which would likely be deemed a good fit for well-intentioned use but could lead to undesirable, negative results under certain conditions.

We further examine the capacity of both human and algorithmic detection of machine generated text to mitigate the fast spread of generated content in the form of news articles and others. Building on previous work that has focused on generating legal texts with a previous generation of NLG tools, we train a more advanced autoregressive transformer model to illustrate ways how such models operate and at what points the operator of the model has a direct or indirect influence on the likely generated output.

In the second part of the article, we examine civil liability issues which may arise when using NLG, particularly focusing on the Directive on defective products and fault-based liability under Swiss Law. Regarding the latter, we discuss specific legal bases that may give rise to liability when NLG is used.[1]

---

[1] *See generally* on the different applications of Machine Learning and AI I.1 - A Oliveira and M A T Figueiredo - Artificial intelligence - historical context and state of the art; I.2 - I Trancoso, N Mamede, B Martins, H S Pinto and R Ribeiro - The impact of language technologies in the legal domain; I.4 - J Gonçalves-Sá and F L Pinheiro - Societal Implications of Recommendation Systems - A Technical Perspective; I.5 - A T Freitas - Data-driven approaches in healthcare - challenges and emerging trends; I.6 - M Correia and L Rodrigues - Security and Privacy; II.2 - E Magrani and P G F Silva - The Ethical and Legal Challenges of Recommender Systems Driven by Artificial Intelligence; II.6 - M S Fernandes and J R Goldim - Artificial Intelligence and Decision Making in Health - Risks and Opportunities; III.4 - W Gravett - Judicial Decision-making in the Age of Artificial Intelligence; III.5 - D Durães, P M Freitas and P Novais - The Relevance of Deepfakes in the Administration of Criminal Justice.

1.2 Risks of Reinforcement Learning

1.2.1 Undesirable Language Generation

A possible way to adapt this and similar model to its users' inputs is by applying reinforcement learning to the model. One such way using the transformer-based model we introduced earlier, is to add relevant user input to the fine-tuning dataset. This allows the operator to adjust the model to the user's behavior and in theory improve upon the overall readability and comprehension.

The potential danger with uncontrolled reinforcement learning utilizing unfiltered user inputs as well using a not carefully vetted data source for the main fine-tuning dataset is shown by undesired outputs from the NLG. Two more prominent recent examples include Microsoft Twitter Bot Tay (Schwartz 2019) in 2016 and IBM's Watson (Madrigal 2013) in 2013.

In the case of Tay, the Bot was training itself on the unfiltered interactions it had with Twitter users that used inflammatory and offensive language. Based on those interactions it would generate inflammatory and offensive language itself even when responding to users that did not use any such language.

One recent approach that is being adopted by OpenAI is content filtering at the input prompt level (Markov et al. 2022). In an environment that requires a high degree of moderation, content filtering can be applied at source to avoid prompts that will likely result in a hateful, violent or otherwise undesirable response. [2] While this does address to a degree the most extreme detectable input prompts, it does not promise an input bias free response, which has to be addressed at the model level.

1.2.2 Code Generation and Vulnerable Code Data

With the advancement of transformer-based text generation it is starting to become possible to train the models on very specific and technically challenging tasks. One such emerging field is automated code generation based on natural language input. The probably most famous and widely used one is Github Copilot which was released in June 2021.[3] It generates code sequences in a variety of languages given some comment, function name or surrounding code.

Copilot is mostly based on the base GPT-3 model that has been then fine-tuned to Github using open-source code (Chen et al. 2021). Since there is no manual review of each entry, Github advises that the underlying dataset can contain insecure coding patterns that are in turn synthesized to generated code at the end-user level. A first evaluation of the generated code already found approximately 40% of the produced

---

[2] OpenAI Content Moderation Tooling, Available: https://openai.com/blog/new-and-improved-content-moderation-tooling/.

[3] GitHub Copilot, Your AI pair programmer. Available: https://copilot.github.com/.

code excerpts to contain security vulnerabilities in scenarios relevant to high-risk Common Weakness Enumeration (Pearce et al. 2021).

The unreviewed generation of potentially vulnerable code would pose a severe risk to the owner of said code, which makes an unreviewed or near-autonomous application of such a tool unlikely to be applied in an autonomous fashion using the underlying models. There are however automated code-review solutions available that inspect a given code passage for any potential quality and security issues (e.g. Sonar [4]). Enabling a non-technical operator to use natural language to generate simple code excerpts that can be automatically scanned for vulnerabilities and deployed in a test environment that would be used for rapid prototyping would seem like the most reasonable semi-autonomous code generation utilization.

1.3 Detection of Machine Generated Text

With the wide availability of cloud computing allowing for the production of machine generated content and social media allowing for the mass distribution of it, the last barrier remains the quality of the generated texts and the ability of regular content consumers to distinguish it from regular produced texts. Based on previous related work, the ability of non-trained evaluators depends to a certain degree on the subject domain as well as the quality of the model itself (Peric et al. 2021). For excerpts that focused on legal language that was sourced from several decades of US legal opinions, the ability to distinguish ranged from 49% (generated by GPT-2) up to 53% (generated by Transformer-XL), both being close to random. Related work also shows that the accuracy improved for the more creative domain of human written stories with the prompt "Once upon a time" where GPT-2 achieved a result already 62% and GPT-3 again a random-guessing value of 49% (Clark et al. 2021). While it is unlikely that we will see machine generated literature ready for mass consumption any time soon, one concerning factor is that the accuracy value for detecting news articles is also at 57% for GPT-2 and a basic random-guess value of 51% for GPT-3.

While most consumers have difficulties differentiating between machine and human generated texts, the same models can be trained to differentiate between those two. If the applied model (GPT-2/Transformer-XL) is known beforehand the rate of detection was 94% to 97% high, while not knowing the model in advance resulted in a detection rate of 74% to 76%. Possible detection would therefore likely be especially hard for models that are not open sourced and cannot easily be replicated. This will likely be increasingly the case as it has been with GPT-3 that has been licensed to Microsoft with the model source code not publicly available.[5]

---

[4] Sonar, Available: https://www.sonarsource.com/.

[5] Microsoft Invests in and Partners with OpenAI to Support Us Building Beneficial AGI, Available: https://openai.com/blog/microsoft/.

1.4 Operator Influence on Output

1.4.1 General Remarks

While setting up tools that generate text content, there are only a few options to influence the output. The first and most basic layer of most NLG algorithms is the basic dataset that is used to train the base model. In the case of GPT-2 with its 1.5 billion it was trained on the data of 8 million Web Pages or 40GB of Internet text. The way the selection was done was partly through selecting outbound web pages from Reddit that received "3 Karma" as a way of somewhat human quality selection. This layer cannot be replicated in most cases from the end-users of the tool and has to be taken as is (while the option to train the model from scratch is present but difficult to implement on a sufficiently sophisticated level for most end-users).

The second and more influenceable layer is the dataset that is used to "fine-tune" the model. This step allows end-users to specialize their output to a certain domain, a certain language style or similar. Here the end-users have the highest degree of influence on the actual NLG output that will be generated. A particular domain area, such as "legal language" for example allows users to specialize the output of the generated language to sound quite similar and even identical to qualified legal language. Current trends for LLMs as well as technical limitations of most operators will make this layer increasingly unaccessible with most models only allowing operator interaction via commercial API. [6] This approach limits operators' influence, but also leaves an auditable utilization trace that can then always be tracked back to the provider of the used model.

The third and most direct change of quality output language can be set at the basic parameter settings of the model. Those are usually and specifically in the case of our example model the desired output text length, the initial text prompt, and the "temperature". The temperature here allows the end-user to increase the likelihood of high probability words and decrease the likelihood of low probability words, which often results in usually more coherent text with a slightly higher temperature (Von Platen 2020). This layer is the most easily modifiable and would be most interacted with on the side of the end-user. Those parameters will likely become less available for most commercialized applications of LLMs, leaving the model provider more influence to optimize parameters and outputs based on existing optimized result lengths and probability scores.

An additional parameter that is also sometimes in place is to exclude any foul language from being generated. This can mean that even if the given text prompt

---

[6] ChatGPT Plus, Available: https://openai.com/blog/chatgpt-plus/.

or underlying training or fine-tuning dataset would contain foul language the model would still never output any words that are considered to be offensive based on a set keyword list.

1.4.2 Data and Methods

To further illustrate the direct impact the parameter setting of the operator has on the output, we trained a GPT-Neo (Black et al. 2021) model on a legal text dataset, that applies some of the methods and data of a previous work, while using a newer and more advanced model (Peric et al. 2021).

Our empirical setting is U.S. Circuit Courts, the intermediate appellate courts in the federal court system. Circuit Court judges review the decisions of the District Courts, deciding whether to affirm or reverse. The judges explain their decision by providing a written opinion. Our corpus comprises 50,000 of these U.S. Circuit Court opinions, uniformly sampled from the universe of opinions for the years 1890 through 2010.1 The sample includes both lead (majority) opinions and addendum opinions (concurrences and dissents). We undertake minimal pre-processing, so that our generator can replicate the original style of the texts. We do remove some metadata and XML markup but keep capitalization, punctuation, etc. We preserve the special legal citation notation used by U.S. courts. The opinions are in general quite lengthy, containing an average of 2024 tokens (words) per article. The average length gradually decreased from the 1890s reaching a minimum in the 1970s. After that, the average length of these opinions has grown steadily until the present day. Notably, it was around 1970 when digital legal research databases came into use. Our approach to representing legal documents is an auto-regressive language model. We are given an unsupervised corpus. We fine-tuned an existing GPT-Neo checkpoint on our legal corpus.

1.4.3 Samples of Operator Influence

We demonstrate how the end-user can interact with the model based on the fine-tuning of the model and based on the parameter selection with the following samples using our reference model. In our first sample (c.) we use the full-sized dataset with the default temperature value applied that generates some meaningful results.

In the other two samples, we used the standard full-sized dataset, but now changed the temperature parameter to 0.9 (d.) and 0.1 (e.) respectively. We observe that the samples set for a higher temperature also have a better readability that doesn't consist of too many listed legal precedents, but rather more natural language.

(a.) Prompt: The Tenth Circuit contravened those settled principles here. Not one of the decisions relied upon (. . .)
(b.) Genuine Ending: (. . .) by the Court of Appeals—Estate of Ceballos v. Husk, 919 F. 3d 1204 (CA10 2019), Hastings v. Barnes, 252 Fed. Appx. 197 (CA10 2007), Allen, 119 F. 3d 837, and Sevier v. Lawrence, 60 F. 3d 695 (CA10 1995)—comes close to establishing that the officers' conduct was unlawful. The Court relied most heavily on Allen. But the facts of Allen are dramatically different from the facts here.
(c.) Full dataset, temperature default 0.7   (. . .) by the majority holds that a defendant who is not a party to a conspiracy cannot be held personally liable for an overt act in furtherance of the conspiracy. To the contrary, the Tenth Circuit held that a defendant is personally liable for an overt act if he "was a member of the conspiracy at the time of the overt act and participated in it in some manner."
(d.) Full dataset, temperature high 0.9   (. . .) by the Tenth Circuit is even remotely analogous to this case. In United States v. Smith, 7 F.3d 1433 (10th Cir. 1993), the court held that a defendant's motion to suppress evidence obtained in violation of the Fourth Amendment was properly denied because the government did not have probable cause to search the defendant's house.
(e.) Full dataset, temperature very low 0.1   (. . .) by the Tenth Circuit in this case is inconsistent with the Supreme Court's decision in United States v. Booker, 543 U.S. 220, 125 S. Ct. 738, 160 L. Ed. 2d 621 (2005). In Booker, the Supreme Court held that the mandatory nature of the Sentencing Guidelines rendered them unconstitutional. 543 U.S. at 244. The Court held that the Guidelines were unconstitutional because they were not "sufficiently reliable to support a finding of 'reasonableness.'" Id. at 245.

2 Legal Aspects

2.1 Introduction to Legal Analysis

The use of artificial intelligence (AI) such as NLG algorithms creates numerous legal challenges, including liability issues. Most AI applications are designed to develop autonomously to deal with problems that their developers did not or could not have considered when programming it. As a result, self-learning AI can evolve in unforeseen ways. In the worst case, an algorithm can cause harm to others through dangerous self-learned behavior.

When using NLG, liability claims can occur in any area where verbal, be it oral or written, communication is used. Hence, a hospital or insurance company using NLG based bots to communicate with patients, a lawyer using NLG to draft briefs, or a news outlet using NLG to redact articles are facing liability claims, if the algorithm's output causes harm to others.

Legal literature that deals with the implications of AI on future tort claims, focuses on the European Council's directive on the liability for defective products

(Directive) and whether new liability provisions are necessary or not.[7] This article further analyzes how verbal communication generated by NLG algorithms can violate personal rights, infringe on intellectual property rights or be the cause of unfair competition claims.

2.2 Liability for Autonomous Actions of AI in General

2.2.1 Unforeseeable Actions of Self-Learning AI as a Challenge for Tort Law

The self-learning ability of AI poses major challenges for developers and operators. On the one hand, AI autonomously develops new solutions to problems. On the other hand, these same characteristics pose a tremendous challenge, as developers and operators are not always able to anticipate risks that self-learning AI might pose to others.

One might conclude that an AI's action adopted from self-learning mechanisms are not foreseeable to the developers or operators of an AI, preventing them from implementing adequate countermeasures (Horner and Kaulartz 2016, p. 7; von Westphalen 2019, p. 889; Gordon and Lutz 2020, p. 58).[8] This perception would shake at the foundations of tort law, as it stipulates the developer's inability to control the risk stemming from AI (Weber 2017, n10).

Scholars have attempted to address the autonomy aspect of AI and have proposed various ideas based on existing liability law, such as analogies to all types of vicarious liability (Borges 2019, p. 151; Zech 2019a, p. 215). As with other new technologies, some argue for a new legal basis to adequately regulate the risks and assign liability to manufacturers and operators (Zech 2019a, p. 214; Gordon and Lutz 2020, p. 61; Säcker et al. 2020, p. 823). Furthermore, some support an entirely new legal concept of e-persons, that makes the AI itself the defendant of a tort claim (Koch 2019, p. 115).

As with most new technologies, it must be carefully analyzed whether they create risks of a new quality or merely change their quantity (Probst 2018, p. 41), as only the first one requires the introduction of new liability rules. Whether the AI qualifies as such has yet to be determined.

---

[7] A lively debate is underway among legal scholars about which existing legal principles are most applicable to liability for harm caused by AI. It is noteworthy that scholars across national boundaries are debating whether different forms of vicarious liability (such as domestic animals) could be drawn upon. See: Eichelberger (2020), n23; Borges (2019), p. 151; dissenting: Grützmacher (2016), p. 698.

[8] Spindler 2019, argues that the deliberate use of products with unforeseeable risks has been happening for a long time and that scholars have not questioned that the person operating such a product is liable for damages.

2.2.2 Respondent to Tort Claim

With AI causing harm to others, manufacturers or software developers will have a more significant role as defendants in tort claims as they are the human minds to which unwanted actions can be accounted to. In the case of NLG algorithms, the output generated is based on the program code developed by the manufacturer of the AI, the person who may be blamed if the output has negative consequences (Conraths 2020, n73).

For AI algorithms, the self-learning phase, when the product is already put into circulation, becomes increasingly important (Grapentin 2019, p. 179). Due to this shift of product development into the post marketing phase, legal scholars argue that not only the manufacturer of the AI bears a liability risk but also the operator (Spindler 2015, p. 767 et seq.; Reusch 2020, n178). For individual software, the operator may also be liable for a manufacturer's actions if the latter can be considered a proxy to the operator and the latter cannot prove that it took all reasonable and necessary measures to instruct and supervise the proxy to prevent the damage from incurring (Kessler 2019, n16). For example, for news outlets that harness NLG, the editor-in-chief or other supervisory staff may be responsible for the proper functioning of the software and be liable in cases the software causes harm to others (Conraths 2020, n81).

2.2.3 Causality as the Limiting Factor of Liability

The fact that self-learning algorithms independently develop after the developer has put it into circulation makes it difficult to delimit each actor's causal contribution to the damage (Ebers 2020, n194). In most cases, self-learning artificial agents (such as NLG) are not standard products but are individually tailored to the operator's needs. Hence, the manufacturer and operator act in concertation when developing and training the AI for the operator to use. Under Swiss law, if two defendants acted together, both are jointly and severally liable for all harms caused (Art. 50 Swiss Code of Obligations ("CO")).

With AI applications and NLG algorithms in particular, the interaction with third parties, such as the operator's customers, becomes increasingly important for algorithms to further develop (Schaub 2019, p. 3). As recent real-life examples have shown, the input generated by customers may have undesired effects on the AI's behavior. In general, a manufacturer must take reasonable measures to prevent an algorithm from using unqualified in-put data (such as hate speech) to adapt its behavior (Eichelberger 2020, n23).[9] But it cannot be expected of a manufacturer to foresee every possible misuse of its product. Under Swiss law, a manufacturer can escape liability if the manufacturer proves that a third actor's unforeseeable actions

---

[9] See above Sect. 1.4.1.

have been significantly more relevant in causing the damage than its own, therefore, interrupting the chain of causality.[10]

Similarly, the Directive sets forth that the manufacturer is not liable if it proves that it is probable that the defect which caused the damage did not exist at the time when the manufacturer put the product into circulation or that this defect came into being afterwards. Some authors argue that the fact that the user's interactions with the AI may be the root cause for harm and therefore, the manufacturer escapes liability.[11]

Apart from these specific challenges, proving causation in any claim for damages is challenging and, in many cases, requires significant resources to establish proof.[12] In many tort cases, not a single cause will be identified to have caused the damage occurred, but various causes will have partially contributed to the claimant's damage (Zech 2019a, p. 207 et seq.). For the claimant, proof of causation will therefore remain a significant hurdle for compensation for damages (Spindler 2019, p. 139 et seq.).

2.3 Directive on Defective Products

2.3.1 General Remarks

Most NLG algorithms will cause economic losses that are not covered by the Directive (Art. 9) or the Swiss product liability law which is congruent with the Directive. Nevertheless, it is conceivable that NLG algorithms will also cause personal injury or property damage. This is the case when an NLG algorithm provides wrong information which causes bodily harm to others (e.g., a doctor receiving a diagnosis from a device that uses flawed NLG to communicate, a communications bot from a private emergency call facility giving false medical advice).

Scholars have extensively discussed whether the Directive applies to software or not (von Westphalen 2019, pp. 890, 892). Despite its ambiguity, most argue that software falls under the Directive.[13] To counter any remaining doubts, the EU Commission has published amendments to the Directive that name software

---

[10] Swiss Supreme Court Ruling 143 II 661, c7.1; specifically for NLG see: Eichelberger (2020), n56.

[11] Gordon and Lutz (2020), p. 58 et seq. and Junod (2019), p. 129 who argues that this defense should not be allowed.

[12] In 2022, the EU Commission published its Proposal for a directive of on adapting non-contractual civil liability rules to artificial intelligence (COM (2022) 496). The proposal introduces disclosure of evidence rules and sets forth presumptions to help the position of the claimant.

[13] *Contra* d II.5 - A T Fonseca, E V Sequeira and L B Xavier - Liability for AI Driven Systems; II.7 - M N Duffourc and D S Giovanniello - The Autonomous AI Physician - Medical Ethics and Legal Liability.

as a product.[14] The following analysis therefore assumes that software qualifies as products under the Directive.

Various aspects of the Directive are discussed in the legal literature, with two standing out: First, it must be determined if the actions of an AI system are to be considered defective within the meaning of the Directive. Second, manufacturers of an AI system may be relieved of liability based on the state-of-the-art defense if they prove that, at the time the product was put into circulation, certain actions of the AI system, particularly those that the system develops through self-learning mechanisms, could not have been foreseen with the technical means and scientific knowledge available at the time.

2.3.2 Defectiveness of an AI System

2.3.2.1 Consumer Expectancy Test

Many scholars struggle with how to determine whether an AI system is defective or not. The Directive considers a product to be defective if it does not provide the safety that a person may expect (Art. 6 (1) Directive). Hence, a product is defective if a reasonable consumer would find it defective considering the presentation of the product, the use to which it could reasonably be expected that the product would be put, and the time when the product was put into circulation. This test based on consumer expectations may not be adequate to determine the defectiveness of cutting-edge technology, as it is hard to establish, lacking a point of reference (Lanz 2020, n745 et seq.). A risk-benefit approach that determines whether a reasonable alternative design would have significantly reduced the occurrence of harm therefore may be more appropriate (Wagner 2017, p. 731 et seq.).[15]

2.3.2.2 AI Challenging the Notion of Defect

Various causes can account for the error of a software. Some of which are easier to prove and do not challenge the definition of defectiveness as set forth in the Directive. Among those figure cases in which the manufacturer caused an error in the algorithm's code, trained the algorithm (before putting it into circulation) with unsuitable data (Eichelberger 2020, n22), or didn't implement adequate measures to prevent that third parties tamper with the code (e.g. hacking) (Eichelberger 2020, n22; Wagner 2017, p. 727 et seq.).[16] But other aspects that complicate the proof of

---

[14] COM (2022) 495.

[15] German Supreme Court Decision VI ZR 107/08 n18.

[16] Spindler (2019), p. 142 argues for a negligence standard to determine if the manufacturer took all necessary measures to prevent hacking vulnerabilities.

defect or challenge the understanding of the concept of defects arise with AI (See also Zech 2019a, p. 204).

From a technical standpoint, it is difficult to analyze the actions of an AI which led to a damage due to the processes taking place in a way not yet perceivable from the outside (black-box problem).[17] Especially in the case of NLG, it may already be difficult for a claimant to prove that the output causing a damage was *artificially* generated, so that the Directive applies.[18]

From a normative point of view, the fact that an algorithm, through self-learning mechanisms, may adopt behavior not intended by its developer, challenges the perception of defectiveness: Scholars discuss various ways to determine the expectations of a reasonable consumer towards AI systems. AI agents outperform the skills of humans for specific tasks. To compare the outcomes of AI algorithms to those of a human does not sufficiently consider the task-limited superior performance of AI compared to humans (Wagner 2017, p. 734 et seq.). Comparing the results of two algorithms to determine the reasonable expectations of customers is not more suitable as its consequence would be that only the algorithm with the best performance is being considered safe, while all others are defective (Wagner 2017, p. 737 et seq.).

Determining the defectiveness of the learning process of an algorithm may further prove to be difficult as it is mainly developing after the product has been put into circulation and happens outside of the control of the manufacturer, in particular with NLG (Binder et al. 2021, n44). The phase where the NLG algorithm interacts with users is particularly challenging the understanding of defectiveness: While the AI is providing its services to the users it simultaneously improves its abilities, therefore raising the question whether the algorithm can be considered defective when it was put into use or not (Binder et al. 2021, n44).

As previous examples have shown, interaction with users can cause an algorithm to develop certain behavior not intended by the manufacturer (Zech 2019b, p. 192). It must be determined whether the manufacturer must provide reasonable measures to prevent the algorithm from evolving in an unintended manner (Eichelberger 2020, n23). Scholars agree that a manufacturer must implement safeguards to prevent an algorithm from incorporating inappropriate or illegal user behavior into its code. This may prove easier in theory than in practice because it is very difficult to predict what user behavior may cause a self-learning algorithm to evolve in a way not intended by the manufacturer. If users interact with the AI in unpredictable ways that cause harm, a product cannot be considered defective (Zech 2019a, p. 213).

---

[17] Zech (2019b), p. 190 et seq., calls it an "intransparency problem"; Casals (2019), p. 204 argues that proof is facilitated since archive logs will likely be available for most AI.

[18] Human generated verbal speech does not fall under the Directive. See also above: Sect. 1.3.

2.3.3 State of the Art Defense

A manufacturer can escape liability if it proves that a defect could not have been detected when the product was put into circulation with the available technical and scientific knowledge. New technologies with unknown negative effects such as AI qualify for the state-of-the-art defense. Scholars therefore propose exempting certain applications from the state-of-the-art defense, as legislatures in various jurisdictions have done for other technological features such as GMOs and xeno-transplantation (See for example: Junod 2019, p. 135; Eichelberger 2020, n20; disagreeing: Zech 2019a, p. 213).

The distinction between conditions that qualify as a defect of a product and those that fall under the state-of-the-art defense when it comes to AI is difficult. Self-learning algorithms may develop undesired behavior that a diligent manufacturer could not foresee. But the fact that a manufacturer cannot foresee the potential harmful behavior of its AI software does not automatically trigger the state-of-the-art defense.[19] Examples from the past show[20] that it is not sufficient that a manufacturer was unable to foresee a *specific* risk of his product. The defense could only be invoked if he was also unable to anticipate a general risk of harm posed by his product (Wagner 2020, § 1 ProdHaftG n61; Zech 2019a, p. 213).

The drafters of the Directive have intended this defense to be applicable to very limited cases. Hence, manufacturers are required to have applied the outmost care and diligence to anticipate negative effects of their product to invoke the defense. Some authors argue that the risk of self-learning AI is already known enough to prevent manufacturers to successfully invoke the defense (von Westphalen 2019, p. 892; Zech 2019a, p. 213).

From a practical perspective the hurdles to invoke the defense are significant as well. A manufacturer that invokes it, would most probably have to reveal business secrets (such as the programming code) to the injured party, therefore making it highly unlikely that the defense will become widely used to defend product liability claims (von Westphalen 2019, p. 892).

Finally, there exists a wide array of possible applications for AI, while not every product category poses the same dangers to consumers. In most cases the imminent dangers of a conventional product represent the greatest risk for harm; enhancements with AI applications of these products do not significantly increase that risk. A general exclusion of AI from the state-of-the-art defense would therefore not consider the individual risk of harm of each product category (Koch 2019, p. 114).

---

[19] Wöbbeking (2020), n10 compares the risk of unforeseeable actions to the dangerous behavior of domesticated animals.

[20] At the beginning of the wide use of asbestos, manufacturers were unable to foresee a general risk for lung cancer. The same was true for HIV being transferred in blood transfusions as there existed no technical means to detect HIV in blood, see: COM (2006) 496 referencing the Hartman v Stichting Sanquin Bloedvoorziening (1999) Amsterdam District Court.

In conclusion, an exemption as proposed by some authors requires more in-depth analysis of the specific risks of AI and their foreseeability. A general call for excluding new technologies from the defense is counter-productive and may hinder manufacturers from investing in products using AI.

2.4 Liability for Negligence

In the absence of a specific provision which allows the defendant to claim compensation for damages, in Swiss law, the general fault based civil liability applies (Art. 41 Swiss Code of Obligations). For NLG, fault-based liability would become relevant if the output generated violates personal rights, infringes intellectual property rights, or triggers the unfair competition act's provisions.

2.4.1 Infringement of Intellectual Property Rights

The output generated by NLG algorithms without human intervention is not protected by copyright due to the lack of creative input (Ragot et al. 2019, p. 574). Reymond 2019; Ebers et al. 2020, p. 9).[21] Hence, output generated by NLG algorithms can be used by other parties without violating copyright laws or paying royalties for its use.

On the other hand, NLG algorithms can rely on sources available on the internet. The risk that they use copyrighted or patented works must be considered by their developers.[22]

2.4.2 Personal Rights Violation

Several examples show that artificial intelligence algorithms for NLG may generate output that violates personal rights of others (defamation, libel etc.). Swiss law provides a victim of personal rights violation with a bouquet of remedies, ranging from injunctions to claim of damages. The autonomy of NLG algorithms does not exclude the operator's civil liability if the output generated by the NLG algorithm violates personal rights of others (Art. 28 (1) Swiss Civil Code).[23] If the claimant proves that the operator of the NLG algorithm was at fault, he may seek monetary

---

[21] Ragot et al. (2019), p. 574; for the German law: Heinze and Wendorf (2020), n63 who argue that for AI which strongly relies on presetting, the programmer of the code may own a copyright to the work produced by the AI.

[22] Heinze and Wendorf (2020), n79; German Supreme Court Ruling I ZR 201/16 (15/2/18); see the recent lawsuit filed against GitHub with the US Federal Court in San Francisco (https://githubcopilotlitigation.com/).

[23] Swiss Supreme Court Ruling 141 III 513, c5.3.

compensation (Art. 28a (3) Swiss Civil Code and Art. 41 Swiss Code of Obligations) (Meili 2018, Art. 28a n16).

News outlets are susceptible to claims if they vastly use NLG algorithms without proper oversight. As news circles are shorter and new players become increasingly important, the risk that output generated by NLG infringes personal rights increases.

News outlets are not the only operators that may see themselves involved in defamation lawsuits when using NLG that does not work properly. In particular, rating portals that use NLG to create comments on businesses (e.g. aggregated from individual feedback form customers) may violate personal rights if the (aggregated) feedback is wrong or violates personal rights of others (Reymond 2019, p. 111, et seq.). If search engines or website owners that provide links to content that violates personal rights of others are also liable, is not yet determined under Swiss law.[24]

2.4.3 Unfair Competition

Output of NLG algorithms may be susceptible to unfair competition claims if in violation of fair competition requirements. Cases in which unfair competition issues involving NLG become relevant are all types of sales activities in which NLG is used to advertise products. This may involve widespread general advertising or automated comparisons with similar products of competitors, or descriptions tailored to individual customers to persuade them to purchase a particular product (Leeb and Schmidt-Kessel 2020, n6). With the advent of rating websites (such as Google Maps, yelp etc.) businesses are taking advantage of good ratings. NLG algorithms may help businesses to easily create fake reviews. The creating or ordering of fake reviews to unjustifiably improve or weaken the rating of a competing business, qualifies as unfair competition, and may give a competitor a claim in damages.

The Swiss Unfair Competition Act sanctions (UWG[25]) various forms of unfair competitive behavior. In particular, the law sanctions actions that mislead customers about the NLG's operator's own products or those of a competitor (Art. 3 (1) UWG).

The law provides for various remedies, such as injunctive relief for the injured persons, for the state or professional associations (Art. 9 and 10 UWG). Injured persons may further claim damages based on the fault-based liability in Art. 41 CO.

2.4.4 Duty of Care

Owners of copyright protected or persons whose personal rights have been violated by NLG output have various legal remedies to act against the violation of their rights. Besides injunctions the injured person may claim damages. The latter is

---

[24] Reymond (2019), p. 114; Swiss Supreme Court Ruling 5A_792/2011, c6.3.

[25] Swiss Federal Law against unfair competition dated December 19, 1986 (UWG).

based on the general fault-based liability provision of the Swiss Code of Obligations (Art. 41 CO). Hence, the claimant must prove, among damages and causality, that the tortfeasor breached the applicable duty of care.

The duty of care is derived from legal or private standards, which for new technologies have yet to be established (Reusch 2020, n301). If specific standards are lacking, general principles for all sorts of dangerous activities apply. Thus, a person creating a risk of harm for others must take all necessary and reasonable precautions to prevent such.[26]

The Swiss Supreme Court has already dealt with cases where links from online blogs led to webpages that violated personal rights. Without in-depth assessment the Court concluded that the operator of the blog could not constantly monitor the content of all webpages linked (Reymond 2019, p. 114 with other references). Similarly, the German Supreme Court concluded that a search engine operator cannot be held accountable for any personal rights violation of autocomplete suggestions generated by its software. The operator of a search engine must only take *reasonable* measures to prevent violation of personal rights. The smooth and efficient performance of the software should not be impeded by rigorous filtering systems.[27] On the other hand, the specific expertise of the manufacturer or the operator which allows them to assess the risk that the AI agent may infringe on third party rights must be considered to set the applicable standard of care (Heinze and Wendorf 2020, n84). Furthermore, the operator is also responsible to regularly control the algorithms datasets which it uses to improve its abilities (Conraths 2020, n69). But despite careful planning, the developer or operator of an NLG-algorithm may not always be able to predict who may be harmed by the algorithm used, hence preventing it to take measures against it (Weber 2017, n22; Binder et al. 2021, n46). Finally, with self-learning NLG-algorithms in particular, developers and operators must prevent that the algorithm takes up harmful behavior from the interaction with its users (Heine and Wendorf 2020, n84).

3 Conclusion

NLG offers a wide array of possible applications. Cutting-edge algorithms allow to create verbal output that cannot be distinguished from human created speech. A cat-and-mouse game is underway between those who program NLG and those who develop algorithms capable of determining whether certain output is human or artificial. As shown, the verification of computer-generated text is crucial from

---

[26] Gordon and Lutz (2020), p. 58 argue that breach of duty is unlikely because harm from AI is not foreseeable to developers. To the contrary: Zech (2019a), p. 198 arguing that the introduction of a high-risk product is negligent if the operator has not taken all reasonable and necessary steps to prevent harm to others.

[27] German Supreme Court Ruling VI ZR 269/12 (14/3/13).

a legal perspective, as the legal bases are only applicable to one or the other respectively.

The self-learning function of artificial intelligence is challenging tort law. Interaction with users can result in unintended behaviors, and in the worst case, even cause harm. This raises delicate questions as to what extent a programmer or an operator of an AI should be liable for its actions as they might not always be able to anticipate future behavior of the AI derived from the interaction with third parties.

Legal research will have to grapple for some time with how to deal with the specific challenges of AI before rashly giving in to the temptation of new legislation.

References*

Binder NB, Burri T, Lohmann MF, Simmler M, Thouvenin F, Vokinger KN (2021) Künstliche Intelligenz: Handlungsbedarf im Schweizer Recht. Jusletter vom 28/06/2021

Black S, Gao L, Wang P, Leahy C, Biderman S (2021) GPT-neo: large scale autoregressive language modeling with mesh-tensorflow. https://github.com/EleutherAI/gpt-neo. Accessed 12 Mar 2022

Borges G (2019) New liability concepts. In: Lohsse S, Schulze R, Staudenmayer D (eds) Liability for artificial intelligence. Nomos, Münster, pp 145–164

Brown T, Mann B, Ryder N, Subbiah M, Kaplan JD, Dhariwal P, Neelakantan A, Shyam P, Sastry G, Askell A, Agarwal S, Herbert-Voss A, Krueger G, Henighan T, Child R, Ramesh A, Ziegler D, Wu J, Winter C, Hesse C, Chen M, Sigler E, Litwin M, Gray S, Chess B, Clark J, Berner C, McCandlish S, Radford A, Sutskever I, Amodei D (2019) Language models are few-shot learners. arXiv:2005.14165

Casals MM (2019) Causation and scope of liability in the internet of things (IoT). In: Lohsse S, Schulze R, Staudenmayer D (eds) Liability for artificial intelligence. Nomos, Münster, pp 201–230

Chen M, Tworek J, Jun H, Yuan Q, Pinto HPO, Kaplan J, Edwards H, Burda Y, Joseph N, Brockman G (2021) Evaluating large language models trained on code. arXiv:2107.03374

Clark E, August T, Serrano S, Haduong N, Gururangan S, Smith NA (2021) All that's 'human' is not gold: evaluating human evaluation of generated text. In: Proceedings of the 59th annual meeting of the association for computational linguistics and the 11th international joint conference on natural language processing (Volume 1: Long Papers). Association for Computational Linguistics, Pennsylvania, pp 7282–7296

Conraths T (2020) Urheberrecht, § 29. In: Ebers M, Heinze C, Krügel T, Steinrötter B (eds) Künstliche Intelligenz und Robotik, Rechtshandbuch. C.H. Beck, München, pp 902–929

Ebers M (2020) Regulierung von KI und Robotik, § 3. In: Ebers M, Heinze C, Krügel T, Steinrötter B (eds) Künstliche Intelligenz und Robotik, Rechtshandbuch. C.H. Beck, München, pp 82–137

Ebers M, Heinze C, Krügel T, Steinrötter B (2020) Künstliche Intelligenz und Robotik, Rechtshandbuch. C.H. Beck, München

Eichelberger J (2020) Zivilrechtliche Haftung für KI und smarte Robotik, § 5. In: Ebers M, Heinze C, Krügel T, Steinrötter B (eds) Künstliche Intelligenz und Robotik, Rechtshandbuch. C.H. Beck, München, pp 172–199

---

* Literature published until the end of March 2022 was considered.

Gordon CA, Lutz T (2020) Haftung für automatisierte Entscheidungen – Herausforderungen in der Praxis. SZW-RSDA 1:53–61

Grapentin J (2019) Konstruktionspflichten des Herstellers und Mitverschulden des Anwenders beim Einsatz von künstlicher Intelligenz. Jurist Rundsch 2019:175–180

Grützmacher M (2016) Die deliktische Haftung für autonome Systeme – Industrie 4.0 als Herausforderung für das bestehende Recht? Comput Recht 32:695–698

Heinze C, Wendorf J (2020) KI und Urheberrecht, § 9. In: Ebers M, Heinze C, Krügel T, Steinrötter B (eds) Künstliche Intelligenz und Robotik, Rechtshandbuch. C.H. Beck, München, pp 304–354

Horner S, Kaulartz M (2016) Haftung 4.0 Verschiebung des Sorgfaltsmaßstabs bei Herstellung und Nutzung autonomer Systeme. Comput Recht 32:7–19

Junod V (2019) Liability for damages caused by ai in medicine. In: Chappuis C, Winiger B (eds) Responsabilité civile et nouvelles technologies. Schulthess, Zurich, pp 119–150

Koch B (2019) Product liability 2.0 - mere update or new version? In: Lohsse S, Schulze R, Staudenmayer D (eds) Liability for artificial intelligence. Münster, Nomos, pp 99–117

Lanz M (2020) Die Haftung beim medizinischen Einsatz synthetischer Nanopartikel. Schulthess, Zurich

Leeb CM, Schmidt-Kessel M (2020) Verbraucherschutzrecht, 10. In: Kaulartz M, Braegelmann T (eds) Rechtshandbuch artificial intelligence und machine learning. C.H. Beck, München, pp 523–538

Madrigal AC (2013) IBM's Watson memorized the entire 'urban dictionary,' then his overlords had to delete it. The Atlantic. https://www.theatlantic.com/technology/archive/2013/01/ibms-watson-memorized-the-entire-urban-dictionary-then-his-overlords-had-to-delete-it/267047/. Accessed 12 Mar 2022

Markov T, Zhang C, Agarwal S, Eloundou T, Lee T, Adler S, Jiang A, Weng L (2022) A Holistic Approach to Undesired Content Detection in the Real World arXiv:2208.03274

Ouyang L, Wu J, Jiang X, Almeida D, Wainwright LC, Mishkin P, Zhang C, Agarwal S, Slama K, Ray A, Schulman J, Hilton J, Kelton F, Miller L, Simens M, Askell A, Welinder P, Christiano P, Leike J, Lowe R (2022) Training language models to follow instructions with human feedback arXiv:2203.02155

Pearce H, Ahmad B, Tan B, Dolan-Gavitt B, Karri R (2021) An empirical cybersecurity evaluation of GitHub copilot's code contributions. arXiv:2108.09293

Peric L, Mijic S, Stammbach D, Ash E, ETH Zurich (2021) Legal language modeling with transformers. In: Proceedings of the 2020 workshop on automated semantic analysis of information in legal text (ASAIL). ETH Zurich, Zürich, pp 1–11

Probst T (2018) Digitalisierung und Vertragsrecht – Probleme des Schutzes der Privatsphäre aus vertragsrechtlicher Sicht. In: Epiney A (ed) Digitalisierung und Schutz der Privatsphäre. Schulthess, Basel, Zurich, Geneva, pp 40–76

Radford A, Wu J, Child R, Luan D, Amodei D, Sutskever I (2019) Language models are unsupervised multitask learners. In: OpenAI

Ragot S, Wigger F, Dal Molin L, Lappert N, Michael AA, Reinle AG, Merz J, Handle M, Gottschalk M, Fischer B, Anthamatten S, Cordoba A (2019) Copyright in artificially generated works. SIC 10:573–579

Reusch P (2020) Produkthaftung, 4.1. In: Kaulartz M, Braegelmann T (eds) Rechtshandbuch artificial intelligence und machine learning. C.H. Beck, München pp 77–153

Reymond MJ (2019) La responsabilité des hébergeurs pour fake news. In: Chappuis C, Winiger B (eds) Responsabilité civile et nouvelles technologies. Schulthess, Zurich, pp 105–118

Säcker FJ, Rixecker R, Oetker H, Limpberg B (2020) Münchener Kommentar zum bürgerlichen Gesetzbuch: BGB, band 7: Schuldrecht besonderer Teil IV. C.H. Beck, München

Schaub R (2019) Verantwortlichkeit für Algorithmen im Internet. InTeR 2019:2–7

Schwartz O (2019) In 2016, microsoft's racist chatbot revealed the dangers of online conversation the bot learned language from people on twitter—but it also learned values. .IEEE Spectrum. https://spectrum.ieee.org/in-2016-microsofts-racist-chatbot-revealed-the-dangers-of-online-conversation. Accessed 12 Mar 2022

So D, Wojciech M, Hanxiao L, Zihang D, Noam S, Quoc VL (2021) Primer: Searching for Efficient Transformers for Language Modeling arXiv:2203.02155

Spindler G (2015) Roboter, Automation, künstliche Intelligenz, selbst-steuernde Kfz – braucht das Recht neue Haftungskategorien? Eine kritische Analyse möglicher Haftungsgrundlagen für autonome Steuerungen. Comput Recht 31:766–776

Spindler G (2019) User liability and strict liability in the internet of things and for robots. In: Lohsse S, Schulze R, Staudenmayer D (eds) Liability for artificial intelligence. Nomos, Münster, pp 125–144

Von Platen P (2020) How to generate text: using different decoding methods for language generation with transformers. https://huggingface.co/blog/how-to-generate. Accessed 12 Mar 2022

von Westphalen FG (2019) Haftungsfragen beim Einsatz künstlicher Intelligenz in Ergänzung der Produkthaftungs-RL 85/374/EWG. Z Wirtsch 40:889–894

Wagner G (2017) Produkthaftung für autonome Systeme. Arch Civ Prax 217:708–764

Weber R (2017) Braucht die digitale Welt ein neues Haftungsrecht? Jusletter 21/09/2017

Wöbbeking MK (2020) Deliktische Haftung de lege feranda, 4.2. In: Kaulartz M, Braegelmann T (eds) Rechtshandbuch artificial intelligence und machine learning. C.H. Beck, München, pp 154–163

Zech H (2019a) Künstliche Intelligenz und Haftungsfragen. ZfPW:198–219

Zech H (2019b) Liability for autonomous systems. In: Lohsse S, Schulze R, Staudenmayer D (eds) Liability for artificial intelligence. Nomos, Münster, pp 187–200

Open Access This chapter is licensed under the terms of the Creative Commons Attribution 4.0 International License (http://creativecommons.org/licenses/by/4.0/), which permits use, sharing, adaptation, distribution and reproduction in any medium or format, as long as you give appropriate credit to the original author(s) and the source, provide a link to the Creative Commons license and indicate if changes were made.

The images or other third party material in this chapter are included in the chapter's Creative Commons license, unless indicated otherwise in a credit line to the material. If material is not included in the chapter's Creative Commons license and your intended use is not permitted by statutory regulation or exceeds the permitted use, you will need to obtain permission directly from the copyright holder.

AI Instruments for Risk of Recidivism Prediction and the Possibility of Criminal Adjudication Deprived of Personal Moral Recognition Standards: *Sparse Notes from a Layman*

Pedro Garcia Marques

Abstract In what follows lies a recount of a concerned criminal lawyer, a layman, as he observes the change foreshadowed by AI in the field of individual risk recidivism assessment for the purposes of criminal penalty imposition on convicted felons. The text will therefore reflect upon the nature of that assessment when promoted by new AI programs based on actuarial-meaning statistically derived-information. It then proceeds to compare that risk recidivism assessment with the one undertaken within the current traditional human paradigm. Identifying the ensuing challenges set by the technological alternatives on the very survival of criminal law's principiological mainstays. A final note will be drawn on what is lacking in the technological proposal, for all its technical upsides and perceived advantages. The approach here changes. From literature one will bring to the fore the very human account that lies at the center of anything resembling judgment. Both the judgment of the individual being assessed and the one of the court doing the assessment. Human as they both are, one heeds the kind of humanity an entire science—that of law—and its specific approach must acknowledge. Exactly that humanity that seems to be lacking in the technological AI proposals.

1 Introduction

Sparse notes, no more, will be found below. Reflections of a criminal lawyer, no doubt sensing the uneasy feeling of redundancy. A layman lead by curiosity and scholarly interest. One that for all his investment is in no doubt that he can only tag along the incessant technological revolution that here as elsewhere creates new

P. G. Marques (✉)
Law School, School of Lisbon, Catholic University of Portugal, Lisbon, Portugal
e-mail: p.marques@ucp.pt

© The Author(s) 2024
H. Sousa Antunes et al. (eds.), *Multidisciplinary Perspectives on Artificial Intelligence and the Law*, Law, Governance and Technology Series 58,
https://doi.org/10.1007/978-3-031-41264-6_18

possibilities and all-encompassing challenges. Challenges of a kind that in order to be properly met will require the one thing that cannot be provided: time for pause.

The following lines are not those of an expert. If expertise is what you, dear reader, are searching, please do look elsewhere. They are, on the other hand, the result of (a small amount of) time to pause and reflect. If, dear reader, you are willing to settle with that then, please, do come in and join me. What I offer are no more than mere reflections. Who knows, maybe your time will in end be well spent.

The immediate object of our attention is be centered around machines and computer programs endowed with artificial intelligence, with particular emphasis on those in which the degree of autonomy is determined by an independent decision-making capacity with the ability to learn, at a level of *deep learning*.[1]

The consideration of predictive tools for the level of risk of recidivism will gain particular importance, namely computer tools for anticipating the risk of recidivism of convicted felons.

Endowed with autonomy in considering the nature and measure of the individual penalties, COMPAS, LSI-R, VRAG and ORAS will be taken as a reference, as they are acronyms of currently available computer programs for "prediction" of *recidivism risk*, each of them dependent on *actuarial-meaning statistically derived-information*.[2]

All of them concern computer programs that, at the present time, calculate, through the attribution of points and ranking definition, the recidivism risk of any certain convicted felon in the commission of crimes in the future.

Offered today as auxiliary tools to judicial decisions, these are not yet programs endowed with autonomous decision-making attributes. Albeit that technological capacity may already be well within reach (Eaglin 2017, pp. 59–122).

At stake in any of these instruments of prediction is, therefore, at the present moment, its claim of capacity to predict future individual behavior. And not just that, but to do it accurately. And always, inevitably, the further claim that *that* judgment of probability, precisely because of its undoubted accuracy, should be able to serve as the criterion and the basis, not only for limiting the individual physical freedom, but also for deciding its severity and nature.

The possibility of criminal adjudication by machines and programs, i.e., by the artifact endowed with artificial intelligence, to any given individual based on any given set of facts of a specific penalty, proposed in a specific form and at a certain level of severity, based on the prediction of his/her future criminal behavior is now

---

[1] On this, please see Eaglin (2017), pp. 59–122.

[2] Acronyms for Correctional Offender Management Profiling for Alternative Sanction (COMPAS), Level of Service Inventory -Revised (LSI-R), Violence Risk Appraisal Guide—Revised (Vrag) and Ohio Risk Assessment System (ORAS), respectively. For the detailed description of these systems, among others, please *see* Eaglin (2017), pp. 59–122. For detailed discussion on risk recidivism assment tools, please see Eaglin (2017), pp. 59–122, Selbst (2017), pp. 96–98, Citron and Pasquale (2014), pp. 1–34, Notes (2017), pp. 1530–1537, Tillers (2002), pp. 1365–1380, and Vervaele (2014), pp. 115–128. In portuguese language, please *see* Rodrigues (2020), pp. 11–58. In Italian language, please *see* Gialuz (2019), pp. 1–23.

upon us. And with it, for the first time, the central role played in the decision-making process of adjudication of criminal guilt and of the assignment of blame by machines. That is, by objects utterly devoid of capability for moral judgment and reflection.

The question will inevitably arise over the possibility and legal justification of individual criminal adjudication devoid of moral recognition.

The absence of which becomes a fact when, in that process of ascription, the machine *calculae* departs from a mere (even if already significant) instrumental role and achieves full autonomy to the point of becoming sole arbiter in the decision-making process of individual adjudication of a criminal penalty. A well-advertised fact in a not too distant future by their respective system's providers (Eaglin 2017, pp. 59–122), as the ongoing development of these instruments and the improvement of their learning capacity will allegedly afford them the kind of algorithms capable of prediction calculations endowed with increasingly smaller margins of error (Eaglin 2017, pp. 59–122).

The moment may come when these instruments for calculating recidivism will become fully capable of replacing the court, the Public Prosecutor's Office and generally the social welfare apparatus in its court's auxiliary capacity, deciding by themselves, by *their own lights*, unaccompanied and unchecked, the nature of the penalty, determining its measure, its duration and the conditions for its completion.

On that day, the decision making process of penalty adjudication will become, not a machine based, not even a machine driven, but rather a machine decision-making process.

The combined consideration of these instruments and their adoption (in their current status and in the near future) will challenge the very existence of an array of traditional principles of criminal responsibility, such as, the personal nature of each individual criminal penalty, the *in dubio pro reo* or the acceptance of free will as the basis for contemporary philosophical justification of criminal individual adjudication.

2 The Predictability of Future Behavior

2.1 The Acceptance of a Judgment of Probability as a Criterion and Basis for Limiting Physical Freedom: Its Implications and Its Consequences

Let us take on each of the challenges one by one. And let us do it *through the lens* of the type of assessment that any of these programs is capable of asserting: one that is undoubtedly based, not on certainty, but only on probability.

Probability of recidivism does not mean certainty of recidivism and risk assessment calculation does not equate to certainty of danger. Therefore, a risk probability judgment, even if rigorously determined in relation to an agent, does not imply that he is actually dangerous.

Thus, the imposition of a penalty based on that calculation may imply:

a. Its enforcement on an agent that, despite the calculated statistical probability, does not actually pose any of the risks calculated as probable;
b. That this negative margin of inefficiency is accepted, meaning that it is admitted as a *cost* of the system that a non-determinable number (since the penalty is applied to all according to a calculated risk calculation validated by the system) of convict felons will be subject to a type of penalty and to a level of severity that, in individual cases, are not justified, due to the non-coincidence between the risk probability calculation and the individual risk that the convicted person *actually* represents.

The penalty or penalties chosen, the measure of their severity, that is, the sentencing to which the accused is subject, subject as it is to a judgment based on a mere probability-based risk calculation, will apply to the individual regardless of the risk that, as mentioned above, *that convicted person actually* represents.

Thus the problem: if the applicable penalty is based on the pursuit of preventive needs, then the risk of justifying a penalty on the basis of a judgment of probability, surely will imply that the deprivation of individual liberty of *that* individual agent may pursue no foreseeable end, legitimate or otherwise. Hence corresponding to a penalty whose imposition no legitimate end can justify.

The abandonment is thus dictated, albeit without conscious realization, of one of the fundamental principles of contemporary criminal adjudication: that of the irrevocable inherently personal nature of each individual penalty.

Probability, risk, that is, doubt—even if supported by calculation—will do. It will suffice for the deprivation of liberty and above all for the imposition of a criminal penalty with the particular kind of acumen that any criminal ascription implies (and is supposed to imply). The convicted felon is blamed, singled out and labeled as dangerous, not because she/he actually is, but because everything *technological*— the machines, a spreadsheet, an algorithm—suggests that she/he is. Even if and even when she/he is not.

The commitment may very well be on the constant refinement of the mechanisms involved in the calculation of probability of risk as the basis for the proposal of— or decision on—the nature and the quantification of severity of the penalty to be applied to each convicted felon.

But that convicted felon will always be regarded by the system as the object of calculation. The object to be targeted with those measures.

Reduced to the condition of object of calculation, the *calculae* on the *rei extensae* involved in the risk assessment necessary for penalty determination will inevitably fail to grasp the absence from the equation of the very person, the individual herself/himself, that forms that *object* of measurement.

Again, one can the swear by the commitment to allow for autonomy in calculation only when the best possible technical conditions are achieved. But with doubt hanging over each risk assessment exercise and with an object rather than a person in view, the perspective adopted is necessarily one of damage limitation in the face of miscalculation by the part of implements that will dispense with any consideration of the person, replacing it by a mere object under measurement.

But, if this is true than one can always argue that probability is precisely at the heart of every assessment the future possibility of recidivist action by convicted felons. Be that the traditional judicial evaluation subject to open court discussion, bearing on the pertinent evidence over the personality of the defendant, as well as her/his family, social and economic standing and conduct before and after the perpetration of the crime; be it the technological cybernetic activation of algorithmically organized parameters that, in all honesty, will bear into the calculus much the same factors and parameters the judge and jury will comb through in order to arrive at a substantiated decision on the sentencing. All of which allowing no more than an estimate. Probability in the end underlies any prognostic judgment on recidivism and sustains any decision on the imposition and enforcement of criminal penalties in each particular case, on each respective convicted felon.

So one can argue that, at least in its technological form these new found methods of criminal recidivism assessment, the issue or rigor or lack of in the calculous of probability becomes expressly thematized. Along with the pledge towards its successful achievement in a measured and verifiable way.

Whereas the traditional judicial form of risk assessment will foster no such ambition as it will not allow for any equivalent capability. For any such close scrutiny will require the kind of mass data treatment and simultaneous differentiated parameter control that will fall quite beneath the scope of capability afforded by the traditional judicial method, human as it is in its nature and form.

Moreover, the treatment of the data and the care taken in its selection in order to properly support the recidivism risk assessment is, one can further argue, no less rigorous, as the traditional *human* method and the new technological *alternative* are set side by side.

This being true it is possible to defend that these new technological possibilities provide the platform for the much-needed criticism and denunciation of traditional systems of risk assessment and ascription—with the inherent blame assignment and individual criminal liability adjudication—for not acknowledging the fact that they, just as much as their cybernetic counterparts, are solely dependent and reliant upon probability. Probability stands for, on one and the other, still as the paradigm.

And by not coming to terms with that realization one can contend that the traditional *human* method will effectively conceal the requirement for the utmost rigor in its calculation of individual risk assessment. Dispensing with the very implements that allow for a thorough and convincing review as well as scrutiny of each individual decision on the penalty. Thus opening the door, without even realizing it, to judicial arbitrariness.

If the criticism is true. And it is. And if we can credit its particular thrust on the very existence today of technological alternatives with their unmatched capabilities; these technological proposals are none the less lacking. And they are lacking where the traditional approaches are not. At the core of their fundamental epistemic option they do fail. And they do fail where the criticized traditional approach, notwithstanding the pertinence of the criticism, does not. The technological models fail in and because of their *epistemic self-sufficiency*.

Self-sufficiency as their epistemic central feature lie, no so much on the fact that the entire calculation model afforded by the ever-adaptable given algorithm is the epilogue of an exercise in probability. Rather, their stapled epistemic self-sufficiency resides on the assumption that probability suffices. No more is needed.

Probability is the exercise on which the cybernetic *calculator* grounds its entire risk assessment. *Doubt* therefore becomes the very thing on which the— every—effort of calculation is based. Henceforth, *doubt*, namely the one that under the persuasion of extraordinary technical capability is reduced to the fringes of statistical irrelevance, will not suffice to merit the reversal, let alone the putting into question of whatever level of risk assessment that has been set regarding *that* individual convicted felon. Despite the doubt, the assertion of statistical probability will suffice.

Ubiquitous as doubt may be on each exercise of calculation, none of that will hinder the imposition of penalty on the convicted felon to the exact measure of the risk that, despite the doubt, he is statistically deemed to represent.

A person is convicted, deprived of he/his freedom—and as mentioned *supra* blamed, singled out and labeled as dangerous—in the face of a justification that may very well be wanting. Since, despite the assessment, in that particular case, that particular person may have, in fact, posed no risk at all.

Of course, one may always turn to the traditional *human way* of going about that risk assessment. Based just as much on probability as its technological counterpart and *craving*, as it were, for the kind of certainty that will provide for its adequate juridical validity. But the *turn* in the analysis will not afford any conceivable answer to the question at hand. *Two wrongs will not make a right*, one would say and the misgivings of the traditional human approach will fall short on providing the kind of improvements the technological one is in dire demand.

But also and above all, albeit underlying a fact, it does not, on the other hand, describe the reality. And the reality of *that* human endeavor is its firm rootedness on the quest for certainty. One that provides an explanation for a penalty grounded on the conviction of that particular judge and through him of the State (and the Commonwealth for those in *those* whereabouts) regarding the specific risk that that individual person *actually* poses. And on the responsibility of the State for those risk assessments provided in error.

In this *human* traditional approach doubt is valued, subject to appreciation, challenged in open court, subject to argument by the parties, contested, reviewed over and over and challenged again. Doubt, even at the fringe of statistical irrelevance, is, even then, doubt. In fact one may say that in this human approach there is no such thing as irrelevant doubt, statistical or otherwise.

The difference in how doubt is handled in each of the *systems* is striking.

And perhaps therein lies the other kind of sufficiency that the technological approach boasts and takes upon itself: the procedural self-sufficiency. Apparently dispensing with discussion of any shape or form, on open court or *in camera* or any other, it calculates and assesses and proposes the end result. It may decide one day by itself on it. In the meanwhile, as it aides the court on delivering its decision, what, may one ask, will the court have in its hands to counteract the *self-sufficiency* of a readymade decision that decides on what is *negligible* doubt, that equates it to sufficient certainty, without ever partaking its rationale, nor allowing for any contradictory discussion on what has already become the machine's sole *actuarial* (using the term on which the machine decides against itself) domain?

Doubt and probability thus fulfill, in the traditional human approach, the part of *costs* of the system They are evidence of its fallibility, the very sources of its injustice. The awareness of what therein lies in palpable threat of unfairness manifest traditional approach's commitment to the principle of presumption of innocence and serves as the backbone of its claim to constitutional validity.

This claim entails the acceptance, as an unquestionable moral assertion of lesser evil, that it is best to acquit a guilty person than to convict the innocent one. And to bring it to bare on the whole exercise of calculation and assessment of recidivism risk of any given convicted person.

Doubt will therefore be brought into consideration in favor of the one being evaluated, accepting risk of error by default. Insufficient weighing of risk assessment serves, in the face of doubt, as the *cost* of a traditional system that, by proclaiming the above mentioned principle of lesser evil, does so as part of its duty towards equal respect and consideration of each individual, recognizing in each and everyone her/his inherent humanity. Such a proclamation is endowed with immediate practical consequences, bringing to the fore the exact principle of which that proclamation and the *traditional* method are their all too human practical translation: that of the *in dubio pro reo*. Precisely the one that the technologic alternative fails to consecrate and to integrate in itself. Precisely the one that avows the constitutional validity of the former to detriment of the latter.

3 The Risk of Technological *Bias*

Furthermore, the linear understanding of prospective behavior at the heart of any technologically autonomous risk assessment will be afford the understanding of human behavior precisely as linear. The feasibility of technological risk assessment becomes possible only insofar as future human behavior is determinable. A determination that, let us remind ourselves, is only made possible through the transformation of doubt over actual risk, when statistically improbable, into *certainty* of risk.

At this level, no room will be afforded to those *rare* moments of regret, desistance, repentance, introspection or epiphany. Back tracking, changing of minds, since statistically highly improbable will equate to nonexistence in the *brave new world* of all too certain technological decisions on risk. Those precise cybernetic decisions that will perform the function, if and only if, the human element is extricated from the equation, utterly ignored from the calculus. Those moments, rare as they are, are as good as nonexistent. Yet human nature and human condition, on those rare moments, stubbornly challenge the machine-like certainty, comforting as it may appear in its alleged accuracy.

If one accepts this *technological* state of affairs, along with the above-mentioned methodological conundrums, a *turn* will be imposed on *the* philosophical premise that sustains and forms the basis for any exercise in criminal adjudication and blame ascription. That of its reliance on the understanding of each person as a free agent. That, in the end, of a commitment to *indeterminism*.

At stake is the abandonment of an indeterministic conception of human action. And at the statistical fringes, where improbability lurks in, the irrelevance of free will is for all intents and purposes accepted. Replaced with a kind of self-appointed statistically plausible determinism, albeit unchallenged and uncritically accepted.

Then there is the risk of perpetuation and promotion of the existing model of social reality in its prejudices and asymmetries. And, with it, the conjunctural set of problems that persist in challenging the credibility of all technological attempts at risk assessment.

Since any exercise will need to take into account data on social environment and provenance of the convicted felon, such an exercise may imply the risk of considering the defendant in terms of a model, and, as such, as a member of a paradigmatic community for statistical purposes. And the risk of bias creeps in.[3]

In addition to the inherent risk of miscalculation, such a model may tend to perpetuate a dominant majority perception of a social reality with the kind asymmetries that feed its underlying prejudices. When lacking critical instruments able to denounce them, the algorithmic model of risk assessment posed by the defendant, instead of being able to ascertain the actual danger that she/he represents as an individual, may undergo the risk of overburdening the exact same persons who, as members of disfavored communities, already suffer the effects of those exact same asymmetries and prejudices.

Even worse. By providing an arsenal of data and methods of calculation that seem to order a necessary conclusion in a logical, plausible and linear way, it will tend to validate and, with that, to legitimize ways of collecting and processing data and consequent proposals for penalties that, underneath that arsenal, replicate—in a fashion that lends itself to be hidden and camouflaged—the precise *bias* that will label those individuals whose risk is being assessed with the same criminogenic factors that affect in a marked way the members of the communities they come from. And for no other reason than the fact that they come from those communities.

Hence, those who, in fact, most often find themselves grappling with justice may, in the logical plausible linear assessment of the machine, find themselves labeled as the personification of danger because mechanical logic demands it. Despite of who she/he individually are and in spite of what a human consideration, under the light

---

[3] The risk of bias in risk predictive assessment tools has a long-standing issue that has merited significant discussion. For detailed analysis on the issue, please *see*, among others, Angwin et al. (2016), Chander (2017), pp. 1023–1045, Flores et al. (2016), pp. 38–45, Spielkamp (2017), pp. 96–98, Temming (2017), pp. 26–29, and Zarsky (2014), pp. 1375–1412.

AI Instruments for Risk of Recidivism Prediction and the Possibility... 347

(a no less) human reasoning, might be able to do in challenging that (machine-like calculated) logic.

4 Conclusion

What is then left out?

Most definitely the consideration of the improbable, although always possible, *change of mind*.

But how so?

We will try to provide an answer in much in the same way as in previous occasions (Marques 2016, pp. 505, 506; Marques 2021, p. 103). The path will be unorthodox. We start with literature.

The kind of *change* that the brazilian writer JORGE AMADO, in his novel *Terras do Sem Fim,* lets us in *in the mind* of Damião, a hired killer (*jagunço*), as he prepares to ambush and kill yet another victim. A change of mind, an epiphany even, that leads him, for the first time, to miss the shot (Amado 1942, pp. 75, 76).

Damião is tormented by the questions he had heard from Sinhô Badaró addressed to another killer (*jagunço*), "Do you think it's good to kill people? Don't you feel anything? Nothing inside?". And now in the ambush, as he was preparing to kill Firmo, an idea emerges. At first, as a mere conjecture—"And suddenly, the terrifying idea cut his head: what if Dona Teresa were pregnant, a child in her belly? (...) He would have been born without a father, the father would have been under the aim" of Damião.

≪And it shudders all over, its huge giant body.

You can see Dona Teresa's face (...) before there was the moonlight, white as milk, spilling over the ground. (...) She is asking him not to kill Firmo, for God's sake he does not kill... On the moonlit floor the black man sees Teresa's face perfectly≫.

What if I didn't kill Firmo? (Amado 1942, pp. 75, 76) [4]

Unpredictable as it may be, therein lies humanity.

And Arendt's words spring to mind: "the fact that man is capable of action means that the unexpected can be expected from him, that he is able to perform what is infinitely improbable" (Arendt 1998, p. 178). And so because man "is unique", since, with each birth, "something uniquely new comes into the world" (Arendt 1998, p. 178).

Every beginning, thus Arendt, every origin bares with it the element of unpredictability. Each moment of *difference* is, therefore, an unexpected and unpredictable moment of novelty, of surprise, confirming both that the "new" "always appears in the guise of a miracle" (Arendt 1998, p. 178).

---

[4] Translation by the author from the original in portuguese.

Here, thought is born as the political condition for action, as the very possibility of language and discourse and, therefore, of a life founded on, because marked by, humanity. And, with that, the word, the thought that reflects it and the judgment that, then, through one and the other becomes possible.

Now, what is at stake here is precisely, with ARENDT, the return of thought to action (Arendt 2005, pp. 188, 189). Of action considered as freedom. Since, when action, that which begets human creativity, is left aside, thought itself, as the "activity of sharing in the difference in which equals are recognized" (Arendt 2005, pp. 188, 189), will be forgotten. And, on that moment, judgment, that on which the very possibility of freedom relies, will disappear from human existence.

Hence, what is definitively left out?

Again, literature.

We turn to PRIMO LEVI in his *Se Questo è un Uomo* (Levi 1989). While captive in Auschwitz he recounts that one day while being escorted by a guard, named Alex, an oiled steel pipe crossed their way. As the guard passed, he leaned on the pipe and accidentally got oil on his hands. "Without hate and without derision", Levi tells us, "Alex wipes his hand on my shoulder, the palm and the back of your hand, to clean it". And concludes Levi, "(. . .) he would be very surprised, the poor and brutish Alex, if someone told him that today I judge him for this act, he and Pannwitz, and the countless people who were like him, big and small, in Auschwitz and elsewhere. " (Levi 1989, pp. 96, 97). [5]

This—human judgment as the essence of *human* thought and the mark of human dignity—becomes forgotten and, as forgetfulness sets in, P. F. TRAWSON's lament becomes our own. A lament that he expresses as follows: "it is a pity that the talk about moral sentiments has fallen out of favor" (Strawson 2008, p. 26). Fallen into disfavor is not only the doubt regarding the restriction of moral concepts into a single, rational origin, but also the perception towards the insufficiency of mere reason as the prime motivational impetus for action.

A lament that serves as the point of departure for the unravelling of his proposed *reactive attitudes of participation*. As those that in the face of each behavior of each one of us trigger common reactive attitudes (ordinary reactive attitudes). The kind of attitudes—participatory in nature—that the Author calls "essentially natural and human reactions", without which "it is doubtful that we have something that we can consider intelligible as a system of human relations, as human society" (Strawson 2008, p. 26).

At stake is the need to take into consideration the network of attitudes and feelings that form an essential part of moral life as we know it, as a perceptible source of the meaning enclosed in the "language of morals", and, as such, of everything we intend to say when we speak of worthiness, responsibility, guilt, condemnation, and justice. Each of them resonates in those attitudes and feelings that constitute the cement of the specific kind of relationship that forms a community. Of the kind of relationship that equate to *life* itself, again with ARENDT, in its ontologically

---

[5] Translation by the author from the original in portuguese.

AI Instruments for Risk of Recidivism Prediction and the Possibility... 349

characterizing *togetherness*. A relationship that, in the end lies, at the very he very foundation of moral responsibility.
That, in the end, is missing. Left out. [6]

References

Amado J (1942) As terras do sem fim (from the 1942 original). Livros do Brasil, Lisbon
Angwin J, Larson J, Mattu J, Kirchner L (2016) Machine bias. There is software that is used across the country to predict future criminals. And it is biased against blacks. https://www.propublica.org/article/machine-bias-risk-assessmentsin-criminal-sentencing. Accessed 8 Sept 2021
Arendt H (1998) The human condition. Introduction by Margaret Canovan. University of Chicago Press, Chicago
Arendt H (2005) Thinking and moral considerations. In: Kohn J (ed) Responsibility and judgment, edition and introduction. Schocken Books, New York, pp 159–189
Chander A (2017) The racist algorithm? Mich Law Rev 115:1023–1045
Citron DK, Pasquale F (2014) The scored society: due process for automated predictions. Wash Law Rev 89:1–34
Eaglin JM (2017) Constructing recidivism risk. Emory Law J 67:59–122
Flores AW, Bechtel K, Lowenkamp CT (2016) False positives, false negatives, and false analyses: a rejoinder to machine bias: there's software used across the country to predict future criminals. and it's biased against blacks. Fed Probation 80:38–45
Gialuz M (2019) Quando la giustizia penale incontra l'intelligenza artificiale: luci e ombre dei risk assessment tools tra Stati Uniti ed Europa. Diritto Penale Contemporaneo 2019:1–23
Levi P (1989) Se questo è un uomo. Einaudi, Turim
Marques P (2016) O juízo crítico da culpa, PhD. Dissertation, Universidade Católica Portuguesa
Marques P (2021) Inteligência artificial e humanismo – prolegomena. In: Sequeira EVD (ed) Católica talks – direito e tecnologia. Universidade Católica Editora, Lisbon, pp 95–114
Rodrigues AM (2020) Inteligência artifical – a justiça preditiva entre a Americanização e a Europeização. In: Rodrigues AM (ed) A inteligência artificial no direito penal. Almedina, Coimbra, pp 11–58
Selbst AD (2017) Disparate impact in big data policing. Georgia Law Rev 52:108–195
Spielkamp MA (2017) Inspecting algorithms for bias. MIT Technol Rev 120:96–98
State v. Loomis (2017) Criminal law-sentencing guidelines – Winsconsin Supreme Court requires warning before use of algorithmic risk assessments in sentencing. 88 1 NW.2d 749. Harv Law Rev 130:1530–1537
Strawson PF (2008) Freedom and resentment. In: Strawson PF (ed) freedom and resentment and other essays. Routledge, London, pp 1–28

---

[6] *See* also, on AI and judicial reasoning, in this book L M Pereira, F C Santos and A B Lopes - AI Modelling of Counterfactual Thinking for Judicial Reasoning and Governance of Law; W Gravett - Judicial Decision-making in the Age of Artificial Intelligence; D Durães, P M Freitas and P Novais - The Relevance of Deepfakes in the Administration of Criminal Justice; and J C Abreu - The "Artificial Intelligence Act" Proposal on European e-Justice Domains Through the Lens of User-focused, User-friendly and Effective Judicial Protection Principles. *See* also, on biases, in this book W Gravett - Judicial Decision-making in the Age of Artificial Intelligence; and D Durães, P M Freitas and P Novais - The Relevance of Deepfakes in the Administration of Criminal Justice. *See* finally, on the COMPAS system, in this book W Gravett - Judicial Decision-making in the Age of Artificial Intelligence.

Temming M (2017) Fair-minded machines–a new drive to revamp artificial intelligence may cut down on bias, Science News, September 16, 2017, pp 26–29

Tillers P (2002) Introduction: a personal perspective on 'artificial intelligence and judicial proof'. Cardozo Law Rev 22:1365–1380

Vervaele JAE (2014) Surveillance and criminal investigation: Blurring of threshholds and boundaries in the criminal justice system? In: Gutwirth S, Leenes R, Hert PD (eds) Reloading data protection Multidisciplinary insights and contemporary challenges. Springer, Heidelberg, pp 115–128

Zarsky TZ (2014) Understanding discrimination in the scored society. Wash Law Rev 89:1375–1412

Open Access This chapter is licensed under the terms of the Creative Commons Attribution 4.0 International License (http://creativecommons.org/licenses/by/4.0/), which permits use, sharing, adaptation, distribution and reproduction in any medium or format, as long as you give appropriate credit to the original author(s) and the source, provide a link to the Creative Commons license and indicate if changes were made.

The images or other third party material in this chapter are included in the chapter's Creative Commons license, unless indicated otherwise in a credit line to the material. If material is not included in the chapter's Creative Commons license and your intended use is not permitted by statutory regulation or exceeds the permitted use, you will need to obtain permission directly from the copyright holder.

The Relevance of Deepfakes in the Administration of Criminal Justice

Dalila Durães, Pedro Miguel Freitas, and Paulo Novais

Abstract Nowadays, it is challenging to distinguish between genuine content created by humans or deepfake created by deepfakes algorithms. Therefore, it is in the interests of society and nations to have systems that can notice and evaluate the content without human intervention. This paper presents the challenges of artificial intelligence, specifically machine learning and deep learning, in the fight against deepfake. In addition, it presents the relevance that deepfakes may have in the administration of criminal justice.

1 Introduction

Deepfakes appeared in late 2017 when an anonymous user on the social network Reddit published videos where pornographic actresses' faces were replaced with celebrities' faces (Europol 2020). The potential of this technique quickly disseminated on the Internet, making it accessible for everyone (Anderson 2018).

Deepfake is one of the most visible malicious uses of artificial intelligence (AI). The name derives from the combination of "deep learning" and "fake media". To create Deepfakes, AI techniques, particularly machine learning (ML), are used to create or manipulate content, which may be audio or video. Content that might be extremely hard for humans or technological solutions alike to distinguish from authentic one (Chawla 2019).

D. Durães (✉) · P. Novais
Algoritmi Centre, School of Engineering, University of Minho, Braga, Portugal
e-mail: dalila.duraes@algoritmi.uminho.pt; pjon@di.uminho.pt

P. M. Freitas
Universidade Católica Portuguesa, Faculty of Law, Porto, Portugal
e-mail: pfreitas@ucp.pt

© The Author(s) 2024
H. Sousa Antunes et al. (eds.), *Multidisciplinary Perspectives on Artificial Intelligence and the Law*, Law, Governance and Technology Series 58,
https://doi.org/10.1007/978-3-031-41264-6_19

2 Deepfake: Definition and Categories

A deepfake is content (video, audio or otherwise) that was either fully or partially fabricated or manipulated from existing content (video, audio or otherwise). However, the most significant cases of deepfake appear in the video format, whose authentication difficulty allows any information since any audiovisual content can be manufactured. Deepfakes emerged from AI applications that combine, mixture, replace or overlay images and videos, creating fake videos so that they look authentic (Maras and Alexandrou 2019; Europol 2020). Deepfake is a clear example of the intricacy and complexity technology used. However, the available applications allow anyone with low computing power and little knowledge to create fake videos (Figueira and Oliveira 2017).

Deepfakes can be legally created to engage or spark critical observations. Nevertheless, deepfakes are also used to commit fraud, deceive, or intimidate people by releasing images or videos without their consent.

There are different categories of deepfakes: face replacement or body-swapping, face reconstruction, face generation, speech synthesis, and shallowfakes. Face replacement or body-swapping substitutes parts of a person for another. Face reconstruction manipulates a part of a person to assemble it seem as if they are expressing something they are not. Face generation lets create synthetic images of convincing but entirely fictional people. Speech synthesis employs training algorithms to generate a deepfake voice or an artificial audio file. Shallowfakes allow the creation of audiovisual frauds by using elementary or basic editing methods (Europol 2020). Table 1 present examples of different deepfakes.

3 AI and Deepfake

As we mentioned earlier, deepfakes are created using AI. But how?

One of the great advantages of AI is that it absorbs a large amount of knowledge from the environment in which it is inserted, learning, and improving its responses day by day.

To better understand the concept of AI, it can be divided into two categories: Artificial Strong Intelligence and Artificial Narrow Intelligence.

Artificial Strong Intelligence includes systems that exhibit human intelligence or even superior in all fields. Furthermore, this type of intelligence can share experience from different domains. Several tests are used to indicate if a given system shows Strong AI, but this has not yet happened, what has led experts to suggest that this is merely an aspiration (Muehlhauser 2013).

Narrow AI or Weak AI includes all systems where there are well-defined right or wrong answers, where there are discernible underlying patterns and structures, and where research and computing speed offer advantages over humans. The existing AI systems are not yet designed to apply abstract reasoning, understand concepts,

The Relevance of Deepfakes in the Administration of Criminal Justice

Table 1 Types and examples of deepfakes (Adapted from (Kietzmann et al. 2020))

Type	Format	Description	Business application
Face replacement or body-swapping	Photo deepfakes	Face and Body-swapping—replacing face or body for someone else.	Cosmetics, eyeglasses, hairstyles or clothes virtuality.
	Video deepfakes	Face-swapping—replacing face to someone else.	Movies, where actor's face are put on body of double.
Face reconstruction (body)	Audio and video deepfakes	Full body puppetry—transporting the body movement from one person to another.	Enterprise directors and athletes can camouflage physical aliments during a video exhibition.
		Lip-synchronism—adjusting the mouse activities and phrases articulated in a talking video.	Institutional videos can be converted into other speeches employing the same spokesperson in the original recording.
Shallowfakes	Video deepfakes	Face-morphing—a face changes into another face through a seamless transition.	Video game participants can introduce their looks to their favorite personalities.
Speech synthesis	Audio deepfakes	Voice-swapping—changing a spokesperson or imitating somebody else.	The spokesperson of narration can be like a young, old, male, or female.
		Text-to-Speech - modifying the audio by writing new content.	Replacing words without the necessity of making a new audio file.
Face generation	Photo deepfakes	Face-generating—generate realistic looking faces.	This can serve as a solution to dispose of photographs without violating the privacy or image rights of any person, since everything has been artificially generated, so no one has been photographed.

or general broad-spectrum problem-solving skills (Krupansky 2017). So, systems in this category have narrow and limited application to solve specific problems.

There are three main different approaches to developing AI systems: Rule-based methods, ML and DL. Of these three approaches, the most used are the last two, which will be addressed in the next section.

4 Machine Learning

ML is a kind of AI that permits software applications to become more trustworthy by improving their capacity to anticipate accurate outcomes (Burns 2021). In ML, the algorithm is presented with a dataset with several data and a tag for the data. In this way, the system will find the common patterns in that dataset. Figure 1 presents the position of ML on AI. The more examples the dataset contains, the more effectively the algorithm responds. In addition, the system learns from its mistakes.

Based on theoretical concepts, ML can be described by a model, which has data as input and prediction as output. Yet, a model is no more than a mathematical formula. A mathematical formula is the result of a ML algorithm implementation. The mathematical formula will measure parameters that can be used for prediction. Models can be trained and learned from training data (Krzyk 2018). Figure 2 presents a diagram visualization of a ML Model.

This is very recurrent in society, allowing companies to investigate trends in the behavior of individuals and patterns in order not only to enhance their product but also to provide a better quality of service to users. Several companies in the world

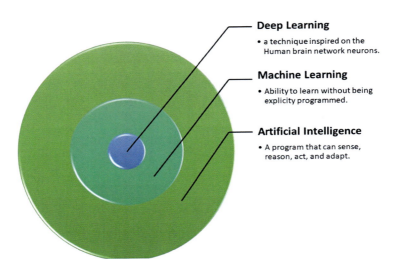

Fig. 1 Position of ML on AI context (adapted from (Cauduro 2018))

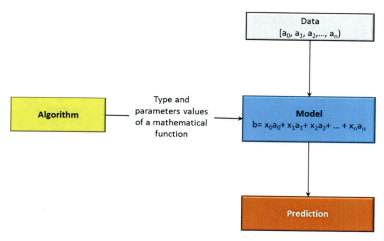

Fig. 2 Diagram visualization of a ML Model

use ML, and it acts as an important differentiating factor between companies. Today, ML is used in many areas and applications. One of the most prominent applications of ML is in recommendation systems, where it allows advising clients on specific topics. Examples are news, games and movies (Burns 2021).

As mentioned, there are several areas in which ML can be applied, and there are several categories in which the different algorithms are grouped based on their objective. As presented in Fig. 3, the three main categories are supervised, unsupervised, semi-supervised learning, and reinforcement learning (Dey 2016; Krzyk 2018). This figure also presents some applications of each type of ML categories.

4.1 Supervised Learning

Supervised learning can be described as a process that uses algorithms capable of producing patterns and hypotheses from given instances, applying them to predict unknown instances. This type of learning tries to predict dependent variables from a list of independent variables. All ML algorithms follow a similar process: dataset, features, algorithms, evaluation, and training.

To use ML models, it is always needed an input dataset divided into training and testing, which must contain millions of data. The larger the dataset, the better is the algorithm's response. The training includes the variable that will be predicted/classified, and it is with this data the algorithm will learn so that it can apply this knowledge in the test dataset and predict/classify that same variable (Dey 2016).

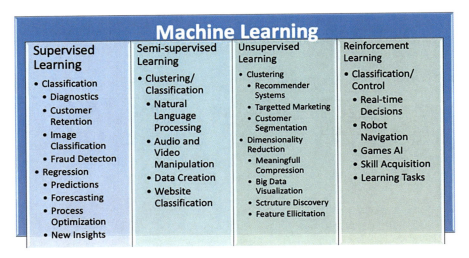

Fig. 3 Machine Learning Methods (Adapted from (Krzyk 2018; Raigon 2020))

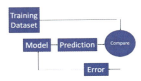

Fig. 4 Supervised learning model

Features are data that will be transformed into a numerical representation so that the algorithm can understand it. The algorithm does not use all the data, because it will learn which one is relevant.

On supervised learning the dataset has several data samples, which consist of pairs of input-output examples that trained the model. When the model is prepared, it will predict the expected label outcome. Then prediction is compared with the label. If there is not a match, we have what is called an error. The error is merely feedback in the model, in which it will be updated. Figure 4 represents the supervised learning model.

Different ML algorithms can be used, namely regression or classification algorithms (Table 2).

Regression algorithms aim to know how one variable evolves concerning others. This type of algorithm predicts a continuous value. Examples of regression algorithm applications are predictions, forecasting, or estimating.

Classification algorithms seek to explain a categorical variable with two or more categories, dividing the data into classes, using common features. Some examples of application classification algorithms are fraud detection, image classification, customer retention and person diagnostics.

The Relevance of Deepfakes in the Administration of Criminal Justice 357

Table 2 Types of algorithms applications

Type	Algorithm name	Description
Regression	Linear Regression	Compares each feature to the outcome to assist future forecasts.
Regression Classification	Decision Tree	Data resource values are separated into branches at decision nodes by a classification or regression model.
	Naive Bayes	It is a group of basic probabilistic classifiers dependent on the application of Bayes theory with strong self-governance of the Naive Bayes features.
	Random Forest	Applies simples' decision based on approach of the most voted. In regression, the prediction is calculated by the average.
	AdaBoost	Employs numerous models to decide but scale is the important measure to obtain precision in forecasting result.
	Gradient Boosting Trees	It focuses on the mistake made by the previous trees and tries to correct it.
	Support Vector Machine	Used for classification task and locates a hyperplane that separates the classes.
Classification	Logic Regression	Quantifies the connection between the absolute variable and at least one free factor by evaluating probabilities using a logistical capability.

4.2 Unsupervised Learning

Unsupervised learning diverges from supervised learning in that none of the data has defined the label. The way the algorithm will create knowledge from the data is done differently, analyzing the affinity between the analyzed objects to detect similarities/differences between their characteristics; from there, labels will be created and assigned (Kotsiantis et al. 2007). This learning results in finding patterns in data that would otherwise be considered noise, not containing helpful information (Ghahramani 2003; Dey 2016).

An advantage of unsupervised learning is that the data does not need to be categorized, making huge amounts of unstructured data accessible for analysis. Algorithms try to draw assumptions from non-labelled data, finding new data patterns. Figure 5 presents the unsupervised learning model.

An important application of unsupervised learning is anomaly detection. In these methods, networks are trained to discover the composition and overall look of a data stream, settling whether one data point looks different from the rest. The application of these methods allows, for example, the detection of cyber fraud attempts in complex transactions.

Unsupervised learning model can be dividing into clustering and reducing data dimensionality.

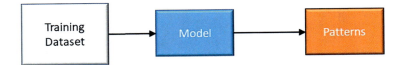

Fig. 5 Unsupervised learning model

Table 3 Algorithms that can be applied for clustering and dimensionality reduction

Type	Algorithm name	Description
Clustering	Gaussian Mixture Model	More flexible in the range and structure of clusters k-means.
	K-Means Clustering	Places the data into a few clusters (k), each having data with equal attributes.
	Hierarchical Clustering	It is a calculation that creates a hierarchy of groups. It begins distributing by groups based on information of each one. Here, two close groups will be in a similar group. This calculation closes when only one group remains.
	Recommender System	Assist to specify the important data for constructing a suggestion.
	K-Nearest Neighbors	It is a direct measure that keeps all available topics and describes new examples dependent on a similitude estimation.
Dimension Reduction	PCA/T-SNE	The processes decrease the number of features to 3 or 4 trajectories with the tallest variances.

Clustering is a technique that splits and groups similar data samples. The groups are called clusters. Examples of clustering are recommended systems, targeted marketing and customer segmentation.

Dimensionality reduction is a method of condensing features into so-called core values that concisely convey similar information. By choosing just a few components, the number of resources is reduced, and a small part of the data is lost.

Table 3 summarizes the algorithms that can be applied for clustering and dimensionality reduction.

4.3 Semi-Supervised Learning

Semi-supervised learning has much use in the digital world, detecting fraud, whether in the news, emails, etc. Algorithms trained in small datasets can learn to label data and be used in translations, allowing algorithms to translate languages using incomplete dictionaries.

The ML model is trained and tested with data present in unequal proportions. The proportion of training data is lower than the ratio of test data. Semi-supervised ML algorithms are located among unsupervised and supervised learning, and unlabeled data can significantly improve learning accuracy (Malapragada et al. 2017).

4.4 Reinforcement Learning

Finally, reinforcement learning consists of teaching a model of ML, defining specific rules that it will have to follow, presenting rewards when the algorithm completes a task well or giving punishments when it behaves wrongly (Burns 2021).

Reinforcement learning differs significantly from the learning as mentioned earlier. In this type of learning, the exchange between the agent and the surroundings in which it works is crucial. In this way, the agent interacts with the environment producing actions that will change the environment causing the machine to receive rewards or penalties (Ghahramani 2003).

It should be noted that the agent is not aware beforehand of the actions needed to take. The decisions it makes will influence future actions (Dey 2016). Figure 6 details the reinforcement learning model.

The machine's goal is to learn to behave in a way that enables rewards (or lessens penalties) over its lifetime. This learning only depends on two criteria: delayed result and trial and error research (Dey 2016; Sutton and Barto 2018). The agent intends to build an optimal policy; however, it solves the problem of studying new states while increasing its overall benefits. This trade-off dilemma is called Exploration versus Exploration. The agent must analyze the two sides of the dilemma and choose the strategy based on the overall results. Hence, to make the best general decision in the future, the agent must preserve information adequately. Examples of reinforcement learning are decisions made in real-time, computer vision, and autonomous driving.

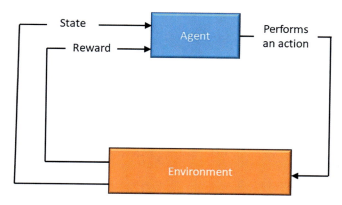

Fig. 6 Reinforcement learning model

There are two different model approach for reinforcement learning, the Markov Decision Processes (MDPs) and the Q-learning model.

An MDP consists of a cluster of finite domain states S, a group of possible actions A(s) in each condition, a tangible reward function R(s) and a transition model P(s', s | a) (Shuweta 2018).

Q-learning is a free of charge method that is applied to make a self-playing PacMan agent. It rotates around revising Q values which represents the value of a behaving a in a state s (Shuweta 2018).

5 Deep Learning

Deep Learning (DL) is a subclass of ML techniques where the systems are comprised of multiple layers to learn representations of data with various levels of conception. Most DL methods use neural network architectures, hence the name deep neural networks. Figure 7 depicts the amount of hidden layers in the neural network. Standard neural networks include 2–3 hidden layers, but deep networks contain around 150 layers (Santos et al. 2021).

The learning of classification tasks from images, text, or sound are performed by DL models (Santos et al. 2021). This learning, on the part of the model, to be done successfully, requires large amounts of labelled data and large computational power, often requiring high-performance GPUs to execute model training (Santos et al. 2021).

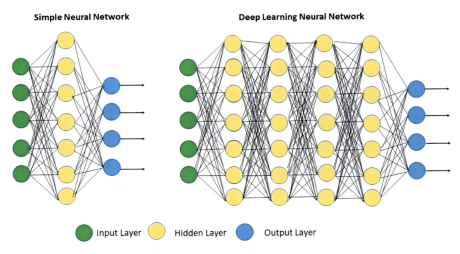

Fig. 7 Comparison between simple neural network and deep learning network (Adapted from (Ceron 2020))

Several areas use DL, but it has had particular success in autonomous driving. The DL is used to automatically detect objects and people in these systems. Another area where the DL is widely used is the Aerospace and Defense areas, *v.g.* satellites detect objects or identify safe zones for troops. These techniques are also relevant in automatic speech translation and home assistants (Mathworks 2022).

Most DL models use the so-called neural networks, inspired by the connections of neurons in the human brain, and can extract/learn features automatically. For example, you can pass images to a network, and this network can extract features from the image without any human intervention. As these networks are trained, they automatically learn to classify/solve problems. One major advantage they have is the ability to improve their classification capacity as the data increases and time goes by (Mathworks 2022).

Many DL applications use the technique of Transfer Learning (TF). TF is a procedure that requires adjustment a pre-trained prototype. The network training starts with an existing dataset. Then, this network is provided with the new data or dataset that contains unknown classes. From there, the network adjusts, transposing the previous knowledge to this new situation. Computation time is shorter in comparison to an untrained network (Mathworks 2022).

As shown in Fig. 8, DL models can be classified as supervised learning or unsupervised learning. In supervised learning DL convolutional neural networks and recurrent neural networks (RNNs) are employed. The RNNs may also be divided into the gated recurrent unit (GRU) and short-term memory. In unsupervised learning DL we have self-organizing map (SOM) and autoencoders (AE) networks. The AE is a restricted Boltzmann machine (RBM) type.

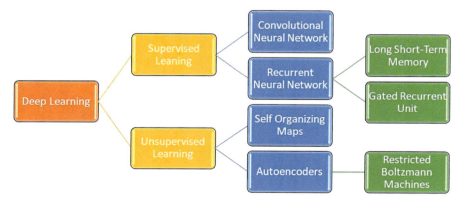

Fig. 8 Deep Learning Models (Adapted from (Madhavan and Jones 2021))

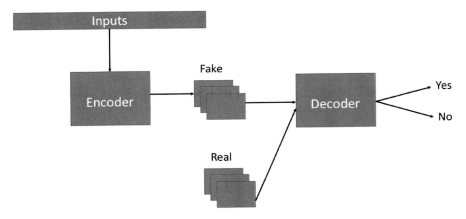

Fig. 9 GAN Architecture

6 Deepfake Generation

Another type of deep neural network are called Generative Adversarial Networks (GANs). These can be used to create deepfakes. They learn from a training dataset and generate a data sample with similar features. GANs have an architecture that is no more than two components of neural networks: an encoder and a decoder. The model uses the encoder to train an extensive dataset in order to generate fake data. The decoder is basically a binary classifier that receives inputs (real or face content) and uses a SoftMax function to identify the authentic data (Fig. 9).

Examples of deepfakes applications are VGGFace (Malli 2017), FakeApp (Malavida 2022), Faceswap (Deepfakes 2022), and CycleGAN (Zhu et al. 2017).

7 Deepfake Detection

Deepfake detection is technology possible, namely in two domains: images and videos.

7.1 Image Detection Models

The literature presents several processes to distinguish the images generated by GAN using deep networks. One of the methods is based on preprocessing procedures to analyze the statistical characteristics of the image and improve the recognition of false appearance pictures made by humans (Li et al. 2018a). Another method is centered on a deep convolutional neural network that identifies

The Relevance of Deepfakes in the Administration of Criminal Justice

false images generated by GANs (Do et al. 2018). Xuan et al. (2019) revealed a convolutional neural network (CNN) based on Gaussian Blur and Gaussian Noise to identify fake human pictures. A hybrid methodology was established to identify fake pictures effectively (Liu et al. 2019; Faceswap 2022).

7.2 Video Detection Models

The video detection models use one of two approaches: biologic or spatial temporal features analysis.

The first approach can be applied to three different methods: catch face fakes, timer for deepfakes, and the relationship between audio and video. The first method is based on the physical aspect of eye blinking. So, this method monitors the eye blinking to catch the fake face. A CNN with an RNN and a binary classifier are used to supervise eye blinking (Li et al. 2018b). The second method is based on the physical aspect of the timer (pulsation) to detect fake videos. This method uses a GAN to compare fake to authentic videos (Ciftci et al. 2020). Finally. The third method is based on the relationship between audio and video. This method uses DL models with a triple loss function which detects fake from authentic videos (Mittal et al. 2020).

The second approach is to use a convolutional neural network (CNN) to extract a feature from a frame. Later, these features can be passed through a LSTM that analyzes the temporal sequence in frames. Finally, the video is classified as real or fake with a Softmax function (de Lima et al. 2020). Also, another approach is Recycle-GAN, which employs dependent generative adversarial networks to combine spatial and temporal data. The evaluation results show that spatial and temporal information can produce a good result in detecting deepfakes (Bansal et al. 2018).

8 Deepfakes and the Administration of Criminal Justice

Deepfakes can have profound negatives impacts by targeting the reputation of individuals, creating false events or content that can result in a wrongful conviction or impact lawsuits, decreasing trust in institutions; and threaten national security or harm international relations if misused by governments (Europol 2020; Meskys et al. 2020; Flynn et al. 2021).

From a criminal justice administration perspective, deepfakes can be quite harmful and dangerous as they create a haze between true and false.

Manipulated videos, pictures, audio or documents can be presented as evidence and deceive judges, lawyers and police officers, "casting doubt on audio-visual evidence as an entire category of evidence" (Trend Micro 2020). Moreover, as the processing power of information systems increases and deepfake technology develops even further, namely in real-time applications, videoconferencing or teleconferencing of witnesses, experts or parties may be manipulated by making them sound, do and act in a manner that did not happen.

Two years ago, the first case of deepfake being submitted as evidence in UK courts made the headlines. In a child's custody case, the mother of the child presented an audio record where the child's father was threatening her (The Telegraph 2020). Later on, the authenticity of the recording was challenged and the court ended up dismissing it. According to the experts that inspected the audio file, it had been tampered with, in order to include words that the father never said (The National 2020).

The court's traditional stance of taking at face value certain type of evidence—video or audio, for example—may have reached its end.

The main question is how the courts and the society in general can adequately protect themselves against the negative effects of deepfake technology.

The suggestion for a Regulation of the European Parliament and of the Council laying down coordinated regulations on artificial intelligence (Artificial Intelligence Act) gives us an idea of what could be the European Union's take on this matter.

Included in its subject matter (article 1(d)) are the rules for AI systems used to "generate or manipulate image, audio or video content". AI systems that are defined in article 3(1) "as software that is developed with one or more of the techniques and approaches listed in Annex I and can, for a given set of human-defined objectives, generate outputs such as content, predictions, recommendations, or decisions influencing the environments they interact with". Among the referred techniques and approaches we find machine learning and deep learning (annex I(a)).

This proposed framework adopts a risk-based approach to artificial intelligence that distinguishes between four different degrees of risk: unacceptable, high, limited and minimal. To better understand the level of risk posed by deep fakes, it is necessary to briefly define each one of them.

Firstly, in the unacceptable risk lie AI uses that are prohibited by the Artificial Intelligence act, as they fail to comply with the EU's values (*e.g.* fundamental rights). AI used for manipulation of human behavior causing harm physical or psychological harm (article 5, 1(a)(b)), social scoring (article 5, 1(c)), and real-time remote biometric identification in in publicly accessible spaces for law enforcement purposes (article 5, 1(d)) is prohibited. Only in specific cases can real-time remote biometric identification occur, more precisely when it is proportionate and strictly necessary to pursue one of three objectives: targeted search of victims, stop a terrorist attack or imminent threat to life and physical safety, or track a suspect or perpetrator of serious crimes (article 5, 1(d) i,ii,iii).

The categorization of an AI system as high-risk means that it is allowed to use, insofar the requirements laid out in article 8 to 15 are fulfilled (*e.g.* up-to-date technical documentation, logging capabilities, adequate transparency, human oversight, appropriate level of accuracy, robustness and cybersecurity) and the providers, users and other parties comply with the obligations foreseen in article 16 to 29, in particular conformity assessment. The European lawmaker includes in this category of risk AI systems in the domain of biometric identification, recruitment tools, credit scores, management of emergency services, among others.

Although the European proposal mentions in the proposal a three-tier risk-based approach (unacceptable, high, and low or minimal), it a fourth level is commonly recognized: limited risk. "Certain" AI systems—recalling the expression used in the proposal—are subject to transparency obligations (article 52). Meaning that their use is allowed, but providers and users must inform the end-users that they are interacting with an AI system or content artificially generated. The range of AI systems covered in this risk level is quite large as it encompasses all AI systems that interact with natural persons, detects emotions, or categorizes based on biometric data, or generates deepfakes.

The AI systems that pose no or low risk fall into the last category of risk. No obligations are imposed to the providers or users of such AI systems. Nevertheless, providers may decide, on voluntary basis, to create codes of conduct and ensure compliance with the requirements set out for high-risk systems (article 69). It is however a decision of the providers of non-high-risk AI systems to apply these requirements, as they are only mandatory for high-risk systems.

Drawing from the aforementioned classification of risk, we can safely affirm the use of deep fakes falls unequivocally into the third category: limited risk. Accordingly, deep fakes would not be prohibited nor deemed as high-risk, but they wouldn't also be classified as low or minimum risk. So, users "who use an AI system to generate or manipulate image, audio or video content that appreciably resembles existing persons, places or events and would falsely appear to a person to be authentic, should disclose that the content has been artificially created or manipulated by labelling the artificial intelligence output accordingly and disclosing its artificial origin" (recital 70 of the proposal). Users of AI systems that produce deep fakes must therefore disclose the artificial origin and nature of the content generated (article 52(3)).

The transparency obligation has however some exceptions.

The European lawmaker tried to reach a balance between the protection of very different values and goals: development, marketing and use of AI systems (recital 1); economic growth and social development (recital 2 and 3); human dignity, health, safety, freedom, equality, democracy, the rule of law, the right to non-discrimination, protection of personal data and privacy, and the rights of children (recital 1 and 15). In doing so, the proposal allows for the dismissal of the obligation of transparency if the deep fakes are used for legitimate reasons. Article 52(3) specifically declares the artificial origin of deep fakes may not be disclosed if it is used with the purpose of detecting, preventing, investigating and prosecuting criminal offences or it is a legitimate exercise of the right to freedom of expression and the right to freedom of the arts and sciences.

Understanding whether deep fakes must be announced or marked as such, or even if they are legal, implies an analysis done case by case. There may be cases where this type of artificial content amounts to a breach of fundamental rights of third parties prescribed as criminal (*e.g.* defamation, extortion, child pornography). In others however it may simply be an expression of creativity. The borders of the freedom of expression, arts and sciences are somewhat difficult to define and curbing the risk of mass manipulation with deep fakes may prove to be a challenge too difficult for law to overcome.

Technological content control or identification tools could be a valuable tool for governments, businesses, and persons alike.

9 Conclusion

The big problem that the administration of criminal justice must solve is enforceability. The current legal framework is unable to tackle deepfakes.

The problem of applying existing legal rules in the case of deepfakes can be summarily described as follows. First, the rapid evolution of technology makes any legal norm quickly out of date. Second, there is an urgent need to define what and how technology should be used. Third, due to the cross-border nature of the technologies, it might be extremely complex to identify the rules that these technologies must comply with; hence they are usually registered in countries with more lenient rules. Fourth, it is difficult to enforce legislation when technology development and usage is not confined to a single country. Fifth, the duties of the parties interested in deepfakes are frequently partial. Sixth, it is possible to circumvent the rules of a given jurisdiction easily (van der Sloot et al. 2021).

AI should assist in identifying and removing problematic deepfakes. In the same way that ML and DL provide the problem, they also have to be part of the solution. Nevertheless, digital literacy should not be neglected, as the pace of technological solutions employed in deepfake creation are frequently ahead of their detection counterparts. There is no real substitute for a critical stance with regard to digital content.[1]

---

[1] *See* generally, on the different applications of Machine Learning and AI, in this book A Oliveira and M A T Figueiredo - Artificial intelligence - historical context and state of the art; I Trancoso, N Mamede, B Martins, H S Pinto and R Ribeiro - The impact of language technologies in the legal domain; J Gonçalves-Sá and F L Pinheiro - Societal Implications of Recommendation Systems - A Technical Perspective; A T Freitas - Data-driven approaches in healthcare - challenges and emerging trends; M Correia and L Rodrigues - Security and Privacy; E Magrani and P G F Silva - The Ethical and Legal Challenges of Recommender Systems Driven by Artificial Intelligence; M Lanz and S Mijic - Risks associated with the use of natural language generation - Swiss civil liability law perspective; M S Fernandes and J R Goldim - Artificial Intelligence and Decision Making in Health - Risks and Opportunities; and W Gravett - Judicial Decision-making in the Age of Artificial Intelligence. *See* also, on the AI Act, in this book P U Lima and A Paiva - Autonomous and Intelligent Robots - Social, Legal and Ethical Issues; A T Fonseca, E V Sequeira and L B Xavier - Liability for AI Driven Systems; M N Duffourc and D S Giovanniello - The Autonomous AI Physician - Medical Ethics and Legal Liability; A Keller, C Martins Pereira and M Lucas Pires - The European Union's approach to Artificial Intelligence and the Challenge of Financial Systemic Risk; J C Abreu - The "Artificial Intelligence Act" Proposal on European e-Justice Domains Through the Lens of User-focused, User-friendly and Effective Judicial Protection Principles. *See* also, on biases, in this book P G Marques - AI Instruments for Risk of Recidivism

References

Anderson KE (2018) Getting acquainted with social networks and apps: combating fake news on social media. Libr Hi Tech News 35:1–6

Bansal A, Ma S, Ramanan D, Sheikh Y (2018) Recycle-GAN: unsupervised video retargeting. In: Ferrari V, Hebert M, Sminchisescu C, Weiss Y (eds) Computer vision – ECCV 2018. Springer, Cham, pp 122–138

Burns E (2021) Tech Accelerator. In: In-depth guide to machine learning in the enterprise. TechTarget. Available via TechTarget. https://www.techtarget.com/searchenterpriseai/definition/machine-learning-ML Accessed 14 Feb 2022

Cauduro A (2018) Medium. In: Deep Learning: o motor dos negócios na era da inteligência artificial. Stay curious. Available via Huia. https://medium.com/huia/intelig%C3%AAncia-artificial-uma-corrida-desleal-80bfa53075ed. Accessed 14 Feb 2022

Ceron R (2020) Blog de Infraestruturas de TI. In: A Inteligência Artificial hoje: dados, treinamento e inferência. IBM. Available by IBM. https://www.ibm.com/blogs/systems/br-pt/2020/01/a-inteligencia-artificial-hoje-dados-treinamento-e-inferencia/. Accessed 14 Feb 2022

Chawla R (2019) Deepfakes: how a pervert shook the world. Int J Adv Res Dev 4:4–8

Ciftci UA, Demir I, Yin L (2020) How do the hearts of deep fakes beat? Deep fake source detection via interpreting residuals with biological signals. In: 2020 IEEE international joint conference on biometrics (IJCB). IEEE, Houston, pp 1–10

de Lima O, Franklin S, Basu S, Karwoski B, George A (2020) Deepfake detection using spatiotemporal convolutional networks. arXiv:2006.14749

Dey A (2016) Machine learning algorithms: a review. Int J Comput Sci Inf Technol 7:1174–1179

Do NT, Na IS, Kim SH (2018) Forensics face detection from GANs using convolutional neural network. ISITC 2018:376–379

Europol (2020) In: Malicious uses and abuses of artificial intelligence. Available via Europol. https://www.europol.europa.eu/cms/sites/default/files/documents/malicious_uses_and_abuses_of_artificial_intelligence_europol.pdf. Accessed 15 Feb 2022

Faceswap (2022). DeepFakes. In: Deepfakes – faceswap. Gihub. Available by Github. https://github.com/deepfakes/faceswap. Accessed 15 Feb 2022

Figueira Á, Oliveira L (2017) The current state of fake news: challenges and opportunities. Procedia Comput Sci 121:817–825

Flynn A, Clough J, Cooke T (2021) Disrupting and preventing deepfake abuse: Exploring criminal law responses to AI-facilitated abuse. In: The palgrave handbook of gendered violence and technology. Palgrave Macmillan, Cham, pp 583–603

Ghahramani Z (2003, February) Unsupervised learning. In: Summer school on machine learning. Springer, Berlin, pp 72–112

Kietzmann J, Lee LW, McCarthy IP, Kietzmann TC (2020) Deepfakes: trick or treat? Bus Horiz 63:135–146

Kotsiantis SB, Zaharakis ID, Pintelas PE (2007) Supervised machine learning: a review of classification techniques. Emerg Artif Intell Appl Comput Eng 160:3–24

Prediction and the Possibility of Criminal Adjudication Deprived of Person-al Moral Recognition Standards – Sparse Notes from a Layman; W Gravett - Judicial Decision-making in the Age of Artificial Intelligence. *See* finally, on AI and judicial reasoning, in this book P G Marques - AI Instruments for Risk of Recidivism Prediction and the Possibility of Criminal Adjudication Deprived of Per-sonal Moral Recognition Standards – Sparse Notes from a Layman; L M Pereira, F C Santos and A B Lopes - AI Modelling of Counterfactual Thinking for Judicial Reasoning and Governance of Law; W Gravett - Judicial Decision-making in the Age of Artificial Intelligence; and J C Abreu - The "Artificial Intelligence Act" Proposal on European e-Justice Domains Through the Lens of User-focused, User-friendly and Effective Judicial Protection Principles.

Krupansky J (2017) Untangling the definitions of artificial intelligence, machine intelligence, and machine learning. https://perma.cc/RVZ4-88NP. Accessed 3 Feb 2022

Krzyk K (2018) Towards Data Science. In: Coding deep learning for beginners. Towards Data Science. Available by Medium. https://towardsdatascience.com/coding-deep-learning-for-beginners-types-of-machine-learning-b9e651e1ed9d. Accessed 17 Feb 2022

Li H, Li B, Tan S, Huang J. (2018a) Detection of deep network generated images using disparities in color components. arXiv preprint arXiv:1808.07276

Li Y, Chang MC, Lyu S (2018b). In ictu oculi: Exposing ai generated fake face videos by detecting eye blinking. arXiv preprint arXiv:1806.02877

Liu F, Jiao L, Tang X (2019) Task-oriented GAN for PolSAR image classification and clustering. IEEE Trans Neural Netw Learn Syst 30:2707–2719

Madhavan S, Jones T. (2021) Deep learning architectures: the rise of Artificial Intelligence In: Artificial Intelligence. https://developer.ibm.com/articles/cc-machine-learning-deep-learning-architectures/ Available by IBM. Accessed 21 Mar 2022

Malapragada P, Jain R, Liu Y (2017) Applying reinforcement learning and supervised learning techniques to play hearthstone. In: 16th IEEE international conference on machine learning and applications (ICMLA). IEEE, Cancun, Mexico, pp 1145–1148

Malavida (2022) FakeApp 2.2.0. In: Malavita. https://www.malavida.com/en/soft/fakeapp/. Available by Malavita. Accessed 28 Feb 2022

Malli RC (2017) Keras-vggface. In: Github. https://github.com/rcmalli/keras-vggface. Available by Github. Accessed 28 Feb 2022

Maras MH, Alexandrou A (2019) Determining authenticity of video evidence in the age of artificial intelligence and in the wake of Deepfake videos. Int J Evid Proof 23:255–262

Mathworks (2022) What is deep learning? 3 things you nedd to know. In: Deep Learning. https://www.mathworks.com/discovery/deep-learning.html. Available by MathWorks. Accessed 28 Feb 2022

Meskys E, Liaudanskas A, Kalpokiene J, Jurcys P (2020) Regulating deep fakes: legal and ethical considerations. J Intellect Prop Law Pract 15:24–31

Mittal T, Bhattacharya U, Chandra R, Bera A, Manocha D (2020) Emotions don't lie: an audio-visual deepfake detection method using affective cues. In: Proceedings of the 28th ACM international conference on multimedia. ACM, New York, NY, USA, pp 2823–2832

Muehlhauser L (2013) The privacy expert's guide to artificial intelligence and machine learning (future of privacy forum, 2018) at 5; "what is AGI? https://intelligence.org/2013/08/11/what-is-agi/. Accessed 2 Feb 2022

Raigon J (2020) Machine learning for fraud prevention keeps TrafficGuard agile. In: trafficguard. https://www.trafficguard.ai/resources/machine-learning-for-fraud-prevention-keeps-trafficguard-agile. Available by trafficguard. Accessed 28 Feb 2022

Santos F, Durães D, Marcondes F, Gomes M, Gonçalves F, Fonseca J, Wingbermuehle J, Machado J, Novais P (2021) Modelling a deep learning framework for recognition of human actions on video. In: Rocha A, Adeli H, Dzemyda G, Moreira F, Correia AMR (eds) Trends and applications in information systems and technologies. Springer International Publishing, Cham, pp 104–112

Shuweta B (2018) Reinforcement learning 101. In: Medium. https://towardsdatascience.com/reinforcement-learning-101-e24b50e1d292. Available by Toward Data Science. Accessed 20 Mar 2022

Sutton RS, Barto AG (2018) Reinforcement learning: an introduction. A Bradford Book, Cambridge

The National (2020) Deep fake audio evidence used in UK court to discredit Dubai dad. In: The National Newspaper. https://www.thenationalnews.com/uae/courts/deepfake-audio-evidence-used-in-uk-court-to-discredit-dubai-dad-1.975764. Accessed 22 Mar 2022

The Telegraph (2020) Doctor Audio Evidence used to damn Father in Custody Battle. In: The Telegraph Newspaper. https://www.telegraph.co.uk/news/2020/01/31/deepfake-audio-used-custody-battle-lawyer-reveals-doctored-evidence/. Accessed 22 Mar 2022

Trend Micro (2020) Trend Micro Security Predictions for 2020. In: Trend Micro Research. Available by Trend Micro. https://documents.trendmicro.com/assets/rpt/rpt-the-new-norm-trend-micro-security-predictions-for-2020.pdf. Accessed 21 Feb. 2022

van der Sloot B, Wagensveld Y, Koops BJ (2021) Summary Deepfakes: the legal challenges of a synthetic society. In: Tilburg Institute for Law, Technology, and Society. https://www.tilburguniversity.edu/sites/default/files/download/Deepfake%20EN.pdf. Availablen by Tilburg University. Accessed 3 Mar 2022

Xuan X, Peng B, Wang W, Dong J (2019) On the generalization of GAN image forensics. In: Sun Z, He R, Feng J, Shan S, Guo Z (eds) Chinese conference on biometric recognition. Springer International Publishing, Cham, pp 134–141

Zhu JY, Taesung P, Isola P, Efros AA (2017) Unpaired Image-to-Image Translation using Cycle-Consistent Adversarial Networks. In: CycleGAN Project Page. https://junyanz.github.io/CycleGAN/. Available by github. Accessed 28 Feb 2022

Open Access This chapter is licensed under the terms of the Creative Commons Attribution 4.0 International License (http://creativecommons.org/licenses/by/4.0/), which permits use, sharing, adaptation, distribution and reproduction in any medium or format, as long as you give appropriate credit to the original author(s) and the source, provide a link to the Creative Commons license and indicate if changes were made.

The images or other third party material in this chapter are included in the chapter's Creative Commons license, unless indicated otherwise in a credit line to the material. If material is not included in the chapter's Creative Commons license and your intended use is not permitted by statutory regulation or exceeds the permitted use, you will need to obtain permission directly from the copyright holder.

Antitrust Law and Coordination Through AI-Based Pricing Technologies

Maria José Schmidt-Kessen and Max Huffman

Abstract Price is the core element of commercial transactions and an important parameter of competition. One of antitrust law's aims is to ensure that market prices form under the laws of supply and demand, and not after the whims of monopolists or cartelists. Innovations in computer and data science have brought about pricing technologies that rely on advanced analytics or machine learning (ML) techniques, which could strengthen existing bargaining power disparities in part by supporting price coordination among competitors.

Existing research establishes a theoretical framework for competitive harm through coordination, showing that pricing technologies can lead to near-cartel price levels while avoiding anti-cartel prohibitions. This contribution builds on that framework, taking into account up to date empirical, game-theoretic, and computer science literature on pricing technologies to produce a taxonomy of those technologies. We then employ a comparative approach to identify the legal effects of various pricing technologies at a more granular level under EU and US antitrust law. The contribution supports greater understanding between economists and policy-makers regarding the analysis and treatment of AI-based pricing technologies.

1 Introduction

Price is the core element of commercial transactions and an important parameter of competition. One of antitrust law's aims is to ensure that market prices form under free competition, so that the laws of supply and demand operate to maximize consumer welfare. One instance where prices do not result from competition is when

---

M. J. Schmidt-Kessen (✉)
Legal Studies Department, Central European University, Vienna, Austria
e-mail: schmidt-kessenm@ceu.edu

M. Huffman
Indiana University McKinney School of Law, Indianapolis, IN, USA
e-mail: huffmmax@iupui.edu

© The Author(s) 2024
H. Sousa Antunes et al. (eds.), *Multidisciplinary Perspectives on Artificial Intelligence and the Law*, Law, Governance and Technology Series 58,
https://doi.org/10.1007/978-3-031-41264-6_20

there is anti-competitive coordination in a market. Anti-competitive coordination is prohibited under various provisions of antitrust law, most importantly under cartel prohibitions (e.g. Section 1 of the Sherman Act in the US and Article 101 of the Treaty on the Functioning of the European Union) and under merger rules (where mergers producing coordinated effects should be prohibited).

The prevailing opinion in antitrust scholarship and enforcement practice has been that, unless there is explicit coordination between competitors, coordination is unlikely to occur in markets with four or more players (Stigler 1964). When coordination is not explicit but tacit, it will rarely be caught by antitrust rules. Under the current state of the law in both the US and EU, tacit coordination is by definition not caught under cartel prohibitions, since existing rules require some evidence of a meeting of the minds between cartel participants to trigger the application of the prohibition. To show that there has been a meeting of the minds, traditionally, evidence about communication between cartel participants, records of a meeting, or exchange of information through a third party is necessary. While there is reason to believe this limitation on enforcement against coordinated outcomes enables price and non-price effects that harm consumers, to date there is not a broadly accepted approach to preventing these outcomes as a matter of conduct enforcement. Increased likelihood of tacit coordination as a result of a merger could potentially be caught under merger laws, but competition enforcers have rarely prohibited mergers because of their potential coordinated effects. In the instances in which they have tried to block such mergers, they have regularly been unsuccessful due to high legal standards for proving tacit coordination imposed by courts.[1]

The conventional wisdom that anti-competitive coordination in the form of tacit collusion is unlikely to occur is being challenged by recent studies in game theory and rapid technological developments (OECD 2017). Innovations in computer and data science have brought about pricing technologies that rely on advanced analytics or machine learning (ML) techniques, which are thought to be capable of self-learning and sustaining price coordination among competitors. It is uncertain whether antitrust laws would catch such algorithmic price coordination. It would depend on (a) the capabilities of the technology used and their potential for causing competitive harm, and (b) on the interpretation of antitrust law. This chapter aims at bringing more clarity to these two dimensions to contribute to ongoing debates on antitrust law and AI-based pricing technologies.

We start by laying out the state of the art on pricing technology and algorithmic tacit collusion in law, microeconomics and computer science literature. Next, we engage with a variety of AI-based technologies that can be deployed for dynamic pricing. We then assess various technological options from an EU and US antitrust perspective before outlining policy approaches and a future outlook.[2]

---

[1] In the EU, an example is Case Case T-342/99 *Airtours*, where the General Court held that the Commission had not been able to show coordinated effects from a merger that would lead to a blocking of the merger.

[2] The Chapter takes into consideration policy developments until 17 February 2023.

2 Algorithmic Pricing and Collusion

Pricing is a core part of companies' competitive strategy. In settings where prices can be adjusted easily and frequently, as for example in the case of online retail or stationary retail with electronic price tags, companies can optimize their pricing by using dynamic pricing techniques (Den Boer 2013). Dynamic pricing allows companies to rapidly react to changes in demand or inventory levels, and to respond to competitors' behavior and market trends.

Increasingly available amounts of data together with algorithms can support and enhance dynamic pricing. Simple algorithms can implement pre-existing "analogue" pricing rules, such as matching the lowest competitor price. In this case, the use of algorithms allows for the automation of price setting and for faster reactions to a rival competitor's price change (CMA 2018). Alternatively, more sophisticated machine learning algorithms can autonomously choose which data to base pricing decisions on and can learn about optimal pricing strategies (CMA 2018).

The impact of pricing algorithms on market competition is ambiguous. On the one hand, they can have pro-competitive effects, like allowing managers to make faster and better decisions or directly reducing costs by fully automating decision-making (CMA 2018). In addition, they might contribute to markets clearing faster and more efficiently (CMA 2018). On the other hand, concerns have been raised that pricing algorithms might facilitate explicit, tacit, or even unintentional coordination of market behavior, leading to collusive market outcomes and consumer harm (CMA 2018).

Academic literature in antitrust law and policy is split regarding the risks for competition from firms' algorithmic pricing. Some authors suggest that markets are being fundamentally transformed by the use of algorithms, and that the risk of widespread algorithmic collusion is real (Ezrachi and Stucke 2016; Mehra 2016). Ezrachi and Stucke (2016) propose four scenarios in which the use of algorithms in pricing can lead to collusive outcomes. First, in situations in which algorithms are used to support an explicit price-fixing agreement by implementing the agreed conduct or detecting any deviations from it. An example of this is the Amazon poster-sellers' cartel which was prosecuted in the US and the UK.[3] In this case, competitors on Amazon reached an express agreement as to the features of the algorithm to be employed in establishing prices on Amazon, with the effect of price coordination that would not have happened in the absence of the agreement. As the UK Competition and Markets Authority described it, an initial verbal price fixing agreement was later implemented using pricing software. This was contrary to antitrust law. Second, in hub-and-spoke situations in which many market actors delegate their pricing decisions to the same algorithm from a third-party developer, Ezrachi and Stucke (2016) argue that there is a risk of price alignment steered by

---

[3] United States v. David Topkins, Plea Agreement, Crim. No. 15-201 (N.D. Cal. Apr. 30, 2015); Online sales of posters and frames, Case No. 50223 (CMA 12 Aug. 2016).

the hub. Third, in situations where companies unilaterally deploy simple algorithms with predictable actions, e.g. algorithms implementing 'win-continue lose-reverse' rules or algorithms that match competitor prices, price alignment can occur. Last, when advanced machine learning algorithms are designed by companies to achieve a goal, like profit maximization, and are left to themselves to figure out the optimal pricing strategy (autonomous agent schemes), they autonomously could learn to collude. In particular, in the case of autonomous agent schemes, this strand of the literature maintains that current antitrust laws are ill-suited for sanctioning this type of conduct.

The opposite view maintains that the claims about risks from algorithmic pricing in debates on AI and antitrust law are "science fiction" (Petit 2017; Schwalbe 2019). This strand of the literature considers in particular autonomous algorithmic collusion as something that is far removed from present day capabilities of the technology and point to the fact that no empirical evidence of autonomous collusion has been presented so far (Schwalbe 2019; Gautier et al. 2020). In addition, this strand of the literature maintains that the currently possible forms of algorithmic collusion do not pose any fundamental challenges to existing antitrust rules (Gautier et al. 2020). Some critiques might be questioned as continuous technological improvements increase the possibility of theorized outcomes. Furthermore, the line between human-assisted and autonomous algorithmic collusion may not always be easy to draw, thus leaving more grey areas for the treatment of algorithmic collusion under current antitrust law than critics maintain.

Literature in microeconomics echoes this split. For economists, collusion is defined as a situation when firms use strategies implementing a "reward-punishment scheme designed to provide incentives for firms to consistently price above the competitive level" (Harrington 2018). The question as to whether algorithms can learn to engage in collusion and to "punish" deviations from collusive behavior has been discussed both theoretically, empirically, and in simulations. For collusion to occur in markets without algorithms, certain structural conditions can facilitate collusion, such as when there is profit to make from colluding, there are few competitors, players on the market are symmetric, entry barriers are high, there are repeated interactions of market players, there is seller-side homogeneity, and there is a high level of transparency that allows competitors to observe each other's behavior (Stigler 1964; Green et al. 2013). These same structural conditions also support non-collusive coordination, sometimes called tacit collusion, oligopolistic coordination, or interdependent conduct, which has not been treated as violating either US law (Section 1 of the Sherman Act) or EU law (Article 101 TFEU).[4]

An early analysis of this problem is offered by Donald Turner, who concluded that tacit coordination should not be treated as an agreement because it merely reflects the behavior of a rational oligopolist, acting in its independent best interest (Turner 1962, pp. 665–666). In particular, there is no conduct that can be condemned by way of remedying the outcome, short of an injunction operating as a price control

---

[4] *See infra.*

(Kaysen and Turner 1959, pp. 110–119, 266–272).[5] Importantly, Turner identifies as not affected by his conclusion conduct "designed to convert an imperfect oligopoly pricing pattern into a perfect one by eliminating uncertainties" (Kaysen and Turner 1959, pp. 670–673). Richard Posner later advocated for an alternative approach to the problem in which oligopolists "base their pricing decisions in part on anticipated reactions to them" with the resulting "tendency to avoid vigorous price competition" (Posner 1969, p. 1564). Posner took issue with Turner's suggestion that an oligopolist might merely find itself in a market where the profit maximizing activity was to consider its competitor's responses, leading to coordinated outcomes. Instead, Posner identifies a number of features required for successful oligopolistic coordination, including substantial similarity of product and reliable knowledge of other firm prices; because those and other features come about by voluntary action, it is possible to remedy the oligopoly pricing by forbidding those actions (Posner 1969, pp. 1575–1576).

The deployment of pricing algorithms is thought to be able to bring about or to magnify some of the conditions that lead to coordinated outcomes, including: market concentration, speed, efficiency, transparency, and stability. Gal (2019), for example, argues that algorithms' speed allows these algorithms to detect and punish deviations from charging supra-competitive prices faster than humans, thus making collusion more stable. Pricing algorithms also process much higher amounts of data than humans, thus making them more efficient in pursuing a collusive strategy. In addition, the argument has been made that due to algorithms' strategy being "encoded", it would be easier for algorithms to "read" other algorithms' strategies thereby increasing market transparency (Gal 2019). In addition, algorithms' prediction capacity based on past market data might increase transparency in terms of more accurately predicting future demand (Miklós-Thal and Tucker 2019). Lastly, if companies need to rely on pricing algorithms in order to be able to get a competitive advantage on markets, this might raise market concentration, as the development or purchase of sophisticated pricing algorithms is costly and only incumbents and larger players will have the resources to compete (Chen et al. 2016; Dorner 2021).

While there is considerable evidence on firms using pricing algorithms (Chen et al. 2016; European Commission 2017), there is scant evidence showing a causal relationship between pricing algorithms and collusive outcomes. One recent study from the German gasoline market, however, showed that after gas stations adopted algorithmic pricing technology, gradual price rises lead to permanent price increases indicating a decrease in competition (Assad et al. 2020). In this study, the authors show that in the aftermath of algorithmic pricing software becoming available and widely adopted by German gas stations, profit margins in non-monopoly markets

---

[5] Turner does not argue that nothing should be done, instead advocating a structuralist approach of curbing market power by legislation.

and in duopoly markets where both stations adopted algorithmic pricing increased considerably.[6]

Due to the difficulty of finding real-world evidence of tacit algorithmic collusion, with the German gasoline market study being the first and only of its kind to date, several studies have tested learning algorithms' capacity to collude in simulations of repeated games. Calvano et al. (2019, 2020) provided a first experimental study where they could show that two Q-learning[7] algorithms could autonomously learn to collude by implementing a reward-punishment scheme in the framework of a repeated Bertrand oligopoly setting.[8] The results showed that, after several iterations, the equilibrium strategy of the algorithms in the repeated game led to sustained supra-competitive price levels. Klein (2021) provides further evidence on the capacity of Q-learning algorithms to learn how to collude in situations of sequential pricing.

The relevance of these studies for policy, however, has been questioned due to the very slow learning process of Q-learning algorithms, which make their use by businesses unrealistic (Ittoo and Petit 2017; Gautier et al. 2020; Dorner 2021). The studies have also been criticized for being difficult to extend to settings more than two-agents due to problems in scalability and learning in a non-stationary environment where several competitors are adjusting their behavior constantly. Lastly, the studies' inapplicability to scenarios with non-homogeneous goods has been criticized (Ittoo and Petit 2017; Gautier et al. 2020). In other words, the simulations that show the possibility of Q-learning algorithms learning to collude have been criticized for being too far removed from the conditions under which real markets work, thus questioning the policy implications from their findings. Nonetheless, the studies show theoretically that two algorithms that are unilaterally deployed and that are not designed to communicate can eventually learn to tacitly collude and produce coordinated outcomes. In addition, the Swedish Competition Authority recently published a report corroborating the evidence from prior experiments and showed the possibility of collusive outcomes also when a variety of learning algorithms were mixed (Q-learning, SARSA, and PG), and when Q-learning agents were programmed asymmetrically (Konkurrensverket 2021).

It is unclear in how far the findings from simulations with Q-learning algorithms apply to other machine learning techniques (Gautier et al. 2020). Hettich (2021) provides initial evidence for deep Q-learning algorithms (DQN)[9] learning how to collude significantly faster than simple Q-learning algorithms. According to his study, collusion disappears in simulations with more than 7 firms. Furthermore, collusion is not hindered when the other algorithms are simple, rule-based algorithms,

---

[6] The geographic markets for gasoline stations are local, each potentially having a different number of players. The authors drew 1 km radii around gas stations to define the relevant market. This is why there are many separate relevant retail gasoline markets within the territory of Germany in this study that allow for comparisons across them.

[7] We elaborate on Q-learning in the next section.

[8] The Bertrand model of competition describes interactions among firms that set prices, the quantity sold being determined by the choices of their customers based on the set price.

[9] DQN algorithms combine a Q-learning algorithm with a Deep Neural Network.

but is hindered if there are various learning algorithms with different characteristics (e.g. differences in learning pace). More research is needed to understand and measure the risks of collusion stemming from DQNs used in pricing.

In computer science, there is an important literature on the capacity of reinforcement learning algorithms to cooperate in repeated prisoner's dilemma (Schwalbe 2019 for an overview), which is comparable to the setting of two firms in a Bertrand oligopoly. The literature has explored the focus on the connection between learning, communication, and cooperation. In two recent studies modelling prisoner's dilemma situations, two important factors for learning cooperation by self-learning algorithms were identified. First, cooperation is easier to achieve when lower degrees of coordination were needed to achieve the highest reward (Leibo et al. 2017). Second, that cooperation was much more easily achieved if algorithms could send signals to each other through a communication protocol (Crandall et al. 2018). Applying these insights to pricing algorithms, this literature would suggest that collusion is more likely the less complex the algorithms and the environment they operate in are (Schwalbe 2019). In addition, as in the case of human agents, communication between algorithms will increase the likelihood of collusion.

All in all, the uncertainty as to whether pricing algorithms can collude and what level of harm they can cause when they align prices on markets persists. Nonetheless, this uncertainty will likely not have vanished before a competition authority or court might have to deal with a case giving rise to questions surrounding the legality of pricing algorithms that are not a simple tool to implement a cartel as in the Amazon Poster cases discussed above. Furthermore, the literature has already hinted to features in the design of pricing algorithms that, at least in theory, should make algorithmic collusion more or less likely. In the next section we discuss various possible AI-based pricing technologies and their characteristics. Subsequently, we give a possible outline for how to deal with different characteristics of pricing algorithms under antitrust rules.

3 Varieties of AI-Based Pricing Technologies

Dynamic pricing can be implemented with the help of a broad range of algorithms. There are very simple if-then algorithms, or rule-based agents, without any learning capacities. Such algorithms can, for example, implement simple business rules in a non-transient manner, i.e. they will not change their behavior by learning from past interaction. There are third-party developers offering these kinds of simple pricing solutions on the market, and they appear to be the most common form deployed today (CMA 2018).

More sophisticated algorithms that are capable of learning, can be categorized as a form of AI. Artificial Intelligence (AI) can take many forms. The recently proposed EU AI Act[10] defines artificial intelligence systems as "software that is developed with one or more of the techniques and approaches listed in Annex I and can, for a given set of human-defined objectives, generate outputs such as content, predictions, recommendations, or decisions influencing the environments they interact with". Annex I contains three examples of AI systems, the most important for us being machine learning approaches.[11]

Machine learning covers a variety of computer programs that learn from experience (Russell and Norvig 1995). The main fields within machine learning are supervised learning, unsupervised learning, and reinforcement learning. Supervised learning entails teaching an algorithm with example input-output pairs a mapping function that will allow the algorithm eventually to predict outcomes for new input data autonomously. Supervised and semi-supervised learning are applied in many fields where training occurs with labeled data, e.g. in the case of algorithmic content moderation on social media. Supervised learning is also used for regressions, and, when deployed in pricing, can thus enable pricing algorithms to predict future trends.

Unsupervised learning, on the other hand, entails giving an algorithm only input data without output variables. The learning task of the algorithm is then to figure out patterns in the input data. Applications of unsupervised learning include pattern recognition in big data and recommender systems. Unsupervised learning can help in pricing decisions in order to discover new correlations or to gain insights across product or geographic markets. It might, for example, allow a cosmetics seller to have new insights about how a seemingly unrelated event, e.g. the weather, impacts demand for cosmetics.

Lastly, reinforcement learning is the machine learning technique that has been deployed in the repeated game simulations discussed in the previous section. Reinforcement learning trains algorithms to make a series of decisions in a complex environment in order to achieve a certain objective through trial and error. Q-learning is one form of reinforcement learning.[12] It enables agent to implement a reward-maximizing strategy in an unknown environment over time. The agent learns by choosing and performing an action in a certain state, estimating the reward for taking that action, and updating its function based on the positive or negative reward

---

[10] Proposal for a Regulation Laying Down Harmonised Rules on Artificial Intelligence (Artificial Intelligence Act) and Amending Certain Union Legislative Acts, of 21 April 2021, COM(2021) 206 final.

[11] The other two examples are logic- and knowledge-based approaches on the one hand, and statistical approaches, Bayesian estimation, search and optimization methods on the other. This definition, however, is not final yet, and has been criticized by various actors in the policy process, including the EU Council (see https://www.euractiv.com/section/digital/news/eu-council-presidency-pitches-significant-changes-to-ai-act-proposal/).

[12] Other types of reinforcement learning are SARSA and policy gradient (PG) methods, the Swedish Competition Authority provides a comparison between Q-learning, SARSA and PG in its November 2021 Report (Konkurrensverket 2021, pp. 17–19).

received.[13] This process is then repeated over and over until the learning process is stopped. In the simulations by Calvano et al. (2019, 2020) and Klein (2021) this process allowed the algorithms to learn to collude over time.

A different structural form of learning relies on so-called deep neural networks (DNN). DNN were inspired by the neuronal structure of the human brain, and consist of multiple interconnected layers of artificial neurons. In DNN, learning can again be supervised, unsupervised, or reinforced (Nicholson 2021). DNNs can learn differently and faster, by modifying connections between artificial neuros and due to each layer being able to execute a different task. DNN is the underlying AI technology for automatic speech recognition, image recognition, and natural language processing, and can also be deployed for predicting and optimizing pricing. It is sometimes referred to as a "black box" because the processes that yield an output are difficult or impossible to understand.

An alternative to DNN are Random Forests that combine the predictions of many decision trees (Montantes 2020). In comparison to DNN, they require less data and are computationally more efficient. They also tend to be more transparent in comparison to a DNN because they allow to make connections between the variables and the prediction model they generate.

The literature has shown that various characteristics of machine learning algorithms can influence the capacity to cooperate/collude. These include memory of prior interactions, the learning pace, the complexity of algorithms (the more complex, the less likely to collude because behavior is difficult to "read" for other algorithms) (Schwalbe 2019; Hettich 2021), and their capacity to communicate (Schwalbe 2019).

4 Algorithmic Collusion in US Antitrust Law

4.1 The Necessity of "Agreement"

The core requirement for a violation of Section 1 of the Sherman Act is the existence of an agreement among two or more independent economic actors.[14] The agreement requirement is also present in some cases under Section 2, which outlaws "combin[ing] or conspir[ing] to monopolize."[15] (Because there is no meaningful difference between the Section 2 conspiracy and the Section 1 conspiracy, the analysis here does not treat them separately.) The question of agreement is binary:

---

[13] More detailed and technical descriptions of how Q-learning works can be found e.g. in Ittoo and Petit (2017).

[14] United States Code, Title 15, Section 1 ("Every contract, combination in the form of trust or otherwise, or conspiracy, in restraint of trade or commerce among the several States, or with foreign nations, is declared to be illegal . . . .")

[15] Id. Section 2.

conduct occurring by agreement must be analyzed for its legality under either the rule of reason or *per se* analytical approaches, but conduct not occurring by agreement is immune from challenge under Section 1, irrespective of the likelihood of consumer harm.

4.2 Non-Agreement Coordination

Most important for the analysis here is the broad category of non-agreement coordination that fits under the labels "tacit collusion," "tacit coordination," "interdependent conduct," "conscious parallelism," and "oligopolistic coordination." This analysis employs the label "non-agreement coordination", best understood as the outcome that occurs when competitors all recognize their independent best interest is achieved not by full-throated competition but by coordination with competitors. An example, frequently cited, is that of competing gas station proprietors who price in parallel fashion despite a lack of implicit or explicit agreement between them (Huffman 2008, p. 646). The US Supreme Court has repeatedly recognized this reality, in cases including *Bell Atlantic Corp v. Twombly* (2007),[16] and held that coordination among economic actors that is caused by their pursuing their independent best interest does not constitute an agreement (Huffman 2008, at 648–649). Two primary reasons support the approach of treating non-agreement coordination as outside of the prohibitions of Section 1. First is a simple and formalistic matter of statutory interpretation: Section 1 does not outlaw conduct by firms pursuing their independent best interest.

Second is the problem of remedying non-agreement coordination. To prohibit oligopoly conduct, courts or regulators would be required to order economic actors not to pursue their independent best interest, by—for example—not taking into account the effect on competitors (and their likely response) to pricing decisions. A rule against oligopoly pricing would effectively be a requirement of naïve or irrational pricing conduct (Turner 1962, p. 692; Whinston 2006, p. 52).

US law has developed in a series of cases to exempt non-agreement coordination entirely from the reach of the Sherman Act. Hylton (2018) argues that Judge Posner's 2015 opinion in *In re Text Messaging Antitrust Litigation* represents the most definitive statement of this principle—as one remarkable example from that opinion: "[T]he Sherman Act imposes no duty on firms to compete vigorously, or for that matter at all, in price."[17] Notably, *Text Messaging* suggests a complete about-face from Posner's (1969) view that the law might take steps to challenge tacit collusion (Hylton 2018, p. 5).

Courts have developed a system of requiring additional evidence, beyond observed parallel conduct, to differentiate agreement from non-agreement coordination. This "plus-factor" framework is fundamentally an evidentiary or pleading

---

[16] 550 U.S. 544, 553–554 (2007).

[17] *In re Text Messaging Antitrust Litig.*, 782 F.3d 867, 874 (7th Cir. 2015).

burden, meant to indicate conduct subject to liability as distinct from innocent conduct, rather than a substantive rule of law. As outlined by Kovacic et al. (2011, pp. 405–406) a plus factor is an evidentiary fact that reduces the likelihood of a non-agreement explanation for coordinated conduct. In their presence, evidence may be sufficient for circumstantial proof of agreement, which can be remedied by prohibition and sanction. In the absence of plus factors, however, there is no basis to assume actual agreement from an observation of coordination among competitors, leaving unremediable non-agreement coordination as the legally necessary conclusion.

4.3 Hub-and-Spoke

Agreements can also be reached through parallel agreements reached with a third party, acting as the "hub" in a hub-and-spoke enterprise structure (Huffman and Schmidt-Kessen 2021, pp. 8–10). The analysis of a hub-and-spoke enterprise becomes interesting if it is possible to prove an agreement around the "rim", which is horizontal among the various spokes. Recent cases in US courts, including the Seventh Circuit's decision in *Toys 'R' Us* (2000) and the Second Circuit's decision in *Apple e-Books* (2015), find horizontal agreements among competitors when the individual vertical agreements with the hub are reached with an understanding of, and reliance on, competitors' comparable agreements.[18] Hub-and-spoke enterprises have characteristics in common with non-agreement coordination, because these enterprises do not rely on actual communication between the spokes. However, unlike non-agreement coordination, it is possible to remedy the hub-and-spoke through a prohibition of the various vertical agreements.

4.4 Remedying Coordinated Conduct

One approach to remedying non-agreement coordination is to attack it indirectly, through challenging agreements or other conduct that increase the likelihood of coordination. A second is to attack the coordination directly under Section 5 of the US Federal Trade Commission Act, with its prohibition of "unfair methods of competition."[19]

With regard to the prohibition of conduct that increases the likelihood of coordination, courts and enforcement agencies interpreting Section 1 prohibit

---

[18] United States v. Apple Inc., 791 F.3d 290 (2015) (upholding finding of liability for a horizontal agreement among publishers orchestrated by retailer Apple, acting as the hub); Toys 'R' Us Inc. v. FTC, 221 F.3d 928 (7th Cir. 2000) (affirming FTC finding of liability for hub-and-spoke conspiracy).

[19] United States Code, Title 15, Section 5.

agreements among firms to share information where those agreements increase the likelihood of oligopolistic coordination (Clark 1983, pp. 915–918).[20] Clark categories such practices as (1) public announcements of business plans, (2) data dissemination on prices and non-price matters, (3) discount deterring practices including MFN clauses, and (4) standardization of terms of trade (Clark 1983, pp. 919–951). Page (2017) summarizes judicial treatment of the sharing of information among firms as dependent on the audience and the past, present or forward-looking nature of the communications. Broad publication to the market, consumers as well as competitors, has obvious competition-enhancing features - for example, communicating petrol prices to consumers, permitting comparison shopping while driving. Communication to competitors but not to the market facilitates tacit collusion and has limited procompetitive benefits, with typical examples including communications within industry trade associations. With regard to communications' temporal character, present or past information is less likely to be harmful than is future information (Page 2017, pp. 611–612).

Market structure is also linked to concerns for non-agreement coordination, and in merger review courts and agencies broadly consider coordinated effects as a reason to challenge or enjoin a merger. The 2010 *Horizontal Merger Guidelines* identify as coordinated conduct (1) explicit agreements, (2) a common understanding not explicitly agreed to but nonetheless enforced, and (3) parallel accommodating conduct (*Guidelines*, 2010, section 7). The *Guidelines* acknowledge that coordinated conduct includes activity that is not in itself an antitrust violation. Mergers will be challenged if by increasing concentration in a market susceptible to coordination, the incidence and effect of coordination is likely to be exacerbated (*Id.*, section 7.1). Susceptibility to coordination includes, among other factors, price transparency and homogeneity (*Id.*, section 7.2). Merger review stands as a significant protection against the possibility of non-agreement coordination otherwise not subject to challenge.[21] Notably, the US Horizontal Merger Guidelines, last updated in 2010, are as of this publication ripe for revision. Given the FTC's emphasis on technology markets, and the leadership of the EU in its Draft Horizontal Guidelines (*infra*), we anticipate a revision will incorporate algorithmic collusion concerns as a factor to be considered in analyzing coordinated effects. [22]

Remedying non-agreement coordination directly under the FTC Act may in theory be possible (Dibadj 2010, pp. 606–608). The FTC Act's broad prohibition targets "unfair methods of competition," rather than the somewhat more specific

---

[20] Concerns for anticompetitive information sharing can also be found in the *Collaboration Guidelines* (2000, at 21, 26–27).

[21] *E.g. United States v. H&R Block Inc.*, 833 F. Supp. 2d 36, 77–81 (D.D.C. 2011) (identifying market structure conducive to non-agreement coordination as a basis for enjoining merger in tax preparation software market).

[22] Federal Trade Commission and Justice Department Seek to Strengthen Enforcement Against Illegal Mergers, 18 Jan. 2022, available at https://www.ftc.gov/news-events/news/press-releases/2022/01/federal-trade-commission-justice-department-seek-strengthen-enforcement-against-illegal-mergers.

"contract, combination.. ., or conspiracy" under the Sherman Act. And the FTC lacks the power to impose draconian penalties, limiting concerns that criminal penalties or treble-damages liability will disincentivize aggressive competitive behavior (Huffman 2022a). However, the remedial concern of how to address the conduct directly—whether to order competition, or to order pricing at marginal cost, or other outcome—remains. The FTC has not challenged non-agreement coordination directly, instead targeting its prosecutions at facilitating practices that tended to lead to coordination (see Clark 1983, pp. 948–951).

5 Algorithmic Collusion in EU Antitrust Law

5.1 Coordination by Agreement

Article 101 (1) TFEU prohibits "all agreements between undertakings, decisions by associations of undertakings and concerted practices which may affect trade between Member States and which have as their object or effect the prevention, restriction or distortion of competition within the internal market". These include in particular price fixing agreements.[23] The core piece of evidence in order to prove a violation of Article 101 (1) TFEU is that there has been communication between the parties to the agreement or concerted practice that has led to a "meeting of the minds" to fix prices. Similar to the US context, mere parallel conduct cannot be prohibited under Article 101 (1) TFEU.[24]

5.2 Non-Agreement Coordination

The EU Commission has been able to prove an anti-competitive agreement without having evidence of explicit communication between the parties before.[25] The Court of Justice of the EU found in *Imperial Chemical Industries* that "parallel behaviour may not by itself be identified with a concerted practice, it may however amount to strong evidence of such a practice if it leads to conditions of competition which do not correspond to the normal conditions of the market, having regard to the nature of the products, the size and number of the undertakings, and the volume of the said market." The Court went on to say that this was especially the case "if the parallel conduct is such as to enable those concerned to attempt to stabilize prices at a level different from that to which competition would have led". The Court thus opened the

---

[23] Article 101 (1) (a) TFEU.

[24] See e.g. Cases C- 40 to 48, 50, 54 to 56, 111, 113 and 114-73 *Suiker Unie;* Case 172/80 *Zünchner v Bayerische Vereinsbank;* Case T-442/08 *Cisac v Commission* [2013].

[25] Case 48/96 *Imperial Chemical Industries* [1972].

door in this judgment to considering evidence beyond the communication between the parties to contextual elements of the market in question. Nonetheless, as the EU Court of Justice judgment in *Woodpulp* stressed, if there is a plausible explanation for the conduct other than collusion, there is no violation of Article 101 (1) TFEU.[26]

Furthermore, the EU Commission states in its Guidelines on Horizontal Cooperation that it will be vigilant of companies' attempt of making markets more transparent by announcing prices publicly.[27] If several companies make public announcements sequentially, for example, this can be evidence of concertation.[28]

In its new Draft Horizontal Guidelines, [29] the Commission recognizes that the use of algorithms can increase market transparency, too, and with it the risk of a collusive outcome in the market. It notes, however, that for algorithms to bring about such outcomes, further structural conditions are required, like "a high frequency of interactions, limited buyer power and the presence of homogenous products/services". [30]In addition, at least a provable indirect information exchange via an algorithmic tool between competitors would be necessary to consider it a form of coordination that could be caught under Article 101 (1) TFEU. This could be, for example, through a shared optimization algorithm that is marketed by a single IT company and that feeds on sensitive data from various competitors. [31]

5.3 Hub-and-Spoke Coordination

A third possibility to establish that there has been anti-competitive coordination contrary to Article 101 (1) TFEU is when parties that intend to fix prices do not communicate with each other, but through a third party. In this case, the third party, acting as a middleman or hub will ultimately establish a "meeting of the minds" between the spokes (OECD 2017; Huffman and Schmidt-Kessen 2021). This was the case, for example in *AC Treuhand*,[32] where a consultancy facilitated

---

[26] Joined Cases C-89, 104, 114, 116, 117 and 125 to 129/85 *Woodpulp*.

[27] EU Commission (2011). Guidelines on the applicability of Article 101 of the Treaty on the Functioning of the European Union to horizontal co-operation agreements, 2011/C 11/01, 63.

[28] E.g. COMP/39.850 *Container Shipping* where the EU Commission found that regular public announcement of price increase intentions through press releases and specialized trade press made several times a year by various companies was considered a concerted practice contrary to Article 101 (1) TFEU.

[29] EU Commission (2022). Approval of the content of a draft for a Communication from the Commission – Guidelines on the applicability of Article 101 of the Treaty on the Functioning of the European Union to horizontal co-operation agreements, 2022/C 164/01. The Draft Guidelines should have been adopted by 1 January 2023, but at the time of writing (February 2023), the final version had not yet been published.

[30] Ibid, 418.

[31] Ibid, 426.

[32] Case C-195/14 P *AC Treuhand*.

the exchanges of sensitive business information between its clients that lead to alignment of prices on the market.

As mentioned above, especially if several actors in a same market purchase pricing algorithms from the same third-party developer, a hub-and-spoke scenario might ensue. As soon as there is a communication from the third-party developer to purchasers that the algorithm helps to align prices, this could possibly be enough to prove a violation under Article 101 (1) TFEU.[33] At the same time, the fact that these third-party pricing algorithms will have stochastic elements, and might be used to implement different pricing strategies determined by the final user might actually not lead to any pricing alignment (Schwalbe 2019; Dorner 2021).

5.4 Collective Dominance

If there would be increasing evidence of collusive outcomes on markets where algorithmic pricing has become widespread, Article 102 TFEU could also potentially provide an avenue for imposing antitrust law sanctions. Article 102 TFEU prohibits "[a]ny abuse by one or more undertakings of a dominant position within the internal market or in a substantial part of it [. . . .] so far as it may affect trade between Member States". While this provision has most often be applied to a single dominant undertaking, it also prohibits abuse of dominance by several undertakings that collectively hold a position of dominance.

The standard of proof of showing that there is collective dominance has somewhat converged with the requirement of showing coordinated effects or, in other words the likelihood of tacit collusion, from mergers (Mezzanotte 2010; Petit 2012; Jones et al. 2019, p. 284). In order to show that the conditions of collective dominance (or coordinated effects from a merger) can be established and sustained, the EU General Court established in the *Airtours* case three necessary conditions[29,34] First, the degree of transparency on the given market needs to be high so to allow market players to monitor each other's conduct. Second, there needs to be a retaliation mechanism in place that is capable of deterring or punishing deviating conduct, i.e. the undercutting of prices. Third, neither customers nor potential competitors could counteract the collusive strategy. The existence of buyer power, for example could be a factor that would undermine tacit collusion.

In addition, there needs to be an abuse to establish a violation of Article 102 TFEU. Article 102 (a) TFEU gives as an example of abuse "directly or indirectly imposing unfair purchase or selling prices or other unfair trading conditions". If the conditions of collective dominance could be established through pricing algorithms, the charging of supra-competitive prices could then constitute abuse for being an

---

[33] Along similar lines, see Case C-74/14 *Eturas and Others.*

[34] Case T-342/99 *Airtours.* See also EU Commission (2004). Horizontal Merger Guidelines, 2004/C 31/03, 45–57.

unfair price. So far, however, there is very little case law on unfair prices in the EU, and even less so on unfair prices as a collective abuse of dominance (Jones et al. 2019, p. 696).

6 Comparative Legal Analysis of Algorithmic Pricing Situations

When it comes to the assessment of algorithmic pricing, the application of antitrust law both in the US and the EU turns on an appreciation of whether there is coordination by agreement or non-agreement coordination. Easy cases arise where algorithms are deployed by express agreement between competitors, with a design to coordinate price or other competitively sensitive terms. This should in all cases be illegal *per se* (US Law) or a restriction of competition by object (EU law) and, as in the Amazon posters cases, subject to criminal prosecution and appropriate private enforcement.

In the case of coordination by algorithm, just as with non-algorithmic coordination, a proof problem arises. Observed coordination may be by agreement, giving rise to *per se* treatment (above), or by non-agreement, leading both to questions (1) whether non-agreement coordination aided by algorithms is somehow different, and (2) whether coordination by algorithms can rise to the level of agreement, even if not originally animated by agreement. As to this second question, under the current state of US antitrust law, the mere deployment of an algorithm which, through machine learning, engages with another algorithm through a series of exchanges and commitments that can be likened to "agreement," is unlikely to give rise to liability. This situation is similar in the EU, albeit price signaling by pricing algorithms could under certain circumstances be interpreted as a form of concerted action. This is one place where experience and empirical study may highlight features of algorithms that are inconsistent with competitive outcomes, providing a basis for enforcement that does not currently exist. The incremental evidence that is building up from experiments run e.g. by Calvano et al. (2019, 2020) and the Swedish Competition Authority (Konkurrensverket 2021), and others, which try to approximate, step-by-step, real market conditions in which AI pricing tools are deployed are an important component. For now, as oligopoly theory would predict, the symmetry of agents is a factor conductive to collusion, but as the Swedish Competition Authority shows, it is not a necessary condition for algorithmic tacit collusion to arise (Konkurrensverket 2021). In addition, traditional factors in competitive analysis as, e.g., entry barriers remain valid with algorithms: when the algorithm can take threat of entry into account, prices will be lower (Konkurrensverket 2021). All initial evidence seems to point in the direction that cases of algorithmic collusion will have to be treated on a case-by-case basis. Their evaluation will be highly dependent on the strategies or policies programmed into or developed by the algorithms.

As to the first question above, the concerns for coordinated outcomes requires an analysis of how to analyze algorithmic pricing. The remedial problem animating the historic debate over challenging non-agreement coordination is equally relevant in the context of non-agreement coordination through algorithms. The more draconian remedies available under US law, including criminal penalties and treble-damages liability, would be inappropriate if applied to an independent decision to deploy a pricing algorithm. Likewise, analysis under the rule of reason would be appropriate, leaving the burden of showing both harm to competition and—where appropriate—the possibility of a less restrictive alternative, on the agency or private enforcer. Sanctions in government enforcement in this case should be limited to forward-looking injunctive relief (Huffman 2022a). In EU law, with its main focus on public competition enforcement, less radical sanctions could be imposed. Cases involving algorithmic pricing could be initially settled by commitments,[35] wherein the EU Commission could impose behavioral remedies or request changes to algorithmic design. In this way the EU's public enforcement approach, applying more of a regulatory than adversarial lens (Huffman and Schmidt-Kessen 2021), is a better fit for the current state of uncertainty with regard to the novel technologies at issue.

Even under a cautious enforcement approach, however, what forward-looking injunctive relief might be appropriate is unclear. Much as Turner (1962) argued, a prohibition of independent profit-maximizing behavior is problematic. The most promising intervention is to challenge features of pricing algorithms that implicate the most concerning of the facilitating practices, whether information sharing or other, identified by Clark (1983), Dibadj (2010), and Page (2017). Disclosures of competitively sensitive information, whether by human or by algorithm, are correlated with coordinated outcomes and should be subject to challenge, with questions of temporality (future, present, or past) and breadth (public or disclosed to competitors only) animating the analysis. Where those disclosures happen by agreement, they should ordinarily be subject to challenge. Other agreements that increase homogeneity or transparency, facilitating non-agreement coordination by algorithm, are likewise concerning. Cooperation among competitors in selecting and programming an algorithm should be considered a facilitating practice and subject to a high degree of scrutiny, likely leading to a challenge—although as with other discussions of business practices, there may be efficiency justifications that will need to be indulged. As empirical results become available to support this, courts and enforcers should be open to interposing presumptions, shifting the burden to justify a particular use to the firm employing an algorithm.[36] Efficiency consideration would equally play a role under EU competition law, both to determine whether the deployment of algorithmic pricing should be categorized as a restriction of competition by effect under Article 101 (1) TFEU (which would require showing of

---

[35] Article 9 Regulation 1/2003.

[36] This is an application of what in the US system is called the "quick look" or "abbreviated rule of reason."

anti-competitive effects on the market from the conduct) and whether it can benefit from an efficiency exemption under Article 101 (3) TFEU.

Merger review provides an opportunity to check changes in market structure or other impacts that may facilitate coordination by algorithm, which is otherwise not subject to challenge under the Sherman Act. In the US, such review should follow the existing analysis outlined in *Horizontal Merger Guidelines* Section 7. In particular, structural presumptions exist as a check on concentration levels (*Guidelines*, section 7.2). As empirical evidence is developed, it is possible those presumptions will need to be strengthened if the arguments of Gal (2019) that algorithmic pricing leads to collusion more readily than non-algorithmic pricing prove to be accurate. Mergers in markets with a history of collusion or non-agreement coordination are already subject to scrutiny based on that history (*Guidelines*, section 7.2), and in the case of markets characterized by pricing algorithms enforcers should investigate whether algorithms were adopted as a means to facilitate coordination and whether past practice with algorithmic pricing in that industry led to outcomes causing concern. Mergers that tend to eliminate the "maverick," perhaps the firm that continues not to employ industry standard software in its pricing decisions or perhaps the firm that programs its software to compete more aggressively than the industry norm, should be subject to increased scrutiny on that basis as well (*Guidelines*, section 7.2).[37] Reflecting the substantial convergence of merger enforcement policy, the same reasoning would apply under the EU Merger Regulation (Akman and Garrod 2011).[38]

Under EU law, the problems addressed under merger law could alternatively be dealt with under and abuse of collective dominance under Article 102 TFEU. This would allow competition authorities to intervene also in the absence of a merger, but it would require a competition enforcer to show that the market in question has the structural conditions that are thought to be conductive to collusion under the *Airtours* criteria discussed above. If, in the case of a concentrated market, pricing algorithms indeed contributed to more transparency, and there was no significant buyer power or other countervailing factor, the question whether algorithms could engage in retaliation in cases of price cuts would define whether collective dominance can be established. For this to happen, algorithms would likely need to be relatively simple and would need symmetric learning capacities to potentially be able prove a position of collective dominance. The question would then still remain whether there is collective abuse and at which level supra-competitive prices would become unfair prices under Article 102(a) TFEU.[39] In the US, collective dominance, or "shared monopoly,"as a theory of harm has not been seriously considered in more than 40 years; one question will be whether the

---

[37] *E.g., United States v. H&R Block Inc.*, 833 F. Supp. 2d 36 (D.D.C. 2011).

[38] See Regulation 139/2004 and EU Commission (2004). Horizontal Merger Guidelines 2004/C 31/03.

[39] On the difficulty of establishing unfair prices.

efficiency of algorithmic decisions might provide a basis for re-examining such a theory in the coming years.

Given the greater constraints of the Sherman Act relative to Articles 101 and 102 TFEU, a US-law analog is the so-called "stand-alone" action under FTC Act section 5 challenging conduct as an "unfair method of competition." Resort to the FTC Act is a common solution advocated by scholars identifying concerns not subject to challenge under existing law of Section 1 (e.g., Dibadj 2010, pp. 606–608). Such an approach is most frequently identified with the FTC's *Ethyl Corp.* Prosecution.[40] *Ethyl Corp.* was reversed on appeal to the federal court of appeals, which held that independent unilateral conduct by firms did not violate the FTC Act, partly on the basis of insufficient proof of an instance of conduct that led to the observed outcomes. The possibility of identifying adoption of algorithmic terms empirically shown to be uniquely pernicious as a way to satisfy the court of appeals' requirement remains.

7 Voices of Policy Makers and Future Outlook

The issue of algorithmic collusion has not escaped the attention of enforcers and policymakers. Broadly summarized, policy responses, in public reports or submissions to multi-jurisdictional committees, reflect both (1) confidence in existing antitrust rules to attack anti-competitive practices and outcomes caused by use of algorithms, and (2) caution with regard to novel theories of enforcement in the absence of real-world evidence of harm caused by the adoption of algorithms. Based on the strength of the theoretical concerns, but the weak evidence of real-world effects, the right approach will continue to be watchful caution on the part of enforcers and policymakers, who should seek to develop evidence of market-level effects to develop their regulatory toolkits. In addition, the current state of substantial parity of analysis across jurisdictions presents a unique opportunity for inter-jurisdictional cooperation.

Existing communications can be described as more, moderately, and less aggressive in their analysis and anticipated treatment of algorithmic pricing. The Autoridade da Concorrência (2019) report on *Digital Ecosystems, Big Data and Algorithms* may be the most suggestive of need for oversight and intervention. With regard to the most dramatic concerns, exemplified by the laboratory experience of Q-learning algorithms "colluding" without active human intervention, *Digital Ecosystems* correctly notes this has not been shown to have happened in a real-world context, but careful attention is appropriate (Autoridade da Concorrência 2019, pp. 270–275). In particular, *Digital Ecosystems* notes firm responsibility for

---

[40] *In re Ethyl Corp.*, 101 F.T.C. 425 (1983), *reversed, Ethyl Corp. v. FTC*, 729 F.2d 128 (2d Cir. 1984).

effects caused by algorithms they deploy and the possibility of requirements to test and verify to ensure compliance (Autoridade da Concorrência 2019, pp. 274–275).

The UK Competition and Markets Authority (CMA) published a Report in 2021 on Algorithms (CMA 2021). On the issue of possible risks for markets from algorithmic tacit collusion, it concluded that empirical evidence is so scarce that no clear conclusions can be drawn. The report by the French Autorite de la Concurrence and Bundeskartellamt (2019) on *Algorithms and Competition* predicts the success of existing rules and enforcement approaches in most cases, and identifies a lack of evidence for the autonomous coordination concerns, recognizing also that tacit collusion is not subject to challenge under EU law (Autorite de la Concurrence and Bundeskartellamt 2019, pp. 26–60). In summary remarks, *Algorithms and Competition* states that existing competition law regimes are sufficient for the task, prior cases involving algorithms have not taxed authorities' expertise, and legal changes should wait for a clearer picture of the types of cases that may be encountered in the future (Autorite de la Concurrence and Bundeskartellamt 2019, p. V). The Canadian Competition Bureau was an early mover with its discussion paper, *Big Data and Innovation* (2017), where it highlighted concerns for post-merger coordination, perhaps from the acquisition of a maverick, and increased transparency through facilitating practices (Competition Bureau Canada 2017, pp. 20–21). However, the CCB did not see any intervention short of price control that would be appropriate (Competition Bureau Canada 2017, pp. 20–21) and instead noted the enforcement experience where traditional cartel agreements were reached using digital tools, including algorithms programmed by agreement between the cartelists (Competition Bureau Canada 2017, pp. 19–21).

The so-far limited reaction from the US is the least suggestive of need for intervention. In 2018, the US antitrust agencies cooperated in a report to the OECD Competition Committee in which they highlighted their views on algorithmic collusion.[41] The US agencies noted the scholarly interest in collusive outcomes reached by algorithm, and noted one of the particular features – speed of response and adjustment – frequently highlighted in those scholarly analyses (DOJ/FTC OECD, para. 18).[42] Substantial shifts in enforcement priorities following political change (Huffman 2022b, pp. 4–6, 6, 8–9) can be expected to bring a different lens to the problem, but we are still lacking definitive pronouncements showing revised goals.

Multi-jurisdictional committees have much promise in facilitating cooperative development of expertise and rules. Both the OECD and ICN have been engaged in the question of coordination by algorithm. For example, the OECD *Algorithms and Collusion Report* (2017) canvassed literature and enforcement experience with

---

[41] Implications of E-commerce for Competition Policy - Note by the United States, at paras. 18–20 (6 June 2018).

[42] An extensive report by a committee of the US Congress considered algorithms only by reference to concerns for dominance and did not discuss the impact of algorithmic pricing on coordinated outcomes. *See* Judicary Report (2020).

regard to collusive outcomes reached by algorithm and observed, "algorithms may permit firms to replace explicit collusion with tacit co-ordination." (OECD 2017, section 4.3). In light of this concern, the OECD *Report* highlighted the possibility of "revisiting" "the notion of agreement", possibly considering rapid price adjustment leading to monopoly outcomes to be treated as "agreement", as could parallel pricing by algorithms which acts as a signaling device (OECD 2017, section 5.2). In a scoping paper, "Big Data and Cartels" (2020), the ICN identifies the same concerns for non-agreement coordination, based on rapid repeated transactions, as well as the unproven possibility of deep-learning algorithms achieving computerized agreement, and also poses the question whether definitions of agreement need to be revised when algorithms operate autonomously (ICN 2020, pp. 12–17).

Moving early to distill the state of the learning to amendments to guidelines promises benefits. It will enable counsel to better advise firms on their deployment of increasingly sophisticated software. As one example, the Competition Bureau of Canada's newly revised *Competitor Collaboration Guidelines* (2021) recognizes "agreements between competitors to use a common pricing algorithm" as a cartel agreement, adding the caution that "conduct that amounts to conscious parallelism is not sufficient (Competition Bureau Canada 2021, section 2.4.1 & n.15). Empirical research into the effects of pricing algorithms, taking into account both the substantial efficiency benefits and the well-theorized concerns, should be a first priority investment for agencies or multi-jurisdictional groups, perhaps through grants to research teams. Much agency expertise is developed through case investigation and prosecution, and studying the effects of algorithmic pricing as part of merger and non-merger investigations should be a priority. Those agencies that have powers to carry out sector inquiries, like the EU Commission[43] and the National Competition Authorities in the EU Member States, as well as the analogous US FTC Section 6 authority (US Federal Trade Commission 1981),[44] could use these powers to acquire more evidence about the state of the art of pricing algorithms and their market impact (Konkurransetilsynet 2021).[45] Enforcement efforts raising these issues should include technologists to complement the existing reliance on economic and management expertise. After greater experience and understanding is developed, rulemaking or legislation targeting the most pernicious uses of technology, likely to be those that produce transparency among competitors but not in the market generally, should be on the table.

---

[43] Article 17 Regulation 1/2003.

[44] United States Code, Title 15, Section 46. Page (2009) outlines this procedural advantage that is unique to the FTC in US law.

[45] A recent example of such a sector inquiry is a recent Report by the Norwegian Competition Authority surveying the use of monitoring and pricing algorithms on Norwegian markets.

8 Conclusion

Substantial scholarly attention and, more recently, work by enforcers and policy-makers in understanding the effects of broad deployment of algorithms to establish prices has not produced a definitive resolution of the degree of the concern or the nature of the appropriate intervention. Both sides—technical development of pricing software, and the establishment of toolkits for investigation and enforcement, continue to develop. In this chapter we bring to the front several key areas of interest for scholars, advocates, and enforcers.

The question of the impact of algorithmic pricing on market outcomes remains unresolved. Theories advanced by early movers among scholars including Mehra, Ezrachi, Stucke, and Gal, have been broadly recognized as worth serious attention by antitrust authorities and policy-makers. The more challenging questions related to autonomous discovery and response, leading in laboratory experiments to algorithmic collusion, are today not sufficiently proved empirically in real-world settings to give rise to more than cautious concern. Empirical findings are also lacking as to the net effect on competition and consumers of efficiency-enhancing algorithmic decision-making, which also threatens coordinated outcomes. Additional empirical evidence from laboratory and real-world experiments, taking into account the diversity of algorithmic design and the variety in the data sources that could be deployed in the development of algorithmic pricing strategies, is necessary. In particular, a better understanding of the incentives and strategies of developers and adopters of pricing algorithms will improve responses in competition policy and law.

An important observation from our comparative study is the substantial parity in treatment across leading antitrust systems. Jurisdictions on both sides of the Atlantic broadly dislike coordinated outcomes, but recognize the challenge or impossibility of preventing these, if no actual agreement between parties can be proven under the cartel prohibitions (Section 1 and Article 101 TFEU). There are less trodden paths that could be pursued by antitrust enforcers in the US and EU, on the one hand under Section 5 of the FTC Act or through Article 102 TFEU and collective dominance. Nonetheless, without having a sufficient evidence base that would specify if, how, and when pricing algorithms cause competitive harm, it seems premature to consider these potential avenues for antitrust enforcement.

Lastly, the overall observed parity provides substantial opportunity for cross-jurisdictional cooperation in finding successful strategies to combat harm that the law has not historically addressed. Prioritizing these concerns, and employing a mix of study, investigation, prosecution, and reduction to guidelines and law, are the right approaches to ensure both technological innovation and enforcement serves society's interests.

Acknowledgements We would like to thank Raghava Rao Mukkamala for useful conversations about the technical topics in the initial phase of this project and to readers of earlier drafts including Shi Jianzhong and Salil Mehra.

References

Akman P, Garrod L (2011) When are excessive prices unfair? J Compet Law Econ 7:403–426

Assad S, Clark R, Ershov D, Xu L (2020) Algorithmic pricing and competition: empirical evidence from the German retail gasoline market. CESifo Working Paper 8521/2020

Autoridade da Concorrência (2019) Digital ecosystems, big data and algorithms. https://extranet.concorrencia.pt/PesquisAdC/EPR.aspx?IsEnglish=True&Ref=EPR_2019_17. Accessed 22 Apr 2022

Autorite de la Concurrence, Bundeskartellamt (2019) Algorithms and competition. https://www.bundeskartellamt.de/SharedDocs/Publikation/EN/Berichte/Algorithms_and_Competition_Working-Paper.html;jsessionid=273756C5C2CAEA08EA14631B8834F6E7.2_cid378?nn=10739378. Accessed 22 Apr 2022

Calvano E, Calzolari G, Denicolò V, Pastorello S (2019) Algorithmic pricing what implications for competition policy? Rev Ind Organ 55:155–171

Calvano E, Calzolari G, Denicolo V, Pastorello S (2020) Artificial intelligence, algorithmic pricing, and collusion. Am Econ Rev 110:3267–3297

Chen L, Mislove A, Wilson C (2016) An empirical analysis of algorithmic pricing on amazon marketplace. In: Proceedings of the 25th international conference on world wide web. International World Wide Web Conferences Steering Committee, Montréal, Québec, Canada, pp 1339–1349

Clark DS (1983) Price-fixing without collusion: an antitrust analysis of facilitating practices after ethyl corp. Wis Law Rev 1983:887–952

CMA (2018) Pricing algorithms. economic working paper on the use of algorithms to facilitate tacit collusion and personalized pricing. https://assets.publishing.service.gov.uk/government/uploads/system/uploads/attachment_data/file/746353/Algorithms_econ_report.pdf. Accessed 8 Oct 2018

CMA (2021) Algorithms: how they can reduce competition and harm consumers. https://www.gov.uk/government/publications/algorithms-how-they-can-reduce-competition-and-harm-consumers. Accessed 19 Jan 2021

Competition Bureau Canada (2017) Big data and innovation: implications for competition policy in Canada. https://www.competitionbureau.gc.ca/eic/site/cb-bc.Nsf/eng/04304.html. Accessed 22 Apr 2022

Competition Bureau Canada (2021) Competitor collaboration guidelines. https://www.competitionbureau.gc.ca/eic/site/cb-bc.nsf/eng/04582.html#sec03-2. Accessed 22 Apr 2022

Crandall JW, Oudah M, Tennom, Ishowo-Oloko F, Abdallah S, Bonnefon JF, Cebrian M, Shariff A, Goodrich MA, Rahwan I (2018) Cooperating with machines. Nat Commun 9:233

Den Boer AV (2013). Dynamic pricing and learning: Historical origins, current research, and new directions. https://papers.ssrn.com/sol3/papers.cfm?abstract_id=2334429. Accessed 22 Apr 2022

Dibadj R (2010) Conscious parallelism revisited. San Diego Law Rev 47:589–639

Dorner FE (2021) Algorithmic collusion: a critical review. arXiv preprint arXiv:2110.04740

European Commission (2017) Final report on the E-commerce Sector Inquiry, COM(2017) 229 final. https://ec.europa.eu/competition/antitrust/sector_inquiry_final_report_en.pdf. Accessed 10 May 2017

Ezrachi A, Stucke M (2016) Virtual competition. Harvard University Press, Cambridge, Massachusetts

Gal MS (2019) Algorithms as illegal agreements. Berkeley Technol Law J 34:67–118

Gautier A, Ittoo A, Van Cleynenbreugel P (2020) AI algorithms, price discrimination and collusion: a technological, economic and legal perspective. Eur J Law Econ 50:405–435

Green EJ, Marshall RC, Marx LM (2013) Tacit collusion in oligopoly. https://faculty.fuqua.duke.edu/~marx/bio/papers/tacitcollusion.pdf. Accessed 22 Apr 2022

Harrington JE (2018) Developing competition law for collusion by autonomous artificial agents. J Compet Law Econ 14:331–363

Hettich M (2021) Algorithmic collusion: insights from deep learning. https://ssrn.com/abstract=3785966 or https://doi.org/10.2139/ssrn.3785966. Accessed 16 Feb 2021

Huffman M (2008) The necessity of pleading elements in private antitrust conspiracy claims. Univ Pa J Bus Employ Law 10:627–661

Huffman M (2022a) Civil sanctions in antitrust public enforcement. In: Cambridge handbook of competition law sanctions. Cambridge University Press, Cambridge (forthcoming)

Huffman M (2022b) Do today's antitrust institutions accommodate independent expertise? Antitrust Magazing Online Aug. 2022, 1–9

Huffman M, Schmidt-Kessen MJ (2021) Gig platforms as hub-and-spoke arrangements and algorithmic pricing: a comparative EU-US antitrust analysis.. https://papers.ssrn.com/sol3/papers.cfm?abstract_id=3969194. Accessed 22 Apr 2022

Hylton K (2018) Oligopoly pricing and Richard Posner. No. 18-10 Boston University School of Law, Law and Economics Research Paper. https://scholarship.law.bu.edu/faculty_scholarship/272/. Accessed 22 Apr 2022

ICN (2020). Big data and cartels: the impact of digitalization in cartel enforcement. https://www.internationalcompetitionnetwork.org/wp-content/uploads/2020/06/CWG-Big-Data-scoping-paper.pdf. Accessed 22 Apr 2022

Ittoo A, Petit N (2017) Algorithmic pricing agents and tacit collusion: a technological perspective. In: Jacquemin H, De Streel A (eds) L'intelligence artificielle et le droit. Larcier, Bruxelles, pp 241–256

Jones A, Sufrin B, Niamh D (2019) EU competition law: text, cases, and materials. Oxford University Press, Oxford

Kaysen C, Turner D (1959) Antitrust policy: an economic and legal analysis. Harvard University Press, Cambridge, Mass

Klein T (2021) Autonomous algorithmic collusion: Q-learning under sequential pricing. Rand J Econ 52:538–558

Konkurransetilsynet (2021) What effect can algorithms have on competition? https://konkurransetilsynet.no/research/nca-reports/?lang=en. Accessed 22 Apr 2022

Konkurrensverket (2021) Collusion in algorithmic pricing. https://www.konkurrensverket.se/informationsmaterial/rapportlista/collusion-in-algorithmic-pricing/. Accessed 22 Apr 2022

Kovacic WE, Marshall RC, Marx LM, White HL (2011) Plus factors and agreement in antitrust law. Mich Law Rev 110:393–436

Leibo JZ, Zambaldi V, Lanctot M, Marecki J, Graepel T (2017) Multi-agent reinforcement learning in sequential social dilemmas. arXiv preprint arXiv:1702.03037

Mehra SK (2016) Antitrust and the Robo-seller: competition in the time of algorithms. Minn Law Rev 100:1323–1375

Mezzanotte FE (2010) Interpreting the boundaries of collective dominance in article 102 TFEU. Eur Bus Law Rev 21:519–537

Miklós-Thal J, Tucker C (2019) Collusion by algorithm: does better demand prediction facilitate coordination between sellers? Manag Sci 65:1552–1561

Montantes J (2020) 3 Reasons to use random forest over a neural network. https://towardsdatascience.com/3-reasons-to-use-random-forest-over-a-neural-network-comparing-machine-learning-versus-deep-f9d65a154d89#:~:text=Both%20the%20Random%20Forest%20and,are%20exclusive%20to%20Deep%20Learning. Accessed 22 Apr 2022

Nicholson C (2021) A beginner's guide to neural networks and deep learning. https://wiki.pathmind.com/neural-network. Accessed 22 Apr 2022

OECD (2017) Algorithms and collusion. https://www.oecd.org/competition/algorithms-and-collusion.htm. Accessed 22 Apr 2022

Page W (2009) The FTC's procedural advantage in discovering concerted action. http://ssrn.com/abstract=1342783. Accessed 22 Apr 2022

Page WH (2017) Tacit agreement under section 1 of the sherman act. Antitrust Law J 81:593–640

Petit N (2012) The oligopoloy problem in EU competition law. In: Lianos I, Geradin D (eds) Research handbook in European competition law. Edward Elgar, Cheltenham, pp 259–349

Petit N (2017) Antitrust and artificial intelligence: a research agenda. J Eur Compet Law Pract 8:361–362

Posner R (1969) Oligopoly and the antitrust laws: a suggested approach. Stanf Law Rev 21:1562–1606

Russell S, Norvig P (1995) Artificial intelligence: a modern approach. Prentice Hall, Englewood Cliffs

Schwalbe U (2019) Algorithms, machine learning, and collusion. J Compet Law Econ 14:568–607

Stigler GJ (1964) A theory of oligopoly. J Polit Econ 72:44–61

Turner DF (1962) The definition of agreement under the Sherman act: conscious parallelism and refusals to deal. Harv Law Rev 75:655–706

US Federal Trade Commission (1981) A history of section 6 report writing at the federal trade commission, office of policy planning report. https://www.ftc.gov/sites/default/files/documents/reports/history-section-6-report-writing-federal-trade-commission/231984.pdf. Accessed 22 Apr 2022

Whinston MD (2006) Lectures on antitrust economics. MIT Press, Cambridge

Open Access This chapter is licensed under the terms of the Creative Commons Attribution 4.0 International License (http://creativecommons.org/licenses/by/4.0/), which permits use, sharing, adaptation, distribution and reproduction in any medium or format, as long as you give appropriate credit to the original author(s) and the source, provide a link to the Creative Commons license and indicate if changes were made.

The images or other third party material in this chapter are included in the chapter's Creative Commons license, unless indicated otherwise in a credit line to the material. If material is not included in the chapter's Creative Commons license and your intended use is not permitted by statutory regulation or exceeds the permitted use, you will need to obtain permission directly from the copyright holder.

The "Artificial Intelligence Act" Proposal on European e-Justice Domains Through the Lens of User-Focused, User-Friendly and Effective Judicial Protection Principles

Joana Covelo de Abreu

Abstract European e-Justice aims at developing electronic tools to allow national jurisdictions and ECJ to contact through reliable and secure digital channels. The 2019–2023 e-Justice Strategy underlined some new EU general principles directly developed under e-Justice paradigm, deserving particular attention the ones concerning user-focused and user-friendly dimensions. As 2021 is the year where justice digitalization will be under discussion, there is a need to understand how AI will impact on justice fields, not only in MS judicial systems (EU functional jurisdictions, when applying EU law), but also in ECJ, as this disruptive technology is being discussed. The Proposal for an AI Act stresses AI systems intended for the administration of justice should be classified as high-risk, considering their potentially significant impact on effective judicial protection domains. Therefore, this paper intends to understand the need to fully stress AI human-centric approach on justice fields, so effective judicial protection can be deepened through user-focused and user-friendly principles; and to scrutinize, from the e-Justice standpoint, how the Proposal for an AI Act must further address judicial instrumental usage of AI systems, so judicial independence, procedural rights and access to justice are observed in the EU jurisdictional setting.

Integrated member and researcher at JusGov – Research Centre for Justice and Governance (UMINHO), where the author also integrates its Directive Committee. Academic Coordinator of the Jean Monnet Module eUjust "EU Procedure and credits' claims: approaching electronic solutions under e-Justice paradigm".

J. Covelo de Abreu (✉)
School of Law – University of Minho (UMINHO), Braga, Portugal
e-mail: jabreu@direito.uminho.pt

© The Author(s) 2024
H. Sousa Antunes et al. (eds.), *Multidisciplinary Perspectives on Artificial Intelligence and the Law*, Law, Governance and Technology Series 58,
https://doi.org/10.1007/978-3-031-41264-6_21

1 E-Justice Paradigm and the Trend of Digitalization of Justice: The Time Is Now for Tackling Artificial Intelligence Pros and Cons

All European institutions are engaged on further developing European e-Justice. Insofar, the Council has been addressing it, since 2007, in a coordinated way, firstly by setting a Working Party on the theme (See, for further development, Storskrubb 2017, p. 276) and, in sequence, by presenting three Action Plans on European e-Justice: from 2009 to 2013; from 2014 to 2018; and the latter, still being developed, from 2019 to 2023 (see Council of the European Union 2019b).

In this sense, European e-Justice "aims at improving access to justice in a pan-European context and is developing and integrating information and communication technologies into access to legal information and the workings of judicial systems" bearing in mind that "the efficient functioning of the judiciary in the Member States" can also relate to the implementation of digital components and a new technological approach (see Council of the European Union 2019b, p. 1, paragraph 1). Particularly trying to establish future guidelines (to be met until 2023), the Council, under "Evolutivity" domains, understood its Action Plan (see Council of the European Union 2019a) "should be flexible with respect to future developments, be they legal or technical" (see Council of the European Union 2019b, p. 4, paragraph 29), stressing that "[l]egal tech domains such as Artificial Intelligence (AI) [. . .], for example, should be closely monitored, in order to identify and seize opportunities with a potential positive impact on e-Justice" (see Council of the European Union 2019b, p. 4, paragraph 30). In this context, this European institution advanced Artificial Intelligence "could have a positive impact on e-Justice, for example by increasing efficiency and trust" despite acknowledging that "[a]ny future development and deployment of such technologies must take risks and challenges into account, in particular [. . .] to data protection and ethics" (see Council of the European Union 2019b, p. 4, paragraph 31).

In the same sense, the European Commission recently devoted its attention to the matter, understanding that "[a]ccess to justice needs to be maintained and to keep pace with change, including the digital transformation affecting all aspects of our lives" (see European Commission 2020a, p. 1). Focusing on Artificial Intelligence—one of the tools equated in this institutional "toolbox"–, the European Commission understood that "the emergence of new technology brings with it the need for ongoing assessment of its impact, in particular as regards fundamental rights and data protection" (see European Commission 2020a, p. 21). Insofar, despite understanding Artificial Intelligence potential on justice domains, "such as making use of information in new and highly efficient ways, and [. . .] reducing the duration of judicial proceedings", that European institution also stressed that "the potential for opacity or biases can also lead to risks and challenges for the respect and effective enforcement of fundamental rights, including [. . .] the right to an effective remedy and fair trial" (see European Commission 2020a, p. 10). In fact, Artificial Intelligence tools and mechanisms pose several questions, demanding

The "Artificial Intelligence Act" Proposal on European e-Justice Domains. . . 399

further transparency, "human oversight, accuracy and robustness" (see European Commission 2020a, p. 10) so fundamental rights protection, the rule of law and, particularly, effective judicial protection demands are promoted.

In this sense, European e-Justice has, so far, been able to play "a double emblematic role":

- On one hand, "as a means to implement interoperable communication systems, so jurisdictional articulation can be facilitated, in an institutional level" (see Covelo De Abreu 2019, p. 300): under European e-Justice paradigm, the Proposal for a Regulation concerning the e-CODEX system (see European Commission 2020b; See, for further development, Covelo De Abreu 2020) has been presented as a means to further develop interoperable channels between national judicial authorities as long as it also envisaged promoting digital interactions between national courts and the Court of Justice of the European Union (ECJ), through eCuria application (See, for further development, Costeira 2021). These converging trends led to the sediment of a wider notion of European Union Procedure (focusing on both ECJ and national courts' roles in the European legal and jurisdictional order) and an atmosphere of an effective judicial integration, even promoting a greater proximity between judicial cooperation in civil and in criminal matters (Silveira et al. 2020);
- On the other hand, e-Justice has been acting "as a referral to effective judicial protection of those rights given to individuals by the European legal order, through new approaches and updates" (see Covelo De Abreu 2019, p. 300): under that paramount, research must be conducted so Artificial Intelligence potentialities and dangers can be fully understood, particularly by conducting a decisive distinction between (a) Instrumental Systems of Artificial Intelligence and (b) Decision Systems of Artificial Intelligence in judicial domains. Based on this distinction, risk's classification of Artificial Intelligence systems might be conducted in concrete terms, as there must be a clear approach on which systems applicable to justice fields must be submitted to stricter obligations as deemed to those of high-risk. Furthermore, these systems will also have to be understood under Artificial Intelligence human-centric approach, so effective judicial protection must be achieved, questioning whether user-focused and user-friendly principles can deepen its observance.

2 Artificial Intelligence Systems Intended to the Administration of Justice

The use of Artificial Intelligence mechanisms in the justice field can pose beneficial and prejudicial challenges on effective judicial protection. However, the measures must be designed and taken in a European level as it "could avoid duplication of national efforts and create significant synergies" and "[i]t could also ensure interoperability and ultimately transform good pilot projects into EU-wide solutions" (see

European Commission 2020a, p. 10). Furthermore, as Artificial Intelligence systems require relevant data and their training, the European Union level is the perfect setting for achieving their usage "in full compliance with personal data protection rules" (see European Commission 2020a, p. 11).

Departing from the European Commission's sensitivities, despite advantages of introducing Artificial Intelligence-based applications in the justice system are palpable, "there are also considerable risks associated with their use for automated decision-making and 'predictive policing' / 'predictive justice'" (see European Commission 2020a, p. 11).

It is settled that a part of "the work of courts and judges is to process information; parties bring information to the court, transformations take place in the course of the procedure, and the outcome is also information"; i.e., "[n]ot all of this information processing is complex customization" (see Reiling 2020, p. 2 of 10) before court proceedings and there are some scenarios where Artificial Intelligence systems are being developed. In this sense, its general use could be established on three major topics, as it is intended to only focus on effective and / or potential systems that are available before courts and to be used in the procedural course running before them: Artificial Intelligence systems on (1) organising information; (2) mobilising useful pre-existing case-law; and (3) forecasting decision trends.

2.1 Artificial Intelligence Systems on Organising Information

Artificial Intelligence systems can be put into use on "[r]ecognising patterns in text documents and files" (see Reiling 2020, p. 3 of 10).

A similar use (despite extrapolated for further extrajudicial and judicial operations) can be already found in the United States of America (USA): eDiscovery is "an automated investigation of electronic information for discovery, before the start of the court procedure", using machine learning "which [. . .] is capable of extracting the relevant parts from a large amount of information" but demanding parties to agree on "which search terms and coding they use" and depending on the judge's assessment and confirmation of the agreement (see Reiling 2020, p. 3 of 10).

Also focusing on organising procedural information, the Ministry of Justice, in Portugal, was developing (until December 2020) the project "Magistratos", particularly focusing on administrative, tax and judicial courts. This system aimed at delivering "a unique interface for magistrates (including prosecutors), enabling the indexation of documents and information which are part of a judicial case", allowing "fast search of documents and contents" (see European Commission 2020c). "Magistratos" was a pilot-project that could provide several tools on how to organise procedural information.

Furthermore, in this topic—and taking these two systems into account –, it could also be equated the development of a system that was able to detect coincident facts' allegations (in written pleadings) between different parties in the litigation.

The "Artificial Intelligence Act" Proposal on European e-Justice Domains... 401

This would help judges to settle the facts that are agreed between the parties, so they could not be issue of proof in judgement sessions, for instance. This tool would save procedural time and it would allow the judge's control—maintaining and deepening his/her independence and impartiality as s/he could analyse all the parties' pleadings in order to check and complement the algorithm's choices—and the parties possibility of questioning the results, in a due process of law, requesting the correction or the complement of the system's selection.

2.2 Artificial Intelligence Systems on Mobilising Useful Pre-Existing Case-Law

Artificial Intelligence would be useful on determining if there were already previous decisions of different or the same court that is now facing the litigation before a case with similar legal framework. It would help judges to more hastily being able to find pre-existing decisions and to understand if the legal grounding could be mobilised in the present case. In this case, the Artificial Intelligence system could have a more decisive role than the nowadays usual search engines based on Boolean techniques, that sometimes are not accurately thought to devise relevant case-law (based on the terms used in the research of results). Furthermore, it would also allow judges to more efficiently contact with previous jurisprudence that otherwise they could never be able to even know.

This system would be an instrumental tool to the judicial work without determining an affection of judicial independence or other effective judicial protection dimensions as this tool should be used under user-control principle and it would be user-focused and user-friendly, as a vivification of human-centric approach on Artificial Intelligence systems.

2.3 Artificial Intelligence Systems on Forecasting Decision Trends (Predictive Justice)

This might be the most visible feature of Artificial Intelligence use in justice domains since when this technology "claims to be able to predict court decisions attracts a lot of interest". However, the expression "predictive justice" did not go without discussion as "the outcome of the prediction algorithms is neither justice nor predictive" (see Reiling 2020, p. 4 of 10), what determined that latest debates led to preferring the term "forecast" since "[t]he outcome looks more like a weather forecast than like an established fact" particularly because "court proceedings risk having an unpredictable outcome" (see Reiling 2020, p. 4 of 10).

Therefore, there are several applications on forecasting courts' decisions, but they are mainly developed under lawyers' standpoint (See, for an extended list of applications, Faggella 2021). Focusing on the procedural standpoint, some USA experiences implemented in courts might showcase this "technology can have limitations when implemented in the judiciary" (see Cabral 2020, p. 115).

In fact, one of mostly discussed issue concerning Artificial Intelligence is the phenomenon of algorithm bias and/or opacity: "the algorithm presents biased results in a repeated way" which mainly is an outcome of the data set used in the learning process of the machine learning algorithm (see Cabral 2020, p. 115). In fact, what defines machine learning is the machine ability to learn from itself through data that are provided to it or that it can collect from daily interactions (See, for further development, Domingues 2015). It is not difficult to imagine if a biased algorithm trend affects Artificial Intelligence tools being used on justice fields and, particularly, that can directly or indirectly impact on judicial decisions.

Take Correctional Offender Management Profiling for Alternative Sanctions (with acronym COMPAS) for example: many academic studies, in several research fields, have been reflecting on how this tool can have led to some actual discrimination affecting individual freedom. COMPAS was used, in practice, in the USA, by some criminal judges to assess "the recidivism risk of defendants or convicted persons, in decisions on pre-trial detention, sentencing or early release" and it used "data from the criminal record and from a questionnaire with 137 questions" (see Reiling 2020, p. 5 of 10).

However, ProPublica—"an independent, non-profit newsroom" (see ProPublica 2021)—published an article on May 23, 2016 (see Angwin et al. 2016) where it exposed what it perceived as a "machine bias" since COMPAS appeared to lead to a higher rate of recidivism being attributed to African Americans in opposition to Caucasians. There were some publications that disagreed from these conclusions, as NorthPointe, Inc.—the developer of COMPAS—taking the lead (See, for further development, Dieterich et al. 2016; Barenstein 2019).

The point being made is that algorithm bias and/or opacity can be "transversal" and, in judicial fields, "the impact of these [bias / opaque] decisions can affect the most pivotal sphere of citizens' rights" as there is a "deterioration of judicial protection due to the inadequate use of algorithms" (see Cabral 2020, p. 117).

Furthermore, taking into consideration Commission's worries—based on stakeholders' wide participation–, Artificial Intelligence "applications in the justice area as a possible high-risk use case" would be those that could be a "part of decision-making processes" as they could assume "significant effects on the rights of persons" (see European Commission 2020a, p. 10), bearing in mind, particularly, that "[w]here machine learning is used, the risks of biased outcomes and potential discrimination [. . .] are high", paying "special attention [. . .] to the quality of the training data used, including its representativeness and relevance in relation to the purpose and the context of the intended application and how these systems are designed and developed to ensure that they can be used in full compliance with fundamental rights" (see European Commission 2020a, p. 11).

Taking these three main topics under attention, we can come to the conclusion that Artificial Intelligence systems used (1) on organising information and (2) on mobilising pre-existing case-law can be categorised as Instrumental Systems of

The "Artificial Intelligence Act" Proposal on European e-Justice Domains... 403

Artificial Intelligence in justice fields as they play a role in preparing the procedure, its information and, in a more extensive way, a potential draft of segments to be used in the legal grounding (based on previous jurisprudence). However, Artificial Intelligence systems (3) on forecasting decision trends can be understood as a Decision System of Artificial Intelligence as it can directly impact on judicial decision and, furthermore, on the formation of the judge's personal perception of the case brought before him/her.

However, in both concepts, risks can be posed by using Artificial Intelligence, existing the need to understand if those systems can be categorised, under the Proposal for an Artificial Intelligence Act (see European Commission 2021b), as high-risk, fulfilling the obligations steaming from that classification.

3 High-Risk Classification of Artificial Intelligence Systems: Human-Centric Approach at the Service of Effective Judicial Protection Domains

Artificial Intelligence was legally addressed from an ethical approach since it departs from the idea fundamental rights operate as moral and juridical rights whose observance provides promising basis to identify abstract principles and ethical values to be operationalized in its context (See, for further development and reflexion, Silveira et al. 2021, p. 337). The main concern about Artificial Intelligence evolution and impact on legal fields is its potential to affect the "respect and effective enforcement of fundamental rights" (see European Commission 2020a, p. 10) which demands understanding its impact on effective judicial protection, "including [. . .] the right to an effective remedy and fair trail" (see European Commission 2020a, p. 10).

Substantiating the Regulation Proposal for an Artificial Intelligence Act, the Commission stressed "[i]t is in the Union interest to preserve the EU's technological leadership and to ensure that Europeans can benefit from new technologies developed and functioning according to Union values, fundamental rights and principles" as it is a proposal "based on EU values and fundamental rights and aims to give people and other users the confidence to embrace AI-based solutions, while encouraging businesses to develop them" (see European Commission 2021b, p. 1).

It is this worry on fully assuring fundamental rights' protection and proclamation before these new technologies that sediments an human-centric approach to Artificial Intelligence: "[r]ules for AI available in the Union market or otherwise affecting people in the Union should be human-centric, so that people can trust that the technology is used in a way that is safe and compliant with the law, including the respect of fundamental rights" (see European Commission 2021b, p. 1). This Proposal understands that "[t]he use of AI with its specific characteristics (e.g. opacity, complexity, dependency on data, autonomous behaviour) can adversely affect a number of fundamental rights enshrined in the EU Charter of Fundamental

Rights" (CFREU) and it "seeks to ensure a high level of protection for those fundamental rights and aims to address various sources of risks through a clearly defined risk-based approach" (see European Commission 2021b, p. 11).

In this sense, the Proposal for an Artificial Intelligence Act looks to be consistent with the fundamental rights regime steaming from the CFREU and "the existing secondary Union legislation" (see European Commission 2021b, p. 5).

The Proposal addresses effective judicial protection dimensions on direct and on indirect terms. In fact, there are several specifications on personal data protection that will play a fundamental role in allowing courts to fully admitting access to justice rights, defence rights, the right to a fair trial within a due time and before impartial and independent judges, among other dimensions of effective judicial protection. Insofar, on personal data protection, the proposal tries to complement General Data Protection Regulation (GDPR)[1] regime but it also operates alongside with, for instance, Directive 2016/680 on the processing of personal data for the purposes of criminal procedures,[2] as it aims at ensuring "the quality of datasets used for the development of AI systems complemented with obligations for testing, risk management, documentation and human oversight throughout the AI systems" (see European Commission 2021b, p. 4), containing "certain specific rules on the protection of individuals with regard to the processing of personal data, notably [imposing] restrictions of the use of AI systems for 'real-time' remote biometric identification in publicly accessible spaces for the purpose of law enforcement" (see European Commission 2021b, p. 6).

Based on data protection demands, Title III of the proposal, concerning high-risk AI systems, "contains specific rules for AI systems that create a high risk to [. . .] fundamental rights of natural persons"; these systems will be able to enter and circulate in the Union's market but they will be subjected to the "compliance with certain mandatory requirements and an ex-ante conformity assessment" (see European Commission 2021b, p. 13).

On the other hand, there was also a concern on promoting effective judicial protection in direct terms and in all of its dimensions, as steaming from article 47 CFREU, focusing particularly on the right to an effective remedy and to a fair trial: as the proposal creates "obligations for ex ante testing, risk management and human oversight", this will facilitate promoting fundamental rights' protection "by minimising the risk of erroneous or biased AI-assisted decisions in critical areas such as [. . .] law enforcement and the judiciary" (see European Commission 2021b, p. 11). Furthermore, to allow "individuals to exercise their right to an effective remedy

---

[1] See Regulation (EU) 2016/679 of the European Parliament and of the Council of 27 April 2016 on the protection of natural persons with regard to the processing of personal data and on the free movement of such data, and repealing Directive 95/46/EC (General Data Protection Regulation).

[2] See Directive (EU) 2016/680 of the European Parliament and of the Council of 27 April 2016 on the protection of natural persons with regard to the processing of personal data by competent authorities for the purposes of the prevention, investigation, detection or prosecution of criminal offences or the execution of criminal penalties, and on the free movement of such data, and repealing Council Framework Decision 2008/977/JHA.

and to the necessary transparency towards supervision and enforcement authorities", some transparency obligations are predicted without affecting intellectual property rights as it "will be limited only to the minimum necessary information" (see European Commission 2021b, p. 11).

Recital 40 of the Proposal establishes that "[c]ertain AI systems intended for the administration of justice [...] should be classified as high-risk, considering their potential significant impact on democracy, rule of law, individual freedoms as well as the right to an effective remedy and to a fair trial". Furthermore, "to address the risk of potential biases, errors and opacity, it is appropriate to qualify as high-risk AI systems intended to assist judicial authorities in researching and interpreting facts and the law and in applying the law to a concrete set of facts". However, this high-risk classification was thought so it would not be applicable to all Artificial Intelligence systems in administration of justice's fields: "[s]uch qualification should not extend [...] to AI systems intended for purely ancillary administrative activities that do not affect the actual administration of justice in individual cases, such as anonymisation or pseudonymisation of judicial decisions, documents or data, communication between personnel, administrative tasks or allocation of resources". As recitals are used, within the European Union law, as an interpretation referral for articles enshrined in the legislative acts they introduce, there is a need, in this sense, to understand which operations can be outside the scope of this high-risk classification in the administration of justice domains, by conducting a concrete analysis of the legal regime steaming from this proposal.

According to Article 6 (2) of the Proposal and Point 8 (a) of its Annex III, Artificial Intelligence systems on administration of justice are characterised as high-risk. In this sense, high-risk systems have to comply with a risk management system: under Article 9 (2) it consists "of a continuous iterative process run throughout the entire lifecycle of a high-risk AI system, requiring regular systematic updating" and, before the system being placed on the market, the fulfilment of "strict obligations" as there is a requirement for *ex ante* conformity assessments (as one of its great innovative features): (a) "[a]dequate risk assessment and mitigation systems"; (b) "[h]igh quality of the datasets feeding the system to minimise risks and discriminatory outcomes"; (c) "[l]ogging of activity to ensure traceability of results"; (d) "[d]etailed documentation providing all information necessary on the system and its purpose for authorities to assess its compliance"; (e) "[c]lear and adequate information to the user"; (f) "[a]ppropriate human oversight measures to minimise risk"; and (g) "[h]igh level of robustness, security and accuracy" (see European Commission 2021c). When these systems rely on techniques involving the training of models with data, there are particularly demanding terms for training, validation and testing of datasets (Article 10). Technical documentation concerning the system must be drawn up before the system is placed in the market (Article 11) and a record must be kept while the system is operating (Article 12), while fulfilling "transparency [...]; human oversight; and robustness, accuracy and security" (see Maccarthy and Propp 2021) demands. Furthermore, "[a]n additional important innovation is a mandate for a postmarket monitoring system to detect problems in use and to mitigate them" (see Maccarthy and Propp 2021).

Risk classification—adopted in this proposal—was thought to achieve a goal: "to avoid an excessive burden to AI systems and market players associated to them that do not represent a relevant risk on fundamental rights' level" (see Cabral 2021, p. 122).

In this sense, considering Artificial Intelligence systems on organizing information, and taking into consideration the development of the project "Magistratos" by the Portuguese Government, there is a need to understand if the complete system will be classified as high-risk. In fact, accordingly to its institutional description, the project is deemed as an interface available to judges and prosecutors to index documents and information. Taking this part of the system into account, it can be understood as a mere administrative tasks' reliever and, therefore, not needing a high-risk classification. However, "Magistratos" also aims at allowing fast search of documents and contents. Therefore, if these two main operations might be able to impact on how justice is applicable to an individual case, it will be understood as a high-risk system and will have to meet all the requirements steaming from the proposal.

In the same category concerning systems on organizing information, a proposal was advanced: a system that could analyse and detect coincident facts' allegations in the parties' written pleadings, favouring the judge's choice of which facts were already agreed between procedural parties and would not be dependent on further proofs. Conversely, this system ought to be classified as high-risk in the first place because, if perceived by the judge as self-sufficient, it would jeopardize judge's independence and could affect the right to a fair trial. In this context, besides *ex ante* conformity analysis and *ex post* monitoring, high-risk classification would also have an important role to establish stricter rules on transparency, human oversight and accuracy, robustness and security of the system. These features—to be met by the Artificial Intelligence system—are the ones refocusing how the grounding base of legal setting for Artificial Intelligence is its human-centric approach, feature that gains a wider significance when judicial sphere is under discussion. Allowing (and even imposing) human involvement and control, the importance of independent and impartial judges defending the right to a fair trial and the exercise of all procedural rights given to the litigation parties becomes fully accomplished. In the face of such Artificial Intelligence system, this could not be different.

So far, concerning Artificial Intelligence systems on organising information, as Instrumental Systems, they can appear as not posing direct issues to effective judicial protection, particularly because they can be mainly developed to ease administrative burden and to present solutions that mostly impact on administrative functions developed in the judiciary. However, they can also focus on avoiding repetitive and / or mechanic work conducted by judges. When this is the case, those systems (or part of them) might be classified as high-risk; being classified as such, these systems' tonic must be refocused in the anthropological approach of Artificial Intelligence where human-centric model must prevail:

– On one hand, allowing judges to fully exercise their task in independent and impartial terms. This can only be achieved if they are prepared to Artificial

Intelligence systems' use, through active digital literacy because these systems must "be designed with ease of use" and to empower the users, which can only be reached if transparency demands are met and judges are aware of technical operations are conducted (see Council of the European Union 2019b, p. 2, paragraph 11);

- On the other hand, high-risk classification will also allow lawyers to understand the intervention of the Artificial Intelligence systems so, if needed, they can fully exercise the right to action and defence rights of the parties they represent. In this sense, active and passive digital literacy are needed – (i) active literacy to lawyers as they play a vital role as judicial operators, demanding they also understand the functioning behind the Artificial Intelligence system and, insofar, are able to question its "reasoning" in their pleadings and allegations; and (ii) passive literacy to general community so people that can have to go to court also is aware of Artificial Intelligence systems' usage and how they can impact their rights and which means there are to react in proper time. Furthermore, the high-risk classification ought to enhance a trust feeling in the justice system.

Artificial Intelligence systems on mobilizing useful pre-existing case-law were perceived as those systems that could detect previous jurisprudence and, if possible, advance segments of the legal grounding that could be useful to the case pending before a court. In this scenario, Artificial Intelligence system would be classified as high-risk as it could have direct impact on judge's behaviour throughout the procedure and it would only be sufficiently reliable if underwent the assessment before being placed in the market and it was subdued to transparency demands to the users (under Article 13 of the Proposal), human oversight (under Article 14 of the Proposal) and accuracy, robustness and cybersecurity requirements (under Article 15 of the Proposal).

In fact, effective judicial protection—especially the dimension concerning a judgement issued in due time—could be enhanced by a system as this one; but it could only be functional as long judges and parties' lawyers were able to understand how the system works, why those results (and not others) were brought up and that the system was solely acting as a means to organize previous decisions' extracts without undermining judges' whole perception of the litigation and free evaluation of evidence brought before him. Furthermore, the way those extracts are organized—if the system also presents them in this way to the judge—must be intuitively perceptible to the users (in a user-focused and user-friendly approach) and under their control. In this context, organized results could be showcased in an editable format, allowing complete and / or partial dismissal and to be copied and pasted in other file, where the judge's decision was being built from scratch.

Lastly, focusing on Artificial Intelligence systems on forecasting decision trends, European Commission worries must be recalled: it was aware of risks posed by automated-decision making (predictive justice) as it had the most potential on affecting effective judicial protection. As a Decision System, high-risk classification is undoubtably the only possible to set aside those risks as these are systems able to "affect the actual administration of justice in individual cases" (Recital 40 of the Proposal).

Here, human-centric approach of Artificial Intelligence must be recalled as general ethical grounding to Artificial Intelligence legal regime in the European Union. Insofar, decision systems cannot operate as definitive or embedded in utterly and unquestionably truths: these are systems that make decision-making process easier but they do not act as substitutes of human intervention, of human oversight and of general comprehension of the system's functioning. These actions are vital so judicial operators at large can operate and enforce all effective judicial protection dimensions:

– Judges have to control the system, which demands digital skills to be developed and implemented; otherwise, their independence—relevant to the maintenance of a legal order based on a rule of law—can be undermined. Accordingly to the 2021 EU Justice Scoreboard, despite some Member States are still implementing Artificial Intelligence systems in the judicial administration, "[t]he overview confirms the observation that justice reform require time – sometimes spanning several years – from their announcement until the adoption of the legislative and regulatory measures and their actual implementation on the ground" (see European Commission 2021a, p. 5). On the other hand, the system's workings have to be presented in comprehensible terms to them, so user-focused and user-friendly dimensions are fulfilled. Otherwise, judicial operations meant to judges—as interpreting the law, applying it to individual cases and delivering material justice—can be confused with technological ones, which undermines judicial function as one basic function controlling how public power is exercised and on restoring rights that have been breached in the legal sphere of the litigation party;
– Lawyers need to understand the system, through a transparency policy available to them and understandable by them, so they can, if that is the case, exercise defence and appeal rights. These rights, before the implementation of Artificial Intelligence systems in the judiciary, need to be exercised in wider terms so parties' reactions concerning digital challenges steaming from disruptive technologies' use in the judiciary can be also discussed. This demands an actualistic interpretation of those rights' exercise legal grounding so arguments concerning digital challenges can also be addressed. Therefore, user-focused and user-friendly principles can play a mediate role: if the Artificial Intelligence system is understandable and thought to empower its user (the judge), it will also be easier to understand by the lawyer, despite not being its direct user.

4 Conclusive Remarks

As we were able to see, perceiving Artificial Intelligence systems as ethically trustworthy allowed a human-centric legal approach which determines that they must "leave a margin for human choice, which can only be obtained through the guarantee that the human will be able to understand, oversight and control Artificial Intelligence functioning inherent proceedings" (see Silveira et al. 2021, p. 341). In fact, European Union Agency for Fundamental Rights (FRA) understood effective judicial protection (enshrined on Article 47 of the CFREU) as "one of the most often used Charter right in legal proceedings", also covering "decision taken with the support of AI technologies" (see European Union Agency for Fundamental Rights (FRA) 2020, p. 75). In this sense, and after making visible how "[u]sing AI can challenge the right to an effective remedy in different ways", particularly when parties involved have not the information and / or the knowledge to understand the systems' functioning: "[w]ithout access to this information, individuals may not be able to defend themselves, assign responsibility for the decisions affecting them, appeal any decision negatively affecting them or have a fair trial, which includes the principle of equality of arms and adversarial proceedings" (see European Union Agency for Fundamental Rights (FRA) 2020, p. 76).

As previously stressed, these problems can only be overcome if digital literacy is promoted also concerning Artificial Intelligence systems' use in the judiciary. In fact, as FRA mentions, "challeng[ing] decisions based on AI [is] essential for providing access to justice", which can only happen if "people [is] aware that AI is used", "people [is] aware of how and where to complain"; and "AI system and decisions based on AI can be explained" (see European Union Agency for Fundamental Rights (FRA) 2020, p. 76).

Furthermore, human-centric Artificial Intelligence is the dogmatic approach that "gains particular new forms and relevance in legal domains and, particularly, in justice fields where fundamental rights have to be met and enforced, despite the legal order that entails them": therefore, as long as Artificial Intelligence systems are "being thought and implemented, not to substitute judicial operators, but to facilitate their tasks, particularly those of repetitive nature or of comparing settled case law" (see Covelo De Abreu 2019, p. 303), these might not appear as an impediment to effective judicial protection. Difficulties will arise but they must be addressed in a way the systems' workings are directed exclusively to act as mere instruments of the judicial function, not assuming a leading role on its accomplishment – that must continue to be solely conducted by judicial operators, dully supported on transparent information and digitally aware of the systems' shortcomings and potentials.

In this sense, the European Ethical Charter on the use of Artificial Intelligence in judicial systems and their environment, authored by the European Commission for the Efficiency of Justice (CEPEJ) of the Council of Europe, is a useful tool to the European Union path: in fact, the Working Party on e-Law (e-Justice) of the Council had several reunions in Brussels where, addressing the topic "Innovative uses of technology – artificial intelligence", in 2019, that Ethical Charter was presented (see Council of the European Union, ANP—EU Monitor 2019). In this sense, under Article 6 (3) of the Treaty of the European Union (TEU), the protection of fundamental rights in the European Union must follow the minimum standard developed under the European Convention of Human Rights (ECHR) of the Council of Europe, as an interpretation standard. In this sense, this Ethical Charter has been able to influence the way European Union is perceiving Artificial Intelligence systems being used in justice fields.

Insofar, this Ethical Charter was adopted to sensitize "public and private stakeholders responsible for the design and deployment of artificial intelligence tools and services that involve the processing of judicial decisions and data", also engaging "public decision-makers in charge of the legislative or regulatory framework, of the development, audit or use of such tools and services" (see Council of Europe – European Commission for the Efficiency of Justice 2018, p. 5).

In line with what we tested before, this Charter acknowledges that "[w]hen artificial intelligence tools are used to resolve a dispute or as a tool to assist in judicial decision-making or to give guidance to the public, it is essential to ensure that they do not undermine the guarantees of the right to access to a judge and the right to a fair trial" (see Council of Europe – European Commission for the Efficiency of Justice 2018, p. 8).

Furthermore, on non-discrimination, it aims at avoiding that, in judicial proceedings, biases functioning of Artificial Intelligence systems can lead to discriminatory decisions: as Artificial Intelligence methods are still struggling with the problem of reproducing existing discrimination "through grouping or classifying data relating to individuals of groups of individuals", there is a need to "enforce "corrective measures to limit or, if possible, neutralise these risks and as well as to awareness-rising among stakeholders" (see Council of Europe – European Commission for the Efficiency of Justice 2018, p. 9).

On quality and security, CEPEJ underlined that "[d]ata based on judicial decisions [. . .] should come from certified sources and should not be modified until they have actually been used by the learning mechanism" (see Council of Europe – European Commission for the Efficiency of Justice 2018, p. 10). In this sense, these worries were included on high-risk classification, when Article 15 of the Proposal establishes the regime concerning accuracy, robustness and cybersecurity demands. These are particularly aligned with judicial fields since reliable data will promote independent and impartial judges and decisions, leading to the fulfilment of the right of a fair trial.

CEPEJ also portraits transparency, impartiality and fairness as general principles to be met when analysing Artificial Intelligence systems in justice fields: on the matter, despite the need to balance intellectual property demands, these can be met through trade secrets' regime already in place before courts; furthermore, "the best practice could be promoting a digital literacy of justice users and rising awareness of artificial intelligence's impact on justice fields" (see Covelo De Abreu 2019, p. 307) as "[t]he system could also be explained in clear and familiar language by communicating [. . .] the nature of the services offered, the tools that have been developed, performance and the risks of error" (see Council of Europe – European Commission for the Efficiency of Justice 2018, p. 11). Similar approach has been met under Article 13 of the Proposal, when establishing what measures high-risk Artificial Intelligence systems have to fulfil, particularly on making the system clearer to the user (more transparent) and on providing more information to the user.

The "Artificial Intelligence Act" Proposal on European e-Justice Domains... 411

Lastly, CEPEJ also stressed the principle of under user control: it aims at making judicial operators "informed actors and in control of their choices"; in order to achieve it, "[t]he user must be informed in clear and understandable language whether or not the solutions offered by the artificial intelligence tools are biding, of the different options available", which gains particular importance to judicial operators and, mainly, to judges and their independence and impartiality; but also to parties, as they have to understand "s/he has the right to legal advice and the right to access the court" (see Council of Europe – European Commission for the Efficiency of Justice 2018, p. 12). These constructions also explain why the European Commission, in the Proposal for the artificial Intelligence Act introduced, within the high-risk classification regime, Article 13, concerning Human oversight.

In this sense, all these developments helped the European Union to establish, on the administration of justice domains, the high-risk classification as the general trend. In fact, despite all effective judicial protection can be further observed by using Artificial Intelligence systems, there are well-known and hidden problems that can undermine it:

- Access to justice and defence rights can benefit from Artificial Intelligence as long as "digital literacy is well provided and transparency methods are adopted" (see Covelo De Abreu 2019, p. 308) since these disruptive systems might allow both plaintiff and defendant to gather "a certain amount of quantitative information (for example, the number of decisions processed to obtain the scale) and qualitative information (origin of decisions, representativeness of selected samples, distribution of decisions between different criteria such as the economic and social context) accessible to citizens and, above all, to the parties to a trial in order to understand how scales have been constructed, to measure their possible limits and to be able to debate them before a judge" (see Council of Europe – European Commission for the Efficiency of Justice 2018, p. 47).
- On judicial independence and impartiality, Artificial Intelligence systems must not depend on hardware or software that put "judges under any kind of external pressure" (see Council of Europe – European Commission for the Efficiency of Justice 2018, p. 48; Covelo De Abreu 2019, p. 308). In this sense, human oversight steaming from Article 14 of the Proposal, allied with transparency demands, are the best keys to further develop judicial independence and impartially, particularly fundamental to the maintenance of a Union of law.
- Lastly, the right to a fair trial will be fulfilled if parties are able to understand that Artificial Intelligence systems have only acted as instruments to judicial function, but have not, in any moment, operated as substitutes of the court. In this sense, human control of the system allied with user-focused and user-friendly features of the system will allow to create this sensitivity.

Digitalisation is the new trend for justice systems—European e-Justice is a paramount that cannot be overlooked since digital impact also has to reach administration of justice so it can benefit from its advantages. In this sense, the 2021 European Justice Scoreboard underlined that "[o]n the use of digital technology by courts [. . .], the majority of Member states already have different digital tools at [their] disposal", despite understanding "there is still a need for further progress in view of [...] artificial intelligence and blockchain-based tools more widely available" (see European Commission 2021a, p. 39). In this sense, the commission was also able to understand that "online access to court judgements [...] has not progressed, particularly for the publication of judgements at the highest instance" (see European Commission 2021a, p. 40) which can also affect Artificial Intelligence systems operating on previous jurisprudence, despite this Scoreboard was able to devise and analyse some "arrangements in place in the Member States that can help to produce machine-readable judicial decisions" so "an algorithm-friendly justice system" can be enabled (see European Commission 2021a, p. 40): in comparison with 2019, "most Member States reported an improvement in 2020", allowing the timid conclusion that "[j]ustice systems where arrangements for modelling judgements according to standards enabling their machine readability have been put in place seem to have the potential to achieve better results in the future" (see European Commission 2021a, p. 40).

Time will set the fundamental tone for Artificial Intelligence systems' impact on judicial systems; however, some insights were addressed, bearing in mind that human-centric approach of Artificial Intelligence cannot be forgotten since human-control, transparency, accuracy and security are main features to allow effective judicial protection to continue to act, within judicial systems, as their basis and their teleological explanation. In order to achieve it, Artificial Intelligence systems ought to be user-focused and user-friendly, otherwise making harder digital literacy to judicial operators and the community at large. [3]

References

Angwin J, Larson J, Mattu S, Kirchner L (2016) Machine bias. https://www.propublica.org/article/machine-bias-risk-assessments-in-criminal-sentencing. Accessed 1 Nov 2021
Barenstein M (2019) ProPublica's COMPAS data revisited. https://arxiv.org/pdf/1906.04711.pdf. Accessed 28 Oct 2021

---

[3] *See*, on the AI Act, in this book P U Lima and A Paiva - Autonomous and Intelligent Robots - Social, Legal and Ethical Issue; A T Fonseca, E V Sequeira and L B Xavier - Liability for AI Driven Systems; M N Duffourc and D S Giovanniello - The Autonomous AI Physician - Medical Ethics and Legal Liability; D Durães, P M Freitas and P Novais - The Relevance of Deepfakes in the Administration of Criminal Justice; and A Keller, C Martins Pereira and M Lucas Pires - The European Union's approach to Artificial Intelligence and the Challenge of Financial Systemic Risk. *See* also, on AI and judicial reasoning, in this book P G Marques - AI Instruments for Risk of Recidivism Prediction and the Possibility of Criminal Adjudication Deprived of Personal Moral Recognition Standards – Sparse Notes from a Layman; L M Pereira, F C Santos and A B Lopes - AI Modelling of Counterfactual Thinking for Judicial Reasoning and Governance of Law; W Gravett - Judicial Decision-making in the Age of Artificial Intelligence; D Durães, P M Freitas and P Novais - The Relevance of Deepfakes in the Admin-istration of Criminal Justice; and J C Abreu - The "Artificial Intelligence Act" Proposal on European e-Justice Domains Through the Lens of User-focused, User-friendly and Effective Judicial Protection Principles.

Cabral TS (2020) O "Juiz artificial": breves notas sobre a utilização de inteligência artificial pelos tribunais e a sua relação com a legislação europeia de proteção de dados. In: Covelo De Abreu J, Coelho L, Cabral TS (eds) O Contencioso da União Europeia e a cobrança transfronteiriça de créditos: compreendendo as soluções digitais à luz do paradigma da Justiça eletrónica europeia (e-Justice). Pensamento Sábio / Escola de Direito da Universidade do Minho, Braga, pp 114–126

Cabral TS (2021) A proposta de Regulamento sobre a Inteligência Artificial na União Europeia: breve análise. In Covelo De Abreu J, Coelho L, Cabral TS (eds) O Contencioso da União Europeia e a cobrança transfronteiriça de créditos: compreendendo as soluções digitais à luz do paradigma da Justiça eletrónica europeia (e-Justice). Pensamento Sábio / Escola de Direito da Universidade do Minho, Braga, pp 117–130

Costeira MJ (2021) e-Curia, noções e impacto nas interações com o TJUE. In Covelo De Abreu J, Coelho L, Cabral TS (eds) O Contencioso da União Europeia e a cobrança transfronteiriça de créditos: compreendendo as soluções digitais à luz do paradigma da Justiça eletrónica europeia (e-Justice). Pensamento Sábio / Escola de Direito da Universidade do Minho, Braga, pp 55–65

Council of Europe – European Commission for the Efficiency of Justice (2018) European Ethical Charter on the use of Artificial Intelligence in judicial systems and their environment, Strasbourg. https://rm.coe.int/ethical-charter-en-for-publication-4-december-2018/16808f699c. Accessed 2 Nov 2021

Council of the European Union (2019a) 2019–2023 action plan European e-justice. 2019/C 96/05, 13.3.2019. Official Journal of the European Union

Council of the European Union (2019b) 2019–2023 strategy on e-justice. Official Journal of the European Union. 2019/C 96/04, 13.3.2019

Council of the European Union, ANP – EU Monitor (2019) Working party on e-Law (e-Justice), Brussels. https://www.eumonitor.eu/9353000/1/j9vvik7m1c3gyxp/vkuv6fq8v8xv?ctx=vh1am07dxtwk&tab=1. Accessed 2 Nov 2021

Covelo De Abreu J (2019). The role of artificial intelligence in the European e-Justice paradigm – suiting effective judicial protection demands. In: Oliveira PM, Novais P, Reis LP (eds) Progress in Artificial Intelligence, 19th EPIA Conference on Artificial Intelligence, EPIA 2019, Vila Real, Portugal, pp 299–308

Covelo De Abreu J (2020) O sentido amplo de Contencioso da União Europeia e a justiça eletrónica europeia – a tutela jurisdicional efetiva como pressuposto e finalidade: breves apontamentos. In Covelo De Abreu J, Coelho L, Cabral TS (eds) O Contencioso da União Europeia e a cobrança transfronteiriça de créditos: compreendendo as soluções digitais à luz do paradigma da Justiça eletrónica europeia (e-Justice). Pensamento Sábio / Escola de Direito da Universidade do Minho, Braga, pp 8–16

Dieterich W, Mendoza C, Brennan T (2016) COMPAS risk scales: demonstrating accuracy equity and predictive parity. https://s3.documentcloud.org/documents/2998391/ProPublica-Commentary-Final-070616.pdf. Accessed 28 Oct 2021

Domingues P (2015) The master algorithm: how the quest for the ultimate learning machine will remake our world. Basic Books, New York

European Commission (2020a) Communication from the commission to the European Parliament, the Council, the European economic and social committee and the committee of the regions. "Digitalisation of justice in the European Union. A toolbox of opportunities". European Commission, Brussels

European Commission (2020b) Proposal for a regulation of the European Parliament and of the council on a computerized system for communication in cross-border civil and criminal proceedings (e-CODEX system), and amending Regulation (EU). European Commission, Brussels

European Commission (2020c) Study on the use of innovative technologies in the justice field – Final Report. https://op.europa.eu/en/publication-detail/-/publication/4fb8e194-f634-11ea-991b-01aa75ed71a1/language-en. Accessed 29 Oct 2021

European Commission (2021a) Communication to the European Parliament, the Council, the European Central Bank, the European Economic and Social Committee and the Committee of the Regions "The 2021 EU Justice Scoreboard". European Commission, Brussels

European Commission (2021b) Proposal for a regulation of the European Parliament and of the Council laying down harmonized rules on artificial intelligence (Artificial Intelligence Act) and amending certain Union legislative acts. European Commission, Brussels

European Commission (2021c) Shaping Europe's digital future – regulatory framework proposal on artificial intelligence. https://digital-strategy.ec.europa.eu/en/policies/regulatory-framework-ai. Accessed 1 Nov 2021

European Union Agency for Fundamental Rights (FRA) (2020) Getting the future right – Artificial Intelligence and fundamental rights (Report). European Union Agency for Fundamental Rights (FRA), Vienna

Faggella D (2021) AI in law and legal practice – a comprehensive view of 35 current applications, in EMERJ – The AI Research and Advisory Company, Business Intelligence and Analytics |Professional Services | Process Automation. https://emerj.com/ai-sector-overviews/ai-in-law-legal-practice-current-applications/. Accessed 30 Oct 2021

Maccarthy M, Propp K (2021) Machines learn that Brussels writes the rules: the EU's new AI regulation, in Brookings, Techtank. https://www.brookings.edu/blog/techtank/2021/05/04/machines-learn-that-brussels-writes-the-rules-the-eus-new-ai-regulation/. Accessed 1 Nov 2021

ProPublica (2021) About us – the mission. https://www.propublica.org/about/. Accessed 1 Nov 2021

Reiling AD (2020) Courts and artificial intelligence. Int J Court Adm 11:8

Silveira A, Covelo De Abreu J, Froufe PM (2020) Brief insights on e-Justice paradigm and the de facto digitalization of justice in the European Union – answers for the plural crisis (the endemic and the pandemic)? Official Blog of UNIO "Thinking & Debating Europe". https://officialblogofunio.com/2020/12/01/editorial-of-december-2020/. Accessed 1 Nov 2021

Silveira A, Veronese A, Covelo De Abreu J, Cabral TS (2021) Capítulo 15: da construção ética e jusfundamental de uma "inteligência artificial de confiança". In: Guerra FilhoWS, Santaella L, Kaufman D, Cantarini P (eds) União Europeia e os desafios da tutela jurisdicional efetiva. Direito e Inteligência artificial: fundamentos, Volume 1 – Inteligência artificial, ética e direito. Lumen Juris Editora, Brasil, pp 333–352

Storskrubb E (2017) E-justice, innovation and the EU. In: Hess B, Kramer XE (eds) From common rules to best practices in European civil procedure. Hart Publishing, Nomos, Max Planck Institute of Luxembourg for Procedural Law, London, pp 271–302

Open Access This chapter is licensed under the terms of the Creative Commons Attribution 4.0 International License (http://creativecommons.org/licenses/by/4.0/), which permits use, sharing, adaptation, distribution and reproduction in any medium or format, as long as you give appropriate credit to the original author(s) and the source, provide a link to the Creative Commons licence and indicate if changes were made.

The images or other third party material in this chapter are included in the chapter's Creative Commons licence, unless indicated otherwise in a credit line to the material. If material is not included in the chapter's Creative Commons licence and your intended use is not permitted by statutory regulation or exceeds the permitted use, you will need to obtain permission directly from the copyright holder.

The European Union's Approach to Artificial Intelligence and the Challenge of Financial Systemic Risk

Anat Keller, Clara Martins Pereira, and Martinho Lucas Pires

Abstract This piece examines the EU's 'Proposal for a Regulation of the European Parliament and of the Council Laying Down Harmonised Rules on Artificial Intelligence' ('AI Act') with a view to determining the extent to which it addresses the systemic risk created by AI FinTech. Ultimately, it is argued that the notion of 'high risk' at the centre of the AI Act leaves out financial systemic risk. This exclusion can neither be justified by reasons of technology neutrality, nor by reasons of proportionality: neither is AI-driven financial systemic risk already covered by existing (or proposed) macroprudential frameworks and tools, nor can its omission from the AI Act be justified by the prioritisation of other types of risk. Moving forward, it is suggested that the EU's AI Act would have benefited from a broader definition of 'high risk'. It is also hoped that EU policy makers will soon begin to strengthen existing macroprudential toolkits to address the financial systemic risk created by AI.

1 Introduction[1]

Technology and finance have become inextricably linked. Incumbent banks, insurance companies and other traditional financial institutions are increasingly dependent on technology, numerous new companies now specialise in offering

---

[1] This chapter only takes into account developments until February 2023.

A. Keller
King's College London - The Dickson Poon School of Law, London, UK
e-mail: anat.keller@kcl.ac.uk

C. Martins Pereira (✉)
Durham Law School, Durham, UK
e-mail: clara.martins-pereira@durham.ac.uk

M. Lucas Pires
Católica Lisbon School of Law, Lisbon, Portugal
e-mail: martinholucaspires@ucp.pt

© The Author(s) 2024
H. Sousa Antunes et al. (eds.), *Multidisciplinary Perspectives on Artificial Intelligence and the Law*, Law, Governance and Technology Series 58,
https://doi.org/10.1007/978-3-031-41264-6_22

technology-fuelled financial applications and platforms, and even the world's largest information technology companies (the so-called 'BigTechs') have begun to tap into the financial services industry. 'FinTech'—a term often used to describe the innovative use of modern technologies in the provision of financial services[2]—is seemingly everywhere.[3]

With its promised ability to radically improve information seeking and processing, Artificial Intelligence ('AI') stands to revolutionise FinTech.[4] But if AI brings significant promise to the financial services industry, it also presents important perils. Most obviously, AI-fuelled FinTech—like most other types of FinTech—creates operational and cyber risk. More significantly, the use of AI in financial services gives rise to new challenges specifically inherent in current AI technology paradigms like knowledge representation, natural language processing and machine-learning (Expert Group on Regulatory Obstacles to Financial Innovation 2019). Crucially, it is increasingly apparent that AI FinTech specifically poses a singular threat to market stability in the form of financial systemic risk.

It is little wonder then that AI has become such a focal point of interest for policymakers around the world, having already attracted over 700 policy initiatives across more than 60 different jurisdictions.[5] In the European Union ('EU'), these policy initiatives have included, in particular, the General Data Protection Regulation,[6] the Digital Services Act Package which comprises both a proposal for a Digital Services Act (European Commission 2020a) and a proposal for Digital Markets Act (European Commission 2020b)—and, recently, an AI Legislative Package—which includes an ambitious Proposal for a Regulation on a European approach

---

[2] The term 'FinTech' can also be employed to describe the new players in the financial system (often start-ups) whose core business involves using technology in the provision of financial services. Such services can include online lending and deposits ('Neobanking'), as well as the provision of payment solutions, investment services, wealth and asset management services, and insurance services ('InsurTech'). For a discussion, see *inter alia* Jackson (2020), p. 9.

[3] The average adoption rate of Fintech among the markets of Australia, Canada, Hong Kong, United Kingdom, and United States was 60% in 2019, while in 2015 it was just 16%, according to a recent report by Ernerst & Young (2019). A similar trend is found in the European Union; see Schmitz (2019).

[4] Typically, AI refers to the technological developments that allow computer systems to behave autonomously and emulate human intelligence, to the point that human input is significantly reduced or even eliminated. For a discussion of the challenges of defining AI, see Russell and Norvig (2010), pp. 1–27; Casey and Lemley (2020), pp. 287–362; Magnusson (2020), p. 337; and Bringsjord and Govindarajulu (2018).

[5] See the report by OECD AI Policy Observatory (2022). Importantly, the OECD AI Policy Observatory has also produced a set of principles promoting the use of AI that is innovative and trustworthy and that respects human rights and democratic value, available at OECD AI Policy Observatory (2019).

[6] Regulation (EU) 2016/679 of the European Parliament and of the Council of 27 April 2016 on the protection of natural persons with regard to the processing of personal data and on the free movement of such data and repealing Directive 95/46/EC (General Data Protection Regulation), OJ 2016 L 119/1.

for AI (the 'AI Act') (European Commission 2021g).[7] This act is effectively a set of horizontal rules that will govern not just the growing use of AI in the financial services industry, but all uses of AI more broadly. Still, its potential for addressing the risks specifically created by AI FinTech has been noted by the EU.[8]

This piece examines the EU's proposed AI Act with a view to determining the extent to which it addresses the systemic risk created by AI FinTech. Ultimately, it is argued that the notion of 'high risk' at the centre of the AI Act leaves out financial systemic risk. This exclusion can neither be justified by reasons of technology neutrality, nor by reasons of proportionality: neither is AI-driven financial systemic risk already covered by existing (or proposed) macroprudential frameworks and tools, nor can its omission from the AI Act be justified by the prioritisation of other types of risk. Moving forward, it is suggested that the EU's AI Act would have benefited from a broader definition of 'high risk'. It is also hoped that EU policy makers will soon begin to strengthen existing macroprudential toolkits to address the financial systemic risk created by AI.

Our work is organised as follows: Section 2 determines the extent to which the use of AI technology in the financial sector can amplify systemic risk; Section 3 outlines the basic features of the EU's AI Act and evaluates its ability to specifically capture the systemic risk created by AI FinTech; Section 4 concludes by making recommendations for further regulatory and supervisory developments in this area.

2 AI Uses in Finance and Systemic Risk

2.1 The Opportunities and Risks of AI FinTech

Recent years have witnessed an increasing adoption of high-end technologies by the financial sector, with AI sitting firmly at the heart of the FinTech (r)evolution.

Broadly, AI is used both in front-office operations (comprising procedures vis-a-vis consumers, customers, and supervisory entities) and back-office operations (involving procedures within the organizational framework of the company or institution). Examples of AI-powered FinTech include chatbots for answering

---

[7] More recently still, the EU has also proposed a new AI Liability Directive: see Directive of the European Parliament and of the Council on adapting non-contractual civil liability rules to artificial intelligence (AI Liability Directive), COM(2022) 496 final, Brussels, 28.09.2022.

[8] Namely, the Explanatory Memorandum for the AI Act notes that its provisions apply to 'AI systems provided or used by regulated credit institutions' (see Explanatory Memorandum, 1.2). More broadly, the AI Act is set to apply to all providers placing on the market or putting into service AI systems in the Union, irrespective of whether those providers are established within the Union or in a third country, to all users of AI systems located within the Union, and to all providers and users of AI systems that are located in a third country, where the output produced by the system is used in the Union—including when those AI systems are applied in connection to the provision of financial services (see AI Act, Article 2).

client queries, trading platforms hosting or using advanced algorithmic trading mechanisms, the provision of deposits and lending services supported by smart contracts running on blockchain protocols, and the automated submission of regulatory reports by supervised entities. In particular, AI enables financial actors to collect and parse through large amounts of data—which may then be put to multiple uses, from calculating credit and investment ratings, to detecting fraudulent and illicit practices. AI can also be used to improve connectivity between agents in the financial system[9]—and AI-fuelled RegTech and SupTech could radically change compliance, regulatory and supervisory procedures.[10]

These uses of AI in finance create significant opportunities for improving efficiency, fairness, and inclusiveness across the financial system, but they also bring important challenges. Indeed, it has long become clear that many modern technological applications are vulnerable to cyber and operational risks, create data privacy concerns, or can become channels for algorithmic bias—and particular features of AI could exacerbate these risks.[11] More recently, specific concerns have emerged regarding the impact of AI FinTech on financial systemic risk.

2.2 The Impact of AI on the Cross-Sectional and Time Dimensions of Systemic Risk

The traditional classification of financial systemic risk refers to two dimensions. The first is the 'cross-sectional (or structural) dimension' that relates to how risk is distributed within the financial system at a given point in time. To monitor this dimension, macroprudential authorities must address interconnectedness and common exposures in financial markets. The second is the 'time dimension' which relates to the procyclicality of the financial system and is concerned with how aggregate risks and vulnerabilities build up over time and are amplified by interactions within the financial system and feedback between the financial system and the real economy. Financial firms and individuals alike tend to assume excessive risks in the upswing (boom phase) and become risk-averse in the downswing (bust phase). These hidden and under-priced risks normally unfold dramatically, potentially leading to the materialisation of systemic risk (Danielson 2017).

As the use of AI in finance becomes increasingly pervasive, a key question is whether AI-driven technology can amplify these two dimensions of systemic risk.

Regarding the cross-sectional dimension, interconnectedness is a rather intuitive concept to understand and apply in this context. The financial system is a network of interconnected financial institutions and interlinked markets. In normal times, these interconnections facilitate risk-sharing across financial institutions. However, during

---

[9] See the report by EBA (2019).

[10] See the examples provided in the report by the FSB (2020), pp. 37–60.

[11] For an overview of opportunities and risks see Boukherouaa et al. (2021).

The European Union's Approach to Artificial Intelligence and the Challenge. . .   419

a period of stress, the same interconnections can easily facilitate the propagation of shocks and result in a 'domino effect'. A shock hitting one market, or one institution can quickly spread to other markets and institutions that are connected to it and impact a large part of the financial system, or even the system as a whole. Similarly, greater reliance on technology across a broad array of interconnected platforms, firms and third-party partners increases interconnectedness and concentration.

Financial institutions largely outsource the use of AI technologies to a small number of third-party technology and service providers. It is indeed the 'famous five' —Amazon, Google, Microsoft, Facebook, and Apple—and their counterparts in China that dominate the AI market partly by applying a strong strategy of acquisitions and complementary dominance in providing cloud computing services.[12] As noted previously, AI services stands to improve the efficiency of the financial markets. Nonetheless, similar to cloud computing providers, AI providers, such as dominant BigTechs, can become systemically important given their interconnectedness with financial institutions and the lack of readily available substitutes for the services they provide.[13] In principle, AI service providers, much like financial market infrastructures, can be said to act as the 'plumbing of the financial system'[14] in light of their provision of infrastructure and platform AI services to financial markets.[15] Unfortunately, at present, the notion of 'systemically important financial institution' is almost exclusively applied, in practice, to traditional financial institutions such as banks and insurance companies (Carstens 2021). Similarly, the notion of 'systemically important financial market utility' is applied to market infrastructures (Carstens et al. 2021, p. 7). Even where domestic macroprudential authorities have a designation power that can be applied to specific legal entities, such as AI providers, within a BigTech group,[16] it is often met with practical and legal barriers and limitations (Keller 2020, p. 138). This challenge is magnified by the existing concerns of market dominance and systemic footprint of BigTechs in light of their collection of user data and their ability to exploit natural network effects.[17]

---

[12] See CB (2019). On acquisitions see Alcantara et al. (2021). See also, Chakravorti (2021).

[13] According to the FSB-IMF-BIS the three key criteria that are helpful in identifying the systemic importance of markets and institutions are: 'size (the volume of financial services provided by the individual component of the financial system), substitutability (the extent to which other components of the system can provide the same services in the event of a failure) and interconnectedness (linkages with other components of the system).'

[14] Press Release, US Department Treasury, Financial Stability Oversight Council Makes First Designations in Effort to Protect Against Future Financial Crises (18 July 2012).

[15] *Ibid.*

[16] For instance, the FSOC has the power to designate nonbank financial institutions and financial market utilities as systemically important and subject them to heightened supervision and prudential standards. See Dodd-Frank Act ss 113, 804.

[17] On the Data, Network and Activity business model of BigTechs see the report of BIS (2019), p. 62.

In a concentrated environment and without direct regulatory oversight, reliance of financial institutions on third-party AI-providers for their core services could amplify idiosyncratic risks, potentially leading to system-wide disruptions. For instance, if a major provider of AI is exposed to a severe operational disruption, such as a cyber threat, information technology lapses, internal process, or control breakdowns,[18] this could lead to a simultaneous system-wide operational disruption. In an extreme case, market concentration in AI providers could also result in a 'lock-in', where financial institutions are excessively dependent upon a specific AI provider and unable to easily replace its services due to a lack of feasible alternative providers[19] and/or lack of interoperability of the service (Lins et al. 2021, p. 441). AI-providers may themselves depend on the use and services of cloud computing providers, another disruptive sector which could pose risks to the stability of financial systems (FSB 2019, p. 5; Bank of England 2021). Global cloud-computing service providers, such as Amazon and Microsoft, often also provide AI-products and services known as Artificial Intelligence as a Service ('AIaaS').[20] The growth of the AIaaS is exponential and is expected to increase by 41% during 2021–2025.[21] The combination of AI with cloud computing services and the concentration of the providers intensify risks inherent in both disruptive technologies—particularly since these AI providers are often outside the regulatory reach and, therefore, are not subject to micro-prudential regulations that ensure their safety and soundness. Furthermore, the data available to macroprudential authorities on exposures of financial institutions to third-party providers is incomplete. The regulatory perimeter may not yet enable macroprudential authorities to collect timely, comprehensive, and comparable data that can be aggregated for macroprudential analysis. This opacity supports adopting comprehensive and cross-border regulatory frameworks, as noted in Sect. 4 below.

In the cross-sectional dimension of systemic risk, shocks could also propagate via common exposures i.e., exposures of financial institutions towards the same sources of risk. For instance, financial institutions or other companies which provide financial services can be exposed to similar risk factors and risk management practices or models. These common exposures arise because of similarities and homogeneity

---

[18] See Request for Information and Comment on Financial Institutions' Use of Artificial Intelligence, Including Machine Learning A Notice by the Comptroller of the Currency, the Federal Reserve System, the Federal Deposit Insurance Corporation, the Consumer Financial Protection Bureau, and the National Credit Union Administration on 31 March 2021, available at https://www.federalregister.gov/documents/2021/03/31/2021-06607/request-for-information-and-comment-on-financial-institutions-use-of-artificial-intelligence (accessed 15 March 2022).

[19] Similar to the risk of cloud services. See FSB (2019). See also FINRA (2021).

[20] Lins et al. (2021), p. 6, define it as 'cloud-based systems providing on-demand services to organizations and individuals to deploy, develop, train, and manage AI models'. See the World Bank Group report from 2019 available at https://documents1.worldbank.org/curated/en/954851578602363164/pdf/Prudential-Regulatory-and-Supervisory-Practices-for-Fintech-Payments-Credit-and-Deposits.pdf (accessed 15 March 2022).

[21] See ReportLinker (2021).

across financial institutions that create the possibility of joint simultaneous failures. As such, reliance on standardised AI models or algorithms, which are trained on similar data streams, could produce herding and uniformity of predictions and behaviour in financial markets.[22] This is particularly worrisome since financial institutions already use AI systems for asset pricing, credit risk modelling and monitoring of risks[23] and will increasingly rely on these, not as complementary systems but as substitutes to existing, human-monitored ones. Moreover, adopting AI-tailored regulation and supervisory systems could inadvertently lead to common characteristics to AI systems, homogeneity, and model uniformity (Calzolari 2021, p. 33). This is not a theoretical concern as common exposures to similar risk management practices and models have proved to be disastrous in the run-up to the 2007–2009 financial crisis, when the Basel Committee standards of minimum capital for international banks heavily relied on the risk assessment of credit rating agencies. In hindsight, it became clear that these agencies had incentives to inflate credit scoring and their models failed to assess risks accurately (Rivlin and Soroushian 2017).

The use of AI systems could also provide a fertile ground for the build-up of endogenous imbalances in the financial system propagated and reinforced through a feedback loop between data and algorithms. In this scenario, the AI system will generate algorithms' decisions and data which will then be used to update models. These models will generate more data and will adapt their decisions and predictions based on that data in a dynamic and autonomous feedback loop. This unpredictable cycle, in its nature, could be dangerous and amplify risks that are already present in financial markets.

The concern of the feedback loop between data and algorithms is particularly acute for three key reasons. First, research on the effects of the feedback loop is still in its infancy,[24] making it difficult to monitor, let alone control it. This fits in well within a broader concern of scarcity of experts and the challenge of financial institutions and regulatory and supervisory authorities to hire and retain highly skilled personnel (Chui and Malhotra 2018). Second, AI service providers use 'alternative data' such as unstructured data, synthetic data and aggregated data (Bank of England and the Financial Conduct Authority 2021). Processing 'alternative data' and using it to inform policy decisions is, in practice, far from easy. Unstructured data must go through a cleaning process to remove errors and inconsistencies and ensure its effective use; synthetic data must capture and

---

[22] See Gensler and Bailey (2020). On herding results when AI systems perform similar calculations simultaneously, see Buckley et al. (2021), p. 51.

[23] FSB (2017b); and Institute of International Finance (2019), highlighting the lack of understanding from supervisors as a key challenge to implementing Machine Learning in credit risk modelling. See also the EBA (2021) and, in particular, see on p. 66 analysis and case studies of RegTech solutions to creditworthiness assessments.

[24] Malik (2020) shows that the feedback loop between data and money laundering algorithm creates a 'self-fulfilling prophecy' where the ML system overestimates its prediction accuracy, and its (human) users over-rely on the system predictions.

accurately represent the original real data[25] whereas aggregated data must be validated, at times, without knowing its granular structure (Rankin et al. 2020). The absence of tailored-data quality standards for AI further exacerbates the unpredictability of the data-algorithms feedback loop. Third, AI systems are trained on past events. Initial outputs, patterns and indicators set by regulators are shaped by humans who may naturally have narrow and backward-looking views of systemic risk. There is, therefore, a real risk that 'overtraining' on past events will result in new types of risks being left 'off screen'. This concern led economists to warn of the danger that AI systems '... will focus on the least important type of risk, those that are readily measured while missing out on the more dangerous endogenous risk. In effect, it will automate and reinforce the adoption of mistaken assumptions that are already a central party of current crises. In doing so, it will make the resulting complacency even more likely to build up over time.'[26] While this risk may not be unique to AI, most AI systems applied in financial services are untested for an abrupt shock to market conditions, a financial crisis and other stress scenarios.[27] Where the parameters of input data are unfitting to these conditions, models may need retraining (Bank of England 2020). However, retraining is an expensive process and, therefore, financial institutions are likely to suffer from inaction bias and choose to delay it, at the expanse of erroneous methods. As we shall see in the next section, the need for macroprudential regulation (and a supporting legal framework) that can 'force' financial institutions as well as AI providers to internalise these negative externalities has not been addressed by the European Union's AI Act—nor is it currently addressed by any sectoral legislation—and remains vital and urgent.

Another key challenge of AI systems that is prevalent in academic discussion is the black-box problem. In AI-driven algorithmic systems, it is possible to observe input and output (incoming and outgoing) data, but their internal operations are not always very well understood.[28] By way of illustration, AI models are so complex that even their creators are often not able to grasp how decisions have been formulated or interpret the reasoning supporting a given output. (Black and Murray 2019, p. 196) Automated decision-making, therefore, raises a concern of

---

[25] There is evidence of decreases in accuracy in models trained with synthetic data compared with models trained with real data. See Rankin et al. (2020).

[26] Buckmann et al. (2021) therefore suggest that when it comes to predicting crises 'Humans' rich historical, contextual, and theoretical understanding helps us to deal with these unexpected situations.'

[27] European Commission (2021a). On the potential negative impact of a crisis on ML models see Bank of England (2020), The Impact of COVID on Machine Learning and Data Science in UK Banking, Quarterly Bulletin 2020 Q4 available at https://www.bankofengland.co.uk/quarterly-bulletin/2020/2020-q4/the-impact-of-covid-on-machine-learning-and-data-science-in-uk-banking (accessed 15 March 2022), suggesting that '... this is linked to the fact that ML models' performance can change or deteriorate under conditions different to those displayed in the data on which they were originally trained.'

[28] Black and Murray (2019), referring to Pasquale (2015).

explainability[29] or, in other words, a concern that the internal behaviour of the model cannot be 'directly understood by humans (interpretability)' and its explanations (justifications) cannot 'be provided for the main factors that led to its output (EBA 2020).' AI systems also raise concerns of auditability since it is not always feasible to conduct an analytical and empirical evaluation of the algorithm.[30] These features can negatively affect the capacity of financial firms to monitor algorithmic performance and assure ongoing compliance with regulatory requirements.[31] This, in turn, could result in inaccurate credit decisions based on erroneous creditworthiness assessments and unsatisfactory credit and liquidity risk management. Lack of explainability also impinges on the ability of financial institutions to adjust their strategies in times of stress or poor performance (Organization for Economic Co-Operation and Development 2021), potentially leading to market volatility, liquidity shortages and even a gridlock during financial turmoil (Bathaee 2018, p. 889).

Without diminishing the importance of the black-box problem, another danger of AI that has been somewhat overlooked is the disparity and mismatch between expectations and targets, on the one hand and objectives and purposes, on the other. The potential disparity between regulatory aims and the operation of AI systems that are programmed to optimise processes should be acknowledged and monitored. The difficulty, however, to foresee this disparity was illustrated in Yuval Harari's book, Homo Deus:

> Even programming the system with seemingly benign gaols might backfire horribly. One popular scenario imagines a corporation designing the first artificial super-intelligence and giving it an innocent test, such as calculating pi. Before anyone realises what is happening, the AI takes over the planet, eliminates the human race, launches a campaign of conquest to the ends of the galaxy, and transforms the entire known universe into a gain super-computer that for billions upon billions of years calculates pi ever more accurately. After all. This is the divine mission its Creator gave it (Harari 2016).

While this scenario may seem more like science fiction than reality, the point to be made here is that regulatory goals, including stability of the financial system and the safety and soundness of financial institutions, may not be easily reconciled and controlled in AI systems.

Another type of disparity could emerge between the straightforward optimisation target of AI and its users' target. This is particularly the case with off-the-shelf AI service that offers to users AI models that are already trained by the provider or other parties and removes the need to set up, train and actively manage the product. This service offers users 'complexity abstraction' and is cost-effective, but it also

---

[29] See FSB (2017a), and Knight (2017).

[30] See the paper by the Banque De France (2020).

[31] This concern has been raised recently in the US: A Notice by the Comptroller of the Currency, the Federal Reserve System, the Federal Deposit Insurance Corporation, the National Credit Union Administration, and the Financial Crimes Enforcement Network on 4 December 2021, available at https://www.federalregister.gov/documents/2021/04/12/2021-07428/request-for-information-and-comment-extent-to-which-model-risk-management-principles-support (accessed 15 March 2022).

hands over the control and responsibility of the service to the AIaaS provider (Lins et al. 2021, p. 6; Pandl et al. 2021). As such, providers will not know much about the business model, practices and targets of the user and the user, in turn, will not know much (or not at all) about the setup and configuration of the AI system (Pandl et al. 2021). The 'veil' between AI providers and users increases the risk that target optimisation will not meet expectations and inhibit the ability to mould the service to the specific needs of the firm.

Finally, the use of AI can also affect regulators and the compliance of financial firms with regulations. As noted previously, AI systems are increasingly used in policymaking—and while this technology entails a great potential particularly in improving systemic risks surveillance by automating macroprudential analysis and data quality assurance, the use of AI to improve macroprudential analysis comes with a price.[32] Lack of explicability and auditability means that macroprudential authorities may not be able to understand how an AI model has arrived at its decisions or predictions, how undesired events occurred and how to respond and mitigate risks that have materialised or prevent risks from emerging in the future. Accordingly, macroprudential authorities may not be able to communicate to the public or parliament the reasons supporting their policy decisions and thus, their transparency and accountability may be diluted.[33] In addition, although AI can indeed be used by banks to maximise their regulatory compliance, for instance, for capital optimisation and improve their risk profile and safety and soundness,[34] assisting banks to 'game' the system more efficiently can ultimately subdue the effect of prudential regulatory standards. When accumulated, the strategic behaviour of financial institutions could result in negative externalities and destabilise the financial system. Most importantly, these 'gaming' techniques may relieve pressures for banks in the short term but may not necessarily be set with a view to longer-term changes that may yield more sustainable outcomes.

This is only the tip of the iceberg. In reality, the impact of the risks that should be of a concern to regulators go much beyond the financial system. Until now, the regulatory focus on the financial system-real economy nexus was limited to ensuring the continuation of efficient allocation of resources of the financial system in the face of shocks and preventing potential negative effects on the real economy. As AI systems will increasingly power not just the financial system but also energy, military and transport, a breakdown in those systems will be truly systemic and potentially devastating. Risks inherent in AI systems will originate from the real economy and ecosystems (Galaz et al. 2021), spilling over to other segments of the

---

[32] On the use of AI in supervision see Hertig (2022).

[33] Keller (2020), p. 177. Though see Danielsson et al. (2021) arguing that AI models can be more transparent than human regulators who can use strategic ambiguity in their communications.

[34] Though the use of Machine Learning is limited in regulatory areas such as capital requirements for credit risk and for Internal Rating Based approaches—they are largely used as a complementary system to the standard model used for capital calculation. To that effect, the European Banking Authority has published a Discussion Paper on Machine Learning for IRB Approaches, November 2021, EBA/DP/2021/04.

The European Union's Approach to Artificial Intelligence and the Challenge... 425

economy and the financial system. This, rather distant, danger has not gone under the radar of supervisors. The European Systemic Risk Board, for instance, observed that 'AI could be used to attack, manipulate, or otherwise harm an economy and threaten national security through its financial system directly and/or its impact on the wider economy. For instance, algorithms could be manipulated in an effort to transfer wealth to foreign powers, to undermine an economy's growth in an effort to create unrest, or to send wrong signals to trading units to seek to trigger a systemic crisis'[35]—a scenario that is truly a case of 'unknown unknowns'.

In truth, much is still unknown about the real extent of the impact of AI-driven FinTech—and while policymakers, industry players and experts appear alert to many of the risks created by AI, the potential of AI-driven technology for magnifying systemic risk has been receiving comparatively little attention. With the EU taking the lead in AI regulation, the time is ripe to assess whether its AI Act captures the financial systemic risk amplified by AI FinTech.

3 The EU's Approach to AI and the Challenge of Systemic Risk

3.1 One Approach, Two Pillars

The risks associated with the growth of AI technology and the development of an increasing variety of AI applications—in finance[36] and elsewhere[37]—have not gone unnoticed by the EU. Quite to the contrary: as the Union enters what it has dubbed as Europe's Digital Decade,[38] the desire to ensure that AI 'puts people first' sits firmly at the forefront of the EU agenda.

Indeed, the EU's recently published approach to AI expresses clear concerns over the unrestrained development of AI applications and their risks, and has elected 'trustworthy AI' as one of the key pillars of its AI policy.[39] At the same time, the

---

[35] See European Systemic Risk Board (2020); see also 'The Rise of Global Technology Risk' in Arner et al. (2019, p. 69) and Buckley et al. (2019).

[36] In March 2018, an Expert Group on Regulatory Obstacles to Financial Innovation (ROFIEG) was appointed to assist the DG FISMA by providing expertise on FinTech, and its final report—dated 13 December 2019—alerted the European Commission to the fact that AI was set to 'become increasingly relevant for both FinTech and RegTech'. See ROFIEG (2019).

[37] The EU's concern with developing a clear AI strategy dates from as early as 2018, when 25 European countries adhered to a Declaration of cooperation on AI (see Declaration—Cooperation on Artificial Intelligence, 10 April 2018, available at https://digital-strategy.ec.europa.eu/en/news/eu-member-states-sign-cooperate-artificial-intelligence, (accessed 15 March 2022)) in what the EU describes as the first 'important milestone' in the road to a fully-fledged European approach to AI. See European Commission (2018).

[38] See European Commission (2021f) and European Commission (2021d)

[39] See European Commission (2022a).

EU has not failed to recognise the promises of AI, and its desire to create a safe environment for AI users, developers and deployers has come tempered by a sense of urgency in bolstering Europe's ability to compete in the global AI landscape.[40] In addition to 'trustworthy AI,' the EU's policy is to be supported by a second pillar of 'excellence in AI.'

The image used by the EU is evocative: pillars typically offer upright support for superstructures—and multiple pillars intuitively offer more support than one. In that sense, the goal of the EU is to 'build a resilient Europe for the Digital Decade' where, *at the same time,* 'people can enjoy the benefits of AI': in other words, the EU wants to become an AI powerhouse sustained by both innovation and safety. But, unlike most pillars, innovation, and safety are not always complementary: they are often at tension with each other and choices that make AI more trustworthy can come at the cost of AI excellence (and vice versa).[41]

Arguably, the complementarities and tensions at the nexus of the EU's approach to AI stand as powerful explanations for many of the regulatory choices that shape that approach—and namely, for the key option to address differently different types of risks created by AI, and some not at all. Under this framework, identifying and recognising the existence of certain risks—like the AI-driven systemic risk discussed in the previous section—is just the first step in policymaking, and a step that is not necessarily followed by regulatory action to mitigate those risks.

With that in mind, this article proceeds to introduce the EU's approach to AI, discussing the extent to which it captures the financial systemic risk amplified by AI.

3.2 The EU's Approach to AI

It has been noted that the EU's approach to AI rests on a dual notion of excellence and trustworthiness. The idea of excellence in AI has translated into concerns over the development and uptake of AI in Europe, the fostering of an environment where AI is able to thrive 'from the lab to the market,' the encouragement of AI as a force for good in society, and the building of strategic leadership in key sectors; the idea of trustworthy AI, on the other hand, reflects concerns over safety risks specific to AI technology, liability issues pertaining to AI, and the importance of updating sectoral safety legislation.[42]

---

[40] See European Commission (2022b).

[41] Indeed, Brummer and Yadav argue that 'when seeking to (i) provide clear rules, (ii) maintain market integrity, and (iii) encourage financial innovation, regulators can achieve, at best, two out of these three objectives'. See Brummer and Yadav (2019), p. 235.

[42] See European Commission —namely the sub-headings 'A European approach to excellence in AI' and 'A European approach to trust in AI,' respectively.

The European Union's Approach to Artificial Intelligence and the Challenge... 427

In practice, these concerns have led the European Commission to publish an AI package in April 2021 that includes a Communication on Fostering a European Approach to Artificial Intelligence' ('Communication') (European Commission 2021b), an (updated) Coordinated Plan with Member States ('Coordinated Plan') (European Commission 2021c), and the previously discussed AI Act—a compromise version of which has recently been approved by the European Commission.[43]

The Communication lays down the foundations for the EU's approach to AI—expanding upon the notion that AI carries both opportunities and risks and noting that 'certain characteristics of AI... pose specific and potentially high risks to the safety and fundamental rights that existing legislation is unable to address'—but ultimately offers very little detail into how the EU plans to deal with the so-called 'two sides' of AI.[44] By contrast, both the Coordinated Plan and the AI Act provide important insights into what the EU has in store for AI.

Broadly, the (updated) Coordinated Plan encapsulates the commitment to foster Europe's ability to compete in the global AI landscape,[45] provides an overview of what has already been done and proposes a plan for future action. Crucially, it notes the importance of developing a policy framework to ensure trust in AI systems—and highlights the publication of a White Paper (European Commission 2020c) proposing an EU Regulatory Framework on AI ('AI White Paper').[46] This regulatory framework is set to include a number of measures adapting the European liability framework to the challenges of new technologies (including AI),[47] several

---

[43] The current version of the proposed AI Act is now awaiting adoption by the European Parliament.

[44] See European Commission (2021d) —where the European Commission recognises both 'AI's potential' and the fact that 'the use of AI also creates risks that need to be addressed.'

[45] This Commitment had already been expressed in the original version of the EU's Coordinated Plan on AI. European Commission (2018).

[46] Other notable outputs include the Independent High-Level Expert Group on Artificial Intelligence's Ethics Guidelines for Trustworthy Artificial Intelligence and the Assessment List for Trustworthy AI produced by the High-Level Expert Group on AI'—available, respectively at https://digital-strategy.ec.europa.eu/en/library/ethics-guidelines-trustworthy-ai and at https://digital-strategy.ec.europa.eu/en/library/assessment-list-trustworthy-artificial-intelligence-altai-self-assessment (accessed 15 March 2022)—as well as the EU Cyber Security Strategy for the Digital Decade, produced by the Commission and the High Representative of the Union for Foreign Affairs and Security Policy, and available at https://eur-lex.europa.eu/legal-content/EN/ALL/?uri=JOIN:2020:18:FIN (accessed 15 March 2022).

[47] The EU aimed to propose these measures sometime between the last quarter of 2021 and the first quarter of 2022 (see European Commission 2018) and it is likely that they will include a revision of the Product Liability Directive, as well as a specific proposal regarding the liability of certain AI systems. See European Commission (2021b).

revisions to existing sectoral safety legislation[48]—and, notably, the aforementioned AI Act.

It is this AI Act that offers the clearest glimpse into how AI is set to be regulated within the EU. At over 80-articles long it is meant to secure Europe 'a leading role in setting the global gold standard' for AI and sets itself to address the risks generated by specific uses of AI technology. Roughly, this is to be accomplished through a horizontal regulatory framework that lays down harmonised rules for introducing and using AI systems in the EU across industries and sectors.

Cross-sectoral horizontal rules are inherently ambitious, but the ambition behind the EU's proposal has come tempered with important concerns for balance. Such concerns are not misplaced; rather, they illustrate the inherent tension between the two pillars in the EU's approach to AI—excellence and trustworthiness—and, more broadly, the inherent tension between innovation and safety that so often underlies regulatory policy. However, it is worth determining whether the EU's AI Act resolves this tension satisfactorily, in a way that allows it to address the impact of AI on the financial system, namely by preventing or mitigating the financial systemic risk demonstrably amplified by AI.

3.3 Missing the Opportunity to Regulate the Systemic Risk Amplified by AI

The Regulatory Framework for AI proposed by the EU currently does very little to specifically address the impact of AI on the financial system. As it stands, the one proposal made by the EU within this framework—the AI Act—targets only one aspect of that impact: the risk of discrimination created by AI systems that evaluate the creditworthiness of natural persons ('algorithmic credit scoring').[49]

This is not necessarily an oversight. The impact of AI technology on the financial system has been expressly acknowledged by the EU on more than one occasion—and it does not necessarily follow that the EU must approve new rules to address that impact. It all comes back to the tension between excellence and trustworthiness—innovation and safety—which the AI Act resolves through two principles: technology neutrality and proportionality.

The idea of technology neutrality[50] is firmly present in the April 2021 Communication that laid down the foundations for the EU's approach to AI,[51] and reflects the

---

[48] The revisions of existing sectoral safety legislation were originally planned for the second quarter of 2021 (see European Commission (2022c)), and are likely to include adaptations of the Machinery Directive, of the General Product Safety Directive, of the Radio-Equipment Directive and of the product legislation that might follow the approval of the proposed AI Act (see European Commission (2021d)).

[49] AI Act, Recital (37) and Annex III, 5(b).

[50] For a discussion of the principle of 'technology neutrality,' see, ia, Greenberg (2016), p. 207.

[51] See European Commission (2021b).

The European Union's Approach to Artificial Intelligence and the Challenge. . .   429

notion that regulation should neither impose nor discriminate in favour of the use of any specific technology.[52] Any rules should focus on regulating the risks created by a particular technology, instead of on the technology itself. This means two things for the EU's approach to AI: first, that any regulatory approach approved by the EU to mitigate the risks created by AI technology should be risk-based (as opposed to technology-based); second, that new rules are only required if and to the extent that AI technology creates risks that are not already adequately addressed within the EU.

Accordingly, the AI Act endorses a risk-based regulatory approach to AI that limits regulatory intervention 'to the minimum necessary requirements to address the risks and problems linked to AI' and tailors it 'to those concrete situations where there is a justified cause for concern, or where such concern can reasonably be anticipated in the near future.'[53] Additionally, it is noted—both in the EU AI White Paper and in its AI Act—that there is currently 'an extensive body of existing EU . . . legislation, including sector-specific rules, further complemented by national legislation' that is 'relevant and potentially applicable to a number of emerging AI applications.' Such rules are fully applicable in these sectors, regardless of whether AI technology is involved, and will only require adjustments if—and only if—they cannot 'be enforced adequately to address the risks that AI systems create (European Commission 2020c).'

Likewise, the notion of proportionality is embedded across the various documents that comprise the EU's approach to AI[54]—culminating in Recital (14) of the AI Act, which underlines the need to introduce 'a proportionate and effective set of binding rules for AI systems.'[55] More broadly, the EU rejects solutions that are 'excessively prescriptive,'[56] or impose 'disproportionate burdens'[57] in favour of solutions that 'facilitate . . . innovation and thus enhance European competitiveness,'[58] namely by avoiding 'unnecessary restrictions to trade (European Commission 2021e).' Specifically, this proportionality is to be achieved by distinguishing between varying levels of risk, by regulating different AI applications

---

[52] The idea of 'technology neutrality' is not new, nor is it exclusive to the EU's approach to AI. For example, technology neutrality is one of the key principles of the European Regulatory Framework for Electronic Communications (see Directive 2002/21/EC of 7 March 2002, recital (31)).

[53] See chapter 1 of the European Commission's Explanatory Memorandum for the Proposal for a Regulation of the European Parliament and of the Council Laying Down Harmonised Rules on Artificial Intelligence (Artificial Intelligence Act) and Amending Certain Union Legislative Acts, 2021/0106(COD), available at https://eur-lex.europa.eu/legal-content/EN/TXT/?qid=1623335154975&uri=CELEX%3A52021PC0206 (accessed 15 March 2022).

[54] See, in particular, European Commission (2021b); and European Commission (2018).

[55] AI Act, recital (14).

[56] *Ibid.*

[57] *Ibid.*

[58] *Ibid.*

differently and according to their perceived level of risk—and, crucially, by leaving those AI applications perceived as less risky essentially unattended.[59]

At the end of the day, the ideas of technology neutrality and proportionality combine in the EU's AI Act to give rise to a 'risk-based approach' to AI that specifically focuses on 'high risk' applications.[60] In other words, even though the AI Act endorses an ambitious, cross-sectoral, horizontal regulatory approach, that approach is limited by the idea that only unregulated AI risk needs to be addressed—and, even then, only 'high' AI risk. The result is a regime that prohibits only a limited number of AI practices,[61] and that only imposes additional requirements and obligations on those AI systems that are considered by the EU to be 'high risk'[62] (and on participants in the production and distribution chains of those systems[63]—all the way down to final users).[64]

Does this 'high risk approach' to AI adequately address the change brought by AI to the financial system? As noted previously, only one aspect of the impact of AI on the financial system is currently covered by the EU's AI Act—the risk of discrimination created by algorithmic credit scoring systems[65]—but the generalised exclusion of the risks posed by other AI systems to the financial system and its players can only be deemed an oversight if it cannot be properly justified under the technology neutrality and proportionality principles that underlie the EU's high risk approach to AI regulation.

On the one hand, there is no question that the EU wants to create a regulatory environment encouraging of 'trustworthy AI;' on the other hand, there is no question either that overreaching laws and rules could come at the expense of the EU's ability to compete with countries like the United States and China for a place at the forefront of the global market for AI technology. And it could be argued that most risks posed by AI to the financial system and its players

---

[59] Notably, the AI Act includes a series of articles whereby the Commission and Member States undertake to encourage and facilitate the adoption of voluntary codes of conduct for the providers of non-high-risk AI (see AI Act, article 69). Also, non-high-risk AI systems may nevertheless be regulated by other rules within the broader EU and national regulatory frameworks—although most legal regimes currently in force in the EU fail to specifically address the risks newly created or enhanced by the development of AI applications.

[60] See the European Commission's White Paper, where the European Commission expressly states that 'to strike this balance [between achieving its regulatory objectives without being excessively prescriptive], the Commission is of the view that it should follow a risk-based approach' European Commission (2020c).

[61] AI Act, article 5.

[62] AI Act, articles 8–15.

[63] AI Act, articles 16–28.

[64] AI Act, article 52. Notably, additional requirements may apply to AI systems intended to interact with natural persons—which may be cumulatively subject to the requirements and obligations that pertain to 'high risk' AI systems (see AI Act, article 52(4)).

[65] AI Act, Recital (37) and Annex III, 5(b). Importantly, AI systems put into service by small scale providers for their own use are exempted from the regulation.

are already broadly captured by its existing financial regulation framework[66]—particularly following recent efforts to expand the scope of that framework.[67] For example, the most recent version of the EU's Markets in Financial Instruments Directive ('MiFID II') contains a series of requirements specifically applicable to firms, engaging in, facilitating, or hosting algorithmic trading,[68] and the 2014 EU Market Abuse Regulation includes express references to algorithmic-driven market manipulation[69]—showing a willingness to address algorithmic-driven (if not explicitly AI-driven) change.

Ultimately, a full discussion of whether the EU's high-risk approach to AI adequately addresses the impact of AI on the financial system far exceeds the scope of this piece. The scope of our enquiry is much narrower: does the high-risk approach to AI endorsed by the EU address the many ways in which AI-driven technology has amplified systemic risk and, if not, are any limitations in scope justified by technology neutrality or proportionality concerns?

Determining the extent to which the EU's approach to AI—and, namely, its AI Act—can address the new sources of systemic risk created by AI requires analysing the notion of 'high risk' at the centre of the AI Act. According to articles 6 and 7 of the AI Act, the classification of a particular type of AI system as 'high risk' depends essentially on its intended use (*see* article 6(1)(a) and 7(1)(a)) and on its potential for posing a 'risk of harm to the health and safety, or a risk of adverse impact on fundamental rights' of individuals (*see* article 7(1)(b))—with no regard for its potential for creating losses and contagion channels that can reach the wider system populated by those individuals. Indeed, this focus on the 'protection of . . . individuals' is made clear in Recital (10) of the AI Act and permeates most of its provisions.[70]

Some solace can perhaps be taken in the fact that article 7 (2)(d) of the AI Act suggests that 'risk assessments' conducive to updating the list of 'high risk' systems already identified by the European Commission[71] should take into account

---

[66] A discussion of the extent to which the EU financial regulation framework does a good job of capturing all the financial activity taking place within its Member States falls outside the scope of this article, although concerns over the system's ability to capture non-bank financial intermediation (sometimes known as 'shadow banking')—particularly as both small FinTech start-ups and larger technological companies ('BigTechs') increasingly position themselves as new entrants in the financial industry—are likely justified.

[67] For example, MiFID II expanded the scope of MiFID to capture proprietary traders that apply 'high frequency trading' techniques. For a discussion, see, ia, Gullifer and Payne (2020). Notably, the EU is in the process of reviewing its current algorithmic trading regime, but ESMA's final report on the matter fails to address the risks created by AI-driven algorithmic trading (see ESMA (2021))—although ESMA's more recent TRV Risk Analysis on Artificial Intelligence in EU Securities Markets does acknowledge the threat of 'possible systemic risks arising from the use of AI in algorithmic trading, as well as algorithmic bias and overfitting' (see ESMA (2023)).

[68] See, in particular, MiFID II, articles 17 and 48.

[69] EU Market Abuse Regulation, article 12(2)(c).

[70] AI Act, recital (10).

[71] AI Act, Annex III.

'the potential extent of [the harm or adverse impact to individuals] in terms of its intensity and its ability to affect a plurality of persons,' but even a broad interpretation of this formula fails to capture the true nature of systemic risk— which, as noted in the previous section, does not just include the risk that individual losses might affect a large number of agents at the same time, but, crucially, the risk that individual losses might propagate from just one individual agent and spread across an increasingly interconnected system—or that the use of similar models may result in common exposures that can facilitate the propagation of shocks.

It seems then that the AI Act struggles to capture the cross-sectional dimension of 'systemic risk' in its definition of 'high risk'—and, in that way, to address it. Given the significant propensity of AI for amplifying systemic risk discussed in the previous section, this could be seen as a significant overlook, but can this exclusion be justified under principles of technology neutrality or proportionality?

Technology neutrality requires regulators to adopt a risk-based—as opposed to technology-based—approach to regulation and intervene only when they identify risks that need mitigating. Now, the previous section has already covered the vast number of ways in which AI-driven technology amplifies financial systemic risk, and while some of these ways have been specifically addressed by recent regulation—namely, MiFID II when it comes to algorithmic trading[72]—others have not received the same regulatory attention.[73] It could, of course, be argued that AI-driven systemic risk is already covered by existing macroprudential frameworks, but the European Systemic Risk Board has recently acknowledged that technology-driven financial systemic risk (or 'systemic cyber risk') creates threats that 'require further work by macroprudential authorities (ESRB 2020).' And AI technology—as it evolves—can be a whole new ball game.

Alternatively, it could be argued that excluding systemic risk considerations from the definition of 'high risk' is justified by proportionality concerns and the relative lesser importance of this type of risk, but that would go against the growing consensus around the significance—and, indeed, the desirable prioritisation—of financial stability as a regulatory goal (Armour et al. 2016). From that perspective,

---

[72] MiFID II, articles 17 and 48.

[73] It is true that the Digital Services package also addresses concerns with AI and its impact on 'systemic risk'—but the Digital Services Act limits the idea of systemic risk to three main categories of risk that do not reflect the macroprudential concerns that underlie the narrower concept of 'financial systemic risk' used in this piece: a first category concerning 'the risks associated with the misuse of their service through the dissemination of illegal content, such as the dissemination of child sexual abuse material or illegal hate speech, and the conduct of illegal activities, such as the sale of products or services prohibited by Union or national law, including counterfeit products;' a second category concerning the impact of services 'on the exercise of fundamental rights, as protected by the Charter of Fundamental Rights, including the freedom of expression and information, the right to private life, the right to non-discrimination and the rights of the child;' and a third category concerning 'the intentional and, oftentimes, coordinated manipulation of the platform's service, with a foreseeable impact on health, civic discourse, electoral processes, public security and protection of minors' (see Proposed Digital Services Act, Recital (57)).

The European Union's Approach to Artificial Intelligence and the Challenge... 433

it is hard to understand why the EU has used its AI Act to address the AI-driven discrimination risks created by a phenomenon like algorithmic credit scoring, while leaving bigger picture systemic risk implications entirely unaddressed (including those that pertain to algorithmic credit scoring).[74]

Thus, it appears not only that the EU approach to AI, in general—and its new AI Act, in particular—fail to capture the systemic risk newly created by AI, but also that such failure is hard to justify under the principles of technology neutrality and proportionality that appear to guide such approach.

4 Conclusion

As the world of finance enters a new age of technological progress, regulators and supervisors across the globe have been brought to a crossroads: how can the financial system harness the benefits of AI while guarding against its risks? Answers are rarely obvious when it comes to algorithmic technology, but that has not stopped the EU from leading the way to shape the global regulatory agenda on AI.

The EU's regulatory aspirations go far beyond addressing the impact of AI on the financial system and its players: a bold new proposal for a horizontal AI Act targets high risk AI applications across industries and sectors. At the same time, the Union's ambitions have been moderated by concerns over its ability to compete in the global AI arena: AI trustworthiness and safety are important, but so are AI excellence and innovation. In the end, the EU's regulatory approach to AI readily acknowledges the impact of AI on the financial system—and, in particular, the risks created by algorithmic credit scoring systems—but leaves the financial systemic risk created by AI seemingly unaddressed.

This might be a significant overlook: this article has demonstrated that AI has been transforming both the financial system and the way in which that system is regulated and supervised, creating new—and still largely understudied—sources of systemic risk. And while the EU's decision to exclude systemic risk from the definition of 'high risk' that underpins its new AI Act could be justified by reasons of technology neutrality or proportionality, neither reason holds water. Neither are these new sources of systemic risk already addressed by existing macroprudential regulatory and supervisory approaches—as recently acknowledged by the EU's own

---

[74] As noted by Aggarwal, the fact that algorithmic credit scoring is a post-crisis phenomenon and the fact that algorithmic credit scoring systems have been trained in a benign macroeconomic environment is potentially worrisome. Relatedly, Aggarwal also expresses concerns over 'the impact of algorithmic credit scoring on the overall volume of household debt and the rate of credit expansion in the economy – particularly to vulnerable consumers for whom debt can quickly become unaffordable' (see Aggarwal (2021), pp. 42–73). The DNB, for instance, also acknowledges the systemic risk implications of AI-driven solutions and concentration of actors under the 'Soundness' principle included in its 'Principles for the Use of Artificial Intelligence in the Financial Sector'. See De Nederlandsche Bank (2019).

European Systemic Risk Board—nor is this type of risk less significant than the risks identified and covered by the AI Act.

It could be argued more convincingly that perhaps the EU's AI Act was not the right type of instrument for addressing this type of risk.[75] But it is nevertheless worrisome that horizontal rules that have the ambition of laying down harmonised AI rules across sectors and industries—and which even address the risks inherent in particular financial activities and services, like algorithmic credit scoring—entirely ignore the specific type of risk that most clearly conveys potential threats to the stability of that system. The tendency to focus on the micro—instead of on the macro—is not new, but episodes like the 2007–2009 financial crisis have taught us the importance of prioritising big picture considerations.

Additionally, it could be that the EU's AI Act actually does a disservice to the goal of mitigating the systemic risk created by AI. Most obviously, the AI Act could contribute to the false notion that the most significant risks created by AI have already been addressed—either in sectoral regulations, in the case of algorithmic trading, or in the AI Act itself, in the case of algorithmic credit scoring—at the same time that AI-driven systemic risk has actually escaped the regulator's radar. Second, the fact that the EU has chosen to address the risks created by AI by proposing a horizontal framework codified in a Regulation (instead of a Directive) ensures that similar regulatory requirements will apply to AI systems across sectors and across Member States, with very little room for variation. To the extent that such requirements may encourage the development of similar products subject to similar control and safety mechanisms, the AI Act could create a degree of uniformity and homogeneity that is itself a new source of systemic risk (Calzolari 2021).

In the end, the risk-based approach at the centre of the EU's approach to AI is an understandable attempt to address the technology neutrality and proportionality concerns that reflect existing tensions between the goals of 'excellence in AI' and 'trustworthy AI'—innovation and safety. But regulatory compromises and trade-offs require a clear understanding of the opportunities and risks that arise from the object of regulation. And underestimating or ignoring the potential of AI for amplifying systemic risk necessarily limits the EU's ability to strike the right balance when regulating AI.

Looking ahead, it is clear that more research is required into the systemic risk created by AI. It is also clear that the high-risk approach adopted by the EU in its AI Act could benefit from a broader definition of 'high risk': one that does not just focus on harm to individuals (or even many individuals) but also considers the broader structural and systemic impact of AI. Additionally, it is hoped that regulators and supervisors will soon begin work on strengthening existing macroprudential toolkits to ensure that they can handle the new systemic risk created by AI.[76] In this regard,

---

[75] See Whittlestone et al. (2021) noting that 'there is an open question as to whether systemic risks can be addressed via the same regulatory processes as more direct and easily identifiable harms'.

[76] See, in particular, the discussion in ESRB (2020).

The European Union's Approach to Artificial Intelligence and the Challenge. . .

some inspiration may be drawn from the EU's algorithmic trading regime and its requirements for stress testing and circuit breakers.[77]

Finally, it is worth underlining that systemic risk can easily travel across borders, and new regulatory and supervisory approaches looking to address the impact of AI on the financial system should acknowledge this international dimension of systemic risk (Keller 2020, pp. 295–296). It is therefore hoped that the EU's meritorious efforts to build a strategy for innovative and safe AI can eventually lead the conversation around the development of a more integrated cross-border approach to AI—and one that more readily acknowledges the important implications of AI for financial systemic risk.[78]

References

Aggarwal N (2021) The norms of algorithmic credit scoring. Camb Law J 80:42–73

Alcantara C, Schaul K, De Vynck G, Albergotti R (2021) How big tech got so big: hundreds of acquisitions. The Washington Post, April 21. https://www.washingtonpost.com/technology/interactive/2021/amazon-apple-facebook-google-acquisitions/. Accessed 15 Mar 2022

Armour J, Awrey D, Davies P, Enriques L, Gordon JN, Mayer C, Payne J (2016) Principles of financial regulation, 1st edn. Oxford University Press, Oxford

Arner DW, Buckley R, Zetzsche D (2019) The rise of global technology risk. In: Arner DW, Avgouleas E, Busch D, Schwarcz SL (eds) Systemic risk in the financial sector: ten years after the great crash. McGill-Queen's University Press, Montreal, pp 69–82

Bank of England (2020) The impact of COVID on machine learning and data science in UK banking, quarterly bulletin 2020 Q4. https://www.bankofengland.co.uk/quarterly-bulletin/2020/2020-q4/the-impact-of-covid-on-machine-learning-and-data-science-in-uk-banking. Accessed 15 Mar 2022

---

[77] For a summary of the EU's algorithmic trading regime, see Conac (2017).

[78] *See* also, on Ethics, in this book P U Lima and A Paiva - Autonomous and Intelligent Robots - Social, Legal and Ethical Issues; A T Freitas - Data-driven approaches in healthcare - challenges and emerging trends; M C Patrão Neves and A B Almeida - Before and Beyond Artificial Intelligence - Opportunities and Challenges; E Magrani and P G F Silva - The Ethical and Legal Challenges of Recommender Systems Driven by Artificial Intelligence; M S Fernandes and J R Goldim - Artificial Intelligence and Decision Making in Health - Risks and Opportunities; M N Duffourc and D S Giovanniello - The Autonomous AI Physician - Medical Ethics and Legal Liability; and R Nogaroli and J L M Faleiros Júnior - Ethical challenges of artificial intelligence in medicine and the triple semantic dimensions of algorithmic opacity with its repercussions to patient consent and medical liability. *See* also, on the AI Act, in this book P U Lima and A Paiva - Autonomous and Intelligent Robots - Social, Legal and Ethical Issue; A T Fonseca, E V Sequeira and L B Xavier - Liability for AI Driven Systems; M N Duffourc and D S Giovanniello - The Autonomous AI Physician - Medical Ethics and Legal Liability; D Durães, P M Freitas and P Novais - The Relevance of Deepfakes in the Administration of Criminal Justice; and J C Abreu - The "Artificial Intelligence Act" Proposal on European e-Justice Domains Through the Lens of User-focused, User-friendly and Effective Judicial Protection Principles. *See* also, on Fintech, in this book K Yordanova and N Berterls - Regulating AI - Challenges and the Way Forward through Regulatory Sandboxes.

Bank of England (2021) Financial stability report. https://www.bankofengland.co.uk/-/media/boe/files/financial-stability-report/2021/july-2021.pdf. Accessed 15 Mar 2022

Bank of England and the Financial Conduct Authority (2021) Minutes from the artificial intelligence public-private forum - second meeting. https://www.bankofengland.co.uk/-/media/boe/files/minutes/2021/aippf-minutes-february-2021.pdf. Accessed 15 Mar 2022

Banque De France (2020) Governance of artificial intelligence in finance. https://acpr.banque-france.fr/sites/default/files/medias/documents/20200612_ai_governance_finance.pdf. Accessed 15 Mar 2022

Bathaee Y (2018) The artificial intelligence black box and the failure of intent and causation. Harv J Law Technol 31:889–938

BIS (2019) Big tech in finance: opportunities and risks. https://www.bis.org/publ/arpdf/ar2019e3.pdf. Accessed 15 Mar 2022

Black J, Murray AD (2019) Regulating AI and machine learning: setting the regulatory agenda. Eur J Law Technol 10:1–21

Boukherouaa EB, AlAjmi K, Deodoro J, Farias A, Ravikumar R (2021) Powering the digital economy: opportunities and risks of artificial intelligence in finance. IMF departmental paper. https://www.elibrary.imf.org/view/journals/087/2021/024/article-A001-en.xml?ArticleTabs=fulltext. Accessed 15 Mar 2022

Bringsjord S, Govindarajulu NS (2018) Artificial intelligence. Stanford Encyclopaedia of Philosophy. https://plato.stanford.edu/entries/artificial-intelligence/. Accessed 15 Mar 2022

Brummer C, Yadav Y (2019) Fintech and the innovation trilemma. Georget Law J 107:235–307

Buckley RP, Arner DW, Arner DW, Zetzsche DA, Selga E (2019) The dark side of digital financial transformation: the new risks of fintech and the rise of techrisk. European Banking Institute Working Paper 2019/54

Buckley RP, Zetzsche DA, Arner DW, Tang BW (2021) Regulating artificial intelligence in finance: putting the human in the loop. Syd Law Rev 43:43–81

Buckmann M, Haldane A, Hüser A-C (2021) Comparing minds and machines: implications for financial stability. Bank of England staff working paper no. 937. Oxford University Press, Oxford

Calzolari G (2021) Artificial intelligence market and capital flows: artificial intelligence and the financial sector at crossroads. https://www.europarl.europa.eu/RegData/etudes/STUD/2021/662912/IPOL_STU(2021)662912_EN.pdf. Accessed 15 Mar 2022

Carstens A (2021) Public policy for big techs in finance. Webinar 'finance as information'. Asia School of Business Conversations on Central Banking, Basel

Carstens A, Claessens S, Restoy F, Shin HS (2021) Regulating big techs in finance. BIS Bull 45:9

Casey B, Lemley M (2020) You might be a robot. Cornell Law Rev 185:287–362

CB (2019) Insight AI trends report. https://interactives.cbinsights.com/artificial-intelligence-acquisitions-by-famga/. Accessed 15 Mar 2022

Chakravorti B (2021) Big Tech's stranglehold on artificial intelligence must be regulated. Foreign Policy Magazine, 11 August 2021. https://foreignpolicy.com/2021/08/11/artificial-intelligence-big-tech-regulation-monopoly-antitrust-google-apple-amazon-facebook/. Accessed 15 Mar 2022

Chui M, Malhotra S (2018) AI adoption advances, but foundational barriers remain. https://www.mckinsey.com/featured-insights/artificial-intelligence/ai-adoption-advances-but-foundational-barriers-remain. Accessed 15 Mar 2022

Conac PH (2017) Algorithmic trading and high-frequency trading (HFT). In: Busch D, Ferrarini G (eds) Regulation of the EU financial markets: MiFID II and MiFIR. Oxford University Press, Oxford, pp 469–485

Danielson J (2017) Artificial intelligence and the stability of markets. https://voxeu.org/article/artificial-intelligence-and-stability-markets. Accessed 15 Mar 2022

Danielsson J, Macrae R, Uthemann A (2021) Artificial intelligence and systemic risk. https://papers.ssrn.com/sol3/papers.cfm?abstract_id=3410948. Accessed 15 Mar 2022

De Nederlandsche Bank (2019) Principles for the use of artificial intelligence in the financial sector. https://www.dnb.nl/media/voffsric/general-principles-for-the-use-of-artificial-intelligence-in-the-financial-sector.pdf. Accessed 15 Mar 2022

EBA (2019) Artificial intelligence in the era of open banking. https://www.abe-eba.eu/thought-leadership-innoation/open-banking-working-group/management-summary-artificial-intelligence-in-the-era-of-open-banking/. Accessed 15 Mar 2022

EBA (2020) Report on big data and advanced analytics. https://www.eba.europa.eu/sites/default/files/document_library/Final%20Report%20on%20Big%20Data%20and%20Advanced%20Analytics.pdf. Accessed 15 Mar 2022

EBA (2021) Analysis of RegTech in EU financial sector. https://www.eba.europa.eu/sites/default/documents/files/document_library/Publications/Reports/2021/1015484/EBA%20analysis%20of%20RegTech%20in%20the%20EU%20financial%20sector.pdf. Accessed 15 Mar 2022

Ernst and Young (2019) Global fintech adoption index. https://assets.ey.com/content/dam/ey-sites/ey-com/en_gl/topics/financial-services/ey-global-fintech-adoption-index-2019.pdf. Accessed 15 Mar 2022

ESMA (2021) MiFID II final report on algorithmic trading. https://www.esma.europa.eu/press-news/esma-news/esma-publishes-mifid-ii-review-report-algorithmic-trading. Accessed 15 Mar 2022

ESMA (2023) Artificial intelligence in EU securities markets. https://www.esma.europa.eu/sites/default/files/library/ESMA50-164-6247-AI_in_securities_markets.pdf. Accessed 15 Feb 2023

ESRB (2020) Systemic cyber risk. https://www.esrb.europa.eu/pub/pdf/reports/esrb.report200219_systemiccyberrisk~101a09685e.en.pdf. Accessed 15 Mar 2022

European Commission (2018) Communication from the commission to the European parliament, the European council, the council, the European economic and social committee and the committee of the regions – coordinated plan on artificial intelligence, COM (2018) 795 final. https://eur-lex.europa.eu/legal-content/EN/TXT/?uri=CELEX%3A52018DC0795. Accessed 15 Mar 2022

European Commission (2020a) Proposal for a regulation of the European parliament and of the council on a single market for digital services (digital services act) and amending directive 2000/31/EC, COM/2020/825 final

European Commission (2020b) Proposal for a regulation of the European parliament and of the council on contestable and fair markets in the digital sec-tor (digital markets act), COM/2020/842 final

European Commission (2020c) White paper on artificial intelligence – a European approach to excellent and trust COM (2020) 65 final. https://ec.europa.eu/info/sites/default/files/commission-white-paper-artificial-intelligence-feb2020_en.pdf. Accessed 15 Mar 2022

European Commission (2021a) Artificial intelligence market and capital flows. https://www.europarl.europa.eu/RegData/etudes/STUD/2021/662912/IPOL_STU(2021)662912_EN.pdf. Accessed 15 Mar 2022

European Commission (2021b) Communication from the commission to the European parliament, the council, the European economic and social committee and the committee of the regions fostering a European approach to artificial intelligence, COM (2021) 205 final. https://digital-strategy.ec.europa.eu/en/library/communication-fostering-european-approach-artificial-intelligence. Accessed 15 Mar 2022

European Commission (2021c) Coordinated plan on artificial intelligence 2021 review – annex to the communication from the commission to the European parliament, the council, the European economic and social committee and the committee of the regions fostering a European approach to artificial intelligence, COM (2021) 205 final. https://digital-strategy.ec.europa.eu/en/library/coordinated-plan-artificial-intelligence-2021-review. Accessed 15 Mar 2022

European Commission (2021d) Europe's digital decade: digital targets for 2030. https://ec.europa.eu/info/strategy/priorities-2019-2024/europe-fit-digital-age/europes-digital-decade-digital-targets-2030en. Accessed 15 Mar 2022

European Commission (2021e) Explanatory memorandum for the proposal for a regulation of the European parliament and of the council laying down harmonised rules on artificial intelligence (artificial intelligence act) and amending certain union legislative acts, 2021/0106(COD). https://eur-lex.europa.eu/legal-content/EN/TXT/?qid=1623335154975&uri=CELEX%3A52021PC0206. Accessed 15 Mar 2022

European Commission (2021f) Proposal for a decision of the European parliament and of the council establishing the 2030 policy programme 'path to the digital decade' 2021/0293 (COD). https://digital-strategy.ec.europa.eu/en/library/proposal-decision-establishing-2030-policy-programme-path-digital-decade. Accessed 15 Mar 2022

European Commission (2021g) Proposal for a regulation of the European parliament and of the council laying down harmonised rules on artificial intelligence (artificial intelligence act) and amending certain union legislative acts COM/2021/206 final

European Commission (2022a) Artificial intelligence. https://digital-strategy.ec.europa.eu/en/policies/artificial-intelligence. Accessed 15 Mar 2022

European Commission (2022b) The digital services act package. https://digital-strategy.ec.europa.eu/en/policies/digital-services-act-package. Accessed 15 Mar 2022

European Commission (2022c) A European approach to artificial intelligence. https://digital-strategy.ec.europa.eu/en/policies/european-approach-artificial-intelligence. Accessed 15 Mar 2022

European Systemic Risk Board (2020) Artificial intelligence in finance: putting the human in the loop. https://www.esrb.europa.eu/pub/pdf/reports/esrb.report200219_systemiccyberrisk~101a09685e.en.pdf. Accessed 15 Mar 2022

Expert Group on Regulatory Obstacles to Financial Innovation (2019) 30 recommendations on regulation, innovation and finance – final report to the European commission. https://ec.europa.eu/info/sites/default/files/business_economy_euro/banking_and_finance/documents/191113-report-expert-group-regulatory-obstacles-financial-innovation_en.pdf. Accessed 15 Mar 2022

FINRA (2021) Cloud computing in the securities industry. https://www.finra.org/sites/default/files/2021-08/2021-cloud-computing-in-the-securities-industry.pdf. Accessed 15 Mar 2022

FSB (2017a) Artificial intelligence and machine learning in financial services. https://www.fsb.org/2017/11/artificial-intelligence-and-machine-learning-in-financial-service/. Accessed 15 Mar 2022

FSB (2017b) Financial stability implications from FinTech supervisory and regulatory issues that merit authorities' attention. https://www.fsb.org/wp-content/uploads/R270617.pdf. Accessed 15 Mar 2022

FSB (2019) Third-party dependencies in cloud services considerations on financial stability implications. https://www.fsb.org/wp-content/uploads/P091219-2.pdf. Accessed 15 Mar 2022

FSB (2020) The use of supervisory and regulatory technology by authorities and regulated institutions. https://www.fsb.org/wp-content/uploads/P091020.pdf. Accessed 15 Mar 2022

Galaz V, Centeno MA, Callahan PW, Causevic A, Patterson T, Brass I, Baum S, Farber D, Fischer J, Garcia D, McPhearson T, Jimenez D, King B, Larcey P, Levy K (2021) Artificial intelligence, systemic risks, and sustainability. Technol Soc 67:101741

Gensler G, Bailey L (2020) Deep learning and financial stability. https://ssrn.com/abstract=3723132. Accessed 15 Mar 2022

Greenberg BA (2016) Rethinking technology neutrality. Minn Law Rev 207:1495–1562

Gullifer L, Payne J (2020) Corporate finance law, 3rd edn. Hart Publishing, London

Harari YN (2016) Homo Deus: a brief history of tomorrow. Harvill Secker, London

Hertig G (2022) The political economy of AI-driven financial supervision. ECGI Working Paper 621. European Corporate Governance Institute, Brussels, Belgium

Institute of International Finance (2019) Machine learning in credit risk. https://www.iif.com/Portals/0/Files/content/Research/iif_mlcr_2nd_8_15_19.pdf. Accessed 15 Mar 2022

Jackson H (2020) The nature of the fintech firm and its implications for financial regulation. Wash Univ J Law Policy 61:9

Keller A (2020) Legal foundations of macroprudential policy. Intersentia, Cambridge

Knight W (2017) The dark secret at the heart of AI. MIT Technology Review. https://www.technologyreview.com/2017/04/11/5113/the-dark-secret-at-the-heart-of-ai/. Accessed 15 Mar 2022

Lins S, Pandl KD, Teigeler H, Thiebes S, Bayer C, Sunyaev A (2021) Artificial intelligence as a service. Bus Inf Syst Eng 63:441–456

Magnusson W (2020) Artificial financial intelligence. Harv Bus Law Rev 10:337–382
Malik N (2020) Does machine learning amplify pricing errors in housing market? Economics of ML feedback loops. https://papers.ssrn.com/sol3/papers.cfm?abstract_id=3694922. Accessed 15 Mar 2022
OECD AI Policy Observatory (2019) OECD AI Principles overview. https://oecd.ai/en/ai-principles. Accessed 15 Mar 2022
OECD AI Policy Observatory (2022) National AI policies & strategies. https://oecd.ai/en/dashboards. Accessed 15 Mar 2022
Organization for Economic Co-Operation and Development (2021) Artificial intelligence, machine learning and big data in finance opportunities, challenges and implications for policy makers. https://www.oecd.org/finance/financial-markets/Artificial-intelligence-machine-learning-big-data-in-finance.pdf. Accessed 15 Mar 2022
Pandl K, Teigeler H, Lins S, Thiebes S, Sunyaev A (2021) Drivers and inhibitors for organizations' intention to adopt artificial intelligence as a service. In: Proceedings of the 54th Hawaii international conference on system sciences, Koloa, Hawaii, 4-8 January 2021
Pasquale F (2015) The black box society: the secret algorithms that control money and information. Harvard University Press, Cambridge
Rankin D, Black M, Bond R, Wallace J, Mulvenna M, Epelde G (2020) Reliability of supervised machine learning using synthetic data in health care: model to preserve privacy for data sharing. JMIR Med Inform 8:e18910
ReportLinker (2021) Global artificial intelligence-as-a-service (AIaaS) Mar-ket 2021-2025. https://www.reportlinker.com/p05647182/Global-Artificial-Intelligence-as-a-Service-AIaaS-Market.html?utm_source=GNW. Accessed 15 Mar 2022
Rivlin AM, Soroushian JB (2017) Credit rating agency reform is incomplete. https://www.brookings.edu/research/credit-rating-agency-reform-is-incomplete/. Accessed 15 Mar 2022
ROFIEG (2019) 30 recommendations on regulation, innovation and finance – final report to the European commission. https://ec.europa.eu/info/sites/default/files/business_economy_euro/banking_and_finance/documents/191113-report-expert-group-regulatory-obstacles-financial-innovation_en.pdf. Accessed 15 Mar 2022
Russell S, Norvig P (2010) Artificial intelligence: a modern approach. Prentice Hall, Upper Saddle River, NJ
Schmitz C (2019) How FinTech is fuelling an ecosystem future in Europe, Ernst and Young. https://www.ey.com/en_gl/banking-capital-markets/how-fintech-is-fueling-an-ecosystem-future-in-europe. Accessed 15 Mar 2022
Whittlestone J, Belfield H, Éigeartaigh SÓ, Maas M, Hagerty A, Burden J, Avin S (2021) Comment on the EU's world-first AI regulation: 'an historic opportunity'. https://www.cser.ac.uk/news/eus-world-first-ai-regulation. Accessed 15 Mar 2022

Open Access This chapter is licensed under the terms of the Creative Commons Attribution 4.0 International License (http://creativecommons.org/licenses/by/4.0/), which permits use, sharing, adaptation, distribution and reproduction in any medium or format, as long as you give appropriate credit to the original author(s) and the source, provide a link to the Creative Commons license and indicate if changes were made.

The images or other third party material in this chapter are included in the chapter's Creative Commons license, unless indicated otherwise in a credit line to the material. If material is not included in the chapter's Creative Commons license and your intended use is not permitted by statutory regulation or exceeds the permitted use, you will need to obtain permission directly from the copyright holder.

Regulating AI: Challenges and the Way Forward Through Regulatory Sandboxes

Katerina Yordanova and Natalie Bertels

Abstract Financial industry was the first filed where it became clear that we needed a new type of regulation, an evolutionary and anticipatory approach that can at least stand chance to mitigate the new risks posed by disruptive technologies such as artificial intelligence (AI). This approach took the shape of various tools, none of which has showed more prominence than the regulatory sandboxes. This rather young approach to regulation spread across various sectors and jurisdictions from FinTech to privacy and healthcare.

The European Commission recognised the potential of the regulatory sandboxes as an increasing compliance mechanism but also as a way to facilitate innovation and thus included them as part of the draft regulation on artificial intelligence (the AI Act). In this article we analyse the potential of the regulatory sandboxes for regulating AI in the format envisioned in Article 53 and 54 from the draft AI Act and the challenges this approach could face based on the experience from earlier regulatory sandboxes involving AI products or services. We also aim to suggest some tailor-made solutions that would mitigate potential disadvantages of the regulatory sandboxes for AI, including how to balance the emerging 'Innovation Principle' and the protection of human rights.

1 Introduction

One of the key figures in modern day engineering, Dean Kamen, believes that "[e]very once in a while, a new technology, an old problem, and a big idea turn into an innovation" (Sorvino 2016). Nowadays people keep testing the limits of technology and creativity, striving to invent the next big thing and change humans' lives. This highly competitive race to the top is certainly fascinating, but changing lives often leads to some unexpected consequences and could create unexpected

---

K. Yordanova (✉) · N. Bertels
KU Leuven Centre for IT and IP Law at KU, Leuven, Belgium
e-mail: katerina.yordanova@kuleuven.be; natalie.bertels@kuleuven.be

© The Author(s) 2024
H. Sousa Antunes et al. (eds.), *Multidisciplinary Perspectives on Artificial Intelligence and the Law*, Law, Governance and Technology Series 58,
https://doi.org/10.1007/978-3-031-41264-6_23

risks. One of the primary roles of regulation is risk mitigation. In the words of Prof Karen Yeung, regulation is an "organized attempt to manage risks or behaviour in order to address a collective problem or concern" (Yeung 2017). The problem with regulating disruptive technologies such as AI, however, originates from a combination of the largely unpredictable and dynamic nature of the said technologies and the traditional approach to legislation which is reactionary and too slow to be adopted and amended. Another big issue is technological opacity which highlights the need of involving a variety of people with specific expertise in drafting legislation that could be comprehensive and serve the basic need of any law, namely, to ensure legal certainty (Kaal 2016).

That's why the long-anticipated White Paper on AI adopted by the Commission in the beginning of 2020 was met with criticism[1] for not reflecting on the need of novel approach to regulating new technologies, especially when individual member states have already been implementing it, predominantly in the form of regulatory sandboxes.[2] It was also surprising due to the fact that regulatory sandboxes, in particular, have been pinpointed on a number of occasions[3] as a prominent tool to facilitate innovation and promote trust in new technologies and especially AI. The omission of the White Paper, however, was attempted to be remedied through the adoption of draft regulation on lying down harmonised rules on artificial intelligence and amending certain union legislative act (the AI Act). Title V provides first comprehensive glance at what regulatory sandboxes for AI are deemed to be and how they are supposed to be implemented.

This chapter aims to outline the key issues policymakers are facing in their attempts to regulate AI and how those issues are addressed through the introduction of regulatory sandboxes as a tool of a novel emerging type of regulation. In order to achieve this, we are going to first explain the nature of the approach and observe if and how it could be applied to AI technologies in a variety of sectors from financial law to health services and if its multidimensional nature is adequately reflected in the draft AI act. Finally, we are going to identify some challenges this regulatory tool faces and conclude whether it lives up to the expectation of being indeed a breakthrough in regulation.

---

[1] See for example (CIPL Response to EU Consultation on AI White Paper 2020) and compare to (Federal Government of the Federal Republic of Germany 2020).

[2] For example, the (ESMA 2019) discusses five operational regulatory sandboxes only in the field of FinTech which regularly deal with AI as demonstrated, for instance, by (UK Financial Conduct Authority 2021).

[3] Outside the area of FinTech regulation, noticeable examples are the Communication from the Commission on Artificial Intelligence for Europe from 25.4.2018, as well as the European Parliament's resolution of 12 February 2019 on a comprehensive European industrial policy on artificial intelligence and robotics.

2 The "Taming" of AI by the Law

As already mentioned, the primary aim of creating laws is to mitigate certain risks arising from objects or relations in society. To illustrate this point, we can look at an object which we are very much familiar with but that was once new and unfamiliar—the car. Its specifics in terms of mechanics and control brought up a number of concerns associated predominantly with people's lives and health. This led to adoption of legislation setting up rules that every driver needs to comply with for their own safety and the safety of other drivers and pedestrians. Later on, the legislator obtained more information which showed necessity of rules governing mandatory driving licenses and insurance. As the development of automobile industry and design progressed further, it became apparent that manufacturers also need to be regulated in order to ensure that new cars are being produced following certain safety standards. With automobiles becoming the most common means of transportation (European Commission and Eurostat 2000), their impact to the environment and urban spaces became obvious which exposed additional risks, leading to further legislation in an attempt to mitigate them.

This simplified example demonstrates the relationship between technology, risk and law. Why, then, would traditional way of legislation not work on another type of technology such as AI? Firstly, arguably an AI technology is much more complicated and has the potential to affect society in more domains than a car. It is often categorized as a disruptive technology[4] and as such it possesses risks that are hard to be predicted. Secondly, AI technologies are much more opaque compared to automobiles. Indeed, an ordinary user may not know exactly the purpose of the many elements composing a car, but someone with sufficient knowledge of mechanics does and hence the predictability, compared to AI that may sometimes act in unexpected ways. Another key difference is the so-called pacing problem of regulation related to AI. The pacing problem is the significant contrast between the pace of AI innovation and innovation of regulatory tools used to govern it (Marchant et al. 2013) Last but not least, in order for legislation to be adequate and to serve its function of risk mitigation, its object needs to be clearly defined. It is important since a well-written and serviceable legal act ultimately needs to cover as broad a range of real-life situations as possible. This is ensured by precise usage of legal terminology and detailed definitions of every term used in the act itself, via references to other acts, through applying the rules of legal interpretation, or through judicial decisions. It also contributes to achieving legal certainty.[5]

---

[4] Disruptive technologies do not have a commonly accepted definition, but they are often characterized by their refinement, ground-breaking nature, and ability to create new industries.

[5] The authors recognise the different theoretical standpoints in defining legal certainty (Van Meerbeeck 2016). Nevertheless, for the purpose of the present research it is to be understood as a quality of a certain legal system that allows people to predict the legal consequences of their actions/the actions of others/the results of certain events and to adjust their behavior according to these predictions.

Turning back to our example, if a regulator wants to adopt a legal act dealing with certain aspects of motor vehicles, a first step would be to define what a motor vehicle is. Looking at Directive 2007/46/EC for instance, we find the definition straight away in Article 3.[6] Reading the definition, a reasonable person would easily conclude that her vehicle with 3 wheels is clearly not a motor vehicle within the scope of the Directive and is therefore not subject to its rules, which is of course possible due to existence of a comprehensive legal definition of a motor vehicle. Returning to the problem at hand, it follows that prior to creating any sort of legislation related to AI and subsequently regulating it, there must be a legal definition that is acceptable for serving the purposes of the AI Act but also not contributing to overregulation of the subject.

This definition has been a hot topic for a while not only in the legal field but also in computer science.[7] This taxonomy issue was highlighted in the discussion that was formed after the High-Level Expert Group on Artificial Intelligence (HLEG) adopted, together with an additional report on the topic, a definition of AI, aiming to "avoid misunderstandings, to achieve a shared common knowledge of AI that can be fruitfully used also by non-AI experts, and to provide useful details that can be used in the discussion on both the AI ethics guidelines and the AI policies recommendations" (High-Level Expert Group on Artificial Intelligence 2019). There was a number of issues that were raised regarding that particular definition ranging from some excluding self-replicating machines from the scope of the definition, through adoption of "created by humans" criterion to having "one size fit all" approach regarding weak and strong AI regardless (Center for Data Innovation 2019).

The aforementioned problems were partially solved through the definition adopted in Article 3(1) of the draft AI Act which covers AI systems and describes them as "software that is developed with one or more of the techniques and approaches listed in Annex I and can, for a given set of human-defined objectives, generate outputs such as content, predictions, recommendations, or decisions influencing the environments they interact with." This new definition, however, also reveals some weak points, for example, not demonstrating clearly what is the difference between AI and AI systems, not reflecting current standardization efforts in EU and being so broad it practically encompasses "even the simplest search, sorting and routing algorithms" (BDVA/DAIRO 2021).

What is of vital importance for this definition is Annex I which contains particular types of AI techniques and approaches such as reinforced learning, symbolic reasoning, etc. and which can be updated through delegated acts in accordance with Article 4 in conjunction with Article 73 of the draft AI Act.

---

[6] A 'motor vehicle' means any power-driven vehicle which is moved by its own means, having at least four wheels, being complete, completed or incomplete, with a maximum design speed exceeding 25 km/h.

[7] Compare the different approach to the definition through the lenses of parallels between human and artificial intelligence proposed by (Norvig and Russell 2010) with the one based on the degree of "self-understanding and autonomous self-control" proposed by (Goertzel and Pennachin 2007).

Regulating AI: Challenges and the Way Forward Through Regulatory Sandboxes

This would allow better reaction time in case of scientific development that has not been covered by the regulation and is intended to address the pacing problem, although it still might not be agile enough considering the time a delegated act still takes to enter into force. In its briefing to the European Parliament, the European Parliamentary Research Service acknowledges the need for better addressing the pace problem and suggests "flexible instruments such as delegated acts, sunset clauses and experimental legislation" (Kritikos 2019).

These new regulatory tools are not a novelty and they emerged long before regulating AI became a task at hand (Ranchordás 2014). They have many names and are often used in various combinations but they do have several things in common: they are more dynamic compared to traditional legislation, allow participation of broader circle of stakeholders and provide valuable feedback to the regulator allowing better understanding of the object that needs regulation and the risks and benefits it involves. Undoubtedly, one of the tools that generated the most hype are regulatory sandboxes which are going to be examined in the following sections.

3 Playing in the Sand

The term 'regulatory sandbox' sometimes creates confusion. It is rather similar to the notion of sandbox environment in computer science. Despite the similarities, however, the two terms are not equivalent. A sandbox is a testing tool, while a regulatory sandbox is a regulatory tool and a process which regulates different risks compared to its namesake (Yordanova 2019).

The financial sphere was the first area in which regulatory sandboxes were tested. The financial crisis of 2008 resulted in a major global crisis of regulation (Armstrong et al. 2019). The financial sphere has always been very much affected and evolved with the evolution of technologies, often referred to as FinTech.[8] Several periods of evolution of FinTech have been identified, starting with the use of the telegraph to reach to what is nowadays considered FinTech 3.0 (Arner et al. 2016). It is characterized by the use of rapid developing technologies often leading to inclusion of new actors in addition to traditional financial product/service providers or automation of processes that may have unexpected and undesired consequences, for example, algorithmic bias leading to discrimination. The variety of ways disruptive technologies could be utilised for the purpose of FinTech creates the necessity of some form of regulation. On the other hand, overregulating innovation just to be safe every possible risk scenario is covered may hinder innovation since developing technologies in accordance with the corresponding legal requirements would me time-consuming, costly and involving increased liability. Therefore, innovators may 'shop' for jurisdiction that is less prompt to regulate the financial sector.

---

[8] Currently there is not a completely unified definition of FinTech but here we would define it as a new technology aiming to automate and improve financial products and services.

These concerns demonstrated the need of a new approach to regulation that would position the regulator as a partner and a guide rather than an enemy for companies willing to innovate. In 2014, the UK Financial Conduct Authority (FCA) started Project Innovate and officially created the first regulatory sandbox. In October 2017, FCA published its "Regulatory sandbox lessons learned report" (UK Financial Conduct Authority 2017) which assessed positively the result of the regulatory sandbox application. This has led to the establishment of a growing number sandboxes under different financial jurisdictions and attempts to transfer the use of the regulation tool to other sectors such as data protection (UK Information Commissioner's Office 2019) or aviation (Civil Aviation Authority 2019).

The potential of regulatory sandboxes for regulating disruptive technologies and especially AI has already been recognised. A number of states such as Finland (Ministry of Economic Affairs and Employment of Finland and Steering Group of the Artificial Intelligence Programme 2017) include the use of sandboxes as a means to build a comprehensive legal framework for AI. The trend is supported by the EU which sees regulatory sandboxes as innovation facilitators (ESMA 2019) and recognizes them as important tool in future regulation activities regarding AI (European Commission 2018).

This trend was further reinforced via including regulatory sandboxes in the European Commission's Better Regulation Toolbox[9] and instrumentalizing it in such further initiatives like the future pan-European blockchain sandbox (Council of the EU 2020) and the draft AI Act as a way to both promote innovation and support SMEs (European Commission 2020). At the same time other jurisdiction outside the EU are already implementing regulatory sandboxes for testing AI-based products, services and business models either through specific AI-dedicated sandboxes[10] or under the framework of another type, for instance, in the area of finances or healthcare.[11]

In this context in order to better understand the nature and the process behind regulatory sandboxes, it is only logical to look at those applied in the filed of FinTech due to their number, geographical distribution and the fact it was the sphere where regulatory sandboxes first appeared in.

Granted there is no universal definition of the term, the European Securities and Markets Authority regards regulatory sandboxes as "schemes to enable firms to test,

---

[9] TOOL #21 from Research & Innovation, Better Regulation Toolbox; European Commission; 6783/20 (COM (2020)103).

[10] For example, Norway's Data Protection Authority has already started a pilot of AI regulatory sandbox in March 2021 initially with a small number of participants chosen from 25 applicants https://www.datatilsynet.no/en/news/2021/25-applications-for-the-sandbox/ while other countries like Chilly are currently working on similar projects (Ministerio de Economía and Fomento y Turismo 2021).

[11] According to data from the World's Bank Key Data from Regulatory Sandboxes across the Globe, at the end of 2020, there were 73 existing regulatory sandboxes in 57 jurisdictions https://www.worldbank.org/en/topic/fintech/brief/key-data-from-regulatory-sandboxes-across-the-globe.

pursuant to a specific testing plan agreed and monitored by a dedicated function of the competent authority, innovative financial products, financial services or business models" (ESMA 2019). The definition highlights several points. Regulatory sandboxes are deemed essentially a testing ground for innovation products, services or business models where their potential risk is mitigated but also where the relevant supervisor may provide certain leeway from the general rules for the purpose of the testing.

On the other hand, the Council of the EU came up with a slightly different definition, presenting regulatory sandboxes as.

> concrete frameworks which, by providing a structured context for experimentation, enable where appropriate in a real-world environment the testing of innovative technologies, products, services or approaches – at the moment especially in the context of digitalisation – for a limited time and in a limited part of a sector or area under regulatory supervision ensuring that appropriate safeguards are in place (Council of the EU 2020).

There are already some differences between the first two definitions, the second one being broader and encompassing various sectors but also putting emphasis on the need for appropriate safeguards during the testing period. Then the draft AI Act provides a further definition for specific AI regulatory sandboxes in its Article 53(1). It is envisioned that AI regulatory sandboxes are.

> established by one or more Member States competent authorities or the European Data Protection Supervisor shall provide a controlled environment that facilitates the development, testing and validation of innovative AI systems for a limited time before their placement on the market or putting into service pursuant to a specific plan. This shall take place under the direct supervision and guidance by the competent authorities with a view to ensuring compliance with the requirements of this Regulation and, where relevant, other Union and Member States legislation supervised within the sandbox (European Commission 2021).

This specific definition provides some additional and novel elements. First of all, it explicitly emphasizes the possibility of a multi-jurisdictional regulatory sandboxes. The feasibility of this type of sandboxes had been questioned before we even started talking about specific AI sandboxes. It was argued that "the fact that the service lacks the standardization associated with regulation makes the sandboxed activity unfit for cross-border provision of services" (Zetzsche et al. 2017). It is yet to be found out how this barrier could be overcome. Furthermore, the scope of the regulatory sandboxes for AI is significantly broadened, encompassing development, testing and validation and therefore combining the traditional function of a regulatory sandbox with those of other tools such as testing and pilots. It is important to note that there is an existing debate on the exact relation between the terminology used to describe these defined 'safe spaces' for testing innovation with or without certain authorities being involved. What is agreed on is that "there is an inherent connection between a regulatory sandbox on the one side, and testing and piloting on the other" (Zetzsche et al. 2017) and also that usually jurisdictions "with a sandbox approach put certain piloting and testing activities inside the sandbox since this is more convenient" (Zetzsche et al. 2017). This probably contributes to the spawning of numerous other terms, for example 'living labs', 'regulatory testbeds', etc., which are used as synonyms and ultimately addressing "areas in which to trial innovation and regulation" (Federal Ministry for Economic Affairs and Energy 2019). Nevertheless, the definition of the draft AI Act seems to incorporate certain testing and piloting elements[12] in addition to the regular sandbox activities, which could be a beneficial element only if it really 'facilitates' the development of innovation and ultimately reduces the 'time to market' which has been the primary goal of the tool to begin with (Ringe and Ruof 2018).

In question about the manner and the degree of the facilitation element of the regulatory sandboxes for AI as envisioned by the European Commission, however, remains open. Going back to the original source and examining the already existing examples of sandboxes for FinTech we can deduct several key elements for a successful sandbox creation and operationalization. First, the sandbox operates for a limited amount of time and under certain test parameters, allowing a pre-determined number of participants. In the interest of transparency and fairness, the sandbox's entry requirements need to be clearly defined and publicly available. They may vary from jurisdiction to jurisdiction, but the most common ones are genuine innovation,[13] consumer benefit and need for testing within the sandbox (UK Financial Conduct Authority 2017). In general, the sandbox is not limited to just SMEs, although some jurisdictions decide to deny entry to regulated entities, supporting only unlicensed companies, which are mostly SMEs (Ringe and Ruof 2018).

On a second place, after a company has been accepted into the sandbox, usually a case officer is appointed to its case in order to provide regulatory expertise and assess if sandbox tools to facilitate the testing are needed in the particular case (UK Financial Conduct Authority 2017; Mangano 2018). The sandbox tools are numerous and offer a wide range of possibilities from the 'never say no' approach applied by the Monetary Authority of Singapore (Agarwal 2018) to the comfort from enforcement and letters of negative insurance on exit offered by FCA. Naturally, when a sandbox is created in a domain that is heavily regulated by EU law, the matter of leeway becomes more complicated due to the fact that the national regulator cannot provide any exemptions from the rules established by the European Union (Ringe and Ruof 2018). It needs, however, to set parameters for the testing phase, for example, restriction on disclosure, limited number of clients to use the product, service or business model, etc.

A third vital element is guaranteeing sufficient customer protection during the test as one of the most important tasks for the regulator, and especially for regulatory sandboxes testing technologies that may put individuals' rights to a significant risk, such as innovation in the area of healthcare. The means to achieve this are dependent on the particular case, but probably the most common are clear and

---

[12] The difference between tests and pilots is regarded as tests being a one-time event the outcome of which determines the subsequent development of a product/service/business model, while a pilot is a final test which aims to ensure some missing data before the product/service/business model is finally released to the market.

[13] Genuine innovation should be understood as new solution significantly different than all the existing ones.

detailed communication about the nature of the test, allowing consumers to make an informed decision on every topic related to the tested product or service, combined with testing parameters that mitigate risks such as testing being limited to non-retail clients. The companies should also ensure compensation or another redress measures in case of harm suffered in context of the test (ESMA 2019).

After the preparation phase has finished, providing answers and solutions to all of the questions discussed above, the testing phase begins. It encompasses constant communication between the company and the regulator. One could say that this phase most completely illustrates the symbiotic nature of the regulatory sandbox. The regulator does fulfil its role of monitoring the test and ensures compatibility with the necessary standards, but it also observes the tested technology and realizes better how it works, its potential risks, and which approach is better to mitigate them.

Finally, the last phase and element is the evaluation phase that requires submission of the final report to the authority, following predetermined parameters during the preparation phase, and assessment of the success of the test.

These common elements are justified by the available data showing high performance results and relatively few unsuccessful tests (UK Financial Conduct Authority 2017). The numerous advantages of the regulatory sandbox model, however, are what make it an increasingly popular choice for regulating disruptive technologies, especially AI. Firstly, a regulatory sandbox demonstrates the regulator's willingness to facilitate and stimulate innovation which is a sign of good business opportunities in the respective state. Secondly, an increase in the level of knowledge for both the participants and the regulator is clearly noticeable. This enables regulators to better perform their functions and gain vital insight of emerging technologies, making them less reliable to outside expertise (Scherer 2016). Furthermore, the time to market is reduced, combined with the assurance that the new products/ services have all the appropriate safety standards built-in. It also allows innovators to have early warning about possible problematic features of their product/ service, as well as the assurance that they would not break any existing regulatory requirements during the test phase.

Would that be enough to draw the conclusion regulatory sandbox is the most appropriate tool in regulating AI? The answer is not so simple. Despite the enthusiasm demonstrated by States and international organizations in creating and applying regulatory sandboxes, there are some challenges that need to be addressed and assessed. Some of the challenges are common for all kinds of regulatory sandboxes: the lack of a complete regulatory framework for a certain product/ service might seem too risky for consumers to engage in the testing; it also means that there would be lack of standardization. Standardization is important due to its implications to cross-border implementation of the products/services. Furthermore, in some cases the risk of an innovation might not be significant enough to require regulation of any kind. In such cases it would simply hinder innovation (Zetzsche et al. 2017). In other cases, the innovation might not be mature enough to be tested in a sandbox, thus a wait-and-see approach could be more suitable (Jenik and Lauer 2017). It is also true that the limited number of participants in the sandbox may not provide the necessary representative sample needed to fully determine the effect of a certain technology. The companies themselves might not be too willing to participate either because they want to grow faster, and the sandbox would limit this ability (Zetzsche et al. 2017) or because they are not stimulated enough by the leeway offered by the regulator, especially in the European context where the sandbox tools are much more conservative compared to other jurisdiction. Last but not least, the participating companies might be reluctant to participate in an environment where potentially trade secrets could be discovered by the competition.

Another category of challenges is related specifically to regulatory sandboxes for AI. The Coordinated Plan on AI stipulates that the envisioned testing facilities for AI "may include regulatory sandboxes ... in selected areas where the law provides regulatory authorities with sufficient leeway." It is rather confusing due to the fact that until now regulatory sandboxes have been created not to test a specific technology, but innovations in a particular field, for example, in the financial sphere. This approach does not limit the technologies that are used but their purpose and application. To illustrate our point, there was an AI-based solution being tested in the FCA's regulatory sandbox as part of its 5th cohort.[14] Its purpose is to help SMEs applying for loans by using AI to increase effectiveness of credit scoring and improve the risk assessment simultaneously reducing costs.

Secondly, the level of effect an AI technology could have might not fall only under the scope of one regulator. For example, an AI technology might be intended to be used only in the banking sector and thus being regulated by the financial authority but at the same time it may occur that it has significant implications to personal data and thus assistance from the data protection authority must be provided. This is problematic from both organisational and administrative point of view. Regulators usually do not have experience in coordinated with each other on such matters which would lead to chaos and inefficiency (Ausloos et al. 2018). It also worth noting that an AI technology is designed to learn, hence, to change. This would mean that an AI technology, exiting the sandbox labelled as compliant, might not be compliant for a long time. Such turn of events might undermine the whole process and ultimately legal certainty (Yordanova 2019).

4   The Way Forward Through the AI Act

The inclusion of the regulatory sandboxes for AI in the draft AI Act signifies the EU's new approach to regulating disruptive technologies but we need to take into consideration all the challenges outlined in the previous section. It is evident that despite the many novel opportunities and advantages offered by regulatory

---

[14] The list with the description of the admitted products and services is regularly updated from the regulating authority for transparency purposes https://www.fca.org.uk/firms/regulatory-sandbox/cohort-5.

sandboxes compared to traditional (reactive) way of regulation and governance, they are not a panacea but a tool and a building block to a new approach to regulation of a data-driven society.

Nesta has carried out detailed research on the features this new regulation model needs to possess and its key characteristics (Armstrong et al. 2019). Building on the work of Geoff Mulgan (Mulgan 2017) and his analysis on elements of emerging regulatory tool kit, Nesta outlines six principles of the new anticipatory regulation which it should possess in contrast to the traditional reactive approach.

Anticipatory regulation needs to be inclusive and collaborative, engaging the public and a variety of stakeholders which also ensures better democratic legitimacy of this kind of regulation. It should also be future-facing[15] and proactive.[16] The next principle is iterative, described as "taking a test-and-evolve rather than solve-and-leave approach to novel problems" (Armstrong et al. 2019). The last two principles are outcome-based and experimental nature. They both show the much more pragmatic and solution-oriented character of the new approach to legislation.

Following these principles, regulators could find the best regulatory tool or a combination of tools for their particular needs. In addition, a regulator should not be hesitant to combine all the opportunities provided by anticipatory regulation with tools and approaches from other modes of regulation such as advisory or adaptive regulations (Armstrong and Rae 2017).[17] It is important to stress that this classification is just an example of a system that is suitable to deal with emerging technologies and AI in particular. We can also consider regulation depending on whether it is based on principles, risks, the market or reliance on internal management (Black 2010).

Despite the chosen classification, the ultimate challenge before regulators remains the mitigation of risk in high-risk AI technologies (Guihot et al. 2017). Regulatory sandboxes certainly offer such a capability, but the result does depend on the nature of the risk and its level. A rather more conservative tool is implementation of sunset clauses in regulation (Vermeulen et al. 2017), although it would not offer the same amount of feedback as a sandbox. Another tool that is certainly looked at is standardization. A proposed solution is AI systems certified as safe to enjoy limited tort liability compared to uncertified ones (Scherer 2016).

These are just some examples of the palette of tools a regulator has at its disposal when regulating AI. The choice of one or another, or even a combination between several should be as customised as possible and supported by constant efforts in improving the regulators' capacities by providing them with best practices and skill

---

[15] By 'future-facing' Nesta understands approach that first identifies what is changing, then analyse possible impacts of the change and subsequently creates scenarios, predicting how different changes may interact with each other.

[16] This principle encompasses regulators proactively engaging innovators on an early stage of development of the innovation, thus ensuring greater predictability.

[17] The three modes differ by their goals, desired outcome and participants, anticipatory regulation being the most future-oriented.

building (Armstrong et al. 2019) especially in the light of the interdisciplinary nature of the AI research (Moses 2011).

The draft AI Act set the scene for regulatory sandboxes to be the centre of attention as the ultimate innovation facilitator. This approach raises at least three different groups of concerns. Firstly, the issues we discussed in the current previous sections regarding regulatory sandboxes in general and those specifically dedicated to AI have not been solved in the current version of the provisions in Article 53. Secondly, the design of the regulatory sandboxes for AI, as described by the text of the regulation, does not seem to provide many incentives for joining such sandboxes. One of the elements that usually attracts the most innovative products/services, namely the weaver of certain rules, is not touched upon. It is vital to be "clear whether Member State authorities will be able to offer regulatory waivers or other types of regulatory arrangements for AI experiments" (Ranchordas 2021). Furthermore, national regulators might not be able to offer any significant waiver due to the fact that they would not have had such competences regarding EU law provisions (Ringe and Ruof 2018).

The only possible waiver of rules we currently know about stems from the text of Article 54 and concerns personal data protection rules. Indeed, participants in the regulatory sandboxes for AI would be able to process personal data, "lawfully collected for other purposes" in order to develop and test "certain innovative AI systems in the sandbox". This exception to personal data protection rules, however, is subject to a rather large number of cumulative conditions acting as guarantee towards the individuals' rights and freedoms. The conditions include the purpose of the innovative AI systems ("safeguarding substantial public interest" in one or more of predetermined areas such as public health for instance), the data being necessary for complying with the high-risk AI systems' requirements, the existence of effective monitoring system for identification of arising of high risks to the fundamental rights of the data subjects. Furthermore, "any personal data to be processed in the context of the sandbox are in a functionally separate, isolated and protected data processing environment" and should not be "transmitted, transferred or otherwise accessed by other parties". In addition, any processing of personal data shall not lead to measures or decisions affecting the data subjects, needs to be deleted "once the participation in the sandbox has terminated or the personal data has reached the end of its retention period" subject to logs of processing also having retention period and purpose limitation. There are also strict transparency requirements in the form of "complete and detailed description of the process and rationale behind the training, testing and validation of the AI system" and "short summary of the AI project developed in the sandbox, its objectives and expected results published on the website of the competent authorities." The burden of satisfying these requirements appear to significantly outweigh the advantages of the waiver offered in the context of the sandbox.

The third group of concerns is related to the lack of clearance on the scalability of the regulatory sandboxes for AI as well as their place in the system of tools for anticipatory regulation. From a practical perspective adopting a smart mix of tools for facilitating innovation is considered the best solution, in which regulatory sandboxes are just one piece of the puzzle. For example, in 2019 UK Civil Aviation Authority (CAA) launched an Innovation Hub and a regulatory sandbox specifically targeting AI innovations (UK Civil Aviation Authority 2021). This combination between innovation hubs and regulatory sandboxes has already been considered as a way to solve some of the scalability issues of the sandboxes (ESMA 2019; European Commission 2020). Furthermore, combining different tools of anticipatory regulation is deemed highly beneficial for the further establishment and development of the Innovation principle (Renda and Simonelli 2019). Additionally, the Council of the EU has already connected regulatory sandboxes with experimental clauses, understood as "legal provisions which enable the authorities tasked with implementing and enforcing the legislation to exercise on a case-by-case basis a degree of flexibility in relation to testing innovative technologies, products, services or approaches" (Council of the EU 2020). This relation, however, is currently lacking from the draft AI act where the role of the regulatory sandboxes as contributing to the creation of evidence-based policy making is currently not present.

5 Conclusion

In 1996 Richard Susskind expresses the opinion that "we are on the brink of a shift in [the] legal paradigm, a revolution in law" (Susskind 1996). Events such as the global financial crisis from 2008 and the US elections in 2016 proves that we need a radically new approach to the world and the way we regulate it. This approach is still under development, and we are far from completing the transition from reactive regulation to anticipatory one.

Regulatory sandboxes are certainly a step forward. They provide a relative safety and degree of control, helping regulators to better understand AI and other disruptive technologies before deciding if and how they should be regulated. After all, "regulation is a mere tool. Where helpful for society, it must be used, where not it is best removed" (Zetzsche et al. 2017).

There are also many questions regarding how to overcome the challenges outlined in the present chapter and what evolution regulatory sandboxes are going to go through in order to stay relevant and answer the needs of the society and dynamic nature of AI. There are already some ideas about Sandboxes 2.0, incorporating access to innovative finding methods (Ringe and Ruof 2018) and guided sandboxes, attempting to resolve the conflict of national and supranational/federal levels with respect to their interaction in a regulatory sandbox.

Currently, there are more questions than answers on how to regulate AI. Global powers outline different approaches in an attempt to become the most attractive investment destination, but ultimately the most successful would be the one that can stabilise the 'shifting sands' of regulatory sandboxes and use them as a cornerstone for building a new way of regulation. [18]

References

Agarwal K (2018) Playing in the regulatory sandbox. Nyujlb (blog). https://www.nyujlb.org/single-post/2018/01/08/playing-in-the-regulatory-sandbox. Accessed 20 Apr 2022

Armstrong H, Rae J (2017) A working model for anticipatory regulation, NESTA, https://media.nesta.org.uk/documents/working_model_for_anticipatory_regulation_0.pdf. Accessed 20 Apr 2022

Armstrong H, Gorst C, Rae J (2019) Renewing regulation 'anticipatory regulation' in an age of disruption. NESTA. https://media.nesta.org.uk/documents/Renewing_regulation_v3.pdf. Accessed 20 Apr 2022

Arner DW, Barberis JN, Buckley RP (2016) The evolution of fintech: a new post-crisis paradigm? Georget J Int Law 47:1271–1320

Ausloos J, Heyman R, Bertels N, Pierson J, Valcke P (2018) Designing-by-debate: a blueprint for responsible data-driven research & innovation. In: Ferri F, Dwyer N, Raicevich S, Grifoni P, Altiok H, Andersen HT, Laouris Y, Silvestri C (eds) Responsible research and innovation actions in science education, gender and ethics. Springer International Publishing, Cham, pp 47–63

BDVA/DAIRO (2021) BDVA/DAIRO position paper in response to the European Commission's proposal for AI regulation. https://www.bdva.eu/sites/default/files/BDVA_DAIRO%20response-feedback%20AI%20Regulation_Final.pdf. Accessed 20 Apr 2022

Black J (2010) The rise, fall and fate of principles based regulation. LSE legal studies working paper no. 17/2010. http://ssrn.com/abstract:1712862. Accessed 12 Nov 2011

Center for Data Innovation (2019) Recommendations to HLEG on AI on its draft ethic guidelines. http://www2.datainnovation.org/2019-hleg-ai.pdf. Accessed 20 Apr 2022

Civil Aviation Authority (2019) The CAA innovation hub | UK civil aviation authority. https://www.caa.co.uk/Our-work/Innovation/The-CAA-innovation-hub/. Accessed 20 Apr 2022

Council of the EU (2020) Council conclusions on regulatory sandboxes and experimentation clauses as tools for an innovation-friendly, future-proof and resilient regulatory framework that masters disruptive challenges in the digital age, 2020/C 447/01. Council of the EU, Brussels

ESMA (2019) ESMAs joint report on regulatory sandboxes and innovation hubs. https://eba.europa.eu/-/esas-publish-joint-report-on-regulatory-sandboxes-and-innovation-hubs. Accessed 20 Apr 2022

European Commission (2018) Coordinated plan on artificial intelligence. COM (2018) 795 Final). European Commission, Brussels

European Commission (2020) Communication from the commission on an SME strategy for a sustainable and digital Europe. https://eur-lex.europa.eu/legal-content/EN/TXT/PDF/?uri=CELEX:52020DC0103&from=EN. Accessed 20 Apr 2022

European Commission (2021) Proposal for a regulation of the European parliament and of the council laying down harmonised rules on artificial intelligence (Artificial intelligence act) and Amending certain union legislative acts. COM (2021) 206 Final. European Commission, Brussels

---

[18] *See* also, on Fintech, in this book A Keller, C Martins Pereira and M Lucas Pires - The European Union's approach to Artificial Intelligence and the Challenge of Financial Systemic Risk.

European Commission, Eurostat (2000) EU transport in figures statistical pocket book. https://www2.uni-mannheim.de/edz/pdf/2000/transstat.pdf. Accessed 20 Apr 2022

Federal Government of the Federal Republic of Germany (2020) Comments from the federal government of the Federal Republic of Germany on the white paper on artificial intelligence - a European concept for excellence and trust. Federal Government of the Federal Republic of Germany, Germany

Federal Ministry for Economic Affairs and Energy (2019) Making space for innovation: the handbook for regulatory sandboxes. Federal Ministry for Economic Affairs and Energy, Germany

Goertzel B, Pennachin C (2007) Artificial general intelligence. Cognitive technologies. Springer, Berlin

Guihot M, Matthew A, Suzor NP (2017) Nudging robots: innovative solutions to regulate artificial intelligence. Vanderbilt J Entertain Technol Law 20:385–456

High-Level Expert Group on Artificial Intelligence (2019) A definition of AI: main capabilities and disciplines. High-Level Expert Group on Artificial Intelligence, Brussels

Jenik I, Lauer K (2017) Regulatory sandboxes and financial inclusion. CGAP, Washington, DC

Kaal WA (2016) Dynamic regulation for innovation. SSRN Electron J https://doi.org/10.2139/ssrn.2831040

Kritikos M (2019) Artificial intelligence ante Portas: legal & ethical reflections. Eur Parliament Res Serv, Brussels

Mangano R (2018) The sandbox of the UK financial conduct authority as win-win regulatory device? Bank Finance Law Rev 34:31–40

Marchant G, Abbott K, Allenby B (2013) Innovative governance models for emerging technologies. Edward Elgar Publishing, Cheltenham, UK

Ministerio de Economía, Fomento y Turismo (2021) Sandbox regulatorio de inteligencia artificial En Chile. https://www.economia.gob.cl/wp-content/uploads/2021/09/PaperSandboxIA.pdf. Accessed 20 Apr 2022

Ministry of Economic Affairs and Employment of Finland, Steering Group of the Artificial Intelligence Programme (2017) Finland's age of artificial intelligence (Objectives and recommendations for measures). http://julkaisut.valtioneuvosto.fi/bitstream/handle/10024/160391/TEMrap_47_2017_verkkojulkaisu.pdf?sequence=1&isAllowed=y. Accessed 20 Apr 2022

Moses LB (2011) Agents of change: how the law 'copes' with technological change. Griffith Law Rev 20:763–794

Mulgan G (2017) Anticipatory regulation: 10 ways governments can better keep up with fast-changing industries. Nesta (blog). https://www.nesta.org.uk/blog/anticipatory-regulation-10-ways-governments-can-better-keep-up-with-fast-changing-industries/. Accessed 20 Apr 2022

Norvig P, Russell SJ (2010) Artificial intelligence: a modern approach, 3rd edn. Prentice-Hall Series in Artificial Intelligence. Pearson Education, Upper Saddle River

Ranchordás S (2014) Constitutional sunsets and experimental legislation: a comparative perspective. Elgar monographs in constitutional and administrative law series. Edward Elgar, Cheltenham, UK

Ranchordas S (2021) Experimental regulations for AI: sandboxes for morals and mores. Morals Mach 1:86–100

Renda A, Simonelli F (2019) Study supporting the interim evaluation of the innovation principle. Centre for European Policy Studies, Brussels, Belgium

Ringe WG, Ruof C (2018) A regulatory sandbox for Robo advice. 14. ILE working paper series. University of Hamburg, Institute of Law and Economics, Hamburg, Germany

Scherer MU (2016) Regulating artificial intelligence systems: risks, challenges, competencies, and strategies. Harv J Law Technol 29:353

Sorvino C (2016) One of America's most successful inventors Dean Kamen talks segway, clean water and robotics. Forbes https://www.forbes.com/sites/chloesorvino/2016/06/09/dean-kamen-inventor-success-segway-water-purification-toyota/. Accessed 20 Apr 2022

Susskind R (1996) The future of law: facing the challenges of information technology. Clarendon, Oxford

UK Civil Aviation Authority (2021) Flylogix BVLOS sandbox report. https://publicapps.caa.co.uk/modalapplication.aspx?catid=1&pagetype=65&appid=11&mode=detail&id=10859. Accessed 20 Apr 2022

UK Financial Conduct Authority (2017) Regulatory sandbox lessons learned report. https://www.fca.org.uk/publication/research-and-data/regulatory-sandbox-lessons-learned-report.pdf. Accessed 20 Apr 2022

UK Financial Conduct Authority (2021) List of admitted participants to the UK FCA's regulatory sandbox. https://www.fca.org.uk/firms/innovation/regulatory-sandbox. Accessed 20 Apr 2022

UK Information Commissioner's Office (2019) Sandbox beta phase discussion paper. https://ico.org.uk/media/2614219/sandbox-discussion-paper-20190130.pdf. Accessed 20 Apr 2022

Van Meerbeeck J (2016) The principle of legal certainty in the case law of the European court of justice: from certainty to trust. Eur Law Rev 41:275

Vermeulen E, Fenwick M, Kaal W (2017) Regulation tomorrow: what happens when technology is faster than the law. Am Univ Bus Law Rev 6:561–594

Yeung K (2017) Are human biomedical interventions legitimate regulatory policy instruments? In: Brownsword R, Scotford E, Yeung K (eds) The Oxford handbook of law, regulation and technology. Oxford University Press, Oxford, p 11

Yordanova, K (2019) The shifting sands of regulatory sandboxes for AI. Centre for IT and IP law blog. https://www.law.kuleuven.be/citip/blog/the-shifting-sands-of-regulatory-sandboxes-for-ai/. Accessed 20 Apr 2022

Zetzsche DA, Buckley RP, Arner DW, Barberis JN (2017) Regulating a revolution: from regulatory sandboxes to smart regulation. Fordham J Corp Financ Law 23:31–104

Open Access This chapter is licensed under the terms of the Creative Commons Attribution 4.0 International License (http://creativecommons.org/licenses/by/4.0/), which permits use, sharing, adaptation, distribution and reproduction in any medium or format, as long as you give appropriate credit to the original author(s) and the source, provide a link to the Creative Commons license and indicate if changes were made.

The images or other third party material in this chapter are included in the chapter's Creative Commons license, unless indicated otherwise in a credit line to the material. If material is not included in the chapter's Creative Commons license and your intended use is not permitted by statutory regulation or exceeds the permitted use, you will need to obtain permission directly from the copyright holder.

Printed in the United States
by Baker & Taylor Publisher Services